Elementary Mathematics Is Anything but Elementary

Content and Methods from a Developmental Perspective

Damon L. Bahr
Brigham Young University

Lisa Ann de Garcia
Brigham Young University

WADSWORTH
CENGAGE Learning

Australia · Brazil · Japan · Korea · Mexico · Singapore · Spain · United Kingdom · United States

WADSWORTH
CENGAGE Learning

Elementary Mathematics Is Anything but Elementary: Content and Methods from a Developmental Perspective
Damon L. Bahr, Lisa Ann de Garcia

Acquisition Editor: Christopher Shortt

Marketing Manager: Kara Parsons

Development Editor: Julia Giannotti

Associate Media Editor: Ashley Cronin

Assistant Editor: Diane Mars

Assistant Editor: Caitlin Cox

Editorial Assistant: Janice Bockelman

Marketing Coordinator: Andy Yap

Senior Content Project Manager, Editorial Production: Margaret Park Bridges

Art and Design Manager: Jill Haber

Manufacturing Buyer: Arethea L. Thomas

Senior Rights Acquisition Account Manager: Katie Huha

Text Researcher: Karyn Morrison

Production Service: Graphic World Inc.

Senior Photo Editor: Jennifer Meyer Dare

Cover Design Manager: Anne S. Katzeff

Cover Image: © Don Hammond/Design Pics/ Corbis

Compositor: Graphic World Inc.

For product information and technology assistance, contact us at **Cengage Learning Academic Resource Center, 1-800-423-0563.**
For permission to use material from this text or product, submit all requests online at **www.cengage.com/permissions.**
Further permissions questions can be e-mailed to **permissionrequest@cengage.com.**

Library of Congress Control Number: 2008929480

ISBN-13: 978-0-618-92817-0

ISBN-10: 0-618-92817-0

Wadsworth
10 Davis Drive
Belmont, CA 94002-3098
USA

Cengage Learning products are represented in Canada by Nelson Education, Ltd.

For your course and learning solutions, visit **www.cengage.com.**

Purchase any of our products at your local college store or at our preferred online store **www.ichapters.com.**

Printed in the United States of America
1 2 3 4 5 6 7 13 12 11 10 09 08

CHAPTER **6**

Instructional Models: Inquiry-Based Teaching with Single-Digit Multiplication and Division | 157

CHAPTER **7**

Lesson Design: Learning How to Create Inquiry Lessons Using Multidigit Multiplication and Division | 188

CHAPTER **15**

Technology Integrations and Data Analysis and Probability | 450

The title of our text is *Elementary Mathematics Is Anything but Elementary*. Its subtitle is *Content and Methods from a Developmental Perspective*. Let's talk about these titles and the context in which this text was written.

Equity and Math Phobia

You are choosing to teach children in a very interesting time in history. Today we know more about how children learn mathematics than we have ever known before. For example, we now realize that children are capable of far deeper mathematical thinking than had previously been thought and that, fundamentally, children *think* differently than adults do.

It is a troubling time, too, however. Recent research indicates that a majority of American adults fear mathematics (Burns 1998). While there may be several root causes for this anxiety, we, the authors, believe that mathematics can be an engaging, exhilarating, self-actualizing endeavor and that *everyone is* capable of the creative, meaningful work known as mathematics. We further believe that we as teachers must examine the ways that we teach to ensure that in our teaching we are not perpetuating math phobia.

There is an additional side to this math phobia phenomenon. If failure is a consistent result of instruction, it causes many caring teachers to wonder if all children are really capable of deep mathematical thinking and learning. In other words, if some of your students don't do well mathematically despite your very best efforts, it is easy to be tempted to believe that some children are just not cut out to do math. As soon as teachers begin to doubt theirs students' abilities, expectations are lowered, and when expectations are lowered, achievement drops.

Knowing and Learning Mathematics Deeply and in a Balanced Way

How about the theme of "balance" that is so central to this book? Education, as in most human endeavors, suffers from the "pendulum swing" phenomenon. This phenomenon refers to the consistent pattern of adopting some new idea, taking it to its extreme through overuse, then discarding it while "swinging" to a stance that is opposite the new idea, but just as extreme. The NCTM (2000) *Principles and Standards for School Mathematics* as well as other important reform documents, such as *Adding It Up* (2001), espouse a more balanced approach to conceptualizing matters related to the teaching and learning of mathematics. Therefore, this text addresses these extremes and adopts a **balanced** stance, capitalizing upon the best of seemingly disparate positions, in a manner similar to those whose visionary leadership produced the widely held literacy pedagogy known as balanced literacy.

Where did we get the idea for the title *Elementary Mathematics Is Anything but Elementary*? In her groundbreaking work *Knowing and Teaching Elementary Mathematics*, Liping Ma (1999) sought to investigate the reasons for differences in the mathematical achievement of children in the United States and of children in higher-performing countries, such as Singapore or China. She states that fundamental, or elementary, mathematics is a deep, complicated subject that requires thorough study in order to comprehend and teach. In fact, she states that teachers should possess a "Profound Understanding of Fundamental Mathematics," or "PUFM." As she explicates this position, it becomes very clear to the reader that elementary mathematics is anything but elementary. For example, she asked many teachers in the United States such questions as, "Why do we borrow in subtraction?" or "Why do we invert and multiply when dividing fractions?" or even, "What does it mean to divide fractions? Can you create a word problem that involves dividing fractions?" She discovered that most of the U.S. teachers she surveyed had very little understanding of elementary mathematics, that all they basically knew were some rote rules, facts, and procedures, with little knowledge of the deep, connected nature of fundamental, or elementary, mathematics that characterizes the knowledge of teachers in higher performing nations.

Integrating Content, Pedagogy, Development, and Student Thinking

The subtitle of our book, *Content and Methods from a Developmental Perspective*, suggests that as you read and learn from this book, we are expecting you to **integrate** the mathematical content and mathematical pedagogy or methods you acquire as you examine how children develop mathematically. The next several paragraphs describe the theory behind this integration.

As mathematics teacher educators in an era of reform we are engaged in both providing and investigating the professional development of preservice and inservice teachers. We developed a theoretical framework to guide our efforts in both endeavors, by studying our own work and the work of others similarly involved. This framework serves to define for us what we hope will be the end result of our professional development efforts and to frame our investigations of that work. Here is a summary of both how we derived the framework and its current structure and content.

Our framework's conceptual underpinnings stem from the work of Wood, Nelson, and Warfield (2001) in their seminal publication *Beyond Classical Pedagogy*. They suggest that research investigating the processes by which teacher change occurs has been conducted from four positions, each with its own set of theoretical roots. We have not only studied the effects of our own professional

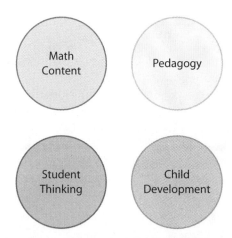

Figure 1. Four Positions from Which Teacher Change Is Investigated

development work from all four positions, but have also found them to be a useful guide in providing that professional development. Those four positions are summarized as follows and are graphically depicted in Figure 1:

1. Carpenter, Peterson, and Fennema (Carpenter, Fennema, Peterson, & Carey, 1988; Carpenter, Fennema, Peterson, Chiang, & Loef, 1989; Peterson, Carpenter, & Fennema, 1989) suggest that change in teaching is brought about by changes relative to perspectives about the development of student thinking.

2. Schifter, Simon, and Fosnot (Schifter, 1996a, 1996b; Schifter & Fosnot, 1993; Schifter & Simon, 1992) suggest that teacher change occurs as teacher perspectives relative to the nature of learning mathematics change. We call this a *developmental position.*

3. Cobb, Wood, and Yackel (Cobb et al., 1990; Wood, Cobb, & Yackel, 1991) view teacher change as stemming from a renegotiation of the social norms that characterize classroom pedagogy.

4. Ball, McDiarmid, Wilson, and Shulman (Ball, 1988; McDiarmid & Wilson, 1991; Shulman, 1986, 1987) posit that change occurs as the nature of a teacher's mathematical content knowledge changes.

We are not unique in designing a theoretical framework incorporating the four positions. Darling-Hammond (2006) has suggested a similar framework that describes her vision of teacher development that incorporates three of the four positions. A graphic representation of that vision appears in Figure 2.

Note that the only position she does not include is student thinking and that she views each of these positions as overlapping. We have adapted her graphic and placed student thinking in its center (see Figure 3) because we believe that the student thinking position is unique among the four positions. Steinberg, Empson, and Carpenter (2004) have demonstrated that a focus on student thinking opens the door to teacher change relative to the other positions. In addition, a careful examination of the professional development work and investigations performed by the researchers that are associated with the other three positions reveal that they all significantly emphasize student thinking. (See the references related to the positions summary located at the beginning of this section.)

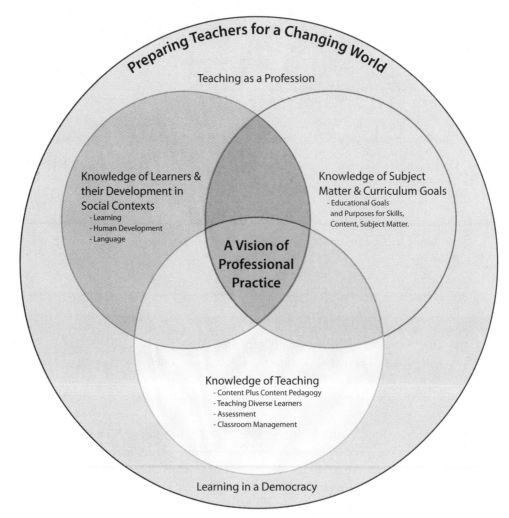

Figure 2. Darling-Hammond Graphic. (Darling-Hammond, L. (2006). Constructing 21st century teacher education. *Journal of Teacher Education* 57(3), 304. Reprinted by permission of Sage Publications.)

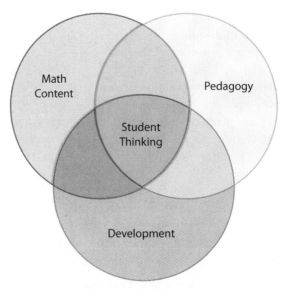

Figure 3. Theoretical Framework for Investigating and Documenting Mathematics Reform

Exactly how did we design the text to encourage such an integration? Here's a list of text structures and features that facilitate integrating content, pedagogy, child development, and student thinking:

1. Each chapter has a pedagogy section followed by a content section, with student thinking and developmental issues interwoven into both (more about this later in the list).

2. The opening chapter listing of main ideas lists both content and pedagogy.

3. Each chapter also begins with a "Conversation in Mathematics" that emphasizes student thinking and illustrates both the pedagogy and content of the chapter.

4. This "Conversation" is then discussed in the chapter introduction from both a content and a pedagogical perspective.

5. The pedagogy section is frequently illustrated with scenarios, examples, and situations that incorporate the mathematical content of the chapter.

6. The introduction to the content section always reminds the reader that although the focus of the section is on content, the pedagogy inherent in those content discussions will be primarily the pedagogy of the chapter.

7. The chapter conclusion summarizes the content and pedagogy in an integrated way.

8. The video analysis assignments associated with each chapter invite readers to examine both the content and pedagogy inherent in the video.

9. The student interview assignment and the classroom application assignment also invite examination of both content and pedagogy.

10. Resources for the teacher at the end of each chapter will provide both content and pedagogy resources.

11. Developmental issues are a key component of both sections. In the pedagogy section, fundamental developmental psychology that underlies the pedagogy is discussed in a way to lay a conceptual foundation for the pedagogy. In the content section, a clear explanation is made of how young children develop the fundamental notions of the particular mathematical content. These developmental summaries could easily serve as scope and sequence guides for curriculum and instructional design.

12. Student thinking is at the core of every aspect of the text. In essence, the text consistently addresses the question of how children think mathematically and how pedagogy can be used to enhance that thinking.

13. Actual lesson plans exemplify the pedagogy and incorporate the content featured in each chapter.

Other Text Features

There are other text features that should also serve to enhance your use of the book. All content sections are based on the five NCTM content areas: Number and Operations, Algebra, Geometry, Measurement, and Data Analysis & Probability (*Principles and Standards for School Mathematics, 2000*). The key notions common to most state curricula relative to these strands for grades pre-K through 6 are presented and discussed via a discussion of the relevant sections of the NCTM *Curriculum Focal Points* and mathematical BIG IDEAS.

There are little "time outs" from general text flow in the form of simple technique or teacher move advice. These include "Struggling Students Support"; "Special Needs Students Support"; "Rule of Thumb," which are self comprehension checks; and "Language Tips," for facilitating the use of language in the classroom, including among ELL/multicultural students.

Each chapter includes video, interviewing and classroom application assignments. We feel these application opportunities will help to solidify text content into the minds and hearts of teachers using our text.

Instructor Ancillaries

- Online Instructor's Resource Manual contains sample syllabi, chapter outlines, and teaching strategies and tips.

- The Cengage Learning Testing CD offers a computerized test bank with multiple-choice questions, short-answer questions, and essay questions for each chapter.

- Cengage Learning's powerful, customizable, and interactive online learning tool, Eduspace, offers a convenient, user-friendly platform to manage, customize, create, and deliver course materials online. In addition to its gradebook, discussion board, and other course-management tools, Eduspace provides text-specific interactive components such as videos, reflective journal questions, test items, and additional materials to aid students in studying and reflecting on what they have learned.

- PowerPoint slideshows accompany each chapter.

Student Ancillaries

- Videos: Using student interviews, teacher interviews, and classroom lessons, the videos cover topics such as:
  - Multi-digit subtraction in a second grade classroom
  - Activities based on place value
  - Mathematical routines in the classroom
  - Activities in the classroom around adding, subtracting, multiplying, and dividing fractions
  - Use of math language in the classroom

- The Student Website offers additional tools to help students connect with textbook material. Features include ACE self-quizzes, a review of key topics in each chapter, glossary flashcards, and the videos.

Acknowledgments

Who in their right mind would ever volunteer to write a textbook? Like most of life's worthwhile ventures, the task of writing this book took on a life of its own. At times it was difficult to determine who was really in charge of the project, the authors or the book itself—and most of the time the latter condition was more true than the former. So why did we choose to do this?

We love elementary mathematics, the teaching of elementary mathematics, and the teaching of elementary mathematics teaching. We felt like we had something to say about those three endeavors, and say it in a way that might be unique and helpful to the elementary mathematics world. There are some great books out there: content books, methods books, and some that address both. What does this book have to offer that others don't?

We believe that great teachers of elementary mathematics must possess beliefs and knowledge, and engage in classroom practice that relates to four issues: mathematics content, pedagogy, child development, and student thinking *in an integrated way*. That is to say, great mathematics teachers possess a view and engage in a practice of teaching that integrates important notions about content, pedagogy, development, and student thinking. Therefore, we designed this book in a way that we think fosters such an integration.

There are three potential users of the book who will appreciate it for varying reasons. First, university content and methods instructors can rely upon it because it is research-based. Second, preservice students can rely upon it because not only is it research-based, its pages are full of both theoretical and practical advice that we ourselves have used in teaching children. Third, inservice teachers can rely upon it because although it contains theory and research, it is, in some respects, a handbook that can guide her or his daily mathematics teaching.

We would be remiss in our responsibilities as authors if we did not acknowledge some very important people who have contributed to this effort. Damon has been greatly influenced professionally and personally by Dr. Randolph Philipp, of San Diego State University. In addition, two of Damon's colleagues at Brigham Young University, Dr. Eula E. Monroe and Dr. Nancy Wentworth, contributed greatly to the theoretical framework that guides this book. Damon would like to thank his co-author, Lisa Ann de Garcia, for her tireless efforts. Finally, Damon wishes to express his undying affection for his wife, Kim, who is a dynamite kindergarten mathematics teacher in her own right. Her support has been pivotal in this project, as well as in every important aspect of his life.

Lisa Ann would like to thank the San Diego Unified School District for providing her the training and opportunities that have made her the person she is today. With the vision of Kris Acquarelli and others from the math department, the role of math demonstration teachers (math lab teachers) and math coaches (math resource teachers) were put into play in the district. Both of these roles allowed Lisa Ann to gain the experience that is shared throughout the pages of this book. Shelley Ferguson, coaching mentor and professional developer, also played a significant role in Lisa Ann's learning and understanding of coaching, as well as her belief that change is built upon the foundation of relationships. She would also like to acknowledge the leadership of Jennifer White, principal of Webster Elementary, for her endeavor for providing quality, student-centered staff development, as well as all the teachers at that site, and others who have assisted Lisa Ann with parts of this book by allowing her to videotape classroom episodes, from which she has learned tremendously.

Lisa Ann would also like to show deep appreciation for her co-author, Damon, for his confidence in her ability to assist him in this amazing work, and for the staff at BYU for giving her the opportunity to shape the minds of aspiring teachers. Finally, she would like to extend endless gratitude for the unconditional teamwork on the part of her husband, Moises, and for what she learns every day from her three children, Adrian, Joshua, and Andrew.

Last of all, we express appreciation to Shani Fisher and Julia Giannotti, along with the other folks at Houghton Mifflin, for their help and advice.

About the Authors

Damon L. Bahr is an Associate Professor of Teacher Education at Brigham Young University. Damon has held several leadership responsibilities with the Association of Mathematics Teacher Educators and was president of the Utah affiliate of that organization in 2002. His current research interests include mathematical discourse, public school–university partnerships, and math coaching. Damon is happily married, the father of four and grandfather of two, and enjoys scuba diving, swimming, golfing, and spending time with his family.

Lisa Ann de Garcia currently teaches math methods courses in the Teacher Education department at Brigham Young University. She comes from San Diego Unified School District, where she was an elementary bilingual classroom teacher as well as a math coach/staff developer. She is an active member of both NCTM and NCSM, as well as Utah Association of Mathematics Teacher Educators. She is a mother of three and enjoys traveling and spending time with her family.

Mathematical Literacy: Acquiring the Big Ideas While Doing Mathematics

PEDAGOGICAL CONTENT UNDERSTANDINGS

Pedagogy   *The Processes That Characterize Doing Mathematics*

- Problem Solving
- Communication
- Reasoning and Proof
- Representation
- Connections

Content   *Curriculum Focal Points and Big Ideas in Mathematics Grade by Grade*

....

Science is built up with facts, as a house is with stones. But a collection of facts is no more a science than a heap of stones is a house.

Jules Poincaré, Mathematician, *1908*

CONVERSATION IN MATHEMATICS

Teacher: Suppose you had 42 water balloons, then you gave 15 to your friend. Now how many water balloons would you have?

Student: 27.

Teacher: How did you get 27?

Student: Well, 40 take away 10 is 30. Then 2 take away 5 is −3. And 30 plus −3 is 27.

Teacher: Where did you get −3?

Student: I just sort of played around with the numbers. I know that 5 is larger than 2, so when you subtract 5 from 2 you have to get a negative number. If I think about it on a number line, I start with 2 and go left 5 spaces, which is 3 spaces below the zero mark, which is −3. And 30 plus −3 is 30 subtract 3, which is 27.

Teacher: I see just what you did.

What does it means to be literate, both generally and in terms of mathematics? Francis Bacon said, "Knowledge is power." All knowledge has some value, and some types of knowledge are more valuable than others. However, it would be difficult to find many pieces of knowledge in any field, including mathematics, that are so vital or essential that every literate person must know them. Certainly there are fundamentals, such as knowledge of the place-value system, that the general population should possess, and there are context-dependent fundamentals that various occupations require— for example, the mathematics that engineers use. All mathematical knowledge has value, but not all of mathematics is essential for all nonmathematicians to know. Can people live meaningful lives without knowing the Pythagorean theorem, or the quadratic formula, or Pascal's triangle? Of course, they can. Most people do. However, to be literate about mathematics, an educated person must have the ability to ask and answer questions about mathematics in a mathematically valid way.

Thus, rather than an exclusive mastery of mathematical content knowledge, literacy also requires the development of intellectual abilities—thinking. Content is not unimportant; it provides the stuff with which we think, Poincaré's "stones," that students can mentally manipulate to develop their thinking and reasoning. However, the creation of large mental storehouses of mathematical content knowledge is not the exclusive goal or the only measure of mathematical literacy. For example, possessing a quick recall of the times tables is not essential for using math, although it does speed up the process of problem solving and is desirable. We have taught children who were incredible mathematical thinkers yet who struggled with learning all the times tables. However, knowing how and when to use multiplication to solve real-life problems is an essential capability of any mathematically literate person. Interestingly, a quick recall of the multiplication tables is likely to develop naturally through consistent and authentic opportunities to solve problems that require multiplication.

The fundamental point of this argument is that "literacy in any field implies that an individual has the potential for deeper learning in that field. Literacy isn't committing a particular set of facts to memory, but the ability to use resources to find, evaluate, and use information in a manner that reflects that field" (Wright 2007). We often expect students to gain these intellectual abilities on their own, simply as a result of learning the mathematical content, and we are disappointed when they do not. Wright (2007) goes on to say, referring to the opening quote of this chapter, "Like Poincaré's stones, such unconstructed, disconnected knowledge is the antithesis of literacy."

In the opening "Conversation in Mathematics," it is clear that the child possesses a reasonable understanding of an important "big idea" in mathematics: place value. But that content knowledge becomes useful, lively, and apparent through a series of teacher prompts that *invite* the child to "process" that knowledge. Those processes included solving an important problem, explaining and justifying the strategies used to solve the problem, representing the thinking associated with the solving in multiple ways, and explicitly describing the connections among those representations.

Thus, in a balanced mathematics classroom, there is balance between the emphasis placed on learning mathematical content (i.e., mathematical knowledge) and the emphasis placed on the processes of mathematics (i.e., the mental activities that characterize doing mathematics). In this chapter, we structure our pedagogical discussion around these processes and their implications for your classroom. We then segue into a general discussion of mathematical content by looking at the big ideas that should be the emphasis of the content side of your instruction. Finally, we look at the grade levels at which those big ideas should be taught as recommended by the National Council of Teachers of Mathematics' (NCTM's) *Curriculum Focal Points for Prekindergarten through Grade 8 Mathematics: A Quest for Coherence* (2007).

Processes That Characterize Doing Mathematics   PEDAGOGY

Learning Theory

How mathematical literacy is defined depends on how we define mathematics itself. As Alan Schoenfeld (1992, p. 343) has stated,

> **Goals for mathematics instruction depend on one's conceptualization of what mathematics is, and what it means to understand mathematics. Such conceptualizations vary widely. At one end of the spectrum, mathematical knowledge is seen as a body of facts and procedures dealing with quantities, magnitudes, and forms, and the relationships among them; knowing mathematics is seen as having mastered these facts and procedures. At the other end of the spectrum, mathematics is conceptualized as the "science of patterns, an (almost) empirical discipline closely akin to the sciences in its emphasis on pattern-seeking on the basis of empirical evidence. . . .**
>
> **What one thinks mathematics is will shape the kinds of mathematical environments one creates, and thus the kinds of mathematical understandings that one's students will develop. . . .**
>
> **There has been a significant change in the fact of mathematics . . . and in the community's understanding of what it is to *know* and *do* mathematics. . . . There is a major shift from the traditional focus on the content aspect of mathematics . . . (where attention is focused pri-**

marily on the mathematics one "knows"), to the process aspects of mathematics (what is known as "doing mathematics"). (italics added) (Schoenfeld 1992. *Learning to Think Mathematically.* New York: MacMillan, p. 343. Reprinted by permission of Information Age Publishing, Inc.)

School mathematics curricula tend to focus on lists of content objectives. Even *Principles and Standards for School Mathematics* (NCTM 2000) contains a list of five content standards: number and operations, algebra, geometry, measurement, and data analysis and probability. It is quite common for these curricula to include as many as 100 objectives. There is no doubt that these objectives interrelate hierarchically with one another, but many textbooks do not attempt to organize the objectives in ways that enable the foundational big ideas to become apparent to students. In addition, the structure of these curricula often result in applications of mathematical ideas being viewed as end-of-unit activities (i.e., a set of word problems at the end of the chapter) rather than being valued as the fundamental contexts for learning.

We believe in the importance of maintaining the distinction between content and process if a mathematics classroom is to reflect the balance inherent in legitimate mathematical work. This distinction reflects something fundamental about human mental activity. All languages possess grammatical structures that differentiate between nouns and verbs, thus expressing the distinction between objects and actions carried out by or on these objects. The content–process distinction in mathematics is nicely described by the words *object* and *action*. What are the mathematical objects we wish to deal with? This is mathematical content. What are the mathematical actions we carry out with these objects? These are the mathematical processes. Mathematical processes are different from content in that they overarch the subject and are not thought of as hierarchical. In the next section, we discuss five fundamental mathematical processes that should characterize the work in which we engage children.

Application to the Learning and Teaching of Mathematics

The five fundamental processes that characterize "doing" mathematics are problem solving, communication, reasoning and proof, representation, and connections (figure 1.1; NCTM 2000).

Problem Solving

Problem solving means becoming involved in a task for which the solution method is not known in advance. To find a solution, students must use previously acquired knowledge and, through this process, gain new mathematical understandings. Thus, problem solving becomes the context in which mathematical understanding is acquired and should not be an isolated part of the mathematics program. Problem solving should be integral to investigating mathematics in all five of the content areas described earlier. Problems can be drawn from everyday experiences, from applications from the sciences, or from the world of work. A good problem tends to integrate several mathematical topics and focuses students upon the big ideas of mathematics.

To ensure that a particular problem facilitates the achievement of specific mathematical targets, the teacher must carefully analyze the problem, along with its numerical or quantitative complexity. The teacher must be able predict

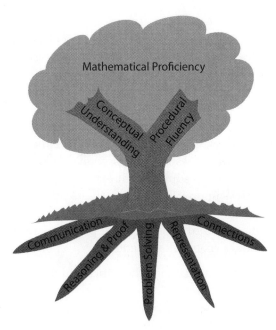

Process of "Doing Mathematics"

Figure 1.1. The five processes of "doing mathematics."

the mathematical ideas that will underscore the students' problem-solving efforts and anticipate the kinds of questions that might promote deeper mathematical inquiry.

Promoting problem solving means more than posing problems or tasks. It also means creating an environment in which students feel they can safely explore, take chances, share both successful and unsuccessful conjectures and strategies, and argue perspectives with one another. Such safe environments promote student dispositions to engage in problem solving, persist in the face of challenging tasks or initial disequilibrium, and view themselves as capable mathematical thinkers.

As a safe problem-solving environment is established, instructional attention can be devoted to specific problem-solving strategies, or *heuristics* (Polya 1957), including simplifying the numerical complexity of a problem, developing a diagram or picture, identifying patterns, listing possibilities, guessing and checking, and working backward.

There is also a metacognitive component of problem solving. Students who successful solve problems first work to ensure that they understand the problem, both its components and its question. They plan their solving activity, and they consistently monitor their progress according to their plans and their internal mathematical sensibilities. If that monitoring reveals a lack of progress, good problem solvers are flexible enough mentally to adjust their strategies or revamp their approaches.

Teachers promote this level of thoughtfulness by asking questions that encourage metacognitive reflection, such as "What do we know from the information in this problem?" "What information does it ask for?" "Is there any missing information that might make solving the problem easier?" "What shall we do first, second, etc.?" "Are we getting closer to a solution?" "Should we try something else?" "Why is that true?" Such questioning places the responsibility for problem-solving success squarely upon the shoulders of the students.

Comprehension Check

- What is problem solving?
- What is the role of problem solving in mathematics instruction?

Communication

Mathematics is a language, and the use of language is a foundation of mathematical proficiency, or "being mathematical" (Ball and Sleep 2007). Indeed, the communication of mathematical ideas is both a means of transmission and an important component of what it means to "do" mathematics. Although communication is at the heart of mathematical proficiency, it is not an entirely natural thing to do. Teachers have to provide an environment in which students can risk expressing their fledgling efforts to communicate their thinking. Teachers must be tolerant and patient, especially as young children first use informal language. They must learn to support that expression without imposing their own mental frameworks upon it.

The NCTM lists communication as one of its standards for school mathematics. According to this standard, "instructional programs from prekindergarten through grade 12 should enable all students to

- organize and consolidate their mathematical thinking through communication;
- communicate their mathematical thinking coherently and clearly to peers, teachers, and others;
- analyze and evaluate the mathematical thinking and strategies of others; [and]
- use the language of mathematics to express mathematical ideas precisely" (NCTM 2000, 60).

When students are invited to share their ideas, those ideas become the focus of discourse and analysis and great cognitive and dispositional benefits result. Those benefits include the following (NCTM 2000):

- The building of meaning and permanence of important mathematical ideas
- Clarity of thought and precision of expression during mathematical discourse
- The development of understanding while listening to others' explanations
- The making of connections while varied representations and strategies are shared and compared
- The enhancement of mathematical understanding as solutions are justified in the face of differing points of view
- Informal assessments that guide ongoing lesson development and occur when ideas are shared and discussed

Communication is fundamental to the work of mathematicians. Mathematical ideas are validated when communities of mathematicians recognize a proposed idea or proof is correct. Classrooms can become informal mathematical communities when students test their ideas on one another to see whether they are sensible and whether their arguments are justified. Such public display of mathematical thinking allows meaningful assessment by the teacher (Lampert 1990), and all students benefit from engaging in the discussion. In this way, argument and logic become the sources of mathematical "rightness" or "wrongness," rather than the teacher serving as the authority.

To promote this type of classroom discourse, a genuine sense of community must be established. This sense enables students to feel free to express their ideas. Younger children need significant scaffolding, or support, from their teachers to share their ideas. A wise use of probing and prompting questions, as well as restating those ideas and representing them visually, is useful to scaffolding. In the lower grades, teachers must also assist students in responding to the sharing of ideas. Inviting them to ask questions of the student who shared her idea is a powerful way to begin the response process. In the middle grades, students learn to assume more responsibility for the classroom discourse and respond to one another without as much teacher orchestration. When a student shares a math idea or strategy, teachers should assign the other students to listen specifically so that they can describe that idea or strategy, compare it to their own, evaluate it, and possibly even gently argue about flaws in thinking.

Writing in mathematics is a useful yet underused method that can also help students enhance the precision of their thinking. Subsequent rereadings often reveal a sense of progress as the students discover that their mathematical abilities have changed since the initial writing.

There is a similar "developmentalness" to developing written communication. As students begin to communicate in written form during the primary grades, they may rely on means other than words, such as drawing pictures. Gradually, they learn to write words and eventually sentences. In the middle grades, you should encourage students to be more elaborate through sequencing and adding details. There should be a mixture of informal writing using ordinary language and drawings, along with more formal mathematical communication using precise vocabulary and symbols. The bottom line is that writing about mathematics is like writing in any content area—you have to teach children how to do it.

Reasoning and Proof

It is not uncommon in traditional classrooms to find opportunities for reasoning and proof limited to a single lesson devoted to problem solving within a textbook chapter. Reasoning is a habit of the mind and, like problem solving, should provide a context for developing important mathematical ideas in all elementary grades.

Questioning is key to helping students, from their earliest classroom experiences on, learn that ideas and conjectures require validation—validation based on sound reasoning. Asking questions such as "Why do you think it is true?" or "Why did you say that?" helps students see that mathematics is endeavor based on the presentation of evidence. Central to placing a high premium upon reasoning is the students in the class coming to an agreement about what constitutes an acceptable mathematical argument.

When a problem is presented and solved, interest in that problem is high if the reasoning behind its solution is made apparent. Consider this "magic trick" borrowed from *Principles and Standards* (NCTM 2000, 56):

> **Write down your age. Add 5. Multiply the number you just got by 2. Add 10 to this number. Multiply this number by 5. Tell me the result. I can tell you your age.**

Students mathematical abilities would be significantly enhanced if they were invited to discover why dropping the final zero from the number you are given and subtracting 10 results in the person's age. Mathematics is an inherently creative activity and therefore involves discovery. Inviting students to make *conjectures,* or informed guesses, is an invitation to discovery. Even the youngest ele-

Comprehension Check

- What is communication?
- What happens to a child's mathematical knowledge when he is invited to verbally communicate that knowledge and how it was obtained?

mentary children can learn to create, refine, and evaluate conjectures in elementary school. Questioning is key as well. Consider asking questions such as "Is there a pattern?" or "What might happen next?" In addition, how a task is presented can enhance the development of conjecturing. Instead of saying, "Find the result of dividing 1/2 by 1/8," you might ask, "Why does multiplying two fractions result in the inverse of the result of dividing those same two fractions?"

You can also enhance the development of reasoning by inviting students to explore their own conjectures and those of other students with concrete materials and pictorial representations. For example, base 10 blocks or graph paper could be used to verify that $12 \times 3 = 36$.

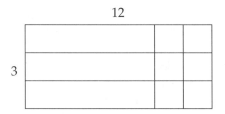

As students develop, they can begin to use technology such as calculators. In this case, they could add 12 three times to obtain 36. Eventually, they could use more formal mathematical representations and tools:

$$12 \times 3 = (10 + 2) \times 3 = (10 \times 3) + (2 \times 3) = 36$$

It is quite common for students to conjecture problem-solving strategies that only work in some contexts. At that point, you should invite students to see whether those strategies work in other contexts. For example, students may conceptualize two-digit multiplication as shown in figure 1.2.

When asked to invent a more efficient strategy, we heard students say, "Multiply the tens ($10 \times 1 = 10$), add the ones ($2 + 3 = 5$), then multiply the ones ($2 \times 3 = 6$) = 156." We then had a wonderful exploration in determining whether that strategy always worked and, if not, under what circumstances it would work.

It is often best to encourage students to start with what they know. The strategy known as a *derived fact* (Carpenter et al. 1999) is an example of such reasoning. If a child is presented with a problem involving $8 + 9$ and knows her "doubles," she could think about using $8 + 8$ and adding 1 or using $9 + 9$ and

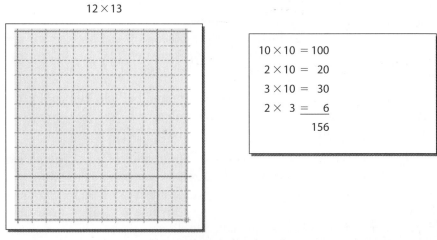

Figure 1.2. 2-digit multiplication.

removing 1. Such an invented strategy would depend on a deep understanding of number and the addition operation.

Young children are capable of verifying their thinking through contradiction. For example, a first grader reasoned that an odd number plus an odd number is an even number in this way: "An odd number has one left over. When you add another odd number to it, the two leftovers combine and there is no leftover. A number with no leftover cannot be odd, so adding two odd numbers must be an even." Students are also capable of disproving conjectures through counterexamples. In the two-digit multiplication example shown previously, students found that the invented algorithm did not work when neither of the two numbers had a 1 in the tens place.

Encouraging students to look for patterns is also a great way to promote reasoning. For example, pictorially representing 1/2 ÷ 3 and 1/2 × 1/3 can lead to the creation of invert and multiply procedures (figure 1.3).

Comprehension Check

■ What are the similarities and differences between communication and reasoning and proof?

Representation

You are using the process of representation to full advantage when you ask students to show a mathematical idea in more than one way. Fundamentally, there are five ways to represent thinking (Lesh, Post, and Behr 1987): manipulative models, static pictures, written symbols, spoken and written language, and real-world situations, or contexts. Figure 1.4 shows the connections among these representations.

Of these five means of representation, real-life contexts may be the most surprising to you. It is actually a useful teaching strategy to present a mathematical idea symbolically and ask your students to create a word problem (i.e., a real-life context) to which that symbolic representation applies. For example, write "12 × 3" on a whiteboard, and a student might say, "I have three egg cartons with 12 eggs in each. How many eggs in all?"

Real-life contexts are a powerful means of representation for an even more fundamental reason than the one just described. Children do not think about mathematics in the same way adults do (Philipp et al 2007). Symbols can support an adult's thinking, whereas they do not usually support the thinking of young children. They come to school used to having their thinking supported by real-life contexts. Consider a kindergarten teacher who writes "2 × 3" on the whiteboard. The 5-year-olds in his classroom would have little comprehension of the meaning of that abstraction, let alone be able to solve it. But if that teacher

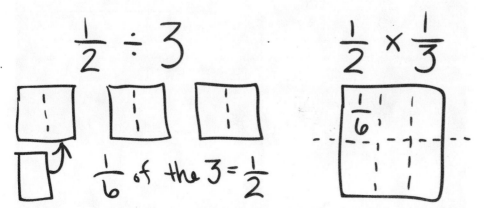

Figure 1.3. Pictorially representing division and multiplication of fractions to create the "invert and multiply" procedures.

Multiple Representations

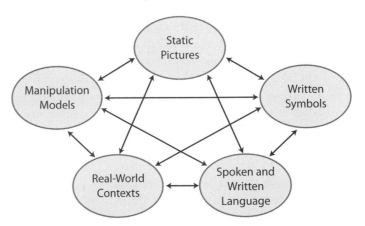

Figure 1.4. Lesh's model for multiple representations.

were to say that he had two bags of candy each with three candies inside and that he would give those candies to the child who could tell the total number of candies, he would break his budget giving candy to all the students who could tell him "Six." The balanced elementary mathematics classroom embeds the learning in real-life contexts because, as we said previously, children first come to school used to thinking about mathematics in such contexts.

All five means of representation would appear in a scenario such as this:

Suppose that in Mr. Wonka's (Dahl, 19) Chocolate Factory all caramels are packaged in tens—whenever there are 10 of anything, they must be packaged. Now suppose his invoice department always shows its caramel orders in five ways: with the actual caramels in the box and then on the paper invoice with pictures, numerals, expanded numerals, and words. Here are the caramels for one order. Now show the four ways on the invoice.

Showing 35 as a model, pictures, numbers and words.

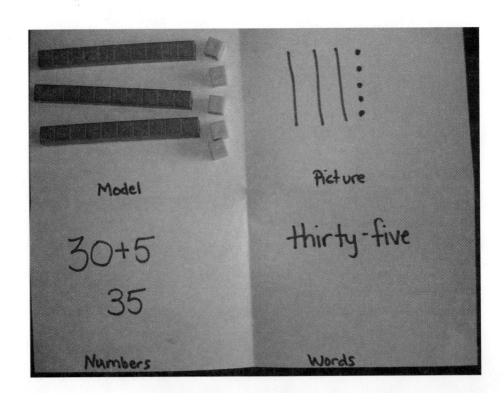

The preceding scenario was a problem involving place value, so for words, the student just wrote out the amount. However, in problems involving computation, there would be more of a written explanation of how the problem was solved. An example of this might look like this:

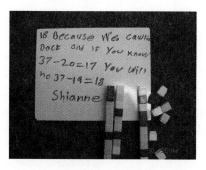

Using a model, numbers and words to explain how to solve a problem.

The wise choice of tasks can lead to the creation of valuable representations, which can then be generalized to not-so-obvious situations. Consider two common multiplication representations, the number line and the array. Are there some tasks embedded in real-life contexts that would lead to children inventing a number line or an array representation? How about "If you were playing 'Simon Says' and Simon told you to jump two times, and then two times again, and then two times again, how many jumps would that be?" It is quite possible that students would represent their thinking with a number line (figure 1.5).

Now imagine this task:

A miniature checkerboard has six rows of five squares each. How many squares in all?

It would be surprising if at least one child did not create the following representation.

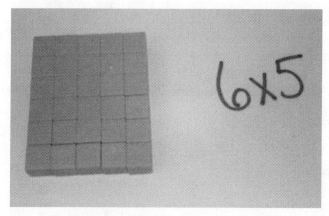

Representation of 6 × 5 using an array.

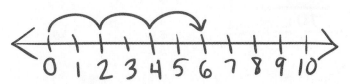

Figure 1.5. Representation of 2 × 3 on a number line.

Thus, representations are used by children first to display the problem context, then to find a solution to that problem, and finally to make those representations models and tools to solve similar mathematical problems.

Connections

The word *connection* is overused in education. It has so many meanings that the word has almost been rendered useless. This is too bad, because it is a powerful word with deep implications for the teaching and learning of mathematics. Anna Sierpinska (1994) defines connecting as the experience of mentally relating one object to another. It refers to the mental relationships that occur between thoughts. Liping Ma (1999) talks about teachers and students developing profound understandings of fundamental mathematics. That profound understanding is characterized by deep, multichanneled mental connections among mathematical ideas of varying degrees of power or significance. Indeed, the balanced math teacher believes that mathematics is a "web of concepts and procedures" (Philipp et al 2007, p. 475). Six types of connections are distinguished by what thoughts are being connected: representations, problem-solving strategies or conjectures, prior and current math learning, mathematical topics, mathematics and other subjects, and mathematics and real-life situations. We describe each type.

Mathematical understanding consists of the connections among representations (Lesh, Post, and Behr 1987). It is one thing to invite students to represent their mathematical ideas in multiple ways, but it is more effective to then invite them to describe the connections or relationships among those representations. Consider the two-digit multiplication example discussed previously in this chapter, 12 × 13. We were observing an upper-grade multiplication lesson and invited a student to share her thinking with us. She drew a graph paper representation and performed the standard multiplication algorithm.

We asked her to explain how the graph paper representation and her numerical representation connected with each other, and she drew a blank. So we asked her what the 6 in the ones place meant and she said, "6 ones."

We then asked, "Are there 6 ones on the graph?" She pointed to them.

Then we asked, "What does the 3 mean?" She replied, "3 tens, or 30."

We asked, "Are there 3 tens or 30 on the graph paper?" She got that look that on her face that is more rewarding than a pay raise, and we knew that she had made the connection.

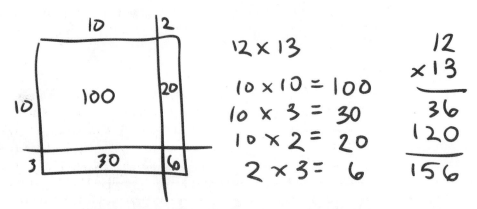

Figure 1.6. Representation of 12 × 13 using an open area model.

Encouraging mental connections between problem-solving strategies accelerates your students' mathematical reasoning abilities. One of the roles you should ask students to assume while you are orchestrating discourse is to compare their strategies with those that are being shared. Are they the same? Are they different? How are they the same or different? For example, if one child solves 3 + 5 by counting from the 3 and another child solves it by counting from the 5, then a child who connects those two strategies develops the understanding that addition is commutative.

Promoting connections with prior mathematical learning is essential to the success of any current lesson. One of the problems that characterizes early instruction in two-digit addition or subtraction involving *composing tens* or *decomposing tens* (terms that are more descriptive and mathematically accurate than *carrying* or *borrowing*), such as 27 + 45, or 61 − 38, comes from the lack of prior knowledge to which problems of this type can be connected. If lower-grade teachers would teach composing tens when teaching children the addition facts that result in two-digit answers, like 8 + 7, and teach decomposing tens when teaching children the subtraction facts that begin with a two-digit minuend, like 15 − 8, then two-digit addition and subtraction would be easier. Such connections are made with great success in other countries (Ma 1999).

Connecting mathematical topics makes learning about those topics synergistically more powerful. For example, inherent in the array representation for multiplication discussed earlier is the length × width algorithm for determining the area of a rectangle. When students use the array to represent 6 × 7, they are laying the foundation for determining the area in square feet of a 6 × 7 foot piece of carpet.

Curriculum integration in a mathematical context is nothing more or less than connecting learning in two or more subject areas, usually simultaneously. Children do not think in subject areas. They learn about the world in integrated ways, and balanced mathematics instruction seeks to legitimately help children see the connections among subject areas. For example, how much mathematics is inherent in a science experience in which students use protractors to measure the angles of incidence and reflection of reflected light?

However, a great deal of poor curriculum design occurs under the guise of integration. Whenever legitimate integration occurs, and thus legitimate connections among subject areas, meaningful learning goals must be facilitated in both subject areas. Using a work of children's literature to introduce a math lesson is not integration. It is only when the reading of that literature simultaneously promotes enhanced reading ability and mathematical conceptualization that true integration occurs, and thus real subject area connections are formed.

The last type of connection is concerned with connecting mathematics with real life. The use of real-life contexts has been discussed in several places in this chapter. However, one observation bears discussing here. In our work with future teachers, we consistently ask them about their previous mathematical learning experiences. In every one of those discussions, at least one teacher brings up the obstacles that obscured his or her mathematical learning because the teacher failed to indicate how mathematics could be applied in real life. One of the best ways to embed mathematics instruction in real-life contexts is to capitalize on the inherent meaning derived from the curriculum integration notions discussed in the previous paragraph. When mathematics is consistently used to solve problems in other subject area contexts, connections to real life occur consistently.

Special Needs

It is essential that students with special needs make connections just like their general education peers. In fact, it is even more important for them to do so, because they may not be able to retrieve information as easily. However, the connections might not come as naturally or incidentally as with other children. For example, students with autism tend to only use one sense at a time, so special attention needs to be placed on providing experiences in which the other senses can be involved. We never know which tool or experience is needed to make the concept click.

CONTENT

Curriculum Focal Points and Big Ideas in Mathematics Grade by Grade

Take another look at the conversation that opened this chapter. What mathematical content knowledge is inherent in the responses and representations produced by the child? He knows that the value of a digit depends on its place, that the value of each place is a multiple of 10, that the value of one place is 10 times greater than the value of the place to the right, and that the total value of a number is the sum total of each of its place values. He also knows that a mathematical idea can be represented in multiple ways that are equivalent. This suggests that he has a solid understanding of some of the big ideas of mathematics. The notion of "big ideas" has been around awhile, and the NCTM has produced a new publication, *Curriculum Focal Points for Prekindergarten through Grade 8 Mathematics: A Quest for Coherence* (2007), designed to provide guidance about what the big ideas of elementary mathematics are. A little history may help you make sense of the role of the *Curriculum Focal Points* guide in today's mathematics education climate.

Traditionally, education in the United States has primarily been the purview of the individual states. Therefore, virtually all states have their own mathematics curriculum documents, each specifying the mathematical content that should be taught at various grades. Although quite common in some ways, they are diverse in others. The notion of a national mathematics curriculum, something quite common in many nations, is a foreign one to the American psyche.

In 1989, a new movement toward what might be termed a national curriculum was launched with the NCTM's *Curriculum and Evaluation Standards for School Mathematics.* Although not a national curriculum in the fullest sense of the term, this was the first real nationally recognized standards document to appear from any content area group. Numerous standards documents in science, literacy, the arts, and so on, appeared shortly thereafter. This document attempted to specify in general terms the kinds of experiences students should have in the mathematics classroom, and it divided its expectations into grade bands consisting of multiple grades (K–4, 5–8, 9–12) rather than specific grade levels. There was a mixture of process and content expectations, and those expectations for kindergarten through fourth grades are listed here as a hint to the document's structure:

■ Mathematics as problem solving, communication, and reasoning

■ Mathematical connections

■ Estimation

■ Number sense and numeration

■ Concepts of whole number operations

■ Whole number computation

■ Geometry and spatial sense

- Measurement
- Statistics and probability
- Fractions and decimals
- Patterns and relationships

Therefore, *Curriculum and Evaluation Standards* was not a national curriculum in the usual sense of the word *curriculum,* but it was a nationally recognized document that provided guidance about the nature of school mathematics. Almost immediately, most leading text publishers gave recognition to this quasi-national curriculum.

In 2000, the NCTM released *Principles and Standards for School Mathematics,* an updated version of the original 1989 document, which provided an even more comprehensive vision of school mathematics and again received widespread national attention. It also fell short of specifying specific content expectations for each grade, but it did provide a clear set of general guidelines, albeit semibig ideas, in narrower grade bands than its predecessor (pre-K–2, 3–5, 6–8, 9–12) with a more well-defined distinction between mathematical processes and mathematical content. The process standards consist of problem solving, reasoning and proof, communication, representation, and connections—a list nearly identical to the process portion of the 1989 standards—and the content standards consist of number and operations, algebra, geometry, measurement, and data analysis and probability.

In the meantime, mathematics curriculum experts became increasingly concerned with the incredibly specific nature of state curriculum documents. All but 1 of the 50 states have mathematics curriculum frameworks that contain anywhere from 30 to 100, and sometimes more, expectations for any given grade level. This can be frustrating for teachers. In addition, it often leads to the "checklist" approach to mathematics instruction, in which teachers teach one specific objective, mark it off their list of curricular responsibilities, and never help children see the larger mathematical ideas or how those narrow mathematical objectives fit within the larger mathematical picture. This American curriculum approach is often characterized as "a mile wide and an inch deep." In contrast, the national curricula of nations whose students vastly outperform American students typically focus on big ideas, a "less is more" approach in which students study a few fundamental mathematical ideas deeply.

As discussions continued in the United States regarding the need for a clearly defined set of big ideas, considerable effort was expended to determine what those big ideas of school mathematics were and how those big ideas played out across the grades. The need for a reasonable and comprehensive list of big ideas resulted in the production of several expositions of ideas. We choose to focus on two: a National Council of Supervisors of Mathematics listing (Charles 2005) and the NCTM's *Curriculum Focal Points.*

In the Spring/Summer 2005 *NCSM Journal,* Randall Charles produced a list of 21 big ideas to guide curricular and instructional decision making. We present his list here:

1. *Numbers.* The set of real numbers is infinite, and each real number can be associated with a unique point on the number line.
2. *Base 10 Numeration System.* The base 10 numeration system is a scheme for recording numbers using digits 0–9, groups of 10, and place value.

3. *Equivalence.* Any number, measure, numerical expression, algebraic expression, or equation can be represented in an infinite number of ways that have the same value.

4. *Comparisons.* Numbers, expressions, and measures can be compared by their relative values.

5. *Operation Meanings and Relationships.* The same number sentence (e.g., $12 - 4 = 8$) can be associated with different concrete or real-world situations, *and* different number sentences can be associated with the same concrete or real-world situation.

6. *Properties.* For a given set of numbers, there are relationships that are always true. These are the rules that govern arithmetic and algebra.

7. *Basic Facts and Algorithms.* Basic facts and algorithms for operations with rational numbers use notions of equivalence to transform calculations into simpler ones.

8. *Estimations.* Numerical calculations can be approximated by replacing numbers with other numbers that are close and easy to compute with mentally. Measurements can be approximated using known referents as the units in the measurement process.

9. *Patterns.* Relationships can be described and generalizations can be made for mathematical situations that have numbers or objects that repeat in predictable ways.

10. *Variables.* Mathematical situations and structures can be translated and represented abstractly using variables, expressions, and equations.

11. *Proportionality.* If two quantities vary proportionally, that relationship can be represented as a linear function.

12. *Relations and Functions.* Mathematical rules (relations) can be used to assign members of one set to members of another set. A special rule (function) assigns each member of one set to a unique member of the other set.

13. *Equations and Inequalities.* Rules of arithmetic and algebra can be used with notions of equivalence to transform equations and inequalities so that solutions can be found.

14. *Shapes and Solids.* Two- and three-dimensional objects with or without curved surfaces can be described, classified, and analyzed by their attributes.

15. *Orientations and Locations.* An object in space can be oriented in an infinite number of ways, and an object's location in space can be described quantitatively.

16. *Transformations.* An object in space can be transformed in an infinite number of ways, and those transformations can be described and analyzed mathematically.

17. *Measurements.* Some attributes of objects are measurable and can be quantified using unit amounts.

18. *Data Collection.* Some questions can be answered by collecting and analyzing data. The question to be answered determines the data that needs to be collected and how best to collect it.

19. *Data Representation.* Data can be represented visually using tables, charts, and graphs. The type of data determines the best choice of visual representation.

20. *Data Distribution.* Special numerical measures describe the center and spread of numerical data sets.

21. *Chance.* The chance of an event occurring can be described numerically by a number between zero and one inclusive and can be used to make predictions about other events. (21 Big Ideas to guide curricular and instructional decision making. Randall, Charles I. (2005). Big Ideas and Understandings as the Foundation for Elementary and Middle School Mathematics. *NCSM Journal* (Spring/Summer 2005) 9–21. Reprinted by permission of Charles I. Randall.)

Recognizing the need to promote instruction focused on such big ideas, NCTM released *Curriculum Focal Points for Prekindergarten through Grade 8 Mathematics: A Quest for Coherence* (2007). As then–NCTM President Skip Fennell stated, "This document of fewer than 50 pages presents three major topics of emphasis at each grade level, pre-K–8. The publication is intended to serve as a catalyst for important discussions and decision making on curricular frameworks at the state and local school district levels." The three major topics emphasized at each grade level are selected from the five content stan-

NCTM FOCAL POINTS

Prekindergarten	**Kindergarten**	**First Grade**	**Second Grade**
Number and Operations: Develop an understanding of whole numbers, including concepts of correspondence, counting, cardinality, and comparison.	**Number and Operations:** Represent, compare, and order whole numbers and join and separate sets.	**Number and Operations:** Develop an understanding of whole number relationships, including grouping in tens and ones; understanding of addition and subtraction and strategies for basic addition facts and related subtraction facts.	**Number and Operations:** Develop an understanding of the base-10 numeration system and place-value concepts, quick recall of addition facts and related subtraction facts and fluency with multidigit addition and subtraction.
Algebra: Recognize and duplicate simple sequential patterns.	**Algebra:** Identify, duplicate, and extend simple number patterns and sequential and growing patterns.	**Algebra:** Identify, describe, and apply number patterns and properties when developing strategies for basic facts.	**Algebra:** Use number patterns to extend knowledge of properties of numbers and operations.
Geometry: Identify shapes and describe spatial relationships.	**Geometry:** Describe shapes and space.	**Geometry:** Compose and decompose geometric shapes.	**Geometry:** Compose and decompose two-dimensional shapes.
Measurement: Identify measurable attributes and compare objects by using these attributes.	**Measurement:** Order objects by measurable attributes.	**Measurement:** Measure by laying multiple copies of a unit end to end and then counting the units by using groups of tens.	**Measurement:** Develop an understanding of linear measurement and facility in measuring lengths.
Data Analysis and Probability: Learn the foundations of data analysis by using objects' attributes that they have identified in relation to geometry and measurement.	**Data Analysis and Probability:** Sort objects and use one or more attributes to solve problems.	**Data Analysis and Probability:** Represent discrete data in picture and bar graphs.	**Data Analysis and Probability:** None

(Continued on following page.)

(NCTM Focal Points, continued)

Third Grade	Fourth Grade	Fifth Grade	Sixth Grade
Number and Operations: Develop an understanding of multiplication and division, strategies for basic multiplication facts and related division facts, and an understanding of fractions and fraction equivalence.	**Number and Operations:** Develop quick recall of multiplication facts and related division facts, fluency with whole number multiplication and division, and an understanding of decimals, including the connections between fractions and decimals.	**Number and Operations:** Develop an understanding of and fluency with division of whole numbers with addition and subtraction of fractions and decimals.	**Number and Operations:** Develop an understanding of and fluency with multiplication and division of fractions and decimals, and connect ratio and rate to multiplication and division.
Algebra: Create and analyze of patterns and relationships involving multiplication and division and develop understanding of functional relationships by describing relationships in context.	**Algebra:** Identify, describe, and extend numeric patterns involving all operations and nonnumeric growing or repeating patterns.	**Algebra:** Use patterns, models, and relationships as contexts for writing and solving simple equations and inequalities.	**Algebra:** Write, interpret, and use mathematical expressions and equations.
Geometry: Describe and analyze properties of two-dimensional shapes.	**Geometry:** Extend understanding of properties of two-dimensional shapes in the context of finding the areas of polygons and use transformations to design and analyze simple tilings and tessellations.	**Geometry:** Describe three-dimensional shapes and analyze their properties, including volume and surface area.	**Geometry:** Find areas or volumes from lengths or find lengths from volumes or areas and lengths.
Measurement: Develop facility in measuring with fractional parts of linear units, analyze attributes and properties of two-dimensional objects, form an understanding of perimeter as a measurable attribute.	**Measurement:** Develop an understanding of area and determine the areas of two-dimensional shapes.	**Measurement:** Connect work with solids and volume to earlier work with capacity and weight or mass.	**Measurement:** Same as Geometry
Data Analysis and Probability: Construct and analyze frequency tables, bar graphs, picture graphs, and line plots and use them to solve problems.	**Data Analysis and Probability:** Solve problems by making frequency tables, bar graphs, picture graphs, line plots, and stem-and-leaf plots.	**Data Analysis and Probability:** Construct and analyze double-bar and line graphs and use ordered pairs on coordinate grids.	**Data Analysis and Probability:** None

dards of *Principles and Standards* (NCTM 2000) mentioned earlier. Although not touted as a national curriculum, it immediately instigated work on major curriculum framework revisions all over the country, and we predict that its content will become the backbone of most state curricula. A national curriculum? Almost.

In the content section of each chapter in this book, we share a comprehensive cross-grade analysis of the expectations communicated in the focal points related to the mathematical topic of the chapter. This enables you to see what big mathematical ideas are appropriate for deep study at each grade level and how those ideas progress across the grades. As an introduction to that analysis, the Focal Points table lists the three major topics of emphasis at each grade, along with the other connections to the focal points, all organized according to the five content standards of *Principles and Standards* (NCTM 2000). Notice that the list of big ideas presented previously is inherent in this focal points summary.

CONCLUSION

As you examine the Focal Points table, we hope you can make connections vertically and horizontally. This means that you can see the connections across strands or topics, as well as the connections within a topic across the grades. As you read the content sections within this book, you might find it helpful to refer back to this figure to remind yourself of the larger curricular picture.

In a balanced mathematics classroom, emphasis is placed on the learning of mathematical content and process, on knowing mathematics, and on doing mathematics. Indeed, the doing promotes the knowing. It is interesting that at the top of each grade-level expectation associated with the focal points is this statement: "It is essential that these focal points be addressed in contexts that promote problem solving, reasoning, communication, making connections, and designing and analyzing representations." Therefore, if we ask the question "Does the learning of mathematics mean learning to engage in mathematical processes or acquiring mathematical knowledge?" we would answer, "Both."

▶ Interview Video with an Eye on Content

You are going to watch five video interviews. Determine which big ideas and which Focal Points are the focus of the tasks presented to the children.

▶ Interview a Child

1. Find a particular topic in your state's mathematics curriculum that seems to be represented at multiple grade levels in varying degrees of complexity. For example, you could look at the topic of two-dimensional shapes and find out what expectations are listed at each grade level for shapes. Then design some questions or tasks associated with each grade level's expectations. These questions and tasks should invite a child to engage in the five process standards.

2. Present these tasks and questions to a third grader. Record the responses, and then determine at what grade level the child seems to be functioning relative to your topic.

▶ Classroom Video with an Eye on Pedagogy

Watch a classroom episode. Your focus should be on looking for ways in which the teacher invites the children to engage in all five process standards.

1. What process standard or standards does this scenario exemplify? Why?

    _____

    _____

    _____

    _____

2. List all five process standards, and give one way in which the teacher invited the children to engage in each standard.

    _____

    _____

    _____

    _____

    _____

    _____

    _____

    _____

▶ Classroom Application

Observe any mathematics lesson. Observe which process standards are being emphasized. List them, and describe how the teacher specifically invited the children to engage in those processes.

▶ Resources

NCTM site for curriculum and professional standards, including process standards, http://standards.nctm.org

Curriculum Focal Points for Mathematics in Prekindergarten through Grade 8, http://www.nctmmedia.org/cfp/focal_points_by_grade.pdf

The Foundation of All Math Learning: Representations of Early Number Concepts

PEDAGOGICAL CONTENT UNDERSTANDINGS

Pedagogy *Mathematical Tools: Concrete and Abstract Representations*

- What Are Tools?
- Constructing Meaning for Tools
- Making Connections between the Concrete and the Abstract
- Misconceptions, Pitfalls, and Difficulties Associated with Tool Use

Content *Early Number Concepts*

- Number Sense
- Developmental Phases for Numbers
- Emergent Phase
- Matching Phase
- Quantifying Phase
- Assessments

The tools we use influence the way we think about the activity. . . . When students use old, familiar tools to solve new problems, the tools help students connect the new activity with what they have done before. Students who use one set of tools may develop somewhat different understandings than students who use another set of tools.

Hiebert et al., Making Sense, 1997

CONVERSATION IN MATHEMATICS

Students in a first-grade classroom are solving the following problem using a variety of tools. Each table has a basket with two-sided counters, a number line, a 100 chart, cubes, and a blank 10 frame.

> *There are 50 students in the room. Imagine that 4 of them leave. How many students are left in the room?*

One student was observed using cubes. He was putting them into groups of five. Thinking that this was an efficient counting strategy, the teacher asked him to explain his thinking:

Teacher: Talk to me about what you are doing.

Student: I saw the 5 in 50, and it made me think about putting them into groups of five: (Begins counting.) 1 . . . 2 . . . 3 . . .

Teacher: You put them into groups of five, so let's count by fives: 5 . . . 10 . . .

Student: 15, 20, 25, 30, 35, 40, 45, 50. (Takes 4 away, recounts, and gets 46 as an answer.)

Wanting to see whether he was able to use another tool to solve the problem, the teacher asked him to use a 100 chart.

Student: (Puts his finger on 50.) I take away (counts 4 squares), and it is 47.

Teacher: What answer do you think you will get if you used a different tool, like the number line?

Student: Maybe 48!

The classroom teacher decided to bring this up to the class when summarizing the lesson. She asked the children what they thought about getting two different answers if they used two different tools. There was no clear response, but most seemed OK with this notion. She decided to let them think about it while creating some good experiences for them to address this issue.

The preceding conversation introduces you to an important pedagogical issue, as well as an important mathematical content area. First, you should notice that the children were using two-sided counters, a number line, a 100 chart, and 10 frames. These are some important tools used to help children think mathematically. In the pedagogical section of this chapter, we discuss how you can use tools to enhance your mathematics instruction.

You should also notice in the preceding conversation that the child was struggling with counting back. Counting back is an important component of early number conceptualization. In the content section of this chapter, we discuss how children develop a sense for numbers and their meanings.

When designing a lesson, the set of tools needed to carry out that lesson is one of the teacher's most important considerations. The kinds and amounts of concrete experiences and support needed for students to understand and internalize a concept or big idea must be carefully planned. Perhaps the goal of the lesson is to work on a more abstract level. The tools are mostly pencil, paper, and the conversations students have with one another. However, if the lesson is too abstract, students may be quickly lost and thus may disengage. Oftentimes, teachers work at the extremes, either providing *only* concrete experiences or working *only* at the abstract level, and do not allow students make connections between these extremes. So how does the teacher know how or when to move from the concrete to the abstract? This chapter discusses not only the kinds of tools found in a mathematics classroom and the difficulties associated with them but also how to make those connections between concrete and abstract representations.

This chapter also looks deeply into the developmental phases children pass through when learning about numbers in the earliest grades. It clearly shows how critical tools are in developing number sense and in making generalizations for even the most basic facts. By the end of this chapter, you should know how to identify which phase a child is working in and how to nudge that child to the next level.

Mathematical Tools: Concrete and Abstract Representations   PEDAGOGY

Learning Theory

It is a bit like the age-old question "which comes first, the chicken or the egg?" There is debate as to whether concrete or abstract thinking precedes the other. Constance Kamii, Lynn Kirkland, and Barbara Lewis (2001) found that math instruction progresses from concrete, to semiconcrete, to abstract symbols. Watching children learn new concepts confirms this to be true. However, the materials do not necessarily convey the intended mathematical meaning to children. The children must impose relationships upon the materials to give them meaning. Therefore, children must have some level of abstract thought before using concrete materials. Once the materials carry some type of meaning, they can help children develop a more abstract idea. This might be more clearly illustrated in figure 2.1.

Take base 10 blocks, for example. If a child is just learning how to count, she probably uses this tool to develop counting with one-to-one correspondence. As the child matures and develops more abstract ideas, she will be able to use this tool for more sophisticated counting using tens and ones. At this point, this

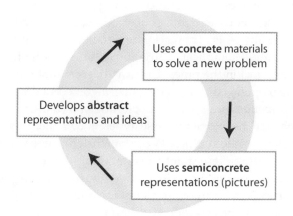

Figure 2.1. The cycle of moving from concrete to abstract representations and ideas.

tool can help support this child's understanding of addition with regrouping.
Later, when the child understands parts of a whole, base 10 blocks can be
supportive in learning tenths and hundredths. "Concreteness is now seen as
necessary and unavoidable only as a stepping stone for developing abstract
thinking—as a means, not as an end in itself" (Vygotsky 1978, 89).

Manipulative tools are important for students of *all* ages and in all mathematical strands. They help students construct mathematical concepts and promote meaningful learning. They are also documented to increase retention and
problem-solving abilities (Clements and McMillen 1996). Studies have also
shown that students who use these tools to learn abstract math concepts out-
achieve students who do not (Sowell 1989; Suydam 1984).

Application to the Learning and Teaching of Mathematics

What Are Tools?

One dictionary's definition for *tool* is "something used in the performance of an
operation; an instrument" (*American Heritage College Dictionary,* 4th ed. Reprinted
by permission of Houghton Mifflin Company.). This is also true in mathematics. You may have more commonly heard tools referred to as *manipulatives*. The
intent of these physical objects is to demonstrate mathematical ideas and construct mathematical understanding. They give children valuable and engaging
firsthand experience with mathematics and give them a way to make abstract
ideas concrete (Burns and Sibley 2000). Tools, however, are more than just
physical materials. According to Hiebert and colleagues (1997), they also
include oral language, written symbols, and skills that students have already
acquired. This chapter focuses on the physical materials; the rest is covered
elsewhere in this book.

Types of Tools

"Basically, any material can be used as a tool—providing that children under-
stand its use and that the tool enables them to solve problems" (Carpenter et al
1999, 92). Probably the most common tools found in a classroom are cubes.
There are two types of interlocking cubes: ones that only interlock at the ends
(Unifix) and ones the can connect from each of the six faces (e.g., Multilink,
Snapcubes, and Popcubes). Each of these two types serves a different purpose.
Many primary teachers prefer Unifix cubes because they tend to be easiest for
small hands to put together. They also are not as distracting for children who
would otherwise build complicated structures during exploratory lessons with
the cubes that interlock on all sides. Unifix cubes tend to be the cube of choice
when children are engaged in activities that involve building tens. Multilink,
Snapcubes, or Popcubes are ideal for explorations that involve creating three-
dimensional objects. Each one of these types is 3/4 inch. Every elementary
classroom should have both types. When purchasing cubes, it is important to
test the ease of putting them together and taking them apart, because some
brands are easier to handle than others. Even upper-elementary students shy
away from using cubes that are hard to put together.

Other essential materials include 100 charts, number lines (−10 thru 110), 10
frames, base 10 blocks (including centimeter cubes), 1-inch color tiles, pattern

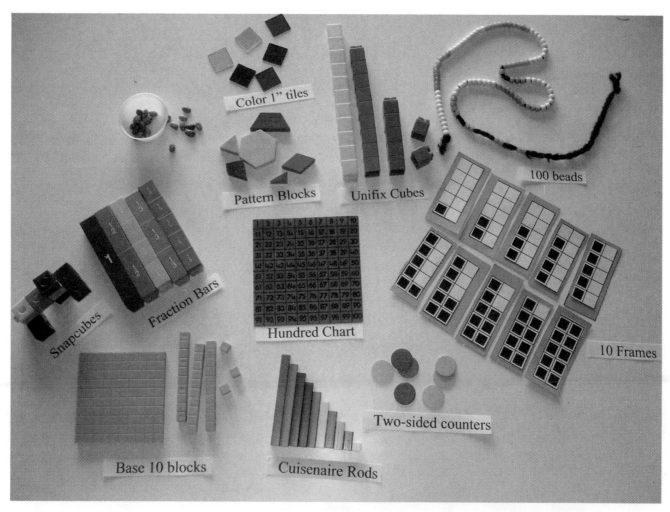

Some common tools used in math lessons, grades K–6.

blocks, geoboards, pan balances, two-sided counters, measurement materials (such as rulers, tape measures, protractors, and a variety of cups), dice (dotted and numbered), geared clocks, Cuisenaire rods, fraction towers, fraction circles, tangrams, calculators, cards, and lots of objects to count in the youngest grades. The use of many of these materials is described in the content sections of this book.

Introducing and Handling Tools

All students are capable of using tools, and tools should be a part of their math experiences—even throughout high school. Commonly, upper-grade teachers do not like to use tools because they feel such use causes behavior problems or that students think they are babyish. In schools where students have been consistently using tools in class, they come to expect them in subsequent years. Children do not complain about tools because they truly know how to use them as problem-solving devices.

If children have not been exposed to tools for a while or the teacher is introducing a new tool, it is important that the children have enough time to explore the materials before the lesson. This gives them a chance to satisfy their curiosity before the lesson begins. Sometimes this is not enough time, and it may be necessary to carve out some time each day for a while to let the children explore the materials.

Children do need structure as to how to handle tools. This includes knowing where to find them, how to pass them out, and how to collect them in ways that are efficient and not distracting to the lesson or the rest of the class. Time spent upfront on minilessons teaching the children the routine of handling the materials goes a long way the rest of the year. In classrooms where structure is clear and children (including kindergarteners) know where and how to get the tools, there is the maximum amount of learning time. As much as 10 minutes can be wasted merely passing out materials when there is no structure in place.

The most effective classrooms have tools prepared and stored in tubs or bags for the number of small groups or partnerships in the classroom. Some have enough tubs to permanently store them in groups, and others use the same tubs for all materials, rotating them depending on the lesson. Some primary teachers have tubs or baskets prepared with enough of each material for use during the exploration activity yet allow children to use other tools if necessary. Others have a tub with one type of tool on each table and students are allowed to go to the table of their preference to solve the problem. If students are encouraged to solve the problem with more than one tool, they would have

Storage of tools easily accessed by students.

to move to different tables. This structure depends on what the teacher is comfortable with and what seems to work with the particular students at that time. Having the materials passed out ahead of time prevents large interruptions in the middle of the lesson. If materials are in closed bags or containers, students are not as tempted to play with them as they would be if the materials were just in a pile in front of them. Gallon-size Ziploc bags also work nicely and can hold a significant amount of base 10 blocks, pattern blocks, color tiles, and so on, for each group.

Teachers use various ways to store and display their math materials for easy accessibility for their students.

Group buckets with assortment of tools to use while exploring.

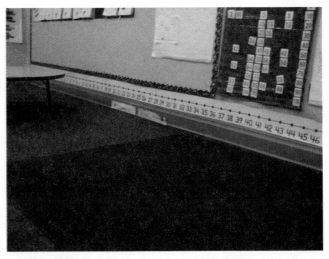

Number line down on the ground for easy access for young children.

Constructing Meaning for Tools

We cannot assume that students come to us knowing how to use any tools. The use of most tools seems obvious to us, as adults, but we already have an understanding of how numbers behave. Children, however, need lots of experiences with tools to develop meaning for them and so that they can subsequently use the tools to solve problems. Even the most basic tool, fingers, must be discovered. It is common to see first-grade children, when adding 2 + 4, count each number out on each of their hands. Teachers think that students should know how to show two and four fingers on their hands without counting, but that comes with lots of experiences. Once the numbers become larger, fingers become harder to use and other tools become more useful (Carpenter 1999)—but only if children have built meaning for them by constructing relationships.

The best way to learn about any new tool is to use it for a real purpose (Burns 2000). Catherine Twomey Fosnot and Maarten Dolk (2001a–c) suggests that, through problematic experiences, tools need to be constructed before they are useful to students in solving other problems. For example, a number line can be complex. Opportunities that allow students to build the number line help create meaning to it and thus help them to use it to solve future problems. A simplistic version might include placing the name cards of each of the students in the class horizontally across the whiteboard. Students would then number themselves in the order that they appear on the board. Lines could be drawn to connect each of the numbers. When the names are eventually removed, the number line is left.

Building 100 charts should be by cutting a number line into tens and taping these groups under one another. It is surprising to hear students' amazement when they realize that the number line and the 100 chart are related. The number line is essential in exploring patterns when skip counting and learning to add and subtract 10 and multiples of 10, 9, and 11.

Tally marks are another tool that needs to be constructed. Students often make five vertical lines and then use the diagonal line to group them. To teach students about tally marks, give small groups of students lots of popsicle sticks to count. The students will place a long row of sticks as they attempt to count them but will usually lose count. After letting them struggle a bit, suggest that every fifth stick be placed across the other four. This helps the students visually by creating groups of five. Children readily agree that this representation is helpful in not losing track. After this experience, most students will have internalized tally marks and will not confuse the notation. This, however, may not be helpful for students who cannot yet count by fives and thus would not use the notation as a counting strategy.

The base 10 blocks are tools that require lots of experiences. Many teachers argue about the appropriate time to introduce these blocks. Using this tool requires students to have some sense of "10-ness." The 10 stick has little lines that suggest it is composed of 10 ones "glued together," as children say. Many children learn to count them by tens without truly understanding that they are made up of 10 ones. This is evident when a student has 3 tens and 2 ones and, when asked how many there are, responds, "10, 20, 30, 40, 50."

Kathy Richardson argues that, in first and second grades, students need their initial experiences building these tens with Unifix cubes. The process of physically constructing helps reinforce the idea of tens. In classes that allow students to have access to many tools (that have all been introduced and explored to some extent), we notice that struggling students tend to gravitate to the cubes as they inherently need to construct. As they begin to internalize tens and their need to construct lessens, they start selecting beans and cups (each small cup can hold a maximum of 10 beans) and then graduate to the base 10 blocks. Allowing children to go through these stages on their own ensures that they are successful in using the tools. If we push too quickly, many students will be using tools that they are not developmentally ready for and thus will be unable to use the tools to solve problems.

Free Choice or Teacher-Initiated Use of Tools?

Marilyn Burns and Robyn Sibley (2000) argues that a variety of materials should be available for students at all times. Having access to a variety of materials helps students learn when a material is and is not appropriate for a specific problem. When children are allowed to choose their materials, they tend to choose what is developmentally appropriate to them and to move to more abstract tools when they are ready.

However, is it ever appropriate to direct students to use a specific tool? Sometimes students need to be "forced" to explore a tool that is out of their comfort zone. Not all students like to relinquish their tool of choice. At times, classroom discussion needs to occur regarding the difficulties children are having using a tool, like the number line. When a tool has been explored as a class, it can be added to the repertoire of tools that the class uses during problem solving, although it does not mean that students have mastered its use.

Sometimes it is important to establish some common language for a specific tool. Students may not come to class with lots of experiences with certain materials. Base 10 blocks are a good example. What may be seen when students who have little or no experience with base 10 blocks are asked to show the number 24 with their blocks?

One student in the class in which the photo was taken did show the quantity of 24 correctly. There was a discussion as to which way showed *quantity*. The class came to a consensus that two 10 sticks and four small cubes actually showed 24. The teacher stated that from now on, when asked to show a number, that is how they are to represent it. The students no longer tried to "draw" the number with their blocks.

The typical response when asked to build the number 24 with base ten blocks.

Choice of Tools

Some tools lend themselves to counting strategies (i.e., 100 chart and number line), and others help reinforce the base 10 system (base 10 blocks and 10 frames). As teachers, we need to know which strategies are more likely to be developed with a specific tool. Many students have difficulty constructing strategies that are alternatives to the one they initially developed (Hiebert et al. 1997). Continuously encouraging students to solve problems with different tools helps them make connections among the tools. They can also begin to see which tool is more efficient in solving a problem. For example, using interlocking cubes may not be efficient in solving a problem like 43 + 68. Children tend to look for tools that prove more useful as problems become more difficult. When students are sharing their strategies, the efficiency of tools can be compared. Some students may be ready to move on to more efficient tools, but others may need more time with the basic ones.

Teachers tend to be eager to wean their students from tools, wanting them to quickly work in the abstract (sometimes by the second day of a series of related lessons). As students gain plenty of experiences problem solving with tools and creating algorithms, they begin to wean *themselves* from the materials. They find it more cumbersome to use the materials when they have generalized strategies and can work with only the numbers either on paper or mentally. As problems become more difficult or too abstract, students tend to revert to tools to help them make sense of the new problem types (Carpenter et al. 1999). Over time, students should experience a spiral from concrete models, to abstract thinking, and back to concrete models as the types of problems become more difficult. When looking through a K–6 perspective, students in all classes should be working with tools but for different purposes. Pattern blocks, for example, might be used in kindergarten and first grade to create patterns, sort, and explore geometry. In fifth and sixth grades, they might be used in exploring division of fractions. Base 10 blocks can help young children understand about regrouping in addition and subtraction, and older children may use them to regroup decimals.

One example of this spiral of working between the concrete and the abstract in exploring addition and subtraction is illustrated in figure 2.2. In this illustration, kindergartners are building numbers but later develop knowledge of their combinations and are able to add and subtract these numbers in their heads without building. When the addition and subtraction problems are using numbers that they cannot solve mentally, they revert to modeling. This spiral keeps growing as the numerical complexity increases.

Special Needs Support

Students with special needs progress through this spiral the same as general education students. In fact, it can be argued that they need it more. Many students with learning problems have trouble thinking abstractly and need lots of concrete experiences before being able to make generalizations and connections.

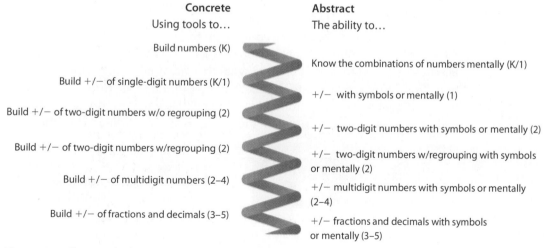

Figure 2.2. The spiral of moving between concrete and abstract representations as numerical complexity increases in addition and subtraction throughout the grades.

Making Connections between the Concrete and the Abstract

Something that takes lots of skill and practice is guiding students to make connections between the concrete and the abstract. Once, during a lesson study, students in a fifth-grade class were solving a problem involving multiplication of fractions using pictures, numbers, and words. First, they were instructed to solve the problem by drawing pictures or using tiles. Then they were instructed to solve it using numbers (an algorithm). When we watched closely, we discovered that the students were solving the problem differently with the algorithm than when they built their models or drew their pictures. The different solving methods are shown in figure 2.3.

These students were not deriving or connecting their algorithm with the tools that they used or models that they had made. They had learned the algorithm on the side, not through their representations. If they had learned from their tools or models, their numeric representation would have been $2/3 \div 2 = 1/3$. Discussions about these two algorithms help students make the connections between multiplication and division of inverse fractions.

Children need help representing on paper what they are doing with materials. It might seem that they should be able to record their work, but doing so takes practice. When first asked to make a picture or record of their construction, children tend to make works of art. They draw every line on the base 10 block or try to make three-dimensional-looking pictures. They need to learn that drawing what they built and art are two different things. The younger they start, the easier it will be for the children to represent their work. This needs to begin in kindergarten. At first, it may be frustrating that young children are not drawing what they did, but through lots of practices and specific feedback, their drawings will begin to look like their work. Such feedback might include sharing different students' drawings and comparing them to the actual model. Other students can comment on whether they understand what was drawn or not. Asking the students to explain how their picture shows their steps helps them see whether they have put down enough information. Also, it is important to tell the children what you understand by looking at their illustrations.

Initially, students need practice just building and recording, or drawing, one number. This may take a couple of days. At first, they may make huge and elaborate drawings. It takes a few times for their pictures to become more efficient. When students share their work, they discuss which ways are most efficient and why. Then, children need to begin to try to draw what they do with the tools in an addition or subtraction problem. This also takes some practice. Finally, they need to begin to record what they are doing using symbolic notation. To do this, they need to do one action with the tools, record with a picture, and then record with numbers. They then need to keep doing one action and recording. This ensures that the students are recording what they are

$$\frac{1}{2} \times \frac{2}{3}$$

Picture:
The student thinks, "half of two-thirds" and draws a picture to match.

Numbers: $\quad \dfrac{2}{3} \times \dfrac{1}{2} = \dfrac{2}{6} \div \dfrac{2}{2} = \dfrac{1}{3}$

Figure 2.3. How a pictorial representation is disconnected from the traditional algorithm.

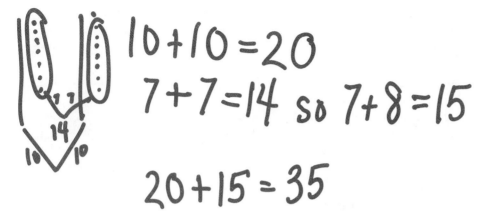

$$17 + 18$$

$$10 + 10 = 20$$
$$7 + 7 = 14 \text{ so } 7 + 8 = 15$$
$$20 + 15 = 35$$

Figure 2.4. Second grade recording of addition with base 10 blocks.

building. An example of this is shown in figure 2.4. See the website for more examples.

Designing Effective Recording Sheets

Students from about second grade and up can usually record their work on blank sheets of paper after some practice. The younger students, however, tend to need more structure when it comes to recording what they are doing with their tools. In kindergarten and first-grade classes, teachers may spend a lot of time discussing and designing recording sheets that help students stay focused on the task at hand, organize their work, and encourage the use of multiple tools.

Oftentimes, the intended mathematics did not come out at the end of the lesson because of ineffective recording sheets. Young students may have difficulty drawing; therefore, the entire math time could be spent in frustration trying to draw the cubes. Two different recording sheets intended for the same lesson are shown. On the first sheet (figure 2.5), students were to draw the equations they built with cubes of two different colors. The second one (figure 2.6) was designed after the first one was used in a lesson. It was noted that because of the students' inability to draw well, it was difficult for them to see the patterns of doubles and doubles plus one.

This second recording sheet was a better scaffold for young students who are just learning how to record their work. The mathematics of doubles and doubles plus one was more obvious, and a stronger discussion about it took place during the lesson's summary. See the website for more information.

Figure 2.7 is an example of a recording sheet designed to record strategies using multiple tools. The teachers who designed this recording sheet found that by providing different areas to record different tools, students were more likely to use more than one tool during the explore time. They wanted a way for students to show what they did with the 100 chart because so many were using it but having difficulty explaining what they did to find their answer. By using this recording sheet, many students were more likely to try a tool they

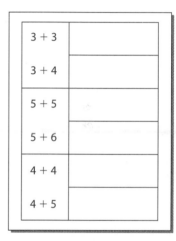

Figure 2.5. Recording sheet for doubles plus one with space to draw what students built with their cubes or tiles. This may not be supportive for first graders who cannot draw well.

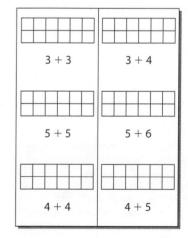

Figure 2.6. More supportive recording sheet for doubles plus one with individual space students can color. This allows them to clearly see relationships.

Figure 2.7. In response to the following problem: My book has 48 pages. My partner's book has 78 pages. How many more pages does my partner's book have than mine?

did not normally use. Many young children do not like to leave blank areas on their papers.

By using a recording sheet that allows for multiple tools, it is easier to see which tool children have command of and which tools are still developing. In figure 2.7, this partnership seems to have a good grasp of tens and ones but did not show clearly how they used the 100 chart. The teacher would have to question the students for more information. This teacher probably would also make sure that this pair would pay attention, during the summary, to other partnerships that used effective recording strategies for their use of the 100 chart.

The long-term goal is for students to record their own math thinking on their own paper, so teachers have to be conscious of how much scaffolding is too much. Perhaps some students need a more structured sheet for a longer period. Depending on the activity, older students may need a structured recording sheet as well. Sometimes a little structure keeps the students focused on the lesson and on the math at hand.

Comprehension Check

■ What are some advantages of letting students choose their own tool to solve a problem? When might you want to direct the tool the students use?

■ What are the steps in moving your students from directly modeling a problem with tools to solving it abstractly with an algorithm?

Misconceptions, Pitfalls, and Difficulties Associated with Tool Use

As pointed out in the initial conversation, young children are content with the notion that they could arrive at a different answer by using different tools to solve a problem. It takes lots of experiences with multiple tools for children to believe that there are many ways to get to one answer. These experiences and follow-up class discussions need to be carefully orchestrated by the teacher.

As alluded to earlier, base 10 blocks can be problematic. Through careful questioning, teachers can assess whether or not students have internalized unitizing, or that 10 of one object makes a new group. Children need lots of opportunities building tens with Unifix cubes before moving on to base 10 blocks. This is the one area in which most teachers are faked out by the students. I think that we want to believe that our students can count by tens, so when we see them counting the rods of the base 10 blocks, we think that they understand what they are counting. A simple way to test children's understanding is to give them five rods (tens) and three small cubes and watch them count. Figure 2.8 shows how many students count.

If they count 53, they probably have developed, or are close to developing, unitizing and probably understand that what they are counting is how many are in each group. They are not just putting labels on them.

Another tool that causes problems is the number line. Ask any first-grade teacher: counting on or back on a number line is no easy task. Why, when counting up 3 from 5, do students land on 7? By counting the 5, they do not understanding what they are counting. The number line seems concrete enough, but it is still abstract. Creating real contexts for the number line helps students realize that they are counting three additional objects. Perhaps the class acts out a problem on a life-size number line. Then on individual number lines they use small centimeter cubes to represent the students. After enough opportunities, they will no longer need the cubes to represent the real-life objects and they will know to start counting on the next number (or previous number if subtracting).

All students should be exposed to a number line beginning with about -10 to numbers past 100. One day, in first grade, the son of one of the authors asked whether infinity goes on forever. He had heard about infinity from friends at school. As his thought was being affirmed, he quickly interjected, "except when you count backwards." He believed that numbers began at zero and only traveled in one direction. It was realized that at home the rulers and number lines all began with zero. Usually questions or discussions about negative numbers do not surface until about third grade, but if posted in the classroom, students recognize that they are there. If asked, many will say -2 is "minus 2." Suppose

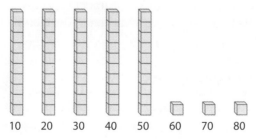

Figure 2.8. How children might count using base 10 blocks before they have internalized unitizing.

students are miswriting their fact families in first grade by stating $3 - 5 = 2$. If there are no negative numbers in the classroom, when the class tries to prove this calculation on a number line, they end up thinking the answer is zero.

Although the 100 chart is closely related to the number line, students have trouble knowing what to do when they reach the end of the row. Some children need more work than others connecting the number line to the 100 chart. It would seem that children should just "get it" that adding 10 is simply going to the number beneath. However, we see students continuing to count when we ask, "What is 25 and 10?" No matter how many times we may *tell* them, they just count. They need to discover through pattern exercises that each time the answer is under the number with which they started.

What If I Do Not Have Enough Materials?

More often than not, a new teacher walks into a classroom barren of materials. If materials are scarce at the school site, teachers should try to pool their resources to create class sets that they can share. Most likely, different grades need certain materials, such as three-dimensional blocks, at different times in the year. Most curriculum kits tend to come with only one set of these blocks, making it difficult to provide the correct amount of exploratory experiences needed to internalize features of three-dimensional figures. If every teacher puts a set into a pool, there should be enough for a couple of classroom sets of one per partnership.

Many essential materials have been around for many adoptions. More than likely, if teachers search storage closets around the school or the classrooms of veteran teachers, valuable materials will be found. For example, Cuisenaire rods may have been used in old adoptions and then forgotten about by many. How many schools have more Multilink cubes than they know what to do with? As teachers learn about how to incorporate materials more effectively into their math lessons, they will want to rediscover these "old" tools.

Comprehension Check

Solve $35 + 28$ using at least three different tools. Record in pictures, numbers, and words (written explanation) how you solved the problem so that it would be easy for another student to replicate it. Did you use the same or different solving strategies with each of your tools? If you used different strategies, why were they different? Which one was easiest to record? Why?

CONTENT   *Early Number Concepts*

We now transition from a pedagogical discussion about tools to a discussion about a mathematical content area, early number concepts. As we do, notice the important role tools play in enabling children to develop these concepts.

Big Ideas and Focal Points

Even when children are just starting to learn about numbers, we want them to begin to understand some big ideas about number concepts. We do not want them to merely learn to rote count but, rather, want them to understand what counting means. NCTM's *Principles and Standards for School Mathematics* (2000, p. 32) state that it is expected that all students to "understand numbers, relationships among numbers and number systems." This understanding begins in kindergarten and continues throughout the grades as children learn about different sets, or types, of numbers. The following examples of some big ideas about early number concepts should be kept in mind when designing children's first experiences:

- Counting tells how many items there are altogether. When counting, the last number tells the total number of items; it is a cumulative count (Charles 2005, 12).

- There is a number word and a matching symbol that tell exactly how many items are in a group (Charles 2005, 12).

- The distance between any two consecutive counting numbers on a given number line is the same. Numbers can also be used to tell the position of objects in a sequence (e.g., third) (Charles 2005, 12).

- The numbers are related to each other through a variety of number relationships (Van de Walle 2004, 115).

The Focal Points table outlines the NCTM focal points (2006) that address early number concepts from prekindergarten through first grade. Although this text primarily addresses kindergarten through sixth grade, it is important to note the prekindergarten standards and expectations, because many children

NCTM FOCAL POINTS

Prekindergarten	Kindergarten	First Grade
Develop an understanding of the meanings for whole numbers	Use numbers, including written numerals, to represent quantities and to solve quantitative problems, such as counting objects in a set or creating a set with a given number of objects	Relate counting with addition and subtraction
Recognize the quantity of objects in small groups with and without counting		Counts on
		Compare and order whole numbers (at least to 100)
Understand that number words refer to quantity	Compare and order sets or numerals by using both cardinal and ordinal meanings	Develop an understanding of and solve problems involving the relative sizes of these numbers
Use one-to-one correspondence to solve problems by matching sets and comparing number amounts and to count objects to 10 and beyond		Understand the sequential order of the counting numbers and their relative magnitudes
Understand that the last word students state in counting tells "how many" (cardinality)		Represent numbers on a number line
Count to determine number amounts and compare quantities (using language such as "more than" and "less than")		Recognize numbers 11–19 as one group of 10 and particular numbers of ones (10 and some more)
Order sets by the number of objects in them		

enter kindergarten without the advantage of having attended prekindergarten. Many may also come from disadvantaged backgrounds, in which case they may not come to school as ready as their peers. In these situations, it is important for the kindergarten teacher to begin with the most emergent skills to provide the most solid foundation as possible. Ignoring, or being unfamiliar, with the emerging skills can create holes in student learning in the first year of school.

Number Sense

In 1989, Hilde Howden eloquently defined number sense as "good intuition about numbers and their relationships. It develops gradually as a result of exploring numbers, visualizing them on a variety of contexts and relating them in ways that are not limited by traditional algorithms" (p. 11).

Developing strong number sense requires lots of exploration and activities that allow students to make connections. This exploration starts when children enter school and needs to continue throughout their school experience. Children who are identified by their teachers as having weak number sense have not had enough opportunities to explore and play with numbers and quantities.

It is typical that as children reach the upper grades they are no longer made to think about the relationships of numbers in their new operational contexts (multiplication and division). The consequence is that children make unreasonable errors that are not noticed because of the lack of understanding of what is happening to the numbers. Many of these students also do not develop fractional number sense; it also tends to be taught void of context.

Although number sense grows and develops throughout all of mathematics, this chapter focuses on those initial experiences that are so critical to the foundational development of strong number sense.

Developmental Phases for Numbers

Western Australia's Department of Education and Training (Willis et al 2006) has summarized six developmental phases of elementary school students for numbers and operations. Those phases are outlined in figure 2.9. The original descriptors were compiled by Western Australia's Department of Education and Training and formed a comprehensive list. We have taken just the main points and have recategorized each phase to include counting, number rela-

Phase	Description	Typical Grade in which Instruction Is Found in U.S. Curriculum
Emergent	Emerging skills with numeracy and realizing that numbers signify quantity	Prekindergarten and kindergarten
Matching	One-to-one correspondence for sharing and counting	Prekindergarten and kindergarten
Quantifying	Using part-part-whole relations for numerical quantities	Kindergarten and first grade
Partitioning	Using additive thinking or thinking in tens and ones	Late first and second grades
Factoring	Thinking additively and multiplicatively about quantities	Late second and third grades
Operating	Thinking of multiplication and division in terms of operators with whole, fractional, and decimal numbers	Fourth, fifth, and sixth grades

Figure 2.9. Summary of developmental phases for numbers and operations.

tionships, and numbers as tens and ones, integrating Kathy Richardson's developing number concepts with these existing phases and relating them to U.S. curriculum. We talk about the first three phases in this and the following chapter. Chapters 4 and 5 cover concepts related to the partitioning phase, Chapters 6 and 7 cover concepts related to the factoring phase, and Chapters 11 and 12 cover concepts related to the operating phase. A complete table with indicators for each phase as we have modified it can be found in Appendix A; you can use this table to easily see how each phase builds on the next.

These phases and their indicators match fairly well with the focal points. It is important to familiarize ourselves intimately with these indicators so that we are meeting the instructional needs of our students. So, even though as a class we are working on using part–part–whole relationships, there may be children who have not mastered one-to-one correspondence. Ignoring that need for one-to-one correspondence does those children a great injustice, because relationships may never truly make sense. In other words, in the long run, it is best to stick to where the children are at and work through the developmental phases rather than skipping steps.

So, if you are a second-grade teacher, how do you know what skills your students have or are lacking and whether or not they are ready to tackle the work expected in second grade? This calls for the following:

- Knowledge of the standards and developmental stages for all previous grades
- Lots of informal observations during the first weeks of school
- Assessment when a problem is suspected or more information is needed

We next outline some of these phases of number with more detail to give a precise understanding of what the youngest learners need to know, particularly in relation to early number concepts. We also give suggestions for assessments to identify struggling areas and activities to help strengthen those areas.

Emergent Phase

Children are normally functioning in the emergent phase while in prekindergarten or kindergarten, depending on their experiences before entering school. Indicators of what children will be doing at the end of the emergent phase are discussed in the next section. When these indicators are in place, children are beginning to move on to the subsequent phase.

Numbers Signifying Quantity

Until this phase, children have been labeling their world and perhaps adding adjectives for how things appear (e.g., shiny, blue, hot). Now there are new adjectives that describe how many. This understanding is a child's first leap into the world of mathematics.

Rote Counting

During this time, children learn how to rote count 1–10, and maybe even higher. Rote counting does not indicate an understanding of numbers or that they know, for example, that 3 stands for three objects. However, practice with rote counting is essential so that the child can add the correct labels to those connections as they are made.

Identifying by Sight One to Five Objects

Through counting, small children naturally are able to identify by sight one to three objects. As they gain more experience with building and counting quantities, they will be able to identify by sight larger quantities, especially in patterns such as those found on dice. Children in this stage need to be building quantities on the 5 frame to learn to instantly recognize quantities on this tool. Doing so supports number recognition in later phases. We have found it to be a red flag for possible problems when children nearing the end of kindergarten cannot recognize 4 without counting.

Differentiating Written Numerals from Letters

During this phase, children are recognizing written numerals as different from the letters in the alphabet and are beginning to write them. As with letters, many students struggle for some time with number reversals and invented ways to write numbers. These typically straighten themselves out over time. Children should have a variety of experiences when learning to write numbers (as well as letters) such as tracing, drawing in sand, outlining sandpaper letters, using fat markers or sidewalk chalk, easel painting, using stencils, using body movements, tracing with their finger on different parts of their body (such as the palm of their hand or thigh), and having others write on their backs to guess what was written.

More, Less, or Same

Emergent mathematicians are able to tell whether a quantity will get larger, get smaller, or stay the same with adding or taking away a given amount. They are not yet able to tell by how much it has grown, just that it is larger. Because they have not developed conservation, they think that a cracker broken into two is more than the one cracker. They focus not on the size of the piece but on the number to determine amount.

An activity to help with this concept might be to show a card with a given number of dots and have the students make an arrangement with the same number of counters. They could then be instructed to make a pile with less dots or a pile with more.

Comprehension Check

■ What are some indicators that a child is functioning at the emergent phase?

Matching Phase

Kindergarten tends to be defined by counting, counting, and more counting. One way to practice counting is through building numbers, generally to about 30, in many different ways—but especially on a 10 frame. This is building off the emergent phase in helping children instantly recognize numbers. This will also be supportive later for part–part–whole relationships and addition and subtraction. Number relationships are also beginning to evolve during this phase. These number relationships are the foundational pieces for addition and subtraction with understanding.

Counting in the Matching Phase

Rote Counting to Double Digits Children continue to learn to rote count well into the double digits, and some even to 100. Still, they do not develop much conceptual understanding of quantities beyond 20, and they only understand double digits to 20 with focused and structured activities. While rote counting, children are probably picking up the pattern of counting within a 10 but may forget the order of the tens.

Teachers may count the days of school, the number of seconds it takes the class to settle down, or the number of children present. Teachers must model lots of counting, and children must have lots of opportunities to count. Many teachers may fall into the habit of only counting to 10 or 20, but it is important to model counting beyond 20, because children tend to not know what to say after they reach 20.

Although counting backward is not necessarily indicated in this phase, teachers need to model counting backward from both 10 and 20 (and possibly 25 to cross the 20). After assessing many children in first grade at one school, it was noted that most could not count back from 20 but were proficient in counting back from 10. In discussing this with the kindergarten teachers of these children the year before, it was realized that they rarely modeled counting back from numbers higher than 10.

Lots of Collections In a prekindergarten or kindergarten class, there should be lots of different interesting things to count. Children need authentic and concrete experiences to count. Many things that the teacher might count may be too abstract (such as the number of seconds it takes to line up). Effective kindergarten teachers have myriad tubs filled with lots of fun things to count, such as dinosaurs, keys, buttons, socks, action figures, and stones.

Countable collections.

One-to-One Correspondence One-to-one correspondence is an important yet difficult skill for children. In developing one-to-one correspondence, children first learn to keep track of objects through moving, touching, and then pointing or learn other visual ways to keep track, such as bobbing their head up and down. Students do not automatically move objects to keep track of them, yet we cannot necessarily impose this strategy on them. When students count by pointing and loose track repeatedly, their teacher might ask whether maybe there is something that they can do to keep track of what they have already counted (figure 2.10). Simply moving them may still be too abstract (figure 2.11). Perhaps they need to place their

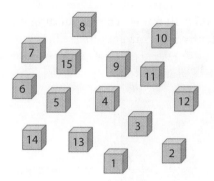

Figure 2.10. Counting with no way of keeping track of what was counted.

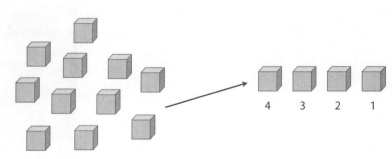

Figure 2.11. Counting by moving.

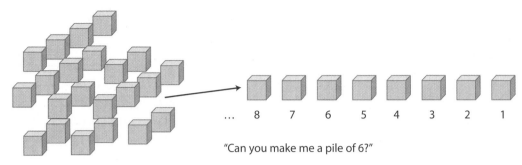

"Can you make me a pile of 6?"

Figure 2.12. Counting an amount and forgetting how much was asked for.

objects in or on something more structured, such as a numbered 10 frame, egg carton, paper plates, or number line.

Some activities that help with one-to-one correspondence are placing pencils on sheets of paper to see whether there are enough pencils, putting cards in envelopes to see whether there are enough envelopes, and passing out paper towels to the students in class.

Another important aspect of one-to-one correspondence is the ability to count out a number of objects without passing the desired number (figure 2.12). For example, if the teacher asks a student to give her six cubes, can that student count out six cubes from a large pile and stop at 6? Students who are developing counting skills cannot.

One big factor in counting is the amount being counted. Children may be able to count by moving or pointing with a smaller amount of objects than with a larger amount. They may be able to count out a small amount and stop on the desired number, but when asked to produce a larger amount, they may forget how many they were suppose to count. The level of numerical complexity can be the difference in how successful a student is in performing many mathematical tasks, not just counting.

Counting All or Direct Modeling Children in the matching phase are using counting and direct modeling as their primary strategies for problem solving. Direct modeling is described in more detail in chapter 3, but basically it is when children model a situation to solve it. In the beginning, they may need to use actual objects, because cubes or other counters may be too abstract. For example, when finding out how many cookies each child should receive, the class may use either real cookies or plastic toy cookies. Classes often model with real students passing out the cookies. Over time, students are able to substitute real

Substituting cubes for actual objects.

objects for other counters that represent those objects. They are also able to begin to record their work by perhaps drawing circles with hair to resemble people and drawing cookies next to each person.

Once children have directly modeled a problem, they find out how many objects there are by counting all. Suppose there were two cookies on one plate and four cookies on another. The children would need to count all cookies to find the total, "1, 2, 3, 4, 5, 6." This might be done with fingers, which are a good counting tool.

Most students initially count their fingers by touching their chin. They then graduate to bending the fingers down one by one, and then they are able to just look at them. It is a red flag when older children are still touching their chin to either count all or count on.

Solving the problem using pictures by "dealing out" cookies.

Cardinality Principle The cardinality principle is in effect when children realize that the last number counted represents the total number in the set. This is identifiable if you ask a child to show you 10 and he shows you all 10 he just counted. If he points to the 10th cube, he is labeling the cubes rather than finding out how many. Using a number line or 100 chart can aid in this misunderstanding, so lots of talk needs to focus on quantity in relation to counting.

This misunderstanding can resurface in the upper grades when students learn about fractions. When using a number line to label fractions, children often believe that 1/2 is a point on the line between the zero and the one, not the entire space between the zero and the middle line. It is also evident in measurement when children think that 1 inch is one line on the ruler and not the entire space.

Discrete versus Continuous Counting Children in this phase learn that some things can be counted using numbers, like students, cookies, and cubes. This is discrete counting. Other things cannot be counted discretely, such as length, area, volume, temperature, mass, and time. This is considered continuous counting. "How many?" would be a question used in discrete counting, whereas "How much?" and "How long?" are questions asked in reference to continuous counting.

Number Relationships in the Matching Phase

How Many More or Less The language for the ideas of more and less is difficult. Students have a harder time talking about the concept of less than that of more. It is hard for children to talk about something that is not there. When comparing, they eventually look at the extra ones in the larger amount to describe what is missing in the smaller amount.

During the matching phase, students line up objects of different sets to find what is leftover. They may make towers with cubes, put them side by side, and break off the extra pieces of the larger group. They may line up the objects and fill in the missing spaces to find out how many more are needed to make the two groups equal.

It is especially important at this stage that students use concrete objects to figure out more and less problems. Providing as many real-life situations as possible is helpful. Consider these examples:

"How many more boys than swings are there?"

"How many more hats do we need so that we all have one?"

"How many fewer girls than boys are present today?"

"Some kids are absent today, and not everyone has a reading partner. What do we need to do so that everyone has a partner?"

Knowing One More and One Less without Counting Just because children can rote count does not mean they realize that the next number signifies one more being added. This understanding must be constructed by the student, and lots of experiences need to be given to assist in this construction. Once children have the vocabulary for more, less, and same, they need to have experiences that help them notice that one more is the next number. Presenting a train of cubes and adding one cube, or taking one away from that train, is a way to help students conceptualize the notion of one more and one less. Another way is to hold up two trains, let's say one of three cubes and one of four cubes, side by side, one of which the students have already counted, then ask how many are in the second train. Some students will count, some might just see that it is four, and some will just know that it is one more. During this discussion, all strategies should be shared aloud. The next time, someone might try to take on the strategy of a friend.

Activities in which students have to build all the towers (1–10), match them to number cards, and then put them in order helps some students see that the towers make "stairs." They see that these stairs are going in number order, like the numbers on a number line. Sometimes, when comparing two of the towers and how they know, they prove it by counting even if that is not how they knew. They still need practice using the language for one more and one less. The teacher might ask, "Did you just know?" After affirmation, she might then ask, "So you knew that the second tower was 8 because it was one more than 7?" She would probably have the child repeat that to help that language sink in.

Language Tip

When presenting and discussing these activities, precise language is the key. Sometimes using many different ways to ask the question is necessary for all students to understand what is being asked.

"How many more is 9 than 7?"

"If you have five candies and your brother has eight candies, how many more candies do you need to have the same amount?"

"If you have five candies, what do you need to do to get eight candies?"

If students speak little or no English, put two towers next to each other and simply ask, "More?" with a quizzical look on your face. When they point to the bigger tower, ask, "How much more?" Emphasize the words *how much*. If they do not understand your question, break off the extras, repeat "How much?" and count them.

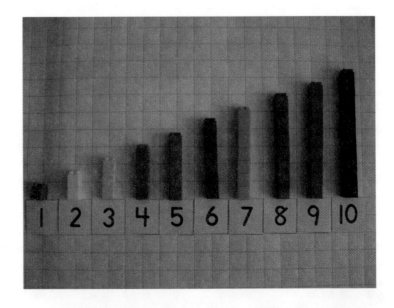

Once students see that one more is the next counting number and they have generalized it, they are able to solve problems involving plus one without the tools. They are able to apply this rule to any number they know how to count.

After one more and one less would come two more and two less. These are the first generalizations children make in learning their facts to 18.

Spatial Relationships and Beginning Estimation   Studies show that success in math is correlated with spatial ability, which leads to more successful abstract thinking. It is a shame, but large urban districts across the United States have eliminated many activities that naturally enhance spatial abilities in children, such as mazes, block designs, and block building. These are critical activities, and they need to be present in a kindergarten program.

An effective activity that helps children develop these spatial skills, as well as estimation skills, is visually seeing how many tiles would fill a shape. This is called *Shape Puzzles* from the book *Developing Number Concepts: Counting, Comparing and Pattern* (Richardson 1999a, 60). Make and trace or cut out shapes by putting any number of color overhead tiles together, and put it on the overhead or document camera. Have the students make estimates as to how many tiles it would take to fill the shape. It is quite amusing to hear some of the outlandish estimates given, especially when this task is new. After gathering some estimates, add one tile to see whether any students change their estimate. Do this until there is only one space left, and you will be surprised by how many students still think that two more are needed. Lots of practice helps students make more reasonable estimates.

Shape Puzzles is an activity that can later be put into a learning center. Do not forget about numerical complexity when doing this activity. The size of your shape makes a big difference. As a class, you may want to gradually increase the size of your shape, but when you add this to the math centers, you may want to print different-size shapes on different-colored paper and assign your students to work using a certain color, depending on their number range (3–6, 7–10, 10–20). This range may be determined by observations or assessments, such as the *Counting Assessment* (Richardson 2003a), discussed later in this section.

Some shapes might look like figure 2.13.

Relating One Number to Another   Children at this stage are beginning to relate numbers to one another. When asked to change one quantity to another, they know whether they need to get more or take some away. Suppose they have five counters and the teacher asks what they need to do to have seven counters. In the matching phase, they probably recount all the counters that they have and then add more to reach the desired amount. If the amount of

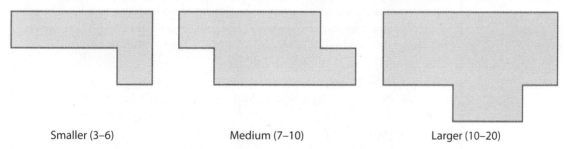

Smaller (3–6)   Medium (7–10)   Larger (10–20)

Figure 2.13. Examples of different sizes of shape puzzles.

Comprehension Check

■ What are some indicators that students are functioning at the matching phase?

■ How can changing the number size affect how children solve problems?

change is small (e.g., 1–3), they may know it without counting and may just get the desired amount. Knowing how many to get would be an indicator of part–part–whole relationships, which is found in the next phase, quantifying.

Quantifying Phase

The quantifying phase is identified by the students' abilities to use part–part–whole relationships to identify quantities. Both counting and number relationships are becoming more sophisticated as students are developing more efficient strategies for problem solving. This probably begins toward the end of kindergarten and the start of first grade. By completion of this phase, students should also have developed conservation of number, the understanding that no matter how the objects are arranged, or counted, there is always the same amount. Students also begin to use symbolic notation by writing number sentences (or equations) to record their work using addition and subtraction. When dealing out objects, students understand that the groups are equal; the students may no longer do one-to-one matching but, rather, can partition out several at one time.

Counting in the Quantifying Phase

Counting On and Counting Back Convincing students to leave the comfort of counting all and move to counting on can be challenging. Many students stop seeing the need to count an amount they already know, and they just count the added amount. Counting on is an important skill, because it is a step to generalizing basic facts. Others need to be coerced into trying this out. Whole-class discussions on problem-solving strategies bring to the surface counting on, because inevitably some students are already using it on their own. Sharing this strategy gives others the idea of trying it on, and the strategy might stick for some students. Others need to keep counting all. Remember, these are developmental phases, and we cannot force students to move from one phase to another. We just need to know what comes next so that we can help support their learning by giving them lots of opportunities for counting two groups.

> **CAUTION** Counting on and counting back have their difficulties. When using abstract tools, such as the number line and 100 chart, it is common for students to start counting on using the first number and not start with the next. This means that children do not understand what they are really counting. Look at figure 2.14.
>
> Using the number line and 100 chart as tools for counting on needs to be more connected to concrete experiences. It is helpful to place small cubes on each number to represent seven objects (figure 2.15). Then, when the students count on by adding cubes, they can see that the first number they should cover is the one following 7.
>
> Once children have made the generalization that when counting on or counting back it is necessary to start with the next number or previous number (depending on which way they are counting), they are ready to use these abstract tools without the concrete support.

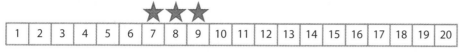

Teacher: "What is 7 plus 3?"   Student: "7, 8, 9"

Figure 2.14. How many children often count on a number line.

Figure 2.15. How to make the number line more concrete.

One way to have students practice counting on is through the numbers they have built on a 10 frame. By now, students should have had lots of experiences building numbers 11–20 on their 10 frames, and once they are comfortable with 10, they stop counting the individual objects on the filled 10 frame on their own. Also, having one number written on an index card and pictures of cubes on another can encourage students to say the first number and count on the rest.

At first, children start counting from the first number, but one generalization that we like students to make is the notion that it is more efficient to start with the larger of the two numbers, or amounts, and count on the smaller. Again, this has to make sense to the students, and perhaps structuring activities that are overexaggerated, such as adding one very large amount to a very small amount (4 + 85), can help them discover this efficiency.

Skip Counting As with one-to-one counting, children learn to rote skip count before they understand what it means. In kindergarten and first grade, teachers typically have students practice chanting by fives and even twos during calendar and other routine activities. However, just because the students can *chant* all their fives to 100 does not mean that they know doing so refers to counting out groups.

For rote counting, one of the most successful methods is counting using rhythm. This is where children are clapping, snapping, tapping, and so on, as they count. For example, counting by twos might be clap, snap. The children do not say a number on the clap (except perhaps as a whisper only to themselves) and then say the corresponding number on the snap. Counting by threes might be clap, snap, tap. And so on. Whispering the number to themselves is important for students still trying to learn the sequence of the skip count. It gives them a chance to process the skipped numbers.

Kindergartners generally count by tens; first graders by tens, fives, and twos; second graders by threes; and so on. Whatever grade you teach, incorporating rhythm counting into your skip counting lessons is essential.

Lots of experiences are necessary for children to internalize what is happening during skip counting. These might include building many cube trains of a certain number and then counting them, skip counting on a 100 chart (maybe coloring in two at a time), and jumping on a floor number line. Children love it if you dump a large bucket of cubes on the floor and tell them to count them. Watch what they do. Some might start one by one, some might group into tens or other numbers. Question them as to why they chose a certain strategy. If there are lots of cubes, they soon learn the inefficiency of counting by ones or twos. By the end of the hour, you are sure to see lots of tens. Then counting all

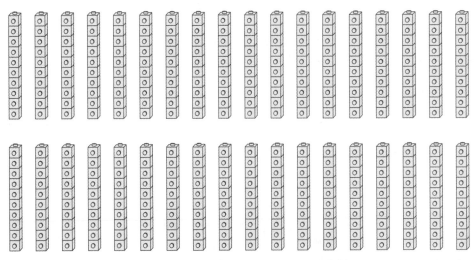

Teacher prompt:

"My, there are sure an awful lot of tens. Is there a way we can organize them to make them easier to count?"

Figure 2.16. How teachers can encourage children to group tens into hundreds.

those tens can be a challenge. Through questioning, push your students to realize that they can group those tens into 10 tens to count by hundreds.

If given a pile of cubes, and asked how many tens they could make, students are likely to give a reasonable estimate. They may even be able to make the piles and count the groups by 10. But, interestingly enough, when asked how many they think there would be if they counted by five, they generally give a larger answer because they are thinking that counting by five means they must call each piece a five. They give an even larger answer if asked to count by twos (figure 2.17). Perhaps they get this idea from counting money. Some pieces can be called 1, others 5, and yet others 10. However, coins can only be counted by their designated value. Cubes should only be counted by their value (a single cube would be a one, in this case). Getting three different answers for three ways of counting cubes shows that students do not have conservation of number.

Ordinal Numbers First graders spend time learning their ordinal numbers (*first, second, third*). Other words that should be included are *next, then,* and *last.* These are seemingly difficult to learn, especially for second-language learners. Lots of modeling from the teacher is needed. Activities in which students have to line themselves up, each holding a sign with the number written on one side and the ordinal number written on the back, are helpful for developing this vocabulary for ordinal numbers.

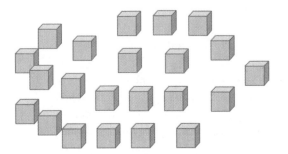

T: How many groups of 10 could you make?
S: 2.
T: How many would that be?
S: About 20.
T: What if you counted them by fives?
S: Then there would be 110.
T: What if you counted them by twos?
S: Then there would be 44.

(Line of questioning taken from Kathy Richardson's *Grouping Tens Assessment*)

Figure 2.17. A teacher questioning to see whether a student understands what it means to count in groups.

Number Relationships in the Quantifying Phase

A Sense of Quantity and Reasonableness Lots of experience building numbers allow students to develop more reasonable estimates regarding quantity. Providing opportunities to estimate weekly with estimating jars and doing lots of counting exercises such as shape puzzles are also beneficial. Throughout the next several years, a sense of quantity will be developing as students gain experience with tens, hundreds, thousands, and beyond. Later, lots of building will still be needed when students are developing their understanding of decimal numbers.

Part–Part–Whole Relationships The second half of kindergarten through first grade should be spent exploring relationships of number within numbers. One big idea we want children to understand is that all numbers are made up of other numbers, the beginning idea of decomposition of numbers. This understanding significantly helps quick recall of basic facts later. Many children see each problem as isolated and unrelated to any other problem, which makes it more difficult to learn their facts.

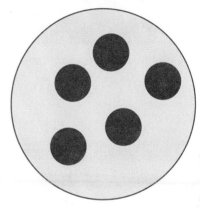

Figure 2.18. A dot card used to encourage seeing numbers within numbers.

Whole-class and independent activities should focus on understanding and learning combinations of numbers through 10. This means *all* numbers, not just 10. An activity to support this would be *Tell Me Fast,* found in *Developing Number Concepts: Counting, Comparing, and Pattern* (Richardson 1999a, 42). Quickly flash a dot card with five dots on it, for example, and ask how students saw the dots (figure 2.18). Some might see them as 4 and 1, as 2 and 3, or just as 5 (because 5 is a recognizable amount for many children).

Depending on the age and developmental level of the child, most children can instantly recognize five or six dots. For amounts above, that they need to mentally combine the smaller groups they see. Therefore, when flashing a card with four dots, if you ask a student how they saw it, you might have to accept that they just knew, because they probably did. If you try to push the issue, you might get a response such as, "I saw 1 and 1 and 1 and 1." Many teachers like to introduce number sentences or equations in this way, because they can be written for what students see, such as 4 + 2 = 6. You may want students to come to the overhead to circle the numbers they saw, such as 2 and 3. Over time, gradually increase the number of dots you show.

Cube trains can also be used to explore number combinations. One experience would be to build a cube train using two colors in different configurations (figure 2.19). This is a great way for students to see commutativity. They also can develop strategies for knowing how they found all possible combinations.

The classic *Hiding Assessment* (Richardson 2003f) is a way to assess where each child is individually in regard to learning number combinations. In this assessment, the teacher uses tiles or cubes and hides some to see whether the child knows how many are missing by seeing how many are left on the table. This is a quick assessment, and it can be done throughout the year to monitor growth.

Start with three tiles (kindergarten) or four tiles (first grade). Ask how many tiles the child sees. Then slyly cover a couple of the tiles up. Ask how many are in your hand. Most children will be able to respond quickly and confidently. For them, this low number of tiles is a way to establish how this activity works. A few children will basically think that this is a magic trick. You may have to do this several times before they understand what is happening. The ones who still think this is magic should use three tiles for their activities.

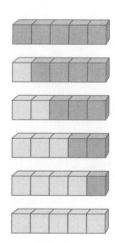

Figure 2.19. Building number combinations with cubes.

The Hiding Assessment.

When children demonstrate knowledge of all combinations, increase the amount by one tile. As soon as you see children start to count on their fingers, count with their eyes, or just take so long that you suspect that they are counting and not knowing, then stop the assessment. The number you were testing becomes the just-right number or the instructional number. They will use this number when doing hiding activities at their independent stations.

There are many kinds of hiding activities that are all variations of the same basic activity. Sometimes just changing the name or manipulative creates novelty and keeps the students excited. *Grab Bag Subtraction*, found in *Developing Number Concepts: Addition and Subtraction* (Richardson 1999b, 62), is an example of such an activity:

The total number of desired cubes is placed in a paper bag. The student then grabs some cubes without looking in the bag, checks to see how many he pulled out, and guesses how many are left inside.

Essentially, the students can play these hiding games all year, as long as the teacher continually assesses them and moves them to higher levels when appropriate. It is important to note if children who are moved on to a new number have forgotten the combinations of the previous number and, if they have, to revert to the previous number. Therefore, periodically check to see that students are still solid with previous combinations.

A sample classroom recording sheet for number combinations might look like the one in figure 2.20.

Student Name	3	4	5	6	7	8	9	10	Knows All

Figure 2.20. Sample sheet for recording the number combinations that students know.

Combining Using Relationships At this point, children are no longer relying on just counting or direct modeling for problem solving. As they develop a sense of quantity and explore relationships, they are able to use this knowledge to solve problems more abstractly. An example of this relationship is doubles and doubles plus one. Children tend to easily learn their doubles, and combined with their understanding of one more and one less, students are able to add numbers such as 4 + 5. They think of it as 4 + 4 + 1. After working with these addends enough, they simply know 4 + 5.

Relating One Number to Another When Changing Numbers We discussed how children in the matching phase should know that when they need more objects in a pile they need to add objects. In this phase, children should know how many would be added or removed to change a pile (figure 2.21). They may start by counting on, but as they develop knowledge of combinations, they move toward just knowing.

Benchmarks of 5 and 10 Children should be familiar with the important benchmark numbers 5 and 10. In kindergarten, there should be lots of initial work with the 5 frame before introducing the 10 frame (figure 2.22). Because 5 is a quantity most students can recognize easily, they tend to learn these combinations quickly. These benchmark combinations will prove invaluable when learning basic facts and making tens to solve double-digit problems.

Special Needs

It is essential that children with learning disabilities use 5 and 10 frames as a way to visualize quantities. This is a supportive mental structure for addition and subtraction for all students.

Desired Student Response:

"To make this a pile of 9, I would need to add 4 more."

Figure 2.21. Sample student response for a question regarding changing one quantity to another.

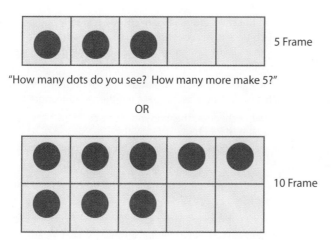

5 Frame

"How many dots do you see? How many more make 5?"

OR

10 Frame

"How many dots do you see? How many more make 10?"

Figure 2.22. Sample 5 and 10 frames used to support number combinations.

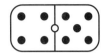 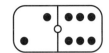 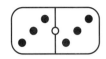 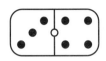

Figure 2.23. Patterns that can support spatial relationships.

Spatial Relationships and Modeling Tens and Ones

We discussed the importance of spatial reasoning in developing abstract thought. There are activities that can help students develop spatial relationships. Through games, many students are able to recognize the patterns of dots found on dice. The teacher can use these learned patterns to help students identify new patterns by showing children how to focus on smaller, known patterns within larger ones. Look at figure 2.23 for an example.

Toward the end of this phase, students are engaged in lots of activities that involve modeling tens and ones and adding using tens in preparation for the partitioning phase, which is centered on being able to break numbers into tens and ones. They may do this through counting lots of cubes by making trains of 10, by gluing 10 beans on a popsicle stick, or by grouping small objects in cups of 10 objects each. They have not necessarily internalized what 10 actually means.

Assessments

In the primary grades, it is imperative that the teacher perform individual student interviews to determine where each child is developmentally. The information gathered from these interviews helps the teacher know how to nudge each child individually and the class as a whole. Not knowing where children are in their understanding of numbers can cause the teacher to be instructing too abstractly or using numbers that are out of the developmental range of the students. This can create gaps in understanding from the start. Developmental student interviews (Richardson 2003a–d, f) that relate to the early number concepts discussed in this chapter are outlined in figure 2.24.

Comprehension Check

Identify some misconceptions that students have when exploring concepts in the quantifying phase. What are some things you can do to help students make the necessary connections to move them beyond these misconceptions?

Counting Objects	Can the child count a pile of cubes accurately and how does he keep track of his counting? Can the child add one to or take one from a pile by just knowing? This assessment identifies the number range that is most comfortable for the child.
Changing Numbers	Does the child know the relative size of numbers, and can he change one number to make another (e.g., change 7 to 10)?
More/Less Trains	Can the child use the amount of one cube train to determine the amount of another?
Number Arrangements	Can the child recognize small quantities within dot patterns?
Hiding Assessment	Which number combinations (to 10) does the child know with ease?

Figure 2.24. Kathy Richardson's developmental interviews that relate to early number concepts.

It is wise to perform a screening in the beginning of each grade to quickly identify children who might need extra support or just to guide your instruction. If necessary, identify key concepts that students should be familiar with from the previous grade. Kindergartners can start the year with the *Counting Objects* assessment. When it is necessary to maximize time, an assessment can be designed to be given in small groups. If seated at a kidney table, dividers should be placed between the students, but in such a way that they all can be seen by the teacher. Students who show high areas of concern need to have individual interviews in corresponding areas to collect more information. An example of a first-grade screening test can be seen on the website.

CONCLUSION

As highlighted in this chapter, tools are not merely something that we put in front of students and expect them to know how to use them to solve problems. The meaning and use of tools need to be created by the student and cannot be imposed by the teacher. Knowing the potential pitfalls inherent in the tools helps the teacher know what to look for when observing students. The teacher's role is to create strategic lessons facilitating the students' ability to make connections among different tools and, as a result, between concrete and abstract representations.

Helping students to move from the concrete to the abstract is not an easy task. Some students take longer than others to internalize concepts with the concrete and thus may not be as ready as others to move on to the abstract. Some tools are more abstract than others and might not be supportive enough. Having students record pictorially and symbolically what they have built is key to making the necessary connections between the concrete and the abstract. Peer modeling, class discussions, questioning, and lots of exposure are all ways we can help those students move on to more abstract representations.

It is important that children have plenty of concrete experiences as they move through the phases of number sense development to assist them in creating generalizations and developing the ability to think abstractly about early number concepts. The emergent, matching, and quantifying phases for numbers and operations are where the foundational activities for building strong number sense are found. Within these phases, some indicators are relevant to counting strategies and others describe number relationships. Some of these indicators continue to develop across phases as the children mature.

It is easy to think that math in the first years is simple, but to a child it is as complicated as calculus might be to us. We cannot assume any understanding on their part and need to constantly ask questions to know what they are thinking. As children become successful in certain areas, all it takes is a slight increase in the number range and the work is again challenging. Likewise, students who are constantly struggling need to be working with smaller numbers to develop those necessary relationships.

▶ Interview Video with an Eye on Content

Watch the videos of student interviews, which focus on early number concepts. In each video, note the following:

Describe the problem.

_____

_____

What developmental phase is the work centered on?

_____

What is the actual concept or skill being discussed?

_____

What tool does the child use to solve the problem?

_____

▶ Interview a Child

Design and give a student interview about an early number concept. Consider which tools you want to provide that may give the child access to the problems. Then write a reflection in which you:

1. Write the specific tasks you asked the child to complete.
2. Write the responses you obtained from the child.
3. Write what number concept phase you think the child is in and why you think so.
4. Write where you would take this child next.

▶ Classroom Video with an Eye on Pedagogy

Watch the video of a classroom episode, which focus on early number concepts. In each video, note the following:

Describe the problem/task.

_____

_____

What developmental phase is the work centered on?

_____

What is the actual concept or skill being discussed?

_____

What tools are the children using to solve the problem?

_____

_____

How does the teacher try to move the students from their current level of representation to a more abstract one?

_____

_____

_____

▶ Classroom Application

1. Observe your cooperating teacher to see how he or she uses tools and their effects on children. As you work with children in the classroom, try to use tools and write about their effects on children.

2. Choose a tool, and collaboratively design and teach a lesson about an early number concept that would allow young students to construct an understanding of that tool. Think about how you can bridge the gap between the concrete and the abstract.

▶ Resources

At the time of writing this book, the best sources for developmental assessments in early number concepts are those designed by Kathy Richardson, *Assessing Math Concepts, Books 1–9*. These are available for purchase from http://www.didax.com.

Richardson has also written a series of three books of activities that support early number development and computation, with an accompanying planning guide. The book that supports the ideas in this chapter is *Developing Number Concepts. Book 1: Counting, Comparing, and Pattern* (1999a), which is also available for purchase at http://www.didax.com.

We also recommend the following books:

Young Mathematicians at Work: Constructing Number Sense, Addition and Subtraction, Catherine Twomey Fosnot and Maarten Dolk (2001)

Mathematics Their Way, Mary Baratta-Lorton (1995)

Minilessons for Math Practice: Grades K–2, Rusty Bresser and Caren Holtzman (2006)

There are lots of companies from which to order math tools. The ones we recommend are listed here:

http://www.enasco.com (in our opinion, the most economical place to buy virtually any math manipulative)

http://www.lakeshorelearning.com (they have 45 stores in 21 different states)

http://www.etacuisenaire.com (another great source for math tools)

http://www.thecontainerstore.com (our favorite clear boxes for storing math tools)

http://www.gamblersgifts.com (the cheapest place, besides Costco, for buying multiple decks of playing cards; you cannot use a credit card or purchase order at Costco)

http://www.dryerase.com (a great selection of individual whiteboards)

▶ Lit Link

There are myriad picture books that focus on early number concepts. Marilyn Burns has written many books, as have other authors, to help teachers introduce a variety of math concepts. Here we list such books, their authors, and the math concept they are trying to target. Creating discovery lessons that use a picture book as a springboard is an engaging way for children to grapple with mathematics, often without them even knowing that they are doing so.

Literature Books to Support Number and Counting

Title	Author
1 to 100 Busy Counting Book	Amye Rosenberg
$1.00 Word Riddle Book, The	Marilyn Burns
Across the Stream	Mirra Ginsberg
Anno's Counting Book	Mitsumasa Anno
Anno's Math Games	Mitsumasa Anno
Aunt Flossie's Hats	Elizabeth F. Howard
Benny's Pennies	Pat Brisson
Blue Willow	Doris Gates
Bug Band, A	Lynette Timothy
Button Box, The	Margarette S. Reid
City by Numbers	Stephen T. Johnson
From One to One Hundred	Teri Sloat
Hund Rhymes	Marc Brown
How Many Bugs in a Box?	David Carter
How Many Snails?	Paul Giganti, Jr.
How Many?	Lucy Floyd
Let's Go Visiting	Sue Williams
Moja Means One	Muriel Feelings
More Than One	Miriam Schlein
Napping House, The	Audrey Wood
One Hundred Monkeys	Daniel Cutler
One Magic Box	Roger Chouinard
One Monday Morning	Uri Shulevitz
Ready or Not, Here I Come!	Teddy Slater
Rooster's Off to See the World	Eric Carle

Seven Little Rabbits	John Becker
Six-Dinner Sid	Inga Moore
So Many Cats!	Beatrice Schenk de Regniers
Ten Black Dots	Donald Crews
Ten, Nine, Eight	Molly Bang
Three Hat Day, A	Laura Geringer
Too Many Hopkins	Tomie dePaola
Two Greedy Bears	Mirra Ginsberg
Two Ways to Count to Ten	Ruby Dee
What Comes in 2's, 3's, and 4's?	Suzanne Aker
Where We Live	Brad Necrason
Who Sank the Boat?	Pamela Allen

 ## Tech Tools

Although most are dedicated to computation and higher math skills, some websites and software are supportive of early number concepts.

Websites

National Library of Virtual Manipulatives, http://www.nlvm.usu.edu

Software

Jumpstart Prekindergarten and *Jumpstart Kindergarten*, Knowledge Adventure

Polygone Explore les Matématiques, Synapse Multimédia

The low emphasis on language makes it appropriate for English Language Learners and Students with Special Needs. Although the language level is low, the mathematics it emphasizes is strong. (The company is French, but the CD is in French and English. The actual website for Synapse Multimédia doesn't sell the CD, but shows aspects of it. Other vendor sites sell it.)

Informing Our Decisions: Assessment and Single-Digit Addition and Subtraction

PEDAGOGICAL CONTENT UNDERSTANDINGS

Pedagogy *Assessment for Instruction*

- Backward Design
- Four Important Assessment Terms
- Traditional Assessments
- Alternative Assessments

Content *Single-Digit Addition and Subtraction*

- Operation Sense
- Problem Types
- Problem-Solving Strategies
- Learning the Basics of Addition and Subtraction
- Practicing for Quick Recall

Evaluate what you want—because what gets measured, gets produced.

James A. Belasco

CONVERSATION IN MATHEMATICS

Teacher: Suppose you had 6 baseball cards and your mom gave you 6 more cards? How many would you have then?

Student: (Makes 2 groups of 6 with Unifix cubes, and then counts all of them.) 12.

Teacher: How did you get 12?

Student: These are 6 cards and these are 6 cards, and I count 12.

Teacher: Now suppose you had 6 baseball cards and your mom gave you 7 more baseball cards? How many cards would you have then?

Student: (Thinks for a few seconds.) 13.

Teacher: How did you get 13?

Student: Well, 6 plus 6 is 12. And 7 is 1 more than 6. And 13 is 1 more than 12. So, 13.

Teacher: Nice work.

We have made no bones about how the type of mathematics instruction espoused in this book is radically different from what many of us experienced in our own schooling. We hope to do our part in continuing to encourage systemwide change in the way mathematics is conceptualized, learned, and taught in schools. Three components promote systemic change: professional development, curriculum materials, and assessment. (Smith and O'Day 1991). Of these, assessment has received the least attention (Firestone and Schorr 2004). It only makes sense that, if we are going to teach mathematics differently, we need to change the way we assess the mathematical progress of our students. Clearly, the teacher in the "Conversation in Mathematics" section was interested in more than just a right answer as she assessed her student's mathematical understanding.

The response of the child to the baseball card task reveals that children are capable of creating some sophisticated strategies for solving problems that involve addition and subtraction, particularly as they use their sense of number and of operation, supported in their thinking by real-life contexts. Operations are powerful vehicles for solving problems. The operations of addition and subtraction are foundational for further work with multiplication and division and are themselves deep mathematical constructs that require time and study to understand and use them effectively. As we look at whole-number addition and subtraction in this chapter, we first look at the NCTM Focal Points which describes the outcomes we should have for our students relative to whole-number addition and subtraction. We next examine the contexts in which we use addition and subtraction. Then, we examine the kinds of strategies children tend to invent to solve problems involving addition and subtraction. Knowing these contexts and strategies enables us to ensure that we provide our students with the kinds of problem-solving experiences that prepare them to deal with those same contexts outside of school and ensure that we possess the kind of deep mathematical knowledge that empowers us to promote genuine problem solving and reasoning among our students. Before this investigation, however, we lay a foundation by discussing an important understanding that, along with number sense, underlies virtually all mathematics—operation sense.

PEDAGOGY   *Assessment for Instruction*

Learning Theory

We begin by listing words often considered to be synonymous with *assess: monitor, evaluate, measure, observe, grade, test, quiz, check.* Although each of these terms has its own meaning, recognizing that all are similar is helpful. A fundamental difference between two of them, *assessment* and *evaluation,* also provide a useful philosophical perspective. One of the ways evaluation is defined includes a focus on what students do wrong, because the root of evaluation includes making value judgments. Assessment, on the other hand, focuses on documenting what students know and can do, with an eye toward building on that knowledge and performance to enhance mathematical proficiency. It is more useful to you to focus on what children know and can do than on what they do not know and cannot do.

Why is assessment an important teaching tool? This question is its own answer. If assessment is a teaching tool, then you cannot teach effectively without a clear understanding of what it is and how and why it is used. Good teachers continually assess students and adjust their teaching. This means that assessment that enhances learning is as important as assessment that documents learning. We suggest, therefore, that you focus on the idea of assessment *for* instruction, in addition to that of assessment *of* instruction. Classroom environments are complex, and consistent assessments inform the decisions made there.

Assessment is the key to establishing an environment in which children understand and feel a sense of responsibility for learning. Indeed, learning is a stewardship that each child possesses. That is not a difficult idea, because humans are programmed for learning. Nevertheless, each child needs to feel a responsibility to learn what is being taught. Assessment provides stewardship accountability. Children take the responsibility to engage in the learning more seriously if they know that there will be frequent and consistent opportunities for them to demonstrate to you, and to others, what they know and can do.

Consistent assessing helps you establish what is important (we assess what we value)—not only what is assessed but also how it is assessed. We seek to provide you with an enlarged vision of what it means to know and do mathematics—that is, to become mathematically literate. This vision is reflective of an international movement (Australian Association of Mathematics Teachers 2002; NCTM 2000) that includes encouraging students toward a balanced acquisition of procedural proficiency and conceptual understanding. Ridgeway (1998, 2) states, "As an issue of policy, the implementation of standards-based curricula should always be accompanied by the implementation of standards-based assessment. In fact, incremental change in assessment systems will foster concurrent improvement in professional and curriculum development."

Application to the Learning and Teaching of Mathematics

Backward Design

For years, good instructional design consisted of determining the instructional goals, planning the instructional activities, then determining how to assess a student's learning at the end. A newer, more sensible approach called *backward design* has proved to be more beneficial in promoting student achievement (Wiggins and McTighe 1998). This approach consists of beginning with "the end in mind" by determining the role of assessment throughout your lesson, especially the assessment you will administer at the end of the lesson. What steps might constitute an instruction or assessment sequence?

1. *Set general learning goals.* These usually refer to the big ideas of mathematics, such as "fractions have no meaning without a reference to the whole."

2. *Design and administer a preinstruction assessment.* Such an assessment enables you to determine whether your students possess the necessary prerequisite knowledge to engage in instructional activities relevant to your goals. For example, if your instruction relates to the goal in step 1, the students should probably know something about sharing or dividing equally.

3. *Determine your specific learning targets.* What targets, or objectives, will you focus on during individual lessons to enable you to help the children reach your goals? In the fraction context, the children should probably know the meaning of fractions when the whole is one whole object, multiple objects, or even part of an object.

4. *Determine acceptable evidence of learning.* This needs to be shown at the end of your lessons. In other words, figure out how you will assess the children at the end of each lesson.

5. *Design an instructional plan.* This includes determining the tasks you will present in conjunction with each lesson.

6. *Conduct interactive instruction or ongoing assessment.* If you use the launch–explore–summarize lesson sequence (discussed in chapters 6 and 7), then you conduct interactive instruction with natural opportunities for ongoing assessment during the lesson presentation.

7. *Administer a postinstruction assessment.* This is critical if you intend to ensure that you avoid the pitfalls of assuming the children learned the intended mathematics and that your students feel a sense of responsibility for learning.

Four Important Assessment Terms

You must know four important terms when learning about assessment: formative, summative, validity, and reliability.

Formative and Summative Assessments

There are many ways to classify assessments. One useful way involves the terms *formative* and *summative*. Formative assessments are used to inform teachers and are often informal. As you interact with children during the progression of a lesson, you can gather a great deal of informal information about how your students are doing if you look for it. Teachers use this information to make decisions about their instruction. Summative assessments, on the other hand, are administered toward the end of the learning (a dangerous thing to suggest, that learning "ends") such as at the end of a lesson or a unit of instruction. Summative assessments have a sense of finality. As with most categorization schemes, a degree of overlap occurs between formative and summative assessments, but distinguishing between them provides you with a sense of the purposes of assessment that will serve you well in your teaching.

Validity and Reliability of Assessments

Two assessment notions must be understood for any assessment endeavor, whether it be reflective of some newer assessment techniques or of more traditional assessments: validity and reliability. *Validity* refers to the degree to which your assessments measure what you think they measure, or rather, the degree to which the interpretations you obtain from your assessments match the kinds of interpretations you hope to obtain. *Reliability* refers to the degree of consistency possessed by the results obtained from your assessments—consistency, or stability, over time; consistency over multiple forms of an assessment; and consistency over multiple parts of the same assessment.

To make sense of these notions, we can refer metaphorically to an assessment device many of us are familiar with—the bathroom scale, that simple device we often step on to obtain an assessment of our weight. While discussing the assessment, or measurement, of body weight, we can consider some nonexamples of validity and reliability.

Suppose you wanted to know how tall you are. Would it make sense to use a bathroom scale to measure your height? Of course not. If you used a bathroom scale, your height measurement, or assessment, would be invalid. Likewise, you would not use an assessment of two-digit multiplication to measure knowledge of single-digit multiplication facts.

Now suppose that your bathroom scale gives you a reading of 140 lbs. at 6 a.m. and a reading of 160 lbs. at 6:05 a.m. You might become horribly depressed, or you might be suspicious of the scale. Your scale would not be reliable if its measurements varied over short periods. This type of reliability is concerned with stability over time and refers to the consistency of results obtained from multiple administrations of the same assessment. It is sometimes referred to as *test–retest reliability*. You would be nervous about your mathematics assessments if you administered them twice without intervening instruction and obtained dramatically different results.

Next, think about two bathroom scales purchased from two stores. Suppose your Wal-Mart bathroom scale says you weigh 140 lbs. and a Kmart scale says you weigh 120 lbs. You cannot be sure which scale, if either, is giving you an accurate measurement. Similarly, if you administer two different performance assessments designed to measure the children's ability to reason and represent place-value notions, with no intervening instruction, then you would suspect the reliability of your assessments. This is referred to as *equivalent forms reliability*.

Two "first cousins" to equivalent forms reliability are applicable to more modern assessment practice. Many assessments require a rater or scorer to assess a child's mathematical performance. You would hope that if two teachers rated the same performance their ratings would be similar. This is referred to as *interrater reliability*. If decisions are made based on those assessments, there would be a similar degree of consistency if two teachers made those decisions. This is referred to as *decision consistency*.

Finally, suppose your bathroom scale has a two "dials," one on the left that says you weigh 120 lbs. and one on the right that says you weigh 20 lbs. Maybe one side of your body weighs a little more or less than the other side, but probably not by much. So, if you asked your students to solve four two-digit multiplication exercises and they did well on two of them and poorly on the other two, you would suspect your assessment results. This type of reliability is concerned with *internal consistency*.

Comprehension Check

■ What are the definitions for these important terms: validity, test–retest reliability, equivalent forms reliability, decision consistency, and internal consistency?

Traditional Assessments

We began this chapter by discussing the need for rethinking the way we assess children if we are going to rethink the way we teach them mathematics. Do not overinterpret this suggestion. Perhaps the "Parable of the Shovel" helps illustrate our meaning.

If you were asked to provide some wood for a wood-burning stove and the only tool you had was a shovel, what would result? You can actually cut wood with a shovel, but it might take you a while. In addition, you might start to build up a little resentment toward the shovel. But is that the fault of the shovel? A shovel is a tool, and it is up to its owner to determine whether it is being used properly and is not being overused.

Traditional assessments, such as short-answer, multiple-choice, and matching items, have taken a bad rap in recent times. They are like the shovel in the parable. Traditional assessments have been overused and misused to the degree that some teachers refuse to use them. However, the best way to find out whether a child knows that $7 \times 8 = 56$ is through a short-answer traditional assessment item. Granted, there is a great deal more to multiplication than knowing basic facts, and that is where alternative assessments come in. But traditional assessments are useful for at least some of the mathematics you teach.

Procedures for Writing Traditional Assessment Items

Multiple-Choice Items Most psychometricians, or assessment experts, adhere to the same procedures when designing multiple-choice items. A multiple-choice item consists of a stem, usually a question, followed by answer choices, or options, which include the correct answer and a few incorrect choices, known as *distracters*. Because a student selects from answer choices, multiple-choice items, along with matching items, are termed *selected response*. Here are considerations when creating multiple-choice questions:

1. Write a clear stem that does not require a reading of the options to be understood.
2. Place most of the wording in the stem. This prevents students from having to select between lengthy answer options.
3. Use positive wording as much as possible. Avoid negative wording, such as *not*, if you can. If you cannot, emphasize it somehow.
4. Make sure the intended answer is clearly the best option.
5. Keep the options grammatically consistent with one another and the stem. This keeps students from making a selection based on grammar rather than on the content of the item.
6. Avoid placing verbal clues in the stem.
7. Make the distracters plausible.
8. Avoid the phrases "all of the above" and "none of the above."
9. Vary the position of the correct answer randomly.
10. Keep each item independent of the other items.
11. Frame the stem as a question. Questions are more cognitively stimulating than statements or incomplete statements.

12. The relative length of the options should not provide a clue to the answer; that is, all answer choices should be the same length.

13. List options vertically.

Matching Items   When you are writing multiple-choice items and you notice that you are repeating the stem multiple times, and possibly some of your options, you should consider using matching items. Here is an example:

   1. *What word refers to the numerals added together in an addition sentence?*
     a. Addend
     b. Product
     c. Sum
   2. *What word refers to the result produced by adding two numerals together in a number sentence?*
     a. Factor
     b. Product
     c. Sum

Notice that the stem structure and the options are repeated. These two items would be better rewritten as part of a set of matching items:

Indicate which term on the right matches each definition on the left.

1. *The numerals multiplied together in a multiplication sentence.*	*a. Factor*
2. *The result produced by adding two numerals together in a number sentence.*	*b. Product*
3. *The result proceeded by multiplying two numerals together in a number sentence.*	*c. Sum*
4. *A number that divides another number.*	

The items on the left are called *premises,* and the options on the right are called *responses.* Here are the procedures to guide your construction of matching items:

1. Keep the list of items relatively short. Lengthy sets of matching items are hard on short-term memory.

2. Keep the responses brief so that when students have to reread responses they do not have a lengthy reading burden.

3. There should be more responses than premises.

4. Keep all matching items on the same page.

Short-Answer Items   Short-answer items are termed *constructed response* because the student has to produce or construct a response rather than select one. Here are few procedures:

1. Construct the item so that only one answer is possible.

2. Frame the item as a direct question.

3. Avoid clues.

   Note: Math facts worksheets are short-answer items.

Recording the Results of Traditional Assessments

Once you have designed your assessment and administered it, you need to record the results. There are four common ways of recording data: raw scores (usually the number correct), percentages, checklists, and rubric scores. We assume you are quite familiar with the first two. Checklists are useful for simple assessment-based decisions in which either a child "has it" or does not. Rubrics are scales with descriptors and are usually used in alternative assessment situations. However, you can use them in traditional assessment situations, particularly with short-answer items. A "quick and dirty" rubric in the alternative assessment section of this chapter can be used for this purpose.

Alternative Assessments

We have been throwing around the terms *traditional* and *alternative* throughout this chapter. How do alternative assessments contrast with traditional? We have given three examples of traditional assessment (multiple-choice, matching, and short-answer items), which is probably the best way to define that term. Alternative assessments, on the other hand, possess these characteristics:

1. They assess both content and process.
2. They invite children to solve meaningful, real-life problems.
3. They elicit demonstrations of higher-order thinking.
4. They connect to past learning.

Designing and Administering Alternative Assessments

Alternative assessments are different from traditional paper-and-pencil assessments. They include open-ended questions, communication, observations, interviews, journals, portfolios, and performance assessments. We discuss each assessment type separately.

Open-Ended Questions Understanding open-ended questions is easier if you know what closed-ended questions are. Closed-ended questions are answered with predetermined and specific responses. For example, "What is the sum of 9 and 7?" is a close-ended question. In contrast, open-ended questions allow for a variety of correct responses and elicit different thinking.

Both types of questions are appropriate for assessing students' mathematical thinking. Closed-ended questions are useful for covering a range of topics, but they do not reveal student thinking in the way open-ended questions do. They involve significant mathematics and usually elicit a range of responses. They should be clearly stated, should require students to communicate their thinking, and should draw out responses that lend themselves to scoring by a rubric.

Here are a couple of examples of open-ended questions:

Julian had some toy bears, and his friend gave him three more. He now has at least six bears. How many bears did he start with?

Suppose I gave you four bags of balls, with three balls in each bag, to play with at recess time. Then you gave five balls to some friends. How many balls would you still have?

Comprehension Check

- What are the three types of traditional assessments?
- What are the four common ways of recording data obtained from traditional assessments?

The first example shows that the problem is open ended because there can be more than one answer. This is definitely a difficult problem, and students used to only having one right answer will struggle with this kind of question. The second example is open ended in that there is more than one way to arrive at the solution.

Communication This type of assessment can assume many forms: oral discourse (conversations, discussion, debates), writing (essays, journals), modeling and representing (manipulativeness, pictures, constructions), and performance (acting out, modeling). Children should learn to communicate with, and about, mathematics (NCTM 1989), so inviting them to communicate in one way or another allows you to assess this ability. Because you are working with children, it is important for you to learn to value informal mathematical language while the students develop concepts and skills. You need to model the use of formal mathematical language.

All students share their personal and cultural perspectives on the uses of mathematical language via communication assessment. Mathematical language can be embedded in the instruction or be an activity itself. Classroom presentations of the children's experiences, perhaps using multimedia aids, provide you with a great assessment vehicle and enhance the learning of other children. This form of assessment encourages children to view mathematics as a tool for communicating ideas. The next chapter details the role communication has in the math lesson.

Observations This assessment procedure is used by many teachers, despite the difficulties associated with collecting and managing assessment information. To use observation assessment effectively, you should observe your students' mathematical performances with a specific goal in mind. The NCTM process standards in *Principles and Standards for School Mathematics* (2000) provide great observational goals, such as representing an idea in multiple ways. Remember that each child does not need to be observed every day and that you obtain the most useful data from learning to assume the role of a participant–observer. In other words, be part of the learning community but also external to it to some degree.

Effective and efficient means for collecting observation information include notepad and pen, checklists, tape recorders, and video cameras.

Measurement, for example, is best assessed using concrete, hands-on tasks. Observations, therefore, are particularly well suited for assessing student understanding of measurement. If you use observation assessment for measurement, here are some goals to guide you: consider looking for use of informal and formal measurement terminology (e.g., long, short, or big), use of arbitrary and standard units, discussions of comparisons (e.g., "Which containers hold more water?"), and use of referents (relating particular measurement units to common objects).

Interviews The wise use of questioning in one-on-one situations enables you to thoroughly assess both cognitive and affective development. Invite children to model mathematical concepts and skills and to communicate them mathematically—in other words, present a good task. Ask probing questions that guide them toward more complex ideas, and ask prompting questions to help children attend to misunderstandings and to increase success to the degree required. We so strongly believe that great insights into how students think are obtained through student interviews that we invite you to design and conduct student interviews at the conclusion of each chapter. By the end of the course, you should have had plenty of interviewing opportunities.

Journals When you assign consistent journal work, you enhance your opportunities to assess the ability of your students to communicate mathematically through writing. Journals allow you to assess the children's reflections of their own capabilities, attitudes, and dispositions. It is important to develop a purpose for journals and to share this purpose with your students. Using notebooks for journaling allows access to previous entries. Journals also create opportunities for dialogue when you respond to them in writing. Allow the children to share their journal entries with one another, and encourage them to review and reflect on their own journal entries.

You might consider using a problem-solving journal. These include problems they want to solve, feelings about being able to solve the problem, solution processes, alternative solution processes and solutions, discussions of the validity of the solutions, and discussions of concepts and skills enhanced by the experience.

Portfolios Portfolios are collections of children's work. Children should be given the opportunity to provide input regarding the portfolio contents, and the type of items selected for the portfolio can be varied to reflect a real sense of the "whole" child.

The contents are developed over time, allowing teachers to obtain information about children's learning patterns—insight into their interpretation of their work, their dispositions toward mathematics, and their mathematical understanding.

A portfolio in geometry might include the following:

- Initial sketches of plane figures (e.g., square and pentagon)
- Interim sketches of plane figures produced during in-depth learning of the concepts
- Final sketches of plane figures created at the end of instruction on the concepts
- Constructions of models
- Written descriptions of plane figures
- Plane figures found in the child's environment
- Classifications of plane figures into groups
- Records of investigations and explorations
- Records of geometry terms and definitions
- Other items chosen by child

As you can see, portfolios are a unique assessment device, one that enables you not only to gauge a child's progress over time but also to assess how well that child can self-assess.

Performance Assessments McMillan (2004, 229–230) describes a performance assessment by providing a list of attributes:

> **[In performance assessments] the teacher observes and makes a judgment about the student's demonstration of a skill or competency in creating a product, constructing a response, or making a presentation.**

They possess several important characteristics:

- **Students perform, create, construct, or produce**
- **Assess deep understanding or reasoning**
- **Involve sustained work**
- **Call on students to explain, justify, and defend**
- **Performance is directly observable**
- **Involve engaging ideas of importance and substance (worthwhile math task)**
- **Reliance on trained assessor's judgments**
- **Multiple criteria and standards are prespecified and public (rubrics)**
- **There is no single correct answer (or solution strategy)**
- **Performance is grounded in real-world contexts and constraints**

Hopefully, you can see that many other alternative assessment processes are incorporated in performance assessments. This is why we call them the "granddaddy of alternative assessments." We have published guidelines on how to design performance assessments elsewhere (Bahr 2008) and include those guidelines in the following paragraphs.

One of the challenges associated with performance assessments is designing them so that they can be delivered on an individual student's level, that is, as developmental assessments (Pegg 2003). In today's classrooms, teachers are usually faced with the responsibility of teaching children with a range of abilities. It is conceivable that a well-designed performance assessment could be administered yet fail to provide useful data if the assessment is delivered at a level that is either too difficult or too easy for the student being assessed. Therefore, here we suggest ways to create such assessments while honoring what is known about the traits that characterize high-quality performance assessments in mathematics.

Because number and operations content forms the cornerstone of the entire mathematics curriculum internationally (Hogan, Murcia, and van Wyke 2004; NCTM 2000; Reys and Nohda 1994), we focus on this content to help you begin to learn to design performance-based assessments for their classrooms.

1. Choose a topic for your grade level, such as subtraction of whole numbers, for which a problem can be developed that leads to the types of concepts you want to develop (e.g., see Ma 1999).

2. Create the performance task. Write an engaging, real-life word problem that incorporates the concepts you have chosen. Craft it so that any size of numbers would make sense in the wording, which allows you to assess multiple levels through one task. For example, here is a second-grade subtraction task:

I have _____ pieces of candy. I gave _____ pieces to my friend. How many pieces do I have now?

Note that numbers of varying numerical complexity can be inserted in the blanks depending on the child's estimated level. The term *level* possesses multiple definitions in mathematics education, but in a number and operations context it often relates to the complexity of the numbers involved in

Level	Number Sense	Addition	Subtraction	Multiplication	Division
A	Rote counting	Joining sets	Separating sets	1 digit × 1 digit = 1 digit (2 × 3 = 6)	1 digit ÷ 1 digit = 1 digit (8 ÷ 2 = 4)
B	One-to-one correspondence	Single-digit addends and sum (3 + 2 = 5)	1 digit − 1 digit = 1 digit (5 − 3 = 2)	1 digit × 1 digit = 2 digits (composing: 2 × 6 = 12)	2 digits ÷ 1 digit = 1 digit (12 ÷ 2 = 6)
C	Single digits < 5	Single-digit addends and double-digit sum (3 + 9 = 12)	2 digits − 1 digit = 1 digit (decomposing) (13 − 5 = 8)	10 × 1 digit (10 × 3 = 30)	1 or 2 digits ÷ 1 digit = 1 digit with remainder (7 ÷ 3 = 2 r 1)
D	Single digits > 5	Multiple single-digit addends (3 + 2 + 4 = 9)	2 digits − 1 digit = 2 digits (no decomposing) (27 − 5 = 22)	10 multiple × 1 digit = 2 digits (20 × 3 = 60)	10 multiple ÷ 1 digit = 10 multiple (no decomposing) (60 ÷ 2 = 30)

Figure 3.1. Hierarchy of numerical complexity for the four operations.

the problem a child is asked to solve. Therefore, one of the ways the level of a problem can be regulated is by controlling the complexity of the numbers in the problem. Teachers with whom we have worked have helped develop a "hierarchy of numerical complexity" relative to number and the four operations to guide them in determining the level at which a child is capable of problem solving. They have found this hierarchy to be quite accurate and useful. Part of the hierarchy appears in figure 3.1. The complete hierarchy appears on the website.

3. Design a quickly administered inventory to estimate level. This inventory should call for the solving of simple exercises of varying complexity in the operation associated with the grade and can be administered to an entire class in written form before administering the performance assessment. A complete inventory for whole-number subtraction appears here:

Second Grade
Operation or Algorithmic Sense Inventory
Whole-Number Subtraction

$5 - 3$ $13 - 5$ $27 - 5$ $27 - 9$

$36 - 24$ $32 - 18$ $406 - 178$ $1,469 - 635$

Note that this inventory is quite procedural in nature. The teachers with whom we have worked have found that procedural performance can be used to find a quick, rough estimate of the level at which the performance assessment should be administered. However, if a child's instructional experience has not included the development of solid connections between concepts and procedures, this estimate is likely to be too high. If the child's responses in the initial stages of the performance assessment indicate that the level estimate obtained from the inventory is inaccurate, the teacher can make an immediate adjustment by readministering the task with numbers of differing complexity.

4. Select criteria to serve as standards for judging the performance. We have found seven criteria to be quite useful in gauging the quality of a student's mathematical performance: five analytical criteria based on the process

Special Needs

Being able to adjust the assessment to the level of the child helps ensure that the assessment is a successful experience.

Rule of Thumb

Inventories are more accurate if children are accustomed to connecting their conceptual and procedural knowledge.

Rubric Level	Problem Solving
4 Independent understanding	Can solve the problem in two ways independently
3 Understanding with minimal help	Can solve the problem in two ways with minimal help or one way independently
2 Understanding with substantial help	Can solve the problem in at least one way with help
1 Little understanding	Cannot solve the problem even with help

Figure 3.2. Comprehensive rubric for scoring the use of NCTM process standards. (T. Proctor, personal communication.)

standards in the NCTM's *Principles and Standards* (2000) in agreement with the earlier suggestions of Dunbar and Witt (1993), and two holistic criteria as suggested by the learning principle, also part of the *Principles and Standards* document. The five analytical criteria are problem solving, communicating, reasoning, representing, and connecting. The two holistic criteria are conceptual and procedural.

Special Needs

Your careful questioning, or scaffolding, is another way to ensure a successful assessment experience for special needs children. Modern assessment theory actually encourages your support of a student's performance as long as the data obtained from the assessment reflects the degree of that support.

5. Design a rubric using those criteria. One way to go about designing this rubric is to create a scoring hierarchy based on the degree of assessor prompting required for a student to experience success in the assessment. In other words, the more assistance a child requires, the lower the rubric score. The incorporation of prompting as factor in distinguishing rubric levels results in a blurring of the line between instruction and assessment in harmony with current assessment philosophy (McMillan 2004). A portion of such a rubric appears in figure 3.2. A complete one appears on the website. 🖱

6. Create questions or prompts to probe student thinking. Appropriate questions ensure that opportunities are provided for students to express themselves verbally, as well as in written form (Dunbar and Witt 1993; Glaser, Raghavan, and Baxter 1992), and that students were invited to display behavior that addresses all analytical criteria, that is, the NCTM process standards (Mewborn and Huberty 1999). In this way, you can be confident that important mathematical knowledge is assessed (Dunbar and Witt 1993; Morgan 1998; NCTM 2000) and that the interpretations associated with the assessment possess construct validity (Messick 1989), particularly in terms of assessing deep, connected conceptual understanding. Some possible prompts and questions for a fifth-grade division assessment are as follows:

a. *Which operation would you use to find the answer? (Problem solving.)*
b. *Explain how you solved the problem. (Communicating.)*
c. *Solve the problem in a different way. Explain or show me. (Problem solving.)*
d. *What would happen to the numbers in the question if you added them? (If student added, ask what would happen to the numbers if the student subtracted them.) (Reasoning.)*
e. *Show this problem as a number sentence. (Representing.)*
f. *Solve this problem using pictures, manipulatives, etc. (Connecting.)*

7. Design a teacher recording form, and create a form for students to record their work on. Examples follow:

Mathematics Performance Assessment	Teacher Recording Form
Name _____ Grade _____ Date _____	
Operation Sense	
_____ Level (number complexity)	Anecdotal Notes:
_____ Problem solving (using multiple ways)	
_____ Communicating (explaining)	
_____ Reasoning (justifying)	
_____ Representing (showing multiple ways)	
_____ Connecting (representing, explaining)	
_____ Procedural understanding	
_____ Conceptual understanding	

Mathematics Performance Assessment	Student Recording Form
Name _____ Date _____ Grade _____	
Worthwhile Mathematical Task:	
I have _____ pieces of candy. I gave _____ pieces to my friend.	
How many pieces do I have now?	
Work Area:	

Recording the Results of Alternative Assessments

There are three fundamental ways of recording data obtained from your alternative assessments: rubric scores, which we discussed previously; checklists, which are used when you simply wish to record whether or not a child can do something; and anecdotal notes, which are used when you want to be descriptive of a child's performance.

As promised earlier, we created figure 3.3, what we call the quick and dirty rubric, which can be used in both traditional and alternative assessment contexts. It does not provide nearly as much information as the comprehensive rubric, which we shared when discussing performance assessments, but it is useful when you are in hurry and need to record some general information about your students' progress.

Figure 3.3. Quick and dirty rubric for scoring the use of NCTM process standards.

CONTENT   *Single-Digit Addition and Subtraction*

In the pedagogical section of this chapter, we detailed how to write and administer different assessments. We now talk specifically about single-digit addition and subtraction of whole numbers while keeping the notion of assessment and student thinking at the forefront. An understanding of how children develop their understandings of addition and subtraction empowers your assessments and enables you to determine where your students are in relation to the developmental continuua we provide you.

Big Ideas and Focal Points

We need to keep in mind a couple of big ideas when thinking about addition and subtraction of whole numbers.

- The same number sentence (e.g., $12 - 4 = 8$) can be associated with different concrete or real-world situations, *and* different number sentences can be associated with the same concrete or real-world situation (Charles 2005, 15).

- Addition and subtraction are connected. Addition names the whole in terms of the parts, and subtraction names a missing part (Van de Walle 2004, 135).

In *Principles and Standards,* the NCTM (2000) states that as a result of its instructional programs, students across all grades should "understand meanings of operations and how they relate to one another" (p. 32). They expand on this by stating that students from pre-K to second grade should "understand various meanings of addition and subtraction of whole numbers and the relationship between the two operations" and "understand the effects of adding and subtracting whole numbers" (p. 78).

The NCTM's *Curriculum Focal Points* give a good indication of what mathematics we can expect children to learn; that is, they enable us to ensure that our grade-level expectations are developmentally appropriate. The *Curriculum Focal Points* give a sense of the kinds of understandings and skills children should develop as they study and use the operations of addition and subtraction and a sense of the grade levels associated with that development. The Focal Points table compares those expectations related to whole-number addition and subtraction across grades.

Operation Sense

In the last chapter, we discussed the fundamental notions of number sense that are so influential in empowering children's mathematical abilities. A companion to number sense, *operation sense,* is every bit as empowering. When we help children develop operation sense, we invite them to develop a deep understanding of the meanings and uses of operations so that they can fully use mathematical operations as important problem-solving tools. There are six components of operation sense (NCTM 2000):

1. Developing meanings for operations
2. Gaining a sense of the relationships among operations

NCTM FOCAL POINTS

Kindergarten	First Grade	Second Grade
Model simple joining and separating situations with objects. Count the number in combined sets. Count backward.	Develop strategies for adding and subtracting whole numbers on the basis of earlier work with small numbers. Use a variety of models, including discrete objects, length-based models (e.g., lengths of connecting cubes), and number lines, for part–whole, adding to, taking away from, and comparing situations to develop an understanding of the meanings of addition and subtraction and strategies to solve such arithmetic problems. Understand the connections between counting and operations of addition and subtraction (e.g., adding 2 is the same as counting on 2). Use properties of addition (commutativity and associativity) to add whole numbers, and create and use increasingly sophisticated strategies based on these properties (e.g., making tens) to solve addition and subtraction problems involving basic facts. By comparing a variety of solution strategies, relate addition and subtraction as inverse operations.	Use understanding of addition to develop quick recall of basic addition facts and related subtraction facts. Solve arithmetic problems by applying understanding of models of addition and subtraction (e.g., combining or separating sets or using number lines), relationships and properties of number (e.g., place value), and properties of addition (commutativity and associativity). Add and subtract to solve a variety of problems, including applications involving measurement, geometry, and data, as well as nonroutine problems.

3. Determining which operation to use in a given situation

4. Recognizing that the same operation can be applied in problem situations that seem quite different (e.g., subtraction is used in more situations than take away)

5. Developing a sense for the operations' effects on numbers

6. Realizing that operation effects depend on the types of numbers involved (e.g., multiplication has a different effect on fractions than on whole numbers)

All six components are interwoven in our discussion of addition and subtraction.

Problem Types

The work of Carpenter et al. (1999), in examining the ways children think mathematically, has resulted in a classification scheme for the problem-solving contexts in which addition and subtraction are used. This scheme is based on the actions or numerical relationships inherent within those contexts. There are four basic classes of contexts, or problem types: join problems and separate problems, which children tend to solve using an action, and part–part–whole problems and compare problems, which involve relating quantities. Join problems involve adding elements to a given set, and separate problems involve removing elements. Part–part–whole problems require the examination of the relationship between a set and its two subsets, and compare problems encourage comparison between two distinct sets. Because join and separate use actions, these problem types are much easier for children to understand and solve.

Within each class of problems are individual problem types distinguished by whichever element of the problem is unknown. For example, join problems have three elements: start, change, and result. If we presented the problem "Sue has 6 gumdrops and Jose gave her 9 more, so how many does she have now?" that would be a join (result unknown) problem. On the other hand, if we presented the problem "Sue has 6 gumdrops. How many more does she need to have 15 gumdrops?" that would be a join (change unknown) problem. Figure 5.2 lists and exemplifies 11 problem types organized by class and by unknown problem element.

Another way to distinguish among problem types is to think about the number sentences that can be used to represent them. Van de Walle (2007) distinguishes between *semantic* sentences, which are listed in the order that follows the meaning inherent in the problem (such as $6 + \_\_\_\_ = 15$ from the preceding gumdrop problem), and *computational* sentences, which isolate the unknowns on one side of the equal sign in the form you would need to use with a calculator ($15 - 6 = \_\_\_\_$). In figure 3.4, we included both number sentence types described for each problem type. Notice that in some cases the sentences in each pair are the same but in other cases they are different in either the order of the numbers or the operations used.

The inclusion of these sentences is primarily for computational-fluent people like you. They are not placed here to encourage you to invite children to represent their thinking in number sentences before it is developmentally appropriate. When children are ready to represent their thinking using abstract number sentences, they will probably use the semantic form. Once they conceptualize the notion of inverse operations, they will naturally develop the more complicated computational form with little direct instruction from you.

Language Tip

Students, especially second-language learners, need a lot of work with the language in the problem types shown in figure 3.4. One of the main reasons certain problems are more difficult is that students are unfamiliar with the wording.

Besides problem type, another way in which these problems can become difficult deals with the numerical complexity associated with them—the size of the numbers. When a child seems confident at solving a problem, just increase the size of one or both numbers to present a new challenge. Likewise, if children are

Easiest   Most
                                                                                                                 Difficult

JOIN

(Result Unknown)   (Change Unknown)   (Start Unknown)
Mike had 4 toy cars. Lynn   Sue has 4 toy cars. How   Betty had some toy cars.
gave him 8 more toy cars.   many more does she need   Philip gave her 4 more toy
How many cars does he   to have 12 toy cars?   cars. Now she has 12. How
have altogether? $4 + \square = 12$ (semantic)   many did Betty start with?
$4 + 8 = \square$ (semantic) $12 - 4 = \square$ (computational) $\square + 4 = 12$ (semantic)
$4 + 8 = \square$ (computational) $12 - 4 = \square$ (computational)

SEPARATE

(Result Unknown)   (Change Unknown)   (Start Unknown)
Michelle had 12 toy cars.   Sue had 12 toy cars. She   Betty has some toy cars. She
She gave 4 to Lynn. How   gave some to Gary. Now she   gave 4 to Philip. Now she
many does she have left?   has 4 left. How many did she   has 8 left. How many cars
$12 - 4 = \square$ (semantic)   give to Gary?   did Betty start with?
$12 - 4 = \square$ (computational) $12 - \square = 4$ (semantic) $\square - 4 = 8$ (semantic)
                                    $12 - 4 = \square$ (computational) $4 + 8 = \square$ (computational)

PART–PART–WHOLE

(Whole Unknown)   (Part Unknown)
Michelle has 4 red toy cars and 8 yellow toy   Sue had 12 toy cars, 4 red and the rest yellow.
cars. How many toy cars does she have?   How many yellow cars does Sue have?
$4 + 8 = \square$ (semantic) $12 = 4 + \square$ (semantic)
$4 + 8 = \square$ (computational) $12 - 4 = \square$ (computational)

COMPARE

(Difference Unknown)   (Compare Quantity Unknown)   (Referent Unknown)
Michelle has 4 toy cars and   Sue has 4 toy cars. Gary has   Betty has 12 toy cars. She
Lynn has 12 toy cars. How   8 more toy cars than Sue.   has 4 more than Philip. How
many more cars does Lynn   How many cars does Gary   many cars does Philip have?
have than Michelle?   have? $12 = 4 + \square$ (semantic)
$4 + \square = 12$ (semantic) $4 + 8 = \square$ (semantic) $12 - 4 = \square$ (computational)
$12 - 4 = \square$ (computational) $4 + 8 = \square$ (computational)

Most
Difficult

Figure 3.4. Classification of problem types with number sentences. (Adapted from Carpenter et al 1999, 12. Reprinted with permission from *Children's Mathematics*. Copyright © 1999 by Thomas Carpenter, Linda Levi, Elizabeth Fennema, Megan Loef Franke, Susan Empson. Published by Heinemann, Portsmouth, NH. All rights reserved.)

having difficulty with solving a problem, the numbers are likely too challenging. Bringing the numbers down allows all students to have access to the problem.

Two levels of difficulty based on numerical complexity are associated with all of these problem types. The easier level involves single-digit numbers. For example, "Mike had 4 toy cars. Lynn gave him 3 more toy cars. How many cars does he have altogether?" or "Michelle had 7 toy cars. She gave 4 to Lynn. How many does he have left?"

The more difficult problems involve one double-digit number, such as "Mike had 4 toy cars. Lynn gave him 8 more toy cars. How many cars does he have altogether?" or "Michelle had 12 toy cars. She gave 4 to Lynn. How many does he have left?" Although both levels of problems involve facts to 18 or fewer problems in a set, the introduction of numbers greater than 10 represents a noticeable increase in numerical complexity that is significant for a young child. It also provides a prime opportunity to incorporate the fundamental

Special Needs

These problems can be made accessible to all students by lowering the numbers.

notions of composing and decomposing that were discussed in a previous chapter. In fact, the incorporation of composing and decomposing at this stage of instruction about addition and subtraction is a fundamental difference between countries that are more successful at mathematics instruction and the United States (Ma 1999), where composing and decomposing are not encountered until multidigit work.

Problem-Solving Strategies

When left to their own devices, children are quite adept at inventing strategies to solve these varied problem types, and there is a "developmentalness" to these strategies. First, children tend to use physical objects (manipulatives) or pictures of physical objects to "directly model" the actions or number relationships inherent in the problem. As they progress, they tend to develop more abstract, and thus generally more efficient, strategies. Direct modeling strategies are replaced by counting strategies, which are then replaced with number facts (figure 3.5). The most commonly recalled number facts, or the facts that seem to be easiest to recall, are the doubles, like 4 + 4, and combinations that make 10, like 4 + 6. Number facts such as these are then used to "derive" the answers to other facts. For example, a child who remembers 4 + 4 = 8 often derives the answer to 4 + 5 by adding 1. Eventually, 4 + 5 becomes a known fact as well.

Figure 3.6 describes and labels the problem-solving strategies children tend to use for each problem (direct modeling and counting). When direct modeling, children use one of the following strategies: joining all, joining to, trial and error, separating from, or matching. The types of counting strategies children use are counting on, counting on to, counting down, separating from, and matching. Please note that the strategies depicted are only one way of solving the problem. Children tend to solve each problem in multiple ways, but the ones pictured are quite common.

Figure 3.7 helps summarize how children develop these strategies.

We mentioned that numerical complexity can make a problem harder, but it also influences the solution strategies that children choose to use. For example, a child might just know 3 + 4 = 7, but when given a problem involving larger numbers, such as 8 + 7, he might use a counting strategy or even a direct modeling strategy, such as using counters. This is why it is critical to know the number range your different students work in. This is also why we come prepared to a student interview with different number sizes. Suppose that you choose to present a separate (result unknown) problem using 7 − 3 = 4 and the child gets the answer quickly, so it is obvious that she just knew. You can choose to either increase the difficulty of the problem type or use the same problem but increase the numerical complexity. It is important to increase one at a time. If you increase both, the child may suddenly use direct modeling and you will not know whether the change in strategy choice results from the size of the numbers or the difficulty of the problem.

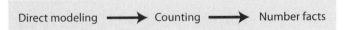

Figure 3.5. Sequence children pass through when developing problem-solving strategies.

Problem Type/ Numerical Complexity	Direct Modeling (graphic)	Child's Wording	Counting/ Keeping Track	Child's Wording
Join (Result Unknown) Mike had 4 toy cars. Lynn gave him 3 more toy cars. How many cars does he have altogether? $4 + 3 = \square$ (semantic) $4 + 3 = \square$ (computational)		**(Joining all)** (Pointing to each block in the set of 4) 1, 2, 3, 4 (then pointing to each block in the set of 7). I put them together and count 1, 2, 3, 4, 5, 6, 7.		**(Counting on)** I have 4 (putting up 3 more fingers and then counting them), 5, 6, 7.
Join (Change Unknown) Sue has 4 toy cars. How many more does she need to have 7 toy cars? $4 + \square = 7$ (semantic) $7 - 4 = \square$ (computational)		**(Joining to)** (Pointing to each block in the set of 4) 1, 2, 3, 4 (then adding one block at a time) 5, 6, 7. (Pointing to the added blocks of the other color) 1, 2, 3. She needs 3 more.		**(Counting on to)** I have 4 (putting up one finger at a time until reaching 7), 5, 6, 7. That's 3 more.
Join (Start Unknown) Betty had some toy cars. Philip gave her 4 more toy cars. Now she has 7. How many did Betty start with? $\square + 4 = 7$ (semantic) $7 - 4 = \square$ (computational)		**(Trial and error)** I start with 1 (block) and count 2, 3, 4, 5 (counting the other 4). That's not enough, so I start with 2 and count 2, 3, 4, 5, 6. That's still not enough, so I start with 3 and count 4, 5, 6, 7. Betty started with 3.		**(Counting on)** She gets 4, then I count up to 7—5, 6, 7—to see how many she must have had.
Separate (Result Unknown) Michelle had 7 toy cars. She gave 4 to Lynn. How many does he have left? $7 - 4 = \square$ (semantic) $7 - 4 = \square$ (computational)		**(Separating from)** 1, 2, 3, 4, 5, 6, 7 blocks. I take away 1, 2, 3, 4. There are 1, 2, 3 left.		**(Counting down)** I put up 7 fingers, put down 4, and have 3 left. I start on 7 on the number line, count back 4, and land on 3.
Separate (Change Unknown) Sue had 7 toy cars. She gave some to Gary. Now she has 4 left. How many did she give to Gary? $7 - \square = 4$ (semantic) $7 - 4 = \square$ (computational)		**(Separating from)** I count (pointing to blocks) 1, 2, 3, 4 and break off that many blocks for Sue. Gary has 3.		**(Separating from)** I left up the 4 fingers that were the cars left. I put down the rest and notice that I put down 3 fingers.
Separate (Start Unknown) Betty had some toy cars. She gave 4 to Philip. Now she has 3 left. How many did Betty start with? $\square - 4 = 3$ (semantic) $4 + 3 = \square$ (computational)		**(Joining to)** Phillip got 4 and Betty ended with 3. If I give Phillip's back, then Betty had 7 to start.		**(Counting on)** I put up 3 fingers and on the other hand count 4 more of the ones she gave Phillip: 5, 6, 7. I start at the 3 on the number line and count 4 more for the ones she gave to Phillip. I land on 7.

Figure 3.6. Examples of how children use direct modeling and counting strategies for problem types.

(Continued on following page.)

Problem Type/ Numerical Complexity	Direct Modeling (graphic)	Child's Wording	Counting/ Keeping Track	Child's Wording
Part–Part–Whole (Whole Unknown) Michelle has 4 red toy cars and 3 yellow toy cars. How many toy cars does she have? $4 + 3 = \square$ (semantic) $4 + 3 = \square$ (computational)		**(Joining all)** (Putting the 4 red and 3 yellow counters together in a pile) 1, 2, 3, 4, 5, 6, 7.		**(Counting on)** I start on the 4, count up 3 more, and land on 7.
Part–Part–Whole (Part Unknown) Sue has 7 toy cars. 4 red and the rest yellow. How many yellow cars does Sue have? $7 = 4 + \square$ (semantic) $7 - 4 = \square$ (computational)		**(Joining to)** (Pointing to the red counters) 1, 2, 3, 4 (then pointing to the yellow counters, adding one counter at a time) 5, 6, 7. She has 3 yellow cars.		**(Counting on to)** I put up 4 fingers on one hand and on the other hand count up to 7. I have 3 fingers on the other hand, so there were 3 cars that are yellow.
Compare (Difference Unknown) Michelle has 4 toy cars and Lynn has 7 toy cars. How many more cars does Lynn have than Michelle? $4 + \square = 7$ (semantic) $7 - 4 = \square$ (computational)		**(Matching)** (Making two trains) 1, 2, 3, 4 and 1, 2, 3, 4, 5, 6, 7. (Putting them together to compare and breaking off extra cubes) 1, 2, 3. Lynn has 3 more cars than Michelle.		**(Matching)** (Making two trains) 1, 2, 3, 4 and 1, 2, 3, 4, 5, 6, 7. (Putting them together to compare and counting extra cubes) Lynn has 1, 2, 3 more than Michelle.
Compare (Compare Quantity Unknown) Sue has 4 toy cars. Gary has 3 more toy cars than Sue. How many cars does Gary have? $4 + 3 = \square$ (semantic) $4 + 3 = \square$ (computational)		**(Matching)** Sue has 4, so Gary has 4 and then 3 more. That's 4, 5, 6, 7.		**(Matching)** Sue has 4, so Gary has 4 and then 3 more. That's 4, 5, 6, 7.
Compare (Referent Unknown) Betty has 7 toy cars. She has 4 more than Philip. How many cars does Philip have? $12 = 4 + \square$ (semantic) $12 - 4 = \square$ (computational)		**(Matching)** I make 7 cars for Betty and 7 cars for Philip, but because Betty has more, Philip must have less. So I take the 4 extra cars from Phillip to get 3.		**(Matching)** I make 7 cars for Betty and 7 cars for Phillip, but because Betty has more, Phillip must have less. So I take the 4 extra cars from Phillip to get 3.

Figure 3.6, continued

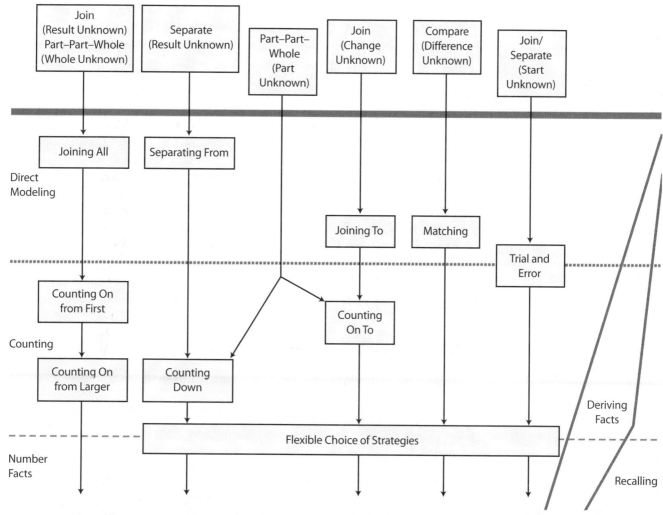

Figure 3.7. Strategy sequence chart. (Reprinted with permission from *Children's Mathematics*. Copyright © 1999 by Thomas Carpenter, Linda Levi, Elizabeth Fennema, Megan Loef Franke, Susan Empson. Published by Heinemann, Portsmouth, NH. All rights reserved.)

Learning the Basics of Addition and Subtraction

Marilyn Burns (2000) defines the basics of arithmetic as learning to compute and the application of computational skills to solve problems. Up to this point, this chapter has discussed how we use skills to solve addition and subtraction problems. This section focuses on the aspect of learning to compute.

It is no secret that teachers as high as eighth grade are frustrated because their students do not have quick recall of addition or related subtraction facts. Struggling students in the upper grades can be observed using tic marks as they attempt to solve multidigit problems. This counting all strategy seems to be the only strategy some children have in relation to addition, yet it proves ineffective almost every time because the numbers are too large for these students to keep track off their tic marks. Surely, if they would just memorize their facts, many say, they would be more accurate. There is some truth to this, but the problem is deeper rooted than just knowing their facts.

The students described in the previous paragraph are still in the counting stages. They have not learned any strategies beyond that. Older students probably understand that addition is combining but do not have enough foundation in the base 10 system to develop more efficient ways of combining. For these students, it would be a crime to make them just memorize their facts. They need to go back and have experiences with tens and ones and building numbers so that they have an opportunity to generalize patterns. These generalizations will support their quick recall of facts and, consequently, will be applied to larger numbers.

Generalizations

What are the generalizations students make that support computation and quick recall? And how do students develop such generalizations?

The following are some big ideas that support flexible thinking and quick recall, which we want students to generalize:

One more or one less

10 more or less

Combinations of all numbers to 10 (part–part–whole relationships)

Commutativity

Doubles or near-doubles

10 and some more

Making tens

The steps in which such generalizations are developed appear to be as follows:

1. Concrete, hands-on experiences

2. Using a model as a visual

3. Using symbols as a visual

4. Making mental calculations with the model in the head

5. Making mental calculations using a generalized rule or known fact ("I just know it")

Struggling Learner

When students do not know their basic facts, test to see whether they are missing any of these generalizations.

After children have plenty of hands-on experiences with a related idea, they tend to still need to refer to that model visually when trying to apply generalized rules they have been developing. Sometimes when the visual is removed, children are observed going back to their counting strategies. This means that they have not internalized the rule and the visual is not yet "stuck in their brain." When we begin hearing children say, "I see the 10 frames in my head," we know they are trying to directly model inside their brain what they did with the concrete items. In time, with enough practice, they will stop relying on the mental images of the models and will be using the generalized rule.

The idea of one more or one less and combinations of all numbers to 10 were discussed in detail in chapter 2 as part of the matching phase. In chapter 4, we explore 10 more or less as part of understanding place value. This section describes developing understanding for commutativity, doubles, 10 and some more, and making tens.

Commutativity

Understanding the commutativity of numbers, or that numbers can be added in any order, helps students by allowing them to start with whichever number they feel would be easier. Children explore the notion of commutativity through story problems and using counters. They come to realize that because

	1	2	3	4	5	6	7	8	9
1	1 + 1	1 + 2	1 + 3	1 + 4	1 + 5	1 + 6	1 + 7	1 + 8	1 + 9
2	2 + 1	2 + 2	2 + 3	2 + 4	2 + 5	2 + 6	2 + 7	2 + 8	2 + 9
3	3 + 1	3 + 2	3 + 3	3 + 4	3 + 5	3 + 6	3 + 7	3 + 8	3 + 9
4	4 + 1	4 + 2	4 + 3	4 + 4	4 + 5	4 + 6	4 + 7	4 + 8	4 + 9
5	5 + 1	5 + 2	5 + 3	5 + 4	5 + 5	5 + 6	5 + 7	5 + 8	5 + 9
6	6 + 1	6 + 2	6 + 3	6 + 4	6 + 5	6 + 6	6 + 7	6 + 8	6 + 9
7	7 + 1	7 + 2	7 + 3	7 + 4	7 + 5	7 + 6	7 + 7	7 + 8	7 + 9
8	8 + 1	8 + 2	8 + 3	8 + 4	8 + 5	8 + 6	8 + 7	8 + 8	8 + 9
9	9 + 1	9 + 2	9 + 3	9 + 4	9 + 5	9 + 6	9 + 7	9 + 8	9 + 9

Figure 3.8. Addition chart to demonstrate commutativity.

the two amounts are essentially being pushed together it does not matter which order they are adding in; the total is the same. This becomes helpful when developing counting strategies, such as counting on from the larger number. This property is also important because it means that children only have to know half of the existing facts; that is, 3 + 7 is the same as 7 + 3 (figure 3.8). If using an addition table, then half of the facts are eliminated.

Doubles or Near-Doubles

When looking closely at the addition chart in figure 3.8, you can see that the addition facts located diagonally across the chart are the doubles. For some reason, children seem to learn the sums to doubles facts easily. Doubles are easily explored through fingers and 10 frames. When children are using the doubles as an addition strategy, then they can explore the relationship of doubles plus and minus one.

"If 4 + 4 = 8, then 4 + 4 + 1 = 9 or 4 + 5 = 9"

It is helpful for students to have visuals for things that comes in doubles to help them remember their sums. For instance, a carton of eggs can be represented by 6 + 6 = 12.

10 and Some More

This big idea refers to 10 + 5, and so on. Initially, when asked this to solve this problem, young children respond by either counting all or counting on. Once children have experiences building numbers 11–20 using 10 frames, they typically notice that 10 and 5 are 15. For subtraction, show a frame of 10 and a frame of 5 and ask how much there would be if you took away 5 or if you took away 10. Create a chart of the equations to match the problems, for example, 10 + 4 = 14. After gathering a substantial list of similar equations, have the students discuss what they notice. These discussions will help students just know that 10 and 4 is 14. Depending on the quality of the experiences a child has, this generalization typically solidifies in first grade.

Making Tens

This is probably the most powerful addition strategy. When students take what they know about combinations of number and use this knowledge to make tens, they are creating easier problems to solve. This shows flexibility and efficiency. Even though teachers can do whole group activities or discussions about making tens, unless a child can add 10 and some more (10 + 5) with ease, making tens will not make a problem any easier; thus, she will just see it as something different to do with the numbers.

We start by adding 9 and some more. The 10 frames tend to be the best tool for this activity. When we show a 9 frame and 4 frame on the board and ask the class what is 9 and 4 more, we see a lot of strategies. They may be counting all, counting on, or making tens. If a child is still counting all, we want to first get her to the counting on stage, not making tens. A child who is making a 10 will say, "I moved a dot from the 4 into the empty square to make a 10, and I know 10 and 3 are 13." As a teacher, your job is not to show the strategy but to get your students to come up with it on their own. When they do, they are better able to internalize the strategy.

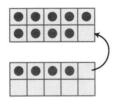

Initially, when children orally share out this strategy, other children cannot mentally see what they are talking about because it is too abstract. Therefore, it is important to act it out with counters. This helps a child see what someone else did but is not useful until he understands 10 and some more.

Once children seem to be using this making tens strategy, try showing only the 9 frame and saying the second number. It is interesting to see how many students revert to counting on. This just implies that they still have to see both visuals and the strategy is not internalized yet. Over time, you will be able to show just the 9 and then eventually you will not need to show either number. A few students may jump to a generalization with no visuals ("1 less than 4 is

3, so 13"), but initially most will see the dots in their head and move them as they did with the visual model. With practice, they will begin to generalize.

Toward the end of first grade and the beginning of second grade, most students are developmentally capable of using this strategy, although this capability varies with individual children and depends on their previous experiences with numbers. After 9 and some more, children need practice with 8 and some more and then 7 and some more, using the same steps with the visuals first. It is interesting to watch students who can generalize the 9 and some more strategy revert to counting on to 8 and some more. They have established a rule for the nines but have not fully generalized the notion of breaking apart numbers to make a 10.

Ultimately, we want our students to be able to use this strategy with any number, so once they are making tens (e.g., 8 + 4), the next step is to ask them what 18 + 4 would be. Most can use the strategy with single digits but do not apply it to multidigit numbers without further experiences.

Here is a summary of the steps children pass through in generalizing making tens:

1. Recognizes individual quantities of the 10 frames
2. Knows 10 and some more (may or may not know a number minus 10)
3. Counts on for 9 and some more
4. Moves counter to make a 10
5. Moves dot mentally to make a 10
6. Moves dot mentally when only sees 9 and hears another number
7. Moves dot mentally when hearing both numbers
8. Generalizes a rule for adding 9
9. May revert to counting on when introducing 8 and some more and 7 and some more
10. Generalizes the idea of breaking apart numbers to add two-digit numbers

Figures 3.9 and 3.10 show approximations of where work for student-developed generalizations falls in grades K–2 and activities that might support such development, respectively. Teachers need to consider the work in the grades under them to determine what needs to be done in their own class. For instance, a second-grade teacher may have to begin at concrete models in relation to 10 more and 10 less if her students lack concrete experiences.

Practicing for Quick Recall

Once students have developed strategies and sufficient conceptual knowledge about the preceding areas, it is appropriate for them to practice what they know. If you refer back to the addition chart, you will notice that once children learn plus one and two, their doubles, and making tens facts (with nines and eights), only a few facts remain for them to learn. One of the most fun and effective ways for practicing facts is through games. Some games are competitive, or against a partner, and some are solitary. Games make wonderful homework assignments and encourage family involvement.

One of the games children enjoy most is *Addition War*. In this simple game, two or more students play, each turning over two number cards. The one with the highest sum wins all the cards. This game could also be played so that the first one getting the correct sum of his pair of cards wins all the cards.

Comprehension Check

- What are the steps students pass through when making a generalization?
- Describe some generalizations students make as they learn their basic addition facts.

Kindergarten	First Grade	Second Grade
One more or one less		
■ Concrete		
■ Visual (direct model or symbolic)		
■ Mental (generalized)		
10 more or 10 less	**10 more or 10 less**	**10 more or 10 less**
■ Concrete	■ Concrete	■ Visual (direct model or symbolic)
■ Visual (direct model)	■ Visual (direct model or symbolic)	■ Mental (direct model or generalized)
■ Mental (direct model)	■ Mental (direct model or generalized)	
Combination of Nos. to 10	**Combination of Nos. to 10**	**Combination of Nos. to 10**
To 6 or 7	To 8 to 10	To 10
■ Concrete	■ Concrete	■ Concrete
■ Visual (direct model or symbolic)	■ Visual (direct model or symbolic)	■ Visual (direct model or symbolic)
■ Mental (direct model or generalized)	■ Mental (direct model or generalized)	■ Mental (direct model or generalized)
How many more make 10? (10 pairs or combinations of 10)	**How many more make 10? (10 pairs or combinations of 10)**	**How many more make 10? (10 pairs or combinations of 10)**
■ Concrete	■ Concrete	■ Concrete
■ Visual (direct model)	■ Visual (direct model or symbolic)	■ Visual (direct model or symbolic)
	■ Mental (direct model or generalized)	■ Mental (direct model or generalized)
	Commutativity	
	■ Concrete	
	■ Visual (direct model or symbolic)	
	■ Mental (generalized)	
	Doubles or Near-doubles	**Doubles or Near-doubles**
	■ Concrete	■ Visual (symbolic)
	■ Visual (direct model or symbolic)	■ Mental (symbolic or generalized)
	■ Mental (direct model or generalized	
	Making a 10 (9+)	**Making a 10 (9+, 8+, 7+)**
	■ Concrete	■ Visual (direct model or symbolic)
	■ Visual (direct model or symbolic)	■ Mental (direct model or symbolic generalized)
	■ Mental (direct model or generalized)	

Figure 3.9. Grade-level generalizations that students make when learning addition facts.

Special Needs

Allowing students to play games and sing songs to practice basic facts reduces stress and frustration of memorization. Allow students manipulatives and study aids while playing.

Depending on the level, it might be helpful to have a third student verify the accuracy of the playing students.

Another fun game is *Guess Your Number.* This game focuses on missing addends or subtraction. Two students have a card that they place on their forehead so that only the opponent can see the face. A third student adds up the amounts and announces the sum. Each student has to quickly guess what card she is holding on her forehead. The first one to guess wins the round.

Kindergarten	*First Grade*	*Second Grade*
One more or one less ■ Building a staircase ■ Comparing towers ■ Building numbers on 5 frames or 10 frames (+/− 1)		
10 more or 10 less ■ Using 10 frames to record the days in school	**10 more or 10 less** ■ Using 10 frames to record the days in school ■ Building and counting 10 trains ■ Tell me fast: Using multiple 10 frames	**10 more or 10 less** ■ Building and counting 10 trains ■ Using 100 chart patterns ■ Building and recording numbers to 100 ■ Using base 10 blocks

Combination of Nos. to 10
■ Hiding games (at individual level)
   – Grab bag subtraction
   – Snap it
■ Number arrangement activities
■ Dot and other arrangement cards: Tell me fast
	Combination of Nos. to 10
	■ Hiding games (at individual level)
	   – Grab bag subtraction
	   – Snap it
	■ Number arrangement activities
	■ Dot and other arrangement cards: Tell me fast
		Combination of Nos. to 10
		■ Hiding games (at individual level)
		   – Grab bag subtraction
		   – Snap it

How many more make 10? **(10 pairs or combinations of 10)** ■ Using 10 frames to record the days in school	**How many more make 10?** **(10 pairs or combinations of 10)** ■ Participating 10 frame discussions	**How many more make 10?** **(10 pairs or combinations of 10)** ■ Playing hiding games ■ Participating 10 frame discussions ■ Rewriting 10 in different ways (e.g., 7 + 3)
	Commutativity ■ Building addition problems and exploring properties of combining ■ Doing mental math addition activities using commutativity (2 + 9 = ____; children solve as 9 + 2 because it is easier to solve)	
	Doubles or Near-doubles ■ Building doubles or near-doubles with 10 frames ■ Exploring fingers ■ Making mental images of doubles ■ Doing mental math activities	**Doubles or Near-doubles** ■ Tell me fast: Making images with doubles or near-doubles ■ Doing mental math activities
	Making a 10 (9+) ■ Using 10 frames to model ■ Solving model problems with blocks	**Making a 10 (9+, 8+, 7+)** ■ Using 10 frames to model ■ Exploring patterns on 100 chart ■ Solving model addition problems with blocks

Figure 3.10. Continuum of activities and tools used to support students to make generalizations relating to learning their basic addition and subtraction facts.

Comprehension Check

- What are some ways students can practice learning their basic addition and subtraction facts?

Hundreds of math games can be played with cards, with dice, on the computer, or online. Games are a way for every student to have access to math practice. For students who have not developed strategies or generalizations, they may need extra support during games, such as counters. It tends to work better when students are similarly grouped while playing games, because they tend to be working on similar strategies. The quick pace, feedback, and "win" element of games makes them a fun and positive way to learn math facts.

CONCLUSION

Assessment that enhances learning is as important as assessment that documents learning. Thus, you should focus on the idea of assessment for instruction, in addition to that of assessment of instruction.

Assessment is the key to establishing an environment in which children understand and feel a sense of responsibility for learning. Assessment creates accountability for that responsibility. Children take the responsibility to engage in the learning more seriously if they know that there will be frequent and consistent opportunities for them to demonstrate to you, and to others, what they know and can do.

Consistent assessing helps you establish what is important (we assess what we value)—not only what is assessed but also how it is assessed. Therefore, as you work to teach mathematics in the ways described in this book, it is important to rethink the ways you assess the learning that occurs as a result of your teaching.

Addition and subtraction are deep, complicated subjects that require thorough study to understand and use them properly. It would be easier to simply tell children to memorize basic addition and subtraction facts and learn standards algorithms, so why bother with this complicated stuff? First, we want children to learn to use mathematics to negotiate their own real worlds. Indeed, real-life contexts support their thinking, whereas abstract symbols do not (Ambrose et al. 2004). Therefore, if we want children to "get" addition and subtraction, then we should encourage their work with those operations in ways that mimic how they are used in real life, which means we need to understand those real-life applications ourselves. Second, children think differently than adults expect them to, and they develop in different ways and at different rates. We should therefore understand how children develop problem-solving strategies and how mathematical problems can become more difficult. We must then use our understanding of these issues to inform our instructional and curricular thinking as we assess and guide children. Is this hard work? You know it. Is it worth it? Yes, if you think children are worth it.

▶ Interview Video with an Eye on Content

Watch a series of videos in which problems are presented to children and they solve them. In each video, determine the type of problem presented, the problem category, and the specific strategy used to solve it. Record your work in the tables provided. The first one is done for you.

Problem No.	Problem Type	Problem Category	Problem-Solving Strategy
1	Join (result unknown)	Addition	Direct modeling, joining all

▶ Interview a Child

Create a word problem for each problem type at the single-digit basic fact level, then describe in words and pictures how a child might solve each type. Use direct modeling for four of them, counting for four others, and derived facts for the other three. Be sure to label the problem types and strategies being described.

1. Using the problems from step 1, interview a child in first or second grade.

2. Write a report about it that contains two parts: individual problem analyses and overall summary.

3. In the individual problem analyses section, each problem you pose should include the following:
   a. The problem type
   b. The problem (underline the numbers used)
   c. A complete description of the child's response
   d. An analysis of the child's response, which includes the following: general strategy, specific strategy, way or ways of keeping track

   Sample analysis of an interview problem:

Problem 1: Join (result unknown)

Problem: Carolee had 3 trading cards. Her sister gave her 9 cards from her collection. How many trading cards did Carolee have altogether? (12)

Response: Margo said "6" and counted "7, 8, 9," extending one finger at a time as she counted. She then repeated "9."

Analysis: Margo employed a counting strategy, counting on from larger, and used her fingers to keep track.

4. In the overall summary, briefly describe what you learned about the child's mathematical thinking, including the following points:

   a. The types of problems the child successfully solved and those she struggled with

   b. The range of numbers with which the child was familiar (number size)

   c. The types of strategies demonstrated (general strategies, specific strategies, and ways of keeping track)

▶ Classroom Video with an Eye on Pedagogy

Observe this class of children exploring addition. As you observe, note the following:

1. Watch for the role of assessment at each stage of the lesson: How did the teacher assess? What was the purpose of those assessments? What did the teacher learn?

2. Note the types of problems presented, the range of numbers used, and the types of strategies demonstrated, both general and specific.

▶ Classroom Application

Observe an addition or subtraction lesson in a first- or second-grade class. Note the following, similarly to what you did in observing the video:

1. Watch for the role of assessment at each stage of the lesson: How did the teacher assess? What was the purpose of those assessments? What did the teacher learn?

2. Note the types of problems presented, the range of numbers used, and the types of strategies demonstrated, both general and specific.

▶ Resources

Classroom Discourse: The Language of Teaching and Learning, Courtney Cazden (2001)

Differentiated Assessment Strategies: One Tool Doesn't Fit All, Carolyn Chapman and Rita King (2005)

Developing Number Concepts. Book 1: Counting, Comparing, and Pattern, Kathy Richardson (1999a)

Developing Number Concepts. Book 2: Addition and Subtraction, Kathy Richardson (1999b)

▶ Lit Link

Literature Books to Support Addition and Subtraction

Title	Author
10 Kangaroos	Jane Manners
12 Ways to Get 11	Eve Merriam

Title	Author
3 Ants	Fay Robinson
Bears Can Share	Betsy Franco
Cats Add Up!	Dianne Ochiltree
Centipede's 100 Shoes	Tony Ross
Getting to Sleep	Rozanne Lanczak Williams
Let's Go Visiting	Sue Williams
My Counting Garden	Sarah Holliday
Napping House, The	Audrey Wood
One Duck Stuck	Phyllis Root
One Gorilla	Atsuko Morozumi
One Monday Morning	Uri Shulevitz
Pigs Will Be Pigs: Fun with Math and Money	Amy Axelrod
Quack and Count	Keith Baker
Roman Numerals I to MM: Mumerabilia Romana Uno ad Duo Mila	Arthur Geisert
Six-Dinner Sid	Inga Moore
Sled, The	Linda Cave
Ten Black Dots	Donald Crews
Ten Friends	Bruce Goldstone
Ten Sly Piranhas: A Counting Story in Reverse	William Wise
Two of Everything	Lily Toy Hong
Under the Picnic Tree	Rozanne Lanczak
Where the Sidewalk Ends	Shel Silverstein
Who's at the Zoo	Jane Finn

▶ Tech Tools

Websites

National Library of Virtual Manipulatives, http://www.nlvm.usu.edu

NCTM: Illuminations, http://illuminations.nctm.org/WebLinks.aspx

SpeedMath, http://education.jlab.org/smadd/index.html

The Little Animals Activity Centre, http://www.bbc.co.uk/schools/laac/numbers/chi.shtml

Software

Math Blaster, Knowledge Adventure

Math Flash, Fast Rabbit Software

Deepening Understanding through Communication and Numeration

PEDAGOGICAL CONTENT UNDERSTANDINGS

Pedagogy *Collaboration and Reflection through Communication and Discourse*

- Collaboration through Accountable Talk
- Teacher and Student Roles
- Reflection through Writing
- Assessing Teacher and Student Communication

Content *Numeration: Understanding Place Value*

- Number Systems
- Hindu-Arabic Number System
- Understanding Place Value
- Working with Larger Numbers
- Assessments

If you want students to understand, then be sure they are reflecting on what they are doing and communicating it to others.

Hiebert et al., *Making Sense, 1997*

CONVERSATION IN MATHEMATICS

Teacher: I would like you to think about the number 352. How many ways can you think of to show that number?

Student: (Grabs the base 10 blocks and shows 3 hundreds flats, 5 tens long rods, and 2 singles units.)

Teacher: How does that show 352?

Student: (Pointing to each manipulative while counting.) The 3 flats are 300: 100, 200, 300. The 5 long rods are 50: 10, 20, 30, 40, 50. And there are 2 units: 1, 2.

Teacher: Will you show me that same number with a picture?

Student: (Draws the following picture.)

Teacher: How are the blocks and your drawing the same?

Student: The number of flats is the same, the number of long rods is the same, and the number of units is the same.

Teacher: Now show me 352 with numerals.

Student: (Writes 352 in columns corresponding with his pictures.)

Teacher: How did you get that?

Student: I counted the number in each group—three flats, five longs, and two units.

Teacher: Now write the number of units in each group.

Student: (Writes 300, then 50, then 2.)

Teacher: Can you take the calculator and do something with 300, 50, and 2 so that you get 352?

Student: (Types in 300 + 50 + 2.)

Teacher: Why don't you write the signs that go between 300, 50, and 2?

Student: (Does so.)

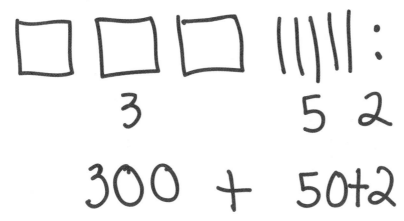

The child in the preceding conversation is demonstrating a level of mathematical literacy involving place value and our number system. He uses multiple representations (pictures, numbers, and words) and has made connections between them to show a deeper understanding of the number 352. He also was able to communicate this understanding to the interviewer. If you recall from chapter 1, representation, connections, and communication are three of five mathematical processes (the other two are reasoning and proof and problem solving) outlined by the NCTM (2000) that characterize what it means to "do" mathematics. This chapter takes an in-depth look at the process of communication and its role in helping a student become mathematically literate.

Communication can take place in both oral and written forms. Teachers need to carefully orchestrate discourse focusing on the content at hand. This discourse is often referred to as *quality talk* or *accountable talk*, where students are accountable not only to their learning community but to knowledge and standards of reasoning as well. The purpose of this discourse is to reach a new level of understanding of the mathematics. However, as critical as social interaction is for learning, students also need time to think on their own and reflect on their work. When reflecting on something, we turn thoughts and ideas over in our head and try to make sense of what we just experienced. It is important that writing be a large part of the reflecting process. So, when is it appropriate to allow students to work alone and reflect versus work together, discuss, and collaborate? In this chapter, we explore the different components of communication and how they are established in the classroom.

For students to be able to successfully communicate their thinking about a given content area in mathematics, they need to have plenty of experiences and opportunities to make connections in that area through multiple representations. The content section of this chapter examines various components of our number system and the experiences children need to be able to make these deep connections.

Collaboration and Reflection through Communication and Discourse

Learning Theory

As stated in his social development theory, Lev Vygotsky viewed purposeful talk as when the best learning occurs. When the child is in his "zone of proximal development," talk helps her negotiate meaning, thus reaching a new level of learning (Vygotsky 1978). Jean Piaget also felt that communication produced the need for "checking and confirming thoughts" and that reflective thought arises "from the interactions between the child and persons in her environment" (Vygotsky 1978, 90).

So, not only do we reflect and then talk, but it seems that talk helps us reflect. This communication spiral (figure 4.1) must then grow as the ideas communicated and reflected become more sophisticated.

Two types of learning result from talk: direct and indirect. *Direct learning* refers to ideas, relationships, strategies, procedures, facts, and other content knowledge. *Indirect learning* refers to social norms and learning environment, such as how to talk to a partner and respect someone else's ideas.

Application to the Learning and Teaching of Mathematics

Collaboration through Accountable Talk

Children seem to talk all day long, everyday. But at school, what are they talking about? If you were to stand back while students were working, would you hear meaningless chitchat or talk focused on the task at hand? Or, is the classroom so controlled that no one is ever talking? We know that talk is important in the learning process, but not all talk supports learning. We do not need to teach children how to talk, but we do need to teach them how to talk for *purpose*.

When a class is engaged in a discussion of a topic, what does it sound like? Does the teacher ask a question, a student dutifully reply, only for the teacher

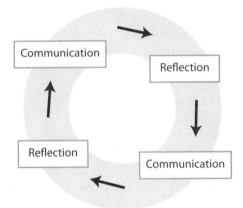

Figure 4.1. Spiral of communication and reflection. The act of reflecting helps us to communicate more clearly. Communication can stimulate a deeper level of reflection.

to respond with approval or disapproval? When a teacher leads a discussion in such a fashion to elicit correct responses from individual students, it allows the rest of the class to be disengaged from the discussion. Students are not using the collective intelligence of the class to learn. They are waiting for their turn to have the right answer (or trying hard to not be called on).

Students engaged in accountable or purposeful talk are not talking "at" one another; rather, they are using talk as a tool for learning. They are the ones asking the questions and thinking about the questions of their peers. They are seriously considering and synthesizing what they know with the ideas shared by others. They are constructing and negotiating meaning together. They are using the conversations to gain both conceptual and procedural knowledge (Chapin, O'Connor, and Anderson 2003).

Goals

According to Suzanne Chapin, Catherine O'Connor, and Nancy Anderson (2003), the goals of talk in the classroom are as follows:

- To strengthen and expand students' reasoning
- To learn mathematical content
- To help students develop their spoken and written language abilities

> **Language Tip**
>
> **Accountable talk is the perfect venue for second-language students or any other student who needs to develop a stronger vocabulary about a subject. Students can hear academically focused language being used and can be encouraged by the teacher to try some new language. Language issues are discussed further in chapter 12.**

When students begin to discuss ideas and what they know, rather than just answer closed-ended questions, teachers can hear how they think and what misconceptions they may have. Hearing how their peers think about a problem can help students realize whether their thinking is faulty or not. Students learn to live the lives of mathematicians, testing "their ideas on the basis of shared knowledge in the mathematical community of the classroom to see whether they can be understood and if they are sufficiently convincing" (NCTM 2000, 61).

What Do We Talk About?

Whole-group, small-group, and partnership discussions should always be focused and centered on the content at hand. In the mathematics classroom, six central themes discussed (Chapin, O'Connor, and Anderson 2003), each of which is described in various chapters in this text. See the website for more information. 🖱

- Mathematical concepts
- Computational procedures
- Solution methods and problem-solving strategies
- Mathematical reasoning
- Mathematical terminology, symbols, and definitions
- Forms of representation

Orchestrating Discourse

If talk is to be child centered rather than teacher centered, then the one most important consideration for talk is seating. Whether students are seated on the floor, in chairs, or at their desks, they must be facing one another in a way that they can carry on a conversation. Traditional seating involves the teacher in

Figure 4.2. Seating where all students face the teacher.

front and the students facing him. This only encourages teacher-to-student dialogue. Consider the seating arrangements in figures 4.2 and 4.3.

Which way allows maximum discussion? When teachers are the focal point, the students tend to either ask questions of the teacher, or answer questions that the teacher has asked. When there is no focal point, then students are directing questions toward the entire class, which elicits response from the entire class. At first, it may be necessary for the teacher to quietly step back from the group to force children to direct their questions and comments to one another.

The mere positioning of children is not the entire solution. When classes begin to gather in a circle, the dialogue pattern may look like the one in figure 4.4.

Figure 4.3. Seating where all students are facing the teacher and one another

Figure 4.4. Students facing one another, but talk is teacher–student.

In this case, the only thing that has been resolved is that everyone can see one another and may be more accountable to what the teacher is saying.

However, the goal should be something like the pattern shown in figure 4.5:

In this scenario, the teacher is not doing all the talking; rather, the students are contributing the most. The teacher's role is to question the children's thinking. If you are unsure who is doing the talking during a discussion, have a trusted colleague come in to chart the pattern of discourse. First, she should outline the seating arrangement, possibly labeling B for boy and G for girl (figure 4.6). Writing down the seating arrangement allows you to study where the boys and girls are sitting and whether they are unevenly dispersed.

Figure 4.5. Student talk is directed toward other students.

Figure 4.6. Charting a seating arrangement to notice speaker patterns.

Every time someone speaks, the observer should draw an arrow from the speaker to the listener. At the end of the day, the teacher can analyze who the talkers were. Perhaps most of the discussion is stemming from the right side of the room or at the front near the teacher. This valuable feedback can help the teacher decide how to correct discourse problems in the classroom.

Getting the class to converse in such a manner is not simple. First, there needs to be some classroom norms in place. Many norms may depend on the teacher's and students' personalities. Some possible classroom norms for discourse are as follows:

■ *The goal of talking is to gather and use new ideas or information.* The focus of having discussions must be clear; otherwise, children are concerned only with what they are going to say and not with what others are saying. They have to understand that they (including the teacher) are collectively building understanding and that every one of them has something to contribute. The teacher is not the holder of all knowledge.

■ *Give the speaker attention with eye contact and appropriate body language.* Focusing on the speaker may seem basic, but many students have to learn how to properly attend to the speaker. On the other side, speakers need to learn how to wait for their peers' attention before speaking. Children often talk even though it is obvious that no one is attending to them. Children can learn to give their peers wait time and even call on their peers to politely demand attention.

So often in partnerships, two children share their strategies, but they do not push back on each other's thinking or say something when the thinking is flawed. Children have to be taught to attend, to listen to the thought process of their partner, and to compare it to that of their own. At times, teachers have to literally turn a child's head so that he is looking at his partner and force him to listen to what his partner is saying.

■ *No hand raising.* Adults do not typically raise hands in group conversations; most know how to insert our ideas, or add to someone else's, as soon as someone has finished speaking. Many teachers want to teach their students how to interact in this fashion. If a child has a question for the rest of the group, it displaces the flow of the discussion if she has to call on someone to answer. Teachers tend to reserve hand raising for lessons that involve more direct instruction.

■ *Only one person speaks at a time, and he must project his voice for all to hear.* Children cannot learn from one another if the speaker is not heard. If an idea gets a buzz from the class, the teacher would probably have the class members take a minute to talk to their partners about what they are thinking.

■ *Students should be responsible for their own learning.* Students must position their bodies so that they can see and hear. Oftentimes, attention is split between a speaker on the rug and an example on the board. Students need to be in charge of themselves so that they can learn, but this takes time and practice. At first, you might sound like a broken record, but for some time it will be necessary to keep directing the students' focus on the speaker. You

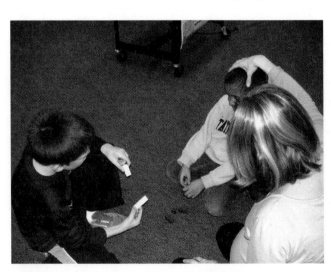

Teacher assisting a partnership to engage in discourse.

will probably say things like, "Turn and look at the speaker" and "Can anybody explain what she just said?"

- *Be respectful.* The focus should always be on the mathematics and methods for solving problems. If this is so, then students should be respectful of other ideas, even if they seem silly to them. There should be no put-downs, just words of encouragement. The way one student responds to another usually determines the likelihood of that student ever sharing again. Many children need examples of what to say in certain situations. At first they may seem a bit contrived, but students begin to use them, or their own words, in more authentic ways. Here are some examples:

"I would like to add to your idea . . ."

"I didn't really get what you mean, or I wasn't listening. Could you explain it again?"

"I'm not sure I agree with you because . . ."

More than likely, you will need to consider who is sitting next to whom in your discussion circle, small groups, or partnerships. Students are easily distracted, and it is usually wise to separate them from friends who are distracting to them. Being aware of strengths and weaknesses, as well as gender, is important when assigning partners. If children are allowed to sit wherever they want, most likely the girls will all end up on one side and the boys on the other. If students have assigned spots in the circle, then transition time is minimized and learning time is preserved.

Teacher and Student Roles

The words and actions of the teacher play a critical role in discourse, and students obviously have an important role in discourse because they are the ones talking.

Teacher Roles

According to the NCTM professional teaching standards (1991, 35), the teacher's role is as follows:

- Posing questions and tasks that elicit, engage, and challenge each student's thinking

- Listening carefully to students' ideas

- Asking students to clarify and justify their ideas orally and in writing

- Deciding which of the ideas that students bring up during a discussion should be pursued in depth

- Deciding when and how to attach mathematical notation and language to students' ideas

- Deciding when to provide information, when to clarify an issue, when to model, when to lead, and when to let a student struggle with a difficulty

- Monitoring students' participation in discussions and deciding when and how to encourage each student to participate

Most of these standards include the word *decide.* Teachers are constantly making decisions, and those decisions are based on the current teaching goals and the particular needs of their students. Not all students need to share all the time. Experience helps them know, for example, which ideas are best to present to the class. Sometimes it is a solid example, and sometimes it is an error. Year to year, each group of children is different. Sometimes you might have a group that just needs more direct instruction compared to the groups of other years.

Talk Moves Chapin, O'Connor, and Anderson (2003) identify five fundamental talk moves made by teachers while orchestrating discourse:

- *Revoicing: "So you're saying that . . ."* The teacher restates what the child has said in an attempt to clarify his thinking for the rest of the students to understand. This is effective when the child has good thinking but is having a rough time articulating his thoughts. This is also good for a timid student who otherwise would not share. Teachers need to be cautious with this talk move because it can be overused. Students will learn to expect the teacher to repeat what a peer has said. This causes them to tune out their peers and to pay attention to the teacher. When this happens, a dialogue pattern of student–teacher–student is taking place.

- *Asking students to restate someone else's reasoning: "Can you repeat what she just said in your own words?"* Restating is an effective way to get someone's thinking clarified by someone else. This is meant to give other students a chance to internalize what someone else has said and match it to their own thinking. If the reasoning cannot be restated by a peer, then the student should be asked, preferably by the peer, to explain again. Sometimes teachers use this talk move to check how much students are paying attention, but that should not be the main use of this move.

- *Asking students to apply their own reasoning to someone else's reasoning: "Do you agree or disagree, and why?"* Before students are comfortable with carrying on their own discussion, this move will be used often by the teacher. Children are not used to comparing their own thoughts with those of someone else. They may feel that it is rude to disagree with someone else. They are also used to just waiting for their turn to share and not mentally engage with someone else's thinking. By asking this question, teachers are neither confirming nor rejecting a student's response. Rather, the student needs to think about what is being said and make sense of it.

- *Prompting students for further participation: "Would someone like to add on?"* Pushing for a discussion to continue flowing encourages students to expand on someone else's thinking and connect their thoughts to those of another student. It is typical at first for conversations to be isolated facts with a lot of connections, so it is necessary for the teacher to link ideas. After a while, students naturally begin to add to what their classmates say.

- *Using wait time.* Waiting might be the most powerful talk move a teacher can use during discourse. It is basically doing and saying nothing. Many teachers find this hard to do, because they feel that they should always be doing something. Allowing students a chance to think after posing a problem or asking a question gives them time to process the information and formulate thoughts. Some students are usually quick to answer, and others stop trying once they see hands in the air. Telling the students to put a "quiet thumb" by their chest when they have an answer lets the teacher know when each one is ready. Wait time is also used when just one student is trying to formulate a thought during a discussion or a question is just thrown out to the group and the teacher wants someone to respond. The longer the teacher is silent, the greater the students' discomfort and the inevitability they will speak out.

Scaffolding *Scaffolding* is defined by Pauline Gibbons (2002, 10) as "the steps taken to reduce the degrees of freedom in carrying out some tasks so that the child can concentrate on the difficult skill she is in process of acquiring." These are temporary structures to assist the child in successfully completing a task (Gibbons 2002; Maybin, Mercer, and Stierer 1992). If students are having difficulty completing the task, rather than simplifying the problem, it is best to restructure the scaffold. This keeps the expectations high.

Carole Greenes and Jenny Tsankova (2004, 60) state:

Scaffolding is an excellent approach for improving discussion and reflection. Scaffolding involves the use of prompts (e.g., "Keep talking." "Tell me more.") that do not interrupt the child's thinking and probing questions (e.g., "How did you decide what to do first?") that encourage the children to reflect on what was done before, to elaborate on their observations and conclusions, and to build on prior knowledge.

Questioning Questioning is one of the most important scaffolding techniques used by teachers. When used consistently, children often pick it up and use it on their peers. However, many teachers find that asking just the right question is difficult. Some questions are asked to elicit more information, whereas others are asked to help get students to the next step and support their thinking. This latter type of questioning calls for a deep understanding of the mathematics at hand and the big ideas that encompass it.

Although some general sets of questions can be used in most situations, the deeper your mathematical content understanding, the better and more precise your questions. The NCTM professional teaching standards (1991, 3–4) give the roles of questioning, which we follow with some examples:

- Helping students work together to make sense of mathematics

  "Do you agree? Disagree? Why or Why not?"

  "Does anyone have the same answer but a different way to explain it?"

  "Can you convince the rest of us that this makes sense?"

- Helping students rely more on themselves to determine whether something is mathematically correct

  "How did you reach that conclusion?"

  "Does that make sense?"

  "Can you make a model and show that?"

- Helping students learn to reason mathematically

  "Does that always work?"

  "Is that true for all cases? Explain."

  "Can you think of a counterexample?"

  "How could you prove that?"

- Helping students learn to conjecture, invent, and solve problems

"What would happen if . . . ?"

"Do you see a pattern? Explain."

"Can you predict the next one? What about the last one?"

- Helping students connect mathematics, its ideas, and its applications

"How does this relate to . . . ?"

"What ideas that we have learned were useful in solving this problem?"

The preceding list is not meant to be a checklist of any kind but, rather, is meant to give you a sense of what types of questions elicit what types of responses and thinking. Most of these questions can be used in any mathematical content area and even outside of mathematics.

Student Roles

The NCTM *Professional Standards for Teaching Mathematics* document (1991, 45) identifies the roles students play in the discourse as the following:

- Listen to, respond to, and question the teacher and one another

- Use a variety of tools to reason, make connections, solve problems, and communicate

- Initiate problems and questions

- Make conjectures and present solutions

- Explore examples and counterexamples to investigate a conjecture

- Try to convince themselves and one another of the validity of particular representations, solutions, conjectures, and answers

- Rely on mathematical evidence and arguments to determine validity

As you can see, discourse is more complicated than just talking and listening. In fact, listening is difficult for children. They think that because they can hear one another they are listening, but listening involves thinking about what they are hearing. None of the preceding roles come naturally to children and need to be taught explicitly and continually.

Reflection through Writing

Writing is an important part of the math day. Through writing, students can explain procedures, justify their reasoning, and reflect on their thinking. It is a tool to help students think, gather, organize, and clarify thoughts. Students who have a chance to write and articulate thoughts on paper can be more successful during discussions, because they have had a chance to "rehearse" their thinking. Through writing, students have a written record of their learning throughout the year and are able to go back to previous thinking and refine or apply it to new situations.

Writing also gives teachers insights into students' understanding. They can see what students have learned, whether the reasoning is strong or weak, and whether there are gaps in understanding. By evaluating student's written explanations, teachers are able to make more informed decisions for future lessons. Usually, similar errors or misconceptions surface, which influences teachers' next steps.

Student math journals are also ideal for sharing student understanding with parents. Scores on tests do not always reflect what children understand, but examples of their explanations do. Students may contribute greatly to classroom discussions, but that contribution may be a bit intangible if there is no written record of those contributions.

Prompts for Writing

Journals and logs are ways for students to keep ongoing records about what they are doing and learning in mathematics. They are able to write about what is easy and what is difficult about solving a particular problem and to have the opportunity to explain why their answer makes sense.

Writing is often seen as a reflective piece to take place either right before or after the discussion. Some teachers want to give students a chance to write what they are thinking before the discussion, and others want them to write after the ideas have surfaced in the discussion. Perhaps students should write both before and after discussions, although it is unrealistic to expect them to have time to do so for the same discussion or even every day.

A written prompt is ideal for a homework assignment in which the students must solve a problem, similar to one present in class, and explain their reasoning for the solution. A small college bluebook works well for this type of assignment. Every day, assign one problem, which the students copy down in their bluebook. Typically, one bluebook is perfect for all the prompts in a single math unit. You may find it useful to mark the homework complete or incomplete daily, but once a week take them home to make explicit comments regarding both the math and the student's ability to write explanations.

Figures 4.7 and 4.8 are examples of homework response questions in a third-grade classroom studying a unit of division. For more examples, visit the website.

In the beginning, students are not strong at writing about what they learned, but with explicit instruction and daily practice they greatly improve. After a few students share their reflections or some homework responses, give them feedback as to what is expected and how they can improve their explanations.

For the first month or so, when asked to reflect on their learning, children undoubtedly will write what they liked doing that day. They need to be constantly reminded that this is not a time to write a list of the daily events but a time to write what was learned and what is still confusing.

Other writing assignments may be creative writing, poems, or songs that involve mathematics. Students who are stronger in literature may need this venue to process some of the mathematics they are learning. They could also write about parts of the math day, such as how they cooperated with their partners, what they enjoyed in a particular unit, and other topics that are responsive to how they perceived their learning experience.

Assessing Teacher and Student Communication

Reflective teachers evaluate themselves often. Videotaping yourself teaching a lesson and having a colleague whom you trust come in and script what you say are effective means for taking an honest look at how you are communicating with students. When analyzing your own teaching, it is possible to measure wait time, count how many times certain children talk, and notice to whom your comments are directed. To read more about this, visit the website.

Language Tip

Some students, especially English-language learners, need more of a scaffold to know how to start an entry. In classes for which teachers daily write the purpose of the lesson on the board, some students rewrite that purpose as a way to begin their prompt: (e.g., "Today we learned about different characteristics of triangles."). Other teachers may use starters such as the following:

- "Write about what you learned." (Today I learned . . .)
- "Write what you are still confused about." (I'm not sure . . .)
- "Write what you are still wondering." (I'm wondering . . .)
- "Show how to solve the following problem in two ways."
- "Write what you know" (e.g., subtraction).

Comprehension Check

- What are some ways to incorporate writing into the math day?

Explain how to share 32 pennies with four people.
Draw a picture to support your explanation.

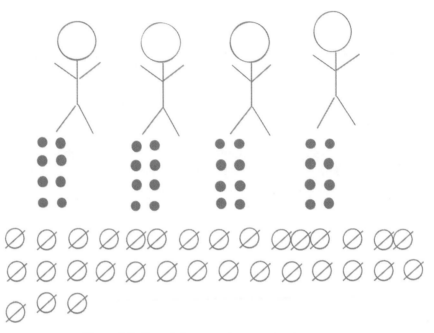

You could pass out 1 penny to each person until all the
pennies are gone. Each person should have the same
number of pennies or it is not fair.

You could also give 5 pennies to each person. That
would be 20. Then two more to each and that would be
28 and then give 1 more to each until they are gone.

Figure 4.7. Sample homework prompt and response.

Day	Problem
1	Explain how to share 32 pennies with four people. Draw a picture to support your explanation.
2	Explain how multiplication and division are related and give examples.
3	Explain how you can use multiplication to solve 30 ÷ 5. Draw a picture to support your explanation.

Figure 4.8. Sample homework response problems for third-grade division.

CONTENT   *Numeration: Understanding Place Value*

As we move into the content section, consider the opportunities for communication on the part of the teacher and students. Pay particular attention to questions you might need to ask your students to help them make the connections
needed to develop a solid foundation in place value and the base 10 system, as
well as the types of responses you expect to receive that would demonstrate
mathematical understanding.

Big Ideas and Focal Points

As you might recall from chapter 2, according to the NCTM's *Principles and Standards for School Mathematics* (2000, 32), an expectation is that all students "understand numbers, relationships among numbers and number systems." The part of this statement that pertains to this chapter is "number systems."

Here are a few of the big ideas about number systems that we need to keep in mind as we are designing meaningful experiences for our students:

> **For any number, the place of a digit tells how many ones, tens, hundreds, and so forth.**
>
> **Each place value to the left of another is 10 times greater than the one to the right.**
>
> **You can add the value of the digits together to get the value of the number (Charles 2005, 13).**

The Focal Points table shows the NCTM (2006) focal points as they pertain to the understanding of place value and the base 10 number system. Second grade is the only grade that specifies understanding of these ideas; however, understanding place value is not something that starts or stops here. Second grade is typically where a lot of work is devoted to this understanding, but there needs to be work slowly building up to it; subsequently, all operations depend on a good sense of place value and the base 10 system. If you teach grades 3–6 and notice that some students are struggling with operations, it is almost guaranteed that their understanding of place value is weak and remediation needs to begin at this level.

Number Systems

A *number system* is the way a society records and communicates ideas about numbers. It consists of a set of elements called *numbers*, and basic operations can be performed on those numbers. Throughout history, societies have developed many ways to try to record numbers and operations.

The people of Papua New Guinea have at least 900 counting systems. Many of them involve counting body parts and involve more than their fingers. They also use body parts such as the nose to refer to different numbers. The Babylonians counted in base 60. They used finger segments of one hand to total 12, and the other hand was used for double counting, or keeping track of the number of 12s they counted (figure 4.9) (Ball 2005).

The Chinese and Egyptians used separate symbols to represent the ones place, the tens place, the hundreds place, and so on, and thus were able to mix up the symbols while preserving the values. These were similar to a symbolic notation of colored counters, where each color stood for a different grouping. If, for instance, red represents ones, blue represents tens, and yellow represents hundreds, then the amount in figure 4.10 would be 368.

Most ancient number systems were either inefficient for recording large numbers or ineffective for showing calculations. By 300 BC, Indians had already begun using symbols to represent 1–9. By AD 600, they had invented a place system and zero (Ball 2005). This Indian number system reached the Arab world. Mathematician al-Khwarizimi began to spread this number system through the rest of the world through the many math books he wrote. Fibonacci, an Italian mathematician, wrote a book to explain to Europeans

NCTM FOCAL POINTS

Second Grade

Develop an understanding of the base 10 number system and place-value concepts (to at least 1,000).

Understand that the base 10 number system includes ideas of counting in units and multiples of hundreds, tens, and ones.

Understand number relationships, such as comparing and ordering numbers.

Understand multidigit numbers in terms of place value, recognizing that place-value notation is a shorthand for the sums of multiples of powers of 10 (e.g., 853 as 8 hundreds + 5 tens + 3 ones).

Reprinted with permission from *Curriculum Focal Points for Prekindergarten Through Grade 8 Mathematics: A Quest for Coherence,* copyright 2006 by the National Council of Teachers of Mathematics. All rights reserved.

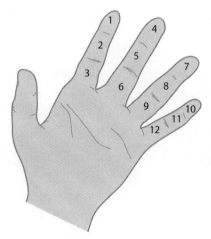

Figure 4.9. The ancient Babylonian counting system.

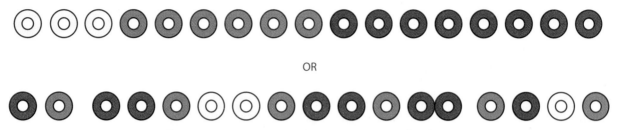

OR

Figure 4.10. An ancient counting system using colored counters.

how this Indian number system worked. It is believed that when one of al-Khwarizmi's books was translated to Latin, a misinterpretation of the translation of his name eventually became our current word *algorithm*. This number system is now referred to as the *Hindu-Arabic number system.*

Hindu-Arabic Number System

This number system comprises a *digit system,* which is a set of numbers represented by certain symbols. In our system, 10 symbols represent the quantities 1–9 and zero. Five basic characteristics define the Hindu-Arabic number system (Cathcart et al. 2001):

- Base 10
- Place value
- Multiplicative principle
- Additive principle
- Zero as the placeholder

Base 10

Objects can be grouped in many different ways. As a society, we have chosen to group objects by tens, based on the number of fingers we have. This is called *base 10.* Some ancient societies grouped objects by 20 for the amount of fingers and toes, which would be base 20. To represent base 20, there would need to be different symbols to represent 1–19 objects and zero. In base 20, the number written as 1 tens unit would represent one group of 20.

If a base 4 system used our Arabic numerals, for example, the only numerals would be 1, 2, 3, and 0 (figure 4.11). Every four items would be grouped as a

30 objects in base 4; written as 132

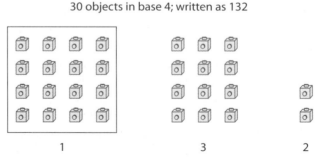

Figure 4.11. Example of a base 4 system using 30 objects.

new unit. This base would be inefficient, because the number to represent a large quantity would be long.

Place Value

Unlike the Egyptian system, where a character, or symbol, determines the amount, in our system, the position of the numeral determines its amount. Changing the order of the numerals changes the amount or quantity of the entire number.

369 is much different from 963

The numeral 3 means 300 in 369, whereas it simply means three in 963. The numerals represent the number of groups. There can be 1–9 groups in any one place before they need to be "regrouped" into another place. Once there are 10 of any group, they must be bundled; for example, 10 tens are grouped into 100, and 10 hundreds are grouped into 1,000.

Multiplicative Principle

In the base 10 system, each numeral to the left of another has a value 10 times greater than the numeral on the right. In other bases, the values are also multiplicative, but they are multiplicative by their base root. In base 5, the number written as 1 tens unit would represent 5 objects. The number written as 1 hundreds unit would represent 25 objects, and 1 thousands unit would represent 125. Thus, each grouping is multiplicative by 5.

Additive Principle

In number systems with an additive principle, the values of the digits can be added together to determine the quantity. With Roman numerals, the amounts represented by the symbols are added together to arrive at a total: CXIV would be 100 + 10 + 4 = 114. In the Hindu-Arabic system, the values of each position are added together to arrive at a total:

372 = (3 × 100) + (7 × 10) + 2

or

372 = 300 + 70 + 2

Zero as a Placeholder

The zero was invented in India in AD 600. Before that, the Babylonians had just left spaces between marks to show a lack of quantity. Most other societies found dealing with the idea of zero to be complicated and useless, because there was little need to count nothing. The circle was incorporated because the Indians used pebbles when calculating and the circle was the shape left by a missing pebble (Ball 2005).

We saw that the Chinese designed a character to follow a numerical symbol that shows which place it refers to. Our number system allows the zero to be the placeholder when there is nothing to count in a particular place. This way, we still know what the value of a particular numeral is by its location within the number.

Comprehension Check

■ **Write the amount of stars shown in the following bases:**

Base 10

Base 12 (you have to invent some new symbols)

Base 5

Base 3

Understanding Place Value

The work related to partitioning and tens and ones is what makes up most of the second-grade math curriculum. Partitioning can be thought of as the ability to break numbers into different amounts that still equal the original number. Take 37 as an example:

$$30 + 7 \qquad 20 + 17 \qquad 10 + 27 \qquad 25 + 12$$

These are all different ways we can break up the quantity 37. As teachers, we need to be careful that we are not teaching this idea in isolation of computation. Students need a reason to break up numbers. We partition numbers to make addition and subtraction easy and efficient.

As alluded to earlier, our current place-value and notational system is a sophisticated structure that took centuries to develop. Early scholars spent many years grouping numbers and figuring out the most efficient way to represent them and computations on paper. Young children need to go through a similar process to construct their own place-value relationships. When we expose children to place-value notation as early as first grade, we are imposing on them an already-constructed and sophisticated system. Because number systems are about number relationships, just telling students how it works is not sufficient for understanding.

There are two types of place-value representation: proportional and non-proportional. Proportional is the kind used most often and thus is the focus of the rest of this chapter. With proportions, the place is represented by the actual quantity. For example, 2 tens will be represented by 20 cubes or perhaps two 10 sticks. Nonproportional is when a place is represented by a different object or color. For instance, red is ones, blue is tens, and yellow is hundreds, as described earlier. We might even think of coin counting as nonproportional because a penny represents 1 cent, a nickel 5 cents, and a dime 10 cents. The learner must assign meaning to these different objects or colors and able to hold on to those quantities when adding the total amount. Some students develop this system on their own when counting or adding, but it is not common.

In 1989, a study was done by Sharon Ross to find out at what age students expressed an understanding of place value to the extent of knowing that the number in the tens place represented that value (e.g., the 3 in 36 represents 30). The results were that 33% of third graders and 50% of fourth graders could articulate such understanding. She also found no significant difference between children with experience working with the manipulatives. Her argument was that natural mental maturity plays a role in understanding place value.

Although maturity and cognitive development play significant roles in the ability to fully understand place value, the question raised with the preceding study is what exactly were the experiences the children had with the manipulatives. As shown in chapter 2, having and using manipulatives, or math tools, is not the same thing as using them to construct understanding. We argue that precisely planned activities should assist students in constructing number relationships and making connections to the standard number system that we use today. To read about acquisition stages for place value, visit the website.

The following sections elaborate on issues and activities that pertain to the acquisition of place value.

Struggling Learners

Most struggling learners in the upper elementary grades have a huge gap in their understanding that is rooted in place value.

Reading and Writing Numbers to 100, 1,000, and Beyond

In English, we have a general pattern for the way that we read or say numbers. However, that pattern does not really begin until 20. The numbers 11–19 can be tricky because they do not have obvious values in the words. The number 29 is read "twenty-nine," which means 20 and 9 more. The word *twelve* does not imply any such value. In other languages, such as Chinese, these patterns begin at 11 with a name that means "10 and 1." Studies of Asian students find that young children do not have the same difficulty with place value as children in the United States. Precision in language regarding the values of the numbers plays a significant role in students' understanding. As teachers, we should always be using different labels to refer to the same amount to emphasize the quantities (such as 2 tens and 9 ones).

Equally challenging can be writing numbers. Young children may be observed writing teen numbers in the way that they are spoken, for instance:

Fourteen   41

Because all other numbers are written in the order in which they are spoken, it is no wonder that children become confused. These are just conventions that children have to learn and memorize, but teachers need to anticipate such errors so that they can be explicit in their teaching.

Most students have continual access to tools such as a number line to 100 and a 100 chart. Probably for this reason, it is common to see few errors in writing numbers from 20 to 100. However, beyond 100, many students begin to make errors. This is a direct reflection of their level of understanding of the place-value system. It is far too common to see a second grader write 248 in the following way:

200408

Why would a child write a number in such a fashion? She is essentially writing the way she hears it and has not established a sense of place value. Many novice teachers might not expect their students to write numbers in such a way because these same students would almost certainly *read* 248 correctly.

Recognizing Numbers as Tens and Ones

Although young children may be able to count well beyond 100, they do not readily see each number as groups of tens and ones. Teachers need to provide a lot of experiences for grouping and building numbers so that children can begin to see that numbers can be broken into different parts and that grouping objects by tens is an efficient way to count and compute.

Grouping Numbers and Objects Initially, when asked to model a two-digit number, say 32, children create a train or pile of 32 cubes or other objects. We want to give them lots of opportunities to build these two-digit numbers by grouping objects in many different ways. When grouping, the same amount of objects need to be in each group so that the children express the amount as groups and leftovers. This will not only help strengthen conservation of number, but these activities also support repeated addition and early multiplication ideas. An example of this is in figure 4.12.

Language Tip

The language around grouping will be tricky, especially if the students are English Language learners. "How many groups" and "How many in each group" are very language-impacted questions. It is very important that the students articulate both orally and in writing the notion of the number of groups. Students who are asked how many cubes are in a group, may say 32, thinking of the entire amount as one group. One way to rephrase this question is to ask, "How many cubes in each circle?" When the child responds with the appropriate amount, you can then reply, "So there are 4 cubes in each group." This way, the idea is understood, and the appropriate language follows. The child should then be asked to tell you, using the correct language, how many groups there are and how many in each group.

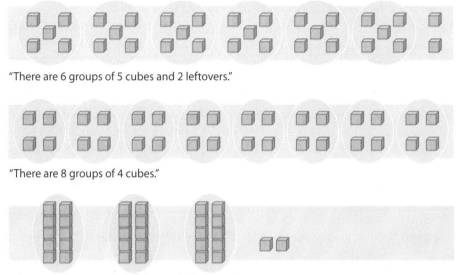

"There are 6 groups of 5 cubes and 2 leftovers."

"There are 8 groups of 4 cubes."

"There are 3 groups of 10 cubes and 2 leftovers."

Figure 4.12. Sample of ways to group 32 objects.

When children are recording the ways to group a set number of items, they need some way to organize their work. A sample recording sheet might look like the one in figure 4.13.

When the students have done many of these, through small-group and whole-group conversations they will begin to discover that, when objects are grouped in tens, the number of groups and extras are the same as the way the number is written, therefore grouping by tens makes counting easy.

Building Numbers An important activity, which helps children conceptualize quantities and reinforces the notion of tens and ones, is to build numbers into the hundreds, found in *Developing Number Concepts. Book 3: Place Value, Multiplication, and Division* (Richardson 1999c, 34). This seemingly tedious task is actually enjoyable to students. In this activity, students work in partnerships. Student A builds a number, and student B records the quantity. After so many

Total Number: 32		
Number in Each Group	Number of Groups	Extras
5	6	2
4	8	0
10	3	2

Figure 4.13. Sample recording sheet filled out for grouping 32 objects.

numbers, the partners can switch jobs so that they each have a turn building and recording.

The builder uses a place-value mat, and the recorder uses a long strip of cash register tape. The builder puts one cube, or bean, on the ones side of his mat, and the recorder writes "01" because there is nothing on the tens side and one cube on the ones side. The builder adds a cube, and the recorder writes "02" underneath her first number, and so on. The recorder should not get ahead of the builder, because they are building and recording simultaneously.

When the 10th cube is to be added, there is always confusion about what to do. Many students just put it on the ones side as the recorder writes "010." This is a perfect time to stop the class, because many students will reach this point about the same time, and discuss some rules about how many digits can be in each place and what they think they should do now. Students should put their cubes in a small cup and place the cup on the tens side. At this stage, it is wise to not use 10 sticks unless the students are older and this is just a reinforcing activity.

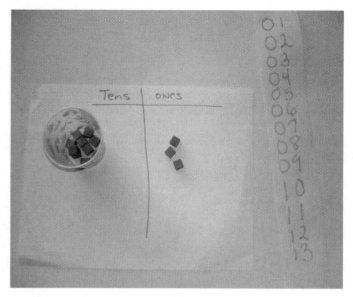

Building numbers on a place value chart.

When they get to 100, another conversation can be had about what to do. The 10 cups may be stacked and a hundreds column added to their chart. This activity should extend over a few days so that students have a chance to build numbers far beyond 100.

After the building activity, the class should come together to look at their register tape to see what patterns that they notice. They will notice things such as the ones are always 1, 2, 3, 4, 5, 6, 7, 8, 9, and 0; the tens column has the same numeral 10 times; and so on. These discussions help students understand the value of each place.

This activity is also good when building decimal concepts, using pennies, dimes, and dollars. The place-value chart would be modified to reflect the appropriate places and include a decimal point.

Building a 100 Chart An extension of building a number line would be building a 100 chart (Richardson 1999c, 36). Although students probably already have experience using a 100 chart, it is always a good idea to build the tools to make stronger connections between concrete and abstract models. Visit the website to see a sample 100 chart.

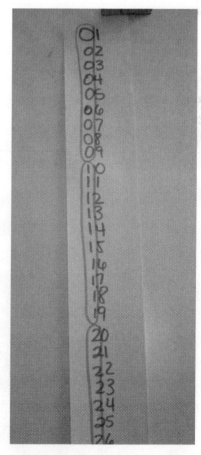

Individually, students should again build the numbers one by one, this time filling in the amounts in a blank 100 chart, but the teacher should not tell the children what they are making. When the entire chart is full, have students talk about what they notice and what tool they created. It is always interesting to hear students' reactions when they discover what they created. These 100 charts can be cut into strips and taped together to create a 1–100 number line. Many students have never made the connection between the 100 chart and the number line.

Finding Patterns on a 100 Chart After children have created their own 100 chart, it is good to spend time exploring patterns on it like looking at multiples of 2, 3, 4, etc. (figure 4.14; Richardson 1999c, 37). Even as this activity

Looking for patterns after building numbers.

100 Chart with Skip Counting Circles

1	2	3	4	5	6	7	8	9	10
11	12	13	14	15	16	17	18	19	20
21	22	23	24	25	26	27	28	29	30
31	32	33	34	35	36	37	38	39	40
41	42	43	44	45	46	47	48	49	50
51	52	53	54	55	56	57	58	59	60
61	62	63	64	65	66	67	68	69	70
71	72	73	74	75	76	77	78	79	80
81	82	83	84	85	86	87	88	89	90
91	92	93	94	95	96	97	98	99	100

3 6 9 12 15 18 21 24 27 30
33 36 39 42 45 48 51 54 57 60
63 66 69 72 75 78 81 84 87 90

Figure 4.14. Finding patterns on a 100 chart.

helps strengthen skip counting, it reinforces patterns that occur in the base 10 system.

Using a Place-Value Mat Using a place-value mat in additional activities is a must after the building activity asnot all children will have yet generalized a sense of tens. When individually working with children to help them see the relationship between what they are building and how they read the number, one activity is to put an amount of cubes and cups on the place-value mat and have each child write the numbers of cups underneath the cups and the numbers of singles underneath the singles. Have him read the number aloud and then count to confirm the quantity.

Whether the students are still using the cups to hold 10 cubes or are now using the base 10 rod, a great game to reinforce the notion of trading up is *Race to 100*. A game that reinforces trading back is *Race to Zero* (Richardson 1999c, 98).

These games can be played to any desired quantity and with different-size dice, depending on the number size the student is working with. Two players play against each other using their own place-value mat and set of cubes or beans. In

Using the place value mat to make connections.

"I have 34 altogether. I need 6 more to make another ten. I might be able to get it on the next roll." Race to 100.

Race to 100, one player rolls the dice and puts that many cubes in her ones spot. She then says how many more she needs to make 10 and whether she thinks she can get it on her next roll. Player 2 takes a turn, and so on. Every time a player adds more cubes, that player needs to say the new total and whether there are enough ones to make a 10. If so, the player says how many leftovers there are. If not, the player says how many more are needed.

Special Needs Support

For students who are having trouble remembering when to regroup, it may be useful to structure their place-value mats with a blank 10 in the ones so that when it is filled students know to trade. A variety of place-value mats that provide various levels of support are available on the website.

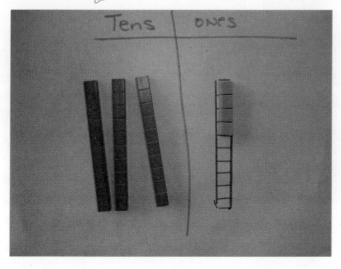

CAUTION Trading

In the beginning, many students do not always understand that they are trading for equal value. If they have 12 ones and want to trade for tens, they might take all their ones and trade for a 10 because they have enough. However, trading issues are not normally evident until computation, especially subtraction. Suppose the problem is 34 − 17. The student might have built his 34 with cubes like this:

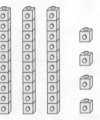

When he wants to take away 7 ones, he will see that he only has 4. He will realize that he needs 3 more. When asked what to do, he will probably say that he needs to break a 10. At this point, it is common for the student to take a 10 and get 3 ones, knowing that he needed 3 more to take away the 7. There need to be conversations about what trading means. This misconception tends to be more prevalent when using base 10 blocks as opposed to interlocking cubes. If equal trading is an issue, it is better to have students work with interlocking cubes.

When playing *Race to Zero*, or trading down from 100, it is always amusing to have children start with a 100 flat and see what they do when they roll their first amount. It takes a long time for them to realize that they have to break the flat into 10 tens and break a 10 into 10 ones so that they can take some away.

Base 10 Riddles   Riddles are a fun way to reinforce any concept. When using riddles to reinforce place value, it is helpful to use a number line and, either as a class or in partnerships, have students help keep track of which numbers are not included in the riddle. When numbers are guessed, the responder should tell whether the number guessed is too high or too low. Keeping track, with

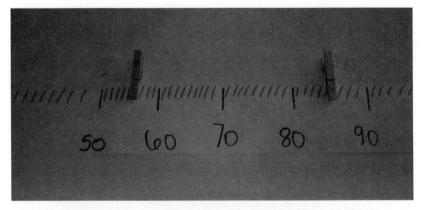

"I am more than 5 tens and 6 ones; and less than 8 tens and 5 ones." Base 10 riddles using a number line.

either clothespins or sticky notes, can help focus children's guesses so that they are not randomly picking numbers.

Here are some other good clues:

- I am a number between ____ and ____.
- I am a double.
- I am a multiple of 5.
- I have at least ____ tens and ____ ones.
- I am less than half of 100.
- I am a multiple of 10.

Knowing and Using Expanded Notation

Expanded notation is related to the multiplicative principle we mentioned earlier. It is the way to record the value of all digits in a given number. For example:

537
a. $500 + 30 + 7$
b. $(5 \times 100) + (3 \times 10) + 7$
c. $(5 \times 10 \times 10) + (3 \times 10) + 7$
d. $(5 \times 10^2) + (3 \times 10) + 7$

Second and third graders would be expressing a number as shown in example a. Upper-grade students would be working with larger numbers and using exponential notation, such as in example d. Students who have a solid foundation of tens and ones, and are able to read and interpret expanded notation in the younger grades, will be able to easily extend their understanding when working with larger numbers in the upper grades.

The ability to break numbers into hundreds, tens, and ones helps children when they are combining and separating amounts. We should not be teaching expanded notation in isolation of computation. Without a reason, or need, to break apart numbers, it just seems like another procedure to perform on numbers.

Closely linking concrete objects with the written notation is essential. However, some students will still have difficulties when transferring from the models to just the numerals. When asked to write 5,938 in expanded notation, a struggling third-grade student may write "50 + 90 + 30 + 8." When asked to add those numbers, the student realizes that it does not total 5,938 but is still not sure how to write it out correctly. Commercial products can help bridge the gap from concrete to abstract understanding of expanded notation, but a homemade product, such as the following, is just as effective:

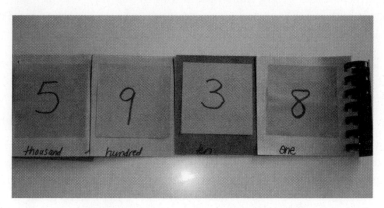

A homemade tool to represent expanded notation.

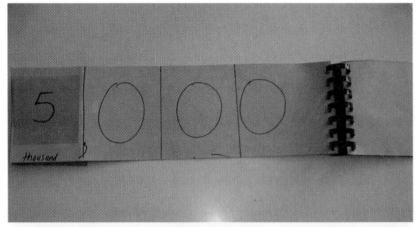

Using the tool to model the expanded notation for 5,938.

Using sticky notes, write the numerals and attach them to the desired place. The child attempts to write the number in expanded notation and then flips the pages to confirm.

Usually within one session, students start to make the connection that there are the same number of zeros as digits.

Knowing 10 More or Less for Any Two-Digit Number

As students are learning 10 more or less for any number, like any other skill, they begin with concrete experiences and move to more abstract ones. For this understanding, they do the following:

More abstract

- Use cubes
- Use 10 frames
- Use the 100 chart
- Just know

Using Cubes Cubes, base 10 blocks, and beans and cups are all tools children use to learn what happens when they add 10 to any number. Using any one of the mentioned tools, have the children model a given number, for instance, 43. Have them add a 10 and then tell how many (figure 4.15). Keep doing this, adding and taking away tens. The generalization that they should be making is that

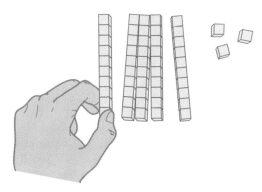

Figure 4.15. Using tens and ones to generalize the idea of adding a ten.

the ones stay the same and that the numeral in the tens place is increasing or decreasing by one.

Using 10 Frames A 10 frame can be used to easily add and subtract 10. When moving away from concrete tools, the 10 frame is nice because it still shows quantity but is easier to manage because it is just paper. A 10 frame should only be used if students have had experience building numbers with it and are familiar with their quantities; otherwise, most students will probably be counting all or counting on to determine the amounts.

Using 10 frames to generalize the idea of adding a 10.

Using the 100 Chart A 100 chart is quite abstract. A given number on the chart does not simply represent that spot but also represents the total amount of squares up to that point.

Exploring the pattern of ±10 using a 100 chart takes a lot of time and may be frustrating for teachers, because it a pattern that seems obvious to us and is not obvious to students. Many teachers will want to tell children that to add 10 to a number the answer is found just below that number, but until the students discover this for themselves they will not trust it.

Exploring these patterns is typical in second grade and should be done throughout the year, because some students will be ready later to discover what is really happening. Simply, on a whole-group 100 chart or on individual ones have students find a number you give them and put a blue centimeter cube on that number. Ask them to find 10 more than that number (watch how many students need to count) and place a blue centimeter cube on the answer. Tell them to find 10 more again; do this four or five more times. Have a discussion, in partnerships and then as a whole group, about what they notice. Ask them if they think that this will happen all the time. Try this with several different numbers.

The 100 chart is also a great tool to explore ±9 and 11. Once children understand the 10-ness of the chart, they will be able to see that 11 is 10 and 1 more. A good reinforcement activity for understanding the relationship of numbers on the 100 chart is to take a partially filled out chart and cut out pieces (figure 4.16).

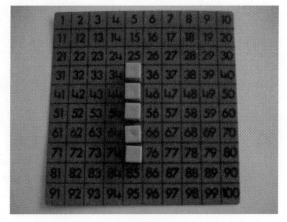

Using a hundred chart to generalize plus ten.

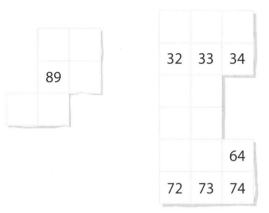

Figure 4.16. Using cut-outs of the hundred chart to practice number relationships.

> ## Common Misconception
>
> In third grade, it is common to explore lots of patterns on the 100 chart and to do lots of skip counting activities. One pattern a student will describe is "When you go down, all there is are sevens," referring to the ones place. If you ask her to say the numbers she is referring to, she will read, "7, 17, 27, 37, 47, ..." If you ask her what she is counting by, she will probably answer, "Sevens." This is an indicator that she does not understand what it means to *count by* a number and activities need to be created to explore that concept.

Then have students fill in the empty boxes based on their relative location to the numbers are already there.

Just Knowing Once children have discovered patterns with the blocks, 10 frames, or 100 chart, they will have generalized rules and can begin to be able to visualize these tools in their head and then solve for ± 10 without using tools. This transition from tool to mentally computing is different for every child, so do not assume that because they can articulate what they are doing with the manipulative that they automatically can transfer to mental computation. When children do start computing mentally, ask them how they know. More often than not, they will say, "I can see the (a specific tool) in my head."

Comprehension Check

- What are the steps that students pass through while learning place value?
- What are some activities that support each of these steps?

Working with Larger Numbers

The larger the number, the less experience children have with that number. We rarely deal with large numbers when counting. Once students are in the fourth grade, they are required not only to read and write in numbers through the millions but also to compute with these numbers. Most fourth graders have a difficult time reading such large numbers, let alone computing using them. Rounding is also another big obstacle. Ample time needs to be spent on understanding how the periods are constructed, on practicing saying numbers, and on building large amounts to develop a sense of magnitude estimates.

It is difficult to find things that are in large quantities and are worth counting, but the time needs to be invested. A million seems like an enormous amount of something, but as inflation keeps creeping up, we find that it is not much.

Before continuing, take a moment and think about how much space in your classroom would it take to house 1 million centimeter cubes.

Now, think about how you would build 1 million of these cubes. We always do this activity with our fourth-grade students. First, if we made a row of 10 hundreds flats, that would be 1,000 cubes. 10 rows of that would be 10,000 cubes. If we wanted to stack them 10 high, that would be 100,000 cubes (that would be like using the 1,000 block for each 100 flat, and we would have a large square of blocks). And if we stacked that 10 high, that would be 1 million cubes. That would be $100 \times 100 \times 100$ cm or 100 cm^3, which is 1 cubic meter (because 100 cm is 1 meter). Now that does not seem like much. And you probably estimated that 1 million cubes would fill half the room.

Granted, you probably would not have this many cubes in your classroom, even if you borrowed from your colleagues, but you would have enough to get started and the students are old enough that they can visually fill in the missing cubes if you help them visualize the outline with the tools you have. This building activity is a good introductory activity into exploring number periods.

When we built 1 million, there was a pattern with the type of block used. The three shapes were cube, rod, and flat. These were used three shapes repeatedly until we reached 1 million. If we create a chart, we can see how that pattern fits with number periods (figure 4.17).

Children might notice that every time there is a one, a cube is used. The same can be said about the tens and hundreds with the rod and the flat. This is not the only pattern that can be made with the cubes. You could guide them to predict what 100 million might look like. When they understand about the different places in the number periods, students have an easier time learning about where the commas are suppose to go.

Students have a considerable amount of trouble learning to read such large numbers. They should learn that the amount within any period is read in the same way and that the comma gives the name.

Because it is not reasonable to count out millions of items, estimation activities help in developing understanding of magnitude of numbers. One activity is called *How Many Beans* (Bresser and Holtzman 1999, 141). Have a large jar whose items you are periodically changing. Beans, jelly beans, macaroni, and so on, are good items to estimate. Have students make estimates as to how many of that item would fill the jar and record the range of those estimates on the board (this activity strengthens data and analysis as well). Pass out one scoop of the item to each group and have them count exactly how many were in their scoop. Record the different amounts each group counted. Have the

Million	*Hundred Thousand*	*Ten Thousand*	*Thousand*	*Hundred*	*Ten*	*One*
1,000,000	**100,000**	**10,000**	**1,000**	**100**	**10**	**1**
$10 \times 10 \times 10 \times 10 \times 10 \times 10$	$10 \times 10 \times 10 \times 10 \times 10$	$10 \times 10 \times 10 \times 10$	$10 \times 10 \times 10$	10×10	1×10	1
10^6	10^5	10^4	10^3	10^2	10^1	10^0
Cube	Flat	Rod	Cube	Flat	Rod	Cube

Figure 4.17. Patterns through the millions.

Comprehension Check

■ **Draw a sketch of what 1 million cubes would look like.**

class find an average amount that the scoop holds. Using that average, count out how many scoops of the item filled the jar. As you reach different points of filling the jar, ask the class to readjust their estimates. The closer you get to the top, the closer their range will be.

After doing this activity with a few different items, students become more realistic with their estimates.

Assessments

At this stage, the main thing you want to see is whether your students can break numbers into different units, including tens and ones. Can they count by groups and know their leftovers by the amount in each group? In other words, if they broke their amount into six groups of five and have three leftovers, do they count, "5, 10, 15, 20, 25, 30, 31, 32, 33"? Or do they say," 5, 10, 15, 20, 25, 30, 35, 40, 45"? Some students may even count them one by one, even though they broke them into groups. Kathy Richardson's *Grouping Tens* and *Ten Frames* assessments target these skills.

Grouping Tens assessment	Can the child to think of numbers as tens and ones?
Ten Frames assessment	Does the child think of numbers as tens and leftovers?

CONCLUSION

There is no better way to know what students think about a concept or what connections they are making than by asking questions and engaging them in dialogue. Students and teachers benefit equally from interactions that take place during discourse, which creates opportunities for students to convince their peers, for teachers to help children gain better mathematical understanding, and for students to internalize concepts that they have learned. When discourse is a common event in the classroom, students develop a sense of shared responsibility in the learning.

Teachers must also build in plenty of time for reflection, both before and after discussions. Reflection includes thinking aloud and silently and recording thinking both numerically and through writing. Writing in math is a skill. It entails a special language, representations, explanations, and proofs. It needs to be explicitly taught for students to be successful with it.

The process of communication and reflection is essential as children are trying to make connections while learning place value. The base 10 system is sophisticated and, although full of patterns, was developed by scholars over hundreds of years. It is a system that seems obvious to us as adults, but it is not obvious to young children. Its understanding needs to be constructed by the learner through grouping objects in ways that make sense to them and then through structured activities so that they can discover which groupings match the way we read and write numbers.

▶ Interview Video with an Eye on Content

Watch the videos of student interviews related to place value. In each video, note the following:

Briefly describe the task the student is asked to solve in the video.

_____

_____

_____

What understandings does the student have around place value?

_____

_____

What supportive evidence do you see?

_____

What would be the next steps for this child in terms of developing his understanding of place value?

_____

_____

_____

▶ Interview a Child

Design a student interview about an area of place value. What would you like to student to be able to say about that area? Consider the questions you ask to elicit the desired responses. What are some alternative questions you may have to ask that might be more supportive? What tools do you need to give your student access to? In a written summary, write:

1. The specific tasks you asked the child to complete.

2. The responses you obtained from the child.

3. What you think the child understands around place value and why you think so.

4. Where you would take this child next.

▶ Classroom Video with an Eye on Pedagogy

Watch the video of a classroom episode focusing on place value and note the following:

Briefly describe the task the students are asked to solve in the video.

_____

_____

_____

What understandings do the students have around place value and how do you know?

_____

_____

Elaborate on the teacher and students' role in communication in this video. How did the discourse support the learning process?

_____

_____

_____

▶ Classroom Application

1. Observe your cooperating teacher and note how discourse is conducted in the classroom. What types of questions does the teacher ask? Does the conversation flow teacher-student or student-student?

2. Collaboratively design and teach a lesson about a place-value concept. As you work with children in the classroom, focus on promoting mathematically rich discourse during your lessons. You may want to start with a small group rather than the whole class as you get used to questioning and encouraging participation of all students.

▶ Resources

Assessing Math Concepts: Books 1–9, Kathy Richardson (2003)

Developing Number Concepts. Book 3: Place Value, Multiplication, and Division, Kathy Richardson (1999c)

Math By All Means: Place Value Grades 1–2, Marilyn Burns (1994)

Developing Number Sense: Grades 3–6, Rusty Bresser and Caren Holtzman (1999)

Classroom Discourse: The Language of Teaching and Learning, 2nd ed., Courtney Cazden (2001)

▶ Lit Link

Literature Books to Support Place Value

Title	Author
Can You Count to a Googol?	Robert E. Wells
Counting Family, The	Jane Manners
King's Commissioners, The	Aileen Friedman
Math Talk: Mathematical Ideas in Poems for Two Voices	Theoni Pappas
Million Fish . . . More or Less, A	Patricia C. McKissack
More Than One	Miriam Schlein
My Counting Garden	Sarah Holliday
My Little Sister Ate One Hare	Bill Grossman

Title	Author
Recess Races	Betsy Franco
Roman Numerals I to MM: Numerabilia Romana Uno ad Duo Mila	Arthur Geisert
Who's at the Zoo?	Jane Finn

Tech Tools

Websites

National Library of Virtual Manipulatives, http://www.nlvm.usu.edu

Gamequarium, http://www.gamequarium.com/placevalue.html

AAA Math, http://www.aaaknow.com/plc.htm

Funbrain, http://www.funbrain.com/tens/index.html

Mathwire.com, http://www.mathwire.com/numbersense/placevalue.html

Mrs. Bogucki's 5th Grade Class, http://mrsbogucki.com/aemes/resource/apps/placeval/default.htm

Dositey, http://www.dositey.com/addsub/tenoneex.htm

Software

Grouping and Place Value, Sunburst Technology

Polygone Explore les matématiques, Synapse Multimédia (This software uses little language, and the mathematics it reinforces is strong. The low emphasis on language makes this software appropriate for English-language learners and students with special needs. The CD is in French and English. The Synapse Multimédia website does not sell the CD; it just shows aspects of it. Other vendor sites sell the CD.)

Learning with Understanding: Concepts and Procedures and Multidigit Addition and Subtraction

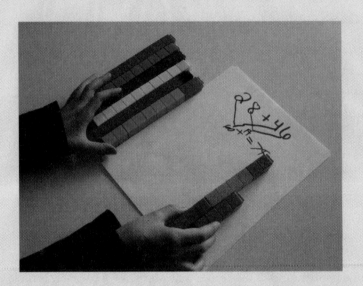

PEDAGOGICAL CONTENT UNDERSTANDINGS

Pedagogy *Concepts and Procedures*

- Conceptual versus Procedural Knowledge
- A Balanced Set of Beliefs about Mathematics
- Types of Concepts and Related Procedures
- Constructing Mental Concepts
- Developing Procedural Fluency
- Standard versus Alternative Algorithms

Content *Multidigit Addition and Subtraction*

- Invented Algorithms
- Standard Algorithms

"Because understanding is synonymous with seeing relationships, emphasizing relationships helps to develop understanding."

Carpenter et al., Children's Mathematics: Cognitive Guided Instruction *(1999, 99)*

CONVERSATION IN MATHEMATICS

Imagine a second-grade student who learns mathematics in a classroom where the teacher is in the habit of helping students learn mathematics with understanding, that is, teaching them why mathematics works, as well as how to do the math. In an exception to that norm, her teacher shows her the procedure for subtracting two whole numbers each with two digits where decomposing, or regrouping, is involved without first developing a conceptualization for doing so. Here is what might happen as the child's thinking is probed in an interview:

Interviewer: I am going to ask you to subtract these two numbers, 62 − 48.

Child: OK. We did this before. But I don't exactly remember it as well, because I didn't figure it out for myself. So . . .

Interviewer: What do you mean?

Child: Well, when I figure things out for myself, it helps me remember it longer.

Interviewer: How about if we go ahead and try this subtraction?

Child: The way that my teacher taught me to do it was to borrow from the 2 and make it a 1, then change the 6 to 7. Then I do 8 take away 1 is 7, and 7 take away 4 is 3, so the answer is 37.

$$
\begin{array}{r}
{\scriptstyle 7\ 1} \\
\not{6}\not{2} \\
-\ 48 \\
\hline
37
\end{array}
$$

Interviewer: Can you think of another way of doing it?

Child: Well, I could draw 6 longs (tens) and 2 units (ones). I am supposed to take away 8 units, which means I don't have enough. So I break apart one of the longs and now I have 5 longs and 12 units. I take away 8, and that leaves 4 units. I take away 4 longs, and that leaves 1 long. And 1 long and 4 units is 14. Wait a minute, I got 37 doing it the other way.

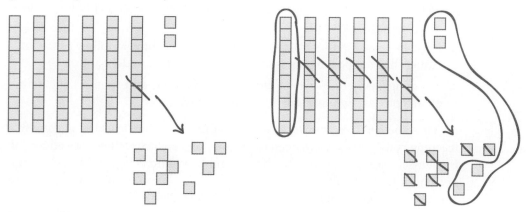

Interview: Which answer do you think is correct?

Child: I think 14 is.

Interviewer: Why?

Child: Because I can see what is going on with the numbers when I draw it out. It makes sense to me.

Interviewer: I noticed that when you first tried to solve the problem, you still wanted to go to the rule that your teacher taught you, even though you didn't quite remember it the right way.

Child: Yeah.

Interviewer: Why do you think you did that?

Child: Well, because I was taught that first.

Interviewer: If you had your choice of which lesson you could have learned first, which one would you have liked to have learned first?

Child: This one (pointing to the manipulatives) because I would have remembered how to do it the right way, and the correct way.

This young student has powerful things to say about the nature of mathematics and about learning mathematics with understanding. When she tried to remember a procedure without learning about its conceptual foundation, her remembrance of that procedure was confused. She says that she likes to figure things out for herself, and when she figures out why things work, the answer stays in her head. She expressed a personal preference for learning concepts before procedures, and when she conceptualized the problem with pictures she was able to invent an efficient procedure herself and justify it mathematically.

Many of us who engage in mathematics education research focus on the beliefs held by the teachers with whom we work (Civil 1993; Pajares 1992; Vacc and Bright 1999), beliefs about the nature of mathematics and about how mathematics is learned and taught. Beliefs are often defined as dispositions to act (Cooney, Shealy, and Arvold 1998). A landmark study demonstrated that the following beliefs are commonly possessed by teachers (Ernest 1989):

1. Mathematics is a set of rules to be learned rather than a body of interrelated and connected concepts.

2. Teaching mathematics consists of telling students how to follow procedures rather than supporting students as they attempt to understand.

3. Learning mathematics is a process of practicing and memorizing rather than a process of reasoning and making sense.

These beliefs have powerful effects on the decisions teachers make while teaching math. Widely held even today, they still shape mathematics education in many classrooms (Fuson, Kalchman, and Bransford 2005). Most of us would not find it too difficult to remember one or more of our math teachers whose teaching methods implied that they held these beliefs.

If we are to teach mathematics with understanding, however, we must begin to think differently about the nature of mathematics and what it means to learn it and to teach it. The NCTM's *Principles and Standards for School Mathematics* (2000) calls for a more balanced approach when it comes to learning both procedures, or "how" to do math, and concepts, or "why" the math works the way it does. In other words, learning mathematics with understanding. The NCTM states that "students who memorize facts or procedures without understanding often are not sure when or how to use what they know, and such learning is often quite fragile" (2000, 20). This phenomenon was nicely illustrated in the opening conversation of this chapter. When the student was taught a procedure she did not understand, her recollection of it was uncertain.

Proficiency in mathematics includes flexibility with knowledge, or the ability to apply what is learned to different settings. It also comprises conceptual understanding, factual knowledge, and procedural facility.

After our discussion of concepts and procedures, we resume our treatment of addition and subtraction, this time building on the big ideas of chapter 3 and moving on to multidigit numbers. Our purpose is to help you develop your own concepts, or operation sense, about multidigit addition and subtraction and to connect those concepts to the procedures that follow from them, including the standard algorithms you learned as a child.

Concepts and Procedures   **PEDAGOGY**

Learning Theory

We can remember learning mathematical procedures like borrowing in subtraction, or long division, or even inverting the second fraction when dividing fractions and wondering why those procedures produced a correct answer. Many teachers we have taught have remarked that when they asked their math teachers why a certain procedure worked, their teachers were reluctant or unable to offer an explanation. This type of experience has lead many of us to say, altering the famous line from *The Charge of the Light Brigade,* "Ours is not to reason why, ours is to invert and multiply." Interestingly enough, learning psychologists have been telling us for years that such meaningless teaching and learning is less than effective.

In the later part of the nineteenth century, Hermann Ebbinghaus (1885) devised some rather sophisticated experiments involving the presentation and recall of nonsense syllables to investigate the three basic memory tasks of recognition, recall, and relearning. It was discovered that some nonsense syllables were easier to learn than others. Nonsense syllables were selected to avoid the meaning associated with ordinary language, yet some of them produce meaningful associations. A syllable that resembles a real word has some of the associative strength of that word. Therefore, nonsense syllables such as *kup, sec,* and *pek* are more easily recalled than, say, *min, siv,* and *sen.* A scale of meaningfulness was established based on association. Subjects were presented with a nonsense syllable, such as *piv,* and asked to think of an association to that word. If 5 of 15 subjects gave associations to the nonsense word *piv,* and 10 subjects provided associations to *dax,* Ebbinghaus could conclude that *dax* is more meaningful than *piv.* Meaningfulness of material does affect its ease of acquisition. Ebbinghaus estimated that learning such material takes only about one tenth of the effort required to learn comparable nonsense material. Note that *meaningfulness* as defined here refers to associative strength. It does not indicate whether the material is "relevant" in the subject's life or deeply "felt" by the subject.

In a more recent study (Chase and Simon 1973), a chess master, a class A player (good but not a master), and a novice were given 5 seconds to view a set of chess pieces from the middle of a chess game. After 5 seconds the board was covered, and each subject was invited to reconstruct the board position on another board. The master player correctly placed many more pieces than the class A player, who in turn placed more than the novice. However, these results occurred only when the chess pieces were arranged in configurations that mimicked meaningful chess patterns. When chess pieces were randomized and presented for 5 seconds, there was no difference in the recall among the three subjects. The apparent difference in memory capacity results from a difference in pattern recognition. What the expert can remember as a single meaningful pattern novices must remember as separate, unrelated items.

The authors of *Adding it Up: Helping Children Learn Mathematics* (Kilpatrick, Swafford, and Findell 2001, 118) write:

> **Scientists have concluded that competence in an area of inquiry depends upon knowledge that is not merely stored but represented mentally and organized (connected and structured) in ways that facilitate appropriate retrieval and application. Thus, learning with understanding is more powerful than simply memorizing because the organization improves retention, promotes fluency, and facilitates learning related material . . . having a deep understanding requires that learners connect pieces of knowledge, and that connection in turn is a key factor in whether they can use what they know productively in solving problems.**

Application to the Learning and Teaching of Mathematics

Conceptual versus Procedural Knowledge

Concepts are defined as topics or mathematical ideas, whereas *conceptual knowledge* is defined as the "quality of one's knowledge of the concepts" (Starr 2005) and "knowledge about facts, [generalizations], and principles" (Baroody, Feil, and Johnson 2007, 123; cited in de Jong and Ferguson-Hessler 1996, 107).

Procedures are the "step-by-step routines learned to accomplish some task" (Van de Walle 2004, 28), whereas *procedural knowledge* is knowledge of the symbols to represent the mathematical ideas and knowledge of the rules and procedures for solving mathematical problems (Hiebert and Lefevre 1986; Starr 2005). It is also defined as "mental 'actions or manipulations' including strategies, and algorithms, for completing a task" (Baroody, Feil, and Johnson 2007, 123; cited in de Jong and Ferguson-Hessler 1996, 107).

Hiebert and Lefevre (1986) defined conceptual knowledge as being rich in relationships and referred to the amount of connections made. Many math educators use this definition. Therefore, when describing a child with conceptual knowledge, or understanding, they may be referring to *deep* conceptual understanding. Subsequently, when speaking of procedural knowledge, many educators may be referring to a *superficial* level of knowledge, one that is not rich in connections.

Actually, both conceptual knowledge and procedural knowledge can be viewed as either superficial or deep (Star 2005). It is possible to have weak conceptual knowledge and weak procedural knowledge or deep conceptual and

Knowledge Type	Example
Weak conceptual knowledge	Child can only represent an idea in one way. **Example:** Only represents 25 + 36 using tally marks: /////////////////////// /////////////////////////////////
Strong conceptual knowledge	Child can represent an idea in multiple ways. **Example:** Understands that subtraction is represented as take away, and compare, and can model subtraction with different tools, such as cubes, a number line, a 100 chart, a 10 frame, and base 10 blocks.
Weak procedural knowledge	Child either inaccurately or inflexibly uses rules, strategies, or algorithms. **Example:** Subtracts 43 − 27 and gets a result of 24.
Strong procedural knowledge	Child can flexibly use rules, strategies or algorithms depending on the situation of the specific problem and can recognize an unreasonable error. **Examples** Adds 29 + 25 by thinking of quarters, so adds 25 + 25 and then adds the remaining 4 to get 54. Adds 29 + 25 by taking 1 from the 25 and adding it to the 29 to make 30, then adding 30 + 24 to get 54. Adds 29 + 25 by adding 20 + 20 to get 40 and 9 + 5 to get 14, then adds 40 + 14 to get 54. Adds 29 + 25 by adding 9 + 5 to get 14, then the 10 with the 20s and adds 10 + 20 + 20 to get 50 (puts the 5 in the tens place next to the 4 in the ones place).

Figure 5.1. Examples of levels of conceptual and procedural knowledge.

deep procedural knowledge, but a student is unlikely to have weak conceptual and deep procedural knowledge, or vice versa (Baroody, Feil, and Johnson 2007). Baroody and colleagues argue that there is an interconnectedness between deep conceptual and deep procedural knowledge and that one cannot exist without the other, although one may be stronger than the other.

The table in figure 5.1 outlines what this might look like in the math work of a child.

Deep procedural knowledge includes not only knowledge of procedures but flexibility and critical judgment as well. It is the ability know how to solve a problem based on the particular set of numbers in the problem. It is efficiency, and it is accuracy.

Children's procedural knowledge is limited by their conceptual knowledge. Many children appear to have great facility with numbers, but if they lack concepts they are limited to what they can do with those numbers. Just because a child can accurately subtract 1,000 − 999 with regrouping does not mean that he should. Children with strong concepts and procedures can step back from the problem and realize that the answer is simply 1. The goal for our students, therefore, is to develop both deep conceptual and deep procedural knowledge and understanding.

A Balanced Set of Beliefs about Mathematics

Rebecca Ambrose and colleagues (2004) organized the beliefs held by teachers who possess a more balanced perspective about learning mathematics with understanding under two headings: belief about mathematics and beliefs about learning mathematics, knowing mathematics, or both:

Belief about mathematics

1. Mathematics is a web of interrelated concepts and procedures.

Beliefs about learning mathematics, knowing mathematics, or both

2. One's knowledge of how to apply mathematical procedures does not necessarily go with understanding of the underlying concepts.

3. Understanding mathematical concepts is more powerful and more generative than remembering mathematical procedures.

4. If students learn mathematical concepts before they learn procedures, they are more likely to understand the procedures when they learn them. If they learn the procedures first, they are less likely to ever learn the concepts.

We discuss these beliefs in detail in the sections that follow.

Belief 1: A Web of Interrelated Concepts and Procedures

Students who possess a conceptual understanding of a particular mathematical topic possess an integrated grasp of the ideas associated with that topic that is more than an isolated collection of facts and methods. The importance of mathematical ideas and the contexts in which they can be applied are understood. They organize their knowledge into well-connected packages, which allows them to acquire new knowledge by connecting it to what they already know.

Deep conceptual understanding is demonstrated when a student can represent mathematical situations in different ways and knows how different representations can be applied in varied situations. Deep understanding, however, consists not only of the ability to produce multiple representations but also of the mental connections that exist between those representations. A measure of conceptual understanding consists of the quality and quantity of those connections.

For example, if we wish to know how deeply a student conceptualizes the subtraction operation, we would expect her to use pictures, concrete objects, or both to show its meaning. She might then use a number line and a number sentence to further represent the operation, explaining the relationships among them all. Finally, she might represent the number sentence as a story problem.

Liping Ma (1999) discusses the notion of a knowledge "package" in her research about the differences that characterize American and Chinese elementary mathematics teachers (figure 5.2). She quotes a teacher who was involved in her study about the assumption that "mathematical learning is a sequence that goes step by step." This teacher states:

> **I would rather say that learning a mathematical topic is never isolated from learning other topics. One supports the other. . . . For example, the meaning of subtraction, etc. The operation of subtraction with decomposition (we might inaccurately call this "borrowing") is the application of several ideas rather than a single one. It is a package, rather than a sequence, of knowledge. . . . There is not a firm, rigid, or single right way to "pack" knowledge. . . . You should see a knowledge "package" when you are teaching a piece of knowledge. And you should know the role of the present knowledge in that package. You have to know that the knowledge you are teaching is supported by which ideas or procedures, so your teaching is going to rely on, reinforce, and elaborate the learning of these ideas. (Ma 1999, 17–18)**

She states that the rectangle represents an important mathematical topic. Then:

> **The ellipses represent the related knowledge pieces. The shaded ellipses represent the key pieces of knowledge. An arrow from one topic to another indicates that the first topic supports the second. . . .**

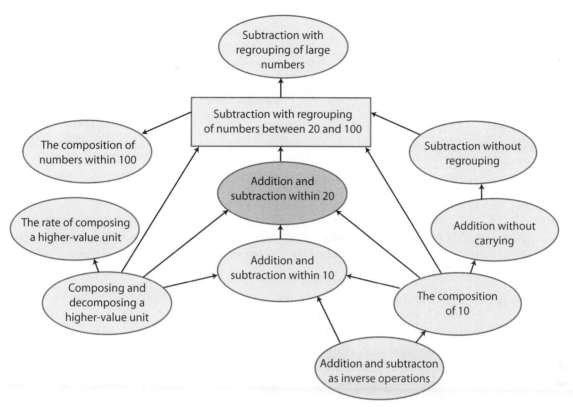

Figure 5.2. Subtraction learning packaged. (Lipping Ma, *Knowing and Teaching Elementary Mathematics: Teachers' Understanding of Fundamental Mathematics in China and the United States.* Mahwah, NJ: Lawrence Erlbaum Associates, p. 19. Reprinted by permission of Copyright Clearance Center.)

Besides the central sequence, the knowledge package also contains a few other topics. Directly connected to one or more links in the sequence, directly or indirectly, these topics encircle the sequence.

The purpose of a teacher in organizing knowledge in such a package is to promote a solid learning of a certain topic. It is obvious that all the items in the subtraction package are related to the learning of this topic, either supporting or supported by it. Some items, for example, subtraction without regrouping, are included mainly to provide procedural support. Other items, for example, composing and decomposing a higher-value unit, are considered mainly as a conceptual support. Still others, for example, the concept of inverse operation, were referred to as conceptual support as well as procedural support (Ma 1999, 18–19).

Belief 2: Knowledge of How to Apply Procedures versus Understanding of the Underlying Concepts

Ma (1999, 22) contrasts the knowledge packages previously discussed with those of teachers who possess only a procedural understanding, using subtraction as an example:

The knowledge packages of the teachers with only a procedural understanding of subtraction contained few elements. Most of these elements were procedural topics directly related to the algorithm of subtraction with regrouping. A brief explanation was usually included, but it was not a real mathematical explanation. For example, when a

Figure 5.3. Procedural understanding of a topic. (Lipping Ma, *Knowing and Teaching Elementary Mathematics: Teachers' Understanding of Fundamental Mathematics in China and the United States.* Mahwah, NJ: Lawrence Erlbaum Associates, p. 23. Reprinted by permission of Copyright Clearance Center.)

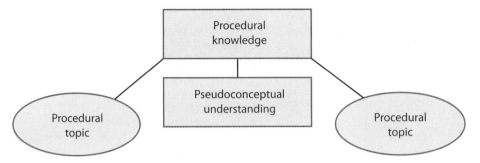

teacher told his or her students that the rationale of the algorithm is just like their mother goes to a neighbor to borrow some sugar, this arbitrary explanation doesn't contain any real mathematical meaning.

Figure 5.3 illustrates this type of knowledge package.

Procedural knowledge of the algorithm is represented by the top rectangle, related procedural topics are represented by the two ellipses, and pseudoconceptual understanding is shown by the trapezoid.

This shallow, narrow type of knowledge that is acquired when students learn a procedure without understanding results in at least four pedagogical problems.

First, it means that students need extensive practice to retain the steps in memory. If students learn a procedure with understanding, they are less likely to need lengthy practice to prevent forgetting critical steps and are more likely to be able to reconstruct those steps if some forgetting occasionally occurs. Thus, an emphasis on learning with understanding enhances the acquisition of fundamental skills.

Second, when children learn without understanding they usually separate what happens in a school context from what happens elsewhere. They do not see the relationship between procedures they use for solving problems in school and those they use for solving problems in other contexts. Without this connection, students' ability to solve real-life problems is hindered.

Third, students who learn procedures without understanding typically cannot adapt or modify those procedures for easier use. For example, students who only possess a procedural knowledge of subtraction would ordinarily need to use a paper-and-pencil algorithm to subtract 402 from 698. However, students with a deep conceptualization could think of the problem as 700 subtract 400, then subtract 4 more. As Kilpatrick, Swafford, and Findell (2001, 123) have stated:

> **When skills are learned without understanding, they are learned as isolated bits of knowledge. Learning new topics then becomes harder because there is no network of previously learned concepts and skills to link a new topic to. This practice leads to a compartmentalization of procedures that can become quite extreme, so that students believe that even slightly different problems require different procedures. That belief can arise among children in the early grades when, for example, they learn one procedure for subtraction problems without regrouping and another for subtraction problems with regrouping.**

Finally, when learning procedures without understanding, there is a danger that students will practice those procedures incorrectly. For example, how many intermediate-grade teachers have seen students solving two-digit subtraction problems requiring regrouping, or "decomposing," such as $71 - 36$, by subtracting the smaller digit from the larger digit in each column to obtain 45 as a result. A deeper conceptualization of subtraction would preclude this error.

Belief 3: Understanding versus Remembering

A substantial body of research (NCTM 2000) indicates that if students learn concepts before procedures that relate to those concepts they learn the procedures faster, remember them longer, and are better able to apply them to real-life situations. In addition, they are better able to invent, or generate those procedures for themselves. We address each of these benefits more specifically.

Why does conceptualizing enable faster learning of procedures? We have previously discussed the role of learning "packages," so consider a package students might develop for adding whole numbers that would empower them to learn the basic addition facts. Students can reduce the number basic facts to learn if they conceptualize that addition is commutative. Also, children tend to learn doubles (e.g., $4 + 4$) fairly easily. A deep conceptualization of addition would allow them to quickly acquire doubles plus one ($4 + 5 = 4 + 4 + 1$) because they recognize the relationships between similar problems. Thus, students are generating new knowledge rather than relying on rote memorization, which pays dividends in terms of the time required for learning.

Conceptual understanding also promotes retention. Connected facts and algorithms learned with understanding are mentally connected and are therefore easier to remember and use. Also, they can be regenerated if forgotten. When students understand a procedure, they are less likely to remember it incorrectly. They also metacognitively manage what they are learning. They know that mathematics is a sense-making endeavor and their efforts in this area deepen the connections among the elements of their learning packages.

Because inquiry often begins in the context of real-life application, and because students are consistently asked to represent their conceptualizations in multiple ways, including representing them in real-life contexts, it is easy to see why a balance of conceptual and procedural learning promotes application. Children come to school with much informal mathematical understanding supported by real-life contexts. Instruction embedded in real-life contexts wisely extends the natural abilities most students possess.

Conceptual understanding provides the basis for generating new knowledge and for students actually inventing procedures for themselves. For example, students who have a thorough sense of number and of the multiplication operation can conceptualize multiple algorithms for multiplying two numbers each with two digits using graph paper and can record that pictorial representation numerically in a way that mimics any of several algorithms. With the confidence in the result generated by that conceptualization, students can be invited to manipulate the numerals mathematically so that they eventually generate those algorithms.

Belief 4: Concepts Should Precede Procedures

Without a balanced perspective, procedural fluency and conceptual understanding can be viewed as competing considerations in school mathematics. However, this is a false dichotomy. As we have discussed, the two are interwoven. Learning concepts makes skills acquisition easier and more efficient. Conversely, procedural knowledge is required to help strengthen and develop important mathematical concepts. For example, developing a concept for multidigit calculations is difficult if students have not acquired a fundamental knowledge of single-digit calculations. On the other hand, if students have learned procedures without the conceptualizations that underlie them, it can be challenging to motivate them to participate in activities that invite them to go back and develop those conceptualizations. In an experimental study (Pesek and Kirshner 2000), fifth-grade students who first learned procedures for calculating area and perimeter and then received instruction on understanding those procedures did not perform as well as students who participated in activities that promoted understanding of area and perimeter.

We should say that the word *balance* does not refer to equal amounts of instructional time. A balance of conceptual and procedural is achieved when students develop knowledge packages that connect a large collection of related mathematical concepts and procedures in sensible ways.

Types of Concepts and Related Procedures

There are three types of concepts and related procedures: systems, operations, and algorithms.

Systems

The first type of concepts is concerned with systems. For example, the Hindu-Arabic number system, or base 10 system, is an important one about which students should have a deep understanding. In fact, the conceptualization of our number system has a special name, *number sense,* which was discussed in detail in chapter 2.

The type of procedures that come from system concepts are called *rules.* For example, when a child knows that the second place from the right in a whole number is the tens place, that child knows a rule. Other systems about which children should have deep understanding include the notions of graphing data; of physical attributes that can be measured and what it means to measure those attributes; of spatial configurations, sometimes called *shapes,* in two and three dimensions and the transformations of those configurations; and of patterns and functions.

Operations

The second type of concepts is concerned with operations: addition, subtraction, multiplication, and division. The name associated with this type of concept is *operation sense,* and this concept was discussed in chapter 3. Conceptualizations of operations lead to the acquisition of basic facts, like the addition facts or the times tables.

Algorithms

The third type of concepts is concerned with algorithms and results from connections between system and operation concepts. For example, for a child to understand the standard "subtraction with decomposing" algorithm for two-digit numbers, she has to conceptualize two-digit numbers, a system concept. Then she must understand that subtracting a larger number from a

Comprehension Check

- How do these four beliefs compare with the three beliefs discussed in the introduction of this chapter?

- Which set of beliefs characterizes most of your experience as a student learning mathematics?

smaller number is not possible when working with whole numbers (although it is possible when working with integers, and using integers in subtraction situations of this type is an efficient alternative algorithm), an operation concept, so she must decompose a higher-value unit, a system concept. Then she must be able to apply her understanding of the meaning of subtraction, an operation concept, to the numbers in each place column. Obviously, the knowledge of how to perform an algorithm would result from this type of concept.

Constructing Mental Concepts

In looking at how children construct mental concepts, we must go back to the learning theories of Jean Piaget and Lev Vygotsky. They did not believe that teachers are able to "teach" a concept; rather, they believed that children built their own understanding through real-world experiences, interactions with their environment, and open-ended activities and questions—in other words, in situations that cause children to think and to inquire about their world.

Rosalind Charlesworth and Karen Lind (2007) outline three learning situations in which concepts are acquired:

- *Naturalistic learning (Piaget).* The adult role is to provide an interesting environment, and the child controls his choice of activity and actions.

- *Informal learning (Vygotsky).* There is some adult intervention, but the child is still in control of the activity. This is where the teacher acts on those "teachable moments."

- *Structured learning (Vygotsky).* The adult is in control of the activity and gives direction to the child's action.

Equilibration

Piaget believed that children do not absorb knowledge passively from the environment but rather construct it through interactions between their mental structures and their environment (Labinowicz 1980). These mental structures, or ways of thinking that we all possess, are called *schema*. When everything we run across fits into our existing schema, we are considered to be in a state of *equilibrium*, or balance. However, our schema is challenged when we run across new ideas. When we cannot assimilate, or fit, a new idea into one of our existing schema, we become unbalanced, or enter a state of *disequilibrium*. At this point, we need to solve the conflict using our own mental activity to accommodate the new information and to regain our balance or equilibrium. Consider the following scenario:

> *A 6-year-old understands the concept that in addition he is able to combine the quantities in any order and write the result symbolically as such (commutative property of addition). When given a task to write the inverse operation of 3 + 4 = 7, he writes 3 − 7 = 4. When challenged by the teacher to prove his answer through use of a number line, he is perplexed when he lands at zero without having counted back all 7 spaces. He struggles for a few minutes and realizes that he needs to start at 7 and go back 3. After several similar problems, the teacher asks what he notices. He states that when subtracting, "the bigger number needs to go first."*

In the preceding scenario, the child had a schema about how addition works. When confronted with subtraction, he tried to *assimilate* this new information into his existing framework. But when he was unable to make his new information fit, he had to *accommodate* this new information by creating a new category in his schema—like adding a new file when a document will not fit in any other file. No doubt, in a few years this new schema will again be challenged when exploring integers.

Equilibrium is the balance between assimilation and accommodation. If we were to assimilate all new information, we would end up with just a few large categories and would not be able to distinguish different inputs; however, if we were to accommodate all information, then we would have too many categories and would have trouble generalizing (Labinowicz 1980).

The processes of assimilation and accommodation allow us to reach higher states of equilibrium (Labinowicz 1980). Each new state of equilibrium brings with it more complex internal structures. Every time we go through this process, we refine and add to our existing thinking pattern. The more opportunity we have to interact with our environment, the more opportunity we have for stimulation to develop our internal structures. "Thus, intellectual development may be visualized as a continuous spiraling process, with equilibration being the driving force behind this adaptation of the individual to his environment" (Labinowicz 1980, 41).

Learning takes place when the child recognizes that there is a problem or is aware that there are contradictions in her thinking. For this to happen, the task must be within reach of her existing framework. At this point, she must do something to solve her problem, which begins the equilibration process.

Equilibration is also known as *self-regulation* because the child takes an active role in the process. This process is thought of as the coordinator of three other factors that affect intellectual development: maturation, physical experience, and social interaction.

As children mature, their brains develop and are able to think of their environment in more sophisticated ways. Children with physical experience have seen objects influence the way they think about and understand those objects, like growing up on a farm versus growing up around boats. Social interaction encourages children to think of things from someone else's perspective, as well as to develop social knowledge of things such as local customs and norms (Labinowicz 1980). None of these factors in isolation are sufficient in developing intellectually. Children who grow up in isolated circumstances void of experiences are not intellectually the same as children of the same age who grow up in rich social and learning environments.

Zone of Proximal Development

Vygotsky's work also strongly emphasized the factor of social interactions and personal experiences. In his view, "social and cognitive development work together and build on each other" (Mooney 2000). He believed that the social interactions and personal experiences were inseparable.

One of Vygotsky's biggest contributions in understanding how children learn is the notion of the *zone of proximal development*. This was defined by Vygotsky as the "distance between the most difficult task a child can do alone and the most difficult task a child can do with help" (Mooney 2000, 83). When children are on the edge of learning a new concept (or in Piaget's state of disequilibrium), Vygotsky believed that they can benefit from the adults or peers in their environment. This "help" should be evident in the form of careful questioning, or *scaffolding*, rather than just telling. Telling students what the answer is or how to do it does not allow them the opportunity to make sense of the problem and work toward a new state of equilibrium. Scaffolding involves giving the students just enough supportive information for them to solve the problem on their own. Sometimes we need to provide many layers of scaffolds before children are able to "get it." As teachers, we do not always know how much support to give, so it is always best to provide minimal support and add layers as necessary.

Consider the following dialogue during a student interview:

The interviewer gives the student the following problem: "A cookie recipe calls for ⅔ cup of sugar, but I don't have enough milk so I need to cut the recipe in half. How much sugar am I going to need?"

The student solves the problem using numerical representations and gets 1 cup as an answer.

Interviewer: Does that make sense?

Student: Um . . . I'm not sure.

Interviewer: If you were going to visualize that I needed ⅔ cup of sugar and now I only need a half of a recipe, does a whole cup of sugar make sense?

Student: (Nods yes.)

Interviewer: Because?

Student: I divided the 2 by 2 and got 1 . . . and divided the 3 by 2 and got 1 and ½.

Interviewer: So you are trying to figure out what that number means?

Student: (Nods.)

Interviewer: Why don't you try solving this with a picture and see whether that helps you better.

Student: (Draws picture.)

I got a different answer this time . . . 4/6.

Interviewer: And 4/6 is how much I am going to use or how much I should have used?

Student: Well it's the same thing as ⅔.

Interviewer: That's how much the recipe wants me to use, so I need to figure out what's half of that.

Student: Well, where I got the 4/6 is that I had the whole and cut it into three pieces, so then I decided to cut them again into half so that the denominator would be 6 and there were four parts shaded.

Interviewer: But does that change the amount of sugar that I had in that drawing right there?

Student: No.

Interviewer: So if it doesn't change it, how is 4/6 related to ⅔?

Student: Because if you simplify it, it would be the same thing as ⅔.

Interviewer: So it is an equivalent fraction. Right? So, since we're kind of stuck in the numbers and we aren't really sure, and with the picture we are a little bit stuck, I thought I would bring you a cup and go get some water to pretend its sugar. What I would like you to do first is mark where you think ⅔ should be and go fill it up with water and do what ever you need to do to figure out what half of that would be.

Student: (Marks the cup with two marks but says that the top one is ⅓ and the bottom is ⅔. Comes back from the sink with the water to the first bottom mark.)

Interviewer: Is this where you think ⅔ is?

Student: (Looking at cup) No! (Goes to sink to readjust.)

Interviewer: So, tell me about what you are thinking and why you changed your mind.

Student: First I filled it up to here and that was ⅓. But because this is ⅓, this is ⅓, and this is another ⅓, two of them would equal ⅔.

Interviewer: So, if that is how much sugar I am supposed to have, how much sugar am I going to put since I need to cut my recipe in half?

Student: (Goes and pours out ⅓.) I had this much and I took out half of it.

Interviewer: So how much do you have now?

Student: ⅓.

Interviewer: Can you go back to your picture and draw a new picture to show how to get . . .

Student: So make it into ⅓?

Interviewer: Well, I want you to go back to the beginning and draw your ⅔ and figure out how you would draw a picture to show what happened. And you might want to think about what you did with the water to help you draw a picture.

Student: (Draws a new picture and quickly crosses out one of the thirds in a manner that says "I got it.")

In this dialogue, the student is obviously confused about what is really happening in the problem. She does not understand what her numbers mean in relation to the problem and cannot figure out how to solve this problem with a picture. In the dialogue, her thinking is at times logical and other times illogical. Piaget describes these rapid shifts in judgment as increasing the probability of internal reorganization (Labinowicz 1980).

At different times during the interview, the student was close to getting the right answer, and it would have been tempting for the interviewer to have pointed out where her answer was in her numerical work or to just tell her how to finish drawing her picture, but this would not have helped her create her own meaning. The interviewer was careful to scaffold, using reflective questions such as "Does that make sense?" These questions allowed the student to reflect on her own work and realize that there was a problem, thus entering the state of disequilibrium. It also gives the interviewer a better sense of the student's thinking about the problem.

The interviewer first let the student tackle the question with no assistance. Observing the student, the decision was made to provide the suggestion of creating a pictorial representation. The interviewer thought that this would be sufficient for the student to figure out the answer. Because the student still seemed unable to use the picture as a means for solving her problem, she was guided to use a more concrete representation. With this representation, she was able to solve the problem and make an appropriate connection back to the picture and, later, back to the numbers (not shown).

Concepts versus Models

Conceptual knowledge of mathematics is referred by Piaget as *logico-mathematical knowledge* (Kamii 1985, 1989; Labinowicz 1985; Van de Walle 2006). As Labinowicz (1980) notes, "We only see what we understand." Because conceptual knowledge is constructed in the learner and it is knowledge that it is understood, not everyone sees the same relationships and ideas that might be inherent in some manipulative tools. The pedagogical section in chapter 2 discussed some problems that children might have when working with certain tools, for example, base 10 blocks and the number line. Teachers may use these tools to help children develop the concepts of the base 10 system, for example. However, if children have not yet developed those concepts, they are not going to be able to see that relationship with that tool. When using base 10 blocks, the teacher may have said 50 times that the "long" is a 10, but to the child it is a label until he has built enough tens to impose that relationship on that particular tool. This is evident when he counts the longs and the small cubes all by tens. When the child is older, he may begin to see the long as a tenth when working with decimal numbers. In other words, teachers need to allow children to construct the meaning of the tool so that it can become a meaningful support in helping develop further concepts.

This is true for ideas as well. If the teacher posed a problem that implies multiplication yet the child does not have the concepts of multiplication, he will never see that relationship in the problem. He will solve the problem through his existing concept: addition. It is the teacher's job to then link what he already knows (addition) with what she wants him to know (multiplication).

Developing Procedural Fluency

As previously stated, a student who possesses procedural fluency has a knowledge of rules, facts, or algorithms and knows when and how to use them with accuracy, flexibility, and efficiency.

Russell (2000, 154) defines each of these abilities in the following way:

- *Efficiency* implies that the student is not bogged down in many steps and does not lose track of the logic of the strategy. An efficient strategy is one that the student can carry out easily, keeping track of subproblems and using intermediate results to solve the problem.

- *Accuracy* depends on several aspects of the problem-solving process, including careful recording, the knowledge of basic number combinations, and concern for double-checking results.

- *Flexibility* requires the knowledge of the more-than-one approach to solving a particular kind of problem. The student needs to be flexible to be able to choose an appropriate strategy for the problem at hand and to use one method to solve a problem and another method to double-check the results.

In the content area of number and operations, for example, procedural fluency includes more than the performance of paper-and-pencil computations; it also refers to mental methods and the prudent use of calculators, computers, and even manipulatives.

A flexible use of rounding as a vehicle for estimating computational results is also an important component of procedural fluency. For example, not every situation involving multiplication requires the standard paper-and-pencil algorithm. Students could multiply by multiples of 10 or powers of 10. Likewise, finding the sum of 299 and 48 or the product of 26 and 4 could be performed more efficiently using mental arithmetic. Also, many situations do not require an exact answer, such as determining the tip for a restaurant bill. And who would dream of completing a complicated tax form without a calculator or computer? Thus, procedural fluency includes skill with a variety of computational methods and knowing how to select the right method for a given situation.

Accuracy is still the goal of solving a math problem. Children who are fluent in math have a higher rate of accuracy than those who are not. This is largely because they are able to make reasonable estimates. They are able to step back from their work and know when an answer does not make sense. It is essential to constantly encourage children to make estimates before solving a problem so that they are able to compare their answers to see whether they make sense. Sometimes students become caught up in the numbers and lose sight of the reasonableness of an answer.

Fluency is developed through both conceptual and procedural understanding. "On one hand, computational methods that are overpracticed without understanding are often forgotten or remembered incorrectly. . . . On the other hand, understanding without fluency can inhibit the problem-solving process" (NCTM 2000, 35).

Children who develop, record, explain, and critique one another's computational strategies are able to generalize strategies for different numbers, which supports flexibility. Over time, they make connections from their invented strategies to more efficient standard algorithms. Because these children possess flexibility, they may not always choose to use a standard algorithm, which may not prove to be the most efficient way to solve a particular problem (such as 1,000 − 999).

Standard versus Alternative Algorithms

When solving problems, children use three strategies: direct modeling, invented procedures, and algorithms (standard and alternative). As described in chapter 3, direct modeling refers to acting out the situation in the problem to find the answer. Children as young as kindergarten are able to solve division problems

Rule of Thumb

Children are ready to move to more efficient procedures when they do not need direct models to support all of their thinking. They often make this move without you encouraging it.

through direct modeling if the context and numerical complexity are supportive enough.

Invented procedures or strategies are generated when children no longer need to or are able to directly model the problem as the numbers become larger and harder to model. Invented strategies may be using blocks or drawing a picture in a way that is not representative of the action in the story, making mental calculations, or inventing a paper-and-pencil procedure (Chambers 1999).

Many times, through their invented procedures, children end up reinventing an alternative algorithm, although at other times children's invented procedures are convoluted and hard to replicate in other situations. Through careful scaffolding, the teacher can help the children record more efficiently and connect their ideas to algorithms that follow their same line of thinking. When the concepts are solid, then the children's thinking is usually connected to the standard "traditional" algorithm. Students with strong conceptual knowledge may never choose to use a standard algorithm because they find an alternative one more efficient.

Standard, or Traditional, Algorithms

An algorithm is a set of rules for solving a particular kind of problem. The standard algorithms we talk about are standard for our country. Many other countries use different algorithms. Students who arrive from other countries may have a different way of solving computational problems. It is important to understand how they work so that we can help students make connections between them. Because accuracy is the goal, forcing students to use a specific algorithm is not necessary. It is more important that students understand why what they are using works.

For example, in Mexico, students hold more information in their head when doing the division algorithm. They do not write every step as we do. It shows mental strength to be able to remember so much while solving, yet many U.S. teachers insist that students "show all their work." In our opinion, such teachers are handicapping children by forcing them to write every step to each problem. Writing should be used as a tool, not as a burden. If children can solve the entire problem mentally, then they should. But they should also be able to record their thinking for class discussions so that others can follow the thought process.

Many students may come to class already knowing the standard algorithm from home. This shows that supportive and well-meaning family members are ready to help them. We know from earlier discussions in this chapter that it is difficult to go back and learn concepts when a formal operation is in place. Most teachers faced in this predicament simply tell their students that they are happy they already know how to use the traditional algorithm but that to use it they must understand why it works and how it connects to other representations being explored in class (such as the blocks or drawings). They are also invited to use the standard algorithm as a way to check their answers. This usually takes care of the situation in a respectful way.

Look at what is usually said when solving a common subtraction problem:

Language Tip

Inviting children to show their thinking in multiple ways is a natural way to help children with limited English proficiency.

$$\begin{array}{r} 72 \\ -35 \\ \hline \end{array}$$ Student: *"You cannot take the 5 from the 3, so borrow 1 from the 7 and make it a 6. Put the 1 by the 2 to make it a 12. Now, subtract the 3 from the 6 to get 3."*

One problem with this explanation is that it does not preserve place value. The 7 is not a 7 but a 70. The student is borrowing not a 1 but a 10 (and really breaking up 72 from 7 tens and 2 ones to 6 tens and 12 ones). Technically, the student can subtract a 5 from a 2. The notion that children think they cannot subtract a larger number from a smaller number hurts their flexibility and their ability to transition into integers later, which is why it is important to expose children early to the negative number line. Children who are fragile in their computational knowledge of subtraction may even be caught subtracting the 2 from the "7" and other random computational acts.

It is critical that when children are exposed to a standard algorithm that place value is preserved ("subtract 30 from the 70") and that the process is connected to what the child already knows about that operation.

Alternative Algorithms

Growing up in this society, we may be unfamiliar with ways to solve computational problems other than the one we learned. Where a standard algorithm has lots of shortcuts, many alternative algorithms are more directly connected with what children do with the models.

Take, for example, addition. When given base 10 blocks and asked to add $37 + 48$, children will almost undoubtedly take the tens and add them together and then take the ones and add them together. They will either put the 10 from the 15 with the 70 or just add 70 and 15, because it is within their mental capacity to do so. Student's initial recording might look like this:

$$37 + 48$$

$$70 + 15 = 85$$

The following algorithm shows this process:

$$
\begin{array}{r}
37 \\
+\ 48 \\
\hline
70 \\
+\ 15 \\
\hline
85
\end{array}
$$

This algorithm is known as *partial sums*. It is a powerful first algorithm for young children because it preserves place value and it matches what most children do with their blocks. Each of the content sections of this book dedicated to computation explores different nontraditional strategies and how they connect to student thinking.

As children become more consistent with their strategy, teachers might either guide them to connect their strategy with the preceding algorithm or challenge them to record vertically what they did horizontally to see whether they reinvent the partial sums algorithm. Most children will realize that partial sums is a clearer way to present their thinking over their invented way.

It is important to emphasize here the difference between the students coming up with a written strategy, and then guiding them to link it with someone else's strategy or an existing algorithm, and the teacher showing the students how to do any of these algorithms, even if it is connected with some kind of concrete material, and asking them to mimic them. If they are shown, even with a block model, the algorithm will just be a procedure void of meaning. Children need to make sense of the problem to attach meaning to the procedure.

Multidigit Addition and Subtraction   CONTENT

As we examine multidigit addition and subtraction in this chapter, we first look at the big ideas and the NTCM's *Curriculum Focal Points for Prekindergarten through Grade 8 Mathematics: A Quest for Coherence* (2007). We then discuss in much detail the algorithms children invent to solve problems of this type, which we introduced to you in the previous section. This discussion is followed by some guidelines for assessment and some sample inquiry lessons. Although the focus of this section is mathematical content, we help you create your own connected mental webs about the concepts and procedures that characterize addition and subtraction.

The primary focus of your instruction with children in the early stages of learning about addition and subtraction is to enable them to develop deep, rich conceptualizations of those operations, that is, operation sense, as we discussed in chapter 3. As this sense is developed, children are in an excellent position to learn to recall basic addition and subtraction facts. As they are learning those facts, they should move on to multidigit addition and subtraction. The problem types for these larger numbers are the same as those for smaller numbers. For example, a join (result unknown) problem is a join (result unknown) problem regardless of the size of the numbers. However, the problem-solving strategies children use and invent are different as they encounter multidigit numbers and invent multistep strategies. Multistep computational strategies have a special name, *algorithms,* so the algorithms that children invent without direct instruction are called *invented algorithms* (Carpenter et al. 1999).

Big Ideas and Focal Points

Several of the big ideas we discussed in chapter 1 are indirectly or directly related to the learning of multidigit addition and subtraction. The first six and the ninth lay a foundation, and then ideas 7 and 8 become the focus.

1. *Numbers.* The set of real numbers is infinite, and each real number can be associated with a unique point on the number line.

2. *Base 10 Numeration System.* The base 10 numeration system is a scheme for recording numbers using digits 0–9, groups of 10, and place value.

3. *Equivalence.* Any number, measure, numerical expression, algebraic expression, or equation can be represented in an infinite number of ways that have the same value.

4. *Comparisons.* Numbers, expressions, and measures can be compared by their relative values.

5. *Operation Meanings and Relationships.* The same number sentence (e.g., $12 - 4 = 8$) can be associated with different concrete or real-world situations, *and* different number sentences can be associated with the same concrete or real-world situation.

6. *Properties.* For a given set of numbers, there are relationships that are always true. These are the rules that govern arithmetic and algebra.

7. *Basic Facts and Algorithms.* Basic facts and algorithms for operations with rational numbers use notions of equivalence to transform calculations into simpler ones.

8. *Estimations.* Numerical calculations can be approximated by replacing numbers with other numbers that are close and easy to compute with mentally. Measurements can be approximated using known referents as the units in the measurement process.

9. *Patterns.* Relationships can be described and generalizations can be made for mathematical situations that have numbers or objects that repeat in predictable ways. (Charles 2005)

The NCTM's *Curriculum Focal Points* touch lightly on multidigit addition and subtraction in first grade and suggest a strong emphasis on them in second and third grades (Focal Points table).

NCTM FOCAL POINTS

First Grade	Second Grade	Third Grade
Children will use mathematical reasoning, including ideas such as commutativity and associativity and beginning ideas of tens and ones, to solve two-digit addition and subtraction problems with strategies that they understand and can explain.	Children will solve arithmetic problems by applying understanding of models of addition and subtraction (such as combining or separating sets or using number lines), relationships and properties of number (such as place value), and properties of addition (commutativity and associativity). They will develop, discuss, and use efficient, accurate, and generalizable methods to add and subtract multidigit whole numbers. Students will select and apply appropriate methods to estimate sums and differences or calculate them mentally, depending on the context and numbers involved. Students will develop fluency with efficient procedures, including standard algorithms, for adding and subtracting whole numbers; will understand why the procedures work (on the basis of place value and properties of operations); and will use them to solve problems. They will add and subtract to solve a variety of problems, including applications involving measurement, geometry, and data, as well as nonroutine problems.	Students will develop understanding of numbers by building facility with mental computation (addition and subtraction in special cases, such as 2,500 + 6,000 and 9,000 − 5,000), by using computational estimation, and by performing paper-and-pencil computations.

Invented Algorithms

When beginning to add two-digit numbers with tens and ones, children invent four types of algorithms in a developmental sequence:

Direct modeling with ones

Directly modeling with tens and ones

Incrementing

Combining tens and ones

Making tens

Compensating

In all cases, the child naturally begins with the place on the left, as opposed to the ones place, as in the standard algorithm—just like we tend to count money. When children are left to their own devices, they usually start by combining larger amounts first.

Direct Modeling with Ones

The approach children use when given the following problem depends on their knowledge of place value:

> Mike had 27 toy cars. Lynn gave him 38 more toy cars. How many cars does he have altogether?

Many children will take interlocking cubes and build a long train of 27 and 38 cubes. The problem that the child begins to face is that now the numbers are larger and he can no longer keep track of his train, so he loses count. If asked by the teacher if this strategy is working for him, he will probably reply, "No." If asked what might be a better way to organize his cubes so that he does not lose count, he may state that he could group them by twos, fives, or other smaller groupings. He should be allowed to try these different groupings, because he will find that this is probably not as efficient as he thought; many children who struggle with number sense have a hard time counting by groups of two, three, five, and so on.

Directly modeling addition by making a single train.

The child will soon realize that tens would probably be the best way to group the cubes because he is sure to know how to count by tens. Many times, the child's partner will quickly let him know that tens are easier to count and teacher intervention is minimally necessary. Note that if the child is unable to count by tens, this strategy will not be helpful.

At this stage, the student should be using a tool that allows him to build tens (not base 10 blocks, because they do not allow for this construction) until he has internalized tens and ones. The teacher will know when he has internalized this because the student no longer wants to build all the tens; he will find it too cumbersome and interfering with the problem-solving process.

Direct Modeling with Tens and Ones

During this stage, a child would use cubes, base 10 blocks, beans and cups, or other manipulatives that can be grouped into tens to show 2 tens and 7 ones in one group and 3 tens and 8 ones in another group. Then, either physically or

Adding by creating tens and ones.

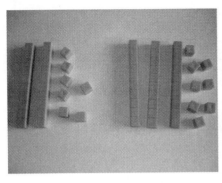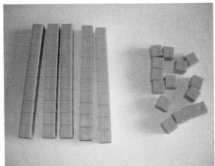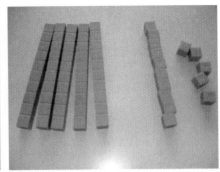

Directly modeling with tens and ones.

mentally, the child would combine the two groups, count the tens, "10, 20, 30, 40, 50," and then add the ones, "51, 52, 53, . . ., 63, 64, 65." A child with a little more number sense might actually combine 10 of the ones into an additional 10 and redo the count accordingly.

As discussed in previous chapters, at this point, students should be learning to record their work so that they can transfer their work with blocks to pictures and numeral representations. A student's recording of the preceding problem would look like the images shown in figure 5.4.

Incrementing

This strategy is called *incrementing* because the child begins with one of the two numbers in the problem without having to create the number mentally through counting or modeling and then incrementally adds on or removes the second number. If a child were presented the toy car problem, she might say, "37, 47, 57," adding the tens to one of the original numbers, followed by the ones: "58, 59, 60, 61, 62, 63, 64, 65." She should be able to record this thinking on an open number line, like this:

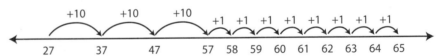

Incrementing for join or separate (result unknown) is easier for children than incrementing for change (result unknown). The problem for children, and even adults, is that they forget what answer they are looking for. They can count up to the number but have lost track of how much they counted. Suppose that the preceding problem said the following:

> *Mike had 27 toy cars. Lynn gave him some more toy cars. Mike now has 65 toy cars. How many did Lynn give him?*

In this instance, a child would be starting at 27 and counting up to 65. He may say, "37, 47, 57, 58, 59, 60, 61, 62, 63, 64, 65. Lynn gave him 65 cars." In this case, he has lost what he was looking for. He has forgotten that he was to keep track of his increments and that his answer should be the amount he incremented.

Making Tens A special type of incrementing involves making tens. As we stressed in chapter 3, success in computation rests in the ability to make tens. Being able to break apart numbers to make tens is a powerful and efficient mental strategy. A student with the ability to make tens would probably solve the toy car problem (27 + 38) as shown in figure 5.5.

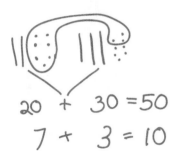

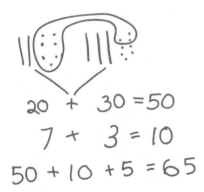

Figure 5.4. Student pictorial and numerical recording of direct modeling with tens and ones.

$$3 \quad 5$$
$$27 + 38$$
$$27 + 30 = 57$$
$$57 + 3 = 60$$
$$60 + 5 = 65$$

Figure 5.5. Student recording while using make a ten strategy.

$$27 + 38$$
$$50 + 15 = 65$$

$$27 + 38$$
$$27 + 30 = 57$$
$$57 + 8 = 65$$

Figure 5.6. Student numerical recording of combining tens and ones.

He would want to break the 8 to smaller numbers so that he can make another 10. It is easier to land on tens than to cross over when solving problems mentally.

Combining Tens and Ones

This strategy is similar to the direct modeling strategy, but the child is either mentally or numerically solving the problem. When a child uses this strategy, she mentally joins or removes the tens, then the ones, and then combines the two results into one result. A student's recording may look like the one in figure 5.6.

> **Rule of Thumb**
>
> Combining tens and ones is the invented algorithm most like the standard algorithm.

Compensating

Compensating involves a child deliberately changing the problem to simpler numbers and then compensating for them at the end. With the toy car problem (27 + 38), a child might say, "38 is close to 40, so 27 + 40 is 67. Then remove 2, and that is 65."

To be able to compensate, the student must have good number sense and understand what is happening with the numbers. A child sharing this strategy may want to come up to the overhead or document camera and demonstrate with cubes in the following fashion:

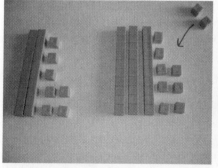
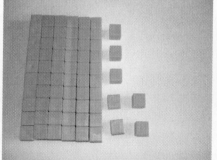
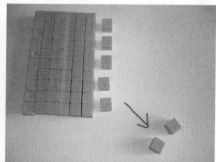

Concrete model to illustrate compensating while adding.

In joining problems, or adding, children have to understand that they are combining two amounts and whatever is added needs to be taken away at the end. However, consider the following problem: $60 - 39 = \square$. Do the same rules apply? Take a few minutes to think about how you would use compensating in this case.

The reason for compensating in this case is to eliminate mental regrouping. You would probably want to change the 60 to a 59 so that it would be easier to subtract the 39. The problem 59 − 39 is easily solved as 20, but what about that 1 you took from the 60? What do you do with that? You would need to add it back to adjust your difference to 21. But what if you wanted to adjust the 39 to 40 by adding 1? What would you do with that 1 you added?

In this case, that extra 1 would need to be added at the end. But that sounds counterintuitive. If you just had two problems where the compensation was to add back something that was taken away, why would you add back something that was added? The answer lies in the model of what is happening when we subtract.

When we subtract, we are really finding the difference between two numbers, or the amount of distance between them on the number line. In the problem 60 − 39, their position on the number line would look as follows:

When you took 1 from the 60, you were decreasing the difference by 1, so at the end, you needed to increase it back.

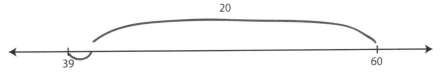

In the second scenario, when you added 1 to 39, you were also decreasing the difference; therefore, you needed to add the 1 back at the end.

If your goal to maintain a *constant difference*, then you would need to add or subtract an equal amount to both numbers. Then you would eliminate the need to compensate at the end. An example would be subtracting 1 from each number to get 59 and 38, which is easily computed mentally to get a difference of 21:

This idea can also be shown with cubes. If two trains are compared next to each other with a difference of 5, then no matter what you do to both of the trains, the difference will remain 5.

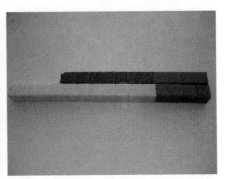

Illustration of the idea of constant difference with unifix cubes.

The ideas of compensating and constant difference are sophisticated and difficult for students to understand at first, depending on their age and developmental level. These strategies should not be taught but explored. Many students will not be ready to try these as their addition or subtraction strategies.

Standard Algorithms

Somewhere in all of this is development of the standard algorithms for adding and subtracting multidigit numbers. Many people have talked about the relative value of these standard algorithms. Some say that they are an important part of our mathematical "heritage" and lead to efficient problem solving. Others argue that they restrict student thinking because they make children give up their own thinking and they "unteach" place value, thereby preventing children from developing number sense (Kamii 2004).

We adopt a middle of the road approach to this issue. On the one hand, we value multiple problem-solving strategies and the mathematical thinking that perspective engenders. In addition, many people, including leading mathematicians, know the standard algorithms but choose to use alternative ones, including the invented ones we discussed in the last paragraphs. On the other hand, the position of the NCTM is clear that standard algorithms should be an important part of a person's problem-solving repertoire, and we agree.

We support the idea of children learning standard algorithms as long as the child's place-value and number sense are strong and they are not taught prematurely, as the only method, or in a rote way that precludes learning mathematics with understanding. In fact, children can be led to discover standard algorithms without being directly taught.

We have had wonderful experiences leading children to discover some complicated standard algorithms, including the addition and subtraction ones, the long multiplication algorithm, and even such challenging algorithms as those associated with adding, multiplying, and dividing fractions. A balanced approach to these issues makes the most sense to us.

Direct Modeling Connections of Alternative and Standard Algorithms

Of all the strategies, or algorithms, that children invent, direct modeling plays a prominent role in the development of efficient computational proficiency. This is true for two reasons. First, it lays the conceptual foundation for all other strategies. Second, it provides a convenient way for that child or other students to communicate the strategies that rely more on mental counting. For example, if a child incrementally solves and shares the solution to the toy car problem by adding the tens to one of the original numbers followed by the ones, not all children listening to that sharing will comprehend the solution. Therefore, you could invite another child to represent that thinking with base 10 blocks or even do so yourself. This alternative representing promotes comprehension of the strategy by enabling children who still think concretely to connect the more abstract,

Comprehension Check

- Add 26 and 48 using the invented algorithms.
- Subtract 39 from 72, also using the invented algorithms.

Struggling Learners

Resist the temptation to move children to the standard algorithm before they understand the mathematics behind it.

Special Needs

We have discovered that special needs children can learn abstract algorithms if they first develop a conceptualization of the underlying mathematics. Avoid moving them to abstract strategies, including standard algorithms, too soon.

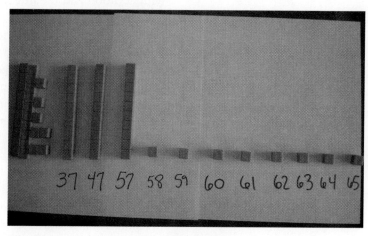

Creating a concrete model of incrementing.

Number Sentence and Description/ Level of Numerical Complexity	Direct Model/ Numerical Recording	Explanation
"What is the total when I combine 23 and 45?" 23 + 45 = ☐ Two digits, no composing	23 + 45 68 	"I represent 23 with 2 tens and 3 ones and represent 45 with 4 tens and 5 ones. I make a set out of the ones and count 8, and I make a set out of the tens and count 6. So, 6 tens and 8 ones is 68."
"What is the total when I combine 27 and 45?" 27 + 45 = ☐ Two digits, with composing	1 27 + 45 72 	"When I put 7 ones and 5 ones together, I get 12, which is more than 10. I make a 10 out of 10 ones and put it with the other tens. That leaves 2 ones. I put all the tens into a set and count 7. The 7 tens and 2 ones is 72."
Partial sums (alternative algorithm) 27 + 45 = ☐ **Note:** This algorithm best connects with most invented strategies and preserves place value	27 + 45 60 + 12 72 	"I add the tens (60) and then the ones (12), which I add together to get 72."

Figure 5.7. Directly modeling multidigit addition (combining).

mental strategies to concrete objects and encouraging them to use the more efficient mental strategies when they are developmentally ready.

Because of the important role that direct modeling plays in laying the foundation for other strategies, we take a closer look at the direct models associated with addition and the three types of subtraction for multidigit numbers, without and with regrouping, or composing, tens (figures 5.7–5.10). Also, we record those direct models numerically in a way that corresponds to the standard algorithms. We do not have enough room in this book to demonstrate all the possible relationships between direct models and all the invented algorithms children create, so we assume that if you can make sense of a standard and popular alternative algorithm by connecting it with a direct model, you can make sense of the other multidigit algorithms children invent.

Comprehension Check

■ **Create some addition and subtraction problems, and practice directly modeling different ways to solve the problem. At the same time, record your work using pictures and numbers.**

Assessments

Many older children who struggle in math really hit a wall once they reach long division. Their weaknesses are inevitably traced back to their understanding of the base 10 system and their addition and subtraction strategies. Almost all of

Number Sentence and Description/ Level of Numerical Complexity	Direct Model/ Numerical Recording	Explanation
"How much is left from 68 if I remove 45?" 68 – 45 = ☐ Two digits, no decomposing	68 – 45 — 23	"I show 68 with 6 tens and 8 ones. I remove 5 ones, which leaves 3 ones. I remove 4 tens, and that leaves 2 tens. And 2 tens and 3 ones is 23."
"How much is left from 72 if I remove 45?" 72 – 45 = ☐ Two digits, with decomposing	72 – 45 — 27	"I show 72 with 7 tens and 2 ones. Since I don't have enough ones to remove 5, I decompose a 10, which means I now have 6 tens and 12 ones. I remove 5 ones, leaving 7 ones, and remove 4 tens, leaving 2 ones. So, 2 tens and 7 ones is 27."
Partial differences (alternative algorithm) 72 – 45 = ☐ **Note:** This can be harder to understand because this algorithm requires students to be facile with negative numbers.	72 – 45 — + 30 – 3 — 27	"First, 70 minus 40 is 30. Then, 2 minus 5 is –3. And 30 minus 3 equals 27."

Figure 5.8. Directly modeling multidigit separation subtraction (take away).

Number Sentence and Description/ Level of Numerical Complexity	Direct Model/ Numerical Recording	Explanation
"What is the difference between 68 and 45?" 68 – 45 = ☐ Two digits, no decomposing	68 – 45 — 23	"I show 68 with 6 tens and 8 ones and 45 with 4 tens and 5 ones. I match and remove pairs of ones (one from the top and one from the bottom) until there are only ones left in the top set (3) and pairs of tens until there are only tens left in the top set (2). And 2 tens and 3 ones is 23."
"What is the difference between 72 and 45?" 72 – 45 = ☐ Two digits, with decomposing	72 – 45 — 27	"I show 72 with 7 tens and 2 ones and 45 with 4 tens and 5 ones. If I match and remove ones, I will still have some leftovers in the smaller set (27), so I decompose a 10, which means I now have 6 tens and 12 ones. I match and remove pairs of ones (one from the top and one from the bottom) until there are only ones left in the top set (7) and pairs of tens until there are only tens left in the top set (2). And 2 tens and 7 ones is 23."

Figure 5.9. Directly modeling multidigit compare subtraction (difference).

Number Sentence and Description/ Level of Numerical Complexity	Direct Model/ Numerical Recording	Explanation
"How much is added to 45 to make 68?" 45 + ☐ = 68 Two digits, no decomposing	68 − 45 ─── 23 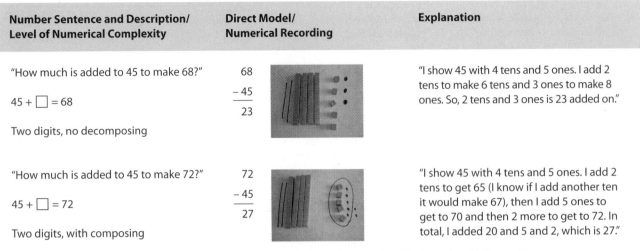	"I show 45 with 4 tens and 5 ones. I add 2 tens to make 6 tens and 3 ones to make 8 ones. So, 2 tens and 3 ones is 23 added on."
"How much is added to 45 to make 72?" 45 + ☐ = 72 Two digits, with composing	72 − 45 ─── 27	"I show 45 with 4 tens and 5 ones. I add 2 tens to get 65 (I know if I add another ten it would make 67), then I add 5 ones to get to 70 and then 2 more to get to 72. In total, I added 20 and 5 and 2, which is 27."

Figure 5.10. Directly modeling multidigit missing addend subtraction (difference).

these students are observed counting all or counting on when trying to add large sums. When given trains of tens, these students might "know" that there are 10 in each train but do not use this knowledge to assist them in computing. When given a "naked number" problem written horizontally, these same students are observed rewriting the problem vertically, either writing with a pencil or tracing with a finger. They almost always are trying to solve the problem using the traditional method and most often get it incorrect because their conceptual understanding is so weak.

When trying to assess an older student to pinpoint weaknesses in strategies and understanding of the base 10 system, Kathy Richardson's *Ten Frames, Grouping Tens,* and *Two-Digit Addition and Subtraction* assessments are good indicators as to how the child deals with tens and leftovers.

Using Inquiry to Teach Multidigit Addition and Subtraction

Here are two examples of inquiry-based lessons that exemplify ways you can teach concepts and procedures in a connected way. You will learn more about inquiry-based lessons in the next chapter.

Second Grade   *Example Lesson 1 (2 cycles)*

Representing two-digit addition, no composing

Launch cycle 1   The teacher reminds students of different problem-solving strategies other students used in the previous day's lesson including using cubes, drawing pictures, and acting out the problem. The teacher gives a prompt: "I have 21 cookies and then received 34 more cookies. How many cookies do I have now?"

Explore cycle 1   The teacher invites the children to solve the problem in at least two ways using whatever tools or strategies they wish.

Summarize cycle 1	Whole group: With teacher assistance, students share strategies—in this approximate order: direct modeling with ones, direct modeling with ones and tens, incrementing, combining tens and ones, compensating. The teacher or the sharing child should make some record or representation on the board or overhead. If the standard algorithm is observed during the explore stage, save it for the next lesson. The teacher assigns the listening students a descriptive role, meaning that the teacher calls on one or more students to describe the shared strategy to the rest of the class.
Launch cycle 2	Whole group: The teacher gives a prompt: "I have 34 cookies and then received 12 more cookies. How many cookies do I have now? This time, I would also like you to make a numerical record of what you did."
Explore cycle 2	The teacher invites the children to solve the problem in at least two ways using whatever tools or strategies they wish.
Summarize cycle 2	Whole group: With teacher assistance, students share strategies. Using the strategies from the previous cycle, the teacher asks students to first share strategies that are similar and then to share any additional strategies. The teacher assigns the listening students a comparative role, meaning that the teacher calls on one or more students to compare the strategies with the numerical record.
Launch for end-of-lesson assessment	Whole group: The teacher gives a prompt: "I have 42 cookies and then received 21 more cookies. How many cookies do I have now? This time, I would also like you to record your work using numbers."

Second Grade   *Example Lesson 2 (2 cycles)*

Solidifying with an eye toward fluency

Launch cycle 1	Whole group: "Yesterday, we worked with some interesting problems. One of them was 'I have 34 cookies and then received 12 more cookies. How many cookies do I have now?' Here are some of the numerical records you made." The teacher shares the strategies based on direct modeling, ensuring that these are reviewed sufficiently so that students understand them, and lists them on the board.
Explore cycle 1	The teacher invites the students to create a way to come up with the solution using numerals only.
Summarize cycle 1	Whole group: The teacher invites the students to share their numeral-only strategies. The teacher assigns the listening students an evaluative role, meaning that the teacher calls on one or more students to state whether or not they agree with the shared strategy—and why.
Launch cycle 2	Whole group: "Now, these are some other strategies that were shared." The teacher shares the strategies that were invented algorithms, and the standard algorithm if shared, and lists them on the board. (The teacher presents the following problem.) "Here's a new problem: 'I have 45 cookies and then received 23 more. How many do I have now?'"
Explore cycle 2	The students choose one of the ways to solve this problem.
Summarize cycle 2	The teacher invites the students to share, following roughly the same sequence as in the previous lesson. The teacher assigns the listening students a descriptive role, meaning that the teacher calls on one or more students to describe the shared strategy to the rest of the class.
Launch for end-of-lesson assessment	Whole group: The teacher gives a prompt: "I have 61 cookies and then received 17 more cookies. How many cookies do I have now? This time, I would also like you to record your work using numbers."

CONCLUSION

Deep conceptual understanding and deep procedural knowledge, or fluency, are equally important in developing mathematical proficiency. Children need to be accurate, efficient, and flexible in their mathematic work. Flexibility and efficiency with algorithms stems from a strong conceptual base. Deep concepts also help students learn their facts for quick recall, which frees their thinking for more complex problem solving.

Children must construct their own meaning for the algorithms they use; otherwise, it can interfere with the child's ability to reason with numbers and they are at risk of forgetting how to carry out the calculation. Once a child has facility with numbers, he may not see a need to even use one set algorithm, because it might just be too much work for certain problems. He probably solves the problems in his head and does not write down all the steps. One of the author's will never forget a child, who usually solved addition and subtraction problems with regrouping mentally, coming home crying from second grade because "I don't know what all those little boxes on top of the numbers mean."

▶ Interview Video with an Eye on Content

In this first set of video clips, determine the type of problem presented, the problem category, and the specific strategy used to solve it. Record your work in the tables provided. The first one is done for you.

Problem No.	Problem Type	Problem Category	Problem-Solving Strategy
1	Separate (change unknown)	Separate subtraction	Incrementing

▶ Interview a Child

1. Create an interview protocol consisting of 11 multi-digit problems based on the problem types of chapter 3 (e.g., join–result unknown). Allow for three levels of numerical complexity in each one:

   2 digits + 2 digits = 2 digits, no composing

   2 digits + 2 digits = 2 digits, with composing

   2 digits + 2 digits = 3 digits, with composing

2. Using the problems you created, interview a child in second or third grade.

3. Write a report about it that contains two parts: individual problem analyses and overall summary. In the individual problem analyses section, each problem you pose should include the following:
   a. The problem type
   b. The problem (underline the numbers used)
   c. A complete description of the child's response
   d. An analysis of the child's response, which includes the general strategy used and how well the child composed or decomposed tens

Sample analysis of an interview problem:

Problem 1: Join (result unknown)

Problem: Carolee had (21, 28, 79) trading cards. Her sister gave her (34, 36, 85) cards from her collection. How many trading cards did Carolee have altogether? (55, 64, 164)

Response: Bobby drew 2 longs and 8 ones then 6 longs and 4 units. He combined 10 of the ones to make another long. Then he counted 6 longs and 4 ones.

Analysis: Bobby used a direct modeling strategy, and he composed an additional 10.

4. In the overall summary, briefly describe what you learned about the child's mathematical thinking, including the following points:
   a. The types of problems the child successfully solved and those he struggled with
   b. The range of numbers with which the child was familiar (number size)
   c. The types of strategies demonstrated

▶ Classroom Video with an Eye on Pedagogy

Watch a video of a class solving a problem that involves a multidigit situation. Your focus should be on how the teacher orchestrates the lesson so that students are able to develop both conceptual and procedural understanding of this problem.

1. Briefly explain the problem and how the students are asked to explore it.

_____

_____

_____

_____

2. What are the different concepts elicited from this problem?

_____

_____

_____

_____

3. What are the different equations students generate to solve this problem?

_____

_____

_____

_____

4. Describe an occasion when the teacher has to scaffold learning for a student.

_____

_____

_____

_____

5. How does the teacher address the different levels of conceptual understanding of the students?

_____

_____

_____

_____

_____

▶ Classroom Application

Watch a classroom involved in solving a problem that involves a multidigit addition or subtraction situation. Your focus should be on how the teacher orchestrates the lesson so that students are able to develop both conceptual and procedural understanding of this problem. You will look for the same aspects in this actual classroom observation as you did in observing the video.

1. Briefly explain the problem and how the students are asked to explore it.

_____

_____

_____

2. What are the different concepts elicited from this problem?

_____

_____

_____

_____

3. What are the different equations students generate to solve this problem?

_____

_____

_____

_____

4. Describe an occasion when the teacher has to scaffold learning for a student.

_____

_____

_____

_____

5. How does the teacher address the different levels of conceptual understanding of the students?

_____

_____

_____

_____

▶ Resources

Young Mathematicians at Work: Constructing Number Sense, Addition, and Subtraction, Catherine Twomey Fosnot and Maarten Dolk (2001)

Developing Number Concepts. Book 2: Addition and Subtraction, Kathy Richardson (1999b)

Assessing Math Concepts: Ten Frames, Kathy Richardson

Assessing Math Concepts: Two-Digit Addition and Subtraction, Kathy Richardson

Assessing Math Concepts: Grouping Tens, Kathy Richardson

▶ Lit Link

Literature Books to Support Addition and Subtraction

Title	Author
10 Kangaroos	Jane Manners
12 Ways to Get 11	Eve Merriam
3 Ants	Fay Robinson
Bears Can Share	Betsy Franco
Cats Add Up!	Dianne Ochiltree
Centipede's 100 Shoes	Tony Ross

Title	Author
Getting to Sleep	Rozanne Lanczak Williams
Let's Go Visiting	Sue Williams
My Counting Garden	Sarah Holliday
Napping House, The	Audrey Wood
One Duck Stuck	Phyllis Root
One Gorilla	Atsuko Morozumi
One Monday Morning	Uri Shulevitz
Pigs Will Be Pigs: Fun with Math and Money	Amy Axelrod
Quack and Count	Keith Baker
Roman Numerals I to MM: Numerabilia Romana Uno ad Duo Mila	Arthur Geisert
Six-Dinner Sid	Inga Moore
Sled, The	Linda Cave
Ten Black Dots	Donald Crews
Ten Friends	Bruce Goldstone
Ten Sly Piranhas: A Counting Story in Reverse	William Wise
Two of Everything	Lily Toy Hong
Under the Picnic Tree	Rozanne Lanczak
Where the Sidewalk Ends	Shel Silverstein
Who's at the Zoo	Jane Finn

▶ Tech Tools

Websites

Dositey, http://www.dositey.com/addsub/as85/add5ar.htm (for practice with the standard algorithm)

Houghton Mifflin Education Place, http://www.eduplace.com/kids/mw/swfs/faf_grade3.html (game to support mental math)

Software

Math Blaster, Knowledge Adventure

Math Flash, Fast Rabbit Software

Instructional Models: Inquiry-Based Teaching with Single-Digit Multiplication and Division

PEDAGOGICAL CONTENT UNDERSTANDINGS

Pedagogy *Instructional Models*

- Behaviorism
- Constructivism
- Components of a Direct Instruction Lesson
- Components of an Inquiry Lesson

Content *Multiplication and Division:* Groups of *and* Shared By

- Understanding Multiplication and Division
- Problem Types and Solution Strategies
- Exploring Multiplication and Division
- Basic Facts

Two kinds of inquiry: Information seeking, which means clarifying, explaining, and confirming. Wondering, which means reflecting, exploring and considering many possibilities.

Carol Lyons and Gay Su Pinnel, Systems for Change in Literacy Education: A Guide to Professional Development, *2001*

CONVERSATION IN MATHEMATICS

On the first day of division in a third-grade classroom, the teacher asked, "what is division?" The students privately wrote what they already knew about division on a sticky note and placed it on the whiteboard. The teacher overheard students' comments as they were writing, referring to division being a "trick." Surprised as to how much they already knew, because she had never taught division lessons, the teacher is now reading the ideas one by one to the class to see whether the rest of the students agree with the thinking written on the notes.

Teacher: (Reads from a sticky note.) "Division is like $1 \div 1 = 1$." What do you think?

Student 1: Not enough explanation.

Teacher: Good start, but it needs a little bit more developing? (Picks up another sticky note.) Let's see if we find more development here. (Reads the note.) "Division is multiplication, but it's backward. The answer is in the front and the problem is in the back." What do you think?

Student 2: I agree.

Teacher: OK, this is what the student wrote down. (Writes $21 \div 7 = 3$ on the board, and points to the problem.) The answer is in the front, but the problem is in the back.

Student 3: It means 3×7 is 21.

Teacher: (Writes it on the board.)

Student 4: But that doesn't work all the time.

Student 5: (Turns to student 4.) Yes, it works all the time because it is going to have all multiplication problems.

Teacher: So, if this were the multiplication problem (pointing to the 7 and the 3), this (pointing to the 21) would be the product? And these (pointing to the 3 and the 7) would be the factors? Is that what you mean?

Student 4: The signs are different.

Student 5: The only thing that they scare you with is the division sign.

Student 4: Oh!

What might be startling as you think about that classroom episode, particularly if you come from a traditional instructional perspective, is that some deep mathematics was exposed and learning took place without the teacher "teaching" anything. She simply posed a question and guided a discussion. By the end of the classroom discussion, students were connecting division to multiplication as an inverse operation, although initially they referred to it as a "trick." This was an important introduction lesson to multiplication and division, because the teacher was then able to better gauge what kinds of experiences she needed to provide her students in the upcoming unit.

There are any number of what is termed *models of instruction*. These are step-by-step guides to lesson, or instructional, design and are based on various philosophical or theoretical perspectives. But when they are all boiled down, just two fundamental instructional models are distinguished by the roles played by teacher and student: either the teacher tells the students what to do or what to know, or the teacher guides the students to discover the learning for themselves. In this chapter, we discuss these two fundamental models of instruction: direct instruction, which might best be characterized as "teaching by telling," and inquiry instruction, which can be thought of "guided discovery." Hopefully you can see that the preceding episode fits into the latter category.

Most of us did not experience guided discovery when we learned multiplication and division as children; rather, we spent lots of time memorizing our times tables. We may have started off understanding that multiplication represented repeated addition but never had the opportunities to explore these operations in depth. A shallow understanding of multiplication can lead to difficulties in algebra, because algebra is generalized arithmetic. The distributive property, one of the key concepts in algebra, is closely connected with multiplication. This chapter explores the underlying concepts for understanding multiplication and division and how inquiry instruction is supportive to these developments.

Instructional Models

PEDAGOGY

Learning Theory

To make sense of the two instructional models, we need to know something about the two basic psychologies of the 20th century: behaviorism and cognitivism/constructivism, or simply constructivism. Some might view these simple classifications as problematic for at least two reasons:

1. It might be an oversimplification.
2. Some learning theorists suggest that cognitivism and constructivism are not the same or that constructivism is a subset, or branch, or cognitivism. Nevertheless, there is sufficient support for our classification to justify its use in guiding our work in this chapter.

Direct instruction is frequently viewed as a logical extension of behaviorism, and inquiry instruction is viewed as a logical extension of constructivism. Truth is associated with both psychologies; therefore, benefits are associated with both types of instructional models.

Behaviorism

Behaviorism is a psychological position based on the proposition that all things organisms do—including acting, thinking, and feeling—can and should be regarded as behaviors. As such, they can be described scientifically without reference either to internal physiological events or to constructs such as the mind. "The central tenet of behaviorism is that thoughts, feelings, and intentions, mental processes all, do not determine what we do. Our behavior is the product of our conditioning. We are biological machines and do not consciously act; rather, we react to stimuli" (Cohen 1987, 71). The key behavior theorists were Ivan Pavlov, who investigated classical conditioning, and Edward Lee

Thorndike, John B. Watson, and B. F. Skinner, who conducted research on operant conditioning.

Obviously, the ethical consequences of behaviorism are great. We certainly do not espouse the extreme behaviorist views of the previous paragraph. However, at least two instructional outgrowths from behaviorism have been shown to be of some instructional use: behavior modification techniques, for correcting extreme aberrant classroom behaviors, and direct instruction. Most people who advocate the latter do not ascribe to the extreme behavioristic perspective, but they have demonstrated that direct instruction is effective in enhancing student achievement.

Constructivism

The basic idea of constructivism is that an individual learner must actively "construct" knowledge and skills. It is founded on the premise that, by reflecting on life's experiences, we construct our own understanding of the world in which we live. Each of us develops our own mental rules and models, which we use to make sense of life. Learning is defined as the process of adjusting our mental models to accommodate new experiences. Constructivists agree that it is through processing environmental stimuli and the resulting cognitive structures that adaptive behavior is produced, rather than from the stimuli itself. John Dewey is often referred to as the philosophical founder of constructivism, with David Ausubel, Jerome Bruner, Jean Piaget, and Lev Vygotsky as its chief theorists.

There are six critical implications of constructivism for the classroom (figure 6.1):

1. Inasmuch as learning is a search for meaning, it must start with the problems about which students are actively trying to construct meaning.

2. Constructing meaning requires comprehending big ideas that encompass subordinate facts and ideas.

3. Good teaching requires teachers understand the mental models students use to make sense of their world and the assumptions underlying that sense making.

4. Because learning is viewed as the process of constructing individual meaning, education consists of more than memorizing someone else's "right answers."

5. Teachers must focus on helping students make mental connections among facts and on fostering new understanding in students. Indeed, understanding is equivalent to the creation of mental connections.

6. Teachers should consistently elicit student responses and use those responses to inform their instructional and curricular decision making. This requires teachers to make extensive use of open-ended questioning and dialogue among students.

Application to the Learning and Teaching of Mathematics

Components of a Direct Instruction Lesson

In a nutshell, direct instruction is an instructional model based on behavioristic principles that emphasizes detailed lessons planned in advance and designed with small learning increments and clearly defined and prescribed teaching

	Behavioral/Objectivist Approach	*Cognitive/Constructivist Approach*
Learning Theorists	B. F. Skinner, R. F. Mager, R. M. Gagné, M. D. Merrill	J. Dewey, J. Piaget, L. Vygotsky
Philosophy	Holds that meaning exists in the world separate from personal experience. Sets goal of understanding, or coming to know the entities, attributes, and relations that exist in this objective reality. Frames instructional goals in specific, behavioral, observable terms. Focuses on immediate, recognizable changes in behavior.	Holds that learners impose meaning on the world and so "construct" their own understanding based on their unique experiences. Frames instructional goals in experiential terms: specifying the kinds of learner problems addressed, the kinds of control learners exercise over the learning environment, the activities in which they engage, the ways those activities could be shaped by leaders or instructors, and the ways in which learners reflect on the results of their activity together.
Learning Outcomes	Describes (1) the conditions under which the behavior is to take place; (2) the task or tasks the learners have been asked to perform; and (3) a series of actions the learners must be able to carry out to indicate understanding, each of which is described using a verb that denotes some observable behavior. Sets a criterion or measure of success that defines what an acceptable level of performance is or how it will be evaluated.	Defines how learners should be able to think or solve problems differently when they are finished and what settings, activities, or interactions instructors predict will lead to these new abilities. States that (1) learners need some opportunity to define for themselves the goals and objectives for the course; (2) focus is more on process and interaction than on what is specifically to be accomplished as a result of the lesson; and (3) outcomes are defined more in terms of a new common perspective than in terms of particular tasks or actions that individuals will be able to carry out. Assumes the learners are motivated by a common interest in some problem or issue.
Instructor Role	Present effectively structured material, and assess students' proper and complete understanding of it. Provide the focus of presentation and interaction. Offer a tutorial relationship to individual students.	Construct a learning environment, and assist students as they explore it by designing experiences that encourage assimilation and accommodation. Suggest that lasting learning comes as a result of activities that are both meaningful to the learners and based in some social context (other learners, colleagues, instructors, clients, etc.). Work as facilitator and architect of learning.
Student Role	Absorb instructional presentations and material, and use them to create performances that indicate attainment of correct mental models.	Explore the learning environment in concert with others, and construct meaning from learning experiences. Apply knowledge in personally meaningful contexts.
Activities	Reading, review, and analysis of provided text and materials. Individual work submitted directly to the instructor for review. Structured assignments directly linked to learning objectives. Little or no cohort discussion.	Emphasis on discussion and collaboration among cohort of students. Application of principles to case studies and projects. Open-ended assignments linked to changing learning objectives. Assignments constructed to reflect real-world conditions and requirements.
Assessment	Individual tests and performances to demonstrate mastery of entities, activities, and processes. Emphasis on a few summative products and performances.	Reporting on active, authentic experiences, activities, and projects. Emphasis on interaction, reflection, and collaboration among a group of learners. Integration throughout the curriculum rather than in final products.

Figure 6.1. The comparisons between behaviorism and constructivism along six dimensions. (University of Washington.)

tasks. Its chief proponents are Siegfried Engelmann and Wesley Becker. Direct instruction is used to describe a lesson in which the teacher has control.

In a direct instruction lesson, the teacher initially spends time lecturing or modeling the desired learning, usually providing simple steps for solving a problem; then the teacher guides the students through a problem similar to the one used in the modeling, with the problem solving again broken into simple steps; finally, the students are given one or many sample problems to practice on their own. You might recognize this as the most common way for math teachers to operate.

Here are the steps that constitute a direct instruction lesson in mathematics:

1. *Anticipatory set.* The teacher assesses student knowledge of relevant prior learning.

2. *Objective.* The teacher states the objective for the lesson in behavioral terms.

3. *Modeling.* The teacher demonstrates and describes the problem-solving process.

4. *Checking for understanding.* The teacher assesses student knowledge of the process previously modeled.

5. *Guided practice.* The teacher invites students to practice solving several problems with guidance. Feedback is provided specifically and immediately.

6. *Independent practice.* The teacher invites students to practice several additional problems independently. Feedback is provided specifically and immediately.

7. *Evaluation.* The teacher invites students to solve more problems independently and assess end-of-lesson accomplishment of the objective. Feedback is again provided specifically and immediately.

At times in a lesson, the teacher might stop the class and have his students focus on a specific strategy, perhaps being used by another student. After some discussion about how that strategy was helpful in solving a problem, the teacher may want to direct the class to try that strategy for one problem. This is not to imply that the strategy is what every student should always use, but perhaps a bigger idea can be found in that strategy. Encouraging all students to try something new helps build those connections among ideas.

Components of an Inquiry Lesson

From a constructivist view, learning is messy and it takes time to explore, make connections, and develop new ideas. Oftentimes, the teacher needs to go through this same process when planning the task to try to predict what the students might do and learn. The students' exploration takes more time than that of an adult, because we already have certain math ideas in place. On the other hand, sometimes our understandings can prevent us from exploring a concept in the same way children can—with a clean slate.

In a classroom where making meaning is the focus, key components of a math lesson are visible. These components may have different names depending on the area in which you live. In many areas, they are known as launch, explore, and summarize (Schroyer and Fitzgerald 1986). These are the names we use in this text. Each of these components is critical and cannot be undermined or shortchanged.

Launch

The *launch* stage is the part of the lesson when the teacher is setting up the task to be explored and the students are meeting as a group. Typically, an introductory activity is presented and worked on individually or in pairs. As a result, some necessary vocabulary might be addressed and students can orient their thinking toward the larger task to come. The stage is being set for learning, and connections are being made to prior learning and previously developed strategies. These connections help build the big mathematical ideas. There needs to be evidence that students understand the purpose, rationale, and expectations of the learning.

The launch period usually lasts 5–10 minutes. Examples of how time might be used during the launch period include the following:

- Summarizing the learning experiences of the students up to that point
- Posing an introductory activity to connect with prior knowledge or prior strategies
- Posing and clarifying expectations of the task to be explored and of issues related to management

In the case of the earlier conversation, the teacher simply launched the lesson by asking, "What is division?"

Explore

During the *explore* part, students go off to work on the proposed task, either in small groups or with a partner. Small groups and partnerships should always be assigned and should remain static for a significant amount of time. Working over time with the same peers allows students to get to know one another mathematically and to build trust with one another. This also helps foster better communication of mathematical ideas. These groupings can be either homogeneous or heterogeneous, but it is usually best to have heterogeneous groupings, because one student can help support the other. Sometimes, students who simply get along with one another need to be paired. Some teachers find that pairing students based on language needs or personality tends to be beneficial as well. Two shy students might be able to talk to each other, whereas a shy student may not participate if paired with a more dominant student. However, some quiet students benefit from a stronger language model.

Students should know exactly what they are to do and where to find materials that they might need to solve the problem. To maximize learning time, the transition from the whole group to small group or partnerships should be minimal. Many teachers choose to have the materials at the tables before beginning the launch stage so that time is not wasted passing things out. When students are allowed use any tool that they are familiar with, the materials need to be easily accessed by students.

As students are working with their groups, the teacher's job is to go around to each table to listen in and question the children. Teachers are developing ideas of where the students are and if the task is too easy or too difficult. Because every class is made up of a range of students, adjusting the task, even for individual groups, may be appropriate.

Teachers are also determining what the common misconceptions or errors are. Teachers can use this information either when orchestrating the summarize part or in designing the next lesson. In the "Conversation in Mathematics" section in chapter 2, during the explore period, the teacher noticed that a misconception about how many answers students could get depending on the number of tools used. This misconception was important enough that it needed to be brought to the attention of all the students, which took place during the summarize period. Because there was no resolution, the teacher had to design subsequent lessons to address this issue.

Rule of Thumb

Keep notes of things students do and say during lessons to be better prepared for the same lesson in a future class.

Teachers who find that they are helping every table, perhaps due to a common unanticipated misconception, may choose to stop the lesson to have a quick discussion about a common problem then send the children back to work. In the literacy world, this is termed the *midworkshop teaching point* by Lucy Caulkins. When a teacher prepares a lesson, it is difficult to anticipate what all students will do, especially if it is the first time the teacher has posed a particular problem. We learn a lot from watching and listening and are often surprised what many students think.

Most tasks require some sort of a product. Considering how we want students to display that product can prove to be critical later in the summarize part. It is difficult to share strategies that are not clearly visible to all students, so many tasks may require creating a group poster that includes multiple representations (pictures, numbers, and written explanations). Students should present their work on transparencies or document cameras so that all the class can easily see their thinking.

The explore period, depending on the age of the students, can last 10–30 minutes. Some problems are problematic enough to require more than one class session to work through. No matter how long it takes, every problem needs to be summarized before the students begin the next task. Because tasks should be connected, the learning that students take from one problem needs to be discussed to assist them in making connections between problems.

Summarize

The *summarize* period is also referred to by Catherine Twomey Fosnot (2001a) as the *math congress*. This is when students get back together as a whole group to discuss their findings and share their strategies, like mathematicians. The teacher's role is to facilitate a discussion in which students communicate their ideas, solutions, and conjectures. We need to decide which idea to focus on, for example, a misconception, a specific strategy, or a way of connecting the model to an algorithm.

This is not the time for each child to share her work; that would be distracting to the focus and goal of the lesson, because some students would ramble on just to hear themselves talk. Also, sharing by too many students causes others to become disengaged. One way to alleviate the potential problems inherent in not allowing every child to share is to invite all students to summarize in small groups before doing so as a class. This provides additional assessment opportunities for the teacher.

During the explore period, the teacher should have been solidifying the focus for the summarize period and selecting which students should share.

Choosing the order in which students should share is critical. A student with a solution strategy that is common to the group might be chosen first, followed by a student with a more sophisticated strategy that might emphasize an idea bigger than the one the teacher had in mind. Choosing sophisticated strategies that most of the class is not ready for or that do not fall within the goals of the lesson only causes students to tune out, and the conversation becomes a one-on-one dialogue between the student and the teacher. We have often found it helpful to have students share directly modeled strategies first, counting strategies second, and more abstract or algorithmic strategies last. This helps students make connections between concrete and abstract representations.

Rule of Thumb

Not everyone shares! If you would like a child who is shy or has language needs to share, it is helpful to ask them ahead of time so they can prepare.

During this time, big math ideas begin to surface, and vocabulary may be assigned to these ideas. For example, in a fourth-grade lesson in which students are exploring factors by making arrays, the students may realize that with certain numbers only one unique array can be built. During the summarize period, after discussing this discovery, the teacher should provide the vocabulary *prime* and *composite numbers*. Had the teacher begun the lesson defining these terms, the students would have never "discovered" this idea and the entire activity would have been merely practice of identifying or sorting prime and composite numbers.

There should be 15–20 minutes dedicated to the summarize period. It cannot be emphasized enough that this is the heart of the math lesson, because this is where the mathematical ideas surface, conjectures are made, and strategies are named. It provides students with the opportunity to mentally "practice" the important mathematics associated with the lesson. Students need to understand that they have a responsibility to contribute to and learn from the discussion. If the summarize stage is sacrificed, the teacher becomes frustrated and is tempted to abandon this style of teaching, feeling that the students are not receiving enough practice. The real issue is that students have not had the opportunities to make the appropriate connections.

To increase the engagement of students while strategies are being shared, we recommend assigning students who are listening to one of four roles then holding them accountable for that role after the sharing:

- *Describing.* "While Karen is sharing her strategy, I want you to listen because I will call on a few of you to tell us how she did it."

- *Comparing.* "While Juan is sharing his strategy, I want you to listen to see how your way is the same as or different from his. I will call on a few of you to tell about your way compared to his."

- *Questioning.* "While Malik is sharing his strategy, I want you to think about some questions you might like to ask him. I will call on a few of you to ask your questions."

- *Evaluating.* "While Maria is sharing her strategy, I want you to ask yourself if you agree or disagree and why. I will ask a few of you to tell us what you think."

Notice that each role assignment included the statement that there would be a chance to demonstrate fulfillment of the responsibility associated with the role after the sharing. If the students have not yet developed the ability to engage in meaningful discourse, it may be best to call on children at random for this.

Language Tip

Providing students with a purpose for listening helps language learners focus auditorily and be more engaged. Providing them with specific phrases of how to respond to their peers helps them participate in the discourse. Teach them to use one of these two statements:

1. "I'm sorry, I can't (describe, compare, etc.) because, even though I was listening, I didn't quite understand what she said. Could you repeat how you did it?"

2. "I'm sorry, I can't (describe, compare, etc.) because I wasn't listening. I apologize and would ask you to repeat how you did it."

Lesson Map

The document in figure 6.2, referred to as a *lesson map*, is a way for teachers to plan for the launch, explore, and summarize stages of an inquiry lesson. Each part is outlined using the previously introduced descriptors. In addition, using areas on this map, teachers can plan the questions that they want to ask the students and can anticipate what students might say and do. They are also able to plan how they might informally assess the students during each part of the lesson.

Look at a multiplication lesson, taking into consideration the specific components of the lesson map (figure 6.3).

Comprehension Check

- List and describe the components of an inquiry lesson.
- Elaborate on the significance of the summarize stage.

Inquiry Lesson Map

Topic:	Time Frame:	Grade Level:	Date:
Goals/Focus:			
State Core/Standard:			

	Task	What Questions Will I Ask?	What Will the Students Be Saying or Doing?	How Will I Assess?
Launch Materials:	• Set purpose • Pose the problem • Clarify expectations			
Explore Materials:	• Students work together to solve the problem • Students record thinking and work in journals • Teachers observe student thinking and ask questions			
Summarize Materials:	• Students share, discuss, and reflect on their thinking • Students question one another and push back on one another's thinking • Students make connections among representations • Teachers carefully select strategies to be shared that build on bigger ideas			

Launch for Assessment (exit slip) A prompt given to students individually to show whether they have taken understanding to a level of independence
Homework /Journal Prompt (if appropriate)

Figure 6.2. An inquiry lesson map.

It is common to build in several spots of personal think time in the launch period and at the beginning of the explore period. We find that personal think time before going off with a partner or small group is essential in helping formulate a plan and come up with some individual thoughts. Otherwise, many students tend to overdepend on their peers.

We have also found that many of our most effective lessons actually repeat the launch–explore–summarize cycle twice and often have a third launch

Launch	Review the meaning of an array. Make an array of 2×3 using color tiles to establish the vocabulary of rows and columns.
Explore	With your partner, make an array of 6×8 using color tiles, then find a way to break the array into two smaller parts that make solving for 6×8 easier.
Summarize	■ Discuss the strategies students used to break up the arrays. ■ On the board, write how students verbalize the breaking of their arrays. Some possibilities will be $(3 \times 8) + (3 \times 8)$; $(6 \times 4) + (6 \times 4)$; $(5 \times 8) + (1 \times 8)$; and $(6 \times 5) + (1 \times 5)$. ■ Ask how breaking up the arrays can be useful in figuring out a multiplication problem to which they do not know the answer.

Figure 6.3. The launch–explore–summarize sequence in multiplication using arrays.

period for independent evaluation or assessment purposes (figure 6.4). Many teachers refer to this launch period for independence as an *exit slip.* Although students are often able to function in a small group environment, they may be riding the coattails of their groupmates. This is an opportunity to see what they have internalized. The teacher uses these small assessments to drive the next lessons.

Oftentimes, the first cycle tends to be a shorter, easier problem than the second. Many ideas that surface from the first cycle are useful as students attack

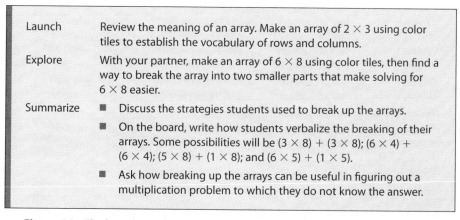

Figure 6.4. A lesson map with two cycles of the launch–explore–summarize sequence.

Cycle 2

Launch	Make a model of 10 × 5 using base 10 blocks. Discuss models and why using rods is more efficient than using unit cubes.
Explore	Make a model of 14 × 5 using base 10 blocks. Find a way to split the model into two smaller parts. Recording what you build using pictures, numbers, and words.
Summarize	■ Discuss the strategies students used to break up the model.
	■ Discuss numerical representations that match how students broke up the model, such as (10 × 5) + (4 × 5). Make the connection to expanded notation.

Figure 6.5. A second cycle of the launch–explore–summarize sequence in the previous multiplication lesson involving arrays.

the more challenging problem. During the first cycle, students typically still work as a whole group but solve the problem with a partner. Once the second problem is given, the students might be sent to their seats or other areas of the room to solve this more challenging problem.

Consider a second cycle for the previously used multiplication problem (figure 6.5).

CONTENT

Multiplication and Division: Groups of *and* Shared By

In the pedagogy section, we discussed the differences between the components of direct instruction and inquiry-based instruction. We also provided an example of an inquiry lesson using multiplication. We now switch to the content section for multiplication and division. As we do, keep in mind how to introduce the related concepts through questioning and investigation rather than teaching by telling. At the end of this section, we provide additional examples of how to teach these concepts through inquiry.

Big Ideas and Focal Points

Randall Charles (2005, 16) identifies some big ideas about multiplication and division, stating:

- **Multiplication facts can be found by breaking apart the unknown fact into known facts. Then the answers to the known facts are combined to give the final value.**
- **Division facts can be found by thinking about the related multiplication fact. . . .**
- **Multiplication can be used to check division.**

NCTM's *Principles and Standards for School Mathematics* (2000, 32) states that students should be able to "understand the meaning of operations and how they relate to one another," as well as be able to "compute fluently and make reasonable estimates."

The NCTM focal points refer to multiplication as early as second grade. The chart in the Focal Points table demonstrates expectations connected with

NCTM FOCAL POINTS

Second Grade	Third Grade	Fourth Grade
Students will solve problems involving multiplicative situations, developing initial understandings of multiplication as repeated addition.	Students will understand the meanings of multiplication and division of whole numbers through the use of representations (e.g., for multiplication, equal-sized groups, arrays, area models, and equal "jumps" on number lines and, for division, successive subtraction, partitioning, and sharing). They will use properties of addition and multiplication (e.g., commutativity, associativity, and the distributive property) to multiply whole numbers and will apply increasingly sophisticated strategies based on these properties to solve multiplication and division problems involving basic facts. They will relate multiplication and division as inverse operations by comparing a variety of solution strategies.	Students will develop quick recall of multiplication facts and related division facts and fluency with whole number multiplication. They will apply understanding of models for multiplication (i.e., equal-sized groups, arrays, area models, and equal intervals on the number line), place value, and properties of operations (in particular, the distributive property) as they develop, discuss, and use efficient, accurate, and generalizable methods to multiply multidigit whole numbers. They will select appropriate methods and apply them accurately to estimate products or calculate them mentally, depending on the context and numbers involved.

multiplication and division of single-digit numbers, otherwise known as the *basic facts.*

Understanding Multiplication and Division

Multiplication is an operation used to count multiple groups. It is a more efficient way of computing than repeated addition. Children need to understand that, when multiplying, each group has the same amount. Division is the inverse of multiplication, just as subtraction is the inverse of addition. As with addition and subtraction, children do not immediately recognize that a relationship exists between the two operations. Through exploration activities, such as using arrays, students begin to see that the two operations are related, and they may even start to use multiplication to solve a division problem. Students who are stronger with their multiplication facts tend to see this relationship faster than those who are not.

Multiplication and addition do have their differences. In addition, for example, two amounts of the same item are being combined. In multiplication, the two numbers are representing two different ideas: groups and the amount of an item in each group. Using numbers to count groups, or *unitizing,* is a big leap for children. They have to keep track of what each number represents in the problem, including the answer.

Struggling Learner

Students who struggle with division generally are struggling with multiplication, and their struggles can usually be traced to poor counting skills.

Properties of Multiplication

Multiplication has five main properties:

- Zero property
- Multiplicative identity
- Commutative property
- Associative property
- Distributive property

The *zero property of multiplication* states that multiplying any number by zero results in zero. No matter how many are supposed to be in each group, if you have zero groups of it, you are left empty-handed. Similarly, if you have six groups of something but nothing in each group, you do not have anything:

$$n \times 0 = 0$$

Multiplicative identity refers to how any number being multiplied by one remains the same. If there are five items per group but only one group, then there are only five items altogether:

$$n \times 1 = n$$

The *commutative property* of multiplication allows students to write the numbers to be multiplied in any order. That is, unlike in division, the order does not matter. In multiplication, this can be easily demonstrated through an array or an area model:

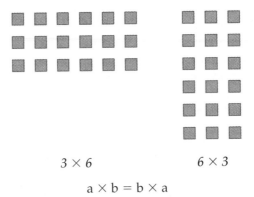

$$3 \times 6 \qquad 6 \times 3$$

$$a \times b = b \times a$$

The *associative property* of addition or multiplication refers to the way the addends or factors are grouped. A group always has at least three numbers, and some of them are within parentheses. These numbers are considered one unit, or are associated together. The sum or product is the same regardless of the grouping.

There are 5 pens in a package and 10 packages in a box. There are 20 boxes in a case. How many pens are in a case?

(5 × 10) × 20 = 1,000, solving first for how many pens are in a box
5 × (10 × 20) = 1,000, solving first for how many packages are in a case

$$(a \times b) \times c = a \times (b \times c)$$

The *distributive property* is critical for the understanding of algebra. In essence, when multiplying two numbers (of at least two digits), the numbers can be broken into smaller parts. These parts can be multiplied by each other and then recombined to find the total product. This is discussed in detail later in the chapter.

23×12

$(20 + 3) \times (10 + 2)$

$20 (10 + 2) + 3 (10 + 2)$

$(20 \times 10) + (20 \times 2) + (3 \times 10) + (3 \times 2)$

$200 + 40 + 30 + 6$

276

Comprehension Check

■ Describe the five properties of multiplication, and create your own example of each.

Problem Types and Solution Strategies

Just as with addition and subtraction, Thomas Carpenter et al. (1999) have identified different problem types and problem-solving strategies associated with multiplication and division.

Problem Types

The problem types can be identified when taking the following problem into consideration:

Adrian made gift bags for his friends. He made 6 bags, each containing 4 toys. There were 24 toys all together.

The preceding problem would be represented in the following way: $6 \times 4 = 24$ (expressed as 6 groups of 4 equals 24). The problem type depends on which part of the problem is the unknown (figure 6.6). If the total amount is unknown, then this would be a standard multiplication problem. If the number of groups is unknown, then this would be a *measurement division* problem. If the number in each group is unknown, then it would be a *partitive division* problem.

$$6 \quad \times \quad 4 \quad = \quad 24$$
$$\uparrow \qquad\quad \uparrow \qquad\qquad \uparrow$$

Measurement   Partitive   Multiplication
division   division

A difference exists between measurement division and partitive division. Students tend to use different modeling strategies for solving each type. Students typically solve measurement division by building each group until they

Multiplication	Adrian made 6 gift bags of toys. He put 4 toys in each bag. How many toys are in all the bags?
Measurement Division	Adrian had 24 toys. He put 4 toys in each gift bag. How many gift bags was he able to fill?
Partitive Division	Adrian had 24 toys. He made 6 gift bags. How many toys was he able to put into each bag?

Figure 6.6. Problem types for multiplication and division. (Reprinted with permission from *Children's Mathematics.* Copyright © 1999 by Thomas Carpenter, Linda Levi, Elizabeth Fennema, Megan Loef Franke, Susan Empson. Published by Heinemann, Portsmouth, NH. All rights reserved.)

arrive at the total number of objects. Partitive division is typically solved by partitioning, or dealing out, the total number into each group.

Solution Strategies

The solution strategies for multiplication and division are the same as those for addition and subtraction. First, students directly model each problem. They then begin to develop counting strategies, and eventually they use number facts (figure 6.7). When students are using either direct modeling or counting strategies, they are unable to consider the whole and the group simultaneously. They tend to create a group and build up to the whole (Fosnot and Dolk 2001a). Counting strategies are harder for children when they are solving for multiplication and division problems, so they do not tend to use them as quickly as they may have in addition and subtraction (Carpenter et al. 1999). Therefore, students typically use direct modeling strategies longer with multiplication and division than with addition and subtraction.

Skip counting is a common counting strategy, but students are at the mercy of their own skip counting abilities. Even though they may know that they have equal groups, if they are not proficient in skip counting by that number, they have to either count by ones or skip count by a smaller number with which they are familiar and count the rest by ones. This is why it is so critical that skip counting of different amounts begins early and continues through proficiency of multiplication facts.

Problem Types	Direct Modeling	Counting	Derived Facts
Multiplication Adrian made 6 gift bags of toys. He put 4 toys in each bag. How many toys are in all the bags?	**Grouping** Makes 6 groups with 4 cubes in each group (groups might be on paper plates). Counts all counters to arrive at the answer.	**Skip Counting** Counts 4, 8, 12, 16, 20, 24 (keeping track of the number of groups by extending a finger; this is known as double counting). **Adding Strategy** "I added 4 + 4 to get 8. And 8 + 8 is 16. That is 4 groups. Another 8 is 24, which is 6 groups.	"I know that 5 groups of 4 is 20, so another group of 4 would be 24."
Measurement Division Adrian had 24 toys. He put 4 toys in each gift bag. How many gift bags was he able to fill?	**Measurement** Breaks the 24 counters into groups by putting 4 into each of the groups. Counts how many groups are made.	**Skip Counting Up** Counts 4, 8, 12, 16, 20, 24 (keeping track of the number of groups until the count reaches 24).	"I know that 3 fours is 12, so another 3 would be 24. That is 6 groups."
Partitive Division Adrian had 24 toys. He made 6 gift bags. How many toys was he able to put into each bag?	**Partitive** Divides the 24 counters into 6 groups by either drawing circles or using paper plates. Deals out the counters one by one until the counters are used up. Counts the cubes in one of the groups to find an answer.	**Trial and Error** (to figure out what to skip count by) "How about 2. So, 2, 4, 6, 8, 10, 12 (uses fingers to keep track of the groups). No, that is not enough. I know that 12 and 12 is 24, so maybe it is 4. That would be 4, 8, 12, 16, 20, 24. Yeah, that works."	"I know that 2 in each group would be 12, so there must be 4 in each group." "I know that 6 times 4 equals 24, so there must be 4 in each group."

Figure 6.7. Direct modeling counting and derived facts strategies for multiplication and division. (Reprinted with permission from *Children's Mathematics*. Copyright © 1999 by Thomas Carpenter, Linda Levi, Elizabeth Fennema, Megan Loef Franke, Susan Empson. Published by Heinemann, Portsmouth, NH. All rights reserved.)

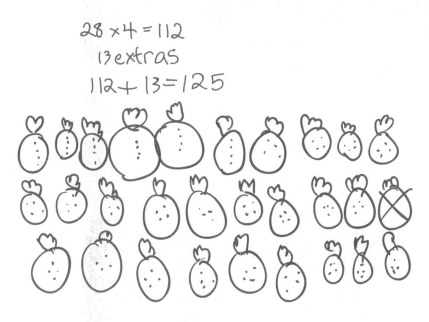

$$28 \times 4 = 112$$
$$13 \, extras$$
$$112 + 13 = 125$$

Figure 6.8. Modeling a division problem using partitive division.

Whereas measurement division is easily solved by skip counting up, the partitive division is not. The number by which to skip count is unknown, so children tend to use trial and error to figure out which number to use. Take the larger problems in figure 6.8 as an example:

> There are 125 candies in a bag. I want to share them with classmates on my birthday by making candy bags. There are 28 students in my class. How many candies can I put into each candy bag.

In figure 6.8, the student started by drawing 28 candy bags but does not know how many candies to put into each one. However, he knows that there should be more than one in each bag. He decides to put 2 candies into each bag. When he is done, he sees enough left to deal out 2 more for each bag. He ends up with 4 candies in each bag and 13 extras.

Additional Problem Types

Multiplication is used in situations besides grouping. Just like in addition, we want to be sure that students are given a variety of contexts and quantities. These additional problem types are rate, price, multiplicative comparison, area and array, and combination (figure 6.9). Whereas the problem types discussed in the previous charts have countable quantities, not all of these additional types do. Some of these concepts are more abstract and are introduced in the upper-elementary grades.

With area, arrays, and combination problems, there is no distinction between the two parts; therefore, they are considered symmetrical. Thus, the two parts play the same role in the problem. For example, in the combination problem, both parts are food items. In the situation of tiling an area, the 10 and the 8 both represent feet. When creating a direct modeling illustration of the area problems, it would be important to know which measurement represented length and which represented width.

Exploring Multiplication and Division

Because children move from counting all to counting groups (before moving on to derived facts), it is important that they are able to skip count, even if only by rote at first.

Comprehension Check

■ Create your own contexts for the problem $7 \times 3 = 21$ using multiplication, measurement division, and partitive division. Directly model each of your problems.

Problem Type	Multiplication	Measurement Division	Partitive Division
Grouping or partitioning	Adrian made 6 gift bags of toys. He put 4 toys in each bag. How many toys are in all the bags?	Adrian had 24 toys. He put 4 toys in each gift bag. How many gift bags was he able to fill?	Adrian had 24 toys. He made 6 gift bags. How many toys was he able to put into each bag?
Rate	A plant grows 3 cm per day. How many centimeters will it have grown in 5 days?	A plant grows 3 cm per day. How many days will it take to grow 15 centimeters?	A plant grew 15 cm in 5 days. How many centimeters did it grow per day if it grew the same amount each day?
Price	Pizzas cost $5 each. How much would four pizzas cost?	Pizzas cost $5 each. How many pizzas would total $20?	Five pizzas cost $20. How much does each pizza cost if each costs the same amount?
Multiplicative comparison	There was three times as much snowfall this year as last year. If last year had 5 total inches of snow, how deep was this year's total snowfall?	This year's snowfall was 15 inches. Last year's snowfall was 5 inches. How many times greater was this year's snowfall compared to last year?	This year's snowfall was 15 inches. It was three times greater than last year's snowfall. How many inches of snow fell last year?
Area and array	Cameron needed to tile an area for an outdoor patio. The area measured 10 feet long and 8 feet wide. How many square feet was the area?	Cameron needed to tile an area for an outdoor patio. If one row used 10 tiles, how many rows would it take to use 80 tiles?	
Combination	The cafeteria offers different ingredients to construct your own sandwich. If it offers three types of bread and four types of sandwich meat, how many different types of sandwiches can be made?	The cafeteria offers 12 different sandwiches choices. It offers three types of bread. If customers are only allowed to pick one type of meat per sandwich, how many choices of meat do they have?	

Symmetrical Problems (label along left side spanning Area and array / Combination rows)

Figure 6.9. Additional problem types or situations for multiplication and division. (Reprinted with permission from *Children's Mathematics*. Copyright © 1999 by Thomas Carpenter, Linda Levi, Elizabeth Fennema, Megan Loef Franke, Susan Empson. Published by Heinemann, Portsmouth, NH. All rights reserved.)

When dealing with a new problem type, it may be necessary for the entire class to act out the story. Young children may have trouble using more abstract objects, such as cubes, to represent cookies or flowers. Using real children and real objects helps children transfer their understandings to other objects. When they are able to directly model the situation, students should be encouraged to represent what they did symbolically. Numerical notation is different when solving a multiplication problem with repeated addition than when using number facts. Over time, the children's numerical representations change in accordance with their solving strategies.

Special Needs Support

Help students connect their tool to the concrete object it represents.

Language Tip

Avoid using clue words! This encourages students to ignore the context and allows them to simply locate some number and apply an often-random operation to the number. Clue words can be deceiving, and many situations do not have any clue words, especially in the upper grades. This means that students need to reason through the situation anyway. In addition, clue words can lead students to solve the problem using the wrong operation. Consider the following situation:

Jason ate three times as many cookies as Mike. Jason ate six cookies. How many cookies did Mike eat?

What operation is indicated by the preceding problem? If a student were to look for clue words, he would see the word *times* and immediately multiply the 3 and the 6 to get a product of 18. However, a closer look reveals that this is really a problem involving division.

As students are developing more sophisticated ways to think about multiplication, teachers need to be precise in their language. Instead of clue words, teachers need to teach children mathematical language. Words like *of* carry a lot of meaning in a math problem, and students typically do not understand its subtle connotations. Misinterpretation of such clue words causes students to be unable to visualize what is happening in a problem. Use words like *groups of* and *shared by,* rather than *times* and *divided by,* to support comprehension of the meaning of the problem.

The multiplication symbol is an arbitrary symbol used in our culture to represent *groups of.* The symbol needs to be formally introduced to children as they have discussions about multiple groups so that they can see that it is a shortcut to repeated addition. The teacher should use the term *groups of* when referring to the symbol, although she may want to interchange it occasionally with *times* so that the children begin to see that both terms are ways to refer to the multiplication sign. *Groups of* preserves the meaning of the operation more than *times* does, and it helps children know what is happening to the numbers. For example:

> "*I see that we have written* 3 + 3 + 3 + 3 + 3 + 3 = 18. *How many groups of 3 do we have? We have 6 groups of 3 to equal 18. We use the* × *symbol to represent* **groups of,** *so we can also write this:* 6 × 3 = 18. *We can also read this as six times three equals eighteen.*"

The same can be said about the division symbol. When students are solving problems for sharing, they want to be introduced to the ÷ sign. The teacher should use precise language and use the phases "shared by," "shared with," or "broken into" when introducing situations using division. This language should carry over even when the number sentence, or equation, is presented without context. The other division symbol, ⌐, is not introduced until children are working with arrays or the area model, where they can develop an understanding of the meaning behind this symbol.

Activities to Develop an Understanding of Counting in Groups

Things That Come in Groups Most educators and curricula suggest initial exploration of groups by encouraging students to make connections to the world around them. Children can consider things that come in groups, such as eggs, cans of soda, shoes, and fingers. They should have opportunities to record multiples of these groups on a function table (figure 6.10). They should then begin to notice that when they count by groups (e.g., of 5) it is like skip counting. When exploring numbers by which they cannot skip count, they may discover what the skip counting pattern for that number would be.

Patterns Time should be spent discovering patterns of these multiples. These patterns can be explored using a list of the multiples and using a 100 chart. Coloring in the numbers on a 100 chart creates a different pattern for each different multiple. Have students visually predict the pattern if they color in all multiples of three, for example. Discussions can be centered on why certain patterns surfaced and how the pattern would change if the number changes.

An everyday example of things that come in groups.

Pack of Soda	No. Cans in a Pack
1	6
2	12
3	18
etc.	

Figure 6.10. Recording things that come in groups as a function table.

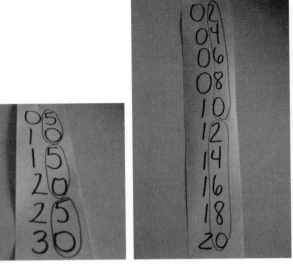

Discovering patterns with multiples.

Models and Recording

This section describes the sequence in which the students learn to model multiplication beginning in second grade and continuing to about fourth grade.

Group   When students are initially solving problems that involve multiplication or division, they begin with grouping. It has been helpful for students to use paper plates, or some other object, to represent the groups and then place the desired number of objects in each group. This is particularly true for division when children are using a dealing strategy to determine the number of groups. Somehow, having boundaries within which the groups should be prevents children from becoming mixed up in their thinking. For example, some students want to divide 12 into four groups, but because they are trying to make equal groups, they may make two piles of six because they found a way to have no leftovers. When nothing represents the piles, they forget that they need a total of four piles.

Array   Moving from grouping to an array model can be a leap for most students. The best way for students to begin using arrays instead of grouping is through an appropriate problem-solving context that elicits such a model, for example, rows of plants in a garden. However, if children are solving problems void of context through grouping, they can be guided to organize their groups in rows, line them up, and talk about what they notice with their model. Keeping their rows somewhat separate helps them see where the individual groups still are. They then benefit from being directed to look for arrays in their environment, such as window arrangements, dots in the ceiling tiles, packages of items, and patterns found on fabric. Two vocabulary words related to arrays (and area) are *rows* and *columns*. A row runs horizontally, and a column runs vertically.

An array using counters.

Area   The area model is similar to an array because the objects are lined up in rows and columns, but the difference is that the objects are squares and they are pushed against one another. This proximity of the tiles to one another can cause the students to lose sight of where the groups are. They may need to temporarily separate the rows or columns to see them again. The area is measured in square units, whether in centimeters, inches, feet, or miles. When working with area problems, students typically use color tiles (each of which measures 1 square inch). When working with this model, it is extremely beneficial to be exploring and discussing area-type problems and using language related to area. This may sound a bit obvious, but too often the area model is used void of problems and context and is just another model. When children begin to explore area and perimeter during measurement in about fourth grade, they inevitably get the two terms confused. Upfront exploration of area during multiplication helps prevent this confusion.

Once children have facility with using area or an array as a model, they can use it to see how multiplication problems can be divided into simpler problems. Once they can see how this works, they can begin to use this idea to mentally solve multiplication problems they do not know. For example, if a child does not know 6×8 but understands that it is the same as $(6 \times 4) + (6 \times 4)$, then he can solve this problem by finding half and doubling. This idea is going to be critical when solving for multidigit multiplication.

When recording the array on paper and labeling the rows and columns, it can become clear why we use the $\overline{}$ symbol to show division. It is unknown whether this is the exact origin of the symbol, but a clear connection can be seen with the model.

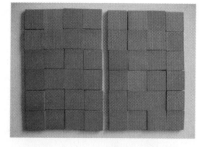

Breaking an area model into two equal pieces.

Comprehension Check

- Identify some initial activities to help students conceptualize the meaning of multiplication and division.

- Explain how students move from a grouping model to a more sophisticated area model and how to connect these models to a number sentence.

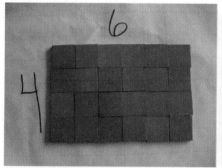 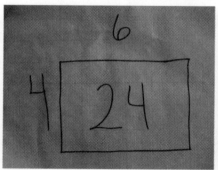 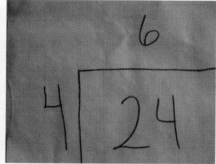

Connecting the traditional algorithmic notation of 24 ÷ 4 with a concrete model.

Basic Facts

As with addition and subtraction, activities that support quick recall of multiplication and division facts should be done only after understanding and concepts are in place. Time should be spent building the multiplication chart so that children do not think that it is some random, or magical, number chart. The building and exploration activities that surround the multiplication chart help children know which facts they really need to study. This construction is appropriate beginning in third grade.

Building the Multiplication Chart

Building a multiplication chart can be a long but important activity. Students need time to build all the arrays of which the 10×10 or 12×12 chart is made. To do this, they need to understand that they always start in the top-left corner. The bottom-right tile indicates the total tiles used. Students remove the bottom-right tile and write the total number of tiles underneath in the corresponding

Building arrays to create a multiplication chart.

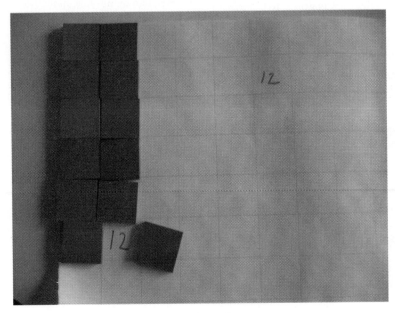

Exploring the commutative property through arrays.

square. When the entire table is complete, or close to it, they notice that it is the same as the multiplication chart. This is a huge revelation to the students. In chapter 2, we discussed how, when a tool is created by the students, it becomes meaningful to them and they can then use it as a tool from which to learn. Most children have difficulty using a multiplication chart because they have little understanding of how it is made. Once they have made the connection to arrays, little teaching needs to go into how to use the chart as a tool.

We like to introduce this activity by having students build all the squares 1–10 (always starting on the top-left corner). As described earlier, students record the total number of squares under the bottom-right tile. This leads into interesting discussions about square numbers and their location on the chart being built. Because the squares are a growing pattern, students can be probed into exploring the relationships of each square to other squares.

Then the students build the rest of the arrays on the same table on which they built the squares. After the arrays have been built and the chart is filled in, the class can go back to explore the relationship that the commutative property has with the chart. If students build 2×6 with tiles on the chart, they can then rotate the array and find that it becomes 6×2. This is essential in understanding that both expressions result in the same quantity. They do, however, represent different situations in a context. By carefully analyzing the chart, students can notice that half the chart is a mirror image of the other because of the commutative property. But what about the square numbers that run diagonally down the center? Why are there not duplicate numbers of them?

Eliminating What Is Already Known

Give each student a multiplication chart. Tell them that they are going to highlight all the facts they already know. This helps them know which facts they still need to learn. Through discussions, they will probably realize that, by now, they know ones facts. They should highlight these facts as known (figures 6.11 and 6.12).

Students that know their addition doubles probably know their twos, so they can highlight these as well. This will probably be followed by their fives and tens, because these are generally the first learned by children. Many students learn their nines by recognizing a pattern, or multiplying by 10 and subtracting one group. For instance, $4 \times 9 = (4 \times 10) - 4$. Patterns should always be explored with concrete objects, such as splitting up arrays, for the pattern to be understood and not be merely a "trick."

Students should go through their table and highlight any fact that they know. Because many students think they know more than they actually do,

1	2	3	4	5	6	7	8	9	10	11	12
2	4	6	8	10	12	14	16	18	20	22	24
3	6	9	12	15	18	21	24	27	30	33	36
4	8	12	16	20	24	28	32	36	40	44	48
5	10	15	20	25	30	35	40	45	50	55	60
6	12	18	24	30	36	42	48	54	60	66	72
7	14	21	28	35	42	49	56	63	70	77	84
8	16	24	32	40	48	56	64	72	80	88	96
9	18	27	36	45	54	63	72	81	90	99	108
10	20	30	40	50	60	70	80	90	100	110	120
11	22	33	44	55	66	77	88	99	110	121	132
12	24	36	48	60	72	84	96	108	120	132	144

Figure 6.11. Highlighting facts that are already known.

1	2	3	4	5	6	7	8	9	10	11	12
2	4	6	8	10	12	14	16	18	20	22	24
3	6	9	12	15	18	21	24	27	30	33	36
4	8	12	16	20	24	28	32	36	40	44	48
5	10	15	20	25	30	35	40	45	50	55	60
6	12	18	24	30	36	42	48	54	60	66	72
7	14	21	28	35	42	49	56	63	70	77	84
8	16	24	32	40	48	56	64	72	80	88	96
9	18	27	36	45	54	63	72	81	90	99	108
10	20	30	40	50	60	70	80	90	100	110	120
11	22	33	44	55	66	77	88	99	110	121	132
12	24	36	48	60	72	84	96	108	120	132	144

Figure 6.12. Highlighting additional facts that are already known.

this may need to be done through testing with the help of the teacher, an aide, or a math partner. With the commutative property, half of the chart is duplicate, so the students can highlight, or eliminate, half of the facts (figure 6.13). A handful of facts remain, which makes the task of memorizing them less frightening.

1	2	3	4	5	6	7	8	9	10	11	12
2	4	6	8	10	12	14	16	18	20	22	24
3	6	9	12	15	18	21	24	27	30	33	36
4	8	12	16	20	24	28	32	36	40	44	48
5	10	15	20	25	30	35	40	45	50	55	60
6	12	18	24	30	36	42	48	54	60	66	72
7	14	21	28	35	42	49	56	63	70	77	84
8	16	24	32	40	48	56	64	72	80	88	96
9	18	27	36	45	54	63	72	81	90	99	108
10	20	30	40	50	60	70	80	90	100	110	120
11	22	33	44	55	66	77	88	99	110	121	132
12	24	36	48	60	72	84	96	108	120	132	144

Figure 6.13. Eliminating half of the multiplication chart of facts that need to be learned using the commutative property.

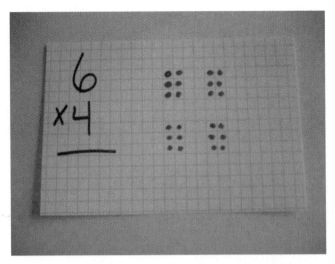

A multiplication flash card with visual support.

Limit the number of facts to learn at one time to three or four. Have students draw arrays or groups to represent the facts they are trying to learn. This helps them continually visualize what the problem is asking and may create a mental structure for thinking about certain facts.

Practicing the Remaining Facts

As long as there is understanding behind the facts the students are trying to learn, they can engage some type of drill to help commit the facts to memory. If students are using derived facts (e.g., $5 \times 6 = 30$, so $6 \times 6 = 36$), then it should not be long before those facts are learned.

If students are having trouble mastering their facts, determine whether they are able to skip count by that number. They may have to go back and learn how to skip count so that they can use it as a tool for solving for these facts. Using a string with 100 beads, alternating colors for every 10, tends to be a good way to reinforce the idea that skip counting is counting out quantities. Exploring multiplicative patterns on the calculator may help students derive skip patterns. If a child wanted to know the multiples of three, they simply have to push "3" on the calculator and the + sign repeatedly. Each push of the + is another multiple of three.

Games are a fun way for students to commit facts to memory without even realizing that they are studying. *Multiplication War* is a classic game in which each student is highly engaged. This game can be played with a number of different rules, depending on the math level of the students. When each student places a card down, the first one to solve for the product keeps both cards. Or, each student puts down two cards, and the one with the highest product keeps both cards. The latter version allows students of different levels to compete, because speed is not an issue. Oftentimes, it is helpful for a third person to verify the product using either a calculator or a times table chart. Students can initially use a chart while playing this game but soon find it inefficient.

The *Array Game*, source unknown, is a fun way for students to connect multiplication with the area model. On a piece of graph paper, outline a 10×10 square. Students compete against a partner. On her turn, the student rolls two dice. She needs to make box within the grid to match her numbers. For example, if she rolls a two and a three, she needs to draw a box that measures two

A string of 100 beads to help promote skip counting.

by three units. She needs to initial her box and write the product inside. Each partner takes turns until a player is no longer able to create a rectangle with her dimensions. At that point, each student adds up her products. The one with the highest amount wins. This game reinforces the idea that a total area can be broken into many parts.

Timed Tests

There have been many heated discussions about whether timed tests should be given in school. The argument against timed tests is clearly articulated by Marilyn Burns (1995b, 408):

> **Teachers who use timed tests believe that the tests help children learn basic facts. This perspective makes no instructional sense. Children who perform well under time pressure display their skills. Children who have difficulty with skills or who work more slowly run the risk of reinforcing wrong practices under pressure. Also, they can become fearful about, and negative toward, their mathematics learning.**

The purpose for giving timed tests must be clear and should be individualized to the child. They do not give the bigger picture of what the child knows and understands, but they put pressure on the child to buckle down and learn the facts. We have seen many students become excited as a class about taking the tests when their individual progress is tracked on a chart. Often the class is rewarded when all, or nearly all, are able to master their facts. Careful attention needs to be given to those students who have difficulty memorizing or taking tests in timed situations. Adaptations such as fewer problems or no time might help make the situation more equitable.

One way to organize individualized tests is to keep a tub with dividers (2–12) with half-sheet tests of each fact. Keep a roster of students, and a record of which fact he is working on. Give each child his corresponding test.

Minimal class time (2 minutes) should be devoted to this. It should be given in the spirit of self-challenge and not meant for punishment. Many classrooms compete against one another, which keeps the motivation high. The bottom line is that third- and fourth-grade teachers want to send their children on knowing their facts, but they want to find a motivating and challenging way in which to do it.

Comprehension Check

- What activities can support the learning and memorization of the basic multiplication facts?

Using Inquiry to Teach Multiplication and Division

If we predominately want to be teaching through an inquiry model, what are some good lessons that can support the development of multiplication and division concepts? The first part of this section described problem types and solution strategies for contextual situations involving multiplication and division. Even kindergartners are able to solve multiplicative situations given the right context. They are not interpreting abstract symbols but use the language to directly model the problem.

We have taken the ideas described earlier for developing a deep understanding of multiplication and division concepts and provided example lesson plans in the table in figure 6.14.

Things That Come in Groups

Launch	▪ From home, provide a few items that come in groups, like an egg carton, a six-pack of soda, and a pair of socks.
	▪ Ask the students what things they know of that come in groups.
	▪ Chart the students' responses.
Explore	▪ In partnerships, have the students come up with as many different items as they can that come in twos, fours, fives, and tens.
	▪ They may use picture books to give them ideas.
	▪ Have the students chart their ideas to share with the class.
Summarize	▪ Have the students share ideas of things that come in groups. Create a class chart and record their ideas.

Patterns

Launch	▪ Review the chart of things that come in groups.
	▪ Pick an item that comes in tens.
	▪ Create a function chart of the total quantity for multiple items.
	▪ "What pattern can we notice with the multiples of 10?"
Explore	▪ Have the students work in small groups to study the patterns for multiples of two, four, and five.
Summarize	▪ As a class, the students discuss the patterns that they noticed with multiples of two, four, and five.
	▪ Create a class chart highlighting the patterns for each of the numbers. (e.g., "When we count by fives, the number always ends in a 5 or a 0.")

Groups of

Launch	▪ Review the previous day's problem-solving strategies from the students (refer to class chart).
	▪ Ask the students to think of a strategy that they might want to try today.
Explore	▪ "Adrian made 6 gift bags of toys. He put 4 toys in each bag. How many toys are in all the bags?"
Summarize	▪ Have the students share modeling strategies for this problem. There might be direct modeling, repeated addition, and derived facts (i.e., 5 bags of toys would be 20, so 6 would be 24). Chart and name any new strategies.

Array and Area

Launch	▪ Show the class an empty egg carton. "What do you notice about its arrangement?"
	▪ Introduce the term *array*.
	▪ Look around the room for other examples of arrays (e.g., windows and tiles in ceiling or floor).
Explore	▪ "In the spring, the farmer planted 6 rows of corn. There were 4 corn stalks in each row. How many corn stalks did the farmer plant?"
Summarize	▪ Share strategies (direct modeling, counting all, skip counting, and derived facts).
	▪ Connect to the problem solved in groups. Is it the same or different?

(A lesson for breaking apart arrays was developed on pages 167 and 168.)

Using a Number Line

Launch	▪ Using a laminated number line, have the students practice counting by twos, threes, and fives with a dry erase marker by making jumps or circling the numbers. Students can also use Cuisenaire rods to count by different amounts.
Explore	▪ "At a traffic light, there were many big trucks waiting. Each truck had a triple trailer. When we passed them, we counted 18 different trailers. How many trucks were waiting for the light?"
Summarize	▪ Students discuss how they solved the problem.
	▪ (After having access to any tool.) "Was one tool more helpful to solve this problem? Which model (of the ones presented in class) matches the problem most? Why?"

Figure 6.14. Example inquiry lessons for different multiplication and division concepts.

Building the Multiplication Chart

Cycle 1

Launch	▪ "Using your color tiles, build a square of three."
	▪ Establish the language related to squares if necessary.
Explore	▪ "With your partner, build all the squares from 1 to 10 on your 10 × 10 grid. Starting in the top-left corner each time, build your square. Then record the total number of tiles in that square under the bottom-right tile."
Summarize	▪ Students discuss what they notice (all square numbers are on the diagonal of the chart) and why they think that happens.

Cycle 2

Launch	▪ "Using the same 10 × 10 grid, make an array showing 2 × 4."
	▪ Establish the guidelines for building the arrays.
Explore	▪ Students complete the grid by building all the arrays. (This may take a couple of days.)
Summarize	▪ "What chart in the room does this remind you of?"
	▪ "I notice that there is a number here and the same number over here (referring to the commutative property). I wonder why that is?" (Encourage students to notice all the double numbers.)
	▪ "But some numbers aren't double. What about these numbers?" (Point to the square numbers.)
	▪ Use an overhead of the multiplication chart and fold it along the diagonal to show how all the numbers on one half are a mirror of the other. "Why is that?" (Try to help students realize that the arrays are just "turned around." With that, introduce the term *commutative property*.)

Figure 6.14, continued

CONCLUSION

Both direct instruction and inquiry instruction are useful, and more importantly, great teachers know both instructional models well and can blend them to meet student needs. Here are two obvious examples:

1. It is common for teachers using direct instruction to ask, amid their modeling and checking for understanding, the deeper-thought questions that characterize an inquiry lesson. This practice *not* an example of being "untrue" or disloyal to direct instruction; such questioning enhances the learning resulting from it.

2. It is common during the summarize stage of an inquiry lesson for teachers to reexplain one student's strategy, engage the class in some kind of group recitation of the strategy, and invite the class to solve another problem using that strategy. In doing so, the teacher is imbedding important components of direct instruction into an inquiry model.

This chapter gave examples of how inquiry-based teaching can be used in learning the foundations of multiplication. In preparation for problems involving large numbers, students need to begin with appropriate explorations to help them conceptually develop understanding of these operations. These experiences begin with problem solving, where students begin to use grouping strategies for both multiplication and division. They model the different types of problems in different ways depending on the context, moving from making groups to a more sophisticated area model. Through classroom discussions and strategic questioning by the teacher, students come to make connections from their models to symbolic notation. Once these connections are in place, it is appropriate to work on committing those facts to memory.

▶ Interview Video with an Eye on Content

Watch a series of videos in which problems are presented to children and they solve them. In each video, determine the type of problem presented, the problem category, and the strategy used to solve it. Record your work in the tables provided. An example is provided.

Problem No.	Problem Type	Problem Category	Problem-Solving Strategy
1	Multiplicative comparison	Measurement division	Skip counting up

▶ Interview a Child

1. Create a word problem for each of the 16 problem types found in figure 6.9 relating to single digit multiplication and division. Include three different number levels: one where both factors are 5 and under, another where one factor is under five and the other is larger than 5, and a third where both factors are larger than 5.

2. Using the problems from step 1, interview a child in the third or fourth grade.

3. Write a report about it that contains two parts: individual problem analyses and overall summary.

4. In the individual problem analyses section, each problem you pose should include the following:
   a. The problem type
   b. The problem (underline the numbers used)
   c. A complete description of the child's response
   d. An analysis of the child's response, which includes the following the general and specific strategy he used.

Sample analysis of an interview problem:

Problem 1: Grouping/partitioning (multiplication)

Problem: Adrian made (3, 4, 6) gift bags of toys. He put (4, 7, 8) toys in each bag. How many toys are in all the bags?

Response: The student drew three circles and then placed 4 counters into each circle. After counting all of them, he responded, "12."

Analysis: Student employed a direct modeling strategy, using a grouping model. He used pictures and counters to create his model.

4. In the overall summary, briefly describe what you learned about the child's mathematical thinking, including the following points:
    a. The types of problems the child successfully solved and those he struggled with
    b. The range of numbers with which the child was familiar (number size)
    c. The types of strategies demonstrated
    d. What recommendations do you have for the teacher, or what would you do with this child if you were to continue to work with him?

▶ Classroom Video with an Eye on Pedagogy

Watch some classroom lessons. Pay particular attention to the lesson structure of each episode. Can you identify the launch, explore, and summarize portions of each video? In which part is the deep mathematical understanding evident?

Video 1

Topic:

Cycle 1

Launch	
Explore	
Summarize	
Cycle 2	
Launch	
Explore	
Summarize	

▶ Classroom Application

1. Observe your cooperating teacher teaching a lesson. Which instructional model does the teacher use? Refer back to the components of the teaching models, and label the different parts of the lesson.

2. Collaboratively design an inquiry lesson about the foundations of multiplication and division that is appropriate for your students. What do your students come to the lesson already knowing? What connections do they still need to make?

▶ Resources

Developing Number Concepts. Book 3: Place Value, Multiplication, and Division, Kathy Richardson (1999c)

Young Mathematicians at Work: Constructing Multiplication and Division, Catherine Twomey Fosnot and Maarten Dolk (2001a)

Lessons for Introducing Multiplication: Grade 3, Marilyn Burns (2001b)

▶ **Lit Link**

Literature Books to Support Multiplication and Division

Title	Author
2 × 2 = Boo!	Loreen Leedy
Amanda Bean's Amazing Dream	Cindy Neuschwander
Anno's Mysterious Multiplying Jar	Anno Mitsumasa
Arithme-Tickle: An Even Number of Odd Riddle-Rhymes	Patrick Lewis
Bananas	Jacqueline Farmer
Counting on Frank	Rod Clement
Doorbell Rang, The	Pat Hutchins
Each Orange Had 8 Slices	Paul Giganti Jr.
Equal Shmequal	Virginia L. Kroll
Grain of Rice, A	Helena Clare Pittman
Great Divide: A Mathematical Marathon, The	Dayle Ann Dodds
Hershey's Milk Chocolate Multiplication Book, The	Jerry Pallotta
Hottest, Coldest, Highest, Deepest	Steve Jenkins
In the Next Three Seconds . . . Predictions for the Millennium	Rowland Morgan (comp.)
King's Chessboard, The	David Birch
Math Curse	Jon Sciezka and Lane Smith
Multiplying Menace: The Revenge of Rumpelstiltskin	Pam Calvert and Wayne
One Hundred Angry Ants	Elinor J. Pinczes
P. Bear's New Year's Party	Paul Owen Lewis
Rabbits Rabbits Everywhere: A Fibonacci Tale	Ann McCallum and Gideon Kendall
Remainder of One, A	Elinor J. Pinczes

Title	Author
Sea Squares	Joy Hulme
Three Messy Dragons	Fay Robinson and Kathryn Corbett
Time Is Better, The	Richard Michelson
Two Ways to Count to Ten: A Liberian Folktale	Ruby Dee
You Can, Toucan, Math	David A. Adler

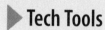 ## Tech Tools

Websites

National Library of Virtual Manipulatives, http://www.nlvm.usu.edu

Math Fact Cafe: The Fact Sheet Factory, http://www.mathfactcafe.com/

NewFreeDownloads.com: Multiplication, http://www.newfreedownloads.com/find/multiplication.html (free downloadable math games)

Choose a Planet, http://www.primaryresources.co.uk/online/moonmaths.swf

Multiplication.com, http://www.multiplication.com

Software

Timez Attack, Big Brainz (High-end video game on multiplication. A free download of the base game can be found at http://www.bigbrainz.com/index.php?PARTNER=krimsten.)

Math Blaster, Knowledge Adventure

Lesson Design: Learning How to Create Inquiry Lessons Using Multidigit Multiplication and Division

PEDAGOGICAL CONTENT UNDERSTANDINGS

Pedagogy *Creating Inquiry Lessons*

- Steps for Planning an Inquiry Lesson
- Lesson Examples
- Planning a Unit

Content *Multidigit Multiplication and Division*

- Multidigit Problems
- Assessment

To begin with the end in mind means to start with a clear understanding of your destination. It means to know where you're going so that you better understand where you are now so that the steps you take are always in the right direction.

Stephen R. Covey, 2004

CONVERSATION IN MATHEMATICS

In this interview, the student is trying to figure out how many candy bags can be made with 150 candies if 5 candies are put into each bag.

Student: (Makes a large circle with 150 written in the center.) If this is the bag of 150 candies. . . . (Draws 10 bags with five dots in each bag.)

Teacher: (Stops student.) How many do you have so far?

Student: 50.

Teacher: How many bags do you have so far?

Student: 10.

Teacher: So if it takes 10 to get 50, how many bags do you think it will take to get 150?

Student: That would be 100 more candies.

Teacher: OK, how many bags would that be?

Student: That would probably be 20 bags.

Teacher: You mean 20 bags more, or 20 bags altogether?

Student: It would be 30 bags actually.

Teacher: Altogether?

Student: Uh-huh. It is 10, and 20 more is 30. So it would be, um, like 3 rows of 10.

$$10 \times 3 = 30$$

30 = 3 rose of ten candie bags

ten & bags = 50 candies

150 candies = 30 bags

$$30 \times 5 = 150$$

$$150 \div 5 = 30$$

As demonstrated in the preceding conversation, young students can make sense of multiplicative situations presented in an authentic context. The student in the preceding conversation begins to directly model this division problem, but when the teacher probes his thinking, he is able to use what he knows about number facts to solve the rest of the problem. Simply providing the problem 150 ÷ 5 would have been too abstract for many students unless they really understand what is happening with division. Many students' only access to this problem would have been through an algorithm, but if this was their first exposure to three-digit numbers, they would have been limited. The task and lesson design are critical in providing all students with access to the math content.

In chapter 6, we discussed the differences between direct instruction and inquiry-based instruction. As you know, the notion of balance is key to the philosophy underlying this book. As with any term, the word *balance* can be interpreted in multiple ways, many of which do not match our usage. *Balance* does not, in the context of this chapter, mean that there should be a balanced amount of direct and inquiry instruction in your classroom. In fact, we believe that a good share of your instruction should be inquiry based. The word *balance* in any instructional context means that you should consistently assess the needs of your students and select whatever instructional strategy meets that need. Therefore, your assessment of students usually suggests that you use inquiry instruction, but sometimes a more direct instructional approach may be warranted. Nearly all of us have grown up learning math through direct instruction. Although writing a lesson using direct instruction still takes some practice, the format is ingrained in our mind. Designing an inquiry lesson is new and different to most teachers; therefore, this chapter is dedicated to learning how to write such a lesson.

We use multidigit multiplication as a mode of writing inquiry lessons, but we also look at examples of content discussed in previous chapters. The key to writing a successful lesson, or series of lessons, however, is truly understanding the content you teach. The content section of this chapter explores the important concepts and connections that students need to develop as they investigate multidigit multiplication and division.

PEDAGOGY   *Creating Inquiry Lessons*

Learning Theory

Research has shown that classrooms in which problem solving was the focus and the teachers made their instructional decisions by listening to students had "significantly higher levels of achievement in problem solving than control classes had" (Carpenter et al. 1999, 109). This model has proved to have significant outcomes on urban students as well (Villasenor and Kepner 1993; Carpenter et al. 1999).

Inquiry is a state of mind (National Research Council 2000b). Ultimately, we want students to generate their own questions and design ways to test them. Inquiry is a central part of the National Science Education Standards. Because it is said that science is the hands-on application of math, it makes sense that inquiry would be central to learning mathematics as well. Inquiry, however, is often misinterpreted to always being a free-for-all approach to teaching. Although we want to get the students to a point where they are asking and finding answers to their own questions, a continuum exists that ranges from highly structured investigations to more opened-ended ones. In mathematics, it is impractical to assume that students are going to generate their questions and discover all there is to know about math. Each teacher has a laundry list of standards to address and a curriculum that is difficult to cover in the school year. Because of these constraints, most learners of mathematics in elementary school are engaging in questions provided by the teachers. However, throughout a consistent inquiry model that includes exploring, analyzing, explaining, and justifying, students naturally come up with their own questions. It is serendipitous when they are the same questions that they were already being prepared to explore in the next lesson.

According to the National Research Council (2000b, 25), the essential features of classroom inquiry are as follows:

- **Learners are engaged by scientifically oriented questions.**

- **Learners give priority to evidence, which allows them to develop and evaluate explanations that address scientifically oriented questions.**

- **Learners formulate explanations from evidence to address scientifically oriented questions.**

- **Learners evaluate their explanations in light of alternative explanations, particularly those reflecting scientific understanding.**

- **Learners communicate and justify their proposed explanations.**

We could easily substitute the word *scientifically* with *mathematically*. But, as discussed in the previous paragraph, inquiry may need to be more guided than the ideal, especially if students have little experience with finding answers for themselves. Inquiries that need more guidance by the instructor are defined by the National Research Council as *partial* inquiries, as opposed to *full* inquiries. This council has organized a chart that outlines the variations of the preceding essential features of classroom inquiry (figure 7.1).

Essential Feature	*Variations*			
1. Learner engages in scientifically oriented questions	Learner poses a question	Learner selects among questions, poses new questions	Learner sharpens or clarifies a question provided by the teacher, materials, or other source	Learner engages in a question provided by the teacher, materials, or other source
2. Learner gives priority to evidence in responding to questions	Learner determines what constitutes evidence and collects it	Learner is directed to collect certain data	Learner is given data and asked to analyze it	Learner is given data and told how to analyze it
3. Learner formulates explanations from evidence	Learner formulates an explanation after summarizing the evidence	Learner is guided in the process of formulating explanations from evidence	Learner is given possible ways to use evidence to formulate an explanation	Learner is provided with evidence
4. Learner connects explanations to scientific knowledge	Learner independently examines other resources and forms the links to explanations	Learner is directed toward areas and sources of scientific knowledge	Learner is given possible connections	
5. Learner communicates and justifies explanations	Learner forms a reasonable and logical argument to communicate explanations	Learner is coached in the development of communication	Learner is provided with broad guidelines to sharpen communication	Learner is given steps and procedures for communication

More — — — — — — — — — — — — — — — — **Amount of Learner Self-Direction** — — — — — — — — — — — — — — **Less**

Less — — — — — — — — — — — — — — **Amount of Direction from Teacher or Material** — — — — — — — — — — — **More**

Figure 7.1. Essential features of classroom inquiry and their variations. (Inquiry and the National Science Education Standards by the National Research Council, 2000, p. 29. Reprinted with permission of the National Academy of Sciences, Courtesy of the National Academies Press, Washington, D.C.)

Application to the Learning and Teaching of Mathematics

Often teachers become frustrated if their students are too dependent and do not try and think for themselves. They deduce that their students cannot handle inquiry teaching. Others comment that the content level of their students is too low and they feel that inquiry takes too much time when they need to be catching their students up. As you can see from figure 7.1, when teaching, it does not have to be all or nothing. We can try to incorporate as many elements from inquiry as possible, or as is practical for our particular students on that particular day, hoping to eventually move as close to a pure model of inquiry as possible. In response to the accusation that inquiry takes too much time, in reality, when math is taught consistently through problematic tasks, we find we get more bang for the buck in that more individual skills are being incorporated than in a direct instruction lesson.

Steps for Planning an Inquiry Lesson

When it comes to planning these inquiry lessons, Grant Wiggins and Jay McTighe (1998), in their book *Understanding by Design*, have outlined three stages of designing a lesson through what is known as *backward planning* or *backward designing:*

- Identify the desired results
- Determine acceptable evidence
- Plan learning experiences and instruction

Planning with the end result in mind means knowing where you are going and what your goals are. We need to determine how to tell when students have met the goals. What evidence do we expect to see? We then need to plan the experiences that would enable students to demonstrate such evidence. When we know the desired outcome at the end of the day or the end of a unit, we can constantly monitor and assess our students to determine whether they are meeting our goals. The following are considerations for planning your inquiry lesson using a backward design (figure 7.2).

The planning needs to begin with the mathematics in mind. Identify the standards that need to be covered. What do the NCTM focal points suggest? Sometimes we become caught up in activities that we enjoy but are not appropriate for the grade level we are teaching.

Planning Steps for a Math Lesson

1. Identify the **standards** or **focal points.**

2. Determine the **big ideas,** mathematical **focus,** and the mathematical **concepts** to be explored.

3. Plan your **summary.**

4. Plan your **assessment** question.

5. Plan your **explore.**

6. Plan your **launch.** How are you going to prepare students for the task? How does previous work connect with what will be explored today? What materials might you need to prepare? How will you determine that all students know what to do?

7. Consider your **accommodations.**

Figure 7.2. Planning steps for a math lesson.

Example standard: "3.a. Use models to represent multiplication of a one- or two-digit factor by a two-digit factor (up to 30) using a variety of methods (e.g., rectangular arrays, manipulatives, pictures) and connect the representation to an algorithm." (Utah State Standard, fourth grade)

Next, identify the objective or focus for the individual lesson. This is the one thing you want to accomplish *today.* The focus should support the development of concepts and big ideas over time, as well as meet state standards; therefore, you need to identify which big ideas and concepts you would like to work on. It is important to also consider the standards and teachings from previous grades about the topic you plan to teach. What do your students already understand about this topic? How can you bridge their understandings with what they need to know now?

Example objective: Teach students to use their understanding of partial products and breaking apart numbers to solve a problem with a multidigit factor.

Then plan the summarize stage. Consider what you would like your students to understand by the end of the lesson. What would you like them to reflect on in their math journal? What conjectures or generalizations do you hope your students make? Thinking of these things now helps you better plan your exploration activity. Note that oftentimes the discussion that takes places during the summarize period is not what was originally planned. When students are exploring, the teacher may notice some general misconceptions, or unexpected strategies, and thus want to change the focus for the summarize stage.

Example summarize: Share an area model a student built, breaking the tens from the ones, and the way the student recorded the model numerically. Make sure to connect the numerical recording with the model and the distributive property, for example, $(10 \times 5) + (4 \times 5)$.

Now that you know what you would like your students to walk away with, how are you going to assess that understanding at the end of the lesson or series of lessons? Students often work well in a group but are unable to take a new skill into independent practice. What quick problem are you going to provide to check this understanding? Are you going to assess this after the lesson or after a series of connected lessons in which all points are embedded in the assessment question? Teachers often refer to a quick assessment as an *exit slip.* Teachers also find it helpful to put this question in a multiple-choice format to help link the exploratory activity to the way the concept may appear on a standardized test.

Example assessment question: Solve the problem 13×7 individually using pictures, numbers, and words.

Next, plan the task that the students will be exploring and what you expect the students do and say as a result of the task. Remember, your explore stage is typically one good problematic task that helps students make the desired conjectures or generalizations. It should be accessible to all students in that it has multiple solutions or multiple ways to find the solution. What problem or problems can you pose that allow students to discover and grapple with the desired mathematics? What strategies might you expect from your students? What questions might you ask them to nudge them toward bigger understandings?

Example task: I want to build a patio behind my house. I want it to be 14 feet by 5 feet. How many 1-foot-square tiles will I need to buy?

When planning your explore stage, consider how you want your students to work together. Do you want them to work in informal cooperative groups or in those with assigned roles? Do you want to provide independent think time before the partnerships or small groups share with one another? What kind of product do you expect the students to turn in, and what guidelines do you want to put on that product? How do you want them to show their work: using pictures, numbers, and words, or are they only building a model? Will you have enough tools to complete the task? How many groups can you have with the amount of tools you can provide? Do the numbers need to be adjusted so that they lend themselves to the tool (especially in fractions)? How are you going to accommodate students who need extra support? Will you keep them with you in a small group, or will you check on them often?

After planning the explore period, consider what activity will help prepare students to tackle the explore task. This is the launch stage. How does previous work connect with what will be explored in this lesson? Do you want to make connections with their background knowledge or strategies they already know? How are you going to introduce the explore task?

Topic: Two-digit multiplication   **Time Frame:** 1 hour   **Grade Level:** 4th

Goals/Focus: Get students to use their understanding of partial products and breaking apart numbers to solve a problem with a multidigit factor

State Core/Standard: Utah Standard 3.a. Use models to represent multiplication of a one- or two-digit factor by a two-digit factor (up to 30) using a variety of methods (e.g., rectangular arrays, manipulatives, pictures) and connect the representation to an algorithm.

	Task	*What Will the Students Be Saying or Doing?*
Launch Materials: Square tiles, pencil, journal	"I am using 1-foot-square tiles to make a small mural. I want the mural to be 6 feet wide and 8 feet long. How many square tiles will I need to buy?"	Students will use square tiles to solve the problem. Some may be making groups, so I will encourage them to create a model that matches the problem. I anticipate that students will be counting all or counting by twos to calculate total tiles. I will ask them, "How can I break up this problem into two simpler problems to help me solve the full problem?"
Explore	"I want to build a patio behind my house. I want it to be 14 feet by 5 feet. How many 1-foot-square tiles will I need to buy?"	Some students might still solve this problem by making groups. I would ask them if their model shows what the problem is showing and ask them to make their model match the situation. Other students might be trying to split their array up into $(5 \times 7) + (5 \times 7)$. I would want to compare that with the solution of someone who split it into tens and ones to determine the most efficient way to solve this problem.
Summarize	Share an area model a student built, breaking the tens from the ones, and the way the student recorded the model numerically. Make sure to connect the numerical recording with the model and the distributive property, for example $(10 \times 5) + (4 \times 5)$.	Students will be engaging in discourse as a class regarding their models and how the models connect to a numerical representation.

Launch for Assessment
Solve the problem 13×7 individually using pictures, numbers, and words.

Figure 7.3. A lesson plan for a multidigit multiplication problem.

Example: I am using 1-foot-square tiles to make a small mural. I want the mural to be 6 feet wide and 8 feet long. How many square tiles will I need to buy?

Notice how this launch problem is similar to the explore problem but uses simpler numbers. The students understand how to model for multiplication, but because the numbers are becoming bigger, the idea is planted about breaking up the problem.

Finally, you need to consider your accommodations. Do you have students with language, learning, or behavior needs? How are you going to ensure that these students have access and are actively engaged?

Figure 7.3 demonstrates how the preceding considerations come together as a lesson plan.

Comprehension Check

- How does the notion of backward design, or planning with the end result in mind, help teachers plan an effective inquiry lesson?

- What is the role of the assessment question at the end of a lesson? How often and in what formats should it be given?

Lesson Examples

Examples of inquiry lessons using the content areas from chapters 2-6 are found in figure 7.4. Each task is considered problematic, although some use "real-life" contexts and some do not. Each of these lessons has a *whole group–small group–whole group* format. Each lesson idea comes from a combination of the required standards and an understanding how concepts are developed. Chapters 10 and 11 elaborate on how to choose and design high-level tasks.

Kindergarten	Example Lesson 1 (One Cycle)
Supporting the Generalization of Plus One	
Launch	*Whole Group:* The teacher builds a tower of _____ cubes and then adds one more and shows one less.
	The teacher asks, "What do you notice?" Students connect the observations to a number line.
Explore	*Small Group:* Students build towers 1–10. They match the towers to number cards and order them. They discuss what they notice with their small group members.
Summarize	*Whole Group:* Students discuss how each bigger tower is the next number on the number line.
	Example Lesson 2 (Two Cycles)
Division through Sharing	
Launch cycle 1	*Whole Group:* The teacher reminds students of different problem-solving strategies other students used in the previous day's lesson, including using cubes, drawing pictures, and acting out the problem.
	The teacher gives a prompt: "I have three cookies, and there are three friends. How many cookies can each friend get if all get the same number of cookies?"
Explore cycle 1	*Partnerships:* One partner solves using cubes, and the other draws on an individual whiteboard. When each has finished solving, they share with each other their answers and how they solved the problem.
Summarize cycle 1	*Whole Group:* With teacher assistance, students share strategies. The teacher focuses on a student who drew a picture but got lost in all the lines, so the class helps that student act out the story.
Launch cycle 2	*Whole Group:* The teacher gives a prompt: "I have six cookies, and there are three friends. How many cookies can each friend get if all get the same number of cookies?"
Explore cycle 2	*Partnerships:* Partners trade tools and solve the problem either using cubes or drawing on a whiteboard. They share solution strategies with each other.
Summarize cycle 2	*Whole Group:* Students share strategies, focusing on a couple of ways some students drew the picture, such as drawing the cookies and then circling them or drawing the cookies, drawing the friends, and drawing lines in a "dealing" fashion.

Figure 7.4. Example tasks in grades K–6. *(Continued on following page.)*

First Grade	Example Lesson 1 (One Cycle)
Difference	
Launch	*Whole Group:* The teacher asks, "Are there more boys or girls in the class? How many more?" The teacher introduces the word *difference*.
Explore	*Partnerships:* Using a cup of two-sided (red–yellow) counters, partners toss and compare how the number of yellow and red counters. They draw and record differences on a recording sheet.
Summarize	*Whole Group:* Two students come up and model how they found the difference of one of their tosses.
	Example Lesson 2 (Two Cycles)
Doubles	
Launch cycle 1	*Whole Group:* The teacher asks students what they know about the word *double* and what a *double fact* would be. The teacher gives the number 6, asks whether this is a number of a double fact, and asks how they know.
Explore cycle 1	*Partnerships:* Students use tools, such as counters, cubes, and pictures, to prove that 6 is or is not the result of a double fact.
Summarize cycle 1	*Whole Group:* Students discuss how they figured out that 6 was a double.
Launch cycle 2	*Whole Group:* The teacher assigns partnerships a couple of numbers each so that the partnerships can determine whether they are doubles or not.
Explore cycle 2	*Partnerships:* Students work together using a variety of tools to figure out whether their numbers are doubles or not.
Summarize cycle 2	*Whole Group:* Students get together to see what they notice about the numbers that are double and numbers that are not. They arrange them in order and discover that every other number is a double. The teacher tells them that all numbers that are doubles are even numbers. A student asks why they are called *even*. Another student comments that maybe it is because when two towers are lined up they are even on the top.

Second Grade	Example Lesson 1 (One Cycle)
Skip Counting	
Launch	*Whole Group:* The teacher leads the class in a skip counting exercise off of the 100 chart. Students begin counting by tens, switch to fives when the teacher gives a signal, and then switch to ones.
Explore	*Small Group:* Students get a handful of coins that they need to find the value of.
Summarize	*Whole Group:* Students discuss strategies they used to find the value of the coins. The teacher focuses on helping students make connections among the different strategies. Students discuss which strategy they feel is most efficient and why.
	Example Lesson 2 (Two Cycles)
Joint Start Unknown	
Launch cycle 1	*Whole Group:* The teacher has students come up with tools they can use to solve problems and with strategies they might consider. The teacher poses the following problem: "Bernie had some cookies. Jennifer gave him 7 more cookies. Now he has 15 cookies. How many cookies did Bernie start with?" The teacher prompts students to try to visualize the problem.
Explore cycle 1	*Partnerships:* Students work together using a variety of tools.
Summarize cycle 1	*Whole Group:* Students share strategies on the document camera, and the teacher charts strategies that are significant and that students may want to use for their next problem.
Launch cycle 2	*Whole Group:* The teacher poses the same situation but changes the numbers to 25 and 46.
Explore cycle 2	*Partnerships:* Students work together using a variety of tools.
Summarize cycle 2	*Whole Group:* Students share strategies on the document camera, and the teacher charts significant strategies that students may want to try another day.

Figure 7.4, continued

Third Grade	Example Lesson (Two Cycles)
Division	
Launch cycle 1	*Whole Group:* The teacher poses the following problem: "There are 36 candies in a box. We are going to make bags for each of the third-grade teachers (there are four third-grade teachers). How many candies can we give each of them if each is given the same number of candies?"
Explore cycle 1	*Small Groups:* Using a variety of tools, students figure out how many candies can go into each bag.
Summarize cycle 1	*Whole Group:* Students discuss how they solved the problem. Efficiency in different strategies is discussed.
Launch cycle 2	*Whole Group:* The teacher says, "Now I want to know how many we can give each of the teachers if there are 50 candies in the box."
Explore cycle 2	*Small Groups:* Students figure out this problem, maybe by trying someone else's strategy. They run into the issue that there are some leftovers.
Summarize cycle 2	*Whole Group:* Students discuss what they should do with the candies that are left over. Some suggest cutting them, some suggest leaving them out, and others suggest just eating them to make the groups even.

Fourth Grade	Example Lesson (One Cycle)
Prime and Composite Numbers	
Launch	*Whole Group:* The teacher poses a question: "What are all the ways I could design a candy box if I needed it to fit four candies in one layer?" After having some partner talk time, the entire class discusses the question.
Explore	*Small Groups:* Each group of students is assigned a few different numbers that they have to create candy boxes for. Groups record results and glue finished designs on a piece of construction paper.
Summarize	*Whole Group:* All groups display their finished designs on the board in number order. The class members discuss what they notice. The ideas that surface are that some numbers can only make one kind of candy box: prime vs. composite numbers.

Figure 7.4, continued

Planning a Unit

Lessons need to be part of a thoughtful sequence to optimally allow students to make the necessary connections between ideas and representations, thus supporting the understanding of big ideas. When designing a string of lessons or looking at a unit of a commercial program, which may be written in a direct instruction format that you want to modify, there are some considerations. Those shown in figure 7.5 help strengthen the connection between ideas and representations.

1. What do the **state standards** say about what needs to be addressed?

2. What are the **big ideas** and **key concepts** of the unit?

3. How do you plan to **assess** the students at the end of the unit?

4. What is the **prior knowledge** of the students? What should they know? What do they actually know? Are there any gaps in their learning? What vocabulary do I need to introduce so that they can talk about the ideas in the lessons? Do I need to do any student interviews to gauge the learning? Can I consult with previous teachers to know how they present certain material and how the children performed in those units?

5. What kinds of **scaffolding** do I need to do to help make my students (with math concept needs or linguistic needs) successful? Will I provide this scaffolding through routines before the unit (chapter 8) or through questioning during the lesson?

Figure 7.5. Considerations for planning a unit.

It is important to focus on student communication and on-task behaviors as a way to assess whether a student is "getting it." The unit guide in figure 7.6 allows teachers to carefully consider what they want the students to be able to say and do as a result of the lessons in a unit.

Many teachers seem to like the weekly planning guide in figure 7.7. (Note that in the figure the previous unit ends (day 16) on Monday and the new unit

Unit _____

Big Ideas:

What do I want the students to be able to articulate or demonstrate at the end of the unit?

Standards: What to Teach	Vocabulary	Prior Knowledge	Scaffolds	Outcomes (How do I know they get it? What will they say and do?)

Figure 7.6. A unit planning guide that focuses on student communication and outcomes.

TEACHING FOCUS: Multiplication   UNIT: 8

Purpose	Routines	Launch	Explore	Summarize
Monday 3/13 (day 16)	Assessment for two-digit addition and subtraction			
Tuesday 3/14 (day 1)	Mental math: 37 + 10 37 + 20 37 + 19	As a class, things that come in two	With small groups, assign one number from 3–10 of what comes in groups	Look at the growing pattern of the number of students' feet. Call students up one by one and count how many feet they have. How is it growing? Ensure that students are counting by two.
Wednesday 3/15 (day 2)	37 + 30 37 + 29 37 + 28	Model circles and stars (Burns 2001b)	Play circles and stars Record addition	What is the same about each of the circles? If you want to know the total number of stars, what should you do?
Thursday 3/16 (day 3)	Estimation of answers (e.g., 38 + 27)	Model circles and stars Model writing with words and connect to symbols (three groups of four is 3 × 4)	Play circles and stars Record addition and multiplication	How does knowing addition help you know multiplication (if it comes up, discuss how two groups got the same number: 12)
Friday 3/17 (day 4)	Is 38 closer to 30 or 40? How can you tell?	Candy box research Design candy boxes	Work with a partner to create rectangular arrays, cut out arrays, glue on paper, and label arrays	What did you notice about multiplication? How did you figure how to write your equation?

Figure 7.7. A weekly planning guide for math in a second-grade classroom.

begins (day 1) on Tuesday.) They generally create a template similar to this one on their computer and type right on it. It is then easier to go back and add notes or make changes. Teachers especially like using this when they plan by grade level, because one teacher can enter the information and print it out, or send it electronically, for the other teachers of that grade level. This form allows room only for the essential components of the lesson, not for the details. Specific vocabulary might be noted in the purpose column, and specific language the teachers want students to use might be added to the summarize column. This is a good planning guide to see an entire unit, or even year, but it does not have room to elaborate on issues such as misconceptions. Notice the column on routines, and refer to chapter 8 to learn more.

Comprehension Check

- What things need to be considered when planning a unit?

- Can the teacher know what prior knowledge the student has about the upcoming concepts?

Multidigit Multiplication and Division

CONTENT

In the preceding pedagogy section, we outlined how to write a lesson plan through backward design, as well as how to design an entire unit. We also provided specific examples of what these lessons would look like in different grades and using content from earlier chapters in the book, including multiplication and division. We spend the rest of this chapter focusing on concepts and understandings as they relate to multidigit multiplication and division.

Big Ideas and Focal Points

The big ideas are the same for single-digit and multidigit multiplication and division. In chapter 6, we outlined the big ideas as follows (Charles 2005, 16):

- **Multiplication facts can be found by breaking apart the unknown fact into known facts. Then the answers to the known facts are combined to give the final value.**

- **Division facts can be found by thinking about the related multiplication fact. . . .**

- **Multiplication can be used to check division.**

Multidigit multiplication and division are discussed in the NCTM focal points for the fourth and fifth grades (Focal Points table). The ideas are extensions of what students were developing in second and third grades.

Multidigit Problems

With the right experiences, many students are able to solve multidigit multiplication and division problems without any formal teaching. Using numbers, such as 25, can help students relate the numbers to quarters, with which they are typically familiar. The number 12 can be thought of as the two sixes. Most students just apply the same strategies they developed with smaller numbers to larger numbers. When taught in terms of quantity, they do not think in terms of the number of digits but, rather, in terms of the relative size of the number. Division in particular is simpler when children consider numbers as an entire amount and not as individual digits. Doing this eliminates a lot of trouble related to long division, like dividing with zeros.

NCTM FOCAL POINTS

Fourth Grade

Students apply understanding of models for multiplication (i.e., equal-sized groups, arrays, area models, and equal intervals on the number line), place value, and properties of operations (in particular, the distributive property) as they develop, discuss, and use efficient, accurate, and generalizable methods to multiply multidigit whole numbers.

Students select appropriate methods and apply them accurately to estimate products or calculate them mentally, depending on the context and numbers involved.

Students develop fluency with efficient procedures, including the standard algorithm for multiplying whole numbers; understand why the procedures work (on the basis of place value and properties of operations); and use them to solve problems.

Students develop understandings of strategies for multidigit division by using models that represent division as the inverse of multiplication, as partitioning, or as repeated subtraction.

Fifth Grade

Students apply understanding of models for division, place value, properties, and the relationship of division to multiplication as they develop, discuss, and use efficient, accurate, and generalizable procedures to find quotients involving multidigit dividends.

Students select appropriate methods and apply them accurately to estimate quotients or calculate them mentally, depending on the context and numbers involved.

Students develop fluency with efficient procedures, including the standard algorithm for dividing whole numbers; understand why the procedures work (on the basis of place value and properties of operations); and use them to solve problems.

Students consider the context in which a problem is situated to select the most useful form of the quotient for the solution, and they interpret it appropriately.

Students apply what is known about multiplication of whole numbers to larger numbers.

By the time students explore multiplication with large numbers, they should have had a lot of exposure to building models with single digits. If they have not had such experience, it is necessary to spend some time building such models to ensure that your students have a conceptual understanding of multiplication and division before exploring larger numbers that can be more complicated to model. The area model becomes predominant in work with multidigit numbers, but other models, such as grouping, should not be forgotten.

When beginning to use two-digit numbers, transition students from color tiles to base 10 blocks. At first, students will probably want to solve problems with base 10 blocks by creating groups. It is natural that when the number complexity is higher the students revert to basic models. Encourage your students to somehow create an area model using their base 10 blocks, predominately through contexts that lend themselves to doing so, like tiling a patio. The first time they attempt to accommodate base 10 blocks in an area model, it will

Modeling 24 × 6 using groups.

An attempt to move from a grouping model to an array.

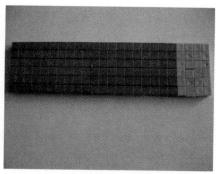

A second attempt to make an array after questioning or context that leads the students to consider the actual dimensions of the problem (24 × 6).

result in a lot of confusion. Oftentimes, they will not create rectangles or their rectangles do not have the dimensions of the original problem. They are simply displaying the total number. When this happens, they are losing sight of what the problem is asking. In this case, ask, "How is this model show the equation?" "Where are the numbers 24 and 6 in your model?" This confusion keeps students at a state of disequilibrium until they figure out how to match the model to the problem.

When it is time to record their work, students should use graph paper and should outline squares exactly as they are shown with their model (figure 7.8). On their paper, they should divide the tens from the ones and label different parts of the problem. They should also write equations to match exactly how they built their model. This supports connection of the concrete with pictures and abstract representations.

Two-digit by two-digit multiplication problems are more difficult to build than two-digit by single-digit numbers, and again they challenge the students. At first, students will use a lot more ones than are necessary when building the model, but through questioning such as "That sure is an awful lot of ones; is there a way you can model this using fewer pieces?" students will see that they are able to trade many of their ones for some tens. After one or two problems

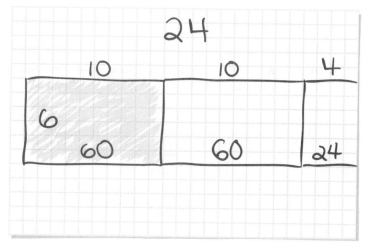

Figure 7.8. Recording pictorially what students built with their cubes.

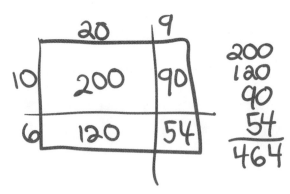

Figure 7.9. Using an open array to model 29 × 16.

of using too much time building with single units, students catch on that they can directly grab the 10 sticks. They will also see that if they have at least one 10 in each number they will need at least a 100 flat. This modeling helps students make better estimates when mentally calculating. Again, students should record their model on graph paper with the exact number of squares shown by the built model, dividing the sections, labeling the parts, and writing the equations that match the model (figure 7.9). Over time, students will no longer need to build the model; this will occur around the time the numbers become too large to draw on graph paper. They will eventually drop the picture using the exact number of squares and move to an open array model in which the rectangle does not have marked units. The children will be able to label the parts and divide the rectangle into the appropriate sections, dividing the tens from the ones (or hundreds, tens, and ones).

Algorithms for Multiplication

The natural algorithm that students develop when using the area model to solve for multiplication is *partial products*. This algorithm essentially breaks the array into hundreds, tens, and ones; solves for those products; and then adds them all together. This is most directly related to the distributive property. In the example in figure 7.9, the parts, or partial products, were 200, 120, 90, and 54. When added together, the product is 464. After building the array, a student would record that numerically as follows:

$$
\begin{array}{r}
29 \\
\times\ 16 \\
\hline
200 \\
120 \\
90 \\
+\ \ 54 \\
\hline
464
\end{array}
$$

Typically, students who have struggled to learn the traditional algorithm gravitate quickly to the use of partial products because it preserves place value and it makes sense. They come to understand that if there are four total digits, for example, then there must be four parts. Many find that drawing the empty array is actually faster and more secure than just solving the problem with numbers. Because they often skip a step when multiplying multiple digits, they prefer to draw the sketch so that they know they did not forget any parts. On scratch paper used for standardized testing, we have seen multiple students use this method.

Next, it is important to relate partial products with the distributive property. Using the preceding problem as the example, the student broke the 29 into $20 + 9$ and the 16 into $10 + 6$. These were multiplied by each other:

$(20 + 9) \times (10 + 6)$

$$20 \times 10 \ = \ 200$$
$$20 \times 6 \ \ = \ 120$$
$$9 \times 10 \ \ = \ 90$$
$$9 \times 6 \ \ \ = \ 54$$

In the initial stages, students may break up all the tens (i.e., $10 + 10 + 9$). This just gives them more parts to multiply. With a little practice, students are able to group all the tens together $(20 + 9)$. Students who can understand how to break the problem apart and put it back together in this way have a more solid understanding going into algebra than those who can only solve the problem through the traditional method.

The picture shown here is an example of a classroom chart connecting the different representations of multiplying with the problem 32×15 with partial products.

Remember that the traditional, or standard, algorithm is a shortcut of the partial products model. When students solve the problem in both ways, the parts found in partial products can also be found in the standard algorithm but are a bit more obscure, especially if the student does not use zero as a placeholder. A common error when using the traditional algorithm is that students only multiply each number once, for example:

$$\begin{array}{r} 29 \\ \times\ 16 \\ \hline 54 \\ +\ 20 \\ \hline 74 \end{array}$$

A classroom chart to show the connections between the open array, partial products, and the distributive property.

In problems like 29×16, why do we multiply the 6 twice? If you are not sure, go back to the pictorial representation.

According to NCTM standards, students should be able to use the standard algorithm, but it should always come after conceptual understanding has been achieved. When students prematurely come to class knowing the standard algorithm (of any operation), teachers tell their students that they can use any strategy that they can explain. After the class has engaged in some level of exploration, then the teacher may bring up this student's way of solving the problem and ask the class to analyze that method, to figure out why it works, and if they can connect it to the models that they have developed. The chart that follows demonstrates making connections between the traditional algorithm and the array model.

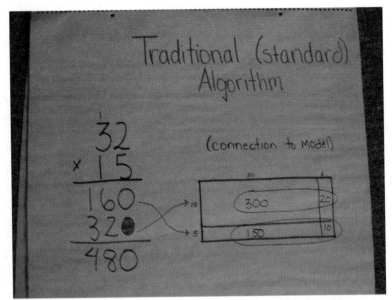

A classroom chart that connects the traditional algorithm to the array model.

Comprehension Check

■ Solve the following problem in two different ways (with grouping and with an area model) using pictures, numbers, and words (a written description to explain your work) to show the connections between each method. Also, write a story problem that would go with each method. Use extra paper if necessary.

32 × 15

A common algorithm not yet mentioned but found in curriculum is the *Lattice Method.* This method dates back to the original book printed by Fibonacci, who introduced several methods using the Hindu-Arabic number system. At the time, Europeans only used Roman numerals, and calculations were ineffective with that number system. In this method, partial products are laid out in a lattice, adding along the diagonals. Investigate this method using the earlier problem of 29 × 16:

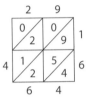

The 29 was written across the top of the lattice and the 16 down the right side. Each square is divided into two sections with a diagonal line. The product is written in these sections, the top diagonal for the tens and bottom for the ones. The sums of the numbers of each diagonal are written on the outside of the lattice, as shown in blue. When regrouping is required, the number is carried into the diagonal above it, as was the case for adding 9 + 5 + 2 = 16. The 6 was placed below the lattice, and the 10 was placed with the 2 and 1 above it.

Every country has its own standard way of computing with the different operations; thus, there are more ways to multiply multidigit numbers. Perhaps one of your students recently came from another country and already has a standard algorithm in place. It is not a bad idea to validate what that student knows and try to strengthen the connections of the other students by exposing them to her algorithm and making the class try to figure out why it works.

CAUTION Although power lies in knowing more than one or two algorithms, especially when strong connections are made among them, there can be a danger in presenting the lattice method prematurely. What tends to happen is that students like this method so much that they generally refuse to use any other strategy to multiply. That means that if the intention of the teacher is to have the students make sense of the problem through models and pictures, it may be too late. Students tend to turn off their desire to make sense of and connections related to the problem once the "shortcuts" are provided. It is important for any shortcuts to be shown only if understanding and connections have been built and it has been strongly suggested that students make connections between the shortcuts and the other strategies they already know. In schools where the mathematical abilities of the students are fragile, it is best to introduce such algorithms only after students have had a few years to develop appropriate understanding.

Algorithms for Division

Division is a bit more complicated because a large amount is being divided evenly and there will probably be some leftovers. Students need to work with the concrete when trying to make sense of such algorithms. When solving problems involving division, they first act out what is happening with their cubes, or base 10 blocks. They should draw each action after they perform it; otherwise, they may forget exactly how they did each step. Eventually, they also need to record each step using numbers. Again, the recording of exactly what was done to the concrete model helps the transition to using a picture as a solution strategy.

Something to work on long before the introduction of division is multiplying by multiples of 10 mentally. The facility of being able to multiply by 10, 100, and 1,000 will prove helpful in division. A warm-up activity could look like the following:

6×10	4×2
6×100	4×20
60×100	40×20
600×100	400×20
$600 \times 1,000$	400×200

This string of problems, or *number string*, is based on a pattern, and from it students generalize the idea that the product has at least as many zeros as there are in the two factors (because $2 \times 5 = 10$, there could be more).

Because division is breaking up a total into a specified number of groups or repeatedly subtracting an amount for each group, the child should pull out as many groups of the divisor as possible; otherwise, the process may take forever. Being able to think in larger quantities, like in the preceding number string, helps the student subtract larger groups.

Partial Quotients *Partial quotients* form an algorithm in which the students try to pull out as many groups of the divisor as possible. They then subtract the amount removed from the total and continue pulling out groups until there are no more numbers or only a remainder is left. This can be modeled with either measurement (repeated subtraction) or partitive division (dealing out), and the context used can greatly affect the model chosen. However, when learning how to connect the pictorial model with the concrete model, it is clearer if you use the model of partitive division.

In the first photo that follows, the student has shown the total amount to be divided with his base 10 blocks (295). He also has written his problem on his paper. In the second photo, the student has decided that at least 10 fifteens are in

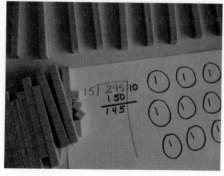

295. He trades his hundreds for tens, and he puts 10 into each of the 15 groups. He then records that action using a picture, drawing a 10 stick in each of his circles. By subtracting 150 (the total number he distributed) from 295 (the original amount), he finds that he has 145 blocks left in his pile.

The student then decides that he does not have enough to pull out 15 more tens. He is not sure how many there are but guesses that at least 5 more fifteens are in 145. He trades his tens for ones and puts five units into each group, as shown in the first photo that follows. He then records this action on his paper, as shown in the next photo. Now he counts by fives and finds out that he has distributed 75 cubes. He subtracts that from the total he had to find that he has 70 left. He decides that he does not have enough to take out another 5, but because it is close, he tries 4. Putting 4 into each group, he finds he distributed 60 and is left with 10, his remainder. He records his actions on his paper, as shown in the final photo.

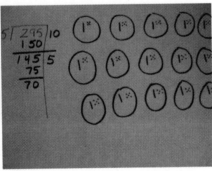
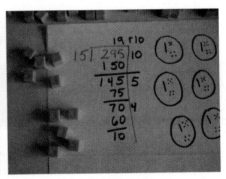

The strength of this model is that students are able to pull out as large of groups as they are developmentally able. More fragile students at first tend to pull out small groups, such as one or two, whereas stronger students are able to pull out groups in tens, multiples of tens, or hundreds. As students grow stronger in their number sense, they are able to think in larger groups, which is reflected in their written recordings. Look at the solution strategies by different students in figure 7.10. What can you say about the students who made each representation?

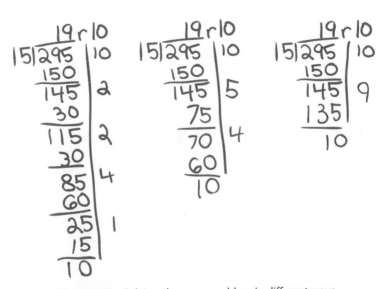

Figure 7.10. Solving the same problem in different ways.

Another strength of this algorithm is that it does not matter whether the dividend has a zero or not. It becomes a nonissue. If the entire quantity is considered, then having zeros may even make solving the quotient easier. Look at this problem:

$$
\begin{array}{r}
201 \\
6\,\overline{\smash{)}\,2106} \\
\underline{12} \\
0 \\
0 \\
6 \\
\underline{6}
\end{array}
\qquad
\begin{array}{r}
201 \\
6\,\overline{\smash{)}\,2106} \;\; 200 \\
\underline{1200} \\
6 \quad 1 \\
\underline{6}
\end{array}
$$

It is common for students, when solving the first way, to forget to bring down the zero and thus to get 21 as an answer.

Traditional Algorithms The *traditional algorithm* for division does not preserve place value. Students who have done well until now may begin to show problems. Many tutors are given referrals because a student is struggling with division. This is an indication that the student does not understand what division is all about, most likely has deeper issues going back as far as an understanding of base 10, and was able to mask this by memorizing traditional algorithms for computation preceding division. If the traditional method continues to be taught, then it should be modified so that students can make some sense of what is happening. Look at figure 7.11, which shows a traditional approach and a modified traditional approach that preserves place value.

In the first problem, the student has to use trial and error to find the exact answer that 15 "goes into" 29, 145 and 106. She also has to remember that they subtract and bring down the next number. Because it does not make sense, it is difficult to remember. If a more traditional algorithm is to be used, in which trial and error is the strategy used to find the exact answer, the student should still see the numbers as entire quantities. For example, 29 is really 2,900. So the student asks, "How many fifteens are in 2,900?" instead of "How many fifteens are in 29?" By subtracting what is left, she essentially "brings down" the rest of the digits.

As in multiplication, all sorts of algorithms show division. In fact, most algorithms used in other countries make students hold more information in

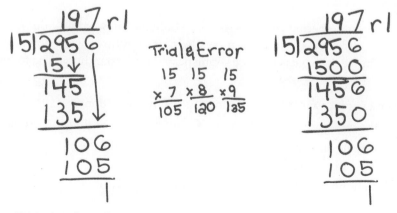

Figure 7.11. A traditional approach and a modified approach that preserves place value.

their head. Our traditional algorithm tends to require handholding, and teachers tend to demand that students show every step. This handicaps the students more than it helps them. The only one who benefits from this is the teacher, because he is able to see exactly where the student made the error. Look at the following algorithm and notation, and try to figure out how it is solved:

$$8 \overline{\smash{\big)}\, 1\ 2\ _4 4\ _4 0} \quad \overset{1\ 5\ 5}{}$$

The subscripted numbers are what students would normally have left after subtracting. For example, if a student thinks 12 ÷ 8, that is 1 with 4 left over. Encouraging students to avoid writing down all steps helps them become stronger with mental calculations. It is frustrating for students if they can hold lots of steps in their head but the teacher forces them to show every step.

What to Do with the Remainder One of the added complexities of division work is knowing how to deal with a remainder. When no context is attached to the problem, the remainder is simply stated. But what about within a context? Students need to carefully think through the problem to decide whether the remainder does one of the following:

- Causes the quotient to be rounded up
- Causes the quotient to be rounded down
- Should be disregarded
- Should be stated as extras
- Should be further divided, resulting in a fractional answer

For example, if the situation refers to how many buses need to be ordered for a certain number of children, it would not be acceptable for the extra children to stay behind. Likewise, if the question relates to many brownies children would receive from a batch, students would want to further divide up extras so that each student is given as much as possible—who wants to throw brownies away? But if you just want to know how many boxes can be filled with a certain amount of an object, then the remainder is not in question.

Comprehension Check

- Solve the following problem using pictures, numbers, and words (a written description to explain your work) showing connections between each. Also, write a story problem that would go with it.

    $82 \overline{\smash{\big)}\, 3495}$

Assessments

It is important to periodically assess your students' knowledge about multiplication and division. These assessments help drive future instruction and help students move from basic to more sophisticated understandings. The following are some things to assess:

- Do they understand the basic language of the operations?
- Can they interpret a problem to be a multiplication or division problem?
- Are they flexible in the way they solve problems (i.e., using multiplication to solve a division problem)?
- Can they build a model to solve a multiplication or division problem in context?

- Can they build a model to solve a multiplication or division problem written only as numbers?
- Can they use an algorithm to solve for multiplication or division?
- Do they understand the algorithm, and are they able to connect it with a model?

Go back to figure 6.9. Pick some of the problem types using numbers that are appropriate to the level of the students you are assessing. An example of the hierarchy of number for multiplication and division in order of difficulty, with a way to model it concretely, is found in figure 7.12. Problems grouped with a blue line have similar modeling strategies and therefore would be considered more difficult if using only pictorial representations, not abstract procedures. It can be interesting to give the problem with no context first to see what kind of connections students make. Then provide the same problem in context. This allows the interviewer to see how the students change their process when they have more contextual support. It is also interesting to note whether the students even notice that the two problems are the same. They usually do not. If they do, you can change the numbers slightly, creating a new problem. Here is an example of providing the same problem in and out of context:

A. 12×8
B. *We want to build a patio for a barbeque. If we build it 12 feet by 8 feet, how many 1-foot-square tiles will we need to buy?*

Other interview questions for multiplication and division might include looking at dot patterns to find out whether students see groups and use those groupings to solve problems. For an example of such questions, please visit the website.

Using Inquiry to Teach Multidigit Multiplication and Division

The pedagogy section of this chapter gave specific examples of how to structure inquiry lessons using number sense, addition, and subtraction, as well as multiplication and division with single-digit numbers. Now that we have discussed different aspects of multiplying and dividing with multidigit numbers, figure 7.13 shows a couple examples of inquiry lessons incorporating these ideas. They are followed by a partial unit plan of multidigit multiplication and division.

Figure 7.14 is a slice of a sample unit centered on building understanding of multiplication of two-digit by single-digit numbers, typically found in grade 4.

Numerical Complexity	Example	Way to Model
1 digit × 1 digit Both factors are 5 or less	2 × 3 = 6	• Grouping (two groups of three) • Array (two rows by three columns)
1 digit × 1 digit One factor is 5 or less One factor is greater than 5	8 × 4 = 32	• Grouping (eight groups of four) • Array or area (eight rows by four columns) broken into four and four rows or five and three rows
1 digit × 1 digit Both factors greater than 5	8 × 9 = 72	• Grouping (eight groups of nine); grouping is becoming more inefficient • Array or area (eight rows by nine columns) broken into four and four rows or four and five columns
10 × 1 digit	10 × 3 = 30	• Area using three 10 rods
Multiple of 10 × 1 digit	40 × 2 = 80	• Area using two rows of four 10 rods each
Multiple of 10 × 1 digit (resulting in three-digit answer)	40 × 6 = 240	• Area using six rows of four 10 rods each
2 digits × 1 digit, no composing	13 × 2 = 26	• Area using two rows (or columns) of 1 ten and 3 ones
2 digits × 1 digit, composing	14 × 3 = 42	• Areas using three rows (or columns) of 1 ten and 4 ones
Multiple of 10 × multiple of 10 = 3 digits	40 × 20 = 800	• Area of 20 rows of four 10 sticks. These trade for eight 100 flats.
Multiple of 10 × multiple of 10 = 4 digits	40 × 60 = 2,400	• Area of 40 rows of six 10 sticks. These trade for twenty-four 100 flats. By now, this model may be too inefficient, because there aren't enough materials, so students move to using an open array model. They may subdivide the tens, depending on their ability to compute with tens.
2 digits × 2 digits, no regrouping	13 × 12 = 156	• Area of 12 rows of 1 ten and 3 ones. The 10 rows of 10 can be traded for a 100 flat, the 10 rows of 3 ones can be traded for three 10 rods, and so on. • Pictorial model begins on graph paper to show one-to-one correspondence.
2 digits × 2 digits, regrouping	23 × 14 = 322	• Area of 14 rows of 2 tens and 3 ones. The 10 rows of 20 can be traded for two 100 flats, the 10 rows of 3 ones can be traded for three 10 rods, and so on. • Pictorial model begins to represent an open array as the numbers become too big for the graph paper.

Figure 7.12. A hierarchy of numerical complexity in multiplication.

Moving from Groups to Area Model in Multiplication

Launch cycle 1	*Whole Group:* The teacher asks students to create two different representations to show 10 × 6 using tools or pictures. The teacher provides graph paper so that they can record their representations.
Explore cycle 1	*Small Groups:* Students work within their small groups to think of a way to model the preceding problem in more than one way.
Summarize cycle 1	*Whole Group:* The teacher chooses a couple of key representations, including an array model. The teacher orchestrates conversation to center on the connections among the different models, focusing on finding where the 6 and 10 are in the model.
Launch cycle 2	*Whole Group:* The teacher asks students to create a representation to show 13 × 6.
Explore cycle 2	*Small Groups:* Students work within their small groups to think of a way to model the preceding problem.
Summarize cycle 2	*Whole Group:* Conversations center on different representations, including which one shows the amounts 13 and 6 and which model (grouping or area) makes it easiest to know the total. The teacher connects this model to the algorithm (10 × 6) + (3 × 6) using the distributive property.

Interpreting the Remainder in Division

Launch	*Whole Group:* The teacher presents a problem: "I am going to order new tables for the classroom. We have 24 students, and each table can seat 4 students. How many tables will I need to order?" The class discusses the problem.
Explore	*Small Groups:* The teacher says, "We are planning a party. We think that 50 people will come. Everyone needs a seat at a table. Each table seats 6. How many tables do we need?"
Summarize	*Whole Group:* Conversation centers on how many tables will be needed at the party. The teacher asks, "What are we going to do about the 2 remainder? What does that 2 represent?"

Figure 7.13. Example lessons for multiplication and division of multidigit numbers.

TEACHING FOCUS: Multidigit Multiplication

Purpose	Routines	Cycle 1	Cycle 2	Final Summarize
Monday • Explore breaking apart as a strategy (using color tiles)	6×10 6×100 60×100 600×100	I am using 1-foot-square tiles to make a small mural. I want the mural to be 6 feet wide and 8 feet long. How many square tiles will I need to buy?	We want to build a patio for a barbeque. If we build it 14 feet by 5 feet, how many 1-foot-square tiles will we need to buy?	Share an area model a student built, breaking the tens from the ones, and the way the student recorded the model numerically. Make sure to connect numerical recording with the model and to the distributive property, like $(10 \times 5) + (4 \times 5)$.
Tuesday • Continue to explore breaking apart using base 10 blocks but with recording a picture	4×2 4×20 40×20 400×20 400×200	Ask students to create two different representations to show 10×6 using tools. Provide graph paper so that students can record their representations.	Ask students to create a representation to show 12×6.	Conversations center on different representations and which one will be the most efficient way to model large numbers (array vs. groups). Discuss difficulties with using base 10 blocks to model 12×6.
Wednesday • Continue modeling two-digit by single-digit problems, but add a numerical representation	In | Out 2 | 5 4 | 9 7 | 15 What's the rule?	14×5. Practice modeling and record as a picture. As a group, record numerically.	22×4. Practice modeling and record as a picture. Also record the problem numerically.	Conversations center on the model and recording. Does the picture look like the model? How do the numbers match the model?
Thursday • Generate a method for multiplying two digits by one digits	In | Out 2 | 6 4 | 10 5 | 12 What's the rule?	25×6. Practice modeling and recording pictorially and numerically.	32×8. Model and record. Try to come up with an algorithm to solve any problem like these.	Discuss models or representations. Discuss the methods students generated for multiplying a two-digit by a single-digit number.
Friday • Try to solve a two-digit by one-digit problem using pictures and numbers (first without regrouping and then with regrouping)	Make a connection between in and out and x and y, and plot it on a coordinate grid.	42×3. Solve using pictures, numbers, and words, but only with a model if support is needed.	45×8. Solve using pictures, numbers, and words, but only with a model if support is needed.	Discuss pictures, numbers, and written explanations. Make explicit connections to the partial products algorithm, because many students should be recording in this way.

Figure 7.14. A sample week of a unit about developing concepts in multidigit multiplication.

CONCLUSION

In this chapter, we extended the topic from chapter 6 regarding instructional models—more specifically, inquiry-based instruction. Using the model of backward planning when designing your lesson is a powerful way to ensure that you are creating the experiences the students need to be able to demonstrate by the end of the unit. This chapter provided specific examples of how to use backward planning when designing both a lesson and a unit with not only multiplication and division but also content discussed in chapters 2–6.

An important consideration when planning a multiplication lesson is that as the numbers increase, students need to move beyond using groups as their exclusive models. Changes in context help support the transition from groups to arrays or an area model, which supports the notion of the distributive property. This understanding is valuable in the upper grades and in Algebra.

Understanding that an array can be broken into smaller parts helps children mentally solve problems and understand what is happening in the multiplication and division algorithms. Essentially, the division algorithm can be thought of as finding one of the missing factors. This can be done by either multiplying up or using a form of repeated subtraction. It is common, when modeling the operation, for students to use a dealing, or partitioning, strategy by using the divisor as the known number of groups. The stronger the child is with thinking about groups, the more groups she can remove from her total number, thus becoming more efficient in using the algorithm.

▶ Interview Video with an Eye on Content

Watch a series of videos in which problems are presented to children and they solve them. In each video, determine the type of problem presented, the problem category, and the strategy used to solve it. Record your work in the tables provided. An example is provided.

Problem No.	Problem Type	Problem Category	Problem-Solving Strategy
1	Multiplicative comparison	Measurement division	Skip counting up

▶ Interview a Child

1. Create a word problem for each of the 16 problem types found in figure 6.9, but now relate them to multidigit multiplication and division. Include three different number levels: two digit by one digit with no regrouping, two digit by one digit with regrouping, and two digit by two digit, or consider the numerical complexity in the chart in figure 7.12 to choose other number levels if more appropriate.

2. Using the problems from step 1, interview a child in the fourth or fifth grade.

3. Write a report about it that contains two parts: individual problem analyses and overall summary.

4. In the individual problem analyses section, each problem you pose should include the following:
   a. The problem type
   b. The problem (underline the numbers used)
   c. A complete description of the child's response
   d. An analysis of the child's response, which includes the following the general and specific strategy he used.

Sample analysis of an interview problem:

Problem 1: Grouping/partitioning (multiplication)

Problem: Adrian made (21, 34, 26) gift bags of toys. He put (4, 7, 18) toys in each bag. How many toys are in all the bags?

Response: The student drew four circles and then placed 2 lines (to represent tens) and one dot (to represent ones) into each circle. He counted all by first counting all the tens, then counting the ones. After counting all of them, he responded, "84."

Analysis: Student employed a direct modeling strategy, using a grouping model. He used pictures that represented tens and ones to create his model.

5. In the overall summary, briefly describe what you learned about the child's mathematical thinking, including the following points:
   a. The types of problems the child successfully solved and those he struggled with
   b. The range of numbers with which the child was familiar (number size)
   c. The types of strategies demonstrated
   d. What recommendations do you have for the teacher, or what would you do with this child if you were to continue to work with him?

▶ Classroom Video with an Eye on Pedagogy

Watch some classroom lessons. Pay particular attention to the lesson structure of each episode. Can you identify the launch, explore, and summarize portions of each video? How are students to demonstrate at the end of the lesson that they have achieved the objective of the day's lesson? How does the lesson structure support this assessment?

Video

Topic:
Cycle 1

Launch

Explore

Summarize

Cycle 2

Launch

Explore

Summarize

▶ Classroom Application

1. Observe a classroom in which students are engaging in a lesson about multidigit multiplication or division. Is there a clear focus for the lesson? What evidence is there that the students have achieved the objective? What do the students understand about multiplication and division as a result of this lesson?

2. Collaboratively design an inquiry lesson using backward planning. Consider how you plan to assess your students and design your lesson to support that assessment. After you teach your lesson, evaluate what your students understood based on their assessment.

▶ Resources

Young Mathematicians at Work: Constructing Multiplication and Division, Catherine Twomey Fosnot and Maarten Dolk (2001)

Lessons for Extending Multiplication: Grades 4–5, Maryann Wickett and Marilyn Burns (2001)

Lessons for Extending Division: Grades 4–5, Maryann Wickett and Marilyn Burns (2003)

▶ Lit Link

Literature Books to Support Multiplication and Division

Title	Author
2 × 2 = Boo!	Loreen Leedy
Amanda Bean's Amazing Dream	Cindy Neuschwander
Anno's Mysterious Multiplying Jar	Anno Mitsumasa
Arithme-Tickle: An Even Number of Odd Riddle-Rhymes	Patrick Lewis
Bananas	Jacqueline Farmer
Counting on Frank	Rod Clement
Doorbell Rang, The	Pat Hutchins
Each Orange Had 8 Slices	Paul Giganti Jr.
Equal Shmequal	Virginia L. Kroll
Great Divide: A Mathematical Marathon, The	Dayle Ann Dodds
Hershey's Milk Chocolate Multiplication Book, The	Jerry Pallotta

Title	Author
Hottest, Coldest, Highest, Deepest	Steve Jenkins
In the Next Three Seconds . . . Predictions for the Millennium	Rowland Morgan (comp.)
King's Chessboard, The	David Birch
Math Curse	Jon Sciezka and Lane Smith
Multiplying Menace: The Revenge of Rumpelstiltskin	Pam Calvert and Wayne
One Hundred Angry Ants	Elinor J. Pinczes
P. Bear's New Year's Party	Paul Owen Lewis
Rabbits Rabbits Everywhere: A Fibonacci Tale	Ann McCallum and Gideon Kendall
Remainder of One, A	Elinor J. Pinczes
Sea Squares	Joy Hulme
Three Messy Dragons	Fay Robinson and Kathryn Corbett
Time Is Better, The	Richard Michelson
Two Ways to Count to Ten: A Liberian Folktale	Ruby Dee
You Can, Toucan, Math	David A. Adler

▶ Tech Tools

Websites

National Library of Virtual Manipulatives, http://www.nlvm.usu.edu

Math Fact Cafe: The Fact Sheet Factory, http://www.mathfactcafe.com/

NewFreeDownloads.com: Multiplication, http://www.newfreedownloads.com/find/multiplication.html (free downloadable math games)

Choose a Planet, http://www.primaryresources.co.uk/online/moonmaths.swf

Multiplication.com, http://www.multiplication.com

Software

Math Blaster, Knowledge Adventure

Fluency through Meaningful Practice: Mathematical Routines and Algebraic Thinking

PEDAGOGICAL CONTENT UNDERSTANDINGS

Pedagogy *Developing Fluency with Mathematical Routines*

- Procedural Fluency
- Algorithms
- Mental Math Activities
- What Are Routines?
- Types of Routines
- Designing a Routine Series
- Planning Routines for the Year
- Assessing Routines

Content *Algebraic Thinking and Reasoning*

- What Is Algebra?
- Algebraic Reasoning
- Making Conjectures and Generalizations
- Justification and Proof
- Integrating Arithmetic and Algebra

· ·

It is an understanding of the relationships that leads to facility with mental computation.

Ruth Parker, Mathematics Education Collaborative, 2002

CONVERSATION IN MATHEMATICS

The following problem was presented to a group of students:

$35 - x = 36 - 20$

After quietly thinking about how to solve the problem, several students shared their strategies, first with their partners, then with the whole class:

Student 1:
Because $36 - 20 = 16$, both sides must equal 16. I knew that $x + 16$ would make 35, so I wanted to take 16 from 35 to find the missing amount:
$35 - 15 = 20$,
take away 1 more is 19.

Student 2:
Since we know that both sides will be 16, I added up from 16 to get to 35:
$16 + 4 = 20$
$20 + 10 = 30$
$30 + 5 = 35$
$4 + 10 + 5 = 19$

Student 3:
$15 + 15 = 30$
$30 + 5 = 35$
And $15 + 5 = 20$, but I added 1 too much, so $20 - 1 = 19$.

Student 4:
$35 - 10 = 25$
$25 - 5 = 20$
$20 - 1 = 19$
(I split the 6 into 5 and 1.)

Student 5:
I subtracted down to get to 16:
$35 - 10 = 25$
$25 - 5 = 20$
$20 - 4 = 16$
$10 + 5 + 4 = 19$

Student 6:
$35 - 16 = x$
I added 4 to each number so that it would be easier to subtract:
$39 - 20 = 19$

Student 7:
$35 - 16$
I can just cancel out 1 ten from each side, and that leaves me with 2 tens. Then I get a -1, so that is 19.

Student 8:

$$\begin{array}{r} 35 \\ -\ 16 \\ \hline 20 \\ -\ 1 \\ \hline 19 \end{array}$$

Student 9:
I know that both sides must be the same. I see that the 36 on the right is 1 more than the 36 on the left, so the 20 on the right must be 1 more than the x on the left. So the difference between the two expressions is the same.

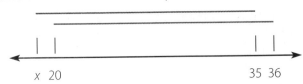

The students in the preceding classroom conversation demonstrate an understanding about numbers far beyond computational ability. They understand equality and the relationship that the numbers have in making the equation true. As a regular activity in the classroom, rather than merely computing, students were expected to look at numbers to determine how they were related to one another. They were encouraged to make conjectures and gener-alizations about how they thought numbers worked.

This activity, referred by Kathy Richardson as a *Number Talk,* is an ongoing, purposeful mathematical routine, which provides meaningful computational practice and helps children develop mental math skills. Number talks are one of a variety of routines that promote flexibility with numbers and other mathe-matical concepts, such as algebraic thinking and reasoning.

In the math education community, some have made a distinction between lit-tle "a" algebra and big "A" Algebra (source unknown). Thus, *algebra* is what the previously discussed students were experiencing in their class. It involves a habit of mind of generalizing, making conjectures, studying relationships, and using functions to model real-world phenomena. And *Algebra* is the formal course offered in middle and high schools. This distinction is made to clarify that teach-ing algebraic concepts in primary grades does not involve solving algebraic equations, for example, as much as it involves providing learning opportunities that build the underlying concepts of equality and number relations.

Algebra is considered the "gatekeeper" to higher mathematics. In addition, according to the National Center for Educational Statistics, students who take Algebra in eighth grade are more likely to apply to college than those who do not. In fact, many districts and states now require that all eighth-grade students take Algebra regardless of their level of preparation. Throwing students who are not ready into Algebra has resulted in failure on a grand scale. When Alge-bra teachers are asked about the factors contributing to students' inability to pass the course, they often respond that students are entering the course with-out adequate understanding of equality and other foundational understand-ings of algebra. A study by Eric Knuth et al. (2006) found a high correlation between the relational understanding of the equal sign and the equation-solv-ing abilities of middle-grade students. They found that even students with no experience with formal Algebra were able to solve equations when they pos-sessed a strong understanding of the equal sign. Students with inadequate understandings of the equal sign appear to not have had any explicit instruc-tion related to this in either elementary or early middle school.

The notion of equality is not the only concept that supports algebraic think-ing and reasoning. This chapter discusses what foundational algebraic concepts are appropriate for exploration in elementary school and how the teacher weaves these ideas into her instruction throughout the year to teach her stu-dents to think relationally about numbers, look for patterns, and generate con-jectures. It also describes exactly what constitutes a routine and outlines some of the most powerful ones that promote numerical fluency.

Developing Fluency with Mathematical Routines   PEDAGOGY

Learning Theory

Ruth Parker, founder of the Mathematics Education Collaborative (MEC) (2002, 127), defines mathematically powerful students as those who do the following:

- Understand the power of mathematics as a tool for making sense of situations, information, and events in their world

- Are persistent in their search for solutions to complex, "messy," or "ill defined" tasks
- Enjoy doing mathematics and find the pursuit of solutions to complex problems both challenging and engaging
- Understand mathematics, not just arithmetic
- Make connections within and among mathematical ideas and domains
- Have a disposition to search for patterns and relationships
- Frequently make conjectures and investigate their validity and their implications
- Have "number sense" and are able to make sense of numerical information
- Use algorithmic thinking and are able to estimate and compute mentally
- Are able to work both independently and collaboratively as problem posers and problem solvers
- Are able to communicate and justify their thinking and ideas both orally and in writing
- Use tools available to them to solve problems and to examine mathematical ideas

A mathematically powerful student possesses both conceptual understanding and procedural fluency, along with a positive disposition toward mathematics. Refer back to chapter 1's illustration of the process standards as being the roots of the tree of mathematical proficiency, and notice that conceptual understanding and procedural fluency are the two main branches of this tree.

Procedural Fluency

We have previously defined *procedural fluency* as knowing rules, facts, or algorithms and knowing when and how to use them with accuracy, flexibility, and efficiency. No one will argue that fluency, or automaticity, with single-digit or multidigit calculations requires practice. The question is, what kind of practice is most valuable? Throughout this book, we reiterate that practice should follow exploration activities that support understanding. When practice, such as drill, is void of understanding, students are not building the conceptual knowledge necessary to make connections between concepts and procedures. This may result in students generating "flawed procedures that result in systematic patterns of errors" (Kilpatrick 2001, 196). Developing proficiency requires more than drill and rote memorization. It is about having myriad computational strategies and being able to select specific strategies depending on the numbers of a particular problem. It is about the ability to reason and to take into consideration quantities, not just digits.

Algorithms

The focus in the classroom should always be on making sense of mathematics, which decreases the chance of students making silly errors. Students can also learn to make sense when learning to use algorithms. If algorithms are "procedures that can be executed in the same way to solve a variety of problems arising from different situations and involving different numbers" (Kilpatrick et al. 2001, 195), then students benefit from spending time figuring out why the algorithms work and which algorithms are most efficient when solving certain problems.

Children can invent their own algorithms for multidigit computational problems, but generally they need good instruction to help them make their procedures efficient. Some students have developed complex ways of thinking about numbers but can become lost in their explanations or recordings. Engaging in conversations with their peers and teachers can help students think about how they can record their work in less convoluted ways. Students also benefit from this dialogue by trying to make sense of someone else's strategy, which enhances the connections between procedures.

Mental Math Activities

Mental math activities give students a chance to develop mental computation procedures, which are often different from procedures they do with manipulatives or pencil and paper. Because it can be cumbersome to hold certain types of numbers in their head, children often look for ways to solve problems that require minimal work. Figuring out what works helps deepen the understanding of operations. As students focus on quantities and relationships, they are more likely to transfer this understanding and way of solving problems to paper and pencil computations. Mental computation activities must be done regularly throughout all grades. If students are not encouraged to develop mental procedures for the computations that they are experiencing in class, they "will be inclined to view the new algorithms as the preferred, possibly the only, methods for computing and will discontinue use of mental procedures even when they are easier" (Kilpatrick et al. 2001, 215). When children realize that they can make sense of and solve math problems using strategies that they understand, they gain confidence and a positive disposition toward math is generated (Kilpatrick 2001; Chambers 2002).

Application to the Learning and Teaching of Mathematics

What Are Routines?

Routines are whole-class, purposefully structured activities that help children develop procedural fluency, as well as reasoning and problem-solving skills, through meaningful practice. Students may be engaged in mental math activities, have access to manipulatives, or be using pencil and paper to solve problems and explore relationships. Students preview new concepts, review concepts that have been previously explored, and practice concepts that have not solidified. The term *routines* does not imply that the activities are mundane and just done because they are part of the schedule; rather, they occur daily and are integrated into the culture of the classroom.

Routines are only 10- to 20-minute activities, depending on the age of the children. They are not intended to be entire math lessons and do not usually tie into the math lesson of the day. Where math lessons tend to be more exploratory, routines tend to be more practical. Instead of isolated events, such as many commercially designed programs, purposeful routines are most successful if they are done in a series, which allows the students to focus on certain mathematical ideas. Initially, the routine may take a little longer, because the goal is to establish the classroom norms in its process and discourse. Once these norms are in place, the focus shifts from the process to the content.

Special Needs

Routines ensure accessibility for all students. Not all students are developmentally ready to take on strategies when they are initially discussed in class, but over time, as they build and strengthen connections, they come to understand how and when to use certain strategies. Most students will not understand all strategies used by their peers, nor will they want to use them as their own, but the persistent discourse allows more students to understand a larger variety of strategies. It is a beautiful thing to watch students choosing to use one of their peer's strategies because they realize it is more efficient than their own or just because they want to try it out.

Types of Routines

Routines in elementary school support the following: development of early number concepts and the base 10 system, algebraic thinking, computational fluency of whole and rational numbers, and data and graphing. Figure 8.1 outlines the types of routines that help support the preceding concepts.

Additional concepts that take more time to learn than is given in the regular curriculum, such as time, money, interpretation of graphs, geometry, and measurement, may also be practiced through routines.

The activities that support early number concepts were discussed in detail in earlier chapters; a brief description of each is provided here.

Early Number Concepts and the Base 10 System

Activities listed in figure 8.1 to help develop and support early number concepts and place value were described in detail in chapters 2 and 4. Before beginning formalized 10 frame routines with the goal of students developing

Develop and support early number concepts and the base 10 system (see chapters 2 and 4)	Dot cards	10 frames	Hiding activities	100 chart	Number riddles	Number of the day
Algebraic thinking	In and out boxes		Concepts of equality		Thinking relationally	
Computational fluency with whole and rational numbers (see chapters 3, 5, and 9–12)	Number talks		Number strings		Number lines	
Data and graphing (see chapter 15)	Coordinate grid activities		Interpretation of graphs		Quick surveys	

Figure 8.1. Routines that support mathematical concepts (on the left). (Partially compiled from Kathy Richardson's early number activities and routines suggested by the San Diego Unified School District.)

3 × 4	6 + 6	Dozen
	:::: ::::	3 + 3 + 3 + 3
36 ÷ 3	Two sixes	Half of 24
10 + 8 + 5 − 3 − 8	Twelve	20 − 8

Figure 8.2. Multiple ways to represent the number 12.

the strategy of making a 10, kindergarten and first-grade teachers use 10 frames as a way to count the days in school. This ongoing daily activity allows children to make connections between tens and ones as they are developmentally ready. As you can see in the photo here, the teacher would also use connecting cubes and numeral cards to record the number of days to help support the idea of tens and ones. This would be in lieu of the common daily activity of counting straws. The act of constructing the tens with blocks when trading seems to be more supportive to many children than bundling 10 straws with a rubber band.

The Number of the Day is another activity that can support not only early number concepts but also number sense in any grade. In this activity, students write as many different ways as they can to represent a number that the teacher has chosen and written on the board. This helps build the connections between representations and supports the idea of the decomposition of number. See figure 8.2 for a variety of ways to represent 12.

Algebraic Thinking

In-and-out boxes, concept of equality, and relational thinking activities are excellent routines and are discussed in detail in the content section of this chapter. Essentially, an *in-and-out box* is a function table that is presented to younger children. In this table, numbers are in the "in" (or *x*) column and the "out" (or *y*) column. Students have to figure out the rule, or what was done to the number in the *in* column to generate the number in the *out* column. These can become quite complicated, and in about third grade, the terms *in* and *out* can be replaced with the variables *x* and *y*. An example is shown in figure 8.3.

Algebraic thinking activities can begin in kindergarten with understanding related to the equal sign. Most curriculum programs only show equations written one way (i.e., 4 + 3 = 7); therefore, students think that writing 7 = 4 + 3 is "backward." It is essential that we send the appropriate message about the meaning behind the equal sign and that we use appropriate language as well, such as "the same as." If we are to ensure that students are comfortable with the ideas related to algebraic thinking, then we need to begin early and be consistent until they reach middle school.

As students grow older, the functions and equations can become more difficult through the use of fractions and integers. However, if your older students

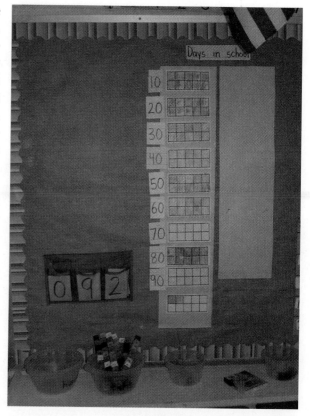

Using 10 frames to count the number of days in school.

IN	OUT
3	5
6	8
4	6
8	10

Rule:

Add 2

Figure 8.3. A function table presented as an in-and-out box.

have no experience with these concepts, you have to begin with simple equations to lay a foundation.

Computational Fluency

Routines to support computational fluency of whole and fractional numbers are typically found in the third- through sixth-grade classroom. These routines occur once ideas have been explored during the regular math lesson and the students have made appropriate connections to a variety of representations.

Number Talks A *Number Talk* is a mental math activity in which students solve computational problems void of context, often referred to as *naked number problems*. It is when everyone takes time to analyze how numbers work. As students share strategies, they might show a pictorial representation or use a concrete model to prove their thinking. Although they are mentally solving problems, sometimes students may make notes with pencil and paper to keep track of their thinking so that they do not lose some numbers in complicated problems, such as long division.

1. Initially, all problems are written horizontally. This is to encourage thinking about the problem as a whole and to discourage solving through traditional algorithms. At first, older children may try to rewrite the problem vertically in the air and solve it traditionally. Once other strategies are discussed, students often no longer need to solve it in this way. This usually takes about a week.

2. Give the class some private think time to come up with a solution. Encourage the students to think of more than one way to solve the problem while you are waiting for all students to have a solution. Students should show that they are ready with a "quiet thumb," a thumbs-up sign next to their chest. This way, other students are not distracted by lots of raised hands. Many children stop thinking when they believe others already have an answer. Those who have multiple strategies can indicate this by putting up as many fingers as strategies.

3. Once everyone has an answer, allow students to have a chance for partner talk and then ask for the answers that students came up with. Make a list of the different answers on the board. At this point, you are not focusing on the strategies but are compiling a list of possible solutions. This way, you can tell the range of answers and you probably can tell, by knowing typical errors, how your students solved the problem. This takes pressure off all your students. This is where discernment is necessary. What is the goal for the routine? Do I want to focus on a common error so that students can figure out why it doesn't work? You are not going to want to go straight to the correct answer, because more learning occurs when errors are exposed. Look at the choices, pick an error, and ask, "Would anyone would like to defend this answer?" Remember, no one is certain yet which is the right answer. When the student shares his strategy, simply say, "What does everyone think about that?" When these are your questions, students are more comfortable, because they learn that they are not under attack and your questions do not automatically mean that they are wrong. If no one wants to defend an answer, maybe because of uncertainty, simply move on to a different answer or ask whether anyone would like to try to figure out how someone found that answer.

40 − 27

Public Recording	Student Explanation	Pictorial Representation
40 − 1 = 39 27 − 1 = 26 39 − 26 = 13	"I subtracted 1 from the 40 to make 39. I did that so I wouldn't have to borrow. Then I subtracted 1 from the 27. I did that so I would keep the difference the same. I then subtracted the 26 from 39 and got 13."	

Figure 8.4. Representing student thinking in different ways.

4. Recording the student strategy is critical during the number talk, whether it is by the teacher or by the student. At first, the teacher needs to model how to record student thinking (figure 8.4), but eventually, students need to learn how to make their own thoughts clear for others to follow.

It is important to consider numerical complexity when deciding on a number talk. It is equally important to choose problems that lend themselves to strategies that you might want to expose. The preceding problem was ideal to elicit the strategy of changing the number to a number for which regrouping would not be required. However, this same problem might elicit many other solution paths. If you would like to expose such a strategy, it is important to listen to the partner talk to see who is using it. Remember that students may not be ready to try a strategy that a teacher might think is obvious. If the students appear ready but no one has made a suggestion, then occasionally it is appropriate to suggest a strategy that a "student from your class last year" used to solve it. Have the class figure out whether it works or not and why.

Number talks are appropriate for addition, subtraction, multiplication, and division. Start with small numbers, even with older children, so that it is easy to prove why things work. When students have a solid understanding of the meaning of operations, even though they have not yet explored multidigit operations they can figure out a way to solve them. For example, a student who understands that $180 \div 9$ means how many nines in 180 can just as easily figure out $180 \div 12$ because it means how many twelves are in 180. When they think about it in this way, children do not realize that this problem is supposed to be any harder than the first.

It is helpful to write the student's strategies on charts and name them. Some strategies are labeled with the name of the student, and others have mathematical names. Sometimes teachers choose to not give a formal name at first to let students have ownership of their strategies. Once many students take on the strategy, teachers may either ask for a name based on what they are doing with the numbers or give it a more formal name. In the previous example of 40 − 27, some students dubbed the strategy used in the pictorial representation as the "move-over" method. This is because they are moving each number over one spot on the number line. This strategy's formal name is *constant difference*. It is a huge mathematical idea in subtraction, but the move-over method was what the students owned and, therefore, was what they were allowed to call it.

Some common strategies to think about when choosing problems for number talks are breaking apart numbers, making a 10, making a 100, thinking of

Language Tip

By initially recording student responses, it helps them become aware of how well, or not so well, they are articulating their thinking. Make sure that you record exactly what the student says and not extra information about what you think he means. This forces the student to be more explicit. If he cannot explain what he is thinking more clearly, usually a peer is able to jump in and explain what his friend is trying to say. For students with limited English skills, have them write numerically how they solved the problem and then model the language to represent their thinking.

quarters, using friendly numbers (numbers such as 10, 25, and 100 that are easy to calculate), adding up, and halving and doubling.

Number Strings A *number string* is a series of related problems, and students develop a sense of pattern and relationships among the different problems. As students explore these patterns, they make conjectures about how numbers work and are able to solve more complicated problems by applying these conjectures.

Number strings typically involve multiplication and division problems and often focus on patterns such as powers of 10 and halving and doubling. Examples of some number strings are in figure 8.5.

When presenting the problems in the number string, just present one problem at a time, giving the students time to solve it. Display the next problem underneath the previous one. After a few problems have been given, have stu-

String	Generalization
$4 \times 2 =$ $4 \times 4 =$ $4 \times 8 =$ $4 \times 16 =$ $4 \times 32 =$ $4 \times 64 =$	As one factor doubles, the product doubles as well.
$2 \times 24 =$ $4 \times 12 =$ $8 \times 6 =$ $16 \times 3 =$	As one factor is halved and the other is doubled, the product remains the same.
$2 \times 6 =$ $6 \times 6 =$ $8 \times 6 =$	The distributive property. One multiplication problem can be split into two smaller problems and the products can be added.
$4 \times 10 =$ $4 \times 100 =$ $4 \times 1000 =$ $40 \times 10 =$ $400 \times 100 =$	The total number of zeros in both factors is the same as the total number of zeros in the product.
$24 \div 24 =$ $24 \div 12 =$ $24 \div 6 =$ $24 \div 3 =$ $24 \div 2 =$ $24 \div 1 =$ $24 \div \frac{1}{2} =$ $24 \div \frac{1}{4} =$	As the divisor is halved, the quotient is also halved.
$3 \times 7 =$ $0.3 \times 70 =$ $0.03 \times 700 =$ $0.003 \times 7000 =$	As one factor is decreased by a power of 10 and the other is increased by a power of 10, the product remains the same.
$21 \div 7 =$ $2.1 \div .7 =$ $0.21 \div .07 =$ $0.021 \div .007 =$	If both the divisor and the dividend are increased or decreased by a power of 10, the quotient remains the same. Note: This is an important generalization to make in understanding why clearing the decimal works in division of decimal numbers.

Figure 8.5. Example number strings and their corresponding generalizations.

dents discuss what pattern they are noticing. This is important, because they are receiving problems that are more difficult and they have to try to apply their pattern to achieve an answer. A good question to ask is whether they think their rule will always work. This can be the foundation for future number strings that investigate the same pattern or principle.

It is important to remember that we are not telling the students the rule or the generalizations that they are suppose to be making regarding a string of numbers; rather, they are suppose to be generating them by studying the patterns.

Number Lines Number lines are a fairly abstract representation of quantity, and students experience lots of difficulty when asked to work on a number line, especially with fractions. Work with number lines has many variations. You may want to be working with a traditional number line with all the numbers labeled. Or you may want to work on an open number line with no marks or, perhaps, one with just the tic marks but no numbers. It all depends on your goals and the level of your students. Open number lines tend to help children focus on the relationships between numbers and understand their relative magnitude.

One activity would be to draw an open, or blank, number line on the board and label the ends with numbers such as 0 and 1, 0 and 2, or 50 and 100. It depends on the level of numbers on which the work is focused. Give several students a sticky note with a number written on it, and let them place their number on the line where they feel it should go (figure 8.6). When all the numbers have been placed, have everyone sit back, examine the placements, and discuss whether they agree or not.

If the number line is completely open, with no marking for a beginning or an end, then have one student at a time come up to the board and give her a number to place where she thinks it should go (figure 8.7). Ask a second student to come up and, in relation to where the first number was placed, place a second number. In this scenario, students do not know all the numbers up front. After a few turns, someone needs to move numbers over, either to make room for new numbers or to redistribute the spacing for the number line to make sense. All students must explain why they put the number where they did. This activity is good for reasoning skills.

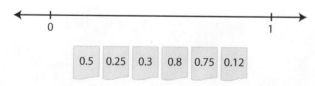

Figure 8.6. An open number line from 0 to 1 and some decimal numbers to be placed on it by students.

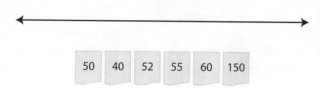

Figure 8.7. An open number line for which the two end points are unknown.

Figure 8.8. An open number line from 0 to 2, with an arrow pointing to a location for which the number needs to be determined.

Another alternative is to create a number line with one or two numbers labeled (figure 8.8). Pointing to a spot on the line can lead students to think about what number would be reasonable at that point.

Data and Graphing

It is important that the class spends an ample amount of time collecting and interpreting data. It is not enough to spend one unit per year addressing this area. Data and graphing are easily integrated into many other content areas. Many teachers consciously collect data every week from what they are working on in science, social studies, and literature to analyze and graph.

Quick Surveys A way to gather data for myriad activities, from data analysis, to graphing, to interpretation, is to do quick surveys. The surveying does not have to be part of your math routines, but the analysis can be. Once a week, have a question written on the board and have students use either a magnetic picture of themselves or a sticky note to answer the question (figure 8.9). This creates a quick graph while students are settling down in the morning or a way to end a day as they leave. The data can be saved for a variety of work throughout the year.

Interpretation of Graphs Interestingly, students spend many years collecting data and creating graphs but little time interpreting graphs. Periodically, students need to look at a graph and make some inferences from the data on that graph. First, they should talk about the facts that they know on the graph to make sure that they understand how to read it. Then questions should be posed, such as "So what does this data tell us about . . . ?" or "Why do you think ____ turned out this way?" Children need to learn early on that graphs

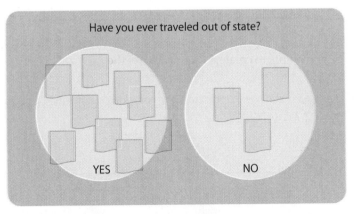

Figure 8.9. A sample survey board upon which students can use a sticky note to quickly record their response.

tell us more than their titles say, and they need to learn how to read between the lines.

Coordinate Grids Routines related to making connections between function tables (in-and-out boxes) and the coordinate grid is a must in fourth and fifth grades. In many states, standardized testing in these grades focuses heavily on this area, yet little emphasis may be placed in the curriculum. This is an abstract concept for children, and lots of time is needed for them to digest what is happening with plotting points and to create equations that correspond to those points. These ideas are discussed in more detail in the content section in this chapter. For purposes of this section, we discuss the stages of connecting the function tables with the graphs to develop effective routines.

We identified 10 stages in making this connection. Each stage takes several days to explore. For fourth grade and above, all 10 stages can be done little by little throughout the entire year, beginning in September. Students younger than fourth grade only explore the first several stages, depending on their age. The terms x and y can usually be introduced at the end of third grade or by the beginning of fourth.

1. Present an in-and-out box all filled in, and ask students to find patterns and what is happening with the numbers, or a "rule" (figure 8.10).

   (*Note:* It is best to arrange the numbers out of order, because students quickly identify patterns in numbers as they go down, or "count by ones," and not across, or "adding 2.")

2. Present an in-and-out box with blank areas in the out column, and have students fill them in and identify the "rule" (figure 8.11).

3. Present in-and-out boxes with blanks in the in column, and have students fill them in and identify the "rule."

4. Have students come up with their own rules and create their own tables.

5. Replace the terms *in* and *out* with x and y, and create an *expression* for the rule: $2x - 1$ (figure 8.12).

6. Replace the terms *in* and *out* with x and y, and create an *equation* for the rule: $2x - 1 = y$.

7. Write numbers for x and y as an ordered pair: (4,7).

8. Learn about the structure of the coordinate grid and plot points from the function table.

9. Plot points on a coordinate grid (one or four coordinates as necessary), connect the points to create a line, and label the line with the equation from the function table (figure 8.13).

10. Starting with a line on a graph, take points from that line and create a function chart. Analyze the function chart to come up with the rule, or equation.

This entire process is more meaningful to students if the data in the function charts is real-life data collected in class. This could be conversions, growth of cubes, rates, and so on. If these connections are not made, then students may well be able to identify the equations on the graphs, but they will never be able to apply them to a useful situation. Collect data throughout the year, and save the charts so that when you come back to the data meaning is still attached to it.

IN	OUT
3	5
6	8
4	6
8	10

Rule:
Add 2

Figure 8.10. An in-and-out box.

IN	OUT
4	7
3	5
6	
5	9
2	

Rule:
Times two, subtract one

Figure 8.11. An in-and-out box with missing "out" numbers.

x	y
4	7
3	5
6	
5	9
2	

Rule:
$x \cdot 2 - 1$ or $2x - 1$

Figure 8.12. The *in* and *out* are replaced with x and y, and the rule is written as an expression.

$x + 1 = y$

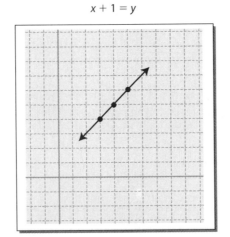

x	y
3	4
4	5
5	6
Rule: $x + 1 = y$	

Figure 8.13. Plotting the ordered pairs on a graph and creating a line.

Students eventually learn the equation for the slope, but it is something that many forget. Understanding this process ensures that they can always generate the equations to create the lines.

Designing a Routine Series

Routines of a given concept should be done in a series to give students an opportunity to explore the mathematics behind the concept in depth, as well as an opportunity to try other students' strategies. Although many of the previously described routines will occur periodically throughout the year, it is helpful initially to develop a series of 3–5 days that focuses on only one routine. When planning this series, you consider what your goals are for the routine and what you would like to have accomplished by the end of the series. Break these goals into manageable chunks for each day.

First consider past concepts that need reinforcing, and then consider concepts that are coming up with which students typically struggle. Once a focus is identified, try to outline 3–5 individual lessons that build on one another and allow students to walk away from the final lesson with a deeper understanding of mathematics. This might mean a conjecture has been identified by the class or new strategies have been developed and explored. An example might be that you notice that your fourth-grade students are struggling with telling time. You also note that telling time is no longer a teaching standard in your grade; therefore, the curriculum is void of lessons about this topic. Figure 8.14 demonstrates an example of a series of quick routines for telling time over a 5-day period.

Planning Routines for the Year

Although each mathematical routine is carefully designed to meet the needs of your students on a given day, you should plan ahead to make sure that certain routines take place at strategic times throughout the year. One grade level's attempt at planning its routines to correspond with their units and assessments is partially shown in figure 8.15. Go to the student website to see this information for grades K–5.

Day 1   Distinguishing between the hour and the minute hands. Telling time to the hour and half hour.

- Using an overhead clock, have a discussion about the function of each hand.
- Discuss why we count numbers by fives when counting minutes.
- Relate the 6 to 30 minutes
- Show different times to the hour and half hour, and have students state what time it is and how they know.

Day 2   Relating the clock to fractions. How do "quarter past" and "quarter to" relate to the clock?

- Using fraction circles, find the halves and quarters and place them over their model clocks.
- Mark ¼, ½, and ¾ on their model clocks.
- Relate a half hour to 30 minutes, a quarter hour to 15 minutes, and three-quarters of an hour to 45 minutes.

Day 3   Telling time to the nearest quarter hour.

- Review the number of minutes in the ¼, ½, and ¾ positions.
- Analyze the position of the hour hand when the minute hand is in these positions.
- Show different times, and have students state what time it is and how they know.

Day 4   Telling time to the nearest 5 minutes.

- Review counting minutes by fives. Point to different numbers around the clock and ask how many minutes each number is. Get students to generalize that the number × 5 is the total number of minutes.
- Analyze what happens to the hour hand as the minute hand moves to different positions on the clock.
- Show different times, and have students state what time it is and how they know.

Day 5   Estimating the time by analyzing only the hour hand.

- Remove the minute hand from the clock. Look at the position of the hour hand to determine the most probable time. Have students discuss how they know which time it most likely is.

Figure 8.14. A sample 5-day set of routines for older students related to the concept of telling time.

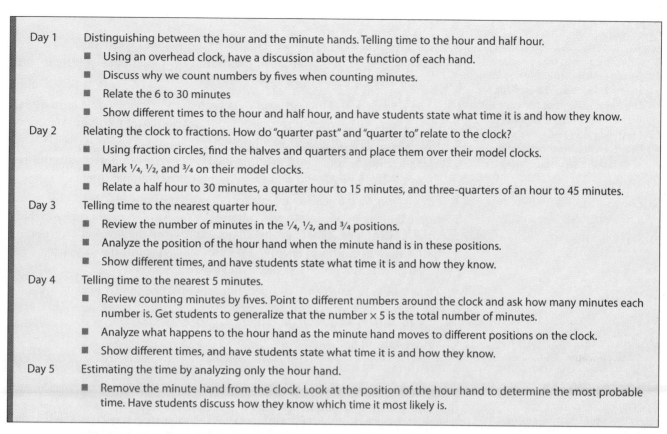

	September (4 weeks)	October (4 weeks)	November (4 weeks)	December (2 weeks)	January/ February (6 weeks)	March/April (5 weeks)	May (4 weeks)	June (4 weeks) (testing)	July (3 weeks)
Math: Routines	*Time *Equality *10 frames (How many more to make 10? 10 and some more) *Dot cards **Centers:** Combinations to 10 (grab bag), story boards, number arrangements, number trains	*Kathy Richardson's *Number Shapes* *10 frames (9+)	*Time *Measuring with nonstandard units *100 chart (+/−10) *10 frames (connect 10 frames to bigger numbers)	*Measuring with nonstandard units *Open number line	*100 chart (starting at any number and adding multiples of 10) *Open number line	*Routines for test: measurement, time, money, graphing, number sense, equality	*Routines for test: measurement, time, money, graphing, number sense, equality	*Mental math (three-digit numbers) *Open number line	*Time

Figure 8.15. A yearlong planning guide of routines for second grade at a year-round school.

Assessing Routines

Periodically, you want to step back and gauge the effectiveness of your routines. When doing a self-analysis of the routines you plan and execute in your classroom, here are some things to consider:

■ *Room environment.* How are students seated and organized? Are materials easily accessible when appropriate? Do transitions to and from routine activities go smoothly and use minimal time?

■ *Planning.* Is the routine clearly planned to develop understanding rather than rote learning? Is the routine building computational fluency?

■ *Opportunity for participation.* Do all students have access to the problem and opportunities to participate and share ideas during routines (private think time, partner talk, whole group share, etc.)? Does the level of questioning allow students to think deeply? Do students feel comfortable sharing even when they only partially know an answer?

■ *Opportunity to articulate thinking.* Students realize that mistakes are sites for learning. Students are held accountable for their thinking and reasoning. Students are expected to articulate lack of understanding, as well as understanding.

Special Needs

Your routines should be able to provide access for all students in your class. Routines that have multiple solutions are ideal, because all students can participate at their own level. Make sure that your higher-level students are not the only ones sharing their thinking. Oftentimes, the other students cannot follow their line of thinking. To encourage other students to share, it is helpful for a student to share how his partner solved it. This is beneficial for two reasons: It can take the pressure off of a student sharing his own ideas, and a quieter student can have his ideas exposed, through his partner, and can gain confidence with his ideas.

CONTENT

Algebraic Thinking and Reasoning

We have just thoroughly explored the role mathematical routines have in the classroom. Some of those routines included algebraic thinking and reasoning but were not elaborated on in detail. We take the rest of this chapter to look at the ideas that encompass algebraic thought. As you read about these ideas, think about how you would be able to incorporate them into your daily routines.

Big Ideas and Focal Points

One of the biggest ideas in algebra is that any number, expression, or equation can be "represented in an infinite number of ways that have the same value" (Charles 2005). These different representations can be shown to be equivalent through use of the equal sign. Most students do not understand the equal sign as showing equality but rather as something that shows what the answer is. Another big idea is the notion of variables being symbols that take the place of numbers (Van de Walle 2004).

According to NCTM's *Principles and Standards for School Mathematics* (2000, 90), all students from prekindergarten to grade 12 should be able to do the following:

- **Understand patterns, relations, and functions**
- **Represent and analyze mathematical situations and structures using algebraic symbols**
- **Use mathematical models to represent and understand quantitative relationships**
- **Analyze change in various contexts**

The Focal Points table shows the NCTM focal points about algebraic thinking throughout the elementary grades. It is interesting to note that these focal points show how block patterns that children build in kindergarten are the foundational building blocks, no pun intended, to more complex patterns, such as functional relationships, in the later grades.

It is equally interesting to note that none of the language is centered on the equal sign. Not until sixth grade is there any kind of language regarding equality. This is important to note, because this could be a contributing factor as to why teachers neglect to explicitly teach these concepts.

NCTM FOCAL POINTS

Kindergarten	First Grade	Second Grade	Third Grade
Children identify, duplicate, and extend simple number patterns and sequential and growing patterns (e.g., patterns made with shapes) as preparation for creating rules that describe relationships.	Through identifying, describing, and applying number patterns and properties in developing strategies for basic facts, children learn about other properties of numbers and operations, such as odd and even (e.g., "Even numbers of objects can be paired, with no leftovers"), and zero as the identity element for addition.	Children use number patterns to extend their knowledge of properties of numbers and operations. For example, when skip counting, they build foundations for understanding multiples and factors.	Students understand properties of multiplication and the relationship between multiplication and division as a part of algebra readiness. They create and analyze patterns and relationships involving multiplication and division. They build a foundation for later understanding of functional relationships by describing relationships in context with statements such as "The number of legs is four times the number of chairs."

(Continued on following page.)

(NCTM Focal Points, continued)

Fourth Grade	Fifth Grade	Sixth Grade
Students continue identifying, describing, and extending numeric patterns involving all operations and nonnumeric growing or repeating patterns. Through these experiences, they develop an understanding of the use of a rule to describe a sequence of numbers or objects.	Students use patterns, models, and relationships as contexts for writing and solving simple equations and inequalities. They create graphs of simple equations. They explore prime and composite numbers and discover concepts related to the addition and subtraction of fractions as they use factors and multiples, including applications of common factors and common multiples. They develop an understanding of the order of operations and use it for all operations.	Students use the commutative, associative, and distributive properties to show that two expressions are equivalent. They illustrate properties of operations by showing that two expressions are equivalent in a given context (e.g., determining the area in two different ways for a rectangle whose dimensions are $x + 3$ by 5). Sequences, including those that arise in the context of finding possible rules for patterns of figures or stacks of objects, provide opportunities for students to develop formulas.

What Is Algebra?

A perhaps overly simplistic answer to the question "What is algebra?" is that algebra is generalized arithmetic. Whereas arithmetic focuses on numerical answers, algebra focuses on the relationships between numbers (Kilpatrick 2001). "If students genuinely understand arithmetic at a level at which they can explain and justify the properties they are using as they carry out calculations, they have learned some critical foundations of algebra" (Carpenter, Franke, and Levi 2003, 2).

Upon entering high school, students should know and understand some key characteristics regarding algebra. The Mathematics Education Collaborative (Parker 2000) has outlined some of key understandings with which students should have had meaningful experiences over time:

Students should

- Know that learning algebra (like all of mathematics) is a sense-making process

- Have a deep understanding of linear algebra, including the use of tables, graphs, and equations, and understand the relationships among the three tools

- Understand functions, and have numerous opportunities to discover functional relationships and, when possible, to describe them as algebraic expressions and equations

- Understand the concept of variables

- Understand that algebra is a tool for determining how things grow, change, or both over time

- Have experience with nonlinear functions, such as quadratic, cubic, and exponential functions
- Understand the relationship between algebra and geometry, and know that geometry can be used to reveal algebraic relationships, and vice versa

Algebraic Reasoning

In support of the preceding understandings, algebraic reasoning in elementary school includes the exploration of equality, inequality, relational thinking, patterns and functions, growing patterns and functions, and variables.

Equality

Ask a random student what the equal sign means, and most likely her response will be "the answer is." Unintentionally, students have been trained to view the equal sign as having this meaning. After all, students generally only see problems for which they have to write their answer to the right of the equal sign (e.g., $4 + 5 = $ ____). It is uncommon for students to have explicit teaching as to what the equal sign represents and for that teaching to be ongoing throughout the elementary grades.

How do you think most students respond to the following problem?

$8 + 4 = \square + 5$

A research study from Karen Falkner, Linda Levi, and Thomas Carpenter (1999) found some startling results after giving this problem to children in first to sixth grades. Students' most common answers were 7, 12, 17, or 12 and 17. Their findings are summarized in the figure 8.16.

Not only was the correct answer given by fewer than 10% of the students in each grade, but fifth and sixth graders scored lower than third and fourth graders. The older children had become less flexible in their thinking. No wonder students are having a difficult time once entering Algebra.

However, this statistic can be easily remedied. Schools that have united to prevent this gross misunderstanding make sure that teachers from kindergarten to sixth grade are using similar language related to the equal sign. Teachers, especially in the younger grades, often read the symbol as "the same as." Children's first experience with the equal sign might be acting out how to make two groups of students the same by either bringing more children into the group or taking some away. Some children might even see that students could be moved from one side to the other to create equal groups.

Response and Percentage Responding				
Grades	7	12	17	12 and 17
1 and 2	5%	58%	13%	8%
3 and 4	9%	49%	25%	10%
5 and 6	2%	76%	21%	2%

Figure 8.16. Student responses to $8 + 4 = \square + 5$ and the percentage correct in the corresponding grades. (Reprinted with permission from *Thinking Mathematically*. Copyright © 2003 by Thomas Carpenter, Linda Levi, Megan Loef Franke. Published by Heinemann, Portsmouth, NH. All rights reserved.)

Number Sentence	Student Response
$4 + 5 = 9$	"True."
$9 = 4 + 5$	"False, because it is backward."
$9 = 9$	"False, because there are only two numbers and no plus or minus sign."
$9 + 0 = 9$	"True."
$4 + 5 = 4 + 5$	"False, because $4 + 5 = 9$." Or "False, because there are two pluses."

Figure 8.17. Possible true/false questions about equality and common student responses. (Reprinted with permission from *Thinking Mathematically*. Copyright © 2003 by Thomas Carpenter, Linda Levi, Megan Loef Franke. Published by Heinemann, Portsmouth, NH. All rights reserved.)

Carpenter et al. (2003) suggests true/false questions to stimulate conversations about the meaning of the equal sign. These same questions can be asked to first graders and to sixth graders. To prove whether or not these sentences are true, younger students benefit from using a balance with cubes, whereas older students are able to think more abstractly. Figure 8.17 is a list of some possible true/false questions and what children typically say in relation to them.

Once students have been given the opportunity to prove the preceding equations, they eventually come to the conclusion that they are all true. They are now ready to explore other equations and solve for unknowns (figure 8.18).

Children in the younger grades need to solve these equations using cubes. Initially, they need a balance to prove that the numbers of cubes on both sides are equal and to figure out how many to add or take away. After some initial work with the balance, they are able to transfer to a more abstract work mat, which represents a balance. An example is shown in figure 8.19.

Cubes are placed on each side of this "balance" as if it were the actual scale.

Kindergarteners need to act out balancing by standing in groups, because the cubes are too abstract. Each group should be given a number card to represent the number of children in their group. Slowly, with guidance, the children are able to use cubes to represent the number of children in each group.

$4 + 5 = 9 + 0$	$4 + 5 = \square$	$4 + 5 = \square + 5$
$4 + 5 = 0 + 9$	$4 + \square = 9$	$4 + 5 = \square + 4$
$4 + 5 = 8 + 1$	$\square + 5 = 9$	$4 + \square = 3 + 6$
$4 + 5 = 10 - 1$	$9 = \square$	$45 + 23 = 45 + \square$

Figure 8.18. Additional equations for true/false questions. (Reprinted with permission from *Thinking Mathematically*. Copyright © 2003 by Thomas Carpenter, Linda Levi, Megan Loef Franke. Published by Heinemann, Portsmouth, NH. All rights reserved.)

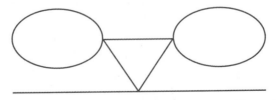

Figure 8.19. A work mat to represent a balance to solve problems about equality.

CAUTION

One thing that we do as teachers, which helps feed the misconception of the equal sign, is record a series of calculations as follows:

$$15 + 5 = 20 - 4 = 16 \times 2 = 32$$

This way of recording only reinforces the idea that the equal sign is a signal that the answer follows. No wonder the older students did more poorly than the younger ones with the research question described earlier. They are most likely used to their teachers recording their thoughts in such a way. Such a string of calculations should be recorded as follows:

$$15 + 5 = 20$$
$$20 - 4 = 16$$
$$16 \times 2 = 32$$

Inequality

Inequalities, such as greater than and less than, are introduced in about first grade with smaller numbers and continue through the grades as students are introduced to larger numbers. Initially, what is difficult about this task is understanding which symbol to use. Later, the difficulty lies in figuring out which numbers are truly larger than the others.

The first word of advice: Kill the alligator story! How many of us try to make children understand what the symbol means by telling a story of how the alligator likes to eat the bigger number? Is this mathematically sound? Is there a reason the alligator likes bigger numbers? We did not know it even ate numbers. In fact, there can be more harm than good in telling these types of stories in mathematics. They take the emphasis off reasoning—in this case, what the symbols represent. Another issue is that not all teachers use the same language for this story. Some teachers say, "The larger number is the one the alligator is pointing to." The problem is that with the > symbol, children do not consider the open space pointing; rather, the side with the vertex is doing the pointing.

Recently, a team of first-grade teachers decided to not tell the alligator story when introducing inequality. They gave their students popsicle sticks and cubes. They had them make two piles of the same number of cubes. Because the students were familiar with the equal sign, they created the sign with their sticks between each pile. Then, students were asked to make one pile bigger than the other. The students had to figure out a way to show that one pile was bigger using their sticks. Oddly enough, some first-grade students essentially created the symbol by themselves. In the summarize, they explained that because when the piles were the same, the space between the popsicle sticks was the same on both sides, but when one pile was larger, the space in the sticks should be larger on that side than the side by the smaller pile.

The teachers, although initially reluctant to not use the story they were comfortable with, all agreed that the students caught on to the symbols faster than any other group they had taught in the past. The students now understood the symbols, and they did not have to remember a silly story.

Relational Thinking

Relational thinking is an extension of children's understanding of equality. Once it has been established that students have a reasonable understanding of the meaning of the equal sign, it is desirable to push children to think about how the numbers are related to each other. The first step would be to get children to write many different expressions that are equivalent to each other (Carpenter 2003), for example, $5 + 3 = 2 \times 2 \times 2$. This reinforces the idea that a quantity can be expressed in many ways.

When presented with a number sentence such as $8 + \square = 7 + 3$, young children initially are going to solve for each side to find out what number needs to replace the variable or fill the empty box. However, over time, they need to be made to step back and see what is happening with the numbers and whether any kind of relationship exists between the numbers in each expression. More often than not, it is necessary to raise the quantities to such a point that they are inoperable for children. This forces them to look at entire quantities. An example might be $58 + 27 = 59 + \square$. Students have to begin to make generalizations about what is happening with the quantities. To prove their conjectures, they have to go back and calculate both sides (perhaps with cubes, the assistance of the teacher, or even a calculator). They can again be presented with numbers within their range to test their conjectures and study what is happening with the quantities using cubes.

In the case of $58 + 27 = 59 + \square$, the conjecture could be made that amounts can be transferred from one addend to the other and the expression remains equivalent. It must be noted, however, that this conjecture does not hold true for subtraction. Look at the following number sentence:

$$58 - 27 = 59 - \square$$

What is the missing number? Many might say that it is 26. But subtraction is a different operation, because $58 - 27$ is 31, but $59 - 26$ is 33. Thus, 26 would not make this true. Reflecting back on what you learned regarding constant difference, if 1 were added to the 58, then 1 should equally be added to the 27 for the difference between the two numbers to remain equal. The point here is that some students, and teachers, make overgeneralizations and try to apply them to number sentences with different operations. When exploring a new operation or a different subset of numbers (such as integers), at the end, both sides need to be calculated as proof of the accuracy of the statements. It is always critical for the teacher to solve the problems before presenting them to students.

The ability to think relationally aids children's ability to learn their basic facts. As discussed, in both the addition and subtraction and the multiplication and division chapters, the ability to see numbers within numbers is helpful in developing quick recall, especially when memorization is difficult for children. Understanding that 6×8 is the same as 6×4 twice, 6×5 and 6×3, or two sixes less than 6×10 allows students access in figuring out problems that are not yet memorized. Otherwise, students may have to resort to skip counting or counting all.

53 = 50 + 3	23 + 45 = 20 + 40 + 3 + 5	0.64 = 0.064
53 = 5 + 3	27 + 45 = 612	0.64 = 0.640
53 = 3 + 50	45 − 27 = 22	
53 = 40 + 13	45 − 27 = 40 − 20 − 5 − 7	
53 = 25 × 2 + 3	45 − 27 = 40 − 20 + 5 − 7	

Figure 8.20. True/false questions that can support base 10 concepts. (Reprinted with permission from *Thinking Mathematically*. Copyright © 2003 by Thomas Carpenter, Linda Levi, Megan Loef Franke. Published by Heinemann, Portsmouth, NH. All rights reserved.)

Base 10 concepts are another aspect of number that can be explored through this notion of true/false statements. When developing your number strings, it is important to include some common errors. This helps students think about and reason why certain errors are inaccurate. Some true/false questions supporting base 10 concepts are outlined in figure 8.20.

Patterns and Functions

Pattern is at the heart of mathematics (figure 8.21). We need to train the children to look for, and to expect to find, patterns in all math work that they do. This starts from their first experiences in school. Sadly, sometimes work with patterns stops in kindergarten or first grade and does not resume until students near middle school. Teachers need to see how the pattern work that they do in the early grades builds on larger ideas. The more students experience building

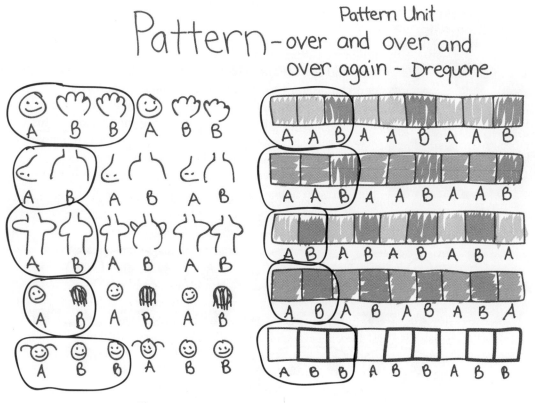

Figure 8.21. A pattern chart in a kindergarten class.

and looking for patterns, the easier it will be for them to find relationships among numbers.

A child's first experience with patterns includes rhythms and physical movements. This may include rhythmic clapping, standing and sitting, people patterns, and physically creating patterns with large objects. The teacher may model or show a picture of a *pattern unit* (the segment of a pattern that repeats) and then have students copy the pattern and *extend* it by repeating it many times. A pattern unit might be as follows:

clap **clap** **snap** **clap**

Children should practice representing these patterns using an alternative tool, such as Unifix cubes.

You may want to have the children build many of the pattern units as separate units. Then have the children stand them up on their ends so that they can compare the units to see that all are built correctly and are not reversed. They then should connect all of the units together and, with their peers, read the entire pattern.

Students should also practice reading patterns in different ways, such as brown–brown–yellow–brown, A–A–B–A, 1–1–2–1, and up–up–down–up. Through these exercises, children learn to represent patterns in more abstract ways.

A dot chart is a wonderful tool with which students can invent their own patterns. It can be used by a whole class or individually in a center. Examples of patterns made from dot charts are shown in figure 8.22.

Just as kindergartners need a lot of counting practice, they need to build lots of patterns. The same objects that they count can be used for the students to create unique patterns. These might be pattern blocks, buttons, toy soldiers, keys, socks, color tiles, and so on. Pattern blocks and objects that can stand on their end can be used to create pattern walls. Creating pattern necklaces, whether inventing a unique pattern or extending a pattern unit, improves pattern making and fine motor skills. This can also be achieved by gluing alphabet pasta patterns to a board or creating patterns using small beans of different colors.

As children develop a more sophisticated eye for patterns, they grow to notice patterns in their environment. These may be

Using common objects, such as socks, to create patterns.

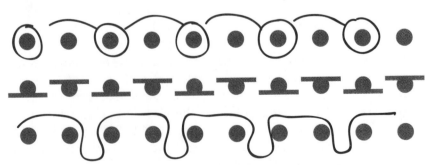

Figure 8.22. Using a dot chart to create patterns. (Baratta-Lorton 1995, 35.)

Figure 8.23. A growing pattern.

natural patterns, such as leaves and petals, or manmade patterns, such as fabric prints. These patterns can inspire them to create their own sophisticated patterns using geoboards, graph paper, or pattern blocks.

Teachers might want to encourage their students to study the leaves on a branch or cut open some fruit and vegetables to see what patterns are hidden inside. Students would be using the skills of observation and prediction (before cutting open a fruit) while studying these natural patterns. They can then create rubbings, make prints, and copy the patterns they see. They can create works of art as they invent more intricate patterns with these natural patterns.

Growing Patterns and Functions

Growing patterns are those that are most associated with functions. Students notice and create patterns growing at a certain rate. Initially, they need to learn to articulate how certain patterns are growing. After some experience, they can attach numerical values to these growths on a more sophisticated function table, or T-chart. An example of a growing pattern is shown in figure 8.23.

A child's response to the way his pattern is growing may be, "I am adding a square tile to each of the three sides." He should then be asked, "By how many tiles is your pattern growing?" to which he would respond, "3."

When doing these lessons as a group, the teacher should ask the students whether they can record each new stage of their pattern so that others can tell how many tiles are in each stage without having to count. Through a discussion, a T-chart is generated in which each stage of building is numbered and the number of tiles it takes to make each stage is recorded. Look at the T-chart, or function table, in figure 8.24, which is recording the pattern illustrated in the previous figure.

The next question is, "How many tiles would be in the fourth stage of my pattern design?" It is at this point that students have to apply some rule of pattern growth that they are noticing. If students are building alongside the teacher, then they may just add the additional three and count all tiles. Others just know that 10 and 3 more make 13. All students have access to this problem.

When analyzing function charts, the amount a pattern is growing between each stage is usually more obvious than figuring out the relationship between the stage and the number of tiles in that stage. Using the preceding chart, a child might say, plus three because she noticed that each stage has three more tiles than the previous one. However, if the teacher asks how many tiles would be in the 10th stage, then the focus is shifted from the growth between each stage to the relationship between the stage and the number of tiles within each stage (figure 8.25). This is a higher level of thinking. Some children continue to build (or imagine building) each new stage and perhaps keep track of all the threes they are using. Others notice that each stage has another three added plus the one at the center of the pattern.

Pattern Stage	Number of Tiles in Each Stage
1	4
2	7
3	10
4	

Figure 8.24. Recording the preceding growing pattern on a function table.

Pattern Stage	Number of Tiles in Each Stage	
1	4	"There is a three plus the one in the middle."
2	7	"There are 2 threes plus the one in the middle."
3	10	"There are 3 threes plus the one in the middle."
4		"So there must be 4 threes plus the one in the middle."
10		"So there must be 10 threes plus the one in the middle."

Figure 8.25. Student explanation of the function table.

The final nudge to get them to make a generalization would be to ask, "How can I figure out how many tiles would be in any stage of my pattern?" This is not a simple question, because it causes children to think hard about the similarities of each stage. After taking some time to explore this further, they will probably respond, "Whatever number of the stage you want, you need that many threes plus the one in the middle." At this point, students are articulating their rule in words. Eventually, they need to be encouraged to articulate their rule using a numerical representation. In the preceding scenario, the rule would be recorded as: $s \times 3 + 1$, where s represents the pattern stage. Older students may record this as $3s + 1$.

It is important to note that seemingly simple patterns can have complex rules, or equations, that describe them. It is important that the teacher takes time to come up with the equation to the growing pattern before introducing it to the children. It could be more complicated than anticipated. Doing so helps avoid a lot of frustration.

Identifying the equations for these patterns is not where it ends. These equations are graphable. Once students are learning about graphs and how to plot ordered pairs, then they are able to graph their equations. Revisit the growing pattern of $3s + 1$. At this point, the labels "pattern stage" and "number of tiles in each stage" can be replaced with the variables x and y. Ordered pairs can then be extracted from the function table. In this case, the ordered pairs are $(1,4)$, $(2,7)$, and $(3,10)$. These ordered pairs can be plotted on a graph, as shown in figure 8.26.

Students could be presented with a line that has coordinates labeled and could work backward to find the equation. Essentially, they would create a T-chart plotting their points and then analyze the relationships between the x and the y to come up with the equation of that line. This process embeds more understanding about slope than memorizing a formula that is easily forgotten.

Special Needs

Growing pattern problems are accessible to students at all levels because there are a lot of entry points and ways to solve them. We do not need to water down the math; instead, we can provide all of our students with rich mathematical tasks.

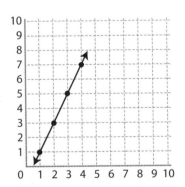

Figure 8.26. Graph representing $3S + 1$.

Try an example. Take the points from the graph and place them on the following table. What rule can be generated?

Quarts x	Gallons y
4	1
8	2
12	3
16	4

A child might easily notice that the x is increasing by 4 or that the y is increasing by 1. However, studying the relationships between the x and the y allows us to generate the equation of $x \div 4 = y$.

When collecting data to graph or studying graphs to analyze, it is important to gather data from real-life contexts. Otherwise, students can become quite competent with graphing and coming up with equations but not understand how these lines and data relate to the everyday world. Some suggestions for pattern studies and data collections are shown in figure 8.27 (note that the complexity varies).

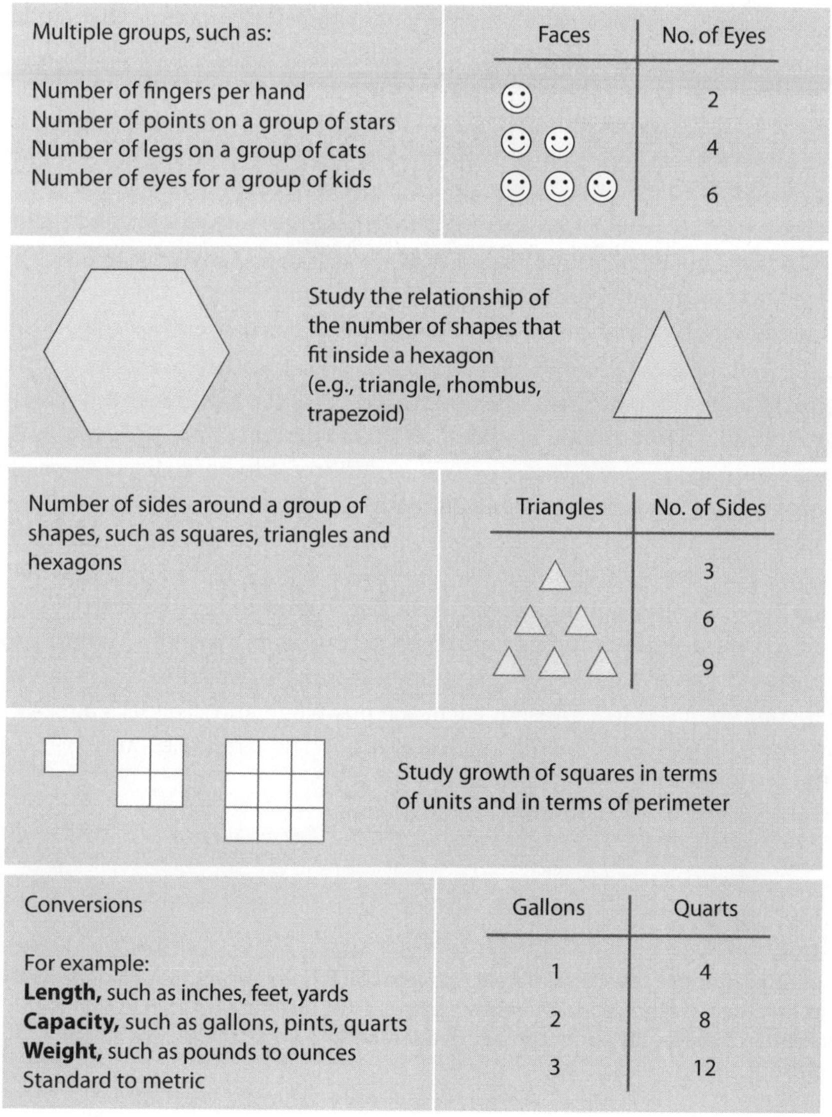

Figure 8.27. Contexts from which relationships can be analyzed and graphed.

Multiple groups, such as:

Number of fingers per hand
Number of points on a group of stars
Number of legs on a group of cats
Number of eyes for a group of kids

Faces	No. of Eyes
☺	2
☺ ☺	4
☺ ☺ ☺	6

Study the relationship of the number of shapes that fit inside a hexagon (e.g., triangle, rhombus, trapezoid)

Number of sides around a group of shapes, such as squares, triangles and hexagons

Triangles	No. of Sides
△	3
△ △	6
△ △ △	9

Study growth of squares in terms of units and in terms of perimeter

Conversions

For example:
Length, such as inches, feet, yards
Capacity, such as gallons, pints, quarts
Weight, such as pounds to ounces
Standard to metric

Gallons	Quarts
1	4
2	8
3	12

After assessing students from different grades at one elementary school for similar types of growth patterns, it was noted that although they were able to study and identify patterns by looking at the pictures, models, and diagrams (such as T-charts), they were unable to figure out a way to organize what they noticed, therefore not allowing them to make some generalization. All students had to be prompted to create a table that would serve as an organizational tool. However, all of these students were in classrooms where they studied and interpreted data on a function table regularly. This interesting finding helped the teachers realize that they spent lots of time having students interpret data to find a rule, or equation, but never had their students generating function tables on their own. This led to a shift in the types of activities that these teachers orchestrated with their students about patterns and functions. They began to connect the data to real-life contexts and have their students study patterns and record these patterns on tables.

Variables

We mentioned variables in our discussion about function tables. A *variable* is the unknown quantity that is to be solved for, and it can change. *Constants* are the numerals in the expression that do not change. For example, two children are 2 years apart in age. Today, the boy is 6 and the girl is 8. How old will the girl be if the boy is 10? The variables are the ages because they change, but the constant is the 2 years difference because that never changes. An equation could be written to represent this problem: $b + 2 = g$. The question might be worded as "If $b = 10$, what is the value of g?"

Three uses of variables in school mathematics have been identified by Zalman Usiskin (1988). These uses are as a specific unknown, as a pattern generalizer, and as quantities that vary.

Unknowingly, children begin solving for an unknown as soon as they begin calculating in kindergarten and first grade. They often see the unknown as an empty box, but the idea is the same. When replacing that empty box with a variable in a later grade, students tend to overreact and suddenly cannot understand the problem. This is why it is important to have discussions along the way about how to represent elements in problems with a single letter rather than lots of words. For example, suppose the age problem was given to a group of second graders. Many students would probably respond that no matter how old the boy is, the girl will be 2 years older. If they were to be asked a way to write a number sentence to represent that, they would probably respond "boy's age + 2 = girl's age." A simple question, such as "What letter could be used to represent each, the boy's age and the girl's age, so that there were no words in the number sentence?" The letters "b" and "g" would be the suggested letters.

Language Tip

Be sure to define the representation of the variable. It is important that students understand that the *b* is representing the boy's age and not just the boy. Myriad things can be represented numerically about the boy in addition to his age, such as his height and weight.

When we encourage students to make generalizations about arithmetic or to derive formulas, variables are used to articulate these generalizations in an equation. For example, when exploring the idea that zero added to any number is the same number, the student explanation may be "When zero is added to any number, the number stays the same." This explanation can be recorded as $n + 0 = n$.

Comprehension Check

- What are components of algebraic reasoning? Give a brief description of each one.

- Why is it important for children to begin experiencing elements of algebraic reasoning in the primary grades?

CAUTION

A misconception that many students have with their first encounters of variables, when not introduced to them in an authentic way, is that letters represent specific values. Some children might think that $a = 1$, $b = 2$, and so on. This misconception is stressful for students because they think they have to somehow memorize values. Another difficulty that can arise related to the understanding of variables is measurements. Students may be used to seeing the first letter of a unit of measurement to label an answer, like "5y" to represent 5 yards. However, algebraically, this would signify five times the number of yards.

Another common error that students make when learning to solve equations is the interpretation of the way multiplication is represented. When presented with the problem "What is $5n$ if $n = 4$?" many students answer 54, thinking that the 4 merely replaces the n with no operation.

Making Conjectures and Generalizations

In previous chapters, we articulated the importance of generalizing mathematics and making conjectures. Students often have an implicit understanding of mathematical properties, but they need teacher-led experiences to make them explicit. The ability to articulate their understandings helps students become metacognitive and more likely to apply what they know to other situations.

A *generalization* is defined as "a mathematical rule about relationships or properties" (Ellis 2007, 196; see also Carpenter and Franke 2001; English and Warren 1995; Lee 1996). When students are making generalizations, they are creating rules that go beyond the problem or numbers they are considering and apply to more general situations. They "lift the reasoning or communication to a level where the focus is no longer on the cases or situations themselves, but rather on the patterns, procedures, structures and the relations across and among them" (Kaput 1999, 137).

Amy Ellis (2007) has created a *taxonomy*, or classification, of generalizing. She distinguished between actions of generalizing (students' activities as they generalize) and reflective generalizations (students' final statements of generalizations).

A teacher recording students' conjectures on a classroom chart.

Actions of Generalizing

The actions students do while generalizing have been identified by Ellis as the following:

- *Relating.* "Students form an association between two or more problems, situations, ideas, or mathematical objects. They relate by recalling a prior situation, inventing a new one, or focusing on similar properties or forms of mathematical objects" (Ellis 2007, 198). For example, a student may recognize the handshake problem (how many total handshakes occur among a certain number of people) and the staircase problem (how many cubes creates a staircase of a given number of floors) as being similar problems (figure 8.28). They both have to do with finding the sum of a series of numbers beginning with 1.

  Students may also invent a new problem that is similar to one being solved. This may help them put the problem into a more real context to help them visualize the situation better.

- *Searching.* "Students engage in a repeated mathematical action, such as calculating a ratio or locating a pattern, in order to locate an element of similarity. Students focus on relationships, procedures, patterns, or solutions when searching" (Ellis 2007, 198). This might be substituting several different values for x to see what can be noticed about y. This also might be hitting the $+$ key on the calculator to come up with a list of multiples for a specific number. Young children might be engaged in building several double towers to determine which numbers are odd and which are even. Upon making a discovery, such as that adding one results in the next counting number, children may test a range of numbers to see whether their rule holds true for all numbers.

- *Extending.* Students extend or apply their generalizations to build other generalizations. For example, students who have generalized the rules that even plus even equals even and odd plus even equals odd are able to then consider what might happen when an odd, odd, and even are added together. "Students who extend widen their reasoning beyond the problem, situation, or case in which it originated" (Ellis 2007, 198).

Reflection Generalizations

Reflection occurs when students identify or state a conjecture or generalization that they have made after engaging one of the previously described actions.

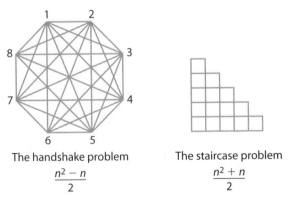

The handshake problem
$$\frac{n^2 - n}{2}$$

The staircase problem
$$\frac{n^2 + n}{2}$$

Figure 8.28. Relating two different mathematical problems to each other.

They may do this while sharing with the whole class or by writing in their math journals. These statements may be an identification of a pattern, property, or rule, or it may be an application of a generalization already identified by the class. Students may also adapt an existing generalization to apply it to a new problem or situation (Ellis 2007).

The more the teacher sets up situations that encourage conjectures and generalizations, the more students naturally come up with them. If it is part of the classroom culture to try to figure out why numbers work as they do, then students begin to take on this habit on their own. Developing a growing conjecture chart helps instill this culture. Oftentimes, students come up with how they think something works but are not certain whether it works for all numbers. The teacher can put their thinking on the conjecture chart and, as the class learns about different groups of numbers, these conjectures can be revisited and retested with different number sets (like negative numbers) to see whether they still hold true. Oftentimes, as students become more sophisticated with their math skills, they need to revise conjectures to include more precision in the definitions.

One example of this is a second-grade class exploring odd and even numbers. The class's original definition was, "Even numbers have partners, and odd numbers do not have partners." Although the children understood what they meant by this, the definition is not clear. On another day, the teacher had the children refine their definition. They did so by saying, "With odd numbers, one object doesn't have a partner where the other objects do" (referring to their double towers). Further exploration allowed the students to conjecture that adding an odd number with another odd number resulted in an even number, although they were not sure that that would work all the time.

Figure 8.29 gives examples of some properties of number operations that are worthwhile for students to explore and to develop their own conjectures and generalizations about. Each of the conjectures can be derived with a true/false question. Whether through using manipulatives or just mentally analyz-

Properties	Generalized Number Sentence	Child's Explanation
Addition and subtraction involving zero	$n + 0 = n$ $0 + n = n$	When zero is added to any number, the answer is the same number.
	$n - 0 = n$	When zero is subtracted from any number, the answer is the same number.
	$0 - n = -n$	When a number is subtracted from zero, the answer is the same number but negative.
	$n - n = 0$	When you take away the same amount from what you have, you are left with zero.
	$a + b - b = a$	When you add one amount to another and take that second amount back, you end up with the amount you started with.

Figure 8.29. Possible conjectures for number properties in numerical representation and child's explanation. See the website for more information. (Reprinted with permission from *Thinking Mathematically*. Copyright © 2003 by Thomas Carpenter, Linda Levi, Megan Loef Franke. Published by Heinemann, Portsmouth, NH. All rights reserved.)

Comprehension Check

- Think about the content sections of the previous chapters. What are some basic generalizations and conjectures we want our students to make about number and operations?

ing numbers, children first come up with a verbal explanation. The trick is to push students to represent their explanations in a number sentence. Writing their explanation in words and then, right below it, writing it with symbols helps them understand how to create these generalized number sentences.

Justification and Proof

If we are to make sense of mathematics, we have to justify the concepts or procedures to ourselves (Carpenter 2003). But often the justifications we have in our head are not easily articulated. Through argument, we are able to clarify our justifications and convince others of our reasoning. Students should be in a habit of justifying all of their work, whether it is how to add three-digit numbers or how to multiply using negative numbers. The summary portion of a lesson is where students engage in this argument and justify their reasoning. Reflection generalization, from the previous section, is essentially the act of students stating their generalizations, or conjectures, and justifying them. A *proof* would be a justification of how a conjecture holds true for all numbers and would include some sort of representation, such as models, diagrams, or a numerical representation, used to convince others.

Carpenter has identified three classes of justification that students engage in. When new to the act of mathematical argument and justification, children may *appeal to authority*. This is when children know that they are right because their teacher, or other authority figure, told them so. When asked, "How do you know that $8 + 3 = 11$?" it is not uncommon to hear, "Because my mother taught me that one at home." At this point, children feel that the adult is always right and they have not learned to question some one else's thinking.

Another way that students justify is through *justification by example*. This is when they argue that something is true because they try testing different numbers and attempt to find a counterexample that would disprove their conjecture. Conjectures may be refined when students learn about a new range or class of numbers that they were unfamiliar with before.

Students then move toward more *generalizable arguments*. They may first just be restating the conjecture in their own words but with no examples because the conjecture may seem obvious. Later, they begin to give concrete examples, using numerical examples or demonstrating the conjecture using concrete objects. They may even build on their conjectures or generalizations to create new ones.

Teachers who expect their students to generalize, make conjectures, and justify their thinking are always probing their class to think more broadly. They do not accept simple answers to math problems. When orchestrating a healthy environment of mathematical arguments and justification, the teacher asks a few key, yet simple, questions to stimulate deeper and broader thinking:

- "How do you know?"
- "Does that always work?"
- "Does that work with all numbers?"
- "How can you be sure?"

Questions such as these put the responsibility of thinking and reasoning back on the student.

Integrating Arithmetic and Algebra

Arithmetic is the act of calculating using one of the four operations. However, teachers can successfully teach algebraic concepts through their arithmetic activities. Throughout this chapter, we outlined how teachers can guide their students into making generalizations of the operations. Students who think about why the operations work develop a deeper understanding of the operation and are more successful with its use.

A *robust* teacher has the ability to weave algebra and arithmetic together by spiraling through certain algebraic themes frequently over a period (Blanton and Kaput 1995). Each time a theme, such as growing patterns, is revisited, the teacher takes the discovery and discussion to a deeper and more complex level. Another characteristic is the ability to develop or adapt existing mathematical tasks to include algebraic reasoning. The average math curriculum adopted by a school or district can be arithmetic oriented. Teachers have to be able to understand the bigger ideas behind the individual lessons to help their students see these big ideas. This often means to think of a unit as a whole and not as the isolated skills in which it was written.

It is imperative that teachers see how the big ideas of arithmetic connect to one another over all the elementary years. Understanding how ideas are connected and where they are headed helps teachers push children to the next level. It prevents teachers from teaching with blinders on and possibly disregarding certain lessons that might seem insignificant. An example of this is the notion of the decomposition of number. Figure 8.30 shows how this big idea is developed from kindergarten through Algebra.

Comprehension Check

- How do strategic teachers weave algebraic concepts throughout the curriculum to avoid teaching in isolation?

- Look closely at figure 8.30. How is the big idea of decomposition of number evident in each of the grades?

Using Inquiry to Teach Algebraic Concepts

In the pedagogy section of this chapter, we discussed ways to integrate algebraic thinking into mathematical routines. We can also give examples of how to use the inquiry model of instruction to teach algebraic thinking and reasoning. Although the following lessons are written with specific grades in mind, they can be adapted to meet the needs of children in any grade. These lessons are not necessarily the first lesson to present the topic but, rather, an example lesson within the topic. Algebraic thinking and reasoning needs to be threaded throughout all grades, and the younger we start, the better.

Equality (Kindergarten)

Launch	The teacher has a chair with a large equal sign (=) taped to it in the front of the room. "What does this sign mean?"
	The teacher invites three students to stand on one side and five students to stand on the other. "Are the two groups equal? Talk to your partner about what we can do to make the two groups equal." (Some students make the suggestion of putting two more children with the group of three, and others suggest removing two from the group of five).
Explore	The teacher has another two groups of students come up to the front.
	All students are given whiteboards and cubes. They draw an equal sign in the middle of their board. With the help of a partner, they try to model with their cubes the students who are in the two groups. They discuss what they should do to make the two groups equal.
Summarize	Students share their strategy for making the two groups the same.

(Continued on following page.)

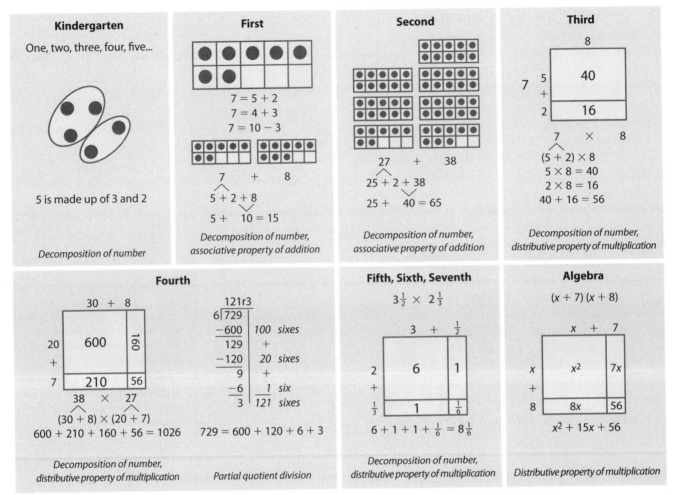

Figure 8.30. The continuum of number concepts, developing from kindergarten through Algebra. Big idea: Numbers are composed of other numbers that, when decomposed, facilitate computation. (Created by Ivan Alba, District Math Resource Teacher, San Diego City Schools, 2007. Reprinted by permission.)

Relational Thinking (First Grade)

Launch	Teacher poses the problem: 5 + ____ = 6 + 8
Explore	Students work with their partners using a whiteboard and cubes.
Summarize	Students share their strategies for knowing that 9 is their answer.

Patterns and Functions (Late Second Grade)

Launch	The teacher shows a cube creature made of some cubes (e.g., 4). "How many cubes is my cube creature made of?" Teacher records responses on a T-chart drawn on the board.
	The teacher shows a second cube creature made of another number of cubes (e.g., 8). "How many cubes is my cube creature made of?" Teacher records responses on a T-chart drawn on the board.
	The teacher asks: "How big do you think my next cube creature will be?" Students talk to their partners about their estimates.
	The teacher shows the third creature (in this case, there is 12 cubes) and records 12 on the T-chart.
Explore	With their partners, students try to figure out how many cubes would make the 10th creature.
Summarize	Students share how many cubes they think the 10th creature will be made of. "What kind of rule could we write to show how many cubes are in any creature?" (creature × 4 = total cubes).

CONCLUSION

The purpose of routines is to provide meaningful practice to help create a mathematically powerful student who enjoys solving problems and is able to clearly articulate his thinking. Someone who is computationally fluent is able to use efficient and accurate methods flexibly for computing (NCTM 2000). For this to occur, the routines need to be precisely designed with a particular group of students in mind. For this reason, almost any commercially prepared product is not an adequate tool to use for this time. To achieve fluency, students need to be able to experiment with a variety of solution strategies and compare the effectiveness of each. They need to be able to judge which is most efficient and whether each truly works all the time for all numbers. They also need to be able to challenge ideas with those of their peers. This level of grappling with mathematics cannot occur with generic warm-up questions, which are generally close ended.

Being able to articulate your own thinking is not easy and takes lots of practice. It can be equally challenging to learn to follow someone else's thinking and to publicly record it. In addition, in the beginning, students may not want to talk about or share their ideas. But after a few weeks, even the most reluctant students begin to open up when they realize that all ideas are equally valued and that they indeed have something positive to contribute to the learning of the entire group.

However, we want students to do more than merely compute. If they are to be successful in middle school Algebra, when they leave elementary school they need to have the habit of mind to reason and make conjectures about how numbers work. They need to expect to find patterns and to know that the numbers they are manipulating in an equation are located within a model. They also need to be able to think relationally and to have developed the ability to make mathematical arguments and justify their solutions by providing counterexamples and representations to prove how properties work with all numbers. This kind of thinking is not come upon by chance but occurs through a concerted effort from all grade-level teachers at a school site. There has to be a schoolwide commitment, as well as a deep understanding by all of how all ideas of each grade level fit together into a bigger picture.

▶ Interview Video with an Eye on Content

Watch videos of different aspects of algebraic thinking and reasoning. Determine what the algebraic focus is, describe the task, and note the student's thinking and reasoning.

Algebraic Focus	Task	Student thinking and reasoning
1		

▶ Interview a Child

1. Design a task for a student interview about a component of algebraic reasoning (equality, relational thinking, patterns and functions, or variables).

2. Using the problems from step 1, conduct this interview with students of different ability and grade levels. What do you notice?

3. Write an overall summary about how your student did. Include recommendations you would make for the child's teacher or what would you do with this child if you were to continue to work with him?

▶ Classroom Video with an Eye on Pedagogy

Watch videos of mathematical routines in different grades. With each routine, identify the concept that the routine is trying to support, a brief description of the activity, and what deeper mathematical understanding students walk away with as a result.

Grade level
_____

Routine
_____

Concept
_____

Describe activity
_____

Mathematical
understanding that
students internalize
_____

▶ Classroom Application

Pick a misconception you discovered during your student interviews and create a series of mathematical routines to help your students make some conjectures and generalizations about the component of algebraic reasoning you tested.

▶ Resources

Thinking Mathematically: Integrating Arithmetic & Algebra in Elementary School, Thomas P. Carpenter, Megan Loef Franke, and Linda Levi (2003)

Lessons for Algebraic Thinking (Grades K–2, 3–5, and 6–8), Math Solutions Publications (Von Rotz and Burns 2002; Wickett, Kharas, and Burns 2002; and Lawrence and Hennessy 2002)

Algebra through Visual Patterns: A Beginning Course in Algebra Volumes 1 & 2, Eugene Maier and Larry Linnen (2008)

Mathematics Their Way, Mary Baratta-Lorton (1995)

San Diego Unified School District's math department, http://www.sandi.net/depts/math/ (under curriculum, choose grade 3 and above, and then scroll down to instructional routines to find a PDF document with descriptions of a variety of routines specific to that grade level)

▶ Lit Link

Literature Books to Support Algebraic Thinking and Reasoning

Title	Author
I Know an Old Lady	Brian Karas
King's Chessboard, The	David Birch
Pattern Bugs	Trudy Harris
Pattern Fish	Trudy Harris
Pet Parade	Maria Velasquez
Six Dinner Sid	Inga Moore
Spaghetti and Meatballs for All	Marilyn Burns
Two of Everything	Lily Toy Hong
What's Missing?	Niki Yektai

▶ Tech Tools

Websites

National Library of Virtual Manipulatives, http://www.nlvm.usu.edu

Cool Math Sites, http://cte.jhu.edu/techacademy/web/2000/heal/mathsites.htm

NCTM: Illuminations, Web Links—Algebra, http://illuminations.nctm.org/WebResourceList.aspx?Ref=2&Std=1&Grd=0

Software

Pre-Algebra World (grades 3–8), Math Realm, http://www.mathrealm.com/CD_ROMS/PreAlgebraWorld.php

Instructional Goals, Number Theory, and Integers

PEDAGOGICAL CONTENT UNDERSTANDINGS

Pedagogy *Instructional Goals*
- Content Goals
- Process Goals
- Disposition Goals
- Social Goals
- Choosing Goals and Objectives

Content *Number Theory and Integers*
- Number Theory
- Integers

The real art of discovery consists not in finding new lands, but in seeing with new eyes.

Marcel Proust

CONVERSATION IN MATHEMATICS

Teacher: Can you tell me what even and odd numbers are?

Student 1: An odd number is a number that doesn't have doubles in it, and it has a number left over. An even number is a number with doubles, like 22 is a double of 11.

Teacher: Is 90 even or odd?

Student 2: Odd, because 9 is an odd number.

Teacher: Can you prove it to me with the blocks?

Student 2: OK. (Puts four 10 sticks in one pile and five 10 sticks in another pile).

Student 1: No, I disagree; 90 is even because it has a double in it, 45 and 45. Actually, every 10 should be even because it has doubles in it.

Teacher: All tens?

Student 1: Yes, because if you have 90, that is 45 and 45. And 50 is 25 and 25. If we use odd tens, you can make a double in it.

Teacher: So if you had an odd 10 and an even 10, what would be the difference?

Student: Because an odd 10, you just have a 10 with a 5. An even 10 you don't. Like 80 is like 8, 4 + 4 = 8, so 40 + 40 is 80, so there would be no 5.

The children in this classroom episode are engaged in some important mathematical work. Not only are they thinking deeply about a topic in number theory, an important point of mathematical *content*, but they also are communicating and justifying their thinking quite expertly, an issue of *process*; they are both quite persistent in the face of a significant mathematical challenge, a *dispositional* issue; and they are "agreeably disagreeing," an important *social* skill.

Children did not come to this classroom equipped with all the *content* knowledge they need, the ability to engage in important cognitive *processes*, a ready-made *disposition* to engage in those processes, or the skills to interact with one another *socially* in a mathematically productive way. They were taught to develop these desirable qualities, and that education was anything but haphazard. In other words, their teacher had clearly defined goals in all four areas suggested by the italicized words—content, process, disposition, and social—and worked diligently to teach those goals. In this chapter, we talk about the importance of goals in your teaching and the types of goals you should set for your students to create a well-balanced classroom.

It is important to remember that the content understanding of the students is limited by that of the teacher. The deeper the understanding of the teacher, the more effectively she is able to push and challenge her students, thus also affecting their disposition. Number theory and integers are two areas that teachers often struggle to understand themselves. This chapter addresses these two content areas. Even though the ideas are related to other topics, such as the four operations, they are more abstract. Nevertheless, they can easily be modeled.

Learning Theory

Lewis Carroll was an English logician and mathematician. In his book *Alice's Adventures in Wonderland* (2004, 83), Alice is faced with a decision:

> One day Alice came to a fork in the road and saw a Cheshire cat in a tree.
>   "Which road do I take?" she asked.
>   "Where do you want to go?" was his response.
>   "I don't know," Alice answered.
>   "Then," said the cat, "it doesn't matter."

That is a lot like teaching. If you do not know where you are headed with your students, it matters little which instructional road you follow. Numerous research studies have demonstrated for years that teachers need to have a clear conceptualization of the outcomes of their teaching. This notion can be traced back to 1934, when Ralph Tyler first conceptualized the notion of an objective. He observed that teachers tended to be far more interested with what they were teaching than with what the students should be able to do with what they were learning. Tyler demonstrated, and was later validated by Frances Fuller (1969), that beginning teachers tended to be preoccupied with concerns about self (e.g., "Can I make it through the day?" "What will I teach next?") to the exclusion of concerns about the results of their teaching on students. Christopher Clark and Penelope Peterson (1986), in four separate studies, discovered that the average amount of planning time devoted to goals and objectives ranged from 2.75% to 13.9%. The most important factor in lack of clarity and task orientation among beginning teachers is the inability to specify or even to conceptualize the learning outcomes resulting from instruction.

Numerous terms in educational circles are used synonymously, or partly synonymously, that have to do with defining what we want to result from our teaching. These words include goals, objectives, outcomes, targets, indicators, and standards. Depending on which author you read, you will find that all of these terms have something to do with figuring out where you want to end up instructionally. The bottom line is this—you do not want to be an Alice in Wonderland teacher. Whether you call them goals, objectives, targets, or whatever, without a clear idea about what effects you want from your teaching, the degree of mathematical learning in your classroom will be woefully low.

The best-known source for conceptualizing objective and outcomes is the *Taxonomy of Educational Objectives, Handbook I: Cognitive Domain* (Bloom 1956). Benjamin Bloom headed a group of educational psychologists who developed a classification of levels of intellectual behavior important in learning. A *taxonomy* is a hierarchal arrangement, so *Bloom's taxonomy* is a way of thinking about, or classifying, objectives according to the level of cognitive complexity they elicit. For example, it is one thing to know that $8 \times 4 = 32$, but it is more complex to know what 8×4 means or to think of a real-life situation in which 8×4 is useful. Bloom identified six levels within the cognitive domain, from the simple recall or recognition of facts as the lowest level, through increasingly complex and abstract mental levels, to the highest order, which is classified as

Level (in ascending order)	Definition	Sample Verbs
Knowledge	Students recall or recognize information, ideas, and principles in the approximate form in which they were learned	Write, list, label, name, state, define
Comprehension	Students translate, comprehend, or interpret information based on prior learning	Explain, summarize, paraphrase, describe, illustrate
Application	Students select, transfer, and use data and principles to complete a problem or task with minimal direction	Use, compute, solve, demonstrate, apply, construct
Analysis	Students distinguish, classify, and relate the assumptions, hypotheses, evidence, or structure of a statement or question	Analyze, categorize, compare, contrast, separate
Synthesis	Students originate, integrate, and combine ideas into a product, plan, or proposal that is new to that student	Create, design, hypothesize, invent, develop
Evaluation	Students appraise, assess, or critique on the basis of specific standards and criteria	Judge, recommend, critique, justify

Figure 9.1. Bloom's taxonomy within the cognitive domain. (Adapted from http://chiron.valdosta.edu/whuitt/col/cogsys/bloom.html. Reprinted by permission of William Huitt.)

evaluation. The taxonomy is presented in figure 9.1, with sample verbs to illustrate each level.

When we refer back to the introduction and the four types of goals or outcomes you can set as you design your instruction that we talked about, hopefully you can see that this cognitive taxonomy is most relevant to goals related to content and process. Bloom, along with David Krathwohl and Bertram Masia (1964), created an affective taxonomy that relates more to social and dispositional goals. It is displayed in figure 9.2.

Application to the Learning and Teaching of Mathematics

There are four types of goals you can, and should, set as you design your instruction: content, process, disposition, and social.

Level (in ascending order)	Definition	Sample Verbs
Receive	Students are open to experience and willing to listen	Ask, listen, focus, attend, take part, discuss, acknowledge, hear, be open to, retain, follow, concentrate, read, do, feel
Respond	Students are ready to react and participate actively	React, respond, interpret, clarify, contribute, question, present, cite, help, write, perform
Value	Students can attach values and express personal opinions	Argue, challenge, debate, refute, confront, justify, persuade, criticize
Organize	Students can reconcile internal conflicts and develop value system	Build, develop, formulate, defend, modify, relate, prioritize, reconcile, contrast, arrange, compare
Internalize or characterize values	Students adopt a belief system and philosophy	Act, display, influence, solve, practice

Figure 9.2. Bloom's taxonomy within the affective domain. (Adapted from chiron.valdosta.edu/whuitt/col/cogsys/bloom.html. Reprinted by permission of William Huitt.)

Content Goals

Content goals are the ones you are most familiar with. If you turn to any curriculum framework in the United States or internationally, you almost always find content goals. It is not uncommon to see those goals defined at varying levels of specificity and arranged hierarchically. Every state seems to have its own way of outlining the content standards. Some states, such as Nevada and Utah, specify one standard for each of the five mathematical content areas (number and operations, algebra, geometry, measurement, and data analysis). But, Nevada's five standards are overarching for all grades, and Utah's are written specifically to each grade, K–6. Other states, such as California, have as many as three separate standards for each content area. Florida, for example, uses the terminology *big ideas* to refer to its content standards. What might be considered a *standard* in one state might be labeled an *objective* in another. An *objective* in one state might be an *indicator* or *specific objective* in another. In other words, it is important that you become familiar with the structure of your particular state's standards and the lingo used to refer to the different aspects of it.

Compare a similar fourth-grade standard, regarding the understanding of decimals, of California, Florida, and Utah. Notice the similarities and differences among them.

California

Number Sense 1.0. Students understand the place value of whole numbers and decimals to two decimal places and how whole numbers and decimals relate to simple fractions. Students use the concepts of negative numbers.

1.2. Order and compare whole numbers and decimals to two decimal places.

1.6. Write tenths and hundredths in decimal and fraction notations, and know the fraction and decimal equivalents for halves and fourths.

Florida

Big Idea 2: Develop an understanding of decimals, including the connection between whole numbers.

MA.4.A.2.1 (math, grade 4, Algebra, big idea 2, benchmark 1). Use decimals through the thousandths place to name numbers between whole numbers.

MA.4.A.2.2. Describe decimals as an extension of the base 10 number system.

MA.4.A.2.3. Relate equivalent fractions and decimals with and without models, including locations on a number line.

MA.4.A.2.4. Compare and order decimals, and estimate fraction and decimal amounts in real-world problems.

Utah

Standard 1: Students will acquire number sense and perform operations with whole numbers, simple fractions, and decimals.

Objective 1: Demonstrate multiple ways to represent whole numbers and decimals, from hundredths to 1 million, and fractions.
    b. Demonstrate multiple ways to represent whole numbers and decimals by using models and symbolic representations.
    c. Identify the place and the value of a given digit in a six-digit numeral, including decimals to hundredths, and round to the nearest tenth.

Objective 2: Analyze relationships among whole numbers, commonly used fractions, and decimals to hundredths.

    d. Identify equivalences between fractions and decimals by connecting models to symbols.

In a previous chapter, you learned about the conceptual and procedural sides of mathematics. It would only make sense, therefore, to have conceptual and procedural objectives. Simply stated, conceptual objectives require students to demonstrate understanding of important mathematics, whereas procedural objectives only require students to "do the math." One of the distinguishing characteristics of many conceptual objectives is that they require students to represent mathematical thinking in multiple ways and to connect those representations. Go back and review the preceding standards, objectives, and indicators, and identify which are more conceptual and which are more procedural. In a balanced mathematics classroom, both types of content objectives are important—conceptual and procedural.

Comprehension Check

■ Locate the mathematics teaching standards for your state. Familiarize yourself with the content standards for the grade you teach or will be teaching.

Process Goals

Process goals are different from content goals in the sense that content objectives describe what students should *know* whereas process describe what students should be able to *do*. In addition, they not only refer to capabilities students should leave your lessons possessing but also describe the mathematical actions, or processes, that students engage in while they learn the content. These mathematical processes, the five process standards, were discussed in a previous chapter but are redefined here:

Problem solving	Inviting students to solve rich problems within mathematics and from real-life contexts in multiple ways
Communication	Inviting students to explain their thinking
Reasoning and Proof	Inviting students to justify their thinking
Representation	Inviting students to show their thinking in multiply ways
Connections	Inviting students to make connections among representations, problem-solving strategies, current and prior mathematical learning, mathematical topics, mathematics and other subject areas, and mathematics and real life

In the objectives of some states, words like *model, connect,* or *represent* imply process, along with content. Some states have incorporated specific objectives for process standards, whereas others have made a conscious effort to integrate the language of the process and content standards. Take a look at the following Florida math content standards, and try to identify the different processes integrated within them:

3.A.2.1	Represent fractions, including fractions greater than one, using area, set, and linear models
3.G.3.2	Describe, analyze, compare, and classify two-dimensional shapes using sides and angles—including acute, obtuse, and right angles—and connect these ideas to the definition of shapes

4.A.1.1   Use and describe various models for multiplication in problem-solving situations, and demonstrate recall of basic multiplication and related division facts with ease

4.G.3.2   Justify the formula for the area of the rectangle: area = base × height

4.A.6.5   Relate halves, fourths, tenths, and hundredths to decimals and fractions

An example of a process standard written separate from the content standards is found in a section of the Utah state standards, *Intended Learning Outcomes*, that specifically defines intended process objectives:

Communicate mathematically
  a. Represent mathematical ideas with objects, pictures, and symbols.
  b. Express mathematical ideas to peers, teachers, and others through oral and written language.
  c. Engage in mathematical discussions through brainstorming, asking questions, and sharing strategies for solving problems.
  d. Explain mathematical work and justify reasoning and conclusions.

Having the processes integrated with the content standards, such as in Florida, is beneficial, because teachers can see how they are directly applied to specific content skills. However, focusing on process standards as a whole can give teachers the bigger picture of how that process should look throughout the everyday curriculum. Nevada is an example of a state that does both, specifies objectives for process standards and weaves the language within the content.

Disposition Goals

Howard W. Hunter said that if we educate the heart all else will fall into place. In *Adding It Up* (2001), Jeremy Kilpatrick, Jane Swafford, and Bradford Findell state that an important consideration for our instructional planning concerns students' dispositions toward real mathematical work. They call it *productive disposition* and define it as the "habitual inclination to see mathematics as sensible, useful, and worthwhile, coupled with a belief in diligence and one's own efficacy" (5).

If students are to do significant mathematical work, they must believe that mathematics is understandable and doable with sustained effort and that they are capable of making sense of it. Students develop such a disposition when a balance exists between conceptual and procedural learning. Conceptual understanding leads to the belief that mathematics is a sense-making endeavor, rather than the confidence-reducing perception that mathematics is a rote memorization endeavor.

Students' disposition toward mathematics is a significant determinant of educational success. Students must perceive themselves as capable of acquiring great mathematical knowledge and of doing great mathematical thinking. American children tend to think that mathematical success is determined by ability, whereas their Asian counterparts view success as stemming from effort (Stevenson and Stigler 1992). You play an important part in affecting the attitudes that your students develop toward mathematics; therefore, we recommend that you set goals in this area.

Language Tip

Designing specific communication goals and objectives during math helps support English-language learners.

Comprehension Check

- Revisit your state standards. Do they address any of the five mathematical processes? Which ones? How are they addressed?

Here is a list of goals to consider focusing on as you design your instruction:

1. Demonstrate a positive learning attitude toward mathematics.
   a. Display a sense of curiosity about numbers and patterns.
   b. Pose mathematical questions about objects, events, and processes.
   c. Demonstrate persistence in completing tasks.
   d. Apply prior knowledge and processes to construct new knowledge.
   e. Maintain an open and questioning mind toward new ideas and alternative points of view.

Social Goals

Current mathematical research and philosophy suggest that mathematical knowledge is socially constructed (Wood et al, 2001). In the videos you have watched in connection with this text, you have seen children interacting with one another as a vehicle for promoting deep mathematical understanding. They do not just walk into your classroom already possessing the ability to engage in that kind of mathematical social interaction—you have to teach them how to do so. Therefore, you need to set goals in this area of your mathematical work as well. What specific social capabilities should children work toward that facilitate their mathematical learning? The following would be examples:

1. Develop social skills and ethical responsibility.
   a. Respect similarities and differences in others.
   b. Treat others with kindness and fairness.
   c. Follow classroom and school rules.
   d. Include others in learning and play activities.
   e. Participate with others when making decisions and solving problems.
   f. Function positively as a member of a family, class, school, and community.

2. Demonstrate responsible emotional and cognitive behaviors.
   a. Recognize own values, talents, and skills.
   b. Express self in positive ways.
   c. Demonstrate aesthetic awareness.
   d. Demonstrate appropriate behavior.
   e. Express feelings appropriately.
   f. Meet and respect needs of self and others.

Previously we discussed an affective taxonomy that incorporated elements relevant to both disposition and social goals. Martin Tombari and Gary Borich (1999) have developed a taxonomy of collaborative skills that can broaden your sense of what it means to act in a socially responsible manner and that can assist you further in setting social goals for your students. It appears in figure 9.3.

Comprehension Check

- Consider the students you are working with and identify a social goal that benefits your class as a whole. What are some objectives that can help your students meet that goal?

Choosing Goals and Objectives

When in the routine of everyday planning, you must decide what your long-term and short-term goals will be and then how you plan to meet them. You will generally be working on more than one kind of goal at one time, such as a content goal and a process goal, each with its own objectives. State objec-

Level (in ascending order)	Definition	Skills or Roles
Basic interaction	Students like and respect one another	Listening, making eye contact, answering questions, using the right voice, making sense, apologizing
Getting along	Students sustain their respect and liking for one another	Taking turns, sharing, following rules, assisting, asking for help or a favor, using polite words
Coaching	Students both give and receive corrective feedback and encouragement	Suggesting an action or activity, giving and receiving compliments or praise, being specific, giving advice, correcting and being corrected
Role-fulfilling	Students fulfill specific roles to create positive interdependency and individual accountability	Summarizer, checker, researcher, runner, recorder, supporter, troubleshooter

Figure 9.3. A taxonomy of collaborative skill. (From Gary Borich, *Educational Assessment for the Elementary and Middle School Classroom*, pages 205–207. Upper Saddle River, NJ: Merrill/Prentice-Hall, 2004. Reprinted by permission of the author.)

Rule of Thumb

Each lesson should have one clear content objective. Teaching too many things at once can be overwhelming to students.

tives, such as "compare and order whole numbers to 10,000," are broad and need many lessons dedicated to reaching this one objective. Generally, the adopted curriculum helps you know how to break these objectives into manageable teaching pieces. This is where knowing what your students know, perhaps through individual interviews, is critical. You need to meet your students where they are and then take them one step at a time toward the goal.

Your daily objective, or focus, should be something that you hope that your students accomplish by the end of that lesson. This keeps you focused and helps you avoid becoming sidetracked by the unexpected ideas that students generate in any given lesson.

CONTENT

Number Theory and Integers

As we shift our focus to the content study of this chapter, we invite you to keep the notion of goals in the forefront of your mind. It is important to be familiar with content goals, not only in your grade but in previous and following grades as well. This helps you add support to fragile understanding or push students deeper when needed. If teachers are only familiar with the expectations of their grade, they become unsure of the experiences their students should have had, thus causing many to start from the beginning of a concept. This prevents students from having continuing deep experiences with math topics. Students should not have the same learning experiences in third, fourth, and fifth grade about a single topic, yet it too often happens.

Process goals help students achieve understanding, which in turn affects their disposition toward mathematics. When reading this next section, think about the five process standards: problem solving, communication, reasoning and proof, representation, and connections; and what you would do to meet each one while teaching number theory and integers.

Big Ideas and Focal Points

Some big ideas that address the topics or ideas discussed in this chapter are as follows:

Number theory

- Every composite number can be expressed as the product of prime numbers in exactly one way, disregarding the order of the factors (Charles 2005, 14).

- Powers of 10 are important benchmarks in our numeration system, and thinking about numbers in relation to powers of 10 can make addition and subtraction easier (Charles 2005, 16).

- Exponential notation is a powerful way to express repeated products of the same number. Specifically, powers of 10 express very large and very small numbers in an economical manner (Van de Walle 2004, 453).

Integers

- Integers are the whole numbers and their opposites on the number line, where zero is its own opposite (Charles 2005, 13).

- An integer and its opposite are the same distance from zero on the number line (Charles 2005, 13).

- The real-world actions for operations with integers are the same those for operations with whole numbers (Charles 2005, 16).

The *Principles and Standards for School Mathematics* (NCTM 2000) states that all students from prekindergarten through 12th grade should understand numbers, ways of representing numbers, and number systems. The expectation of grades 3–5, according to NCTM, is that all students should explore numbers less than zero by extending the number line and through familiar applications. And the expectation of grades 6–8 is that all students should develop meaning for integers and represent and compare quantities with them.

The ideas related to number theory presented in this chapter are extensions of broader topics, such as multiplication and division; therefore, the NCTM focal points do not directly address any of these ideas, except for prime and composite numbers in the fifth grade. In addition, the focal points only formally address integers in the fifth grade.

> **NCTM FOCAL POINTS**
>
> **Fifth Grade**
>
> Students explore prime and composite numbers.
>
> Students explore contexts that they can describe with negative numbers.

Number Theory

The ideas behind odd and even numbers can be explored beginning in second grade. The concept of rounding numbers begins early but continues through the study of large numbers. Square numbers tend to surface in third grade when making arrays for multiplication. The other items related to number theory tend to be explored in about fifth grade.

Odd and Even Numbers

Odd and even numbers form one of the first number theory explorations in which students can participate. Students have to make sense of what is happening with this idea. Some ideas children explore about odd and even numbers are as follows:

- What is an odd or even number?
- What happens when you add two even, two odd, or an even and an odd number together?
- What happens when you multiply two even, two odd, or an even and an odd number together?

What Is an Odd or Even Number? When students are in first grade, they may have their first exposure to odd and even numbers. After a significant amount of time in the school year, the teacher may direct their attention to a chart on which students have been recording the numbers of days in school. This might be on a long register tape or in a 100 chart form. Most teachers have students record the days in two different colors (one for the odd number and one for the even number of days). After gathering this data, teachers might ask children what they notice about the different-colored numbers. At this stage, students might say that every other number is red, for example, or on a 100 chart, that all the numbers in one column are red and all the numbers in the next column are black. Teachers need to have some students pick some black numbers and others pick red ones and build the two numbers using cubes. Then they can ask the students to try to break the numbers into two groups. Students with one type of number will always have two evenly divided groups, whereas the other students will always have one leftover. The teacher can then present the terms *odd* and *even*. Young children can make initial conjectures about odd and even numbers, such as these:

"All even numbers have partners, and all odd numbers do not."

"Even numbers are doubles, and odd numbers are doubles plus one."

These are typical conjectures that young students make, but they need a little refining. Once in the second grade or above, teachers should revisit the definition of odd and even numbers by having students try to prove it with cubes. A more refined conjecture might sound like the following:

"Even numbers can be broken into two equal groups with no leftovers. Odd numbers always have one leftover when broken into two equal groups."

A teacher must not be fooled into thinking that students now understand odd and even numbers. In third grade, teachers should ask students whether 90 is an odd or even number. What do you think they will say? Give them base 10 blocks, and what do you think they will do? To a child, the 9 stands out more than the 10-ness of the number, and they will most certainly say that it is odd. They will prove it by gathering 9 rods of the base 10 blocks and putting 4 tens in one pile and 5 tens in the other pile, stating that there is 1 leftover. However, what they are not considering is that it is 1 ten and that 10 can be further split into ones and divided into the two groups.

This is when students start to discover that, because it is a 10, it can be split in two, no matter whether there is an even number of tens or an odd number of tens. This is the first divisibility rule that students start to make: how to know if a number is even, or divisible by two.

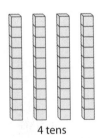

4 tens

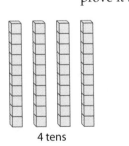

4 tens   1 ten

What Happens When You Add Even and Odd Number Combinations?
Another area of odd and even numbers that children in second and third grades are able to explore is what happens when two numbers are added together. They easily see that two odd numbers make an even number because each odd number has an "extra" and together they make an even number. Two evens also make an even because they did not and still do not have any left-overs. Only an even and an odd are still odd because that extra one does not have anything to partner with.

What Happens When You Multiply Even and Odd Number Combinations?
This idea tends to be explored in about fourth grade, or after multiplication is understood. It can be quite interesting. We want students not only to know what happens but also to be able to articulate why. Two evens have an even product because there were never any leftovers. An even and an odd are even because no matter how many groups of an even you have, the number is still even. An odd and an odd are the only combination that can produce an odd number because if there were an even group of odd numbers the leftovers would be paired. In an odd number of groups, there is still one leftover. Examine this in a model:

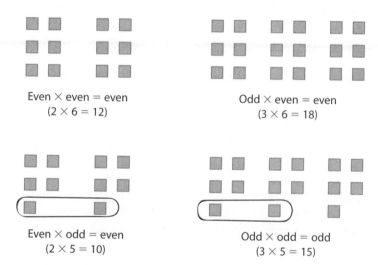

Even × even = even
(2 × 6 = 12)

Odd × even = even
(3 × 6 = 18)

Even × odd = even
(2 × 5 = 10)

Odd × odd = odd
(3 × 5 = 15)

One way to encourage students to explore these two ideas (addition and multiplication) is by deciding whether it would be a fair game if one player got a point for an even sum or product and the other player got a point for an odd sum or product when rolling two dice. Students soon learn that the addition game is fair whereas the multiplication game is not. When approaching the questions from the point of view of a game, sometimes students record all possible solutions. There are many ways to record, but the teacher may want to take this opportunity to introduce a matrix for recording (figure 9.4). Students can then compare its efficiency to the way they had chosen to do it. Visual students tend to like the matrix.

Comprehension Check

■ Make a representation to prove whether 110 is an odd or an even number. Explain your thinking.

Rounding Numbers

It is common for teachers to get a knot in the pit of their stomach when they think about having to teach rounding. Students of all ages have an issue with this, and it just seems painful to teach. Another problem is that rounding and estimation seem to be used interchangeably, which confuses students.

+	1	2	3	4	5	6
1	2	3	4	5	6	7
2	3	4	5	6	7	8
3	4	5	6	7	8	9
4	5	6	7	8	9	10
5	6	7	8	9	10	11
6	7	8	9	10	11	12

×	1	2	3	4	5	6
1	1	2	3	4	5	6
2	2	4	6	8	10	12
3	3	6	9	12	15	18
4	4	8	12	16	20	24
5	5	10	15	20	25	30
6	6	12	18	24	30	36

Figure 9.4. Using a matrix to clearly visualize the fairness of two games.

Rounding aids in estimation. For example, if a child wants to estimate the product for 38 × 11, he would round the numbers to 40 and 10 and then know that the product is around 400.

Rounding tends to be taught in isolation of any practical use, and this may be why so much agony is attached to it. Children need to know the reason rounding is useful. Adults naturally round when telling time and estimating how much they will spend at the store. We round to make some computations easier or just to make approximations when the exact answer is not critical. Estimating helps us know whether an exact answer is probable or not.

Rounding two-digit numbers does not cause as much of a problem as rounding larger numbers, especially if we are rounding to an unnatural place (like the hundreds place of a number in the ten thousands) for seemingly no reason. A need has to be generated for why rounding to that particular place would make sense in a certain situation.

One of the better models that we have seen used in teaching rounding is the "marble on the hill" method. The first things that children have to be able to do when rounding is identify a given number between two "friendly" numbers. Take, for example, 36. A student has to know that 36 falls between 30 and 40.

CAUTION A common error students make is to identify 36 as between 20 and 40. They see the 30 in their target number and go ahead and back a 10. Before even worrying about rounding, some group exercises need to be done just to identify the two end numbers.

Once these numbers are successfully identified, draw that segment of the number line (figure 9.5).

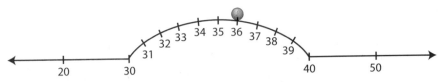

Figure 9.5. Using a marble on a hill to demonstrate the rules for rounding.

A marble is placed at the location of the number, 36, and students need to decide which way this marble is going to roll. Once a number ending in five is presented, students can debate which way it should roll, but the teacher will have to eventually state that the convention is that if it is on the five, or halfway, then it will always roll to the greater number, or round up.

Once children understand rounding of two-digit numbers, it does not mean that they can just apply it to larger numbers. In fact, the larger the number, the more difficult it tends to be. They need to go through the entire process again, identifying the two numbers that the target number falls between. So, if there was a reason that students were trying to round 45,369 to the hundreds place, then they need to identify that this is between 14,300 and 45,400. This idea is extended to decimals as well.

Square Numbers

Square numbers tend to be the biggest "ah-ha" at professional development workshops for experienced teachers. We all know how and what an exponent is, but why is it called *squared*? Greek math was based on geometry, and everything mathematical can be represented in some concrete way. For example, how would 4^2 be represented? It can be rewritten as 4×4, so how is that drawn?

Voilà! A square. So, what can be said about cubed numbers? Exponents are not so scary if students understand how they look when represented concretely or pictorially.

Exponents

Increasing a number to a power of 10 moves the decimal to the right, and taking a number to a power of negative 10 moves the decimal to the left, thus decreasing the amount.

Whereas multiplication is a form of repeated addition, exponents are a form of repeated multiplication. In the elementary grades, students mostly work with the power of two and three because they are easily modeled. Other powers are explored within different contexts, such as with prime factorization.

> **CAUTION** The most common error that students make is to multiply the integer with its exponent. For example 5^2 may be solved by some as $5 \times 2 = 10$ rather than $5 \times 5 = 25$.

When an entire expression is repeated, then the expression is raised by that power:

$$(3 + 4) \times (3 + 4) \times (3 + 4) = (3 + 4)^3$$

Order of Operations

A convention exists for how we solve multistep problems involving different operations. This convention is referred to as the *order of operations*. Even though it is necessary to just tell students what that order is, it is important to have students realize that the answer can be different depending on how they decide to solve the problem. One way to prove this is to hand students two different calculators. Perhaps half the class, or one partner, receives a cheap dime-store calculator and the others are handed a scientific calculator. If you happen to have access to both, use them now to calculate the following:

$$8 + (2 \times 5) \times 3^4 \div 9$$

What were your answers? Did you come up with the same or different answers and why? Scientific calculators are programmed to solve problems using the order of operations. The order of operations is defined as follows:

1. Parentheses
2. Exponents
3. Multiplication or division
4. Addition or subtraction

It seems natural that whatever is in the parentheses be solved first. The exponents also have to be solved to continue with the problem. The area that gives students the most trouble is remembering which comes first, the multiplication or division, or the addition or subtraction. Many teachers teach a mnemonic so that their students remember the order, but we like the students to realize that addition and subtraction are on the bottom of the mathematical totem pole for operations and not to depend on remembering a saying. For some students, however, this is helpful. If that is the case, having them come up with their own mnemonics is more meaningful.

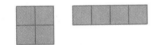

Figure 9.6. Creating different arrays to build a particular number.

Using arrays to understand prime and composite numbers.

Prime and Composite Numbers

It is a lot of fun to see children explore the meaning of prime numbers. One activity, which may take as long as two class periods, is to have students build all arrays for a particular number. For example, 4 can have the arrays in figure 9.6 to represent it.

Have students cut out the arrays for different numbers on graph paper and glue them to construction paper dedicated to just one number. Assign each pair or group of students a few numbers. Have students display all the numbers at the front when they are completed, and during the summary have them discuss

what they notice. They will notice that some numbers only make one array and others can make more than one array. This is when you can introduce the vocabulary *prime* and *composite* for these types of numbers.

Another way to explore prime numbers is through a Sieve of Eratosthenes. Take a 100 chart, and cross out all the numbers that are multiples of two (starting with the first multiple, 4).

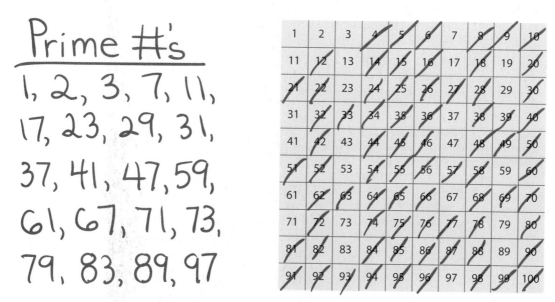

Figure 9.7. Using a Sieve of Eratosthenes to find prime numbers.

Then cross out all the numbers that are multiples of three and so on until you cannot cross out any more numbers. The numbers that are left uncrossed are prime numbers (figure 9.7).

> **CAUTION** A common misconception that children have when first exploring prime numbers is that all odd numbers are prime. If that comes up, have the class explore the idea to either prove or disprove that conjecture.

Prime Factorization

Prime factorization creates another pit in most teachers' stomach. Prime factorization tends to show up briefly in the curriculum, and by state testing all is forgotten, or maybe was never truly understood. Essentially, students have to factor numbers down until they are all prime numbers. If a factor tree is made to find the prime factorization of a number, then it is easy to see all the different factors of a certain number. Take the number 12, for example. You can initially break down 12 in two ways, so try them both:

$$12 \qquad 12$$
$$6 \times 2 \qquad 3 \times 4$$

Then, if any of the factors are still composite, break them down further:

$$12 \qquad 12$$
$$6 \times 2 \qquad 3 \times 4$$
$$2 \times 3 \qquad 2 \times 2$$

As you can see, no matter how you chose to break the number down, the prime factors are the same: 2, 2, and 3. This would be more correctly written as 3×2^2.

When introducing this concept, challenge your students to come up with a way to multiply a string of numbers to find a specific number, using all prime numbers. At the end, have them share their different solutions and strategies and compare their similarities. Some will have forgotten to factor a composite number, so that can be up for discussion.

Divisibility Rules

Knowing some divisibility rules is helpful for knowing what a number can be divided by without a remainder. A student may most commonly use this when working with fractions and trying to find a common denominator. Earlier we discussed how to know whether a number is even or odd. This is the same as knowing whether a number is divisible by two. Figure 9.8 lists divisibility rules

Comprehension Check

■ Create your own numbers that match the divisibility rules given here.

Divisible By	Rule	Example
2	A number is divisible by 2 if it ends in 0, 2, 4, 6, or 8.	34 is divisible by 2
3	When all digits in a number added up to a number divisible by 3, then the initial number is also divisible by 3.	1,434 $1 + 4 + 3 + 4 = 12$ 12 is divisible by 3, so 1,434 is also divisible by 3
4	The last two digits must be divisible by 4 for a number to be divisible by 4.	2,348 48 is divisible by 4, so 2,348 is also divisible by 4
5	The last digit must be either a 5 or a 0 for the number to be divisible by 5.	345 is divisible by 5
6	To be divisible by 6, the number has to be divisible by both 2 and 3. So the numbers have to add up to a multiple of 3, and it has to end in 0, 2, 4, 6, or 8.	1,434 is divisible by both 3 (see earlier rule) and 2, so it is also divisible by 6
7	The last digit is doubled and then subtracted from the rest of the number. The answer will be either 0 or divisible by 7. (If the ending number is too big, you can do this process again.)	553 $3 + 3 = 6$ $55 - 6 = 49$ 49 is divisible by 7, so 553 is also divisible by 7
8	For a number to be divisible by 8, the last three digits are divided by 8.	5,256 256 is divisible by 8, so 5,256 is also divisible by 8
9	For a number to be divisible by 9, the sum of the digits must be divisible by 9.	7,434 $7 + 4 + 3 + 4 = 18$ 18 is divisible by 9, so 7,434 is also divisible by 9
10	To be divisible by 10, the number must end in 0.	450 is divisible by 10
11	■ For factors to 9, the digits will be the same for any number divisible by 11. ■ For any number to be divisible by 11, the sum from every second digit subtracted from the sum of all other digits is 0 or divisible by 11.	121 $1 + 1 = 2$ $2 - 2 = 0$ 121 is divisible by 11 92,939 $2 + 3 = 5$ $9 + 9 + 9 = 27$ $27 - 5 = 22$ 22 is divisible by 11, so 92,939 is also divisible by 11
12	To be divisible by 12, the number is divisible by both 3 and 4.	324 $3 + 2 + 4 = 9$, which is divisible by 3 and . . . 24 is divisible by 4

Figure 9.8. Divisibility rules for numbers through 12.

and gives examples. Some rules are easy for students to explore and come up with the rule themselves, such as for 2, 5, and 10. Others need to be stated, but then students can test them. A list of all rules can be presented, and students can test lots of numbers to figure out which number the divisibility rule proves.

Integers

It is not uncommon for informal discussions about negative numbers to surface as early as first grade, when children are contemplating the idea of infinity and the notion that numbers go on forever. Children seem to be fascinated with that concept but tend to think that numbers only go on forever in one direction, because when they go backward they stop at zero. The first formal introduction to integers tends to be in third and fourth grades. Fifth grade usually begins to address the addition and subtraction of positive and negative numbers, which becomes more thoroughly explored in sixth grade as it is expanded to multiplication and division.

Many school sites and districts are thinking about how and when they introduce children to negative numbers. They are strategically posting a negative number line (-10 to 110) from at least first grade, and sometimes kindergarten. These classrooms are not necessarily formally discussing negative numbers, but sometimes informal conversations occur because of the children's natural curiosity. It is also helpful to have these models as children develop misconceptions, such as thinking that subtraction is commutative and stating that $3 - 5 = 2$. Using a negative number line, they can see that the answer would be less than zero—not exactly zero, as they would think if they only see a positive number line and think that once they reach zero they stop.

Exposing children early to the negative number line, even with no discussion, seems to have a positive effect. We have heard children in second and third grade commenting, while trying to develop alternative algorithms for addition and subtraction, that they remember seeing it in their first-grade class. They are beginning to make connections, and they had remembered seeing the model in the past. Some students are even able to develop problem-solving strategies, such as partial differences, when they have incidentally seen number lines. They do not necessarily know that the ones to the left of the zero are called negative, but they usually call them "minus," so it makes sense to them.

History of Negative Numbers

Negative numbers had a fairly rocky start. This idea was studied and accepted more in the East than in the West. The Chinese are recorded as being able to use negative number in equations in 100 BC–50 BC in their publication of *Nine Chapters on the Mathematical Art* (O'Connor and Robertson 2003). They even had developed the use of red and black rods to represent positive and negative numbers, respectively, which, ironically, is opposite of how we color-code them today in accounting but is how we color-code charges of electricity. The Chinese used this system in commercial calculations and computing taxes. As you may recall, by AD 600, place value and the notion of zero were developed by the Hindu in India. At this time, they even had written rules for multiplication of negative numbers. By AD 1000, the Arabs had acknowledged the negative notion of debt (Bragg 2006).

Europe, however, had a harder time accepting the idea of negative numbers. In the third century, Greece rejected negative numbers as an absurdity. Greek math was based on geometry and did not have a positional system, or place value. When solving equations through drawings, negative numbers never came up (Roney-Dougal 2006). By the 18th century, European mathematicians were beginning to accept the idea of negative numbers, but initially only in the context of debt.

Introducing and Modeling Integers

Interestingly, debt is one of the initial ways that students are exposed to problem solving using negative numbers. After reflecting on the history of negative numbers, it seems that this is a real and practical application. In more recent times, however, society has developed other conventions for which using negative numbers is also practical, such as temperature, sea level, and levels on a high-rise or parking structure that has floors both above and below ground (figure 9.9).

An *integer* is a whole number used to count discrete quantities. These numbers can be positive, negative, or zero, which is neither positive nor negative. Rational numbers can also have either positive or negative values. When dealing with negative numbers in grades K–6, students generally only focus on whole numbers, or integers.

Learning and teaching integers may involve different experiences in different areas of the country. Many of us never remember being formally taught negative numbers, because young children in some parts of the country are more likely to naturally internalize negative numbers from the frigid winters—unlike those who live in warmer climates, where the thermometer rarely falls below 45°F.

Some primary teachers even take the opportunity to use their table point system to informally teach the idea of integers. Students are allowed to earn table points but then have to pay points for specified reasons. The teacher allows students to "borrow" points that they do not have, but now they owe the teacher and, before they can earn their reward, have to return to zero and then earn the designated amount of points.

Before even worrying about the numbers, students need experiences *net change*. Take one of the preceding examples, like the parking structure. If all levels are numbered ground, 1, 2, 3, 4, and so on—and B1, B2, B3, and so on, for the basement levels—then students can be given directions such as "You drive into the ground floor and then go up three levels to find a parking spot. What

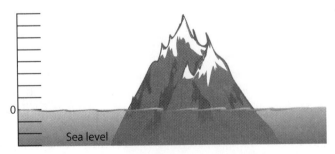

Figure 9.9. Using sea level to understand positive and negative numbers.

is your net change? (+3 floors) When you get there, the parking attendant tells you that spaces remain on B4, so you go down there to park. What is your net change now? (−7 floors)" The positive and negative in the answer of net change represents the direction of the change, up or down. This is a good way to explain *absolute value*. The positive or negative refers to the direction traveled, but there was still a span of 7 floors that were driven.

Once students can think about an entire amount on either side of the zero, they are able to begin to make equations to match their models. In the preceding problem, the equations would be $0 + 3 = 3$ and $3 − 7 = −4$. Generating the equations after they have solved the problem with the model helps them make sense of the symbols.

The preceding scenario leads nicely to the more abstract number line model. Children who think linearly tend to think well on a number line. However, it can become confusing to operate on a number line, especially when subtracting negative numbers. Therefore, using double-sided counters, as explained in the next sections, is highly supportive for conceptually understanding computation with integers, because it is a way to directly model the problems. Initially, adults might find that they have a more difficult time understanding this model as we have already established rules for operating with integers. Children, on the other hand, tend to find this a very clear model and can easily use it to make generalizations about how integers work.

Zero Pairs The first step in being able to use double-sided counters is to be familiar with the idea of zero pairs.

A *zero pair* is created when a negative and a positive are combined. Technically, there are an infinite number of zero pairs. Figure 9.10 shows examples of zero pairs using two-color counters.

When using zero pairs to make a number, simply have students create lots of zero pairs and ask them to show numbers, +4, for example. They will have to remove four negative counters to do so (figure 9.11).

Figure 9.10. Making zero pairs using two-sided counters.

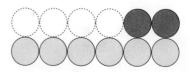

Figure 9.11. Showing +4 using the concept of zero pairs.

Addition and Subtraction of Integers

Once students understand the idea of zero pairs and are comfortable making them and making numbers from them, computation becomes easier to model. However, there are things to be aware of. It is not always as simple as it looks. First, asking a student to model $3 + 4$ would result in the representation in figure 9.12.

Asking the student to model $(+3) + (−4)$ would elicit the response shown in figure 9.13.

If students understand zero pairs, then they would just cancel out the pairs and would be left with one negative counter.

Figure 9.12. Showing $3 + 4$ using two-sided counters.

Figure 9.13. Showing $(+3) + (−4)$ using two-sided counters.

What can be tricky is asking the students to take away something they do not have. For example, consider $(+3) - (-4)$. Children will start by placing the three positive counters and then will not know what to do.

What questions could you ask them to help them figure out what to do? Simply asking "How does what you know about zero pairs help?" is usually enough to start most students thinking about adding many pairs of counters so that they can take away four negative counters (figure 9.14).

They may have some pairs of counters left over, but these cancel each other out. Thus, regardless of how many pairs of counters are added, the remaining amount of seven positive counters does not change.

Contexts for Addition and Subtraction of Integers Perhaps one of the most difficult aspects of teaching integers is to create a real enough context for negative numbers to make sense. We often forget about context once we start dealing with more difficult numbers, such as fractions or integers, and only have students manipulate the numbers. However, context, at least initially, is still vital for problem solving and sense making. Figure 9.15 shows sample contexts for different types of problems.

Figure 9.14. Using the idea of zero pairs to model $(+3) - (-4)$.

Problem Type	Context
Adding a positive and a negative $(+) + (-)$ **or** $(-) + (+)$	■ You balance a checkbook adding your credits, perhaps when you deposit a check, with your debits. ■ You have negative table points and earn points by turning in your homework. ■ You start with one temperature and either add negatives (colder) or positives (warmer).
Adding two negatives $(-) + (-)$	■ You add two debits or debts you have to see how much you spent or owe all together. ■ You travel down three floors on the elevator, and then you go down four more floors. How far down have you gone?
Subtracting a negative from a positive $(+) - (-)$	■ You have $100 in your account after buying a shirt from the store for $20. You find that it has a hole in it and return it to the store. The store refunds your money by crediting your account (removing the debit that you had made). ■ You compare the difference between temperatures (the answer would be in an absolute value form).
Subtracting a positive from a negative $(-) - (+)$	■ The temperature is $-10°F$. It gets colder, and the temperature drops another 5 degrees. ■ You already owe $15, and you just spent $5 more.
Subtracting a negative from a negative $(-) - (-)$	■ You owe your mom $15 for concert tickets that she bought for you until your next allowance. Your birthday rolls around, and she forgives $10 of your debt. ■ You compare the difference between two negative temperatures (the answer would be in an absolute value form).

Figure 9.15. Sample context for addition and subtraction integers.

Problem Type	Generalization
Adding a positive and a positive $(+) + (+)$	"When we add two positive integers together, the answer is larger."
Adding a positive and a negative $(+) + (-)$ $(-) - (+)$	"When we add a positive and a negative together, it is like subtracting. The answer will be smaller than the first addend. The answer will have the sign of the largest number in the problem."
Adding two negatives	"When we add two negatives, it is like adding, but the answer is negative. The absolute value, or distance from zero, is the same, but it is to the left instead of to the right."
Subtracting a positive from a positive $(+) - (+)$	"Subtracting two positives will result in a smaller amount. If you are subtracting a smaller number from a larger number, the answer will be positive. If you are subtracting a larger number from a smaller number, the answer will be negative."
Subtracting a negative from a positive $(+) - (-)$	"When we subtract a negative number from a positive number, the answer gets bigger because we are taking away negatives and making more positives. It is like adding."
Subtracting a positive from a negative $(-) - (+)$	"When we subtract a positive from a negative, it is like adding, because we are making more negatives but the answer is negative."
Subtracting a negative from a negative $(-) - (-)$	"When we take a negative from a negative, we have fewer negatives, so the answer is larger. The answer will be negative if the first number is larger [like $(-5) - (-1)$], but the answer will be positive if the first number is smaller [like $(-1) - (-5)$]."

Figure 9.16. Generalizations we want students to make regarding addition and subtraction with integers.

Do not forget the different problem types discussed in the addition and multiplication chapters. Using integers, and other difficult number types, makes those problem types appropriate for older students.

Generalizations for Addition and Subtraction of Integers Through activities that use one of the earlier concrete or pictorial representations of addition and subtraction with positive and negative integers, we want children to make some generalizations. To make clear conjectures or generalizations, students need to explore the different situations in isolation (figure 9.16).

It is important to help students be able to stand back from the problems and not over analyze the situation. Once, a sixth-grade class was solving different problems involving integers. One student was stuck on $(+5) + (+3)$. The teacher simply asked her, "You don't know what five plus three is?" That was all it took to snap her out of being overfocused and not seeing the obvious.

Multiplication and Division of Integers

As with fractions, we can think of multiplication and division of integers in the same way as we do with whole numbers. It is often helpful to go back and reevaluate what the operation means with whole numbers to understand what it means with integers.

Multiplication is essentially thought of as repeated addition, or adding many groups of the same amount. We can apply that idea to integers. For example, $(+3) \times (-4)$ would be three groups of negative four. Perhaps you bought three T-shirts for $4 and you want to see what your total debit will be. Using chips, this would look like figure 9.17.

So, what about $(-3) \times (+4)$? If a positive group is one that you can see, then a negative group might be one you cannot see, such as one that is missing.

Comprehension Check

- Create a context, or situation, for the following problems. Solve for each using pictures, numbers, and words:
  a. $(+30) + (-4)$
  b. $(-20) - (+3)$
  c. $(-24) + (-15)$
  d. $(+18) - (-13)$

Figure 9.17. Modeling 3 × −4 using two-sided counters.

Figure 9.18. A negative group of positive four would mean that the positive four would disappear, leaving only negatives.

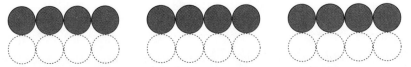

Figure 9.19. Modeling −3 × 4 using two-sided counters.

What if you had three missing groups, or sets, of pens? You would want to know how many pens were missing altogether. You may respond that you have 12 missing pens, or that you have −12 pens. Keeping in mind what we know about zero pairs, this could be modeled as in figure 9.18.

It gets even more confusing. Try (−3) × (−4) (figure 9.20). A scenario for this would be that you had three sets of $4 debits reversed. How much did you gain?

A negative group of negative four would mean that the negative four would disappear, leaving only positives.

Now try division. Keep in mind the differences between partitive and measurement division when thinking about a situation and how to model it. Take the preceding pen scenario. There were 12 missing pens (or −12 pens), and there were 4 pens in each pack (figure 9.21). How many packs were missing? This would be an example of measurement division {(−12) ÷ 4 = −3}.

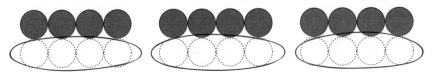

There are three packs of pens missing, or −3 packs.

Figure 9.20. Modeling −3 × −4 using two-sided counters.

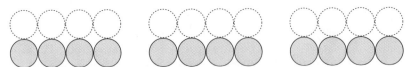

A negative group of negative four would mean that the negative four would disappear leaving only positives.

Figure 9.21. Modeling −12 ÷ 4 = −3 using two-sided counters.

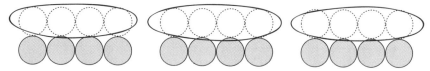

Figure 9.22. Modeling $12 \div -4 = -3$ using two-sided counters.

Look at partitive division. The scenario would become "There were 12 missing pens (or -12 pens), and there were three missing packs. How many pens were in each pack?" The model would look like the one in figure 9.21, but what is being counted is different $[(-12) \div (-3) = 4]$.

Think about the reversed debt scenario given earlier using measurement division. Suppose that the bank credited you $12 for some shirts you returned to the store. Each shirt cost $4, so how many debits do you have $[(+12) \div (-4) = (-3)]$? A model is shown in figure 9.22.

Figure 9.23 gives the generalizations you want children to make and articulate when multiplying and dividing integers (remember, integers are whole numbers). Like all other generalizations or conjectures, they should go on your growing charts in your classroom.

Other Ways to Represent Integers

Red and yellow counters are probably the most popular manipulative used when solving for positive and negative. However, in accounting, "in the red" means debt, or negative, and "in the black" means profit, or positive. Therefore, some curriculum, like Everyday Math, uses red and black for the exploration of positive and negative integers. It is not difficult to cut up a lot of small squares of red and black construction paper for your tools. Another popular tool is the spacers used in tiling. They can be purchased at your local home improvement

> **Comprehension Check**
>
> ■ **Create a context, or situation, for the following problems. Solve for each using pictures, numbers, and words.**
> a. $(+8) \times (-4)$
> b. $(-12) \times (+4)$
> c. $(+36) \div (-9)$
> d. $(-24) \div (-8)$

Problem Type	Context
Multiplying two positives $(+) \times (+)$	"When we multiply two positive integers, the answer is larger and positive because we are making positive groups of a positive amount."
Multiplying two negatives $(-) \times (-)$	"When we multiply two negatives, the answer is larger and positive because we are removing sets of negative numbers leaving positive numbers."
Multiplying a positive and a negative $(+) \times (-)$	"When we multiply a positive and a negative, the answer is smaller and negative because we are making groups of negative numbers."
Dividing two positives $(+) \div (+)$	"When we divide two positive numbers, and the absolute value of the divisor is larger than the absolute value of the dividend, then the answer is smaller and positive because we are finding how many groups of one number are in the total."
Dividing two negatives $(-) \div (-)$	"When we divide two negatives, and the absolute value of the divisor is larger than the absolute value of the dividend, then the answer is larger and positive because we are finding how many groups of one negative number are in another."
Dividing a positive by a negative $(+) \div (-)$	"When we divide a positive number by a negative number, we get a negative quotient because we are finding out how many negative groups were removed to get the total number."
Dividing a negative by a positive $(-) \div (+)$	"When we divide a negative number by a positive, we get a negative quotient because we are seeing how many times a positive number is being removed (repeatedly subtracted) to make the original total."

Figure 9.23. Generalizations for students to make regarding multiplication and division of integers.

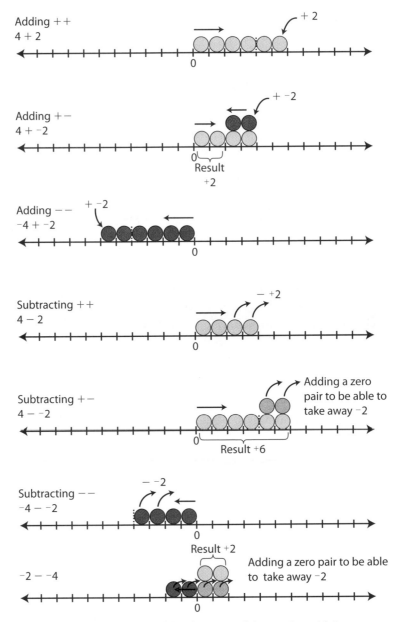

Figure 9.24. Using the number line to model operating with integers.

store and are shaped like positives. They are made of rubber, so to make the negatives just cut off two of the legs.

The use of a negative number line cannot be ignored when discussing ways to model integers. As when dealing with whole numbers in the primary grades, teachers cannot forget that the number line is a more abstract representation than the ones discussed earlier and tends to reinforce counting strategies. All operations using integers can be modeled on a number line, but some are harder to conceptualize than others, such as subtracting a negative. Most adults only have experience with the number line; thus, if teachers use this model as the sole way to teach integers to children, without the proper understanding of what is happening, the students are easily confused. Figure 9.24 shows some basic representations of integers using a number line.

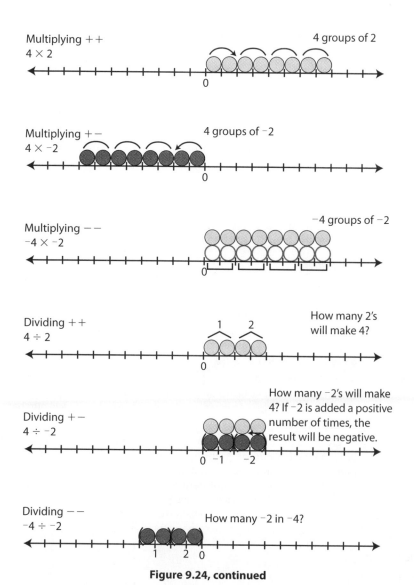

Figure 9.24, continued

Using Inquiry with Number Theory and Integers

Exploring Odd and Even Numbers

Cycle 1

Launch	In partnerships, students talk about what they think makes a number odd or even and discuss their ideas as a class.
Explore	In partnerships, students use cubes to prove their ideas or conjectures, using numbers under 10.
Summarize	Students share how their models prove or disprove their ideas.

Cycle 2

Launch	The teacher asks the class to figure out whether 90 is odd or even using any tool.
Explore	Students work in partnerships to try to prove whether 90 is odd or even.
Summarize	Students share their findings by using their models to support their conjectures.

(Continued on following page.)

Discovering Square Numbers and Their Relationship to the Multiplication Chart

Launch	The teacher describes the task and models procedures for building square numbers on 10 × 10 graph paper with 1-inch squares. Students begin making all squares (1–10) from the top-left corner and record the total under the last tile at the bottom-right corner.
Explore	Students work in pairs, building every square and recording the total number of tiles in that square on their graph paper. When they are done, students discuss in their partnerships patterns and other observations.
Summarize	As a class, students discuss what they noticed. The teacher focuses the conversation on the discovery that the square numbers run diagonally and are the same numbers from the multiplication chart. Students might discuss why there is no mirror number, as with the other arrays, because no matter how you flip the array, or square, it lands in the same place. Students should link that to the commutative property and how the factors are the same in all square numbers.

Exploring Prime Numbers

Launch	The teacher asks students to design candy boxes for a specified number of candies. Each box has to be rectangular and cannot have spaces (is a perfect array). They are to create as many different boxes as possible with their number. The teacher hands each small group 2 or 3 different numbers from 2 to 20. (Groups with smaller numbers may receive more numbers than groups with larger numbers.)
Explore	Students work together to design their boxes, using color tiles or counters. They record their final boxes on graph paper, cut out the shape, and glue it on construction paper. Students glue all possible boxes for one number onto their paper.
Summarize	All groups bring up their construction paper models and arrange them in order on the front board, from 2 to 20. They sit down and talk with their partner or small group about what they notice, and then they share as a group what they notice about the arrays. Some students notice that some numbers were only able to make one type of candy box whereas other numbers made many types of boxes. The teacher then introduces the formal terms of *prime* and *composite numbers* for these ideas.

Exploring Integers

Cycle 1

Launch	The teacher presents the following problem: "Table 4 has −10 points since they had all forgotten to turn in their homework. Table 1 has 25 points. How many points does table 4 need to catch up with table 1?"
Explore	Students work in their groups to solve the problem using any tool they wish. They record their work using pictures, numbers, and words (explanation) on their presentation paper.
Summarize	Students share their solutions and how they solved the problem. The teacher invites the class to write the problem using an equation. The class gives the following equation: $-10 + 35 = 25$. The teacher asks the class members what they think happens when they add a positive and a negative number together.

Cycle 2

Launch	Keeping the cycle 1 idea in mind, the teacher poses several similar equations in which students have to add a positive and a negative number. Sometimes the positive number is the "larger" of the two, and sometimes the negative is.
Explore	Students solve for all the problems, and as a small group they try to generate a more formal generalization of what happens when the two numbers are combined.
Summarize	Students share their ideas, and the generalization is formalized: Adding a positive and a negative is like subtracting. If the positive number is "larger" (or the absolute value of the positive number), the answer will be positive, and if the negative number is "larger," then the answer will be negative.

CONCLUSION

Greg Anderson said, "When we are motivated by goals that have deep meaning, by dreams that need completion, by pure love that needs expressing, then we truly live life" (1995). The setting of meaningful goals to guide our mathematics instruction is such a common sense idea, yet it has been shown that a key difference between those teachers who foster real mathematical progress and those who do not is that the former have the ability to conceptualize the end results of instruction with precision. To truly educate the whole person, we must consider the cognitive content, process, dispositional, and social results of our work with children.

Ideas in number theory and integers can begin to be explored in the primary years but should be revisited often as students mature and their understanding develops. Students can begin to make simple generalizations early on but can refine them by adding more sophisticated ideas and language. Also, as numbers become more complex, students need to revisit ideas, such as odd and even numbers, to extend their generalizations to a new set of numbers. Even though the branch of mathematics is called number *theory,* it does not mean that the explorations have abstract.

▶ Interview Video with an Eye on Content

Watch a series of videos around either number theory or integers. Briefly describe the task and the child's response. What did the child understand or not understand around the question presented?

Task Description	Child's Response	Understandings or Misconceptions
1		

▶ Interview a Child

1. Design a task for a student interview about integers. Use the different problem types and contexts to help you write your questions.

2. Using the problems from step 1, conduct this interview with students of different ability and grade levels. Be sure to provide a variety of tools such as counters, a number line and paper and pencil. What do you notice? Were some problem types harder than others? What were his misconceptions?

3. Write an overall summary about how your student did. Include recommendations you would make for the child's teacher or what would you do with this child if you were to continue to work with him.

▶ Classroom Video with an Eye on Pedagogy

Watch a classroom episode in which the teacher involves children in a task designed to promote their understanding of a concept in number theory or integers. Focus on trying to infer the content, process, dispositional, and social goals that drive the lesson.

Task Description	Content Goals Are they conceptual or procedural? Explain	Process Goals Teacher and student actions to support your inferences	Dispositional Goals What evidence do you see?	Social Goals What evidence do you see?

▶ Classroom Application

1. Observe your cooperating teacher lead a lesson about either number theory or integers. What goals and objectives does the teacher establish for the lesson? Were the students able to meet those objectives?

2. Collaboratively, design a whole group or small group lesson that includes a content, process, and social or dispositional goal and objective about an area in number theory or integers. Determine a way to measure whether those objectives were met by the end of the lesson. If they were not met, what do you feel prevented this from happening?

▶ Resources

How to Encourage Girls in Math and Science, Joan Skolnick, Carol Langbort, and Lucille Day (1997)

Curriculum Planning: A Contemporary Approach, Forrest Parkay, Eric Anctil, and Glen Hass (2005)

Instruction: A Models Approach, Mary Alice Gunter, Thomas H. Estes, and Jan Schwab (2006)

Measurement and Evaluation in Teaching, Norman Gronlund and Robert Linn (1990)

▶ Lit Link

Literature Books to Support Number Theory, Integers, and Disposition

Title	Author
Calculator Riddles	David A. Adler
Fibonacci Fun: Fascinating Activities with Intriguing Numbers	Trudi Hammel Garland
Go Figure: A Totally Cool Book about Numbers	Johnny Ball
Math Curse	Jon Scieszka and Lane Smith
Mensa Number Puzzles for Kids	Harold Gale and Carolyn Skitt
Number Games: Mindgames for Kids Ages 8 and Up	Ivan Moscovich
Phantom Tollbooth, The	Norton Juster
Rabbits Rabbits Everywhere: A Fibonacci Tale	Ann McCallum

▶ Tech Tools

Websites

National Library of Virtual Manipulatives, www.nlvm.usu.edu

Resource Room: Multisensory Teaching: Positive and Negative Integers, http://www.resourceroom.net/math/integers.asp

Explorelearning, http://www.explorelearning.com (select grades 6–8 to find options for integers and number theory)

Funbrain: MathCar Racing, http://www.funbrain.com/osa/index.html

PrimOmatic: The Prime Number Checker, http://www.archimedes-lab.org/primOmatic.html

Software

Pre-Algebra World: Number Sense, Math Realm

High- and Low-Level Tasks and Fractional Number Sense

. . . .

A man is like a fraction whose numerator is what he is and whose denominator is what he thinks of himself. The larger the denominator, the smaller the fraction.

Leo Tolstoy

CONVERSATION IN MATHEMATICS

Teacher: Your mom gave you eight doughnut holes and asked you to give half of them to your sister. Can you show me half?

Student: (Makes two groups of four with the counters.)

Teacher: How many doughnut holes are one-half?

Student: Four.

Teacher: How do you know?

Student: Half means to make two groups of the same size.

Teacher: Nice work.

Student: Teacher, when I make one-half, I also have four-eighths.

Teacher: What do you mean?

Student: There is one big group of eight doughnut holes. Each small group has four, so that means four-eighths.

Teacher: I like the way you thought about that.

Children come to school with a wealth of experience solving mathematical problems in their everyday lives. To be a problem solver, a person needs to have confidence and persistence. The school environment needs to provide a plethora of experiences that allow students to develop mathematical knowledge and strategies by building on the informal mathematical experiences they have outside of school. This means designing problems, or tasks, that invite children to extend what they already know without leaving their "comfort zones" and that incorporate the mathematics you wish children to acquire.

Notice in the conversation that the child was presented with what appears to be a simple task—dividing a set of objects into halves. Yet within that task were some deeper mathematical ideas, such as fractional equivalence, multiplicative relationships, ratios, and proportions. Therefore, we think the task presented was a good one, and as you read this chapter, you will see why. In addition, the task introduces you to the content emphasis of this chapter, fractional number sense. Specifically, this chapter discusses in depth what a task is and how to design a high-level task as part of a daily math lesson. Then we segue into a discussion of how children develop their understanding of fractions.

High- and Low-Level Tasks

Learning Theory

One of the most important findings of current research is something that most of us intuitively believe—children do not all think the same way. In an open classroom environment in which children are allowed to explore a given mathematical problem using their own schema, they work in different ways, use different strategies, and represent their thinking in ways that are both varied and unique. Therefore, a new theory has become popular that incorporates both the idea of precisely defined outcomes and the idea that children engage in legitimate mathematical work in different ways. Marty Simon (1995) has coined the term *hypothetical learning trajectory*. The word *hypothetical* is key because until students begin investigating and exploring a problem, we cannot predict with certainty how they will make sense of the mathematical situations in which they work. Simon (1995, 136–137) uses a sailing voyage metaphor to discuss the notion of a *trajectory* (a term we might add to the list of *outcome* synonyms):

> You may initially plan the whole journey or only part of it. You set out sailing according to your plan. However, you must constantly adjust because of the conditions that you encounter. You continue to acquire knowledge about sailing, about the current conditions, and about the areas that you wish to visit. You change your plan with respect to the order of your destinations. You modify the length and nature of your visits as a result of interactions with people along the way. You add destinations that prior to the trip were unknown to you. The path that you travel is your (actual) trajectory. The path that you anticipate at any point is your "hypothetical trajectory."

Catherine Twomey Fosnot and Maarten Dolk (2002, 23) used to think about hypothetical trajectories as learning *lines* consisting of big ideas, mathematical models, "and the strategies that children construct along the way [as] they grapple with key mathematical topics." However, because real learning is anything but a neat, linear progression (Eleanor Duckworth [1987] calls learning messy), Fosnot and Dolk created three new metaphoric terms in the spirit of hypothetical learning trajectory—landscapes, landmarks, and horizons. They state (2002, 24):

> The big ideas, strategies, and models are important landmarks for [the teacher] as she journeys with her students across the landscape of learning. As she designs contexts for her students to explore, her goal is to enable them to act on, and within, the situations mathematically and to trigger discussions about them. [The teacher] has horizons in mind when she plans—horizons like place value or addition and subtraction. As she and the children move closer to a particular horizon, landmarks shift, new ones appear.
>
> The paths to these landmarks and horizons are not necessarily linear. Nor is there only one. As in a real landscape, the paths twist and turn, they cross each other, are often indirect. Children do not construct each of these ideas and strategies in an ordered sequence. They go off in many directions as they explore, struggle to understand, and make sense of their world mathematically. . . . Ultimately, what is important is how children function in a mathematical environment (Cobb 1997)—how they "mathematize." (quotes added)
>
> It is not up to us, as teachers, to decide what pathways our students will use. Often, to our surprise, children will use a path we have not encountered before. That challenges us to understand the child's thinking. What is important, though, is that we help all our students reach the horizon. . . .

When we are moving across a landscape toward a horizon, the horizon seems clear. Yet we never actually reach it. New objects—new landmarks—come into view. So, too, with learning. One question seemingly answered raises others. Children seem to resolve one struggle only to grapple with another. It helps to have the horizons in mind when we plan activities, when we interact, question, and facilitate discussions. But horizons are not fixed points in the landscape; they are constantly shifting. (Reprinted with permission from *Young Mathematicians at Work,* copyright © 2001 by Catherine Twomey Fosnot and Maarten Dolk. Published by Heinemann, Portsmouth, NH. All rights reserved.)

Deborah Ball (2000) stated that she learned from years of work with third graders that the task we present to children to begin their inquiry matters greatly. The task becomes the instructional embodiment of the mathematical horizon you intend to lead children to. It is where the models, big ideas, and strategies we hope might emerge live embryonically. Models you want developed, big ideas you want conceptualized, and strategies you want created all start with the task.

Application to the Learning and Teaching of Mathematics

What Is a Task?

Tasks are essentially the activities that the students engage in during a math lesson. The goals the teacher has for the students determine which kind of task would be most appropriate for a given lesson. Tasks should not be purposeless activities but, rather, should be connected and linked to a big idea. Student learning is generated from the types of tasks that are given; therefore, it is essential that the teacher carefully considers what these goals are and is aware of the cognitive demands of the task. Mary Kay Stein et al. (2000, 11) argue that "tasks that require students to perform a memorized procedure in a routine manner lead to one type of opportunity for students thinking; tasks that demand engagement with concepts and that stimulate students to make purposeful connections to meaning or relevant mathematical ideas lead to a different set of opportunities for student thinking."

Mathematical tasks that we were perhaps more familiar with growing up might have been memorizing our multiplication tables or solving multiple problems of the same kind after having one demonstrated to us on the chalkboard. These examples, memorizing and practicing procedures without connections, are considered lower-level demand tasks (Stein et al. 2000). They do not invite students to explore relationships or result in high-level engagement. These tasks prove helpful with improving efficiency or preparing for standardized tests. When students become more efficient with their basic facts and other routine problems, their mind is freed to focus on more complex problems. It saddens a teacher to see a student trying to solve a problem that involves complicated long division when that student only knows his twos times tables. When trying to solve the problem and create representations of his work, he is only able to separate out groups of two at a time. Not only might this student not finish his assignment on time, but it adds to his frustration and dislike of math.

Higher-level demand tasks are defined by Stein et al. (2000) as procedures with connections and doing mathematics. Higher-level tasks include verbs such as *construct, predict, explore, investigate, discover,* and *justify.* The key here is giving the students opportunities to make connections and explore relationships between representations. We, as teachers, can point out relationships to children, but they will not make sense until these relationships are discovered from themselves and used to solve problems. One of the things we live for is to see that look on the face of a child who has finally "gotten it." Just because something is obvious to us does not make it obvious to a child. Finding out that the digit in the tens place represents how many 10 sticks the child has can be a huge revelation. Figure 10.1 gives an example of each of the task levels.

According to Marilyn Burns (1998, 69), "doing math has to do with thinking and reasoning about problems or situations that call for applying mathematical ideas and skills." She later said (2000) that arithmetic skills should not be taught in isolation but, rather, in the situations that require those skills. Before skills, such as multiplication facts, are committed to memory through lower-level tasks, the concepts need to be explored and developed using higher-level tasks and alongside experiences related to how numbers work. Once there have

Lower-Level Demands	**Higher-Level Demands**
<u>Memorization</u>	<u>Procedures with connections</u>

Lower-Level Demands

<u>Memorization</u>

What are the decimal and percentage equivalents for the fractions $\frac{1}{2}$ and $\frac{1}{4}$?

Expected Student Response:

$\frac{1}{2} = 0.5 = 50\%$

$\frac{1}{4} = 0.25 = 25\%$

<u>Procedures without connections</u>

Convert the fraction $\frac{3}{8}$ to a decimal and a percentage.

Expected Student Response:

Fraction	Decimal	Percentage
$\frac{3}{8}$	.375	$0.375 = 37.5\%$
	8 ⟌ 3000	
	24	
	60	
	56	
	40	
	40	

Higher-Level Demands

<u>Procedures with connections</u>

Using a 10 × 10 grid, identify the decimal and percentage equivalents of $\frac{3}{5}$.

Expected Student Response:

Pictorial	Fraction	Decimal	Percentage
	$\frac{60}{100} = \frac{3}{5}$	$\frac{60}{100} = 0.60$	$0.60 = 60\%$

<u>Doing mathematics</u>

Shade 6 small squares in a 4 × 10 rectangle. Using the rectangle, explain how to determine each of the following: (a) the percentage of area that is shaded, (b) the decimal part of area that is shaded, and (c) the fractional part of area that is shaded.

One Possible Student Response:

(a) One column will be 10% since there are 10 columns. So 4 squares is 10%. Then 2 squares is half a column and half of 10%, which is 5%. So the 6 shaded blocks equal 10% plus 5%, or 15%.

(b) One column will be 0.10 since there are 10 columns. The second column has only 2 squares shaded, so that would be one half of 0.10, which is 0.05. So the 6 shaded blocks equal 0.1 plus 0.05, which equals 0.15.

(c) Six shaded squares out of 40 squares is $\frac{6}{40}$, which reduces to $\frac{3}{20}$.

Figure 10.1. Examples of lower-level and higher-level tasks. (Reprinted by permission of the Publisher. From Mary Kay Stein, Margaret Schwan Smith, Marjorie A. Henningsen, and Edward A. Silver, *Implementing Standards-Based Mathematical Instruction: A Casebook for Professional Development*, New York: Teachers College Press. Copyright © 2000 by Teachers College Press. All rights reserved.)

been plenty of opportunities to make connections and explore relationships, tasks that focus on accuracy and efficiency are appropriate.

During lower-level tasks, students typically are completing about 10–30 similar problems, whereas higher-level tasks usually consist of 1–3 problems during a math lesson. Constructing meaning is a "messier" process and takes a lot more time than merely practicing a procedure. At first, many teachers are uncomfortable with giving just a few problems. They fear that students are not getting enough practice. Over time, however, teachers come to realize that, if they have selected the right task, not only do students apply previous skills to find a solution, but the math they are learning is more deeply rooted and tends to "stick" better. Practice can then be embedded in any number of other routines, such as homework, games, problems of the day, class openings, and even an occasional worksheet.

Finding the balance between lower-level and higher-level tasks may vary from class to class. The teacher must cautious in assessing the abilities of the students. If students are used to waiting for the teacher to tell them what and how to do problems, it takes a lot of training for them to be able to work on their own. Students might act helpless as a way to convince the teacher to give them hints that take away all of the thinking. Thinking is a lot of work, and they probably will not want to do it at first. If students are learning based on the kinds of tasks they are engaged in, then it is imperative that the teacher pays attention to what kinds of tasks she is mostly assigning. James Hiebert et al. (1997) suggest that students become better and faster at whatever they do the most. If they spend most of their time with worksheet exercises, then that is what they grow comfortable with and they become better at doing worksheets. If they are constantly immersed in rich problematic tasks that are asking them to find patterns and relationships, then they are likely to build new relationships and construct new understanding. Focusing exclusively on lower-level tasks can lead to a limited understanding of what mathematics is and how one does it (Stein et al. 2000; NCTM 1989).

Comprehension Check

- What are the four levels of tasks?
- How do they vary?
- Create an example of each of the four levels using fractions.

Outcomes of a Problematic Task

A problematic task can result in reflection and residue, or a deeper understanding of math.

Reflection and Communication

Mathematical understanding is built through reflection and communication. Reflection is students talking and thinking to themselves about the problem and their solution method, whereas communication is students sharing with one another. For students to want to communicate and share their ideas, there must be something worthwhile to communicate and they must want to find the answer. Ordinary tasks do not usually intrigue the children enough that they want to talk about their findings. Designing a task that is truly problematic compels children to talk to one another about their strategies or where they are stuck.

Communication is reciprocal, both talking and listening. It is easier for a student to share his strategy than to listen to someone else's. We tend to first train the students how to share their thinking while being clear and concise. Many children tend to skip steps, which makes it hard to follow their thinking.

Listening to someone else's thinking, however, takes a lot of effort. Generally, the solution path of someone else is different and requires a student to consider how the other solution path is related to her own.

According to Hiebert et al. (1997), the following are necessary to promote reflection and communication:

- Tasks must allow students to treat the situations as problematic.
- The mathematics, not the situation, should be what is problematic.
- Tasks should allow students to use tools.
- Tasks should give students opportunities to use the skills and knowledge they already possess.

Reflecting and communicating were discussed in depth in chapter 4.

Residue

If the task comprises the preceding elements, then students have a high chance of taking away a deep and lasting learning of important mathematical value. This learning that takes place from solving problems is commonly referred to as *residue* or *lint* (Hiebert et al. 1997). Think of it like drinking a smoothie. When you have finished the glass, smoothie residue coats the inside of the glass. If you were to keep using the glass, the layers would just become thicker. Each layer allows for the next layer to stick to it, creating more residue. Perhaps you would prefer the analogy of lint in a dryer. Once a layer of lint lies in the lint trap, more lint is likely to stick to it, creating a thicker layer of lint. Mathematical residue is not much different. Once students have some experiences and learning that they can hang on to, future learning can, in a sense, stick to it. Over time, this creates a solid mathematical base of understanding.

Hiebert et al (1997) explores two types of residues as (1) insights into the structure of mathematics and (2) strategies or methods for solving problems. Some tasks allow students to discover how numbers work and relationships. For example, work with factors and multiples leads to important fractional understandings. Other tasks allow students to develop specific strategies for solving problems and techniques for organizing and manipulating numbers. When doing so, students are walking away with the ability to construct their own methods (Fennema et al. 1993; Hiebert and Wearne 1993; Hiebert et al. 1997; Kamii and Joseph 1989; Wearne and Hiebert 1989). When students are able to do this, they do not have to memorize procedures for each problem.

We cannot always recall formulas for procedures that we do not use frequently. There are specific problems, however, for which we know we can recreate the formula through manipulation of the problem. Take the handshake problem as an example:

If 10 people in a room had to give everyone a handshake, how many handshakes would have taken place?

This problem is related to a less contextual problem: What is the sum of the numbers 1–10? We may never remember the formula, but every time we are exposed to the problem, we can derive it from drawing part of the picture, just enough for us to remember. Through experiences, we have discovered many situations to which this formula applies, with some minor variations. The more experience we have had with similar problems, the faster we are able to solve them.

Students are not any different from us adults. In fourth and fifth grades, it is common for students to have to work with equivalent fractions, such as in learning the algorithm for finding equivalent fractions, or missing numerators. When it comes to future use of that algorithm, however, many students have it poorly memorized or misapply it. Because little meaning lay behind what they had memorized, they cannot identify when their answer does not make sense. However, when students are taken through a series of meaningful tasks, they develop a deep sense of the meaning underlying the algorithm and are therefore better able to use it for further mathematical investigation.

When selecting the task, the teacher needs to think about what residue is left behind. To ensure deep understanding of a concept, the teacher needs to also consider the residue left for sets, or a series, of tasks. According to Hiebert et al. (1997, 31), "tasks are related if they allow students to see the same idea from different points of view, or if they allow students to build later solution methods on earlier ones." At first it may be difficult to see the bigger picture; the teacher needs to see how lessons connect to help support the development of a big idea. This ability tends to form after the first year in a specific grade level and does not set until after about 3 years teaching in the same grade. The first-year teacher has the disadvantage of not being able to see clearly where the children should be by the end of the school year.

Comprehension Check

■ What are the outcomes of a problematic task? Describe each one.

Designing and Selecting a Problematic Task

How do we design a problematic task that requires students to make relationships and construct understanding? We know from years of experience that simply putting students into groups and asking them to solve a problem using tools does not achieve the level of mathematical engagement required to construct understanding.

Whereas it might have been popularly believed that once a skill is learned it can be applied to a problem or context, Hiebert et al. (1996, 1997) argues that the mathematics is learned as a *result* of solving problems. When solving higher-level tasks, students are focusing on the mathematical ideas, making connections, and exploring relationships. Therefore, contexts should be used not at the end, as a way to apply a learned procedure, but at the beginning, as a way to construct meaning (Fosnot and Dolk 2002).

Another common term for *doing* mathematics is "mathematizing." Fosnot and Dolk (2002, 9) describe this as "organizing information into charts and tables, noticing and exploring patterns, putting forth explanations and conjectures, and trying to convince one another of their thinking." Basically, to create an environment in which students are mathematizing, they need to be constantly immersed in activities in which these actions are contextualized. In other words, students need real-life contexts for their problem solving. This is especially true in the younger grades. Younger children require real-life situations to help them visualize what is happening so that they can impose those actions on their tools. Fosnot further argues that real-life contexts are needed for students to develop meaning for tools used later in other problem-solving experiences (see chapter 3).

Making a task problematic might not always mean creating a real-life situation; rather, it could involve studying how numbers are related to one another. In a class where the Cognitively Guided Instruction program is used, children are often solving mathematical problems that are set in story contexts, but problems could be writing number sentences that equal a certain number or creating conjectures for an odd and an even number (Carpenter 1999).

Figure 10.2 outlines the key elements of a high-level task as identified by several resources.

It is obvious from this list that designing a task in which the student is *doing* mathematics is no easy feat. According to the NCTM (1991), the three areas that teachers need to focus on when designing a task are the content, the students, and the way the students learn mathematics.

Content

As authors, we hope that you walk away with the understanding that teachers must become intimately familiar with the math content they teach. Oftentimes, teachers are pedagogically excellent teachers, but their lessons are limited by their knowledge of the content. If you do not know where you are going or how certain big ideas build onto one another, you do not know how to lead the students into the discovery of big math ideas. Some students share a strategy but

---

Professional Standards for Teaching Mathematics, National Council of Teachers of Mathematics (1991)

- Present sound and significant mathematics
- Develop knowledge of students' understandings, interests, and experiences
- Have knowledge of the range of ways in which diverse students learn mathematics
- Engage students' intellect
- Develop students' mathematical understandings and skills
- Stimulate students to make connections and develop a coherent framework for mathematical ideas
- Call for problem formulation, problem solving, and mathematical reasoning
- Promote communication about mathematics
- Represent mathematics as an ongoing human activity
- Display sensitivity to, and draw on, students' diverse background experiences and dispositions

About Teaching Mathematics: A K-8 Resource, Marilyn Burns (2000)

- Create perplexing situations that students understand
- Promote students' interest in finding a solution
- Prevent students from proceeding directly toward a solution
- Set a solution that requires use of mathematical ideas

Learning Mathematics in Elementary and Middle Schools, W. G. Cathcart et al. (2001)

- Create problems that sometimes contain missing, extraneous, or contradictory information
- Invite the use of calculators, computers, and other technology

Growing Mathematical Ideas in Kindergarten, Linda Dacey and Rebeka Eston (1999)

A developmentally appropriate task in kindergarten:

- Focuses on multisensory experiences
- Focuses on concrete experiences
- Encourages natural development of oral language
- Prompts children to investigate ideas related to conversation of number, length, area, weight, and volume
- Encourages children to represent mathematical ideas generated by their manipulation of physical objects

Designing Groupwork: Strategies for the Heterogeneous Classroom, Elizabeth Cohen (1994)

A multiability task:

- Has more than one answer or more than one way to solve the problem
- Is intrinsically interesting to make different contributions to
- Uses multimedia
- Involves sight, sound, and touch
- Requires a variety of skills and behaviors
- Requires reading and writing
- Is challenging

Figure 10.2. Key elements of a high-level task.

have trouble articulating what they are thinking. Their teachers may politely dismiss the strategies because they cannot see where the students are going mathematically with their thought. The students miss out on seeing how their strategies are connected to something bigger.

It is also important to look closely at what the task is asking the students to do. Is it asking for merely an answer, or must they defend their answer by comparing representations? Sometimes just adding one of the verbs listed earlier (*construct, predict, explore, investigate, discover, justify*) adds a new dimension to the problem. The verbs *compute* and *justify* have a huge difference in meaning and result in different levels of thinking and thus different levels of products. The teacher needs to consider the desired outcome for the lesson when choosing the verb.

A carefully designed task incorporates contexts that promote concept development, as well as problem solving and reasoning (NCTM 1991). Consider a series of tasks taken from Philipp (2007) that promote fractional number sense (figure 10.3). Engage yourself in some of these tasks. Notice what fraction idea is inherent in the task and how each task builds on the previous ones.

Students

You should know a great deal about your students generally, from cultural, sociological, psychological, and political perspectives, and specifically. For example, You should realize what students already know and what they need

Struggling Learner

A good task is designed within the zone of proximal development for all students. As students explore the math inherent in the task, their level of access is self-determined by the tools they select for solving it.

---

4 children share 12 stickers
2 people share 7 cookies
9 bagel pizzas are shared by 4 children

8 children share 9 mini-chocolate pies
4 children share 10 chocolate bars
4 pieces of cake are shared among 3 children
6 divers share 20 bars of gold recovered from the *Titanic* wreckage

3 children share 2 doughnuts
6 people share 8 pancakes
3 apples are shared by 4 children

3 little pigs share 11 ears of corn
2 children share half of a pie
13 licorice sticks are shared among 8 children

4 children share 5 doughnuts (doughnuts all the same)
4 children share 5 doughnuts (doughnuts all different)
4 people share 1 doughnut
2 people share 1 doughnut
3 people share 1 doughnut
3 people share 2 doughnuts

Make a whole in as many ways as you can (using fraction circles, not on paper)

Make whole circles from three colors or fewer, and record your work

How many apples (on a tray with 3 halves, 7 fourths, and 12 eighths)?
How many eighths do we have for the leprechauns?

8 children share 15 candy bars
8 children share 15 candy bars (want large pieces)
8 children share 15 candy bars (all different) (used previously)

20 children each get 3 eighths of a pizza (used previously)
3 children share 4 doughnuts
3 children share 4 brownies at one table
5 children share 8 brownies at another table

22 children each get 2 eighths of a pizza

5 children share 1 pizza at one table
7 children share 1 pizza at another table

Figure 10.3. Tasks involving fractions. (From Philipp 2007. Reprinted by permission of Randy Philipp.)

to work on. In addition, you should take into account your students' interests, dispositions, and experiences if you want to create meaningful tasks.

How Students Learn Math

Knowing the common mistakes that children make in relation to a certain topic can help you set up the task to either address or avoid those pitfalls. Check each content chapter for possible pitfalls. It is also important to collaborate with your colleagues at your grade level to find some of the common mistakes and common difficulties with certain tasks or lessons. This helps ensure that you design the lesson that address these difficulties. This may mean choosing a different set of numbers or providing a larger variety of manipulatives for your students to explore.

Ultimately, tasks need to provide you with a window into your students' thinking (NCTM 1991). Tasks that only require an answer simply tell you whether the student can or cannot solve the problem. They give you no idea how efficient their thinking is or what misconceptions they might have. Knowing how children think on a particular problem helps you adjust future lessons to either target misconceptions or to push their thinking further.

Special Needs

It may be necessary to use some listening comprehension strategies to ensure that all of your students understand the components of the task and the question inherent in it.

Analyzing the Level of a Task

As mentioned earlier, tasks fall into one of two categories: lower-level and higher-level tasks. Lower-level tasks consist of *memorization* and *procedures without connections.* Tasks with higher-level demands consist of *procedures with connections* and *doing mathematics.* Figure 10.4 contains descriptions of each category.

Sometimes it can be difficult to identify the level of a task. Some tasks appear to have higher-level demands because they may require tools, use diagrams, or use real-world contexts (Stein et al. 2000) but may actually be considered lower level because specific procedures may be highly implied. This may depend on how much experience with the procedure students have had up to the point of assigning the particular task. The contrary may also be true. Tasks may appear to be low level but really may be high level if a particular procedure is not implied or if students have not had experience with the procedure. The level of cognitive demand of a task may vary depending on the age or developmental level of the students. What may be low level to a fourth grader may be high level to a second or third grader. Also, the choice of numbers may influence whether a task is low or high level.

Use the following example from a second-grade classroom:

> *Abel had 25 valentines in his bag. He then got 12 more from other children in his class. How many valentines does Abel have all together?*

This, depending on the experience of the children, may be considered a low-level task. It is probably obvious to the children that they have to add and that the numbers they are adding do not pose a challenge. But changing the numbers in this problem to 37 and 16 throws a new twist and provides a problematic situation for students who have not yet had experience with regrouping. However, for first graders who have had little experience with numbers over 10, the original problem would prove to be of high cognitive demand.

THE TASK ANALYSIS GUIDE

Lower-Level Demands	Higher-Level Demands
Memorization tasks • Involve either reproducing previously learned facts, rules, formulae, or definitions or committing facts, rules, formulas, or definitions to memory. • Cannot be solved using procedures because a procedure does not exist or because the time frame in which the task is being completed is too short to use a procedure. • Are not ambiguous—such tasks involve exact reproduction of previously seen material, and what is to be reproduced is clearly and directly stated. • Have no connection to the concepts or meaning that underlie the facts, rules formulae, or definitions being learned or reproduced.	Procedures with connections tasks • Focus students' attention on the use of procedures for the purpose of developing deeper levels of understanding of mathematical concepts and ideas. • Suggest pathways to follow (explicitly or implicitly) that are general procedures that have close connections to underlying conceptual ideas, as opposed to narrow algorithms that are opaque with respect to underlying concepts. • Usually are represented in multiple ways (e.g., visual diagrams, manipulatives, symbols, and problem situations). Making connections among multiple representations helps develop meaning. • Require some degree of cognitive effort. Although general procedures may be followed, they cannot be followed mindlessly. Students need to engage with the conceptual ideas that underlie the procedures to successfully complete the task and develop understanding.
Procedures without connections tasks • Are algorithmic. Use of the procedure is either specifically called for or is evident based on prior instruction, experience, or placement of the task. • Require limited cognitive demand for successful completion. There is little ambiguity about what needs to be done and how to do it. • Have no connection to the concepts or meanings that underlie the procedure being used. • Are focused on producing correct answers rather than developing mathematical understanding. • Require no explanations or require only explanations that focus solely on describing the procedure that was used.	Doing mathematics tasks • Require complex and nonalgorithmic thinking (i.e., there is not a predictable, well-rehearsed approach or pathway explicitly suggested by the task, task instructions, or a worked-out example). • Require students to explore and understand the nature of mathematical concepts, processes, or relationships. • Demand self-monitoring or self-regulation of cognitive processes. • Require students to access relevant knowledge and experiences and make appropriate use of them in working through the task. • Require students to analyze the task and actively examine task constraints that may limit possible solution strategies and solutions. • Require considerable cognitive effort and may involve some level of anxiety for the student because of the unpredictable nature of the solution process required.

Figure 10.4. Characteristics of mathematical tasks at each of the four levels of cognitive demand. (Reprinted with permission from Stein et al, 2000, p. 16. *Mathematics Teaching in the Middle School,* 1998, NCTM.)

Maintaining the Intended Level of a Task

The mathematical task framework (Stein et al. 2000) is a structure that allows analysis of a task. There appear to be three phases of a task that all influence student learning: the task itself, the way the task is set up by teachers, and the way it is implemented by students. Figure 10.5 illustrates these three phases.

We have already discussed the importance of designing or selecting a task, but just because the task is designed with a high level in mind does not mean that it stays that way throughout the lesson. The way the teacher sets up the task to the students plays an important role in to whether or not the level is maintained. Teachers may knowing or unknowingly give hints as to how to proceed with solving a problem. These hints can cause a truly problematic task to become one that just requires the students to use procedures. It is also important to state the expectations of the students, for solving the problem and for displaying their work, up front. Clear expectations help motivate students to stay on task and to make sure that their thinking is clearly articulated in their work.

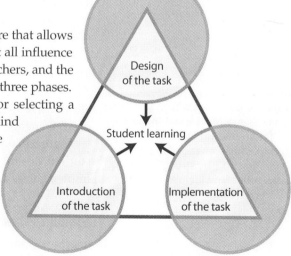

Figure 10.5. Representation of how the three components of a mathematical task affect student learning. (Reprinted with permission from Stein et al, 2000, p. 16. *Mathematics Teaching in the Middle School,* 1998, NCTM.)

Tasks are probably mostly compromised during the implementation phase. Myriad factors may affect the level of the task at this phase. Teachers may be over- or undersupportive during the lesson. It takes time to know how much support is the right amount. When struggling, teachers should ask students questions to gently guide them to see something new without giving the problem-solving opportunities away. Questioning is explored more in a later chapter.

Providing the appropriate amount of time to wrestle with the math is essential for a task to maintain high cognitive demand. When students are rushed, they may never have a chance to make the appropriate connections and synthesize their new ideas. Plenty of time is also needed for discussion, both within small groups and with the entire class. We mentioned earlier that reflection and communication are among the essential outcomes of a problematic task. Sufficient time is necessary for these to occur. Lack of time may also cause the teacher to shift his focus from the process to merely finding the right answer.

On the contrary, providing too much time can cause the class to get off task, and discipline problems may occur. Classroom management, from the way the materials are distributed to the way discussions are led, is an essential component of ensuring the maintenance of high-level tasks.

At times, a teacher realizes that the task she has assigned her class is not appropriate for the understanding that the class possesses. Thus, the teacher may need to make a conscious decision about how she is going to scaffold this lesson to support the students' understanding, and this lesson may well need to drop from *doing mathematics* to *procedures with connections*. These spur-of-the-moment decisions are part of the balance within the task levels.

After analyzing hundreds of lessons in the QUASAR Project in the 1990s, Stein et al. (2000) concluded that high-level tasks were the most difficult of tasks to implement; they were often altered to lower-level tasks because of factors mentioned earlier. Although high-level tasks are difficult to implement, Stein et al. likewise concluded that the classrooms that consistently encouraged high-level student thinking rendered the most significant learning gains.

Teacher and Student Roles during a Task

Teachers have definite responsibilities in ensuring that a task is successful. However, students also have a role to play. Although they may not be involved in the designing of the task, they must take responsibility for their learning and actively engage themselves in the process of making meaning. The teacher needs to set up a supportive environment, but the students need to make efforts, take risks, and try to make their own connections. In other words, they need to engage themselves in active, rather than passive, learning.

Figure 10.6 highlights the various roles played by both the teacher and the student during the three phases described earlier (design, introduction, and implementation) to ensure the success of a task.

Student Work

Teachers want students to show their work in different ways. Some prefer journals, and others want groups to make some kind of collaborative poster to use to present their findings to the class. Different tasks might call for different types of products. If the goal is to make connections among several strategies, then more emphasis is on group-type products that can be seen easily from the entire

Rule of Thumb

If you find yourself tempted to adopt a direct instruction mode for a lengthy period in which your thinking is the key feature, it is probably a sign that your task has become low level.

Language Tip

Nuances associated with cultural differences may make a task inaccessible for diverse populations. For example, children raised in urban environments may struggle with tasks about farm life.

	Teacher Roles	Student Roles
Design	• Have a good understanding of big ideas and student thinking • Know your students (abilities and interests) • Know goals and consciously choose which level of task meets those goals • Consider the residue left by the task and the connections you hope the students will make • Decide how reflection and communication will be incorporated • Select or design an appropriate task for the level of the students • Select or design a series of tasks that are connected • Create a culture of inquiry	
Introduction	• Provide clear and high expectations • Have a clear structure of procedures • Provide careful scaffolding as needed, without doing the thinking for the students • Have appropriate and sufficient materials available	• Ask for clarification, and make sure that the problem is understood
Implementation	• Listen to students' thought processes • Ask questions • Build trust and a safe environment for wrong answers • Invite discussion • Evaluate the appropriateness of the task and adjusting it to fit the needs of the students • Provide enough time to grapple with task, reflect, and communicate	• Actively engage with the problem • Take risks • Use time and materials appropriately • Work collaboratively (in groups or partnerships) • Communicate, share, and discuss ideas and strategies • Defend methods and justify solutions • Try to make connections between strategies • Reflect (i.e., write in a journal) • Explore, investigate, discover, and wonder

Figure 10.6. Teacher and student roles during different phases of a task.

class. On these types of products, students demonstrate their understandings by creating multiple representations (pictures, numbers, and words). Figure 10.7 shows an example of some student work as a result of a problematic task.

Teachers can easily glimpse into student thinking when looking at pieces of work such as these. They are good springboards for conversation and questions between the teacher and the student or the entire class.

Comprehension Check

▪ Reflect on the teacher and student roles during the three phases of a task.

Figure 10.7. Student work sample.

CONTENT *Fractional Number Sense*

One of us once received a T-shirt with the slogan, "5 out of 4 people don't understand fractions." Rote procedural knowledge of whole numbers does little to help children understand the new world of fractions, or rational numbers, particularly if instruction in fractions is also procedural in nature. Indeed, we think many a math phobic had his first real taste of math phobia in the context of studying fractions. The tragedy, therefore, is that many people would not even get the joke inherent in the quote at the beginning of this paragraph.

As we examine the important ideas associated with making sense of fractions in this section, we first look at the big ideas and NCTM focal points. We then discuss in detail the types of fractions used in real-life contexts, including improper and mixed fractions. Lastly, we look at some suggestions for tasks you can use to engage students in the kinds of high-level problem solving that result in deep, connected understanding of fractions.

A reciprocal relationship exists between your understanding of fractions and your ability to produce tasks that allow for the kinds of emergent fractional understandings that help children to use fractions in meaningful ways. We hope you develop understanding as you read this section.

Big Ideas and Focal Points

Several of the big ideas we discussed in relation to whole numbers are indirectly or directly related to learning fundamental notions about rational numbers, or fractions (Charles 2005, 12–16).

- *Numbers.* The set of real numbers is infinite, and each real number can be associated with a unique point on the number line.

- *Equivalence.* Any number, measure, numerical expression, algebraic expression, or equation can be represented in an infinite number of ways that have the same value.

- *Comparisons.* Numbers, expressions, and measures can be compared by their relative values.

- *Operation Meanings and Relationships.* The same number sentence (e.g., $12 - 4 = 8$) can be associated with different concrete or real-world situations, *and* different number sentences can be associated with the same concrete or real-world situation.

- *Properties.* For a given set of numbers, some relationships are always true. These are the rules that govern arithmetic and algebra.

The NCTM's *Curriculum Focal Points for Prekindergarten through Grade 8 Mathematics* (2006) give us a good indication of what mathematics we can expect children to learn; that is, they enable us to ensure that our grade-level expectations are developmentally appropriate. The focal points give you a sense of the kinds of understandings and skills children should develop as learn about rational numbers and give you a sense of the grade levels associated with that development. The Focal Points table compares expectations related to rational number sense across grades.

NCTM FOCAL POINTS

Third Grade	Fourth Grade	Fifth Grade	Sixth Grade
Develop an understanding of the meanings and uses of fractions to represent parts of a whole, parts of a set, or points or distances on a number line.	Generate equivalent fractions, and simplify fractions.	Represent the addition and subtraction of fractions with unlike denominators as equivalent calculations with like denominators.	Make sense of procedures for multiplying and dividing fractions, and explain why they work.
Understand that the size of a fractional part is relative to the size of the whole, and use fractions to represent numbers equal to, less than, or greater than one.		Develop fluency with standard procedures for adding and subtracting fractions.	Use common procedures to multiply and divide fractions efficiently and accurately.
Solve problems that involve comparing and ordering fractions by using models, benchmark fractions, or common numerators or denominators.		Make reasonable estimates of fraction sums and differences.	Multiply and divide fractions and decimals to solve problems, including multistep problems and problems involving measurement.
Understand and use models, including the number line, to identify equivalent fractions.		Add and subtract fractions and decimals to solve problems, including problems involving measurement.	Build on understanding of fractions to understand ratios.
Generate equivalent fractions, and simplify fractions.			Express the result of dividing two whole numbers as a fraction (viewed as parts of a whole).
			Give mixed number solutions to division problems with whole numbers.
			Recognize that ratio tables not only derive from rows in the multiplication table but also connect with equivalent fractions.

Although the *Curriculum Focal Points* do not specify significant teaching about fractions before third grade, it is imperative that some preliminary work with fractions be done with younger-grade children. The child in the "Conversation in Mathematics" section that opened this chapter is in first grade, and kindergarten is not too early to work with parts of a whole.

We should clear up a little confusion about vocabulary first. You sometimes hear the terms *rational numbers* and *fractions* used synonymously. Although these two terms have something in common, they do have different meanings. *Rational numbers* are any numbers than can be expressed as a ratio; therefore,

3 is a rational number because it can be expressed as ¾, ⁶⁄₂, and so on. Three basic types of rational numbers refer to situations in which parts of a thing or a set of things are involved: fractions (e.g., ²⁄₇), decimal fractions (e.g., 0.173), and percentages (e.g., 69%). We concentrate on fractions in this chapter.

To ensure that children are able to use fractions in varied real-life situations, you should know the three fundamental ways to think about fractions: parts of a whole (part–whole), parts of a set (part–set), and division (¾ = 3 ÷ 4).

Part–Whole Fractions

Each of the three kinds of part–whole fraction situations is directly modeled in a different way. The first is linear, or one-dimensional, and relates to distance or length. Rulers are great representations of linear fractions. If, for example, the distance between 0 and 1 on an inch ruler is divided into eight equal sections, then the space between each section is ⅛, and the distance from the end of the ruler to, say, three ⅛ lines is ⅜ of an inch. The pattern of fractional parts repeats for each 1-inch section, but if measuring from the end of the ruler, then a mixed number or mixed fraction is used to represent the distance. For example, if the object being measured is the length of 1 inch and three more eighths of an inch, then the object is 1⅜ inches long.

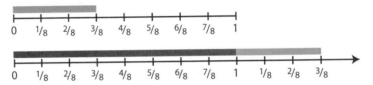

The second part–whole fraction situation is planar (the adjective form of *plane*), or two-dimensional. Rectangles and circles are the most common plane figures used in classrooms to represent planar fractions. In this situation, the total area of a plane figure is divided into regions of equal smaller areas. In each of the following figures, ⅜ of each figure is shaded because each is divided into eight equal pieces and three of those pieces are shaded red.

The most common way children tend to think of planar fractions is using a circular representation, probably because of the popularity of pizza. We have found, however, that rectangular representations are a little easier to manipulate in the classroom. Both models, as well as others, promote flexibility and connections among different representations. The mixed fraction 1⅜ would be represented as shown here:

The third part–whole fraction variation is a capacity, or volume, situation that involves three-dimensional figures. Most of us are familiar with these because of measurement cups used in the kitchen. These figures show ⅓ and 1⅓, respectively.

Note that a linear model is used to help determine the volume in these cup representations.

Three key notions must be emphasized with children. The first is the idea of equal parts. One of our favorite ways to help children with this idea is by showing windows divided into sections and comparing windows with equal-sized sections to those without equal-sized sections. For example, it would be great to talk about why this window is *not* divided into thirds.

The next idea is that the fractional parts have no meaning without reference to the whole. It is common for children to manipulate fractional pieces in the classroom without referring to the whole, and this is a dangerous practice. Although the notion of "parts of a whole" is being solidified, it is essential that children keep the relationship between the parts and the whole in front of them visually.

Here is an activity that emphasizes the importance of defining the whole. Suppose we have two pizzas, one pepperoni and the other cheese, each divided into eight pieces, and you eat two pieces of pepperoni pizza and one piece of cheese pizza. What problems could you come up with for which one answer might be three, another answer ⅜, and another answer ³⁄₁₆? Try this before reading on.

If we asked "How many pieces did you eat?" the answer would be three. If we asked "How much of one whole pizza did you eat?" the answer would be ⅜. And if we asked "How much of all the pizza did you eat?" the answer would be ³⁄₁₆. The first answer has little to do with fractions, but the other two answers differ because the "whole" changes.

Finally, it has been discussed in previous chapters that when children begin to conceptualize multiplication and division they come to understand that one of the numbers in a multiplication or division expression has a new role or job—that is, rather than both numbers specifying the number of objects in a given set or group, one of the numbers refers to the number of groups. For example, in the expression 3×4, the number 3 refers to the number of groups of 4. This is referred to as *unitizing*. A similar mental transition occurs with fractions. The children come to understand the following:

- Each number in a fraction specifies a different kind of quantity.
- The denominator of a fraction refers to the number of pieces of a whole object or the number of objects in a given set.
- The numerator refers to the numbers of pieces or objects under consideration.
- The two numbers work together in an additive way to produce one mathematical idea.

These issues relative to roles are not a new idea for students, if you think about it. Take the number 27. It is really two numbers working together, in an additive way, to produce one mathematical idea (20 + 7), each specifying a different kind of quantity—the 2 specifying the number of quantities of 10, and the 7 specifying the number of unit quantities.

Now consider the number ⅔. This is really two numbers, 2 and 3, working together in a multiplicative or ratio way, to produce one mathematical idea (2 ÷ 3), each specifying a different kind of quantity—the 3 represents the number of pieces of the whole or the number of objects in a set, and the 2 represents the number of those pieces or objects under consideration.

Part–Set Fractions

The second fundamental way to think about fractions involves parts of sets. In this situation, the denominator of the fraction refers not to one whole object divided into a specific number of parts but to the number of objects in one whole set. For example, the 3 in ⅓ involved in a part–whole representation refers to 1 whole thing divided into 3 equal parts. The 3 in ⅓ involved in a part–set representation defines the number of objects in the set, 3 in this case.

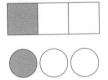

This way of thinking about fractions appears to be relatively straightforward but is difficult for students and can lead to some misconceptions. For example, if students were asked to compare ⅓ and ¼, one might draw rectangular representations and, as long as the "whole" for each was the same and the parts were drawn equally, easily see that ⅓ is larger than ¼.

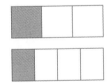

However, if a child drew part–set representations, she might conclude that ⅓ and ¼ are the same because the number of objects shaded in each representation is the same.

Fractions as Division

A third way to conceptualize fractions is to think of them as a representation of division. Consider this problem: Suppose you have two brownies to share equally with three people, Sally, Bob, and Alison. How much will each person receive? Before reading on, try to solve this yourself.

You could draw two brownies and then think to yourself, "I know each person will receive less than one whole brownie, so maybe I'll divide one brownie into three parts and give each person one part and then do the same thing with the other brownie. Each person will receive ⅔."

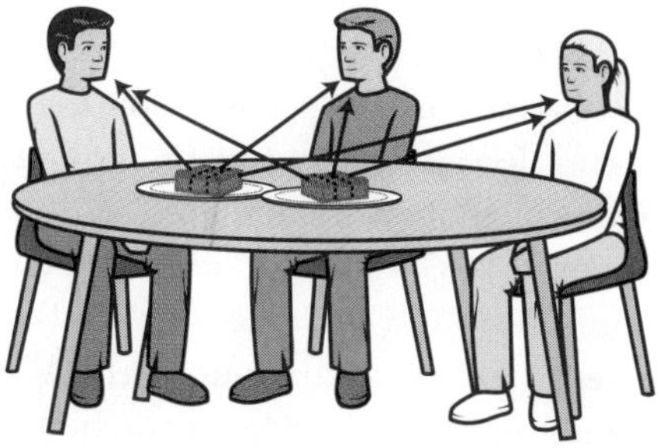

In other words, two brownies divided among three people leaves ⅔ of a brownie for each person. Stated more simply, 2 *divided* by 3 is ⅔. Indeed, the fraction line means "divide," so it only makes sense to think "2 divided among 3." This is a revelation for most people and is an important understanding related to fractions that children should make.

Other Fraction Notions

It will be helpful for you to conceptualize other fraction notions. As in previous content chapters, we discuss these notions in a developmental sequence, encouraging you to understand how children might directly model them and making a record of them in a manner that parallels an algorithm. The notions are (1) relationships between improper and mixed fractions and (2) equivalence, in which we also discuss finding missing numerators, the meaning of simplifying, and the process for simplifying.

Mixed and Improper Fraction Relationships

Suppose you have 1⅔ brownies that you want to serve your guests in serving sizes of ⅓. How many thirds are in 1⅔?

All you have to do is count the number of thirds and discover that 1⅔ = 5⁄3.

Now suppose you served cheesecake at a wedding reception. Each cheesecake was cut into ⅛-sized pieces and placed on plates. At the end of the reception, there were several pieces left over, 27 to be exact. How many cakes were left?

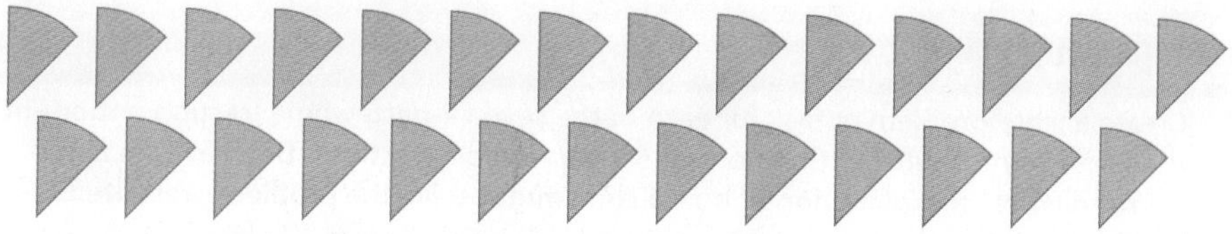

If you put the pieces together to make whole cakes again, eight pieces per cake, you would find 3 whole cakes and another ⅜ of a cake. 27⁄8 = 3⅜.

Invite students to analyze what they do to convert from a mixed number to an improper fraction, or vice versa, and see whether they can come up with an algorithm of how they can do this without using models or drawing pictures. What you will hear them articulate is "There are 3 eighths in 27, so that would make 3 wholes. There would be 3 left over. Those are eighths, so there would be ⅜ left over. That would be 3 and ⅜." They realize that they have to divide the numerator by the denominator and whatever is left over is the fractional piece. Going from a mixed number to improper fraction would sound like this: "There are 8 pieces in each whole, so that is 8 times 3, which is 24. There are 3 extra pieces, so that is 27. There are 27 eighths." Guide them to generalize how they would do this for any number.

Fractional Equivalence

In a previous chapter about early number sense, we encouraged you to invite children to name given quantities in multiple ways, like saying that 5 is also 4 and 1, 2 less than 7, half of 10, and so on. The challenge for young children is to conceptualize that two seemingly different fractions can represent the same quantity or portion. How is it possible that if I mow ⅓ of the lawn and my brother mows ⁴⁄₁₂ of the lawn we actually mow the same amount?

As mentioned previously, four concepts related to fractional equivalence seem to build on one another:

- Equivalence itself
- Finding missing numerators
- The meaning of simplifying
- The process for simplifying

Figure 10.8 provides a sample task, a typical direct model, and possible wording that children might use relative to each of these notions. Note that we are looking exclusively at part–whole fractions and that the three types of part–whole fractions are intermingled in the examples. We look at part–set fractions in the next figure.

Some fraction notions, such as comparison, might be more easily shown with part–whole fractions than with part–set. However, the notions relative to equivalence can be conceptualized quite well using part–set. Figure 10.9 presents those conceptualizations.

Comprehension Check

- Create a word problem or task for each of the seven 4-part–whole fraction notions in the Focal Points table fraction notions for part–whole fractions. Draw a representation and write an explanation of how a child might solve the problem presented.
- Create a word problem or task for each of the four fraction notions for part–set fractions in Figure 10.8. Draw a representation and write an explanation of how a child might solve the problem presented.

PART OF A WHOLE

Fraction Notions	Sample Task	Direct Model	Child's Wording
Equivalence	If you have ²/₃ of a piece of licorice and your brother has ⁴/₆, how could you prove that you each have the same amount?		I divided a line into 3 equal parts and another line into 6 equal parts. I can see that the 2 parts are the same length as the 4 parts.
Missing numerators	If you have ¾ of a pint of milk and your cousin has a pint of milk divided into 12 levels, how many levels of your cousin's milk will it take to have the same amount of milk as you do?		I divided a rectangle into 4 equal parts and shaded 3 of them. I drew another rectangle of the same size, divided it into 4 equal parts, and then divided it into 12ths with 2 lines going across. I shaded 9 12ths to cover the same area as ¾.
Meaning of simplifying	Which fraction is a simpler representation, ²/₃ or ⁸/₁₂?		I showed both fractions. I think ²/₃ is simpler because it covers the same area with the fewest number of pieces and the largest pieces.
Process of simplifying	What is the simplest way to represent ¹²/₁₆?		I used my fraction pieces to show ¹²/₁₆ and then looked for the largest pieces that would cover the same area.

Figure 10.8. Direct models for each fraction notion (part–whole).

Implications in the Classroom

We have discussed the types of fractional representations and how students might think about each one. What activities can be introduced in the classroom to be sure that students have a chance to think flexibly about fractions?

Early Experiences with Fractions

We mentioned that, even though fraction standards do not show up in the NCTM focal points until the third grade, it is important to begin developing this understanding as early as kindergarten. With our youngest students, we tend to provide them with real-life experiences involving sharing, and food seems to be the perfect context. Young children may still focus more on the quantity of an object they have rather than the size. So, if you were to split your snack, they may notice if you had two pieces and they had one but not if you had a bigger piece. Asking them to share multiple objects (part–set) may make more sense initially than splitting one object in two equal parts. This can also be supported by acting out the grouping with either objects or themselves.

PART OF A SET

Fraction Notions	Sample Task	Direct Model	Child's Wording
Equivalence	If you have 6 M&M's, 4 brown and 2 red, can you prove that the fraction that is brown is both 4/6 and 2/3?		I arranged the M&M's in a row. 4 out 6 were brown. If I broke my row into groups of 2, I have 3 groups, 2 of which are brown.
Missing numerators	If you have 4 skittles, 3 that are red and 1 that is purple, how could you maintain the same ratio if you had 12 skittles?		I arranged 4 skittles vertically, the top 3 red. Then I made equal rows of the same color until I had 12—4 rows, 3 of which are red.
Meaning of simplifying	Which fraction is a simpler representation, 2/3 or 8/12?		I showed 8/12 by making the longest rows possible that were the same color and all rows the same length, which means 3 rows, two of which are red. 2/3 is simpler because it counts rows, not individual skittles.
Process of simplifying	What is the simplest way to represent 12/16?		I showed 12/16 by making the longest rows possible that were the same color and all rows the same length, which means 4 rows, 3 of which are red = ¾.

Figure 10.9. Direct models for each fraction notion (part–set).

However, in kindergarten, most students are able to explore this notion of cutting something to equally share it with their friends. The real challenge is with drawing and cutting. We want children to explore strategies for how to know whether they are cutting something into equal groups; however, this is a difficult task. Just remember that these are initial experiences.

Making Fraction Kits

All students, from about second or third grade on, should begin a fraction unit by making their own fraction kits. These kits may or may not be used in other exploratory exercises, depending on the precision when making the kits. If there are little or no other manipulatives in the classroom to support fractional understanding, then this is a critical lesson.

Take a few strips of construction paper, all the same size but different colors. The amount of strips depends on how many fractions you want your students to create. One strip represents the whole, another represents halves, and so on. Have students fold the papers, cut them, and label them. It is important that students figure out how they should make the folds to show equal portions. In the primary grades, you will probably have students make halves, thirds, fourths, sixths, and eighths. In the upper grades, you might include fifths, tenths, and twelfths. You can have the students glue their pieces onto a con-

struction paper so that they can see the relative sizes or keep them in an enve-
lope for future activities, such as playing *Race to One.*

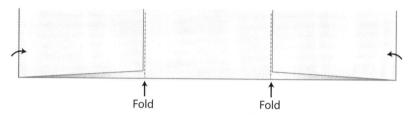

Folding Tricks Not all fractions are easily produced. To fold thirds, you need
to fold the strip like a letter. Not all students have had experience folding letters. Fifths are tricky; the following illustration helps you fold them:

Fold over the two ends until the space in the middle is the same as the two ends,
then fold at the end of each segment as illustrated.

Race to One *Race to One* is similar to playing *Race to 100* or *Race to Zero,* as
described in chapter 4. Using one set of the fractional pieces from the kits that
the students have produced per partnership and a spinner or number cube
with fractions on each space, one player spins or rolls a fraction, finds that fractional piece, and lays it down on his strip that is representing a whole. Both
players do this until the whole is filled. However, if his spin is a fraction that
takes him over the whole, then that student loses his turn. He might also lose
his turn if he runs out of pieces of that size.

Try starting with the whole filled with different fractions and removing
them when the spinner lands on the corresponding part. A fun consideration is
whether or not you can trade pieces so that some can be added or removed.

Number Line

Activities involving the number line are critical because students consistently
demonstrate difficulty in relating fractions with the number line. Draw a number line on the board for the whole class. Hand students a sticky note with a
fraction written on it and have them place it on the part of the number line
where they think it should go. The number line may be labeled or not. A number line with no labels is called an *open number line.* You may want to start with
a number line from 0 to 1 and then progress to a line from 0 to 2. You may or
may not want a number line with the tick marks already present.

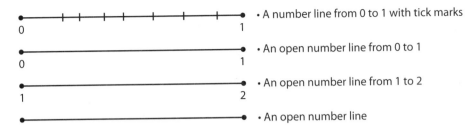

- A number line from 0 to 1 with tick marks
- An open number line from 0 to 1
- An open number line from 1 to 2
- An open number line

When first exploring open number lines, children (and even adults) are more concerned about the order of the fractions than about where they should go in relation to one another. The following is a typical example of how students place their sticky notes on an open number line.

This says a lot in that the students were able to determine the proper order, but they are not considering the placement on this line of 0 to 1. As you can see, ⅞ should be ⅛ away from 1, but the difference between the ⅞ and the 1 is much greater than the difference between the 0 and the ⅛. It is important to have students focus on the relationships between the numbers.

When ordering fractions, students want to begin to consider benchmark fractions, such as 0, 1, and ½. For example, where should ⅗ be placed? In relation to ½, 2½ fifths would equal ½, so 3 fifths must be greater than ½. Fractions that are close to 1 can be compared as to how far they are from 1. Take, for example, ⅞ and ⁸⁄₉: ⅞ is ⅛ away from the whole, whereas ⁸⁄₉ is ⅑ away. Because ⅑ is smaller, it is closer to the whole.

Fraction Circle

A great visual that you can make with your students is a fraction circle. This involves having two circles, one on a white piece of paper and the other on a colored piece. The white page should have marks for specific fractions labeled. The colored page goes on top. Cut the line shown on the illustration here, slip the two circles together, and turn. The fractions are nicely illustrated.

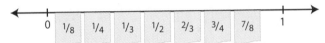

Equivalents

Children can use a lot of tools when working with fractions and equivalents. Some such tools are pattern blocks, Cuisenaire rods, fraction circles, fraction bars, and fraction towers. Another useful tool for comparing fractions, one that is more abstract, is a fraction chart, such as the one in figure 10.10.

To use a chart like this, students place their ruler on it to align the fractions and see which fractional pieces are equal. The teacher needs to be aware that a tool such as this may promote the misconception that the fraction is the point on the line and not the entire length from zero to that point.

Perhaps an easier tool for finding equivalent fractions is a multiplication chart (figure 10.11).

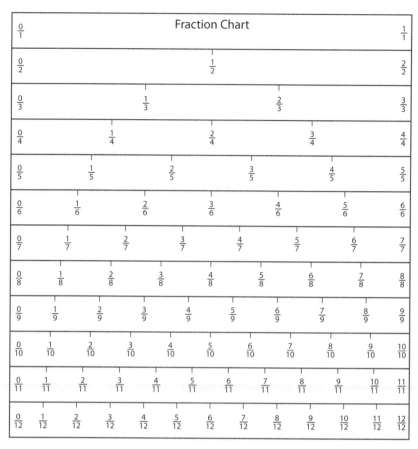

Figure 10.10. Fraction chart. (From The Gatsby Charitable Foundation, http://www.cimt .plymouth.ac.uk/projects/mepres/book7/y7s10act.pdf. Reprinted by permission of Professor David Burghes, CIMT.)

1	2	3	4	5	6	7	8	9	10	11	12
2	4	6	8	10	12	14	16	18	20	22	24
3	6	9	12	15	18	21	24	27	30	33	36
4	8	12	16	20	24	28	32	36	40	44	48
5	10	15	20	25	30	35	40	45	50	55	60
6	12	18	24	30	36	42	48	54	60	66	72
7	14	21	28	35	42	49	56	63	70	77	84
8	16	24	32	40	48	56	64	72	80	88	96
9	18	27	36	45	54	63	72	81	90	99	108
10	20	30	40	50	60	70	80	90	100	110	120
11	22	33	44	55	66	77	88	99	110	121	132
12	24	36	48	60	72	84	96	108	120	132	144

Figure 10.11. Multiplication chart.

On the chart in figure 8.12, you can find ¾ by locating the 2 and the 4 in the same column. If you move both of these circles to the right or left, you can identify all equivalent fractions. This works for numbers that are not touching as well. Find ⅙ by locating the 1 and the 6 in the first column. Move to the right, and you will see ²/₁₂, ³/₁₈, and so on.

Using Inquiry to Teach Fractional Number Sense

Here are two examples of inquiry-based lessons that include some tasks involving fractions.

Example Lesson 1 (2 cycles)

Deciding which fraction is larger

Launch cycle 1	The teacher refers to tools used in previous lessons, such as two-sided counters, fraction towers, fraction circles, and the number line. The teacher asks students to represent some simple fractions using each of the tools. The teacher then poses the following problem: "If you ate ½ of your sandwich and your brother ate ¾ of his sandwich, who ate more? How do you know?"
Explore cycle 1	Students work in partnerships to solve the problem using at least two different tools. They record their work in their journals using pictures, numbers, and words.
Summarize cycle 1	The class members discuss how they proved which amount was larger. They compare strategies and tools used.
Launch cycle 2	The teacher poses a second problem: "If you have ⅔ of a piece of licorice and your brother has ⁴/₆, who has more? How do you know?"
Explore cycle 2	Students work in small groups to solve the problem using at least two different tools. They record their work on their presentation paper using pictures, numbers, and words.
Summarize cycle 2	The class members discuss how they proved which amount was larger. They compare strategies and tools used. The conversation centers on the notion that fractions can have different names, making them equivalent fractions.

Example Lesson 2 (2 cycles)

Equivalent fractions

Launch cycle 1	The teacher reminds students of the previous day's lesson of equivalent fractions. A student asks if there are other fractions for which that happens. The teacher suggests that they try to find out, so they decide to figure out all the ways to make ½.
Explore cycle 1	Students work in partnerships using fraction towers to explore all the ways to make ½.
Summarize cycle 1	The teacher creates a chart of all equivalent fractions students discovered for ½: ²/₄, ³/₆, ⁴/₈, etc. The class looks at all the fractions to find patterns. Some students notice that the numerator doubled is the denominator. The teacher invites the students to try this with other numbers, which they do, such as ¹⁰/₂₀. They come up with the conjecture that because they are using half the number of pieces, the numerator would always be half of the denominator.

Launch cycle 2	The teacher asks students what they think might happen when finding equivalent fractions for ⅓. Students give suggestions.
Explore cycle 2	Students work in partnerships or small groups to find as many fractions as they can that equal ⅓. They begin to formulate conjectures.
Summarize cycle 2	Again, the teacher creates a chart of all equivalent fractions students discovered for ⅓. They look for patterns and share conjectures that they formulated as small groups. They eventually conclude that the denominator would have to be three times greater than the numerator.

Example Lesson 3 (2 cycles)

Whole number division with ½, ¼, and ⅛ remainders

Launch cycle 1	The teacher reminds students of different problem-solving strategies other students used in the previous day's lesson, including using cubes, drawing pictures, and acting out problem.
	The teacher gives a prompt: "Three children share two doughnuts. How many doughnuts does each person receive?"
Explore cycle 1	The teacher invites students to solve the problem in at least two ways using whatever tools or strategies they wish.
Summarize cycle 1	*Whole group:* With teacher assistance, students share strategies in this approximate order: direct modeling with manipulatives, direct modeling with pictures, and other mental strategies. The teacher assigns to the listening students a comparative role, meaning that the teacher calls on one or more students to compare the shared strategy with other shared strategies or with their own strategies.
Launch cycle 2	*Whole group:* The teacher gives a prompt: "Nine pizzas are shared by four people equally. How much does each person get? This time, I would also like you to make a numerical record of what you did."
Explore cycle 2	The teacher invites students to solve the problem in at least two ways using whatever tools or strategies they wish.
Summarize cycle 2	*Whole group:* With teacher assistance, students share strategies. Using the strategies from the previous cycle, the teacher asks for students to share first strategies that are similar and then any additional strategies. The teacher assigns to the listening students a comparative role, meaning that the teacher calls on one or more students to compare the strategies with the numerical record.
Launch for end-of-lesson (exit slip) assessment	*Whole group:* The teacher gives a prompt: "Nine brownies are shared by eight people equally. How much does each person get? This time, I would also like you to make a numerical record of what you did and then raise your hand when you are finished."

Example Lesson 4 (2 cycles)

Whole number divided by a larger whole number

Launch cycle 1	*Whole group:* "Three sheets of paper are shared by four people. How much paper does each person receive?"
Explore cycle 1	The teacher invites students to come up with multiple of ways of thinking about this problem.
Summarize cycle 1	*Whole group:* The teacher invites students to share their strategies in the same order as in the previous lesson. The teacher assigns to the listening students an evaluative role, meaning that the teacher calls on one or more students to state whether or not they agree with the shared strategy—and why—for the rest of the class.

Launch cycle 2	*Whole group:* "Two bagels are shared by three people. How much does each person receive?"
Explore cycle 2	The teacher invites students to solve the problem in multiple ways and to make a numerical record.
Summarize cycle 2	The teacher invites students to share, following roughly the same sequence as in the previous lesson. The teacher assigns to the listening students an evaluative role.
Launch for end-of-lesson assessment (exit slip)	*Whole group:* The teacher a gives prompt: "Four cupcakes are shared by five people. How much does each person get? This time, I would also like you to make a numerical record of what you did and then raise your hand when you are finished."

CONCLUSION

Students need to experience both practicing procedures and "doing" mathematics. A good mathematical task embeds skill practice within it without the student even realizing this. Oftentimes, many skills are required to solve a task. Time dedicated to memorizing some basic facts or procedures is sometimes necessary to improve fluency and efficiency, thus allowing students to concentrate on more difficult problems. This memorization or practice also can take place at home for homework.

A task can be associated with more than one level. The teacher needs to be aware of the characteristics that make up each level and decide which would meet the particular goals she has set. To become successful problem solvers, students need to be immersed in lots of experiences, or problematic tasks, that allow them to develop and apply various skills. A problematic task allows students to reflect and communicate, and it should leave mathematical residue. The design, setup, and implementation of the task all affect student learning and need to be purposefully planned and executed. Through thoughtful questioning, the teacher can assess the students carefully and determine whether the level of the task is appropriate, as well as stretch the students' thinking. A sequence of tasks should connect, building onto bigger ideas.

Many teachers are under the constraints of their districts or states to use a specified commercial curriculum. Most curricula are written in a more traditional way, presenting a specific, new skill each lesson. Experienced teachers know how to take the focus for that lesson and design a meaningful task through which the students can discover and construct the math intended for that lesson.

There is great power in spending the time to help children understand fundamental fraction notions through the designing of well-crafted tasks. Indeed, many children can make sense of complex fraction computations, like adding fractions with unlike denominators, without a lot of difficulty if they are secure in their understanding of the meaning of fractions. You may have to spend some time deepening your own understanding; we guarantee that your students will push you as they do the same.

▶ Interview Video with an Eye on Content

Watch a series of videos in which problems are presented to children and they solve them. For each video, determine the type of fraction that is involved, the fraction equivalence notion involved, and how the child solved it.

Problem #	Fraction Type	Equivalence Notion	Strategy
1			

▶ Interview a Child

1. Create a word problem for each equivalence notion for both fraction types. Describe in words and pictures how a child might solve them using direct modeling. Be sure to label the notions and types.

2. Using the problems you used in #1 above, interview a third or fourth grade child.

3. Write a report about it that contains two parts:
   a. Individual problem analyses
   b. Overall summary

   In the individual problem analyses section, for each problem you pose include:
   a. the equivalence notion and fraction type
   b. the problem
   c. a complete description of the child's response
   d. an analysis of the child's response, which includes the following: general strategy and specific strategy

   In the overall summary, write a **summary** of what you learned about the child's mathematical thinking:
   a. the types of problems the child successfully solved and those she struggled with
   b. the types of strategies she or he demonstrated (General Strategies, Specific Strategies, and ways of keeping track)

▶ Classroom Video with an Eye on Pedagogy

In this classroom video in which students are studying fractions, analyze the level of the task during all three phases: design, introduction, and implementation. Give reasons for your analysis.

Design	
Introduction	
Implementation	

▶ Classroom Application

Observe and/or participate in the planning and implementation of five different math lessons. Analyze the level of the task during all three phases: design, introduction, and implementation of each lesson. Give reasons for your analysis.

▶ Resources

Implementing Standards-Based Mathematics Instruction: A Casebook for Professional Development, Mary Kay Stein et al. (2000)

Lessons for Introducing Fractions, Marilyn Burns (2001)

Young Mathematicians at Work: Constructing Fractions, Decimals, and Percents, Catherine Twomey Fosnot and Maarten Dolk (2002)

▶ Lit Link

Literature Books to Support Fraction Concepts

Title	Author
Apple Fractions	Jerry Pallotta
Eating Fractions	Bruce McMillan
Fraction Action	Loreen Leedy
Fractured Math Fairy Tales: Fractions & Decimals	Dan Greenberg
Funny & Fabulous Fraction Stories	Dan Greenberg and Jared Lee
Give Me Half!	Stuart J. Murphy
Hershey's Fractions	Jerry Pallotta
Inchworm and a Half	Elinor J. Pinczes
One Riddle, One Answer	Lauren Thompson
Parts of a Whole	Kari Jenson Gold
Piece = Part = Portion: Fraction = Decimals = Percent	Scott Gifford
Trouble at the Cookout	Betsy Franco

▶ Tech Tools

Websites

Visual Fractions: A tutorial that models fractions with number lines or circles, http://www.visualfractions.com/

A Tour of Fractions (for teachers and students), http://mathforum.org/paths/fractions/

Who Wants Pizza? A Fun Way to Learn about Fractions, http://math.rice.edu/~lanius/fractions/index.html

Mathematics K–6 Programming Support: Fractions Learning Objects, http://www.curriculumsupport.education.nsw.gov.au/primary/mathematics/k6/programming/program_support/fractions/fract_learnobj.html

NCTM: Illuminations—Web Links, http://illuminations.nctm.org

Software

Jumpstart Math for Second Graders, Knowledge Adventures

Fraction Shape-Up, Merit Software

Curriculum Integration and Fraction Computation

PEDAGOGICAL CONTENT UNDERSTANDINGS

Pedagogy   *Curriculum Integration*
- Reading and Literature Integrations
- Fine Arts Integrations
- Science and Social Studies Integrations

Content   *Fraction Computation*
- Addition and Subtraction of Fractions
- Multiplication of Fractions
- Division of Fractions
- Implications in the Classroom

"Because understanding is synonymous with seeing relationships, emphasizing relationships helps to develop understanding."

Thomas Carpenter et al., Children's Mathematics: Cognitively Guided Instruction *(1999, 99)*

CONVERSATION IN MATHEMATICS

Teacher: As we have watched our tadpole grow and metamorphosize into a frog, we have noticed that it eats more. On Monday, we noticed that it ate about ½ of the brine shrimp disk we fed it. On Tuesday, it ate about ¾ of the disk. How much shrimp did our tadpole eat both days?

Student: (Draws a circle, splits it in half vertically, and shades one section; draws another circle, divides into fourths, and shades three sections.)

Student: It ate 1 and ¼.

Teacher: How'd you get 1 and ¼?

Student: I put the ½ and 2 of the fourths together like this. (Draws another circle, splits it in half vertically, splits one of the halves in half horizontally, and shades all.)

That makes 1 whole. Then I have one more fourth. (Draws another circle, splits it into fourths, and shades one section.)

That makes 1 whole and ¼. The frog at 1 whole shrimp disk and another ¼.

The second-grade child you just read about was never taught to add fractions. Instead, she spent considerable time in a class where she developed a deep number sense for fractions. She developed this knowledge by solving problems that were both personally meaningful and mathematically rich, like this one that related directly to her study of tadpoles. In other words, this problem was meaningful because it reflected an integration of mathematical and scientific inquiry. This chapter teaches you how to create high-level tasks by using the obvious benefits of curriculum integration as a vehicle for enhancing the meaning of those tasks.

The child in the preceding conversation combined the knowledge she gained from engaging in high-level tasks with an understanding of the addition operation and solved this problem. What is so unusual about that? Most of us were taught mathematics procedurally, which works OK for operating with whole numbers. Note we said OK, not good, or great. Many of us "checked out," however, when we were taught how to operate on fractions. In fact, research shows that when most adults are asked why they use common denominators when adding fractions, or what the addition of fractions means, they have no idea. Furthermore, they do not know why multiplying fractions "straight across" works or why inverting and multiplying is an efficient procedure for dividing fractions. When asked to create a problem calling for the dividing of fractions, they often create one calling for multiplying instead. This chapter explains why fraction computations work the way they do.

PEDAGOGY   *Curriculum Integration*

Learning Theory

Curriculum integration has been a popular topic for years. Meaningful learning experiences can be generated when teachers use the natural connections among subject areas or disciplines. However, some methods for integration do not honor the integrity of the disciplines involved and are not, therefore, legitimate curriculum integration. For example, reading a storybook about pizzas and then doing fraction problems using pizzas as models is not real integration.

There are four types of legitimate curriculum integration:

1. *An integration of the cycles that characterize good teaching in both subject areas.* For example, you are now familiar with the launch–explore–summarize teaching cycle. This cycle is not unique to mathematics teaching. Experts in most subject areas espouse an inquiry teaching cycle that begins with the presentation of some problem or task, is followed by an opportunity to explore ways to solve that problem, and ends with an opportunity for students to discuss their solutions with others. The problem might be a scientific one, like why winds blow from regions of cold to regions of warmth; a literature-based one, like why Tommy had the courage to release the midnight fox in Betsy Byars's great children's novel; or even a problem in dance involving the best ways to explore space and show various emotions. Therefore, looking for the commonalities associated with teaching cycles in various subject areas can be a powerful means of curriculum integration.

2. *An integration of the cycles that characterize real learning in both subject areas.* Throughout this text we have used such terms as *develop, solidify,* and *practice.* Mathematical learning tends to first develop, then become more solid, and then become "practiced," in the same sense that a lawyer practices law or that a doctor practices medicine. Thus, develop–solidify–practice is a useful way to think about a mathematical learning cycle. Again, this cycle is not unique to mathematics. When a child learns that the vowel–consonant–silent e (v–c–e) usually results in the vowel having a long sound, that idea first develops through an enriched exploration of words possessing the v–c–e pattern, becomes more solid as the child consistently recognizes v–c–e words, and finally becomes practiced as v–c–e words become automatic. Therefore, looking for the commonalities associated with the cycles that characterize learning in various subject areas is another vehicle to promote curriculum integration.

3. *An integration of the mental processes that characterize cognition in both subject areas.* Throughout this text, we have consistently emphasized the five NCTM

process standards—problem solving, communicating, reasoning and proof, representation, and connections. These five processes characterize good "mathematizing" but are just as characteristic of good science, good reading, good drawing, or good singing. For example, the science process skills that serve as the backbone of good school science inquiry include such processes as observing, communicating, classifying, measuring, inferring, predicting, hypothesizing, and experimenting (Rezba et al. 2007). **Although the five math processes are not specifically mentioned in the science list, with the exception of communicating, a careful examination of them reveals that problem solving, reasoning, representation, and connections are fundamental to them.** Another example—if a child wants to show depth in a landscape drawing, he is trying to *solve* a visual problem. He *reasons* that, when he stands on a hill and looks at the surrounding landscape, objects farther away appear higher in his field of vision and smaller, and he *connects* this observation with a way of organizing the objects in his landscape drawing. He *communicates* depth, therefore, by *representing* distant objects in a similar way.

4. *An integration of the purposes of the tasks, or problems, presented to children.* From a mathematical perspective, this type of integration amounts to the presentation of one of two kinds of tasks: a mathematical task that is solvable using some other curriculum area, or a task from some other curriculum area that is solvable using mathematics. For example, you can present a mathematical problem that might be solved by some creative movement exploration, or you can present a movement problem that might be solved mathematically. In so doing, you authenticate the tasks you present through the connections between mathematics and other subject areas. Children then see mathematics as a useful endeavor because of its relevance to other fields of study. This fourth type of integration is the pedagogical focus of this chapter.

Application to the Learning and Teaching of Mathematics

In the rest of this pedagogy section, we organize our discussion of integration according to task creation and our discussion of selection according to subject area.

Reading and Literature Integrations

Integrating reading instruction with math instruction has become quite popular over the years. Sometimes we use math to solve problems found in literature, and other times we use literature to solve mathematical problems.

Using Mathematics to Solve Literature Problems

Mathematically related problems within literature can be either implicit or explicit. Suppose you are reading *Charlie and the Chocolate Factory* by Roald Dahl with your fourth graders. As you read about the fate of Mike Teavee, the character who is shrunk by Willy Wonka's special transporting television camera and then stretched to a size much larger than his original height, you might pose this task: If Mike Teavee could fit into his father's suit coat pocket, how much did he shrink? Such a problem would lend itself to such math topics as measurement, division, fractions, and even ratios. In this example, the problem is implicit in the reading and solvable by math.

Some works of children's literature explicitly present problems in the context of the reading. In the book *The Doorbell Rang* by Pat Hutchings, Ma makes 12 cookies for her two children to share equally. Then the doorbell rings, and they are joined by two friends. Before they can eat their cookies, two more friends join them, meaning six children now need to share. Then six more friends join them, and each child ends up receiving only one cookie. This is a great example of a literature-based problem explicitly designed for mathematical problem solving.

Using Literature to Solve Mathematical Problems

Suppose you want your students to solve a problem related to the relationships among various geometric shapes. *Sir Cumference and the First Round Table*, by Cindy Neuschwander, could serve as a great vehicle to engage students in a discussion about the characteristics of shapes and how they compare with one another. In one sense, the book provides a vicarious problem-solving experience for students in a geometric context.

Fine Arts Integrations

In this section, we look at the visual arts, music, dance, and drama as we discuss how fine arts and math instruction can be integrated, either by using mathematics to solve fine arts–related problems or by using the fine arts to solve mathematical problems.

Using Mathematics to Solve Problems Related to the Fine Arts

You might be studying ancient Greece (an additional social studies integration) with your sixth graders and want to create simple replications of the Parthenon. Fractions could definitely come in handy as you work to get the proportions right. Students would examine photographs of the Parthenon, compute the fraction relationships associated with each part, and use those fractions to create an accurate replication.

Music provides an obvious context for the use of mathematics in solving fine arts–related problems. When trying to "solve the problem" of how long to hold a note, for instance, it helps to realize that the entire system of notation is based on fractions. In ¾ time, a quarter note is one beat, an eight note is half of a beat, and so on. Or, if a whole note counts as one whole, then a half note is held half the time of a whole note, a quarter note is held a quarter of the time, and so on.

When you involve children in dance and creative movement, it is all about geometry and spatial relationships. For example, as the children express various feelings, their movements vary according to important, fundamental geometry ideas such as high, low, wide, thin, widespread, and concentrated. In folk dance, the patterns through which children would move are all geometric: squares, circles, and so on.

Special Needs

Children with special needs, or otherwise struggling in mathematics, benefit greatly from movement and activities involving spatial relationships.

Using the Fine Arts to Solve Mathematical Problems

Any time you invite children to represent their thinking with concrete objects or pictures, you have the potential to incorporate the visual arts as a vehicle for solving math problems. This does not mean that every manipulative or pictorial representation is also a visual art experience, but reasoning about those representations mathematically lays a foundation for reasoning about them in a visual arts context.

Because most of your mathematics instruction should be embedded in real-life contexts, dramatization can play a vital role in helping children conceptualization a problem and solve it. Good tasks usually tell a good story, and dramatizing the story enhances the meaning associated with and comprehension of those tasks.

Science and Social Studies Integrations

Science and social studies are two subject areas sometimes referred to as *content area curricula.* This means that learning that occurs within these two subjects consists partly of the acquisition of knowledge and concepts (content) and partly of the acquisition of skills related to that content. We have already discussed the relationships between the science process skills and the mathematical process standards. Similar relationships can be drawn between the process standards and the language associated with the Expectations for Excellence: *Curriculum Standards for the Social Studies* produced by the National Council for the Social Studies (1994), which includes such verbs as *compare, explain, articulate, analyze, predict, demonstrate,* and *interpret.* Therefore, we focus on the knowledge acquisition side of science and social studies in an effort to look at the integration between these two subject areas and mathematics. In other words, we do not look at using science and social studies to solve mathematical problems; instead, we discuss using mathematics to solve problems and answer important questions related to these two subject areas.

Two types of mathematical tasks are based on the contexts that social studies and science can provide. First, tasks can be based on mathematical data provided by study in these two areas. For example, if students are studying crocodilians and comparing the relative sizes alligators, crocodiles, gharials, and caimans, the numbers obtained would provide fertile soil for comparative subtraction or work with fractions. Or, if you engage your students in a comparison of the resources available to the Union and Confederate armies during the American Civil War, similar mathematical work could be done.

A second type of task is associated with direct, empirical science and social science inquiry in which the data obtained is mathematical. For example, hands-on investigations about weather usually involve measuring and obtaining mathematical data about which important weather questions can be asked, questions that require mathematically comparing nighttime and daytime temperatures or determining the relative amount of rainfall during the winter. In social studies, it is quite common to engage students in surveys of various types related to political or community issues. Creating graphs and tables that incorporate this data leads students to use mathematics to solve important social studies questions.

Comprehension Check

- Describe what it looks like when mathematics is truly integrated with other parts of the curriculum.

- Create a couple of examples of how mathematics can be integrated into other subject areas.

CONTENT   *Fraction Computation*

Big Ideas and Focal Points

Keep in mind some big ideas, suggested by Randall Charles (2005, 15), in regards to the computation of fractions:

- The real-world actions for addition and subtraction of whole numbers are the same for operations with fractions and decimals.

- Different real-world interpretations can be associated with the product of a whole number and fraction (decimal), a fraction (decimal) and whole number, and a fraction and fraction (decimal and decimal).

- Different real-world interpretations can be associated with division calculations involving fractions (decimals).

- The effects of operations for addition and subtraction with fractions and decimals are the same as those with whole numbers.

- The product of two positive fractions each less than one is less than either factor.

By the time children are in fifth and sixth grades, they are ready to use the fractional number sense they developed in third and fourth grades to begin serious study of operating on fractions. Without that foundation, however, it is difficult for most children to acquire the mathematical achievement specified by the NTCM's *Curriculum Focal Points for Prekindergarten through Grade 8 Mathematics: A Quest for Coherence* (2006), as shown in the Focal Points table.

Unlike previous content chapters, this chapter does not describe problem types relative to fractions to any great degree, with the exception of partitive and

NCTM FOCAL POINTS	
Fifth Grade	**Sixth Grade**
Represent the addition and subtraction of fractions with unlike denominators as equivalent calculations with like denominators.	Make sense of procedures for multiplying and dividing fractions, and explain why they work.
Develop fluency with standard procedures for adding and subtracting fractions.	Use common procedures to multiply and divide fractions efficiently and accurately.
Make reasonable estimates of fraction sums and differences.	Multiply and divide fractions to solve problems, including multistep problems and problems involving measurement.
Add and subtract fractions to solve problems, including problems involving measurement.	Express the result of dividing two whole numbers as a fraction.
	Give mixed number solutions to division problems with whole numbers.

measurement division models. This discussion is organized by operation—addition, subtraction, multiplication, and division—and sequenced by our intuitive sense of problem difficulty based on the mathematical content. In other words, we discuss conceptualizations of operating on fractions from simple to complex to help you develop your understandings and to exemplify a potential curricular structure that can guide your instructional and curricular planning. In doing so, we examine some common ways children might directly model fraction situations, particularly part–whole situations from a two-dimensional, or planar, perspective.

Addition and Subtraction of Fractions

What does it mean to add fractions? When we add ⅕ and ⅖, what does that mean? A useful way to think about it goes back to the fundamental idea of fractions in two-dimensional representations. If we have ⅕ of a single object, like a pan of brownies, that means that pan has been divided into five equal parts and we have one of those parts, so ⅕ answers the question, "How much of . . . ?"

Extend that same thinking to adding fractions. If we have ⅕ of something and then ⅖ of the same thing, *how much of* the total thing do we have? For example, if you frost ⅕ of a pan of brownies and then you frost ⅖ more of that same pan, how much of the whole pan did you frost?

You would have frosted ⅗ of the whole pan of brownies: ⅕ + ⅖ = ⅗. Pretty straightforward. This is not that different from adding tens or hundreds. If you add 10 and 20, you are really adding 1 ten and 2 tens, which gives you 3 tens, or 30. In both cases, you are adding one of something to two of something and getting three of that thing.

Now think about subtraction. We could look at all whole number problem types in which subtraction might be involved, but we stick to separation for now, assuming that you could figure out the direct models that might characterize comparison or the problem types in which an addend is missing. Back to the brownies. Suppose you made a pan of brownies last night. You cut the batch into five pieces but decided to wait to frost it until the morning. When you woke up, you discovered that only ⅗ of brownies were left in the pan, so you frosted that portion. If you now remove one piece, how much of the original pan of brownies is frosted and remaining in the pan? ⅗ − ⅕ = ⅖.

Next, move to mixed fractions. What does it mean to add mixed fractions, like $1\frac{3}{5} + 2\frac{1}{5}$? Again, this is a great deal like adding two-digit whole numbers. Think about it. If a child directly models 23 + 35 efficiently, she might show 2 tens and 3 ones and then 3 tens and 5 ones. Next, she might combine the tens and combine the ones. Then she would combine those two results. Similarly, you can directly model $1\frac{3}{5}$ as 1 whole and $\frac{3}{5}$ and $2\frac{1}{5}$ as 2 wholes and $\frac{1}{5}$. Next, you can combine the wholes, combine the fifths, and then combine those results: $1\frac{3}{5} + 2\frac{1}{5} = 3\frac{4}{5}$.

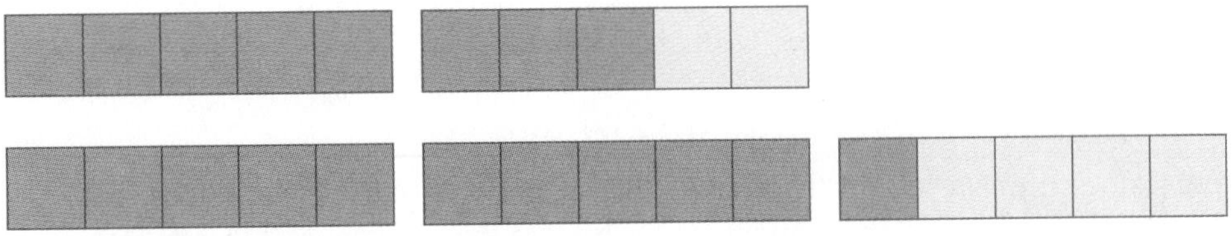

What happens when you add mixed fractions and the resulting fractional total is larger than 1? Basically, you are composing, just like when you composed tens while working with whole numbers. The only difference is that you do not compose to make a 10; you compose to make a whole, and the number of pieces that make a whole depends on the denominator. Suppose you have $1\frac{4}{5}$ pans of brownies and then add to them $2\frac{3}{5}$ pans of brownies. How many whole pans of brownies do you have? $1\frac{4}{5} + 2\frac{3}{5}$. When you combine $\frac{4}{5}$ and $\frac{3}{5}$ that makes $\frac{7}{5}$. Take 5 of the fifths and compose another whole. Now you have $\frac{2}{5}$ and 1 + 2 + 1 wholes, or $4\frac{2}{5}$.

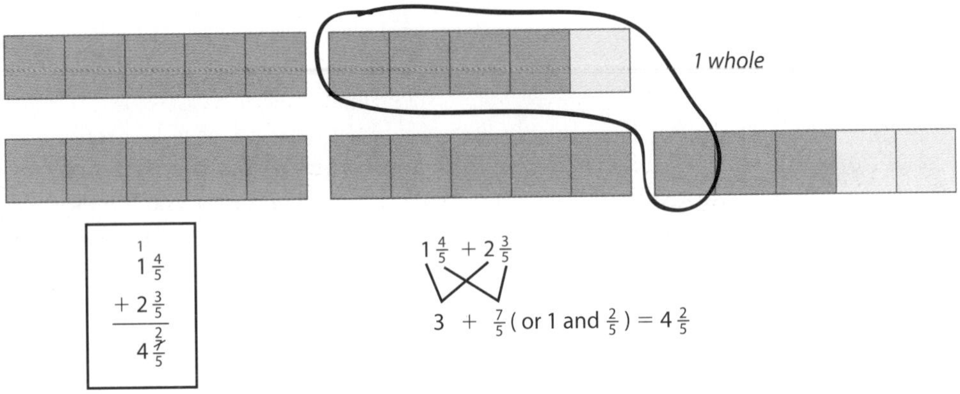

You can decompose a whole to subtract mixed fractions, such as $4\frac{1}{5} - 2\frac{3}{5}$. You cannot remove $\frac{3}{5}$ from $\frac{1}{5}$ without using negative numbers, which would be OK, but for now stay with positives. You can decompose 1 whole so that you only have 3 wholes and a total of 6 fifths. Remove 2 wholes and 3 fifths, and that leaves 1 whole and 3 fifths—$1\frac{3}{5}$.

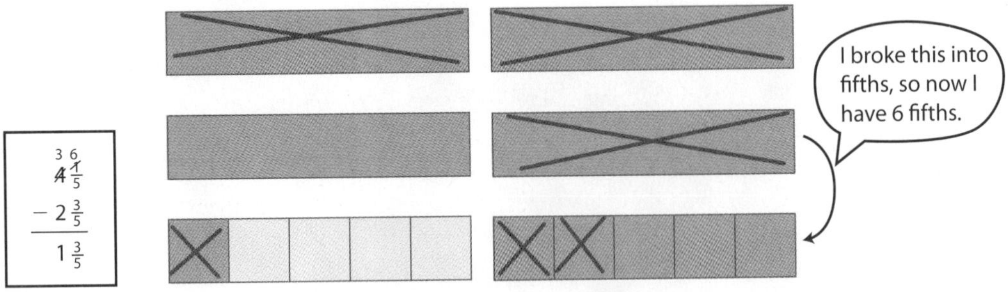

Now for the granddaddy of 'em all—adding and subtracting fractions with unlike denominators. Take, for example, ½ + ⅓. This is an "apples and oranges" situation. By that we mean that you are adding two different things, halves and thirds in this case, and expecting to come up with some reasonable result. That is like asking, "How much is two apples and three oranges?" Unless you establish some commonality between apples and oranges, that question makes no sense. So you could ask, "How many pieces of fruit do I have in my cart if there are two apples and three oranges in it?" The word *fruit* establishes a sense of commonality between apples and oranges. What, therefore, is common between halves and thirds? Is there a way to think about halves mathematically that is like thirds? Is there some other name you can attach to halves that also applies to thirds?

This is where the notion of fractional equivalence from chapter 10 comes in handy. Think about some fraction manipulative, like pattern blocks, that allows you to represent ½ and ⅓. Now look for a smaller piece that could be used to cover the same area as ½ and ⅓. That piece would be ⅙. What do ½ and ⅓ have in common? They both can be represented using sixths: ½ = ³⁄₆ and ⅓ = ²⁄₆. You can combine ½ and ⅓ by combining their equivalents: ³⁄₆ + ²⁄₆ = ⁵⁄₆.

Three basic situations characterize adding and subtracting fractions with unlike denominators based on the relationship between the denominators:

- The denominator of one fraction is a factor of the other, such as ½ + ¼, which means that the lowest common multiple of the two denominators is one of the denominators (4)

- The two denominators have a common multiple that is smaller than the result of multiplying the two denominators, as in the case of ¼ + ⅙ (12)

- The lowest common multiple is the result of multiplying the two denominators, as in ½ + ⅓ (6)

All that remains is conceptualizing various combinations of the preceding situations, which means adding and subtracting mixed numbers with unlike denominators with or without composing or decomposing. Figure 11.1 summarizes this progression of adding and subtracting fractions.

Multiplication of Fractions

As discussed earlier, children should understand that the results obtained from operating on numbers depends on the type of numbers being operated on. For example, multiplying whole numbers usually, but not always, results in products that are larger than the two factors: 2 × 3 = 6. One of the biggest hang-ups for children in their work with fractions occurs when they start to observe that multiplication involving common fractions (fractions less than 1) usually results in a product less than the factors: ½ × 6 = 3 and ½ × ⅓ = ⅙.

Comprehension Check

- For each of the following problems, create a context that would match, and then solve each problem using a model (or pictures), numbers, and words. Be sure to make connections between your numerical and pictorial representations.
  a. ¾ + ½
  b. ⁴⁄₇ + ⅔
  c. 3⅕ − 1⅘

Level	Type	Number Sentence	Direct Model
A	Add like denominators.	$\frac{1}{5} + \frac{2}{5} = \frac{3}{5}$	
B	Subtract like denominators.	$\frac{3}{5} - \frac{1}{5} = \frac{2}{5}$	
C	Add mixed fractions, like denominators, with no composing.	$1\frac{3}{5} + 2\frac{1}{5} = 3\frac{4}{5}$	
D	Subtract mixed fractions, like denominators, with no composing.	$3\frac{4}{5} - 2\frac{1}{5} = 1\frac{3}{5}$	
E	Add mixed fractions, like denominators, with composing.	$1\frac{4}{5} + 2\frac{3}{5} = 4\frac{2}{5}$	

Figure 11.1. Sequence of adding and subtracting fractions.

What then, does it mean to multiply fractions? Go back and think about some meanings associated with multiplying whole numbers. What does 2 × 3 mean? If you recall from chapter 6, it means "two groups of three."

Did you notice the word *of* in that phrase? If 2 × 3 means two groups of three, what, then, does ½ × 6 mean? It means half *of* a group of six. So if I have six erasers and I give you half of them, I would give you three, which is comparable to 6 ÷ 2 partitively. Note that this example requires a part–set fraction definition, have of a set of six. If we have two common fractions, like ⅓ × ½, that literally means ⅓ *of* ½. So if I have ½ of a cake and then frost ⅓ of that ½, how much of the whole cake did I frost? Note that this question references the unit whole and suggests a part–whole fraction definition. We could draw a rectangle cut in half and then cut one of those halves into three equal parts. What does the problem tell us to do next? It

Level	Type	Number Sentence	Direct Model
F	Subtract mixed fractions, like denominators, with decomposing.	$4\frac{1}{5} - 2\frac{3}{5} = 1\frac{3}{5}$	
G	Add or subtract fractions, unlike denominators, for which one denominator is a common multiple of the other.	$\frac{1}{2} + \frac{1}{6} = \frac{3}{6} + \frac{1}{6} = \frac{4}{6}$	
H	Add or subtract fractions, unlike denominators. The least common multiple of the denominators is less than the result of multiplying the denominators.	$\frac{1}{4} + \frac{1}{6} = \frac{3}{12} + \frac{2}{12} = \frac{5}{12}$	
I	Add or subtract fractions, unlike denominators. The least common multiple of the denominators is equal to the result of multiplying the denominators.	$\frac{1}{2} + \frac{1}{3} = \frac{3}{6} + \frac{2}{6} = \frac{5}{6}$	
J	Add or subtract mixed fractions with unlike denominators with or without composing.	(Combinations of above)	

Figure 11.1, continued

tells us to ask how much of the whole these smaller pieces constitute. If we extend the third lines across the rectangle, we can see that ⅓ of ½ is ⅙ of the whole cake.

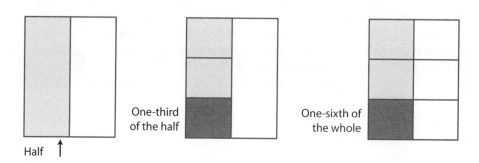

Half

One-third of the half

One-sixth of the whole

Language Tip

Using supportive language aids in conceptual understanding of the meaning of computation of fractions.

Often, if such a problem is given in context, such as "A recipe called for a cup of sugar; I had to cut my recipe in half, so how much sugar am I going to need?" students naturally solve it with a picture by drawing ⅔ and marking out one of the thirds, thus numerically recording ⅔ ÷ 2 = ⅓. These are great places to compare how ⅔ × ½ and ⅔ ÷ 2 are the same. This helps introduce the notion of the reciprocal, which comes in handy when dividing fractions.

So how do children develop their sense for multiplying fractions? In what order might we design tasks that enable them to conceptualize this fascinating

Level	Type	Sample Problem and Number Sentence	Problem-Solving Explanation	Direct Model
A	Fraction with a numerator of 1 times a whole number. The denominator is a factor of the whole number.	I had eight doughnuts and gave half of them to my friend. How many did I give away? ½ × 8 = 4 (Children naturally solve this problem as 8 ÷ 2 = 4.)	I divide the eight objects into two groups, because that is what the 2 means, and then count the number in one group, which is four.	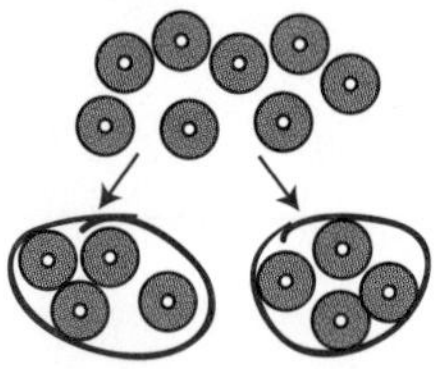
B	Fraction with a numerator of 1 times a whole number. The denominator is not a factor of the whole number.	I had seven cookies and gave half of them to my friend. How many did I give away? ½ × 7 = 3½	I divide six of the objects into two groups, with three in each. I split the remaining one into two equal pieces and give one piece to each group, which makes 3½ for each group.	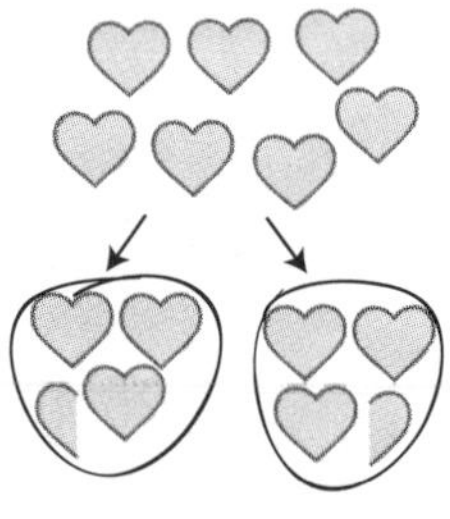
C	Fraction with numerator greater than 1 times a whole number. The denominator is a factor of the whole number.	I had 24 pencils and gave ¾ of them to my friend. How many did I give away? ¾ of 24 = 18	I divide the 24 pencils into four equal groups, because that is what the 4 means, and then count the number in three of those groups, which is 18.	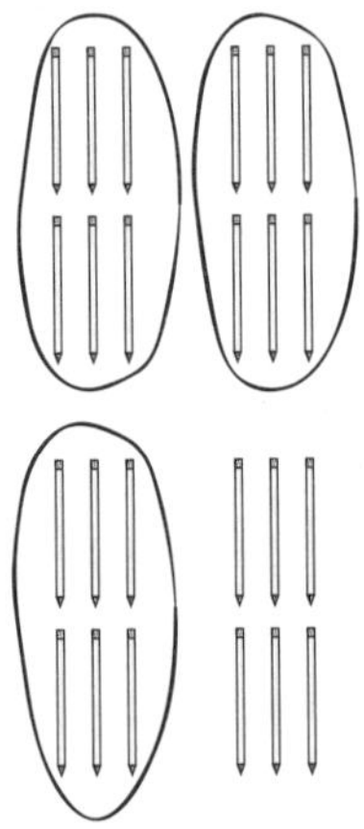
D	Fraction with a numerator greater than 1 times a whole number. The denominator is not a factor of the whole number.	I had three cookies and gave ⅖ of them to my friend. How many did I give away? ⅖ of 3 = 1⅕	The only way I could make five parts of three cookies was to divide each cookie into five parts and then give two of each of those five parts, which is 6 fifths. The 5 fifths makes 1 whole, and then there was 1 more fifth.	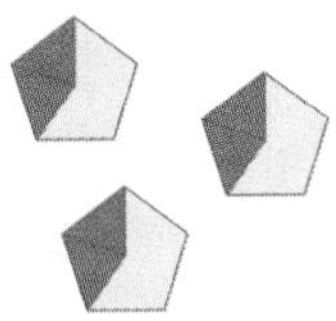

Figure 11.2. Sequence of multiplying fractions.

part of elementary mathematics? Our own research (Bahr and Truscott, in progress) with older elementary children suggests that they develop a conceptualization for multiplying fractions in an order that approximates the sequence in figure 11.2.

If you recall from chapter 7, where we discussed multidigit multiplication, the distributive property was used by separating the numbers into tens and ones and multiplying the parts. This was modeled by creating an area model, multiplying the parts, and adding up the partial products. This same idea can

Level	Type	Sample Problem and Number Sentence	Problem-Solving Explanation	Direct Model
E	Whole number times a fraction. The denominator is a factor of the whole number.	I ate eight sandwich halves. How many whole sandwiches did I eat? $8 \times \frac{1}{2} = 4$	I drew eight rectangles and cut each in half. I shaded half of each rectangle and then counted 1 whole for every 2 halves, which makes 4 whole sandwiches.	
F	Whole number times a fraction. The denominator not a factor of whole number.	I ate five sandwich halves. How many whole sandwiches did I eat? $5 \times \frac{1}{2} = 2\frac{1}{2}$	I drew five rectangles and cut each in half. I shaded half of each rectangle and then counted 1 whole for every 2 halves, which is 2 whole sandwiches and $\frac{1}{2}$, or $2\frac{1}{2}$.	
G	Fraction times a fraction, with 1 in both numerators.	My mom gave me a third of a cake to frost. I frosted half of that. How much of the whole cake did I frost? $\frac{1}{3} \times \frac{1}{2} = \frac{1}{6}$	I drew a rectangle, cut it into thirds, and shaded 1 third. I divided the shaded third in half and colored one of the halves. I extended the half line across the rectangle, which made a total of six parts with one colored, or $\frac{1}{6}$.	
H	Fraction times a fraction, with 1 in only one numerator.	My mom gave me $\frac{1}{4}$ of a cake to frost. I frosted $\frac{2}{5}$ of that. How much of the whole cake did I frost? $\frac{1}{4} \times \frac{2}{5} = \frac{2}{20}$, which is the same as $\frac{1}{10}$.	I drew a rectangle, cut it into fourths, and shaded 1 fourth. I divided the shaded fourth into fifths and colored two of the fifths. I extended the fifths lines across the rectangle, which made a total of 20 with 2 colored, or $\frac{2}{20}$.	
I	Fraction times a fraction, without 1 in the numerators.	My mom gave me $\frac{3}{4}$ of a cake to frost. I frosted $\frac{2}{5}$ of that. How much of the whole cake did I frost? $\frac{3}{4} \times \frac{2}{5} = \frac{6}{20}$, which is the same as $\frac{3}{10}$.	I drew a rectangle, cut it into fourths, and shaded 3 fourths. I divided the each shaded fourth into fifths and colored two of the fifths in each column. I extended the fifths lines across the rectangle, which made a total of 20 with 6 colored, or $\frac{6}{20}$.	

Figure 11.2, continued

be applied to multiplication of mixed fractions. For example, 3¼ is the same as 3 + ¼. So, if we were to multiply this by 2½ (or 2 + ½), then our model might look like this:

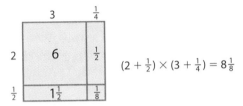

$$(2 + \tfrac{1}{2}) \times (3 + \tfrac{1}{4}) = 8\tfrac{1}{8}$$

If we added up all the partial products, we would get 8⅛ as our product. This may or may not be a more efficient way for solving for mixed numbers than converting them into improper fractions, multiplying, and then reducing the product. However, the connections between multiplication with fractions and whole numbers and the distributive property should be made explicit.

Comprehension Check

- For each of the following problems, create a context that would match, and then solve each problem using a model (or pictures), numbers, and words. Be sure to make connections between your numerical and pictorial representations.
  a. ⅓ × 15
  b. 15 × ⅓
  c. ½ × ⅓
  d. 2½ × 4⅓

Division of Fractions

Division is where the rubber meets the road when it comes to operating on fractions. Do you remember the quote "Ours is not to reason why, just to invert and multiply?" Why do we invert and multiply when dividing fractions? The truth is that you do not have to do so, but multiplying by the reciprocal ("inverting and multiplying") is a handy algorithm. The more fundamental question is, What does it mean to divide with fractions?

Most American adults (including elementary teachers, we are sorry to say, but with no offense intended), when asked to create a word problem that can be solved by dividing fractions, create one that involves multiplying by a fraction instead (Ma 1999). This is because they do not understand how the meaning of an operation changes when the numbers being operated on differ from each other. For example, if we asked you to create a word problem that incorporates ½ ÷ ⅛, you might be tempted to create a problem like "I have ½ of a pie and I eat ⅛. How much of the whole pie did I eat?" Do you see the word *of*? That should be your first clue that such a problem involves multiplying fractions, ½ × ⅛, not dividing. So what is a problem involving ½ ÷ ⅛?

How about this one:

You have baked a cake to feed some dinner guests tonight, and you plan to give each person a serving size that is ⅛ of the whole cake. When you get home from work, you notice, to your horror, that your extremely hungry spouse has eaten half the cake. It is too late to make another cake, so you ask yourself, "How many ⅛-sized pieces of cake can I get out of ½ of a cake?"

You could invert and multiply if you realized that this was a division problem. Or you could simply draw a rectangle and cut it into halves vertically. Then you would draw another rectangle below it, cut the second rectangle into eighths vertically, and ask yourself, "How many of those eighths cover the same area as ½?" (Hear the equivalence thinking again?)

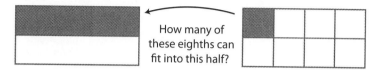

How many of these eighths can fit into this half?

When operating with fractions or decimals, it can be confusing knowing which number goes in which part of an equation. Therefore, it is helpful to consider what is happening in the operations when dealing with whole numbers to know what is happening with the fractions. This is basically a measurement division problem. In measurement division involving whole numbers, like 8 ÷ 2, you are asking how many groups of two are in eight, or more simply, how many twos in eight? Therefore, ½ ÷ ⅛, from a measurement perspective, literally means how many eighths are in a half? Is it possible to think about the division of fractions partitively as well? Yes, it is.

What does 8 ÷ 2 mean partitively? It means divide eight things into two equal groups. The answer is the number in each group, or one group, because each group has the same number in it. In other words, eight in two groups means four in one group. So what does the 8 ÷ ½ problem mean? It means, If there is 8 in ½ of a group, how much is in 1 whole group? Thus, 8 in ½ a group means 16 in 1 whole group.

You can also think about it from a multiplicative perspective. 8 ÷ 2 = ____ means the same as 2 × ____ = 8; that is, two times what equals eight? Therefore, 8 ÷ ½ means ½ × ____ = 8; that is, half of what equals eight? Here is a problem incorporating 8 ÷ ½ from a partitive perspective: If it takes 8 quarts of paint to paint half a large wall, how much paint would it take to paint the whole wall?

Our research (Bahr and Truscott research in progress) suggests that children develop their conceptualization of fraction division in the sequences suggested by figures 11.3 and 11.4.

We begin with measurement division because it seems more straightforward than partitive.

Did you notice the parenthetical statements in the last table? Each one is basically suggesting that, if you think carefully about what dividing with or by fractions partitively really means, you can see that it is mathematically the same as multiplying by the reciprocal. So, "Ours *is* to reason why because now we know why we invert and multiply!"

Note that it is not uncommon for children to think that, because you can multiply straight across to procedurally determine the result of multiplying two fractions, you ought to be able to divide straight across. The truth is, you can. Suppose we are dividing ½ by ⅛. We would do 1 ÷ 1 to get the new numerator (1). We would solve 2 ÷ 8 to get the new denominator (¼). What results is a complex fraction: 1/(¼). You can procedurally determine 1/(¼), or you can remember that the fraction bar means divide and think in a measurement way. How many fourths in one whole? There are four, and that is the answer to ½ ÷ ⅛. We do not recommend this method, but so much for saying you have to invert and multiply.

Level	Type	Sample Problem and Number Sentence	Problem-Solving Explanation	Direct Model
A	Whole number divided by a fraction.	How many half cakes are in three whole cakes? $3 \div \frac{1}{2} = 6$	I drew three rectangles then split them into halves. I counted 6 halves.	
B	Fraction divided by a fraction. The divisor is smaller, with a whole number as the result.	How many $\frac{1}{8}$ cake pieces are in half a cake? $\frac{1}{2} \div \frac{1}{8} = 4$	I drew one rectangle and split it in half. I drew another rectangle and split into eighths. I counted 4 eighths that would cover the same area as 1 half.	 4 of these eighths fit in the half
C	Fraction divided by a fraction. The divisor is smaller, with a mixed fraction as the result.	How many $\frac{1}{3}$ cake pieces are in half a cake? $\frac{1}{2} \div \frac{1}{3} = 1\frac{1}{2}$	I used pattern blocks. I got a trapezoid (half of a hexagon) and then put a rhombus (one-third of a hexagon) onto the trapezoid. I saw that another half of a rhombus would still cover the trapezoid.	
D	Fraction divided by a fraction. The divisor is larger, with the denominator of the divisor a factor of the other denominator.	How much of $\frac{1}{2}$ of a cake is contained in $\frac{1}{6}$ of a cake? $\frac{1}{6} \div \frac{1}{2} = \frac{1}{3}$	I used pattern blocks and got a triangle (one sixth of a hexagon) and put it on top of a trapezoid (one half of a hexagon). I saw that the triangle was $\frac{1}{3}$ of the trapezoid, and $\frac{1}{3}$ of the trapezoid would fit onto the triangle. So $\frac{1}{3}$ of the $\frac{1}{2}$ is in the sixth.	
E	Fraction divided by a whole number.	How much of three cakes is in half of a cake? $\frac{1}{2} \div 3 = \frac{1}{6}$	I drew three circles cut in halves. Since that makes six total parts and half of one whole is one of those six parts, half of one circle is $\frac{1}{6}$ of the total parts.	

Figure 11.3. Sequence of dividing fractions (measurement division).

Implications in the Classroom

As you can see, computing with fractions can be quite complicated. This means students need lots of hands-on experience to be able to make sense of the operations. The idea of multiplication of fractions can be made accessible to even young children through a context that is easily understood by them. Look at the problems in figure 11.5, which were given to first graders.

If young children are able to reason through this problem and arrive at a correct solution, then why do so many fifth graders fail at computation involv-

Level	Type	Sample Problem and Number Sentence	Problem-Solving Explanation	Direct Model
A	Whole number divided by a fraction.	If it takes 3 gallons of paint to cover half of a wall, how much paint is required to paint the whole wall? $3 \div \frac{1}{2} = 6$	I drew a rectangle and split it in half. I drew three cans inside one of the halves to show the amount of paint it takes to cover that half. That means it would take three cans to cover the other half, and 2 threes is six. (That is really $3 \times 2 = 6$.)	
B	Fraction divided by a fraction. The divisor is smaller, with a whole number as the result.	If it takes half a gallon of paint to cover an eighth of the wall, how much paint is required to paint the whole wall? $\frac{1}{2} \div \frac{1}{8} = 4$	I drew a rectangle and cut into eighths. I wrote $\frac{1}{2}$ inside one of the eighths to show the amount of paint it takes to cover that eighth. Because it would take eight of those halves to cover the whole wall, 8 halves is four. (That is really $\frac{1}{2} \times 8 = 4$.)	
C	Fraction divided by a fraction. The divisor is smaller, with a mixed fraction as the result.	If it takes a $\frac{1}{2}$ gallon of paint to cover a third of the wall, how much paint is required to paint the whole wall? $\frac{1}{2} \div \frac{1}{3} = 1\frac{1}{2}$	I drew 1 rectangle and split it in thirds. I wrote $\frac{1}{2}$ inside one of the thirds to show the amount of paint it takes to cover that third. Because it would take three of the halves to cover the whole wall, 3 halves is $1\frac{1}{2}$. (That is really $\frac{1}{2} \times 3 = 1\frac{1}{2}$.)	
D	Fraction divided by a fraction. The divisor is larger, with the denominator of the divisor a factor of the other denominator.	If it takes a $\frac{1}{8}$ = gallon of paint to cover half the wall, how much paint is required to paint the whole wall? $\frac{1}{8} \div \frac{1}{2} = \frac{1}{4}$	I drew a rectangle and cut it in half. I wrote $\frac{1}{8}$ inside one of the halves to show the amount of paint it takes to cover that half. Since it would take two of the eighths to cover the wall, 2 eighths is a fourth. (It means $\frac{1}{8} \times 2 = \frac{1}{4}$.)	
E	Fraction divided by a whole number.	If it takes a $\frac{1}{2}$ gallon of paint to cover three walls (the room is small), how much paint is required to paint just one wall? $\frac{1}{2} \div 3 = \frac{1}{6}$	I drew a paint can and split it in half, shading the lower half to represent the paint. I drew three rectangles of equal size under the half that covered the same area as the half to represent three walls. Each of the three small rectangles divides the half into three parts. If I divide the other half into three parts, I can see that one of the small parts of the half equals a sixths of the whole rectangle that represents 1 whole gallon. (That is really $\frac{1}{2} \times \frac{1}{3} = \frac{1}{6}$.)	

Figure 11.4. Sequence of dividing fractions (partitive division).

ing fractions? The answer is that the problems are presented void of context or language supports to help students conceptualize what is going on. Teachers always need to consider how to make a problem more accessible to children who are struggling.

Just because the students are older does not mean that the problem types from chapters 7 and 9 no longer apply. The operations work in the same way; just the numbers are more complicated. This is the perfect time to be using

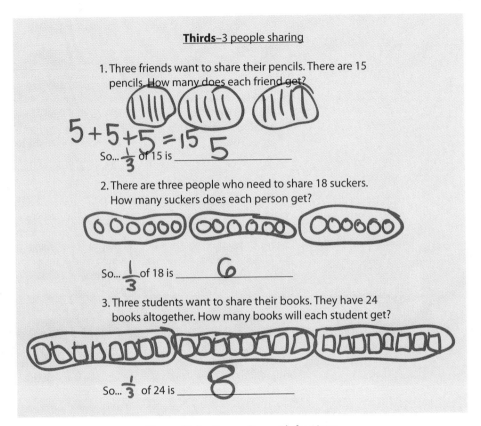

Figure 11.5. Computing with fractions.

these problem types. The contexts will help students directly model these problems, thus giving access to all.

Just as with whole numbers, we want students to be able to increase their strategies by eventually moving beyond direct modeling to more abstract strategies, beginning with pictorial representations. Drawing fractions is not exactly easy for children. They have to go back to drawing pictures of what they are doing with the models so that they can wean themselves from the models. They need exposure to contexts that lend themselves to different kinds of representation, for example, grouping, planar models, and linear models. Remember, it is also important to be recording their actions using symbolic notation. This helps students transfer what they are doing with the tools to numerical representation.

But what generalizations do we want them to make so that they can begin to compute using symbolic notation? With addition and subtraction, we want students to understand that the denominator is just the name of the fraction and that the denominator is not added or subtracted. Early experiences (grades 2–4) should prepare students to fully internalize basic fractions, such as ½, ⅓, and ¼. They should be able to combine these amounts visually and mentally without concern for the difference in denominator. For example:

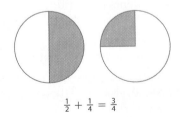

$$\frac{1}{2} + \frac{1}{4} = \frac{3}{4}$$

There is no reason any student should attempt to add these using common denominators. As with whole numbers, students should learn to step back from the problem and think about the quantities.

As opposed to addition and subtraction, the denominator is acted on in multiplication and division. Students need to generalize that, with multiplication, the numbers are multiplied directly across. They also need to experience the inverse of multiplication, the division of fractions. When provided contexts for multiplication of a whole number with a fraction, students often divide by a whole number (see level A in figure 11.2). That is because it is makes more sense to be dividing than to be multiplying when splitting up a group. If students are provided situations in which they have to compare results of what happens when fractions are multiplied versus divided, then they can generalize that taking the inverse of a fraction in a division problem can become a multiplication problem. But children do not make these connections by accident. They need problems that specifically let them notice these connections.

Using Inquiry to Teach the Computation of Fractions

Here are two examples of inquiry-based lessons that exemplify ways in which you can integrate science and social studies with your mathematics instruction.

Fifth Grade	*Example Lesson 1 (2 cycles)*
Creating and interpreting tables and graphs during a science investigation	
Launch cycle 1	The teacher begins with a question: "How is the breathing rate of cold-blooded animals affected by changes in the temperature of their environment?" The teacher invites students to perform an investigation in which they count the number of gill slit openings of goldfish that occur at regular 1-minute intervals. They place ice in the water and measure the temperature of the water during those intervals.
Explore cycle 1	The teacher asks students to create multiple ways to display their data.
Summarize cycle 1	*Whole group:* Students share strategies categorized by numerical (table) and pictorial (graphing) means. Listening students are specifically asked to compare the various displays.
Launch cycle 2	The teacher asks students to create fractions that describe the relationship between the normal number of breaths and the reduced number of breaths: "What fraction could we use to show how the number of breaths in the first interval compares to the number of breaths during the second interval?" (If the fish breathed 24 times in the first time interval and 8 times in the second time interval, the fraction would be $8/24$, or $1/3$)
Explore cycle 2	The teacher asks students to represent their fractions in multiple ways.
Summarize cycle 2	*Whole group:* With teacher assistance, students share strategies. The teacher asks listening students to assume an evaluative, or justifying, role as they listen to the strategies.
Launch for end-of-lesson assessment (exit slip)	*Whole group:* The teacher gives a prompt: "Over the entire time we measured, what happened to the fish breathing rate while the water temperature was lowered?" Students should write and draw their responses.

Sixth Grade	*Example Lesson 2 (2 cycles)*
Fractions and area in the context of social studies	
Launch cycle 1	*Whole group:* The teacher creates a simple map of a fictitious castle on graph paper, making sure that the fractions involved simplify to relatively simple fractions. The teacher asks, "What fraction of the square footage in the castle comprises the king's quarters? What fraction comprises the jester's quarters?"
Explore cycle 1	Students compute the areas, add them up, create fractions, simplify them, and then add them. The teacher monitors their progress.
Summarize cycle 1	*Whole group:* The teacher invites students to share their strategies. The teacher assigns the listening students an evaluative role, meaning that the teacher calls on one or more students to tell the rest of the class whether or not they agree with the shared strategy and why, and a comparative role, in which students look for similarities and differences in the strategies.
Launch cycle 2	*Whole group:* The teacher presents a task similar to the one in the first launch.
Explore cycle 2	The teacher observes how the strategies compare with the previous explore session.
Summarize cycle 2	*Whole group:* The teacher invites students to share their strategies. The teacher assigns the listening students an evaluative role, meaning that the teacher calls on one or more students to tell the rest of the class whether or not they agree with the shared strategy and why, and a comparative role, in which students look for similarities and differences in the strategies.
Launch for end-of-lesson assessment (exit slip)	*Whole group:* The teacher presents one more combination.

CONCLUSION

One of the challenges associated with conducting good mathematical inquiries is coming up with good tasks to present in your launches. We have always found that once a teacher looks to curriculum integration as a vehicle for developing good tasks there seems to be no end to the tasks that can be generated. In fact, you will come up with more tasks than you have time to solve. In addition, your students will never ask why the mathematics they are learning is important, because a meaningful curriculum characterizes your classroom.

There is a great deal of mathematics in this chapter. It is proof that elementary mathematics is anything but elementary. But here is the good news. We have taught young children these notions using a conceptual, inquiry-based approach and know that children are capable of knocking your socks off when it comes to learning how to operate on fractions. We guarantee that you will learn to think deeply about fractions right along with them—a thrilling, rewarding, and renewing experience for them and for you.

▶ Interview Video with an Eye on Content

You will watch a series of videos in which problems are presented to children and they solve them. For each video, determine the type of fraction computation that is involved (using tables 15.1–15.4) and how the child solved it.

Problem #	Fraction Computation Type	Strategy

▶ Interview a Child

1. Create a word problem for each type of fraction computation found in tables 15.1 through 15.4. Describe in words and pictures how a child might solve them using direct modeling. Be sure to label the types.

2. Using the problems you used in #1 above, interview a fifth or sixth grade child.

3. Write a report about it that contains two parts:
   a. Individual problem analyses
   b. Overall summary

   In the individual problem analyses section, for each problem you pose include:
   a. the fraction computation type
   b. the problem
   c. a complete description of the child's response
   d. an analysis of the child's response, which includes the following: general strategy and specific strategy

   In the overall summary, write a **summary** of what you learned about the child's mathematical thinking:
   a. the types of problems the child successfully solved and those she struggled with
   b. the types of strategies she or he demonstrated (general strategies, specific strategies, and ways of keeping track)

▶ Classroom Video with an Eye on Pedagogy

In this classroom video in which students are studying fraction computation, determine the types of curriculum integration present in the lesson. Give reasons for your determination.

▶ Classroom Application

1. Experiment with the four types of legitimate curriculum integration in a real classroom. Comment on your experience in terms of the characteristics of each type found in this text.

2. Also experiment with mathematics integration with literacy, fine arts, social studies, and science. Again comment on your experience in terms of the characteristics associated with integration with those subject areas found in this text.

▶ Resources

Young Mathematicians at Work: Constructing Fractions, Decimals and Percents, Catherine Twomey Fosnot and Maarten Dolk (2002)

Lessons for Extending Fractions: Grade 5, Marilyn Burns (2003)

Lessons for Multiplying and Dividing Fractions: Grades 5–6, Marilyn Burns (2003)

▶ Lit Link

Literature Books to Support Fraction Concepts and Operations

Title	Author
Apple Fractions	Jerry Pallotta
Fraction Action	Loreen Leedy
Fractured Math Fairy Tales: Fractions & Decimals	Dan Greenberg
Funny & Fabulous Fraction Stories	Dan Greenberg and Jared Lee
Give Me Half!	Stuart J. Murphy
Hershey's Fractions	Jerry Pallotta
Inchworm and a Half	Elinor J. Pinczes
One Riddle, One Answer	Lauren Thompson
Piece = Part = Portion: Fraction = Decimals = Percent	Scott Gifford
Trouble at the Cookout	Betsy Franco

▶ Tech Tools

Websites

Visual Fractions: A tutorial that models fractions with number lines or circles, http://www.visualfractions.com/

A Tour of Fractions (for teachers and students), http://mathforum.org/paths/fractions/

Who Wants Pizza? A Fun Way to Learn about Fractions, http://math.rice.edu/~lanius/fractions/index.html

Mathematics K–6 Programming Support: Fractions Learning Objects, http://www.curriculumsupport.education.nsw.gov.au/primary/mathematics/k6/programming/program_support/fractions/fract_learnobj.html

NCTM: Illuminations—Web Links, http://illuminations.nctm.org

Software

Fraction Shape-Up, Merit Software

Primary- and Second-Language Issues in Mathematics and Decimals, Percentages, and Ratios

PEDAGOGICAL CONTENT UNDERSTANDINGS

Pedagogy *Primary- and Second-Language Issues in Mathematics*

- Language Acquisition
- Learning the Language of Math
- Irregularities with Math Vocabulary
- Explicit Teaching of Vocabulary
- Environments That Support Both Language and Concept Development
- Discourse Structures

Content *Decimals, Percentages, and Ratios*

- Decimals
- Percentages
- Ratios and Proportions

....

"It boils down to this: if you can't talk about math, you are unlikely to do it well."

Pat Wingert

CONVERSATION IN MATHEMATICS

Consider the following dialogue with a fourth-grade student:

Teacher: If you took a test with a 100 questions and you got 4 questions wrong, what percentage would you get?

Student: 96%.

Teacher: How do you know?

Student: Because 96 plus 4 is 100, that is 96 right and 4 wrong, and that's how I get 96%.

Teacher: What if you had 50 questions on the test and you got 4 wrong?

Students: 46%. It is the same thing; you have to subtract.

Teacher: What if you had 10 questions and got 4 wrong?

Student: That would be 6, right? So 6%.

Teacher: What if you had 10 questions and 0 wrong?

Student: That would be 10%, which would really be 100%.

Teacher: What do you mean by that?

Student: There are 10 questions. Zero means I got nothing wrong.

Teacher: Are 10% and 100% the same?

Student: No. That would actually be 100%.

Teacher: So, what would 10 questions and 1 wrong be?

Student: It would be 9%. Well, actually, that is 9 out of 10; that is not a percentage.

At first, it seems that the student in the preceding conversation has an understanding of percentages, but when questioned further, his lack of understanding is soon revealed. His misconceptions are not atypical for children who are just beginning to learn about percentages. They only understand it in relation to 100, not as fractional parts of other numbers. One of his misconceptions lies with the mathematical language related to percentages and the connections it has with fractions.

Although it seems as though they should be separate, language is indeed an integral part of understanding math concepts. The language used in mathematics is different from that used in conversation. Children need to be taught the precision and peculiarities of mathematical language. But what happens when English is not the child's native language? This creates both an English-language and a mathematical language problem. This chapter explores the important role that language plays in the acquisition of math concepts and how English-language learners are not the only ones who need support in developing appropriate academic language that centers on mathematics.

A lot of specific language is associated with the concepts of fractions, decimals, and percentages, as well as with ratios and proportional reasoning. Not surprisingly, these are some of the most difficult areas for upper-elementary students. Research suggests that more than half the adult population is not able to think proportionally (Lamon 1999). However, the ability for a student to think across these areas and make connections between them is evidence of computational fluency. As difficult as it may be to teach these ideas to students, it is critical that they have the opportunity to develop as strong of a foundation as possible, because proportional reasoning is "the cornerstone of a variety of topics in the middle and high school curriculum" (Van de Walle 2004, 298), such as fractions, similarity, data graphs, probability, and algebra. In the content section of this chapter, we examine the concepts of fractions, decimals, and percentages, ratios, and proportional reasoning in depth. A deeper understanding of a difficult area helps us, as teachers, have more precision with the language when we teach it, therefore increasing the students' understanding.

PEDAGOGY   *Primary- and Second-Language Issues in Mathematics*

Learning Theory

Each year we are finding increasing numbers of students in our classrooms whose primary language is not English. In 2004, there was a 56% increase from 1994 to more than 5 million English-language learners nationwide. However, we are expected to teach them grade-level content just the same. This is a difficult challenge, and to do so, some basic understandings about language acquisition need to be in place.

Jim Cummins (1984) might be best known for his distinction of two levels of language proficiency: basic interpersonal communication skills (BICS) and cognitive academic language proficiency (CALP). If you can picture an iceberg, BICS is the part of the iceberg that is exposed and CALP would be the much larger part that is hidden (figure 12.1). BICS is that language used informally and in social settings, and CALP is the language used academically. It is more formal and lacks context cues from which to draw meaning.

BICS, or conversational fluency, takes most students about 2 years to acquire. CALP, or academic proficiency in a secondary language, on the other hand, takes about 5–7 years to develop. When students possess conversational fluency, they may easily appear to be fluent in English. However, this is not always the case. Just because a student can converse does not mean that she has obtained cognitive proficiency in English. Students who come to the United States having already developed certain concepts, however, have an easier time transferring what they know into their new language, because there is a common underlying proficiency across languages (Cummins 1981).

According to Stephen Krashen and Tracy Terrell (1983), the natural language approach describes how students naturally acquire their second language in stages, much like that of their primary language. Some stages are shorter in duration than others. These stages are preproduction, early production, speech emergence, and intermediate fluency. Teachers need to use different strategies depending on which stage the child is at. As a whole, these strategies are called *specially designed academic instruction in English* (SDAIE) or sometimes known as *structured English*. These strategies include providing comprehensible input, scaffolding, modeling, background knowledge, contextualization, schema building, and metacognitive development (Walter 1996). Language acquisition is also enhanced when anxiety is low and interaction is high.

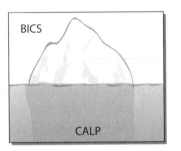

Figure 12.1. The distinction between BICS and CALP as part of English-language proficiency.

Application to the Learning and Teaching of Mathematics

Language Acquistion

Contrary to popular belief, math is not language free or culture free. Leslie Garrison and Jill Mora (2005) explain that English-language learners, such as Latino students, are reported by the California Department of Education as having low achievement in mathematics because of a common misconception that math is "culture free" because it uses symbols. How often have you heard someone refer to math as being "universal"? However, the NCTM (1989) emphasizes the critical role that language has in the development of mathematical concepts. Conceptual understanding, as described throughout this book, requires the use of both concrete materials and language to grow. This implies that perhaps the concepts are universal but that language is essential in the development of those concepts.

As discussed in the learning theory section earlier, second-language learners are often judged by teachers as being more linguistically proficient than they really are. It may appear from their level of general conversations that they have the language skills of a native English speaker, yet they are underachieving in content areas. Cummins (1979) identifies these students as lacking content-specific vocabulary, which prevents them from developing concepts.

English-language learners' low achievement in mathematics, therefore, can more appropriately be attributed to their low levels of English proficiency (Garrison and Mora 2005). But second-language learners are not the only ones struggling in mathematics. Many native English speakers, such as those in lower socioeconomic areas, those with learning disabilities, and those whose learning styles do not fit with the traditional school setting, also struggle, possibly because the language of the classroom is so different from the language used at home. There are different rules for the way we communicate; for example, we may raise our hand in class but not on the playground. We also use different registers, speaking more informally with our family and friends out of the classroom than when discussing academics within the classroom. The language used in the mathematics classroom and the way we use it is even more highly specialized. Many native English speakers struggle with math because the talking used in developing mathematical concepts is not just social chatter but, rather, a language of its own. The "language of math is not acquired effortlessly and naturally through social interaction but rather learned and taught in school as a separate register and often as a consciously memorized vocabulary" (Pilar 2005, 24).

In "UnLATCHing Mathematics Instruction for English Learners" (2006, 14), Leslie Garrison, Olga Amaral, and Greg Ponce write:

> **Part of the reason English learners struggle in mathematics is that rather than being language free, mathematics uses language that is a highly compressed form of communication where each word or symbol often represents an entire concept or idea. In a literature text, readers can comprehend a passage if they are familiar with 85%–90% of the words. The other words and their meanings can often be gleaned through context. Mathematics problems, on the other hand, generally require the student to understand nearly every word as there is seldom enough context provided with the problem to assist with unfa-**

Rule of Thumb

For English-language learners, keep the mathematical expectations high and increase the linguistic support. Edward De Avila and Sharon Duncan (1981) have researched the correlation between language proficiency and mathematics achievement in Latino students who are English-language learners. They found that the low achievement in mathematics was attributed to low levels of English proficiency. These students apparently have had high expectations and received no linguistic support or the expectations of them were lowered so much that they were denied equal access to mathematics (Secada 1992).

miliar words or concepts. **Another problem that English learners encounter is that sometimes they recognize a word, but the meaning they know for the word is different from the intended meaning and therefore does not help them understand the problem.**

Maybe instead of the words "English learners" we can substitute the words "many children," because this seems to be the case even for native English speakers.

When researching best practices for teaching mathematics to English-language learners, it should be noted that these techniques are generally good practices for all learners. Rusty Bresser (2003) has compiled a list of 10 strategies for helping English-language learners:

1. **Ask questions and use prompts**
2. **Practice wait time**
3. **Modify teacher talk**
4. **Recast (interchange) mathematical ideas and terms**
5. **Pose problems that have familiar contexts**
6. **Connect symbols with words**
7. **Reduce the stress level in the room**
8. **Use "think-pair-shares"**
9. **Use "English experts"**
10. **Encourage students to "retell"**

If these suggestions are supportive to both native English-language and second-language learners, how can we take what we know about how we learn a first or second language and apply it to learning the language of mathematics? Some ideas are discussed in the next section.

Comprehension Check

- Consider the 10 strategies for helping English-language learners. Which of these strategies have been discussed in previous chapters? What does this tell you?

Learning the Language of Math

If Krashen's natural language approach suggests that learning a second-language mirrors learning a first language, then we might want to think of learning math similarly. Cummins distinguishes between a context-embedded and a context-reduced environment when referring to concept and language development. A *context-embedded* environment is one rich in linguistic supports, such as modified speech, print-rich strategies, and total physical response. Context-embedded registers are associated with everyday language. A *context-reduced* environment is one that reflects academic learning. It is more abstract, more formal, and less personal (Gibbons 2002). When initially developing math concepts, all students benefit from rich context and linguistic support. Young children need the problems to include their situations and experiences, as well as use their everyday language. Over time, they are able to discuss the same concepts using more abstract representations and language as they make connections, an element of a context-reduced environment.

Marilyn Burns (2006) points out, however, that learning math language is not completely synonymous with learning a second language. Oftentimes, when a second language is learned, we already have the concepts from the first language and we are merely learning the labels of those concepts in the new language. Learning math language involves the development of new ideas.

Some second-language learners come to us with math concepts in place in their primary language, and others do not. Being aware of what types of students you have can help you decide what types of experiences they need to develop their mathematical language.

Throughout this book, we describe a classroom of problem solving, exploring, conjecturing, reasoning, defending, connecting, and reflecting as a means of developing conceptual understanding in mathematics. All of these actions and ways of communicating require language. Mathematical concepts and the language related to these concepts are built using everyday language. The use of this language in the mathematics classroom develops through four stages, as described by Ron Pilar (2005): everyday language, mathematized-situation language, the language of mathematics problem solving, and symbolic language. The descriptors and an example are given in figure 12.2.

Pilar explains that the problem stated using the child's everyday language may not include all important information, such as with how many friends the child wanted to share the cookies. After extracting all pertinent information, the teacher should model the student's problem in a more formal register, the mathematized-situation language, which is clear to all students and in which all information is explicit. As time passes, the students become familiar with how story problems sound and begin to use this formal register, as well as include all relevant information.

As problem solvers, we do not go from a problematic situation to the symbolic notation without some kind of internal dialogue. If we did, then it would not be problematic. This *internal chatter*, as Jennie Bickmore-Brand (1990) calls it, is the internal talk that we have about what a problem means and how to solve it. It is as a result of this internal dialogue that a solution process emerges. It seems that as the complexity of the problem increases, the need for internal chatter is greater. In figure 12.2, it acts as the link between the problem and the symbolic notation that represents it. Young children do not just know how to talk or think about a problem. Teachers must think aloud and model this type of dialogue to their students. With plenty of modeling, students begin to think, reason, and question in a way that is helpful in the problem-solving process.

Everyday Language	Mathematized-Situation Language	Language of Mathematics Problem Solving	Symbolic Language
Language acquired through social interaction (acquired naturally)	Everyday language in which mathematical relations are made more relevant (mostly acquired naturally with some learned and taught terms)	Language used to verbalize mathematical concepts and to talk about them (learned and taught)	Symbolic written language and its oral counterpart (learned and taught)
Said: I brought 15 cookies for my friends. I want to share them at lunch and give each of them the same amount so that it will be fair.	I brought 15 cookies for my three friends. I want to share them equally. How many cookies can each friend get?	I have to take the 15 and split them into three equal groups to find out how much each group will get.	$15 \div 3 = x$ "Fifteen divided by three equals x" or $\frac{1}{3} \times 15 = x$ "One-third of fifteen equals x"
Known but left unsaid: There are three friends.			

Figure 12.2. Four stages of how language develops in the mathematics classroom. (Reprinted with permission from *In Changing the Faces of Mathematics: Perspectives on Latinos* by R. Pilar, copyright 2005 © by the National Council of Teachers of Mathematics. All rights reserved.)

In classrooms where reflective talk is not valued, students do not learn how to think or talk about problems in ways that help them make sense of them. Rather than making meaning, the focus of mathematics discussions are "on remembering and performing the steps in the pattern" (Barnett-Clarke and Ramirez 2004, 59). Teachers often comment that their students do not know how to think, but in reality, they were never *taught* how to think. It is critical that mathematical thinking is modeled for the students.

The last stage of mathematical language is symbolic language. We must be careful and not be fooled by students who use symbolic notation to solve problems without understanding. Kathy Richardson refers to this as the *illusion of learning,* when students seem to know and understand but they do not. This is why questioning is so critical. Students who understand are able to use the language of symbolic notation while understanding all concepts it represents.

So, it appears that we learn to talk about math in context-rich environments and through lots of modeling by those who are already fluent. Classroom discussions allow students who are more "fluent" in mathematical language to serve as models to their peers. As fluency develops in certain areas, context levels in those areas are reduced because concepts have been established. As new concepts are developing, context levels again become enriched. For example, when young children are learning addition, they are immersed in lots of real-life contexts to help them visualize the situations that can be used to solve the problems. As their skills develop and they understand the concepts behind the symbolic notation, they may no longer need the language of the situations to discuss basic addition and subtraction. But as these children work with larger numbers, they need to work in contexts again because the symbolic notation is still too abstract for them when they apply it to a higher numerical complexity.

Comprehension Check

- What are the four stages of language used in the mathematics classroom? Create your own example of what problem solving sounds like for each stage.

Irregularities with Math Vocabulary

Consider the following excerpt from the poem "Isn't English a Trip?" written by José Franco (2005):

I thought it would be easier
when math class started.
Because that's just about numbers,
and circles,
and things like that,
right?

Was I in for a surprise!

When Mrs. Jones started talking about addition,
she used the word plus
like 2 plus 2 equals 4.
Sounds good to me.
But last week she mentioned the word combine,
And she said that meant addition too.

"What, Mrs. Jones?
Could you please repeat your question?
What's the sum of all the elephants?"

Hmmmmm
What did Julia tell me sum *meant?*
Is that the same as some,
like "when some of the kids tease me"?

(Reprinted with permission from Isn't English a trip? Written by Jose Franco [2005]: In Changing the Faces of Mathematics: Perspectives on Latinos. *[21–22]. NCTM.)*

This poem expresses a common experience second-language learners and language-impoverished children have. As teachers, we need to be acutely aware of the irregularities of math vocabulary. We have peculiarities in syntax and differences in meaning between mathematical language and ordinary language.

For example, how do young children tend to read "41"?

Many children, when learning about numbers, read this number as "fourteen." They are reading it the way it is written, and they have not been specifically taught the differences in the way teen numbers are said compared to the rest of the numbers. In China, the number 14 is literally said "10 and 4." As a result, there is little confusion about the quantity of the number.

There are some syntactical issues with some math vocabulary, such as with homonyms: *sum* versus *some* or *whole* versus *hole*. Words that sound the same as a word already in their schema can be confusing when trying to make meaning with the math. There are also many synonyms that teachers may use to refer to the same idea without knowing it, and students tend to think that each word or phrase carries its own idea. For example, *add, plus, combine, increase by,* and *join* all refer to the same idea. How about differences in meaning, such as with the word *odd?* Many students may be walking around thinking that odd numbers are strange numbers. Another example is the word *difference*. When asked what the difference is between the two sets of cubes he made (to show a compare problem), a child typically says that one is red and the other is yellow.

There are also irregularities between the oral names for symbols and their written form. For example, why doesn't it make sense to write 300602 for three hundred sixty-two? Why is ⅘ not written like 4.5 as a decimal? Why is ¾ said "*x* over four" and not "*x*-fourths?"

It is extremely important that teachers be precise with their language when referring to math vocabulary and their related concepts. Imprecision can lead to many misconceptions rather than strengthening conceptual learning. Many teachers say that "decimals are just like whole numbers." Then where are the oneths? Others say that "you cannot take a bigger number away from a smaller number," or "multiplication makes the numbers bigger," but those ideas are inaccurate and lead to huge misconceptions.

Explicit Teaching of Vocabulary

There are two types of knowledge: social and logical. Social knowledge is culture driven, such as what symbols we use to represent ideas and how we label certain ideas. Logical knowledge is constructed by the learner. Vocabulary that surrounds social knowledge cannot be figured out and needs to be explicitly taught. Vocabulary associated with logical knowledge also needs to be taught, but only after an idea has developed. Math researchers, such as Burns, have stressed the need to introduce vocabulary only after developing understanding of the related mathematical ideas, thus connecting its meaning to the students' learning experiences. Intentional, explicit instruction of vocabulary words (Burns 2006) is essential if we expect students to understand and use the vocabulary in their own language.

It is not uncommon for a sixth-grade teacher to complain because her students do not know the difference between perimeter and area. After all, students have been exposed to these terms since about third grade. When analyzing the situation more carefully, it appears that the students were never required to use the vocabulary in their own language during explorations and discussions. This resulted in many students not having internalized such vocabulary. Because they never practiced the appropriate uses of the vocabulary, it did not stick with them.

A couple of years ago, one elementary school decided to research this problem and come up with a solution. Teachers began to pay attention to the way they introduced vocabulary and its use by the students. They realized that they never told the children that they expected to hear them using such vocabulary in their conversations. They began to explicitly teach the vocabulary essential for the exploration activity (such as the names of shapes and attributes), and they told their students, "when you are talking with your partner, I expect to hear you use the words. . . ." Teachers from all grades were astonished when, as early as the first lesson, they began to hear their students use the expected vocabulary. They used it not only during that conversation but also in future lessons. In general, students were increasing their expressive mathematical vocabulary.

This is an example of a kindergarten lesson built around the concept of more and less. The students already know what the words *more* and *less* mean, but the teacher wants the students to use these words to help explain how they know where the number 2 should be placed in relation to other numbers already laid on the floor.

Teacher: When you are talking with your partners, I expect you to be using the words *more* and *less* about where the two should go. (Children discuss.)

Child: (To his partner.) I think that the two should go before the three because it is one less and the three is one more.

A first-grade class was trying to solve a problem in the most efficient way, and the teacher wanted her children to use the term *efficient* in their explanations.

Teacher: My job is going to be to solve this problem in the most efficient way I can. Your job will be to see if you agree, to see if you think I am solving it in the most efficient way. (Solves 16 + 70 using tally marks.)

Children: (Complaining because it is taking too long.)

Teacher: (Solves 16 + 70, but this time drawing tens, as rectangles, and ones, as small squares.)

Children: (Enthusiastically agree that this was is more efficient.)

Teacher: Our word that we have been practicing is *efficient*, so I want you to be using this word when you are talking to your partner. I want to hear which way is more efficient and why. So, I would say to my partner, "I think the first way is more efficient because. . . ." Or "I think the second way is more efficient because. . . ."

Child: (To his partner.) I think that the second way is more efficient because you only have to draw those little rectangles for tens and the little squares for ones.

A fifth-grade teacher wants her students to internalize the terms *prime* and *composite* numbers, so she requires students to use these terms when they share their ideas with their partners.

Teacher: It appears that you have discovered that some numbers can only make one type of array and other numbers can make many arrays. There are special names for those kinds of numbers. Numbers that can only make one type of an array are said to be *prime*, and numbers that can make more than one array are said to be *composite*. Discuss with your math partner what you can say about the factors of prime and composite numbers. I expect to be hearing you using the correct terminology. When you are done, I want you to write in your math journals what prime and composite numbers are and show a couple of examples.

Allowing the child to try these new words with a partner and then explain them in their own words in a whole group setting or in their math journals, rather than just listening to them being presented, helps ensure that they understand the new vocabulary. It also increases the chance that they can begin to use these new words on their own. Researchers have found that for a vocabulary word to become part of someone's personal repertoire it must be used in meaningful ways close to 30 times. This means that the class must include as much focused talk as possible. For that to happen, math has to cross other content areas, such as literature and science. Poetry, stories, and articles can be read and created about mathematics. If science is the real-life application to mathematics, then science should be dripping with math vocabulary.

As teachers, we have to watch how we use terms and symbolic language so that we do not create any misconceptions. For example, we should not write equations as streams of thought; doing so causes students to get the wrong idea about the meaning of the equal sign. For example, a child might solve a problem saying that seven plus seven equals fourteen and one more is fifteen. We should not record that thought as follows:

$$7 + 7 = 14 + 1 = 15$$

That notation is incorrect and partially leads to students thinking that the equal sign means "the answer is" rather than "the same as." The correct notation of this equation should be as follows:

$$7 + 7 = 14$$
$$14 + 1 = 15$$

When referring to changing 23 to 230, many might say that they are "adding a zero." Is zero really being added, or is the number being multiplied by 10? Others might ask, "How many tens in 425?" but really mean, "What is the value for the 2 in 425?"

It may seem that oversimplifying definitions or teaching key words is helpful to students, but this does more harm than good. Teaching key words, such as *in all*, does not teach them to think about what the problem is asking. Students fall into the habit of just looking for numbers and trying to do something to them. In actuality, most problems do not even have these key words, and such key words often are misleading. Consider the following problem:

> *Mateo made four times as many clay pots as Luke. Mateo made eight clay pots. How many clay pots did Luke make?*

In this problem, students relying on clue words would quickly multiply the two amounts found in the story. However, to solve the problem, division is necessary. It may be more typical for traditional key words to appear in the younger grades, but it is in these grades that children are trained how to approach problem-solving situations. If they are trained to look for key words, then they will be looking for them in fifth grade as well, when it is less helpful. On the contrary, if second graders are trained to think and reason, then they will think and reason in the upper grades, too.

Teachers also have to periodically monitor one another's vocabulary, as it is used across the grades, through classroom visits, grade-level planning, staff meetings, and lesson studies. Who is using the term *number sentences?* Who is using the term *equations?* Should we use one instead of the other or both? What do the standards say? What language appears on tests? There is nothing more frustrating than teaching students rich authentic vocabulary and at the end of the year find that the test uses a basic word that is unfamiliar to the children. Are teachers within the same grade using similar language? One third-grade teacher may like to use the term *commutative property,* while the other may feel it is too hard and want to use the term *order property.* The goal should be rich, authentic vocabulary with lots of different ways to express ideas.

The entire staff at a school site should sit down to map out the expected vocabulary at each grade level for certain concepts. Going through the process of mapping vocabulary from K–6 as a site ensures that appropriate vocabulary is taught when it needs to be and that issues related to some chronically difficult areas (such as area and perimeter) can be supported in the lower grades. Figure 12.3 gives an example of a site that went through this process. The staff members wrote down the vocabulary they used as a grade level. They found that in measurement, for example, third through sixth grades focused on area

	Kindergarten	First Grade	Second Grade	Third Grade	Fourth Grade	Fifth Grade	Sixth Grade
Measurement	Longest, shortest, tallest, area, perimeter (when sitting on rug), capacity (at capacity, over capacity), weight (heavy, light, equal, the same)	Units of measurement, estimate, longer than, shorter than, length, weight, capacity, balance, standard and nonstandard units, linear, centimeter, inch, volume	Centimeter, inch, length, pound, kilogram, weight, perimeter, temperature, capacity, ruler, scale, degrees, Fahrenheit, Celsius	Length, inch, foot, yard, mile, capacity, weight, temperature, mass, grams, kilograms, plane figures, volume, area, perimeter	(Capacity), weight, linear units, mass, temperature, Celsius, Fahrenheit negative numbers, coordinate grid, graph an equation, area, perimeter, axis, difference	Area of triangles, parallelograms, surface area, net, volume, relate area and perimeter, customary length, metric units, capacity, weight, mass	Estimate, perimeter, diagram, circumference, customary measurement, parallelogram, trapezoid, surface area, prism, pyramid, volume, cylinder

Figure 12.3. Vocabulary map of one mathematical strand from kindergarten through sixth grade.

and perimeter. They also noticed that kindergarten was addressing this vocabulary, knowing how troublesome it is for upper grades. Kindergarten teachers would have the children sit either on the perimeter or in the area of the rug, depending on the activity, and they used this vocabulary daily. Students had to listen and physically move to part of the perimeter or area. Sadly, there had been no follow through with first and second grades. Creating this chart as a staff made it obvious to these grades that to ensure success they needed to informally reinforce the ideas that kindergarten began to instill until it was formally explored in third grade.

Environments That Support Both Language and Concept Development

Concept development is the goal of math instruction, but the linguistic abilities of the class need to be taken into consideration if we are to provide comprehensible input (Garrison and Mora 2005). We need to balance students' existing conceptual knowledge with their existing linguistic ability in deciding what the goals are and how we are going to meet those goals. The relationship between language and concepts is known as *logological knowledge* (Johnson 1991).

Students who struggle with language, either English-language learners or language-impoverished students, need more context-embedded language or more language support. Students who struggle with mathematics must work more concretely than many students who are strong in math. This may be more easily understood by analyzing the chart in figure 12.4.

According to these quadrants, more linguistic support is given to those who fall on the left side and this support is removed as they move toward the right side in their language competency. If you have students with language needs, a good exercise would be to make a blank quadrant and list your students in the quadrants with which they correspond. Once your quadrants are complete, you can assess whether or not you feel that you are meeting the needs of your students.

Discourse Structures

We discussed the importance of discourse and its use in mathematics class in previous chapters. Classroom talk needs to emphasize precision in mathematical language by you and the students. Students need to read, write, and speak mathematically using words and symbols to develop fluency. You need to be modeling a range of vocabulary, as well as demanding its use by the students.

When new vocabulary or symbols are discussed, they should be written on the board or added to a math language wall that can be accessed easily by all students during math time. Vocabulary should not just have a definition but should be accompanied by a pictorial and a numerical example.

During classroom discussions, students do not benefit from unclear or chaotic speech. Second-language students do not always have the ability to distinguish among all the words

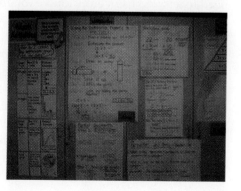

An authentic math language wall accessible to all students.

Comprehension Check

- Give an example of how looking for clue words can be misleading.

- What do the three teachers in the dialogues in this section say to elicit the vocabulary they want their students to use?

Comprehension Check

- Compare the intervention strategies you would provide for students who are low in English and those who are high in English if all are low in math. Refer to figure 12.4 on page 352.

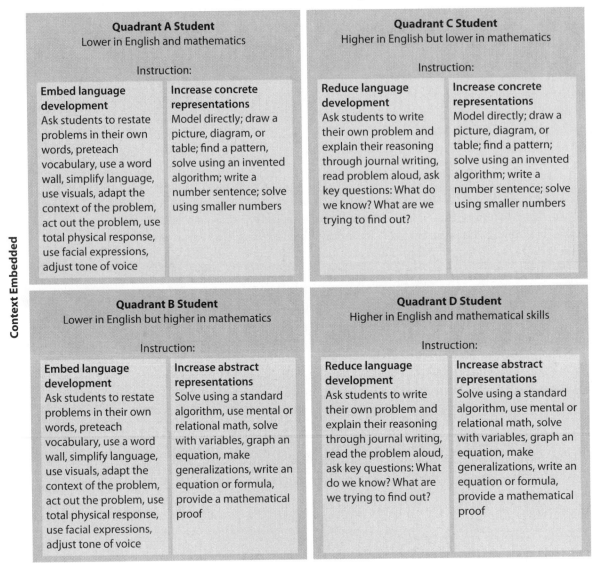

Figure 12.4. Language acquisition and content quadrants. (Adapted from Cummins 1994; Garrison, Amaral, and Ponce 2006.)

Special Needs

Both, students with language needs and those with certain identified learning disabilities benefit when their teacher uses voice inflection, modified speech, longer wait time, body language, and other means to indicate transitions from one topic to another.

quickly enough that they can follow fast-paced conversations. All students need to learn to use voices loud enough for all to hear, as well as to try to clarify their thoughts as much as possible. They also need to learn to talk one at a time and not interrupt one another. It may be necessary for you to rephrase what other students are saying in simpler or more precise speech, but beware of restating students too often. Students with language needs can grow dependent on your support and may never learn to listen to their peers.

It might be necessary to have a student sit next to you during whole group discussions. This way you can whisper into his ear some information that may scaffold his understanding of what is being discussed. You may even want to check in with him before he goes off to explore and make sure he understands the task.

Because it is common to interchange words that mean the same idea as a way of developing vocabulary, it is important that you point out that these different words mean the same thing; otherwise, you may cause confusion. If certain students are missing key vocabulary, then perhaps small-group lessons need to focus on developing that missing vocabulary, and perhaps the concepts behind that vocabulary, before entering a unit that would demand understanding of such ideas.

Just as it benefits any child, small-group work is imperative for students with language needs because it gives them a chance to think and talk with peers, possibly in their primary language, about the problem. Oftentimes, second-language children are quiet because they are shy about trying their new language. Small-group environments provide a reduced-risk atmosphere for students to explain their thinking and allow them to rehearse what they might share in front of the entire group. Chapter 14 describes the nature of complex instruction (Cohen 1994) and its role in eliciting language during the problem-solving process. Second-language classrooms have seen significant improvements in the use of mathematical language because of this approach. Students have assigned roles and a sense of interdependence exists in the design of the task, which creates a need for students to talk about the task at hand.

Decimals, Percentages, and Ratios

CONTENT

We now transition from a pedagogical discussion about language to a discussion about mathematical content areas of decimals, ratios, and percentages and how they help support proportional reasoning. As we do, please notice the important role language plays in enabling children to develop these concepts.

Big Ideas and Focal Points

Decimals, percentages, ratios, and proportional reasoning are broad topics and thus have several big ideas associated with them. The following are some of the bigger ideas related to these topics:

Decimals

- Decimal place value is an extension of whole number place value.
- The base 10 numeration system extends infinitely to very large and very small numbers (millions and millionths; Charles 2005, 14).

Percentages

- Percentages are simply hundredths and as such are a way of writing both fractions and decimals (Van de Walle 2004, 280).

Ratios

- Ratios are multiplicative comparisons of quantities; there are different types of comparisons that can be represented as ratios.
- Ratios give the relative sizes of the quantities being compared, not necessarily the actual sizes (Charles 2005, 13).
- Equal ratios result from multiplication or division, not from addition or subtraction (Van de Walle 2004, 298).

Proportionality

- If two quantities vary proportionally, that relationship can be represented as a linear function (Charles 2005, 18).
- Proportional thinking is developed through activities involving comparing and determining the equivalence ratios and solving proportions in a variety of problem-based contexts and situations without recourse to rules or formulas (Van de Walle 2004, 298).

The NCTM's *Curriculum Focal Points for Prekindergarten through Grade 8 Mathematics* (2006) first address the preceding concepts in fourth grade (Focal Points table); however, some foundational work with tenths is usually done as early as third grade.

NCTM FOCAL POINTS

Fourth Grade	Fifth Grade	Sixth Grade
Students understand decimal notation as an extension of the base 10 system of writing whole numbers.	Students apply their understandings of decimal models, place value, and properties to add and subtract decimals.	Students use the relationship between decimals and fractions, as well as the relationship between finite decimals and whole numbers (i.e., a finite decimal multiplied by an appropriate power of 10 is a whole number).
They understand that it is useful for representing more numbers, including numbers between 0 and 1, between 1 and 2, and so on.	They develop fluency with standard procedures for adding and subtracting decimals.	Students use the relationship between decimals and fractions to understand and explain the procedures for multiplying and dividing decimals.
Students relate their understanding of fractions to reading and writing decimals that are greater than or less than 1, identifying equivalent decimals, comparing and ordering decimals, and estimating decimals in problem solving.	They make reasonable estimates of decimal sums and differences.	Students use common procedures to multiply and divide decimals efficiently and accurately.
They connect equivalent fractions and decimals by comparing models to symbols and locating equivalent symbols on the number line.	Students add and subtract decimals to solve problems, including problems involving measurement.	They multiply and divide decimals to solve problems, including multistep problems and problems involving measurement.
		Students use simple reasoning about multiplication and division to solve ratio and rate problems.
		They extend whole number multiplication and division to ratios and rates by viewing equivalent ratios as deriving from the multiplication table and by analyzing simple drawings that indicate the relative sizes of quantities.

Decimals

A child's first exposure to decimals is when dealing with money, usually in second and third grades. At this time, to the child, the amount on the right of the decimal just represents "cents," not tenths or hundredths. Even though students may have some understanding of fractions, decimals pose to be a new challenge. Careful scaffolding and activity selection are critical in helping students develop a strong foundation in their understanding of decimal numbers.

An understanding of decimals needs to be developed. This can occur by engaging in activities similar to those students used when developing an understanding of place value of whole numbers. Recall the building numbers activities in chapter 4. These helped students understand the different places in our place-value system and how each new place was created when there were 10 groups in the place to its right. You can do these same building activities for the tenths and hundredths place.

Building Decimals

Build a place-value mat with ones, tenths, and hundredths. Third-grade students consider a flat of base 10 blocks to be 100. They may not yet be flexible enough to consider that the flat can represent 1, so you might be more successful if you begin with money. You can choose to use only pennies or pennies and dimes. Ten pennies could be grouped in a small cup and placed in the tenths column, or traded for a dime. Ten cups, or dimes, would be traded for one dollar in the ones column. Play games, such as *Race to a Dollar,* or *Race to One,* which is just like *Race to 100* (see chapter 4). Discussions need to be centered on the connections between the places in whole numbers and those in decimal numbers.

Connecting Fractions with Decimals

At this time, it is also appropriate to connect fractions (tenths and hundredths) to decimals, because they are spoken in the same way.

0.5	5 tenths	$^5/_{10}$	5 tenths
0.05	5 hundredths	$^5/_{100}$	5 hundredths

Helping students make the connection between tenths and hundredths, in about fourth grade, usually involves using base 10 blocks or a 100 grid that students can color. Through the nature of the language, students should know that tenths are part of a whole broken into 10 equal pieces and hundredths are part of a whole broken into a 100 pieces. So, 4 tenths ($^4/_{10}$ or 0.4) and 40 tenths ($^{40}/_{100}$ or 0.40) would be represented as shown in figure 12.5.

Therefore, 0.4 and 0.40 are the same amount. A fraction such as 0.43 can only be represented using the second model because there are tenths and hundredths and the top model only shows tenths.

$\frac{40}{100}$ or .40 would look like this:

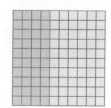

Figure 12.5. Representation of 0.4 and 0.40 using a grid.

Language Tip

Many students, especially English-language learners, have trouble saying the decimals; they tend to say them in the same way as the whole numbers (i.e., hundreds). It is important that the teacher force the students to emphasize the *-ths* endings. It is equally important to stress that we say *and* when we read the decimal point but not in other

parts of the numbers. It is all too common that we say four hundred *and* sixty-two instead of four hundred sixty-two. This is a bad habit and sends a mixed message. If we are careful with our language, we can help students make the connection between mixed numbers and decimals larger than one:

4½   four and a half   *4.5*   four and five tenths

Students can then begin to understand that the 4 in 4.5 is one type of quantity and the 0.5 is another, just like the 4 and the ½ are two types of quantities: a whole and a fractional piece. The *and* separates the wholes from the parts.

When working with decimals greater than one, it is important to model and encourage students to use the proper ways of reading a decimal number. For example, 3.45 is *three and forty-five hundredths,* not *three point four five.* We all are lazy now and then and say *point* when we read numbers. Some industries even use that as part of their vocabulary. However, when we are trying to instill a sense of place value behind these numbers, it is important to support that sense with proper language.

One of the areas of difficulty between fractions and decimals is that in a fraction, the amount of pieces in a whole is stated in the denominator, whereas in a decimal it is stated in its position. It is not obvious to children that the same whole can be broken into different amounts and, thus, compared. So once other fractions, besides tenths and hundredths, are to be compared with decimals, understanding tends to fall apart.

Before any kind of algorithm is used, just like in fractions, it is important that students have more of a global sense of the quantity, for example, ½. If students truly understand what a half is, then they know that no matter how the figure is divided up it is half of that many pieces, or divided by two. So should students be making the connection not only between the equivalent fractions that make up one-half but between the decimals as well: 0.5, 0.50, 0.500, and so on. Using a calculator is another way for children to make the connection between the fraction and the decimal.

Initially, perhaps through calculator use, students should learn the decimal and percentage (discussed later in this chapter) equivalents for benchmark fractions. These fractions are ¼ = 0.25; ½ = 0.5; ¾ = 0.75; and ¹⁄₁₀ = 0.1. They can all be shown on a 100 grid, which helps the connection-making process (figure 12.6). These equivalents are ones we want our students to know without question. They are helpful later when making comparisons.

Students should learn, through their use of the calculator, that they need to divide the numerator by the denominator to find a decimal equivalent. This can be a great segue into dividing decimals by hand (without a calculator). First have your students, through representations, identify what the decimal equivalent should be for a fraction such as ½. Then have them change that fraction to a decimal using division on a calculator and compare the results. Next have

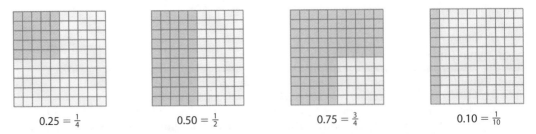

$$0.25 = \tfrac{1}{4} \qquad 0.50 = \tfrac{1}{2} \qquad 0.75 = \tfrac{3}{4} \qquad 0.10 = \tfrac{1}{10}$$

Figure 12.6. Using 100 grids to prove the equivalence of fractions and decimal numbers.

them figure out how they should set up the problem in written form and what they need to do to find the answer.

Comparing and Ordering Decimals

One understanding we need students to have is the meaning of the zero in a decimal. Unlike in whole numbers, the zeros to the left of the key number are significant whereas the zeros to the right are not. Zeros to the right may be disregarded, although when taken into account they can determine how many pieces the whole is broken into. However, although broken into different amounts, the amount remains the same (0.5, 0.50, 0.500, etc.). Just as with whole numbers, it is important for students to model these amounts with either concrete tools or pictures to begin to make the important generalizations regarding ordering decimals, such as the number in the place to the farthest left has the most significance of the entire number in regards to ordering.

> **CAUTION** A common misconception about the role that zero plays can show up when students are ordering decimals. One student may say that 0.30 is larger than 0.5 because 0.30 looks like "30" to her.

Students need to understand that decimals, like whole numbers and fractions, have specific locations on a number line and practicing placing numbers on a number line can help with understanding how they are related to fractions.

The more places that the decimal contains, the more precise it is. Students need to understand that there are infinite ways to make a number more precise but that the context dictates how precise we need something to be. For example, money needs to be calculated to the hundredths, whereas scientists may need precision to the millionths.

Operating with Decimals

The big ideas related to operations with decimals and whole numbers are the same. For example, addition still refers to joining, subtraction to difference, and multiplication to groups. But somehow, the decimal throws a wrench into the operations when it comes to performing computation. The biggest issue is that students are not thinking in quantities and are thinking in isolated digits. When they think this way, they make errors because they are not lining up the decimal point or do not know where to place the decimal point in a product. The following are examples of how to use decimals in each of the four operations.

Addition and Subtraction Children are still able to use their invented algorithms and alternative algorithms when adding and subtracting. Take the problems in figure 12.7.

When students understand what they are adding or subtracting, they no longer have to worry so much about lining up the decimals as they begin to concentrate on what they are adding.

$$0.45 + 3.4 + 2.16 =$$

5 wholes
9 tenths
11 hundredths = 6.01
or 1 tenth and
1 hundredth

$$
\begin{array}{r}
0.45 \\
3.4 \\
2.16 \\
\hline
5.00 \\
0.90 \\
0.11 \\
\hline
6.01
\end{array}
$$

Figure 12.7. Adding a series of three decimal numbers using invented and alternative algorithms that mirror whole number computation.

Multiplication and Division Multiplication and division are the operations for which the decimal can be hard to deal with. There are rules for how to deal with the decimal, but children have little understanding of them and thus usually do not have any idea about the accuracy of their answer. It is critical that they understand what is happening so that they are able to make estimates regarding the size that their answer should be. Most students, when asked, say that multiplying two decimals (as they would two fractions) results in a larger number because when they multiply the numbers always become larger. Multiplying decimals larger than one do indeed result in larger products, because you are also multiplying whole numbers, but decimals smaller than one do not. It all goes back to the language related to the operation:

0.8 groups of 30

That means not even an entire group of 30. If students temporarily ignore the decimal while multiplying using basic facts, then they can see that 30 × 8 = 240. Well, 240 does not make sense because it is much larger than 30, but 24.0 does because it is near 30 but not more. If students are asked to solve several problems like this, they could begin to generalize the rules of multiplying and how many places to move the decimal.

The *Everyday Math* curriculum (2007) uses the term *magnitude estimate* to refer to estimates that determine the place an answer should have. Here is an example:

30.2 × 17.8   *Rounding these numbers to the nearest 10 results in 30 × 20, which is 600. The answer should be in the hundreds place.*

See how we are able to connect this problem to an array model (figure 12.8).

When dividing, we are all familiar with the notion of having to "clear the decimal" to be able to divide. Does anyone understand why that works? Examine the following number string to see whether you can make sense of this rule:

6,000 ÷ 30
600 ÷ 3
60 ÷ 0.3
6 ÷ 0.03
0.6 ÷ 0.003

What generalization can be made from this pattern?

The quotient to all these problems is 200. So what we generalize from this pattern is that if what is multiplied or divided to both the divisor and the divi-

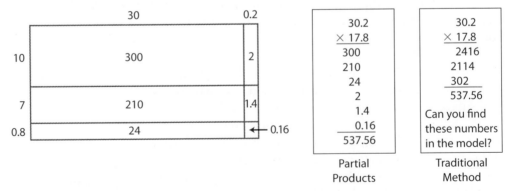

Figure 12.8. Using an array to connect multiplication of decimal numbers to the traditional and alternative algorithms.

$0.4\overline{)434}$ (Remember, it is asking how
                            many 0.4 are in 43.4)

Multiplying both	$4\overline{)434}$	100
sides by 10, we get:	400	
(We are now asking how	34	8
many fours are in 434.)	32	
	2	0.5
		108.5

Figure 12.9. Using partial quotients, an alternative algorithm, to solve for division involving decimal numbers.

dend is the same, then the quotient remains the same. That concept can be applied to the following problem:

$0.03\overline{)6}$

If students understand that $6 \div 0.03$ is the same as $600 \div 3$ through the exploration of number strings, such as the one mentioned previously, then they either choose to make both numbers whole so that they are easier to deal with or decide to leave the numbers alone and just ask themselves, "How many 3 hundredths are in 6?" It is not mandatory that the decimal be cleared, but it is done to make the problem more manageable because considering decimals can be confusing.

Although many teachers embrace certain alternative algorithms because doing so preserves place value, some are not sure what to do with partial quotients when they involve decimals. These teachers tend to go back to teaching the traditional algorithm because of their own insecurities. Although we promote understanding in both alternative and traditional algorithms, we want teachers to choose what they teach based on deep understanding of both algorithms. Look at a division problem involving decimals (figure 12.9).

For the last part of this problem, there was a remainder 2. By now, students are usually encouraged not to leave remainders but to divide through the entire problem. They might say to themselves, "How many fours in two?" which would be a half, or 0.5. They may decide to put a zero to make 2.0 but think of it as a basic fact ($20 \div 4$) and say 5; still, they know that the decimal has to go in front of the answer because there was a decimal in the problem. Regardless, students need to have developed satisfactory number sense to become flexible when dividing with decimals, and this flexibility comes from whole group mathematical routines, such as the previously described number string.

Comprehension Check

- What are some activities that can help students make the connection between fractions and decimal numbers?

- Create problems using decimal numbers for all four operations. What do students have to understand before they can solve these problems?

Percentages

Percentages have several functions. They can be used for statistics, be used to produce a new quantity in a functional relationship, represent part–whole relationships, and make comparisons regarding change over time.

You can see from the initial conversation that understanding the nature of percentages is a difficult concept because whatever is being measured needs to be broken into 100 parts. For example, if one bag of candy had 100 candies and another had 10 candies, the number of candies to show 100% would be different for these two bags. So, if we were to say that we ate 100% of a bag of candy, that

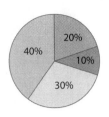

Figure 12.10. A sample graph.

would mean two very different things, as would 50% and 10% of the bags. Students have trouble conceptualizing or translating that understanding of what 10%, for example, represents, especially because percentages are most often illustrated in a circle graph or pie chart. Look at the graph in figure 12.10.

Suppose that this shows the colors of the candies found in a bag. If there were 100 candies, then 40 would be green, 30 would be yellow, 20 would be blue, and 10 would be red. But now suppose that there are only 10 candies in the bag. Then 4 would be green, 3 would be yellow, 2 would be blue, and 1 would be red. Yet the graph remains the same. It is necessary to think of this as a ratio to compare the two bags of candies. Going from a bag of 100 to a bag of 10 is not difficult: there is ¹⁄₁₀ of a bag, so there is ¹⁄₁₀ of each color, and that can be easily computed. But a bag of 35 candies is more difficult to compare, and this is where some computation is necessary.

Finding some percentages, such as 50%, 25%, and 10%, is easier because it can be thought of as dividing the total by 2, 4, and 10, respectively. These are benchmark percentages that we like students to be familiar with. The ability to make such mental calculations for benchmark numbers is useful when finding almost any percentage of an amount. In life, we find ourselves often mentally calculating percentages. Examples of this are tipping, sales tax, and discounts. If our meal was $24.50 and we want to leave a 20% tip, how do we typically solve that? We might take 10% and then double it:

2.45   2.45

To do this, students need to already possess the ability to multiply and divide by 10 and understand how this connects with 10%. If the tip should be 15%, then they would have had to take half of 10% and add it to 10%.

Practical Application of Percentages

Adolescent children tend to like to shop, and discounts should be relevant to their lives. It is not uncommon to see a sale of 10%, 20%, 25%, 30%, 40%, or even 60% off. However, students often do not know how to figure out how much they are saving and how much the item actually costs. They just know that it is "cheaper." This type of problem solving involves multiple steps. If students are not used to having real problems presented to them during math or are used to single-step problems, then they have not had appropriate experiences to prepare them to think and reason about real-life contexts. To find how much a sweater that is 60% off costs requires the following mental calculations:

- Finding 10% of the item
- Either multiplying that amount by six or adding it to half of the total amount (50%)
- Subtracting the amount from the total (100%) to find out what would be left

When shopping, we need to be able to estimate the amount of tax charged so that we know whether we have enough money for the purchase. We tend to mentally calculate tax differently than discounts because discounts are usually in multiples of 10 and tax is a cumbersome percentage: 6%, 7.25%, or more. If tax is 7% per dollar, then multiplying 7 by the amount of dollars usually tells you how many cents the tax is. If the item is $8, then the tax is $0.56. If the item is $80, then the tax is 560 cents, or $5.60.

$$\frac{50}{5} = 10 \qquad\qquad 50 \times 0.20 = 10$$

0.20	0.20	0.20	0.20	0.20
10	10	10	10	10	= 50
$\frac{1}{5}$	$\frac{1}{5}$	$\frac{1}{5}$	$\frac{1}{5}$	$\frac{1}{5}$

Figure 12.11. Different ways of finding 20% of 50.

So what can we learn from the preceding mental calculations that can help us compute more tedious percentages on paper? In the tax example, every time we multiply by the percentage, the decimal appears with two digits to the right. That must mean that when multiplying by 7% we are actually multiplying by 0.07, because 0.07×8 would yield an answer of 0.56. If the term *percent* really means *per hundred*, then 7% is the same as 7 out of a 100, which is $\frac{7}{100}$ or 0.07! Therefore, dividing by 100 or multiplying by 0.01 would "move" the decimal to the left two places.

Also, we can find a percentage through division or multiplication. For example, we want to find 20% of an amount. If 20% is $\frac{20}{100}$, then we know that through reduction it is the same as $\frac{1}{5}$. We can divide the total by five (because 20% is one of five equal parts) to find the amount. We can also say that $\frac{20}{100}$ can be written as 0.20 and therefore multiplied by the total because the language says, "0.20 of . . . ," which we know indicates multiplication (figure 12.11).

The most practical application of percentages for students is when they are trying to convert their raw score to a percentage on a test. If this is done weekly, students can begin to think flexibly with percentages. Tests typically have a number of problems that is not difficult to convert, for example, 20. By having different amounts, students can come up with strategies based on the particular number on the test. For example, if there were 50 questions, then they might deduce that because there are half as many questions there are two points off for each wrong answer. If the number of problems is not quite so nice to mentally calculate, then students should calculate the number correct divided by the total number to receive their percentage. If they divided the number incorrect by the total number, then the answer would have to be subtracted from the total number of questions.

$\frac{45}{62}$ forty-five out of sixty-two $62\overline{\smash{\big)}45}$

This is most practically solved with a calculator. But why does this work? Why can you just divide the numerator by the denominator to find a percentage? This has to do with ratios, which are further discussed in the next section. But take 50 questions as an example. Missing 10 questions in 50 is the same as missing 20 questions for 100, so $\frac{10}{50} = \frac{20}{100}$. They both divide to equal 0.2, or 20% (figure 12.12).

20	20	20	20	20	100 questions
10	10	10	10	10	50 questions
4	4	4	4	4	20 questions

Figure 12.12. Showing 20% using different amounts.

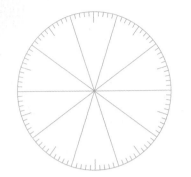

Figure 12.13. A circle graph divided into hundredths.

Creating a Circle Graph

Reading a circle graph, or pie chart, requires the reader translate between the percentage and the total amount. So if it is referring to a population of 10,000, 50% would be 5,000. Sometimes these totals are indicated on the graph. Students do not seem to have as much trouble with the interpretation as with the creation of such a graph. Not only do the students have to calculate the different percentages for the different amounts to be displayed, but they can find drawing the chart to be a challenge. This, however, can be alleviated with computer programs that create charts after data is inputted.

It is hard to create actual fractional pieces of a circle. It is helpful to provide your students with a template that has the hundredths, or at least the tenths, marked off (figure 12.13). These black-line masters can easily be found on the Internet.

Algorithms Involving Percentages

We have already discussed that to find a percentage of a number you need to divide that number by the total number of pieces:

45 out of 50
45 ÷ 50 = 90%

What if you know the percentage but want to find the amount it corresponds to?

If you consider inverse operations, then the preceding equation can also be written as 90% × 50 = 45. So, if you did not know that 45 is 90% of 50, you would simply multiply 90% (or 0.90) by 50:

90% × 50 = 45
0.90 × 50 = 45

What if you knew the fractional piece but not the total number of pieces? Go back to the original problem and consider inverse operations again. You may have to think of whole numbers for a minute to make sure you are plugging the right numbers into the right spot, like 10 ÷ 2 = 5, 10 ÷ 5 = 2, 5 × 2 = 10. When thinking about decimals, fractions, and percentages, sometimes it is easy to become confused about which number goes where.

45 ÷ 90% = 50

Let the language of the problem guide you in setting it up. If the question is, "45 is what percent of 50?" write it out (remember, *is* means "equals" and *of* means "multiply"). Then, through inverse operations—or isolating the variable, as it is often referred to in middle school—you can solve for *x*.

45 = x% • 50.

More Than 100%

Students do not usually think in terms of percentages over 100%, but it is necessary to provide contexts in which they can make sense of this. If 100% is the entire amount of something, then 200% would be double (100% plus another 100%). 150% would then be 100% plus another 50%, or half of the original amount. So, suppose that there was a population of 20,000 people. What would the population be at different percentages?

100% = 20,000
150% = 30,000
200% = 40,000
300% = 60,000
50%   = 10,000

What patterns can be noticed, and what could students generalize as a result? We want students to realize that to find 200%, for example, they simply have to multiply the total by 2. This can help reinforce the idea that 200% = 2.00.

Ratios and Proportions

A ratio is a way to express a relationship between two amounts. This relationship can be expressed in three ways: a to b; a:b; and a/b. When two or more ratios are equal, or name the same relationship, they are considered *proportional*. Proportional ratios can be notated as a:b = c:d or a:b :: c:d.

Whereas fractions show a part–whole relationship, a ratio can show a part–whole, a part–part relationship, or even a relationship between two independent sets. Consider some examples (figure 12.14).

After years of work with fractions, it seems counterintuitive to compare two parts and express the ratio as a fraction. Perhaps using the colon or words initially can help lessen the confusion. Children have to understand that just because the ratio may look like a fraction it does not have the same meaning. Precise language for the way they are read helps with this understanding (6 *to* 4, rather than 6 *out of* 4). The students need to understand that the order of the numbers indicates how the quantities are being compared.

Equivalent ratios are those that name the same relationship, such as 1:2 and 4:8. These ratios would then be considered proportional. The linear relationship between these ratios could be graphed if we assigned x- and y-coordinates for the two numbers. Rate is a good example of this functional relationship. Examples

These color tiles can be compared the following ways:
- Blue to the total tiles
  6 to 10; 6:10; $^6/_{10}$
- Blue to the purple tiles
  6 to 4; 6:4; $^6/_4$
- Purple to the blue tiles
  4 to 6; 4:6; $^4/_6$

When making a recipe, there might be a ratio of two eggs for every cup of milk. This can be expressed as 2:1. This can also be described as the ratio of milk to eggs as 1:2 or ½.

Figure 12.14. Part–whole and part–part relationships between objects.

1 lb	2 lb	3 lb	4 lb	5 lb
0.50	1.00	1.50	2.00	2.50

Figure 12.15. Rate as a functional relationship.

might be cents per pound, inches per foot, and laps per minute. When calculating, students may want to record their thinking as shown in figure 12.15.

Sometimes a ratio is used as an operator rather than to describe the relationship between two sets (Kennedy, Tipps, and Johnson 2008). An example would be determining the size of a miniature replica of some object, like a model airplane. The model might be ½₀ the size of the real plane. Therefore, the scale is 1:20. If the actual plane is 80 feet long, then the model is ½₀ that size, which would be 4 feet in length.

Activities to Develop Proportional Reasoning

A practical application for ratios and proportion is cooking. An engaging way to help students understand the idea of proportional reasoning is that of making juice or lemonade. Students can investigate what a good ratio between sugar and water would be to derive the desired sweetness. Then to maintain that sweetness, they would have to proportionally add water and sugar. Otherwise, they end up with a drink that is too sour or too sweet.

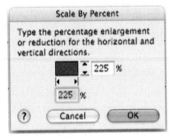

Enlarging and reducing photographs on the computer is a good visual for students who think of the relationship between the ratios as additive versus multiplicative. Take a graphic with original dimensions of, say, 4 × 3 inches on the computer. Drag that image to a size of 8 × 7 inches (adding 4 inches to each dimension). What happens to the photograph? Now drag the original image to 8 × 6 inches (multiplying each dimension by two). Now what happens? The

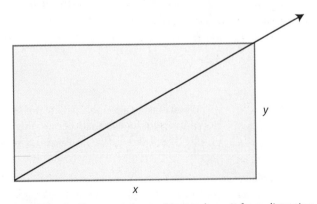

Figure 12.16. How to scale an object to keep it from distorting.

first photo is distorted, whereas the second remains undistorted. Some drawing programs, like Appleworks, allow you to scale an image by a percentage. What happens if you were to put 100% in each box? How about 50%? How about 225%? What would happen if the two boxes had two different amounts? Note that to keep the photo from distorting when you are enlarging it by dragging the corner you are dragging it diagonally, so the slope is equal to the ratio of the two sides (figure 12.16).

Students should try to draw similar shapes. This would be most successful using dot paper (figure 12.17).

This exploration can lead to an activity in which students reduce or enlarge a picture using graph paper and coordinates. They can take a magazine picture or photograph and tape it to graph paper. They should extend the lines of the graph paper over the picture with a pen and label the coordinates. Then they take another piece of graph paper with either smaller or larger squares and label the coordinates on that sheet. Using the coordinates as the guide, they transfer the picture from one sheet to the other. Instead of having two types of graph paper, which may not be available, students can decide what their scale is going to be and draw squares of this new scale on the picture they are going to copy. They could also create a mural on a wall in a similar way (figure 12.18).

Reading and creating maps are other common applications of ratios. Map scales are ratios that compare the distance on a map to the actual distance. The scale is located on the bottom of a map. Have students re-create a map by changing the scale.

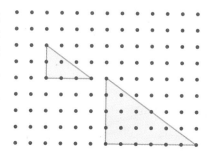

Figure 12.17. Using dot paper to draw similar shapes.

Comprehension Check

- Imagine that you have a pile of red and yellow counters. Facing up, there are 6 red counters and 12 yellow counters. What are all the ways to describe the relationships of these counters?

Figure 12.18. Using different-size graph paper to scale a picture up or down. These squares are 200% bigger than the drawing page. The ratio between the picture and the drawing is 2:1.

Using Inquiry to Teach Decimals, Percentages, and Ratios

The following are some example lessons that use the inquiry model of instruction to teach the concepts of decimals, percentages, and ratios.

Ordering Decimals

Launch	The teacher poses the following problem: Jessica found $0.30 in her pocket. Her brother found $0.08 in his room. Who found the most money, and how do you know?
	Students solve with partners using a variety of tools, including a blank 100 chart, base 10 blocks, and pictures.
	Students share their strategies.
Explore	The teacher poses the following problem that students solve in their small groups: Several students at the lunch table check their pockets to see how much change they have; they want to know if they have enough to buy Otter Pops after school. These are the amounts that the students have: 0.52, 0.83, 0.29, 0.54, 0.09, and 0.20. Who has the most money? Who has the least? Write the amounts in order from least to greatest.
Summarize	Students share their answers and strategies as a whole class.

Relating Fractions to Percentages

Launch	The teacher establishes the language for *percentage* as per hundred.
	Using a blank 100 grid, students color in 1% of the grid and then 10%.
	Students write a fraction to show the same amount.
	Students share how they know the fraction.
Explore	David shared ½ of his cookie with his best friend. What percentage of his cookie did he share?
	He shared ¼ of his sandwich with his sister. What percentage of his sandwich did he share? What fraction and percentage did he keep?
Summarize	Students share their answers and strategies as a whole class.

Ratios

Launch cycle 1	The teacher shows a cylinder and asks, "Which is longer, the circumference or the height?" Students make estimates, and the teacher measures to check.
Explore cycle 1	Students explore lots of cylinders to discover whether there is a relationship between circumference and height by finding the ratio of the two for each of their cylinders. They use a calculator to calculate the ratios and record their findings on a chart labeled cylinder, circumference, height, and ratio.
Summarize cycle 1	Students share their finding that there is no relationship between circumference and height because the height makes no difference as to the diameter of the tube.
Launch cycle 2	The teacher assigns a task in which students determine whether there is a relationship between circumference and diameter.

Explore cycle 2	In small groups, students explore their cylinders. They use a calculator to calculate the ratios and record their findings on a chart labeled cylinder, circumference, diameter, and ratio.
Summarize cycle 2	Students share their finding that there is a relationship between circumference and diameter; it is a little more than 3.
	The teacher introduces the vocabulary of that ratio as *pi* (3.14).

CONCLUSION

There is a correlation between low achievement in mathematics and low levels of English proficiency. But English-language learners are not the only students underachieving in mathematics. Many students whose native language is English also struggle in math. Mathematical language has a specific register that takes time for students to learn. It appears that strategies that benefit second-language learners in content areas such as math are good strategies that support all learners. When teachers habitually use these strategies in their classrooms, they cannot help but support both concept and language development of all their students, no matter what their language needs.

Teachers need to be conscious about the way they are modeling mathematical language. They need to be consistent with their usage of terminology, both individually and as a staff, and to provide a rich vocabulary that helps students make connections between ideas. Watered down vocabulary should not be accepted because it limits students' understanding of concepts. Awareness needs to be given to those words that might be confusing to students, especially second-language learners, such as homophones. Explicit teaching of vocabulary is essential, but only after the development of concepts.

We want students to be able to talk about problems in flexible ways, so we must model mathematical language by thinking aloud. All students need this rich modeling to be able to develop through the stages of mathematical language, as well as to build their conceptual understanding.

As you can see, a lot of math understanding and connections begin to merge when students have to think using decimals, percentages, and ratios. It is critical that the children are able to think flexibly regarding the whole and what they are comparing so that they can become mathematically fluent. Proportional reasoning is developmental and is one of the skills students develop when moving from Jean Piaget's concrete operation to the formal operational stage (Van de Walle 2004). Even though middle school is where ratios and proportions are thoroughly explored, some groundwork can be done in the earlier grades through cooking and geometry. To prevent misconceptions or confusion about proportions and fractions, teachers need to be explicit and precise in their language when addressing these topics. Although difficult, it is critical that students have a proper foundation when studying such ideas as ratios, rates, and proportions; these areas are fundamental in the math they will experience in middle and high school when studying how two quantities change directly together.

▶ Interview Video with an Eye on Content

Watch some student interviews around decimals, percentages, and ratios. Note the task, the child's response, and what his understanding or misconception is around the area. Does the interviewer need to alter the language in any way to make the problem more accessible to the child?

Task Description	Child's response	Understandings or misconceptions	Way language may have been altered
1			

▶ Interview a Child

1. Design a student interview on the concepts of decimals, percentages, and ratios for a fluent English speaker and an English-language learner. Consider the language you want to use in your problems to ensure access to your students. How might these interviews be different?

2. Write an overall summary about how your student did. Include recommendations you would make for the child's teacher or what would you do with this child if you were to continue to work with him. What type of linguistic support does this child need?

▶ Classroom Video with an Eye on Pedagogy

Watch the classroom lessons and think about the language the teachers are using for the concept being taught. Do they make any adjustments for different language abilities? How do they convince their students to try on the new vocabulary?

General description of the task or lesson	
Vocabulary used to support the concept	
Adjustments for different language abilities	

cate, reason, represent, and connect in ways that often surprise and astound their teachers and their regular-education peers. We have even heard some teachers say that they can finally teach grade-level mathematics to their special needs children.

Geometry is one of those areas through which it is easiest to reach struggling learners. Elementary children, especially those who usually struggle in math, seem to prefer geometry because it is a time when they can draw and build shapes and otherwise use their visual skills. Many teachers speculate that struggling learners love geometry because it meets a learning style that seldom is used in traditional-type instruction. Geometry and spatial reasoning are embedded in all other strands of mathematics, yet we do not instinctively incorporate geometry into the other strands as we teach them.

Exceptionality **PEDAGOGY**

Learning Theory

How do we really learn? Our brains are made with at least 100 billion brain cells, or neurons (Nolte 1988). Each cell has little branches called dendrites. Dendrites from different cells connect with one another at gaps, or synapses, to transmit signals or exchange information. Early in life we produce many synapses that require use or they are lost. At first, we overproduce synapses, and then the ones that are stimulated remain while the unstimulated ones die off. However, as we go through life, we are able to create new synapses and modify existing ones through learning experiences. This was observed in laboratory rats; the rats placed in cages in which they had opportunities to learn and explore had altered structures of their cerebral cortex, unlike those who just had opportunities for exercise or no activity (Ferchmin, Bennett, and Rosenzweig 1978; National Research Council 2000a; Rosenzweig and Bennett 1972).

If a child's brain has not had the chance to make the appropriate synapses needed to do a task, then he is not going to be able to easily do it. These synapses need to be built through experiences. If a student already possesses synapses needed for a task, then practice enables these synapses to become stronger. However, if the task is too challenging, the student does not possess the appropriate synapses for the task and "practice" only causes the child to imitate without understanding (Hannell 2005); thus, no new synapses are built.

This understanding tells us that learning is an active process. Being passive learners does not create change in our brain structure. Children who are disadvantaged, socially, linguistically, or cognitively, are generally deprived of stimulation experiences. They more than anyone need a rich and stimulating educational experience.

Application to the Learning and Teaching of Mathematics

Access and Equity

NCTM's *Principles and Standards for School Mathematics* (2000) describe *equity* as the equal opportunity, including high expectations and strong support, for all students to learn mathematics. However, the standards specify that equity does not mean the students receive identical instruction. For students to have equal access to the curriculum and content of mathematics, they all may need different supports. We would never think of denying a child a pair of glasses just because none of the other children are wearing glasses. The same goes for instructional supports. One student may need questions read to them orally because of a visual processing problem, and another may need to dictate a story to the teacher because of issues with fine motor skills. These accommodations should not be considered a crutch; rather, they should be considered a device that gives that child equal access to the curriculum.

Historically, our educational system has imposed stereotypes and low expectations on many minority and special needs learners. Often, these low expectations have manifested themselves in the form of tracking. Tracking has resulted in the "slower growth in achievement of students in the low tracks" (Hill 2004, 127; see also Hallinan 1994). It is difficult for a child to switch to a higher track; therefore, the gap continually widens. This, in essence, creates societies of students who learn less and students who learn more. It is not unlike third-world societies, where the haves oppress the have-nots by denying them access to information. Teachers, as well as the educational system as a whole, must set high expectations for all their students if we are to provide access and equity for all learners. High expectations tend to foster a *Pygmalion effect* or *self-fulfilling prophesy.*

In addition, if we expect all children to learn, then we have to know what kinds of additional accommodations or modifications we need to provide so that all students can achieve success. Many such accommodations require resources and supports. Studies have shown that traditionally underserved children can learn mathematics when provided with the proper supports (NCTM 2000, 14; see also Campbell 1995; Griffin, Case, and Siegler 1994; Knapp et al. 1995; Silver and Stein 1996). These supports, however, are not always easily obtained. Teachers can make modifications in the classroom, but what about supports that are needed from outside the classroom? This might range from resource teachers, aides, and specialists (language, special education, or mathematics) to specialized technology and equipment. These supports may be easier to obtain for students with an individualized education plan (IEP) than for unidentified students. Even so, supports and resources can vary greatly from state to state. Many states or districts do not include items that they feel they cannot fund. This can be frustrating to teachers and parents.

Poor curriculum and instruction are also contributing factors in the lack of success of minority students and those with special needs. Susan Miller and Cecil Mercer (1997, 51) state that "75% to 90% of classroom instruction is based on textbooks, and in most cases, those books define the scope and sequence of the material being taught." This curriculum is meant to meet the generic needs of a grade level but not specific needs of your particular students. The purpose of cognitively guided instruction (Carpenter et al. 1999), described in previous chapters, is to focus on the individualities of each student while developing grade-appropriate concepts and big ideas. Understanding problem types, numerical complexity, and solution strategies has revolutionized the way in which teachers are able to provide access to the curriculum for all learners. Other efforts are being made with various publishers to produce curricular materials that reflect NCTM standards and the processes of doing mathematics; still, the execution of the lesson is left up to the interpretation and experience of the individual teacher.

It is critical that the teacher, whether general or special education, has "knowledge of the normal development of mathematics learning and knowledge of the current individual thinking approaches of students in the class" (Mercer, Jordan, and Miller 1996, 150). It seems that, for the sake of inclusion, a child is often placed in a classroom with age-appropriate peers. Although the teacher may be well versed in the grade-level curriculum, she lacks the strategies needed to meet the individual needs of that child. What seems to happen equally as often is that a child is placed in a self-contained classroom with other students of similar need. The teacher of this classroom may be an expert at individualizing instruction but may not have a deep understanding of grade-level content. These children may not be getting pushed as they should. The general education and special education teachers need to team tightly to create a strong support system for each child.

Role of Assessment

As we explained in chapter 3, it is important that teachers assess in multiple ways and for multiple purposes. Teachers should assess both to evaluate knowledge after instruction and to determine what should be taught. This is especially true with students with special educational needs. The role of assessment is critical for teachers to determine not only what needs to be taught but also how the student best learns. Assessments that seem to best serve teachers, especially those of students with special needs, are developmental assessments that require a one-on-one interview and lots of observation.

Individualized assessments allow teachers to discover what kind of language or other modifications a student might need. Oftentimes, asking a question in a slightly different way yields different results. Teachers start to become more aware of the role precise language has in the assessment process. They often begin to alter the way they ask questions to the class as a whole when they realize that certain phrases or expressions cause confusion.

When assessing students with language or other learning issues, it is important to modify these tests so that it is clear what it being tested. Are you testing language or math skills? If the mathematics is what you are trying to test, make sure that the words are within your student's lexicon to make the problems comprehensible. Modifications might have to be made for a couple of your students or your whole class, depending on their language needs. Word problems are more supportive when they have names of peers and situations and vocabulary that is familiar to the students. Supportive pictures might be helpful, and numbers might need to appear as numerals and not words. Some students need to have the directions read aloud so that they can aurally process them.

> **Rule of Thumb**
>
> It is important to ask students to represent answers using models, pictures, numbers, and words. This should be especially true for students with special needs. They need the opportunity to express what they know in different ways. They may not be able to express the answer in all of these ways, but they are more likely to have success if they have an option of how to show their work.

Differentiating Instruction

When you look at differentiating techniques for students who are advanced learners, those who are struggling learners, and those who have language barriers, it is evident that many differentiating strategies are covered in the different chapters of this book because they are generally good teaching strategies for all learners. These strategies include the following:

- Emphasizing clarity, clear expectations, immediate feedback, and explicitness (Karp and Howell 2004; Tomlinson 2001; http://www.dyscalculia.org)

- Building conceptual knowledge and understanding processes to support the development of underlying skills (Lovin et al. 2004; Miller and Mercer 1997)

- Using scaffolding (Mercer, Jordan, and Miller 1996; Walter 1996)

- Providing a variety of authentic, purposeful, and interesting contexts that enhance learning (Bottage 1999; Hannell 2005; Mercer, Jordan, and Miller 1996)

- Creating a structured environment (Karp and Howell 2004)

- Arranging structured group discussions (Chapin, O'Connor, and Anderson 2003; Mercer, Jordan, and Miller 1996)

- Using cooperative and collaborative learning (Cohen 1994; Hill 2004)

- Setting up flexible grouping (Hill 2004; Leff 2004)

- Designing kinesthetic activities and allowing opportunities for movement (Hill 2004; Leff 2004)

- Using multiple intelligences and many modalities (Hill 2004; Tomlinson 2001)

- Creating visual organization displays (Hill 2004)

- Practicing fluency building over time (Karp and Howell 2004; Mastropieri, Scruggs, and Shiah 1991; Miller and Mercer 1997)

- Using a concrete to abstract teaching sequence (Mercer, Jordan, and Miller 1996; Miller and Mercer 1997; Mastropieri, Scruggs, and Shiah 1991)

- Providing plenty of opportunities for verbalization (Leff 2004; Mastropieri, Scruggs, and Shiah 1991; Miller and Mercer 1997)

Although these strategies greatly increase access for our exceptional students and may appear to function within the confines of our classrooms, we cannot become disillusioned by the myth that "'good teaching' is good teaching for all students" (Karp and Howell 2004, 119). There is still a reason these students have been identified as needing extra support.

As educators, we tend to throw around a lot of labels for children. Whether it is to label a specific learning disability (e.g., attention deficit disorder or autism), socioeconomic status (e.g., low SES), or language level (e.g., early intermediate), we tend to let these labels cloud how we view these children as learners. "Legal labels and diagnoses are often inadequate and misleading" (Montis 2000, 554; see also Lyon 1995). We need to teach to each child based on what we know about what that individual can do (Brodesky et al. 2004; Karp and Howell 2004). Oftentimes, especially in the lower grades, children are not yet diagnosed with a learning disability but exhibit behaviors considered to be red flags. Others may have a diagnosis, but it may not accurately define what the difficulties are. For example, a child may be temporarily diagnosed with attention deficit/hyperactivity disorder as parents and physicians try to determine the underlying causes of the inattentive behavior. After a significant amount of time and a number of additional studies, the diagnosis could be redefined, perhaps to dyslexia, Asperger's syndrome, mild autism, or even hearing loss. Teachers must know how to determine the individual child's strengths and weaknesses and then maximize the strengths and minimize the weaknesses (Brodesky et al. 2004; Karp and Howell 2004).

It is important to gather any information you can, either from a previous teacher or from school records. You need to know right away if you have a beginning English speaker, an advanced learner, or a student with attention problems so that you do not waste instructional time trying to "figure them out." If any of your students have an IEP, make sure that you review it and discuss it with the learning specialist who wrote it. Unfortunately, it is far too common to have a child with an IEP or 504 plan and not know it for a couple of months. Also, speak to parents of any students you may be concerned about. They know better than anyone their child's strengths, weaknesses, likes, and dislikes. At times, you will have a student with a rare diagnosis and will spend the entire year learning all you can about how to support that child. Every year, a teacher's repertoire of instructional strategies increases based on the needs of his students of that year.

Advanced Learners or Gifted Students

Not all advanced learners are gifted, and not all gifted students are advanced learners. Every school district has its own protocol for determining who are the advanced learners or gifted students in its schools. Some districts use a visual–spatial assessment that requires no language to eliminate bias. Others use criteria that include state test scores, academic grades, and other performance-type measures. The first tends to identify a broader range of students than the latter. With the first method, it is not uncommon to have students who are gifted in one area and the polar opposite in another. A student with dyscalculia, an inability to calculate, may be gifted in language and reading. The second method tends to weed out students who just simply do well in school. It is important to know what measures were used to identify your particular student; this knowledge gives you more information about that student's abilities.

Gifted students need differentiation as much as a struggling learner does. The regular curriculum can be boring and nonengaging. The challenge is to tailor the curriculum yet not isolate such students from their peers. Carol Ann Tomlinson (2001) warns of several risks with advanced learners. First, for some students learning comes easily and they have to put forth little effort. An entire academic career of little mental effort produces mentally lazy individuals. We all probably know a few people who scored 1600 on their SATs yet never went to college and ended up in dead-end jobs. A second risk is that some students get the wrong idea about success. They tend to believe that "grades are more important than ideas" (Tomlinson 2001, 11). Many tend to "become perfectionists" (11) and they may "fail to develop a sense of self-efficacy" (12). These students place such a high value on success that they are terrified of failure and avoid it at all costs. These students do not seem to know that failures are a natural process of learning and developing true self-efficacy.

It is our experience that many gifted students are fluent with abstract and mental calculations. Therefore, they tend to like to work alone. However, it is just as important that these students learn to work with one another to develop their communication skills in articulating how they solved problems. Although such students generally have a high verbal ability, their thought processes may be so advanced that they cannot explain exactly what they did. Their explanations tend to be difficult for their peers to follow. In addition, because these students are capable when dealing with raw numbers, they often are unable to make concrete or pictorial representations of their work. As a teacher focuses on creating abstract representations from concrete models with her students, with gifted students, she may find herself forcing them to create concrete models to match their abstract representations. In essence, they started running before they learned to crawl.

At first, gifted students usually complain about having to represent their work with pictures because they feel that it slows them down. However, the slowness generally results from a lack of experience. We have found that once these students have seen the value in creating multiple representations their understanding becomes that much more solid, which makes them powerful mathematicians and role models for their nongifted peers.

Struggling Learners

Students who are struggling are particularly challenging because, although it may be obvious that they are having difficulties, they have not been formally identified with any specific learning disability. These children can easily fall between the cracks as teachers may second-guess the need to refer them to learning specialists for testing. Teachers might pass them on, thinking that they will eventually catch up. However, the reality is that, once fallen behind, they rarely catch up without interventions. Their gap of understanding continues to widen each year, making them fall ever further behind their peers. Therefore, it is critical that all concerned teachers are persistent in creating a paper trail as soon as they suspect that something could be an issue. Just because a previous teacher has brought a student up for assessment without success that does not mean that you should not try again. Sometimes, when the child is older, it is easier to identify certain difficulties.

Not all students struggle because they have a learning difficulty. A great percentage of our students come to school less ready than their peers. That ill-preparedness with basic skills, such as counting, can have a domino effect throughout their entire educational experience. Other students might struggle because the instruction is not engaging or meeting their learning styles. It is our experience that when there are high expectations and the curriculum and teaching are extremely focused and purposeful, gaps and holes in understanding can be prevented, especially if such focus begins in the youngest grades.

Role of Number Sense

It is quite evident that a strong sense of number is critical in preventing holes in understanding in later years. In a quest to identify learning gaps in older students, the San Diego Unified School District (Tash 2005) developed a student interview for third through sixth graders based on the ideas from Kathy Richardson's *Two-Digit Addition and Subtraction* developmental assessment. After interviewing many upper-grade children, the premise was confirmed that struggling students have a severe lack in their understanding of tens and ones and the base 10 system. It was postulated that the sixth graders would feel insulted by such an interview, but the contrary proved to be true. The interview questions, although founded on second- and third-grade concepts, were a struggle for the students. However, because they all had access to the problems, these children did not feel frustrated; rather, the ability to provide an answer in any way they could made them feel successful.

Comprehension Check

- What considerations need to be made when working with gifted students or advanced learners?

Interview questions should be designed so that the interviewer has the opportunity to see how students are able to work with concrete objects, pictorial representations, and abstract numbers and symbols. You may want to do this in or out of a context. Oftentimes, a student solves a story problem much differently from the way in which he solves one with just numbers because there are clues as to how to act it out. Oftentimes, assessing children without a context gives good information regarding to how they handle pure computation.

An example of the hierarchy of the type of questioning you may want to ask using numbers and concrete objects out of context is on the student website. 🌐 These ideas can easily be embedded into a contextual problem.

Intervention Strategies to Strengthen Number Sense   Once it has been determined exactly where the holes are, intervention strategies can be designed to solidify missing concepts. For example, if a student can visually add a 10 train to other trains but cannot add more than 10 without counting on, then she needs work on making tens, and tens, and some more. However, if a student can add by making tens visually with the cubes but once the cubes are removed reverts to a traditional strategy without understanding, then work needs to be done to connect what the child can do with the tools to a more abstract representation. Intervention strategies include explicitly teaching students the following:

- Place value
- System of tens
- Strategies for the operations
- Understanding of relationships

Once ideas are explored and begin to solidify with smaller numbers, gradually increase the numeral complexity to ensure carryover.

Lessons and activities, which target the preceding understandings, are not any different from what has been described in earlier chapters of this text. The point is that if students have not gone through the processes of developing concepts of place value and the base 10 system by the time they are in fourth, fifth, or sixth grades, they must go back and make these connections. Generally, upper-grade teachers are not familiar with ways to support these more primary understandings; as a result, struggling students never have the opportunity to create these original supports upon which the rest of mathematics must be built.

A teacher with this type of student must find a way to carve out a significant amount of time to individually work with that student. Some schools have a before- or after-school math program a couple of days each week. For others, small group instruction is a sacred part of the day. And others support a more individualized tutoring program. To conserve resources, struggling students across different classrooms and grade levels can be pooled because they generally have similar needs. No matter which venue best fits the needs of the particular child and school, it is essential that this teaching be more explicit than pure discovery. At this point, there is no longer time for students to make all the discoveries that we wish they would have made in the primary years. It is necessary to be more explicit; however, explicitness does not imply abstractly telling students what they need to learn. Connections still must be made along a concrete to abstract model. Explicitness is being more direct about which strategies you want them to learn.

> **Example 1:** *Many struggling learners (even in sixth grade) have difficulty counting by groups and have not made the connection that on a 100 chart 10 more is merely the number below the original number. If you ask this child to count by tens on a 100 chart, he may point to 10, 20, 30, 40, and so on. If you then ask him to count by tens beginning at 6, he likely will not know what to do. Merely telling this student the "rule" for finding 10 more will not help his understanding of what it means to count a group of 10. Even though such students are older, they still have to go through the experiences outlined in chapter 4 to make those connections.*

> **Example 2:** *In second grade, a significant amount of time should be spent developing strategies for regrouping in addition and subtraction. Lots of strategies are exposed, and over time some of the more efficient ones, like partial sums, are brought to the surface. In the case of older struggling learners, we want to lead students more directly to the strategies that emphasize place value.*

Although we no longer have the time for struggling learners to explore all strategies, we do not we want to rush and confuse the students with many ways to solve a problem. We want them to develop at least one efficient strategy that they understand.

A 60- to 90-minute block of time, as suggested by the San Diego Unified School District (Tash 2005), before or after school with an older struggling learner may include the following components:

- Work to strengthen foundational understandings (base 10 system, plus 10, plus 9, counting in groups, and other generalizations outlined in chapters 3–5)
- A routine to develop efficiency, accuracy, and flexibility with the different operations
- A story problem using numbers that are in the range of the students' ability to develop computational skills in addition and subtraction and then multiplication and division
- A game that strengthen ideas and provides plenty of practice but is still motivating and engaging to the students

Students who are behind in math but do not have learning disabilities typically can make the connections and develop strategies much quicker than children in the younger grades who are experiencing these ideas for the first time. Many of these older children have some understandings in place about multiplication, division, and fractions, for example. They are mentally more mature than second graders and overall have had more experiences. Therefore, they are able to make connections faster, but they still need the structured experiences, activities, and questions to get those "ah-ha's" that indicate learning.

Comprehension Check

- When working with students struggling in math, what are some areas we need to pay particular attention to? How can we determine the roots of their weaknesses?
- How might working with struggling students be similar to or different from working with those with an IEP?

Students with Specified Learning Disabilities and Attention Deficit/Hyperactivity Disorder

For a child to be considered as having a specific learning disability, there must be a significant gap between intelligence and achievement in one or more of the following areas:

- Oral expression
- Listening comprehension
- Written expression
- Basic reading skills
- Reading comprehension
- Math calculations
- Math reasoning

This lack of achievement cannot be caused by a visual, hearing, or motor disability; mental retardation; emotional disturbance; or environmental, cultural, or economic factors.

Because the process of doing mathematics incorporates all of the preceding skills, any one learning disability can affect a student's ability to do math. It is essential to identify the cause of this underachievement so that the teacher can help remove the barriers and can emphasize the modalities that support the way the child best learns.

The following are possible barriers to learning that students might have (Karp and Howell 2004, 120):

- Memory
- Self-regulation
- Visual processing
- Language processing
- Related academic skills
- Motor skills

It is highly probable that a child in a self-contained (special education) classroom have only experienced traditional math instruction, because special education teachers historically come from a behaviorist background. Many special education teachers say that it is not important for a child to understand what he is doing as long as he can do it. This reasoning is ironic. How are children ever going to apply what they know if they do not understand what they are doing? The act of "spoon-feeding" information to students with special needs, because teachers believe they cannot learn like others, has proved to foster passive learners who become helpless and lack confidence in mathematics (Karp and Howell 2004; Poplin 1998; Pressley and Harris 1990; Seligman and Altenor 1980).

We instead support the idea that because children with specific learning disabilities have normal IQs but a blockage in the way they learn, they need every opportunity to try to make connections and generalizations and to get information into their heads. This includes lots of experiences such as acting, building, drawing, talking, writing, moving, and touching. These experiences promote understanding and encourage students to make connections. Merely practicing discrete, abstract skills, such as "adding with carrying," does not.

Specific Barrier	Possible Indicators	Possible Strategy
Memory (visual memory, verbal or auditory memory, working memory)	■ Inability to retain math facts or new information ■ Forgetting steps in an algorithm ■ Performing poorly on review lessons ■ Difficulty telling time ■ Difficulty solving multistep word problems	■ Use mnemonic devices ■ Use rehearsal strategies ■ Make the students aware of their specific learning strategy and teach them to use it to memorize information ■ Make the calculator, multiplication chart, and other study aids available
Self-regulation (excitement or relaxation, attention, inhibition of impulses)	■ Difficulty maintaining attention to steps in algorithms or problem solving ■ Difficulty sustaining attention to critical instruction ■ Blurting out answers ■ Difficulty waiting for their turn	■ Minimize distractions in the environment ■ Allow students to work in short blocks or on shorten assignments ■ Incorporate more breaks and opportunities for movement ■ Provide a quiet corner in the room where students can go to work ■ Provide constant and explicit feedback (i.e., using a reward system for on-task behavior) ■ Provide visual organizers with important information or directions highlighted ■ Provide oral directions
Visual processing (visual memory, visual discrimination, visual or spatial organization, visual–motor coordination)	■ Losing place on the worksheet ■ Difficulty differentiating between numbers, coins, operation symbols, and clock hands ■ Difficulty writing across paper in a straight line ■ Difficulty aligning numbers and other aspects involving directionality ■ Difficulty using a number line	■ In a story problem, write numbers using words ■ Provide options, written or drawn, so that students can cross them out when they have used them ■ Ensure use of lots of manipulatives ■ Provide many organizational tools to help visualize quantities (i.e., 10 frames, 100 charts, base 10 blocks) ■ Avoid transparencies to present important information (once removed the students is lost) and instead provide information on charts or the whiteboard that can remain posted the entire class

Figure 13.1. Specific barriers to learning and possible strategies to remove them. (Compiled from Karp and Howell 2004; Mastropieri, Scruggs, and Shiah 1991; Mercer, Jordan, and Miller 1996; Miller and Mercer 1997; and personal experience.)

Individualization for these students is defined by Karen Karp and Philip Howell (2004) as removing specific barriers, providing a clear and structured environment, incorporating more time and practice, and providing clarity.

Removing Barriers

Teachers have to understand how each barrier affects student learning. They need to work closely with the resource specialists for their school site or district to learn strategies for teaching students to circumvent the particular disability. Examples of strategies are listed in figure 13.1.

Structuring the Environment

A structured environment is beneficial not only to students with learning or attention disorders but to most children. Care needs to be given, however, to not *overstructure* the environment. Students need to know what to expect in a

Specific Barrier	Possible Indicators	Possible Strategy
Language processing (expressive language, vocabulary development, receptive language, auditory processing)	■ Difficulty with oral drills ■ Inability to count on from within a sequence ■ Difficulty carrying out multistep directions ■ Difficulty with word retrieval ■ Difficulty explaining how they solved a problem	■ Simplify language ■ Maintain quiet, calm environments ■ Allow lots of opportunities to manipulate ■ Act out story problems ■ Explicitly discuss key vocabulary ■ Use cloze sentences or sentence starters (The ____ has ____ and ____.) to help students reflect ■ Encourage lots of talk with partners and small groups
Related academic skills	■ Reading ■ Writing ■ Study skills	■ Allow students to demonstrate understanding in a variety of ways ■ Explicitly teach how to study using different modalities: saying, listening, writing, etc.
Motor skills	■ Writing numbers illegibly, slowly, and inaccurately ■ Difficulty writing numbers in small spaces and aligning columns ■ Difficulty with one-to-one correspondence ■ Difficulty working with small manipulatives	■ Allow a peer to write down the thinking process of the student ■ Provide access to technology ■ Provide larger manipulatives ■ Provide number and symbol cards students can manipulate to show thinking ■ Orally interview the child

Figure 13.1, continued

given math lesson. If every day they are expected to think and then talk about their thinking, they are more apt to engage in thinking. If they only talk about their thinking sometimes, then students are more likely to engage less, almost to gamble that they do not have to participate orally. In classrooms in which the environment is too structured, much of the thinking is done for the child and the result is a teacher-centered environment. In this case, the teacher might model the mathematics rather than the procedure of a particular activity. For example, the class is to perform trials by flipping a coin and rolling a die. They are to predict outcomes and record their results. A teacher would want to model how to handle the materials so that the dice do not fly across the room but might not want to model how to record the results if the goal is for the students to design their own recording device.

Some students, however, may need as an accommodation a template to record their results and organize their thinking. The following are some additional examples of how to structure a learning environment:

■ Create strategy charts that are easily accessible

■ Structure discussions, discourse, and small group interactions

■ Make manipulatives easily accessible and available

■ Remove excess clutter, especially around areas that house math charts, vocabulary, and the current problem for the day

■ Write directions on the board

■ Teach students how to use and write in their math notebooks or journals

■ Provide frequent feedback

Incorporating More Time and Practice

For a variety of reasons, to master concepts and skills, many students with learning disabilities need a lot of repetition (Carnine 1997; Karp and Howell 2004; Miller 1996). Just as with any student, repetition that takes the form of drill must be preceded by significant experiences to develop concepts. Many students with learning disabilities experience difficulties in the area of memory, and drill may prove more frustrating than beneficial. Practice involving repetition must be engaging. Games, songs, and videos are great forms of repetition that can more fully engage the learner.

Students with learning disabilities also need extra time exploring ideas to develop concepts. Units might need to run longer than normal. Increasing the length of the math day, although ideal, may not benefit students who become overloaded quickly. It might be more appropriate to schedule shorter, more frequent math sessions throughout the day that contain the same focus. This might take place as a whole group lesson in one part of the day, some small group explore work in another part, and more individualized work in a third part of the day. Maybe for these students, routines need to more closely mirror what concepts are being taught so that they can practice applying them more quickly. "The spiral approach does not often meet the needs of students with learning disabilities because topics are often covered too quickly and too much time lapses between the repeated coverage each year" (Karp and Howell 2004, 5; see also Miller and Mercer 1997).

Providing Clarity

Providing specific feedback is important to all students, especially those with learning needs. Oftentimes, they do not know what they do not know. Giving them goals is helpful because then they know what to work on. Writing these goals on a goal sheet allows them to have access to them when they need reminders about what to work on. This empowers students and creates accountability for their own learning.

Students with Dyscalculia

Dyscalculia refers to a disorder in calculation. The National Center for Learning Disabilities (2006) defines dyscalculia as "a wide range of life long learning disabilities involving math." Unlike dyslexia, dyscalculia is not a term or condition with which educators are familiar. However, studies have shown that there is an overlap between these two disorders, suggesting that between 20% and 60% of students have both (Butterworth and Yeo 2004; Hannell 2005). As you have discovered in much of this text, language plays a significant role in mathematics. If children are suffering with specific language disorders, their math skills are at risk of suffering as well.

In the previous chapter, we discussed the importance of internal chatter (Bickmore-Brand 1990) for problem solving. Children with dyscalculia may not engage in this internal chatter to "manage the mathematical tasks they are attempting" (Hannell 2005, 6; see also Garnett 1998). Glynis Hannell continues to explain that these children may recite language they do not understand or mimic procedures they see the teachers performing.

Besides language, individuals with dyscalculia may struggle with visual–spatial skills and memory. Visual–spatial skills may be exhibited with difficulty

---

Comprehension Check

- What are some specific learning barriers children might have, and what strategies can help them overcome these barriers?

- How can the environment and specific feedback play roles in assisting students with specific learning disabilities?

in sorting, recognizing patterns, orienting numbers and shapes, telling time, measuring, and visualizing. Memory affects the child's ability to learn to count, recognize numbers, and remember math concepts, formulas, and basic facts. (Hannell 2005; National Center for Learning Disabilities 2006; http://www .dyscalculia.org).

There are multiple domains in mathematics, and students may be able to perform well in some and yet have significant difficulties in others (Geary 2004). On standards-type assessments, these students may not appear to be struggling because their extremely high and low scores average themselves out (Hannell 2005). Perhaps that is one reason it is hard to spot children with this issue.

Like students with other learning disabilities, children with dyscalculia also often have the following issues:

- Insufficient early experience of the number system
- Insufficient instruction in the way the number system works
- Insufficient time and opportunity to gain skills in using the number system
- Being moved on to more abstract work before they understand the basics
- Learning to "muddle through" without understanding
- A defeatist and negative attitude toward mathematics (Hannell 2005, 54)

The assessment and intervention suggestions outlined in the previous section are highly appropriate for students showing symptoms of weak number sense.

Students with dyscalculia may perform inconsistently from one year to the next, suggesting the critical role that the quality of instruction plays (Geary 2004). The key interventions are not unlike strategies already mentioned. The focus for these children needs to be on making sense of the mathematics, making connections, providing tasks in multiple contexts, making generalizations, and moving from concrete to abstract representations (Hannell 2005). These children have trouble making connections, so these connections need to be slow and deliberate.

Students with dyscalculia may need many accommodations, depending on their exact area of difficulty. These range from using graph paper to help line up numbers, to providing extra time on tests, to using a calculator for problem solving. For a more comprehensive bank of strategies, visit http:// www.dyscalculia.org.

Comprehension Check

- What is dyscalculia? Why is it easy for students with this condition to fall through the cracks?

Students with More Severe Learning Needs

There are myriad learning needs that are more severe, such as autism and mental retardation, than those already described. Although we concur that each child must be treated as an individual with her own set of strengths and weaknesses kept in mind, the general principals from this book related to how children learn math can be applied to children with more severe learning needs as well.

As a parent of a young child, Joshua, with autism exhibiting severe language delays, one of the authors of this book has spent a lot of time working to develop his mathematical understanding. Besides behavior and compliance, the biggest hurdle faced is his lack of language. It is necessary to treat him like a second-language learner with beginning proficiency.

It is first important to consider the big ideas of what Joshua is to learn and then to think of all possible connections he could make to develop that big idea. Unfortunately, it is difficult to present new situations in context because his language is too limited. One of his strengths is finding patterns, so for him it is essential to do a lot of modeling and allow him to catch on to the pattern. Using one-word or short phrases when demonstrating a concept is important so that he can attach vocabulary to what is being done. Sticking to the rule of thumb of moving from concrete to abstract is critical for Joshua's ability to make

Generalization		Steps in Achieving Generalization
Plus one		Use many different tools to get the concept across:
Concrete → Abstract	10 frame	• Show a quantity on the 10 frame and add a cube in an empty square, saying, "Three plus one equals four." • Show a quantity and add a cube, saying, "Three plus one equals" (making the student say, "Four"). • Show just the first quantity, saying, "Three plus one equals." • Remove the visual and say, "Three plus one equals."
	Tower of cubes	• Show a tower, say the number of cubes it has, and add one more, saying, "Five plus one equals six." • Show a tower, say the number, and say, "Plus one is" or "One more makes." • Remove the visual and say, "Three plus one equals."
	Number line	• Put a cube on a number and physically move it up one, saying, "Three plus one equals." • Put a cube on a number and say, "Plus one is" or "One more makes."
	100 chart	• Point to a number, say it, and move to the next number while saying, "Plus one is." Repeat many times.
Counting in groups		• Have students rote count on the 100 chart (by 10, 5, and 2). • Have students jump on a floor number line by twos. • Have students count out and make lots of piles of a number using cubes, such as five, and then label each pile with a number card (5, 10, 15, etc.). • Have students count out lots of groups of a number, such as five; build towers; and then count the groups built by giving a verbal cue: "Count all the fives." • Provide towers of a set amount (10, 5, or 2) and say, "Count the cubes." • Give students a pile of loose cubes and instruct them to count the cubes by a set number.
Addition		• Present symbols (3 + 2 =). As you read each step of the problem aloud ("Three . . . plus two . . . equals"), have students grab three cubes and place them on a circle, grab two more cubes and place them on another circle. Hand-over-hand push the cubes together and count the cubes out loud to find the total. • Present a problem (3 + 2 =). Have students draw dots for each number on two different circles and then count all dots out loud to find the total (begin by saying "Three plus two equals" as the students move through the sequence and fade when they can do on their own) • Present a problem (3 + 2 =). Have students draw each set of dots on a blank area and count them to find the total. • Present a problem (3 + 2 =). Teach the students to use fingers, showing each quantity on each hand. • Present a problem (3 + 2 =). Have students solve it mentally or generalize the skill.

Figure 13.2. Developing big ideas and skills while moving from concrete to abstract representations over time.

important mathematical generalizations, even if they happen slower than those made by his neurotypical peers.

Figure 13.2 lists examples of how to support the generalization of plus one, counting in groups, and addition with a child with severe language needs. Each generalization moves through a progression of concrete to abstract. Each bullet would be a stage that may be worked on for some time, depending on how quickly the child is catching on.

When working with children with severe cognitive and language deficits, the stages in making these generalizations can be slow, sometimes over the course of a year or more. In that time, you are working with many concepts and some come more easily than others. Each step tends to be more deliberate and exaggerated than when working with other children. You will probably find yourself doing a lot of hand-over-hand work to help them "get" how to solve the problem using manipulatives. These generalizations cannot remain disconnected from the real world, so you need to think about how to connect these skills to a context. Through working with Joshua, he is ready for stories using just a few words so that we can act them out together, for example, "**Mommy** has **four cookies. Joshua** has **three cookies. How many cookies** do we have?" The verbal emphasis is placed on the words in bold, because these are the words that he knows and that have the most significance in the problem. They are then connected to a numerical representation.

Be careful before using popular commercial products that seem to be a quick fix for students who have difficulties in mathematics. It is essential to analyze whether a product helps support the development of a big idea or is simply helping students learn how to be good counters.

Comprehension Check

■ How is teaching children with severe learning needs similar to and different from teaching other students?

Geometric and Spatial Reasoning   CONTENT

In the pedagogy section of this chapter, we described ways to differentiate the math lesson so that all students have opportunities to make connections and create generalizations. We now shift our focus to geometry and spatial reasoning. Geometry is more than studying shapes. It is a way to visually represent algebra and other higher levels of math. "Many researchers believe that when data and relationships are presented spatially, students are better able to generalize and remember the underlying mathematical concepts" (Chapin and Johnson 2000, 162).

Big Ideas and Focal Points

Three overall big ideas relate to geometry, as defined by Randall Charles (2005, 20):

1. *Shapes and Solids.* Two- and three-dimensional objects with or without curved surfaces can be described, classified, and analyzed by their attributes.

2. *Orientations and Locations.* Objects in space can be oriented in an infinite number of ways, and an object's location in space can be described quantitatively.

3. *Transformations.* Objects in space can be transformed in an infinite number of ways, and those transformations can be described and analyzed mathematically.

In the *Principles and Standards for School Mathematics,* the NCTM (2000, 41) states that by the time students complete grade 12, they should be able to do the following:

- Analyze characteristics and properties of two- and three-dimensional geometric shapes and develop mathematical arguments about geometric relationships
- Specify locations and describe spatial relationships using coordinate geometry and other representational systems
- Apply transformations and use symmetry to analyze mathematical situations
- Use visualization, spatial reasoning, and geometric modeling to solve problems

The NCTM further details each grade's expected outcomes in its *Curriculum Focal Points for Prekindergarten through Grade 8 Mathematics* (2006). These standards are shown in the Focal Points table.

NCTM FOCAL POINTS

Prekindergarten	Kindergarten	First Grade	Second Grade
Children develop spatial reasoning by working from two perspectives on space as they examine the shapes of objects and inspect their relative positions. They find shapes in their environments and describe them in their own words. They build pictures and designs by combining two- and three-dimensional shapes, and they solve such problems as if deciding which piece fits into a space in a puzzle. They discuss the relative positions of objects with vocabulary such as *above, below,* and *next to.*	Children interpret the physical world with geometric ideas (e.g., shape, orientation, and spatial relations) and describe it with corresponding vocabulary. They identify, name, and describe a variety of shapes, such as squares, triangles, circles, rectangles, (regular) hexagons, and (isosceles) trapezoids presented in a variety of ways (e.g., with different sizes or orientations), as well as such three-dimensional shapes as spheres, cubes, and cylinders. They use basic shapes and environment and to construct more complex shapes.	Children compose and decompose plane and solid figures (e.g., by putting two congruent isosceles triangles together to make a rhombus), thus building an understanding of part–whole relationships, as well as of the properties of the original and composite shapes. As they combine figures, they recognize them from different perspectives and orientations, describe their geometric attributes and properties, and determine how they are alike and different, in the process developing a background for measurement and initial understandings of such properties as congruence and symmetry.	Children estimate, measure, and compute lengths as they solve problems involving data, space, and movement through space. By composing and decomposing two-dimensional shapes (intentionally substituting arrangements of smaller shapes for larger shapes or substituting larger shapes for many smaller shapes), they use geometric knowledge and spatial reasoning to develop foundations for understanding area, fractions, and proportions.

Third Grade	**Fourth Grade**	**Fifth Grade**	**Sixth Grade**
Students describe, analyze, compare, and classify two-dimensional shapes by their sides and angles and connect these attributes to definitions of shapes. Students investigate, describe, and reason about decomposing, combining, and transforming polygons to make other polygons. Through building, drawing, and analyzing two-dimensional shapes, students understand attributes and properties of two-dimensional space and the use of those attributes and properties in solving problems, including applications involving congruence and symmetry.	Students extend their understanding of properties of two-dimensional shapes as they find the areas of polygons. They build on their earlier work with symmetry and congruence in grade 3 to encompass transformations, including those that produce line and rotational symmetry. By using transformations to design and analyze simple tilings and tessellations, students deepen their understanding of two-dimensional space.	Students relate two-dimensional shapes to three-dimensional shapes and analyze properties of polyhedral solids, describing them by the number of edges, faces, or vertices, as well as the types of faces or vertices. They find measurements of three-dimensional shapes, such as volume and surface.	Students continue to use geometric shapes to measure and applying new work with equations.

Van Hiele Levels of Geometry

Piere van Hiele and Dina van Hiele-Geldof, two Dutch educators, studied differences in geometric thinking and levels that students of all ages pass though when studying geometry. Their theory of the five levels of geometric thought is known as the *van Hiele levels* (figure 13.3). It is helpful to be familiar with these levels because they make it easier to identify exactly where your students are when working with geometric ideas.

In elementary school, students work mostly on the levels 0 and 1 and start to advance into level 2. Students often enter high school geometry without the foundations of the previous levels. It is easy to see why that would cause failure for those students. It is frustrating when middle school and high school teachers have to do lessons on classification of polygons because students came unprepared.

Like all developmental levels discussed in this book, we need to make sure that we create a strong foundation upon which future levels can rest. The primary years are critical for laying this foundation.

Level 0: Visualization	Seeing shapes as a whole and describe them based on what they look like. Students are able to sort and classify shapes based solely on their appearance.
	"The red shape is not a triangle because it looks different."
Level 1: Analysis	Describing and classifying shapes based on their properties.
	"A square has four sides and four right angles."
Level 2: Informal deduction or abstraction	Developing more abstract and generalized definitions of shapes based on their properties. Students make relationships between properties using if–then reasoning.
	"If a square has four sides and four right angles, then it must be a type of a rectangle."
Level 3: Formal deduction	The level of high school geometry. Students appreciate and understand that the use of theorems, axioms, and postulates is necessary to prove why what they may have believed earlier is true.
Level 4: Rigor	The level of geometry for a college math major. Students study and compare axioms of different geometric systems.

Figure 13.3. The van Hiele levels of geometry. (Burger and Shaughnessy 1986; Van de Walle 2004.)

Four Geometric Systems

Four geometric systems that students learn about during their elementary years are topological, transformational, Euclidean, and coordinate geometry.

Topological geometry	Proximity and relative position
	Things that change or distort yet remain the same
	Place and order
	Mazes and networks
Transformational geometry	How shapes appear as they are moved in space
	Transformations: translations, rotations, and reflections
Euclidean geometry	Two-dimensional figures
	Three-dimensional solids
	Points, lines, rays, line segments, and angles
	Properties: congruence, similarity, symmetry
Coordinate geometry	Location and relationship of points and figures within the Cartesian plane
	Ideas such as slope, distance, and equations, explored on the grid

Topological and transformational geometry are discussed together as spatial reasoning, followed by Euclidean and coordinate geometry.

Spatial Reasoning

Spatial reasoning is at the heart not only of geometry of but all mathematical strands. It involves the ability to think and reason by comparing, manipulating, and transforming mental pictures (Casey et al. 2004). Children may use it when mentally computing, estimating a quantity, measuring, comparing fractions, or considering the relationship of two expressions.

Researchers have found that children who have developed spatial reasoning skills are stronger in mathematics in general than those who have not (Casey et al. 2004). Research has found that young boys (4½ to 6 years old) outperform girls in skills such as mental rotational ability and that these results are sustained over time (Linn and Petersen 1986). Correlations have been made between mental rotational ability and SAT scores (Casey et al. 1995, 2004). The relationship between the SATs and mental rotational ability was stronger than other factors, such as confidence and anxiety (Casey et al. 1997). This could be a reason that more males tend to enter more mathematical professions. The speculation is that when boys are young they spend more time on their own engaged in activities that support these skills, such as playing with Legos or building blocks. Studies have shown that providing rich and focused experiences in the earliest grades, such as teaching geometry through storytelling and the use of tangrams, can improve spatial skills in young girls (Casey et al. 2004), thus possibly closing the achievement gap.

Perhaps this is why some students are able to move from the concrete to the abstract more quickly than others. The girls in the preceding study were found to use manipulatives and direct modeling strategies more often, whereas the boys tended to be able to mentally, or abstractly, manipulate numbers (Carr and Jessup 1997). Boys who used mental strategies were found to be able to equally use manipulatives if asked, whereas girls were unable to use more abstract strategies.

Students who can use visual skills, along with analytical skills, are better and more flexible problem solvers (Chapin and Johnson 2000). If there is indeed a correlation between visualization skills and mathematic ability, then it is imperative that all teachers, especially those of prekindergarten and kindergarten, help foster this ability with any strand of mathematics from the onset. However, this is an area in which many teachers lack experience; therefore, it is often dismissed. How can we support this critical development?

Spatial sense comprises two components: spatial visualization and spatial orientation. *Spatial visualization* is the ability to visually compare shapes that have changed position on the plane (two dimensional) or in space (three dimensional), whereas in *spatial orientation* the student considers a fixed figure from different points of view (Chapin and Johnson 2000; Yakimanskaya 1991).

Spatial Visualization

Movements that children may impose on shapes are flips, slides, and rotations. These movements are referred to as *transformations*. Children who do not yet have conservation might not recognize a shape as being the same after moving it. Here is a classic example of this:

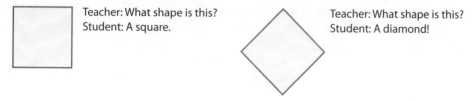

First, just to clarify, a diamond is a mineral. What this child is most likely referring to is a rhombus, even though it is still a square. As discussed in the previous chapter, using proper mathematical terminology is essential. Sadly, even software programs reinforce the term *diamond* when teaching small children their shapes.

The preceding illustration shows how children do not think that the shape stays the same once rotated. They have not generalized a set of rules or definitions for what makes a square a square and therefore are just imposing the way it looks overall as a way to compare them.

The most basic transformation is a *slide*. It may seem basic that a shape slightly moved over would still be that shape, but this is not obvious to young children. Shapes that slide are *congruent* and have the same size and shape. Children often confuse the terms *congruent* and *similar* (have the same basic attributes but are either larger or smaller).

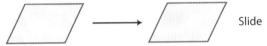

Slide

Flips and *reflections* occur when a shape is flipped across a reflection line.

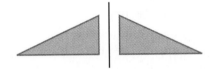

A single shape that can be divided into two pieces that mirror each other is said to be *symmetrical*. The line that divides this shape is called the *line of symmetry.*

Although our face has a line of symmetry, if you put a mirror on half of your face, you can see that your face is not exactly symmetrical. Beauty has been equated to symmetry. Studies have shown that babies prefer faces that are more symmetrical than to those with less symmetry.

Young children can investigate reflections and symmetry by using mirrors. They can take a shape and draw what it would look like flipped, or take a drawing of half a shape and try to draw the other side, and then compare it to its reflection in the mirror. These are initial experiences children have with trying to imagine what a shape looks like in a different form.

Rotating an object is turning it on a rotational point. That point can be inside or outside the shape (figure 13.4). It is most common to see the rotational point in the center of the object (figure 13.5). Children use this visual skill when assembling a jigsaw puzzle as they try to figure out if a piece is going to fit.

When something is rotated 360°, it returns to its original position. If a figure looks like its original self when partially rotated, it is said to have *rotational symmetry*.

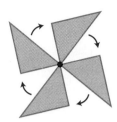

Figure 13.4. A rotational point outside the shape.

Figure 13.5. A rotational point within the shape.

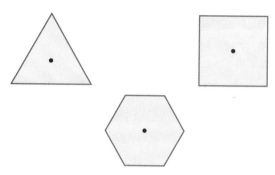

If these regular polygons were rotated on the specified points, how many degrees would it take for them to look like it they were in the original position? Can you generalize a rule for what the rotational symmetry (in degrees) of any regular polygon is?

Tessellations Patterns that surround us often consist of slides, flips, and rotations. One application of such a tiling is creating tessellations. In these cases, the patterns are created by repeatedly sliding a shape so that there are no gaps between each slide. Shapes that can tessellate are those whose interior angle is divisible by 360°, because the shape has to completely fill the plane at the vertex. Triangles, squares, and hexagons are the only regular polygons that can tessellate (figure 13.6).

M. C. Escher is famous for his artwork using slides, flips, and rotations. Children love it when his artwork is included in their study.

A simple creative tessellation can be created by taking a square, cutting out a portion, and adding it to the outside of the square (figure 13.7).

Pentonimoes and Nets Creating pentominoes using five tiles, where only sides can touch, is a good activity for students to use to practice visualizing shapes. Because the basic shape is the same, no matter what the position, students have to look at the shape and mentally rotate and flip it to see whether it matches a shape they have already created.

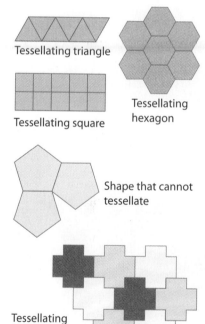

Tessellating triangle

Tessellating square

Tessellating hexagon

Shape that cannot tessellate

Tessellating pattern

Figure 13.6. Shapes that can and cannot tessellate.

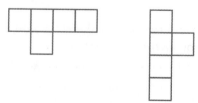

The second figure is both a flip and a rotation of the first. These would be considered the same *pentomino*.

Having young children explore different-shaped boxes, like a shoebox and an oatmeal container, and open them up to see what shapes are created when they are flattened is a helpful activity, as is having them try to create nets of

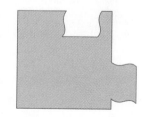

Figure 13.7. How to create a shape that tessellates.

wrapping paper that would be able to cover a shoebox. A *net* is a flat shape, like the preceding pentomino, that when folded would make a three-dimensional figure. Older children benefit from this as well. Look at the following net and determine what would be made when it is folded:

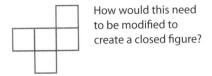

How would this need to be modified to create a closed figure?

Spatial Orientation

Spatial orientation involves analyzing figures from different points of view. When reading or creating a map, we are generally looking at an area from a bird's-eye view. Success in reading and interpreting a map requires knowing how to orient yourself to that map. Students have difficulty with this and need experiences, which help them see things from different points of view. Younger children may draw maps of their bedrooms, as well as of their route around their school campus. They should then describe these routes or maps by relating the location of objects to one another.

Children need to build their language related to directionality, location, and distance. Early grades focus on words such as *in, around, behind, under, to the right of, near,* and *far.* Older children use more formal language, such as *north, south, adjacent, in the vicinity of,* and formal measurements.

Being able to interpret a two-dimensional picture as a three-dimensional structure takes some visual skills. Try to imagine what structures look like from different points of view (figure 13.8). It can be tricky to match different views to a corresponding structure.

Children also need experiences building models and re-creating them on isometric dot paper. This kind of paper allows children to draw three-dimensional pictures. Doing so helps them relate the model to a flat drawing.

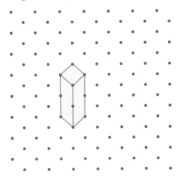

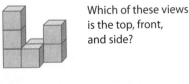

Which of these views is the top, front, and side?

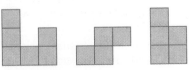

Figure 13.8. Different views of the same three-dimensional model.

Coordinate Grids and Graphing

We may think of coordinate grids when talking about measurement, but the ability to locate points, create paths, and measure distances within a coordinate system requires spatial orientation skills. Whereas younger students visually describe and compare attributes of two-dimensional and three-dimensional figures, older students need to locate and graph points and figures on a plane. They compare distances between points on the Cartesian plane and use its grid system for measurements. Playing games such as Battleship helps students learn to maneuver between points.

Other Activities to Strengthen Visual–Spatial Skills

You can see why kindergarten and first grade should be filled with block-building experiences. Children love to spend time building structures. This should be used not merely as a pastime but as an opportunity to urge children to examine their structures from all perspectives, describe and draw what they see, and test ways in which different structures can fit together. "In order to capitalize on the mathematical nature of block building, teachers should provide more opportunities for block exploration, while providing guidance for what construction might be like" (Casey et al. 2004, 35; see also Casey et al. 2002).

Equally important is work with plane shapes. Creating, copying, and describing their shapes helps students pay attention to attributes of those shapes and how they change when they are transformed. Children should have structured opportunities to build and identify shapes within shapes, for example, two triangles in a square. Work with tangrams, pattern blocks, and geoboards can support this. There are tangram and pattern block puzzles in which the individual shapes are outlined to provide support and others in which they are not.

Give your students shapes, or have them notice some in their environment, and have them visually decide what the figure would look like if parts of it were removed.

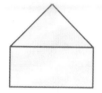

You would be amazed by how many second-grade students do not know that this figure is created by a combination of a triangle and a rectangle. They physically have to cut it to know.

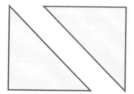

Some students also have a hard time knowing that this figure makes a square when the two shapes are pushed together. It is necessary for the teacher to fold the paper in such a way that they can see what happens when the gap is removed.

Children should also spend a lot of time noticing the shapes and patterns within their environment. Focus their attention on natural and manmade patterns, and analyze how the patterns were created. Does the flower have rotational symmetry? Was a pattern created with rotated figures? Have them mentally move furniture around to see what they think it would look like in the classroom and then try it out.

Richardson's *Tell Me Fast* and *Shape Puzzle* activities from her *Developing Number Concepts* books, described in chapter 2, are helpful in strengthening visualization skills.

Solving and creating mazes is another excellent way to enhance visual skills for learners of any age. Put a maze on the overhead and have students solve it without touching the routes.

Dale Seymour Publications has produced sets of visual thinking cards that promote visual–spatial skills. In districts where Raven's Progressive Matrices are used as the test for gifted students, many teachers know to use these cards with their own children as a way to "prepare" for the test. These sets are highly recommended for your classroom, no matter what age you teach. Some cards are more sophisticated than others, but there are some for everyone. Even stu-

Comprehension Check

- How might early experiences with spatial reasoning affect the way children model computation problems?

- What kinds of activities can help support spatial reasoning?

- Create two different nets to make the same solid figure.

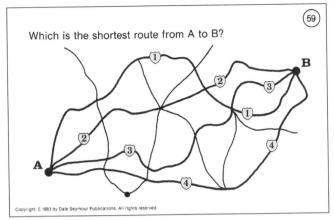

Which is the shortest route from A to B?

Which of these six is the missing piece?

puzzle

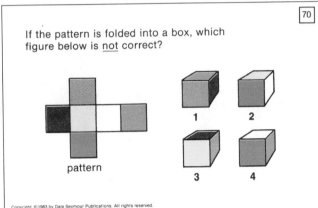

If the pattern is folded into a box, which figure below is <u>not</u> correct?

pattern

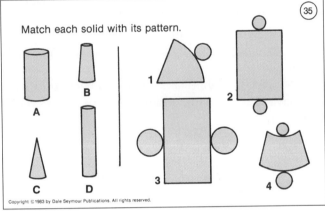

Match each solid with its pattern.

Visual thinking cards. (Copyright © 1983 by Dale Seymour Publications. All rights reserved.)

dents with limited language can solve the cards that do not have complicated directions.

Euclidean Geometry

Euclidean geometry is basically the study of two- and three-dimensional shapes. Students in kindergarten and first grade spent time learning to identify these shapes (van Hiele level 0), and second graders begin to study their properties (level 1).

Two-Dimensional Figures

In the beginning, children tend to learn their basic shapes, like circle, square, and triangle. However, as teachers, we tend to underestimate the ability of young students to learn shapes like hexagon, trapezoid, and rhombus. Another mistake we make is that most of the examples that we show students, or that they encounter in their work, are regular polygons. This is reinforced by shapes that they see in their environment, like traffic signs. With regular polygons, all the sides are the same length. Here are examples:

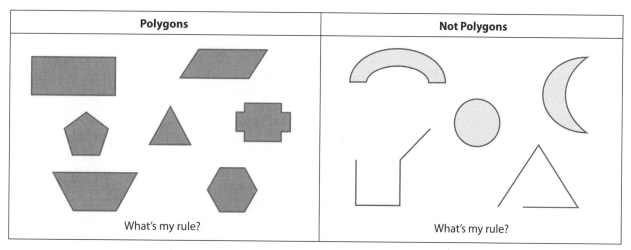

Polygons	Not Polygons
What's my rule?	What's my rule?

Figure 13.9. Creating a class chart to determine what is and is not a polygon.

The problem with this is that when confronted with an irregular polygon the students consider it to be a different shape. The following are examples of irregular polygons.

When students first learn about properties, they begin by learning what makes a polygon a polygon. The definition of a *polygon* is that it has to be a closed figure with no curved sides. Try putting up a chart of examples of polygons and nonpolygons and see whether the students can come up with the definition on their own (figure 13.9).

Once they come up with the basic definition, give them several figures to sort into the categories of polygon or nonpolygon and make them articulate why they put each shape into a particular category.

When learning the names of the different polygons, students begin by paying attention to the number of sides: triangle (3), quadrilateral (4), pentagon (5), hexagon (6), heptagon (7), octagon (8), enneagon (9), decagon (10), hendecagon (11), and dodecagon (12). But at this time, students need to be made aware of corners, or *vertices*. Children should spend time creating a chart of how many corners and sides each shape has (figure 13.10). This, with some structured dialogue, helps them see the relationship between corners, or vertices, and sides.

At this stage, a vertex is easier to identify than an angle. Angles are more abstract and deal with an amount of space rather than a physical feature. Children begin to analyze angles in about the third grade.

They start by learning what is a right angle and then compare other angles to see whether they are more than a right angle or less than a right angle. This work is important building for the older grades when they have to mea-

Name of Polygon	Number of Sides	Number of Vertices
Triangle	3	3
Quadrilateral	4	4
Pentagon	5	5
Hexagon	6	6
Octagon	7	7

Generalization: Polygons have the same number of sides and vertices.

Figure 13.10. Creating a chart to find a relationship between the number of sides and the number of vertices of polygons.

Figure 13.11. Connecting two straws with a twist tie to create a tool to study angles.

Rule of Thumb

Apply vocabulary after students have discovered a mathematical property. The same is true when classifying triangles or other polygons.

sure the angles. Measuring angles with a protractor tends to be problematic because there are two sets of numbers on it. Having a good foundation in determining the size of the angles in comparison to a right angle helps students with estimation later.

Providing the proper terminology from the beginning is important. An angle less than 90° is an *acute* angle, and an angle more than 90° is *obtuse*. Providing examples of other ways in which obtuse is used can help students not only broaden their vocabulary but also remember which kind of angle it is.

Students need lots of opportunities identifying and making angles. Everything has angles, so there can be plenty of opportunities for students to notice angles in their environment. Providing them with some straws and twist ties is an easy way to manipulate and make angles (figure 13.11).

Once students are familiar with angles, they can then start to sort and classify polygons based on their angles. Triangles are usually the first polygons sorted. Have them do sorts and create a rule for their sort. When sorting triangles, common characteristics that students state are that one pile is the "regular" or "normal" triangles, another pile has triangles whose two sides are equal, and the third pile is made up of triangles for which all sides are different.

Some groups of students focus on the type of angles rather than the sides (figure 13.12). These students might still notice the "normal" triangles but then notice the right triangles and then that the other triangles are skinny but one angle is wider than the others.

A teacher could strategically guide students to see whether there are relationships between the types of angles that they notice and the length. Students would discover (through measuring) that the "regular" triangles all have the same length and would see that all the angles are acute. The triangles with right angles have two other angles that are acute; some have two sides that are equal and some have

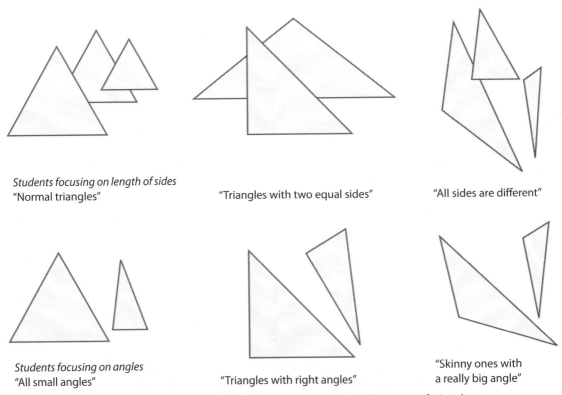

Students focusing on length of sides
"Normal triangles"

"Triangles with two equal sides"

"All sides are different"

Students focusing on angles
"All small angles"

"Triangles with right angles"

"Skinny ones with a really big angle"

Figure 13.12. Possible ways in which students may classify groups of triangles.

sides that are all different, but all three sides are never the same. The group that has an obtuse angle could also have two sides that are equal but never three. When the angle is obtuse, the other two angles are narrow. At this point, the teacher should provide the technical names for the triangles they are sorting:

Normal triangles	▦ Equilateral triangle
	▦ Regular triangle
With two equal sides	▦ Isosceles triangle
All sides different	▦ Scalene triangle
All small angles	▦ Acute triangle
With right angles	▦ Right triangle
Skinny ones with a really big angle	▦ Obtuse triangle

Quadrilaterals are interesting to sort because some seem more triangular and students fail to prove that they are quadrilaterals by counting the number of sides. Sometimes the vertex is inverted and they do not see it as a corner. Still, with emphasis on what the definition of a vertex is (the point where two sides meet), the existence of these strange vertices, or *reflex angles,* can be proved. This makes for a great class discussion.

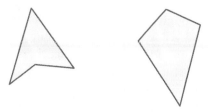

Quadrilaterals that students often mistake as triangles

Points and Lines

Figure 13.13 gives definitions of common terms associated with lines.

The study primary students do related to points and lines precedes their later work with points and lines on a coordinate grid. Primary students work

Point	A nondimensional location in space	•
Line	A set of points that go on forever in both directions	←——————→
Ray	A set of points that go on forever in one direction with a point of origination at the other end	•——————→
Line segment	A set of points with a specific beginning and a specific end	•——————•
Intersecting lines	Two lines that cross	⤫
Parallel lines	Two lines that are equidistant and never cross	←——————→ ←——————→
Perpendicular lines	Two lines that meet or intersect at a 90° angle	↑ ←———•———→

Figure 13.13. Common terms and definitions related to points and lines.

on learning to understand the basic properties of lines; later they use the grid to calculate the distance between points and to show relationships between points and lines.

When studying these terms, children have the most difficult time by far remembering the difference between parallel and perpendicular lines. Teachers should heavily reinforce this vocabulary when it is introduced and insist that their students use these words in context while working. They should have lots of opportunities to make creations composed of both types of lines. Finding and describing pairs of lines in the environment are also essential.

Three-Dimensional Solids

Children can begin to work with solid figures as young as kindergarten (figure 13.14). Solid figures are part of their lives, so for the youngest students, solids should be introduced from items they are familiar with in their environment, such as a ball, cubes, and an ice cream cone. Wise primary teachers introduce solids with small food items. They have the children feel the item with their hands and then, once inside their mouths, feel all around with their tongue. This is a great opportunity to incorporate other senses.

One difficulty with teaching about solid figures, no matter what grade, is that there are seldom enough solid sets for students to explore. Teachers must anticipate what they are going to need when they begin teaching geometry. Oftentimes, lessons are pushed aside because teachers were not prepared with enough materials for all students to explore. One set of wooden solids, common in most curriculum kits, is not enough to provide proper exploration for the entire class. Ideally, there needs to be a set of three-dimensional figures for every two students so that they can explore and talk together.

Solid figures are not taught year round, so half-class sets can be collected among the teachers and passed around when needed. Teachers should also begin to collect everyday items that are good examples of these three-dimensional shapes so that they are always on hand.

Some of the earliest exploration activities involve finding out whether a particular solid rolls or slides. Other activities include counting faces, vertices, and edges. The difference between an edge and a corner is difficult to distin-

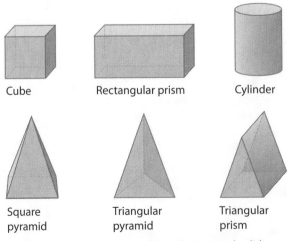

Cube   Rectangular prism   Cylinder

Square pyramid   Triangular pyramid   Triangular prism

Figure 13.14. Common three-dimensional solids.

guish; therefore, the definition of an *edge*, where two faces come together, needs to be explicit. Children often have trouble counting faces, edges, and corners because they fail to keep track of which ones they have counted. Sharing strategies of how they keep track while counting is always a great class discussion.

A class chart should be generated that compares the faces, edges, and vertices to find relationships among them. These relationships would have to be determined within similar classes of solids. An example of such a chart can be found in figure 13.15.

Solid	Number of Faces	Number of Vertices	Number of Edges
Sphere	0	0	0
Cube	6	8	12
Rectangular prism	6	8	12
Cylinder	2	0	0
Square pyramid	5	5	8
Triangular pyramid	4	4	9
Triangular prism	5	6	9

Figure 13.15. Class chart to find relationships between the number of faces, vertices, and edges.

Language Tip

When asking students to practice using the language associated with these solids, have them play games to encourage use of the vocabulary. Place some solids in a bag and instruct one partner to reach in and feel one solid. He has to describe it in detail to his partner, who in turn has to guess which solid it is. This can also be done by the second student asking for a few clues, such as "How many faces does it have?"

Another game to play to reinforce both two-dimensional and three-dimensional figures is to give each student a card with a shape drawn on it but to have them wear it on their back so that they cannot see what card they have. The students walk around asking for clues from their classmates regarding which shape is represented on their back. Their clues have to be about the physical features of the shape, such as "Does it have any curved surfaces?" not "Is it a cube?"

Pythagorean Theorem

We all might recall the formula to finding the length of the hypotenuse of a right triangle, but did we ever understand why it works? If we create squares using the sides of the triangle, it might look something like this:

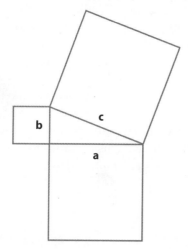

Ancient Greeks discovered that the area of the two smaller squares add up to the area of the bigger square, which is always made by the hypotenuse, because the area of any one of those squares is the side multiplied by itself, or x^2, it can be said the area of square a (or a^2) plus the area of square b (or b^2) equals the area of square c^2. This gives you

$$a^2 + b^2 = c^2$$

Comprehension Check

■ How can we encourage students to discover different properties of shapes rather than just make a list and tell about them?

Special Needs

Create a grid system on the floor using painter's tape. Give students coordinates and have them find their location by standing on the correct spot. They can then try to trace and find the shortest routes to their friends.

So to find the length of box *c*, you only have to take the square root of that area.

Coordinate Geometry

Elementary school students use coordinate geometry to specify locations of points and to describe paths between these points. The coordinate grid is a way to geometrically represent algebra. The grid, often referred to as the *Cartesian plane*, was conceived by René Descartes because he wanted to be able to describe the landing positions of a fly he was observing on a ceiling. He discovered that he was able to describe its positions by comparing it to the distance from the walls of the room.

Younger students work with the grid system through map reading. They engage in activities such as tracing routes from one location to another and identifying the shortest distance between the two points. The grid is made with two number lines, one running horizontally and the other running vertically. Earlier grades may use a grid with both letters and numbers to assist them in finding locations. Because this is how maps are set up, good activities are to have students locate points on local maps. The game Battleship uses both letters and numbers and can give children the initial skills they need in locating coordinates.

As students move from letters and numbers to two sets of numbers, there is immediate confusion as to which number comes first. The two axes are labeled *x* and *y*, and the convention is to begin along the x-axis. An *ordered pair* is the two numbers with which a location is found, such as (3,4). The three is found along the x-axis, and the four is along the y-axis. Students need to engage in a lot of practice correctly identifying and placing points using ordered pairs.

Upper-elementary students begin to calculate the distance between two points, either horizontally or vertically—for example, the distance between points (3,5) and (3,9). This tends to be confusing, but formulas can be generated if students have a chance to make sense of what they are being asked. They need to reason that they are looking for the distance, or difference, between two points, such as the location of the store in relation to the post office. That means students need to understand what difference really is. This can be explored through number talks, found in chapter 8.

Older students can use the coordinate grid to create translations or dilations of figures. When translating a figure, students analyze the points on the grid to re-create the shape or drawing onto another part of the grid. When making a *dilation*, or a scale drawing, they are using ratios to make an image larger. This is a wonderful way to incorporate math and art.

A figure translated onto a different part of the coordinate grid

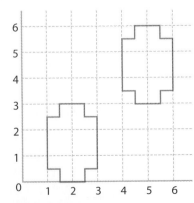

Using Inquiry to Teach Geometric and Spatial Reasoning

Here are some sample inquiry lessons for teaching geometric and spatial reasoning. Although these lessons generally meet the needs of diverse learners, consider your particular students and decide how these lessons would need to be adjusted to meet their individual needs.

Testing Congruency

Launch	The teacher models what *flip, rotate, turn,* and *slide* mean using a shape on an overhead.
Explore	Students test the congruency of different shapes drawn on a paper through the use of flips, rotations, turns, and slides of a shape they can manipulate.
Summarize	Discuss the differences between these different movements.

Creating New Shapes from Triangles

Launch	The teacher establishes rules of creating a new shape, such as putting two triangles together where the two sides completely touch each other (not just corners or partial sides).
Explore	Students make as many different shapes as possible using up to four triangles.
Summarize	Students show and discuss all the shapes that can be made with their triangles, paying particular attention to how two triangles make a rectangle. Students also use language from the previous lesson about flip, rotate, turn, and slide to discuss how the shapes were put together. Students investigate the number of sides of their new shape.

What Is My Shape?

Launch cycle 1	The teacher reviews a chart from a previous activity in which students explored solid figures. The teacher models activity and passes out bags of solid figures to each partnership.
Explore cycle 1	One student reaches in the bag without looking and chooses a solid figure. The partner asks questions, using specific vocabulary, regarding what her partner feels. After a specified number of questions, the student guesses which solid her partner is feeling.
Summarize cycle 1	Students discuss what kind of language was most descriptive and which questions were most specific when trying to guess the shapes.
Launch cycle 2	The teacher tapes a piece of paper on the back of each student. Each paper has a picture of a plane or solid shape. The teacher models the explore activity.
Explore cycle 2	Students walk around the room asking one another questions about what shape is on their back, such as "How many faces does it have?" Students use specific language established in earlier lessons. They have to guess what shape is taped to their back by the clues they are hearing.
Summarize cycle 2	Students discuss which questions helped them discover what shape was on their back.

What Is a Triangle?

Launch cycle 1	The teacher asks students what a triangle is. Each student writes a response on a sticky note and posts it on the board. The teacher reads the different suggestions.
Explore cycle 1	The teacher shows different shapes and asks students to classify them as a triangle or not a triangle. These shapes go on a class chart.
Summarize cycle 1	Students discuss the parameters of what makes a triangle, like three sides and three vertices.
Launch cycle 2	The teacher hands groups of students a bag of different types of triangles. The teacher gives instructions that students are to sort the triangles in any way they can.
Explore cycle 2	Students work in small groups to sort the triangles.
Summarize cycle 2	Students discuss the different ways they sorted triangles. Some groups sorted by types of length of sides (all the same size, two the same size, and all different sizes) and others sorted by the appearance of the angles look. The teacher assigns the proper terminology to the classifications, such as *equilateral, isosceles,* and *scalene triangles.*

CONCLUSION

Many geometric systems are explored in elementary school, such as topological, transformational, Euclidean, and coordinate geometry. Geometry integrates many strands and other content areas, such as algebra, measurement, and art. There is evidence that visual–spatial skills help students develop abstract thought, thus increasing their performance on math tests such as the SAT. It may then be no wonder that struggling students enjoy geometry because it is more hands-on and these students tend to be lacking more abstract thinking abilities. Perhaps it is an indication of how much they still need concrete experiences in all of their math instruction. More research is needed on this correlation. However, the importance of geometry for developing visual–spatial skills cannot be dismissed, and structured activities to help support these skills need to be incorporated from the first years of a child's schooling.

▶ Interview Video with an Eye on Content

Watch some student interviews around each of the geometric systems: topological, transformational, Euclidean, and coordinate geometry. Note the child's response and what his understanding or misconception is around the area. Think about what the next steps might be for teaching this child.

Which geometric system does the question address?	

What understandings does the student exhibit?	
If you were to teach this child, what would your next steps be?	

▶ Interview a Child

1. Design and conduct a student interview around the different geometric systems for a child who seems to be particularly struggling. In which systems do you think your student will perform the best? Why?

2. Write an overall summary about how your student did. Include recommendations you would make for the child's teacher or what would you do with this child if you were to continue to work with him? Does this student have any barriers that might need to be removed that might help him answer the questions more successfully?

▶ Classroom Video with an Eye on Pedagogy

Watch the classroom lessons. How do the teachers make accommodations for their different students with special needs?

Focus for the lesson	
How is the lesson accessible to all students in the class? What accommodations are used for the different students?	

▶ Classroom Application

1. Observe your cooperating teacher and note how the teacher differentiates the lesson to meet the needs of all learners.

2. Collaboratively design and teach a lesson related to an area in geometric and spatial reasoning. Notice if there any gender differences and how the students who generally function lower in the class perform.

▶ Resources

Understanding Geometry, Kathy Richardson (1999d)

Math By All Means: Geometry Grades 1–2, Chris Confer (1994)

Math By All Means: Geometry Grades 3–4, Cheryl Rectanus (1994)

Mathematics Their Way, Mary Baratta-Lorton (1995)

How to Differentiate Instruction in Mixed-Ability Classrooms, Carol Ann Tomlinson (2001)

Teaching Mainstreamed, Diverse, and At-Risk Students in the General Education Classroom, Sharon Vaughn, Candace S. Bos, and Jeanne Shay Schumm (1997)

Differentiated Instructional Strategies: One Size Doesn't Fit All, Gayle H. Gregory and Carolyn Chapman (2002)

Dyscalculia: Action Plans for Successful Learning in Mathematics, Glynis Hannell (2005)

Lit Link

Literature Books to Support Geometric Reasoning

Title	Author
Changes, Changes	Pat Hutchins
Circles, Triangles, and Squares	Tana Hoban
Cloak for the Dreamer, A	Aileen Friedman
Drop of Water, A: A Book of Science and Wonder	Walter Wick
Ed Emberley's Picture Pie: A Circle Drawing Book	Ed Emberley
Grandfather Tang's Story	Ann Tompert
Greedy Triangle, The	Marilyn Burns
Holes	Louis Sachar
Look Around! A Book about Shapes	Leonard Fisher
Marvelous Math: A Book of Poems	Lee Bennett Hopkins
Missing Piece, The	Shel Silverstein
Opt: An Illusionary Tale	A. and J. Baum
Picture Pie: A Circle Drawing Book	Ed Emberly
Sam Johnson and the Blue Ribbon Quilt	Lisa Campbell Ernst
Shape of Things, The	Dayle Ann Dodds
Shapes	R. Kightly
Shapes	Jane Simon

Title	Author
Shapes Game, The	Rogers and Tucker
Shapes, Shapes, Shapes	Tana Hoban
Shapes: How Do You Say It?	M. Dunham
Star in My Orange, A: Looking for Nature's Shapes	Dana Meachen Rau
Tangrams: 330 Puzzles	Ronald C. Read
Village of Round and Square Houses, The	Ann Grifalconi
Wing on a Flea, The: A Book About Shapes	Ed Emberley
What Is a Square?	Rebecca Kai Dotlich
When a Line Bends . . . a Shape Begins	Rhonda Gowler Greene

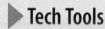 **Tech Tools**

Websites

Geometry in our World, http://www.Faculty.fullerton.edu/crenne/geometry/geometry.htm

NCTM: Illuminations, Web Links—Geometry, http://illuminations.nctm.org/WebResourceList.aspx?Ref=2&Std=2&Grd=0

Software

The Geometer's Sketchpad, Key Curriculum Press (grade 3–college)

Math Blaster, Knowledge Adventure

Geometry World: Grades 3–8, Math Realm (software is compatible with Mac Classic and older PC versions, but there are some features that can be directly accessed and played on website: http://www.mathrealm.com/CD_ROMS/GeometryWorld.php)

Teaching Measurement in a Meaning-Centered Classroom

PEDAGOGICAL CONTENT UNDERSTANDINGS

Pedagogy   *Learning Environments*

- Meaning-Centered Classrooms
- Building an Intellectual Community
- Engaging the Learner

Content   *Measurement*

- Metric versus U.S. Customary System
- Measuring in the Early Years
- Length
- Area and Perimeter
- Volume
- Capacity
- Angles
- Circles

"Children grow into the intellectual life around them."

Lev Vygotsky

CONVERSATION IN MATHEMATICS

A fifth-grade teacher presents the following problem on the board during an opening math activity:

What is the area of the parallelogram?

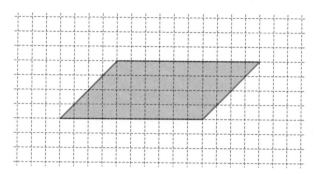

Teacher: During your private think time, I want you to solve the problem on the board. Write your thoughts down in your math journals. (Allows about 2 minutes for students to work silently.) Now, turn and talk to your partner.

Student: (All turn to their preassigned partners sitting next to them and begin discussing.)

Teacher: (Allows another 2 minutes for students to explain their thinking to their partners.) What are the different answers that we came up with? (Writes the students' possible solutions on the board.) So, who would like to defend one of their answers?

The preceding conversation shows a teacher allowing her students a chance to work on the measurement problem first alone, then with a partner, and then as an entire class. This allows the students to contribute to the learning of the entire class and not to depend solely on the teacher.

We might reflect back on our education and remember the teacher standing in front of the classroom at the chalkboard and rows of children facing the front, dutifully echoing what he said or did. There may have been the static reading groups named the blue jays, red robins, and cardinals. The responsibility of the teaching and learning was that of the teacher. The role of the teacher was to fill the students with deposits of information. This is known by Paulo Freire (2003, 72) as the "banking model of instruction." Freire explains that "education thus becomes an act of depositing, in which the students are the depositories and the teacher is the depositor. Instead of communicating, the teacher issues communiqués and makes deposits, which the students patiently receive, memorize, and repeat." This method of teaching was termed by David Perkins (1992) the "trivial pursuit" model of education, where "knowledge is an accumulation of facts and routines" (Nichols 2006, 3).

Jean Piaget's view is that the aim of education should be to create moral and intellectual autonomy rather than to deposit information, as per Freire and Perkins. *Autonomy* is defined as independence and self-government. Autonomous thinking is to critical thinking at the formal operational level. Students who are not encouraged to think at this level and are just given "correct" answers begin to believe that the teacher is the holder of all truth. This becomes apparent if students distrust their answers when questioned about how they solved a problem.

One might think that in Piaget's model the teacher no longer has a role in education and that the students are to teach themselves. There is nothing further from the truth. The teacher's role is even more critical than before. She not only must know her content intimately but also must be able to strategically orchestrate the lesson to create an environment that fosters formal operational thought and intellectual autonomy. This chapter explores how to develop an intellectual community in the classroom and how to possess deep understandings surrounding measurement that are needed to further encourage students to think critically in this area.

PEDAGOGY   *Learning Environments*

Learning Theory

Both Piaget and Lev Vygotsky argue that learning results from social interaction. They believe that learning is a social process and that language plays a significant role in instruction and cognitive growth (Kamii 1984; Vygotsky 1978). Vygotsky (1978, 90) argues that "learning awakens a variety of internal developmental processes that are able to operate only when the child is interacting with people in his environment and in cooperation with his peers." This social interaction is necessary to create the zone of proximal development, but once the process is internalized, the child can use the process independently.

To develop intellectual and moral autonomy, Piaget argues that it is necessary for children to exchange points of view and learn to defend and justify answers. Kamii (1984, 414) states that "children can develop intellectual autonomy only when all ideas, including wrong ones, are respected. Children can develop moral autonomy only when their ideas are given serious consideration in the process of making decisions."

Anne-Nelly Perret-Clermont (1980), studied a first- and a sixth-grade classroom in which children were motivated to think by confronting their ideas to their peers. She concluded that when children challenge and defend one another's ideas for as little as 10 minutes, "higher levels of logical reasoning are often the outcome. Moreover, she found that children could generalize these higher levels of reasoning to areas not covered in the experiment" (Kamii 1984, 414).

Piaget states that, "discussion gives rise to reflection and objective verification. But through this very fact cooperation . . . leads to the recognition of the principles of formal logic" (Kamii 1984, 415; Piaget 1965, 403). Thus, it is apparent that the social environment in the classroom affects to not only the intellectual development, or autonomy, but the social, affective, and moral development as well.

Brain theory explains how our body reacts in different situations. The brain responds to all senses during learning (Gregory and Chapman 2002; O'Keefe and Nadel 1978). When we experience stressful situations, the emotional areas of our brain takes over and the rational thinking part of the brain is not as efficient, which results in decreased learning (Gregory and Chapman 2002, 1): "The neural information the heart sends to the brain can either facilitate or inhibit cortical function, affecting perception, emotional response, learning and decision making." Our heartbeats emit electromagnetic fields that are detectable by our brain waves. The "gut feelings" that we get about people are our neurons registering these electromagnetic fields.

If children sense that their teachers are not sensitive, their rational thinking becomes inhibited and they are less likely to care much about what is being taught. Therefore, the saying is true: People need to know that you care before they care what you know.

Application to the Learning and Teaching of Mathematics

How does a teacher lead a student-led lesson? How does he create such a learning environment? In 1991, the NCTM's *Professional Standards for Teaching Mathematics* recommended shifts in classroom environments, one of which was toward "classrooms as mathematical communities—away from classrooms as simply a collection of individuals" (p. 3). One of the NCTM's six teaching standards is learning environments:

> **[Learning environments] foster the development of students' mathematical power by:**
>
> ■ **providing and structuring the time necessary to explore sound mathematics and grapple with significant ideas and problems;**
>
> ■ **using the physical space and materials in ways that facilitate students' learning of mathematics;**
>
> ■ **providing a context that encourages the development of mathematical skill and proficiency;**
>
> ■ **respecting and valuing students' ideas, ways of thinking, and mathematical dispositions;**
>
> **and by consistently expecting and encouraging students to—**
>
> ■ **work independently or collaboratively to make sense of mathematics;**
>
> ■ **take intellectual risks by raising questions and formulating conjectures;**
>
> ■ **display a sense of mathematical competence by validating and supporting ideas with mathematical argument. (p. 57)**

The first three ideas have been discussed in previous chapters. This chapter explores the remainder of these ideas and how to develop an intellectual community in the classroom.

Meaning-Centered Classrooms

In a meaning-centered classroom, the mathematical purpose is clear and evident in all aspects of the lesson: the content, the teaching and learning, and the environment (figure 14.1). There is much evidence that students are constructing understanding that leads to a realization of the purpose by the end of the lesson.

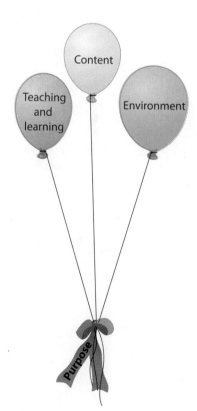

Figure 14.1. The various aspects of a lesson connected by a single mathematical purpose.

- What evidence do students provide that they are developing understanding of the big ideas, or focal points?
- What evidence shows that this is rigorous yet appropriate content to these students?

Figure 14.2. Questions a teacher may ask when evaluating the content in the class. (Beldock, Reggett, and Winters 2005.)

- How are students demonstrating that they are making sense of what is being taught?
- What ideas or concepts seem to be confusing to the students?
- In what ways is it clear that the students are developing ideas and concepts over time?
- What evidence shows that students are independent problem solvers?

Figure 14.3. Questions a teacher might ask while observing students in the learning process. (Beldock, Reggett, and Winters 2005.)

Content

The content is the vehicle through which the purpose is achieved. Math concepts are embedded into purposefully chosen tasks that have clearly stated goals. These tasks are not isolated; rather, they are connected to construct bigger mathematical ideas. It is imperative that teachers have a clear understanding of the content and how it is connected to a clear purpose in developing understanding about a mathematical concept. Understanding of content knowledge by the students can be assessed from their work on tasks. Frequent assessments and analysis of student work help teachers know whether students are developing the bigger ideas embedded in the lesson (figure 14.2). Observing students also determines whether the content is rigorous and appropriate for them. Every group of children is different and enters the grade level with different skills. Tasks that worked last year may no longer fit the needs of this year's particular group of children. Students may come more or less prepared or may have different learning styles.

Teaching and Learning

The mathematical purpose should also be evident in the teaching and learning that takes place during the lesson. The instructional practice should reflect high expectations for learning. The teacher should be leading the learning by choosing purposeful tasks with multiple entry points, questioning to promote and deepen learning, helping students view mistakes as opportunities to learn, providing a variety of tools for student use, and providing specific support to second-language learners. The teacher helps the students connect new learning with prior learning.

Some organizational structures that teachers use in their instruction include purposeful use of student groupings to support learning—individual, small group, and whole class. Evidence shows students have guidance for working in groups when the teacher makes choices to use various groupings. Mathematics is taught daily for at least an hour at elementary school and includes opportunities for students to think, reflect, and connect mathematical ideas and concepts. Providing accommodations for a variety of learning styles is evident in the classroom. Assessment is ongoing, embedded in daily instruction, and used to inform instructional decisions (figure 14.3).

Environment

A supportive learning environment includes a strong intellectual community, which has evidence of high student engagement and other environmental supports. An intellectual community includes an environment in which the classroom norms are listening to one another, as well as the teacher; making student learning public; and viewing mistakes as opportunities to learn. Student who are engaged respond to the teacher's expectation to explain their thinking by communicating strategies, making conjectures and predictions, and extending their thinking. Students are expected to ask questions of one another using the language of mathematics and to listen to one another to develop and deepen their own understanding. They keep written records of strategies and communicate their thinking through writing and talking. Environmental supports include evidence of a meaning-centered classroom, such as the use of charting to record student thinking and representations for solving problems (figure 14.4).

> ■ In what ways are students showing respect for one another's ideas and holding one another accountable for the learning?
>
> ■ In what ways do students use one another's ideas and the materials in the room as resources as they make sense of an idea?
>
> ■ What is the evidence that all students are engaged in thinking and making sense of the mathematical ideas?

Figure 14.4. Questions a teacher might ask when evaluating the learning environment in the class. (Beldock, Reggett, and Winters 2005.)

If we walked into a classroom, what would it look like for students to be constructing understanding? The following is a list of some examples of what we might see and hear, generated by math coaches at the San Diego Unified School District:

- Multiple representations
- Generalizations or applications of skills to new problems
- Accountable talk through which students are explaining their paths to solutions
- Students using math language when explaining their ideas
- "Oh, I get it!"
- Students taking risks and throwing out ideas even if they are not fully sure of their answers
- Students adding onto one another's ideas
- Students figuring out someone else's mistakes
- Active listening by the student and the teacher, including eye contact and responding to the speaker
- "Scrunchy face" (a term used by the Japanese to describe the look a learner has on her face when in a state of disequilibrium and engaged in the problem)

Comprehension Check

■ What evidence exemplifies a meaning-centered classroom?

Building an Intellectual Community

"Ms. Treas, I don't think I can fit all my thinking on just one sticky."

Michelya, a third-grade student

Students' Beliefs about Math

As adults, many of us have the belief that math is about learning a rule and practicing it repeatedly. This is a result of years of holding onto this idea, because beliefs about math are formed early in school. Students' experiences shape their beliefs, which in turn affect the way they approach problems. If they have experience looking for patterns, then they approach problems expecting to find patterns. However, if they experience being told what to do, then they develop a sense of learned helplessness and do not try to reason through a problem. Fourth graders who have not used manipulatives since the early grades believe that they are inappropriate for older children. Often-times, students refuse to use tools other than paper and pencil, saying that they can solve the problem "the other way." This refusal is usually an indication that they do not know what to do with the tools, not that they do not need them.

Students need to believe that they can learn and that what they are learning is useful, relevant, and meaningful. If we as teachers want children to think and reason, then we need to purposefully design the structure of their class to value thinking and reasoning. If we want students to believe that they can do mathematics, then we must provide them with the tools that allow them to make the proper connections and develop the big ideas. Ultimately, we want children to gain confidence in their abilities, to be willing to try and to persevere, and to enjoy doing mathematics.

Benefits of Collaboration and Communication

As discussed earlier, learning theorists believe that the act of collaborating assists in learning. In *Teaching with the Brain in Mind*, Eric Jensen (1998, 93) states that "essentially we are social beings and our brains grow in a social environment. Because we often forge meaning through socializing, the whole role of student-to-student discussions is vastly underused."

During collaboration, there must be a sense of shared understanding. Students have a chance to more deeply understand a problem by seeing different solution paths, hearing different points of views, and talking about why they work. Acts such as talking, sharing, defending, and challenging all take place during collaboration. *Cognitive conflict* is another advantage of collaborative efforts. Piaget describes cognitive conflict as the internal pressures, rather than external pressures, of trying to solve problems. It happens when students present their ideas, question the ideas of others, and justify and defend their solutions (Hiebert et al. 1997).

Questions such as "What does it mean to talk about mathematics?" and "What is a conjecture?" are answered within the interactions of the community (Fosnot and Dolk 2001a). Unlike solely listening to a teacher, interaction benefits children because the "difference in thinking is likely to be within a range that will generate genuine, fruitful conflict. Students can often challenge each other in ways that they can make sense of and deal with productively" (Hiebert et al. 1997, 46; see also Doise and Mugny 1984).

Classroom Norms

Students cannot learn if they are fearful or stressed. To achieve an environment in which students can safely share and defend their ideas, teachers must help establish classroom expectation and norms. Figure 14.5 lists examples of norms written from the student's perspective.

In the article *Never Say Anything a Kid Can Say*, Steven Reinhart (2000, 479) describes the shift in his perception of what is a good teacher from "one who explains things so well that students understand" to "one who gets students to explain things so well that they can be understood." How do teachers shift from one type to the other? Respecting and listening to students' ideas, encouraging and teaching students how respect and listen to one another's ideas, questioning carefully, believing errors are opportunities for learning, and increasing wait time are the key components for this transformation. Most of these ideas are norms for communication, which have been discussed in detail

In Math I will:

. . . be a good problem solver.

. . . write and talk about math.

. . . learn to reason.

. . . share my "path to the solution."

. . . learn that math is important.

. . . explain my thinking.

. . . become competent.

. . . have fun doing math.

Figure 14.5. Classroom norms written from the student's perspective.

in chapter 4. We describe two in detail here: listening to students' ideas, both by the teacher and by other students, and believing errors are opportunities for learning.

Listening to Students' Ideas Teachers need to establish high expectations, as well as beliefs, that problems can be solved in a variety of ways and that their students are capable of coming up with their own solutions. Rather than putting down a solution path that seems convoluted or incorrect, teachers must listen to the students and try to follow their thought process. Generally, teachers are amazed at the complexity and sophistication in their students' thinking. Oftentimes, students are overcomplicating the problem. Listening carefully allows teachers to determine possible misconceptions and erroneous thinking.

This happened to one of the authors during her first year of reformed mathematics teaching. The class was engaged in a mental math activity, and one of the students came up to share her thinking. She had come up with the right answer, but following what she was saying was impossible because her approach to finding the solution did not match the one expected. The student had a convoluted explanation, which made it harder to follow. She had to explain herself four times or so before what she was doing became clear: she was solving half of the answer and then doubling it to get the full result. It was such a different strategy from the one intended that it took longer to get what she was saying.

Listening involves making meaning out of what the speaker is trying to say. Teachers who listen to their students carefully learn from them daily. After a while, teachers become familiar with how children think and can anticipate certain solution strategies. This is important when students are sharing half of a solution that they are not quite sure how to finish. If teachers are familiar with all possible solution strategies, then they most likely recognize the one the students are forming and can help guide them to an answer and hopefully a deeper understanding of that particular concept or bigger idea. When teachers lack experience in listening to strategies, they often dismiss a potential solution even though it is connected to a big idea and merely move on to the next student.

The best way to start listening to student thinking is to chart numerically what the student is saying. This also helps the other children visualize the thought process behind the solution. This is not an easy task. Take the following problem and the student's solution path:

152 + 191

"I took 1 ten away from the 50 and gave it to the 90, so now it is 142, and this 90 turns into 100. Then I added the 100 with the other 100, so now it is 201, and then I added the 2 with the 100, which equals 300. Then I added 40, which equals 340. Plus 1 equals 341. Then I added the 2, and I got 343."

The teacher, and especially the other students, can get lost in this oral explanation. Although ultimately, we would want the student to be up at the board recording their own explanations using efficient recording techniques, initially this process must be modeled. Here would be an example of a way to record of the child's explanation to the above problem:

$$\underset{40 \qquad\qquad 100}{\overset{10}{\diagup\quad\diagdown}}$$

$152 \; + \; 191$

$142 \qquad 201$

$100 \; + \; 200 \; = \; 300$

$\quad 40 \; + \; 300 \; = \; 340$

$340 \; + \quad 1 \; = \; 341$

$\quad 2 \; + \; 341 \; = \; 343$

It is not easy to take a child's thinking and record it for all to understand; however, it is a necessary step in teaching children how to record their own thinking. It takes practice, and over time charting feels more natural.

Believing Errors Are Opportunities for Learning It may be counterintuitive to love a good mistake, but an experienced teacher knows that errors are opportunities for learning. Piaget believes that errors are necessary for the construction of new ideas. When students are in a state of disequilibrium, they tend to bounce between logical and illogical judgments. As their judgments become more logical than illogical, they enter a state of equilibrium. Thus, the period when children are making errors is one of natural steps to understanding. Children who seem the most confused often show the greatest progress toward a deeper level of understanding (Labinowicz 1987). Evidence that students are reaching a state of equilibrium can be found in their confidence level, facial expressions, and body language.

Errors can also be windows into a child's thinking. Sometimes the error is an answer to a different question, which allows the teacher to understand how the child interpreted a problem. When we see children making errors, instead of correcting them, we need to be asking ourselves, "Why are they making this mistake? Is it because they do not understand the context or the language in the question? Are they making silly errors, or are they misunderstanding how to carry out or apply a procedure? Are the numbers too hard? Is more than one student making the same mistake?" Teachers need to decide whether they need to individually conference with a child or bring the error to the entire group.

If the classroom culture is one of mutual respect and mathematics is the center of the discussions, students do not have any problem if a teacher wants to share an error with the class. Still, sometimes it is necessary to consider the fragility of a student whose error you want to make public.

Most errors surface during the summary, when students are sharing their work. If the first question that the teacher always asks the group is "Does this make sense?" then students begin to analyze the solution for the validity of the mathematics and discuss their opinions. If mistakes are "simply outcomes of methods that need to be improved" (Hiebert et al. 1997, 48), then they are a necessary step in building understanding.

Engaging the Learner

To learn, the student must be engaged in the lesson and in his work. At first glance it may appear that the class is engaged, yet when examined more carefully it becomes apparent that a significant percentage of students are often tuned out. Not only does the teacher need to learn how to step back and examine the level of engagement, but she needs to ask herself why certain children are tuning out and how to help them tune back in. If children remain tuned out for significant amounts of time, they quickly fall behind.

Principals in one learning community got together over the 2005–2006 school year to observe children and brainstorm considerations a teacher needs to have when planning for full engagement. They outlined the following six considerations as being essential for maximizing engagement: lesson design, teaching, learning behavior, management, physical environment, and charting.

Knowing the Learner

Before you begin to design curriculum and individual lessons, it is important to know what kinds of students you have. Not all students learn in the same way, and what works one year may not work the next. "We all have different learning styles, process information differently, and have distinct preferences about when, where, and how we learn" (Gregory and Chapman 2002, 19). The most common ways to classify learners are through learning styles, thinking styles, and multiple intelligences (figure 14.6). Other factors to consider are noise level, structure, motivation and persistence, responsibility, and desire to work alone or with peers.

There are a variety of ways to gather this information from students, such as questionnaires, and the information can be used in determining the best entry points for students in lessons.

Music, laughter, and kinesthetic actions are documented ways to increase engagement. Pop music seems to increase brainpower and student achievement (Gregory and Chapman 2002) and Mozart and Baroque music can soothe and calm (Campbell 1998). Silvia Cardoso explains in *Cerebrum* (Gregory and Chapman 2002, 17) that "laughter helps the immune system to increase the number of type T leukocytes (T cells) in the blood. T cells combat damage and infection, and some researchers have even dubbed them 'happiness cells.'"

Learning Styles		Thinking Styles	Multiple Intelligences
(Dunn 1987)	(McCarthy 1990)	(Gregorc 1982)	(Gardner 1983)
▪ Auditory	▪ Imaginative learner	▪ Concrete random thinkers	▪ Verbal or linguistic
▪ Visual	▪ Analytical learner	▪ Abstract sequential thinkers	▪ Logical or mathematical
▪ Tactile	▪ Common sense learner	▪ Abstract random thinkers	▪ Visual or spatial
▪ Kinesthetic	▪ Dynamic learner		▪ Musical or rhythmic
▪ Tactile and kinesthetic			▪ Bodily or kinesthetic
			▪ Interpersonal
			▪ Intrapersonal
			▪ Naturalist

Figure 14.6. Learning styles, thinking styles, and multiple intelligences. (Adapted from Differentiated instructional strategies, Gregory and Chapman, 2002. Thousand Oaks, CA: Corwin Press, Inc. Reprinted by permission of Sage Publications via Copyright Clearance Center.)

Lesson Design

Learning organized around inquiry helps create an engaging environment because student are working together to solve a problem. The directions need to be clear and precise, and students need to be clear about what their job is. When appropriate, teachers need to model what is expected of the learners. This does not mean teachers should model the thinking; rather, teachers should model procedures, such as how to play a game or how to gather materials.

Teachers need to carefully plan their questions and consider at which points during the lesson students might turn and talk, stop and jot, or discuss as a class. This needs to be carefully orchestrated so that all voices are heard.

Proper materials, available in sufficient quantity, help ensure that students are not fighting over tools and that they are able to properly explore a mathematical concept. It is important to avoid wasting class time tracking down more materials because there are not enough to go around.

Teaching

Teaching needs to be lively and personal. Children are most engaged when teachers are dramatic, enthusiastic, and authentic in their responses to children. Teachers show sincerity when they laugh with their students, as well as gasp with amazement and say things like, "Wow! I am amazed at your thinking." Children are also captivated when their teachers tell stories from their lives, so making these connections is beneficial in sustaining a high level of engagement.

Learning Behavior

Student learning behavior may include eye contact, self-monitoring of position so that they can fully see everyone else, and appropriate discourse. Ways that we show that we are listening and engaged to a speaker include leaning in and facial expressions. Being able to enter and exit a conversation without jumping all over one another is an important skill that allows the conversation to remain clear for the entire class.

Normally, fiddling with materials and articles of clothing is a sign of being disengaged. However, when taking into consideration learning styles, there may be students who have heightened engagement when their fingers are occupied. It is important to know who these students are so that you do not reprimand or embarrass them. Schools can buy items from sensory catalogues that are dedicated to helping control fidgeting. Consulting an occupational therapist to learn about sensory issues that might get in the way of learning is recommended.

Many schools in areas of poverty and high second-language populations tend to have issues related to engagement. These issues could be related to language, culture, or a difference in the social class of home and school. School tends to reflect white middle-class values and uses a certain "language." Many students who live outside a middle-class environment do not know how to code-switch between home and school. One elementary school decided to dedicate time to teaching specific learning, or scholarly, behaviors to students. The principal identified four levels of compliance and attitudes children have toward school:

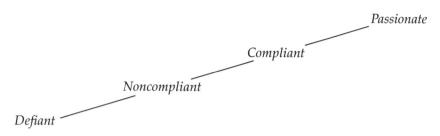

Passionate

Compliant

Noncompliant

Defiant

Her question was, "How do we get the kids up to passionate?" In reality, there were many children at the school who first needed to get to compliant, but how could this be accomplished? What did the teachers not know or understand about their students? How do they teach children how to *live* at school?

As a school site, 12 behaviors were selected and adapted from Ron Clark's *The Essential 55* (2003) as the most important for the school environment. Teachers began to teach these behaviors in minilessons. It was amazing how the climate of the school changed when behaviors such as "no eye-rolling" and "always greet adults when you pass them down the hall" were explicitly taught.

Figure 14.7 is a student reflection chart that was created by a classroom teacher after several staff meetings focused on what scholarly behaviors look like. Scholarly behaviors were broken into three categories: physical behaviors, class conversations, and independent skills. The reflection chart has room for students to write their personal goals. Many teachers have class meetings either daily or weekly, which allow feedback, reflection, and a chance for students to design their goals. In these classes, students are accountable to one another for their goals as they make them public. This process created an awareness of what it means to look, act, and sound like a learner.

Teachers have observed that students can tell you right off what might be amazing about their peers but at the end of a difficult day might ask, "How did I do?" They can be so unaware of their own behaviors. This reflective piece helps students become more self-aware and monitor their behavior and learning.

Management

Management can positively or negatively affect engagement. The unorganized teacher can have too much dead time in his lessons, which is a breeding ground for off-task behavior. Simple things like tightening transitions to 10 seconds or less and ensuring that procedures are in place for passing out materials and for moving from a whole group to partnerships make a big difference to the flow of the lesson and keep children focused.

Transitions and procedures need to be continually taught until the students need minimal verbal cues for what they have to do. When properly trained, children as young as 5 years can respond quickly and quietly to a teacher who merely says, "Meet me on the rug." This kind of training takes persistence and follow-through. Once children learn that they cannot get away with roaming or visiting during transitions, they get what they need and go where they need to be.

Another management tool to maximize engagement is grouping strategies. We have mentioned several times in this book the notion of whole group, small groups, and partnerships. Seamlessly and purposefully moving from one type of group to another keeps children moving and accountable to different members of their learning community. Small groups and partnerships are vital in classrooms with second-language learners.

Language Tip

Teacher proximity is key in supporting students who have more trouble staying engaged, as well as those who need more language support. This might mean that during whole group discussions these students are closest to the teacher so that she can easily check on their understanding. She can also whisper clarifying language to students who needs support when sharing.

Scholarly Behavior Goals Name _____ Date _____				
Scholarly Behaviors	**1** **Never**	**2** **Sometimes**	**3** **Mostly**	**4** **Always**
Physical Behaviors — Gives eye contact at all times				
Manages body: sits tall, moves body to see text and/or speaker				
Is not distracted by materials, clothing, tools, classmates, noises, etc.				
Quickly transitions to the rug or seats with all the materials needed				
Class Conversations — Shows thinking about what is being learned: nods, has expressive face, adds to conversations				
Adds to conversation to make thinking bigger				
Knows when to talk and when to listen				
Speaks in a voice that is easily heard by classmates				
Uses partner for support and to deepen thinking				
Independent Skills — Manages own learning: ignores/handles distractions, solves problems on own, uses classroom charts and other resources				
Completes work				
Can explain what is being learned				

My Personal Goals	
To become more scholarly, I will work on . . .	
To get better at this, I will . . .	

Figure 14.7. Scholarly behavior goals designed by Stephanie Hasselbrink, a fifth-grade teacher at Webster Academy of Science and Research. (Adapted from staff meetings that identified what it means to be a scholarly learner. Reprinted by permission of Stephanie Hasselbrink.)

Allowing students to work with a couple of other children gives them the opportunity to practice expressing themselves in a low-stress environment and increases the chance and success for sharing with the whole class. Teachers should roam the room to listen to these groups and look for ideas to be shared at the end of the lesson. By giving certain children a heads-up that they will be asked to share, these students have an opportunity to collect their thoughts and articulate what they might say before it is their turn.

Whole Groups There are definite parts of the lesson for which the class needs to be together and a general discussion needs to take place, whether to give instructions or to discuss the mathematics explored. Discourse seems to have most of its troubles during this grouping structure. Some students can begin explaining a complicated way of thinking that loses the entire group, and the dialogue ends up being between the teacher and the student.

Small Groups Small groups give students a chance to work together with a few of their peers and allow them opportunities for communication that are rare within a whole group. Small groups may be structured as heterogeneous or homogeneous, depending on the foci of the lesson. Teachers usually have to structure their groups several times until the right fit is achieved.

One small group strategy is known as *complex instruction*. This strategy is found in Elizabeth Cohen's book *Designing Groupwork: Strategies for the Heterogeneous Classroom* (1994). The three principles that make up complex instruction are curricular materials, instructional strategies, and status and accountability. The goals are to create a level of interdependence within the groups in which all students are accountable:

> **When teachers give students a group task and allow them to make mistakes and struggle on their own, they have delegated authority. . . . Delegating authority in an instructional task is making students responsible for specific parts of their work; students are free to accomplish their task in the way they think best, but they are accountable to the teacher for the final product. (p. 2)**

Groups tend to comprise four people, all of whom have a specific role. The teacher specially trains students to successfully carry out their role. There is a specific structure that includes an initial private think time during which each member of the group thinks about how to try to solve the problem, and perhaps begins to solve it, before discussing it as a group. Students are not allowed to summon the teacher for help until every child has the same question, and only an assigned member is allowed to do this.

Teachers who are implementing complex instruction in their classrooms comment that the most challenging aspect is designing a groupworthy task. To create this interdependence, the task must require the participation of each member of the group. Everyone must have something to contribute. This creates a need to communicate. One author has witnessed in second-language classes that have implemented this strategy, the level of engagement and discourse has increased dramatically. Refer to the website for information regarding sample jobs and responsibilities as well as sample directions for group work. 🌐

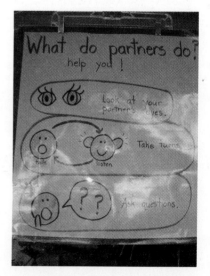

A partnership is a structure within which students can safely discuss and try their mathematical ideas before sharing with the whole group.

Partnerships Partnerships are particularly helpful for second-language learners who need extra rehearsal time before sharing. Partnerships are strategically organized to maximize student learning. Oftentimes, a struggling student is paired with a more proficient student who is sensitive and has the ability to coach the partner in either the mathematics or the language. Sometimes two quiet students benefit from being paired together. When two students spend time in a mathematical relationship, they get to know one another as mathematicians and build a history of mathematical discussions.

Physical Environment

The physical environment of the classroom plays a large part in the distractibility of the students. Students need clean, neat, and orderly classrooms that are uncluttered and not overstimulating. Along with some music, certain colors are calming. Students that naturally have difficulty focusing need an environment that is structured, predictable, and organized. The materials need to be easily accessed, and the charts should be clearly displayed.

The average classroom probably has too much furniture. Classrooms that have minimal furniture are easier to get around; they also have ample room for meeting areas on the floor. Ridding a classroom of excess furniture and other "stuff" can be extremely difficult for teachers, especially if those who have lived in a classroom for any length of time. It is helpful to ask a colleague to come in with an unbiased set of eyes to determine what is unnecessary clutter.

A lucky teacher may be able slowly trade individual desks for round tables. Round tables are best for creating a collaborative atmosphere during small group instruction. At the least, desks should be grouped in small pods to allow for small group work.

Round tables also remove the need for individual seating assignments, which has advantages. Many teachers turn around regular desks to keep students from using the inside of their desks (which can become home to many interesting things). Cubbies or magazine boxes lined up on a bookshelf are sufficient for storage of students' work things.

There should be a large meeting place where the entire class can get together for whole class discussions, or congresses. This means a large rug that fits the entire class (even sixth graders happily sit on the floor) or enough space for a semicircle of chairs. Sometimes you may have a group of students who cannot leave their hands to themselves and need more boundaries. If this is the case, use chairs. Whether children sit in a circle on the rug or in chairs, they should have assigned spots so that transitions are quick and smooth. This takes training, especially with chairs, but it allows all children to see one another and maximizes class discussions.

The presentation board needs to be clear of excess stuff. When studying Japanese lessons, it was noted that they use the board as a place to lay out the story of the math lesson. They spend much time deciding what to put on the board, in what location, and at what time during the lesson. It was discovered

that discipline issues were minimal during these lessons because when students tuned out, which they did, they knew that whatever they missed would still be on the board and they did not lose out on problem or solution strategies. They were able to monitor their own learning.

When someone stands at the door and looks in, it the current learning foci in the classroom should be obvious. In other words, the walls act as supports for current learning, not as a museum on what has been occurring the entire year. The learning charts and math word wall need to be in an area that is easily viewed by students as they tackle their math work.

Charting (to Support Learning Behavior and Content)

Charts support learning behavior, as well as content. They should be cocreated, because they are most meaningful that way. Some teachers cocreate a chart with the students and then rewrite it at night to increase legibility, but all thoughts remain the same maintain its value. Generally, commercially purchased charts and visuals have minimal value because they were not cocreated with the class and students are rarely caught referring to them.

If you are not used to it, constructing charts can be difficult, but they are an important element in student learning. Start by creating strategy charts during mental math activities. Save these charts on a stand, and one day the students will want to remember a computational strategy a fellow student invented a previous day. All they have to do is go back to the chart stand and flip through to find the problem. This provides motivation to construct charts in other parts of the math lesson and other content areas.

Not everything done in class is worth saving, but strategy charts, language charts, and key representations created by students that demonstrate big ideas are important to post in visible areas so that students can refer to them. Posting multiple versions of the same representation is unnecessary.

The following are examples of different kinds of charts and methods for displays:

> **Rule of Thumb**
>
> Critically think about the material that is going on your chart. If the chart or product does not support further learning, then it does not need to go up.

> **Special Needs**
>
> Strategically creating and displaying charts of the learning that takes place can give support to those students who have trouble remembering essential vocabulary or the steps used in solving a problem.

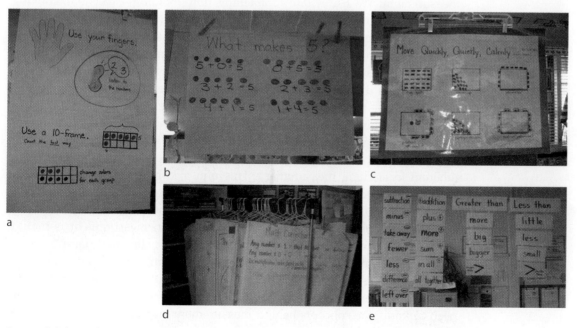

Purposeful charts that support different aspects of a mathematics lesson. a. Strategy chart. b. Early numeracy chart. c. Procedure chart. d. Storing charts for easy access. e. Language charts hung from the ceiling.

Comprehension Check

- What are some different grouping strategies, and what are the benefits of each one?
- Consider the physical environment of your classroom or that of your mentor teacher. What aspects are supportive of the learning that happens during mathematics? What changes might you consider?

CONTENT   *Measurement*

The pedagogy section of this chapter describes what is required to achieve an intellectual community in a meaning-centered classroom. In this next section, keep meaning centered in mind as you learn about the big ideas of measurement and the best ways to teach it to children.

Big Ideas and Focal Points

Randall Charles (2005, 20) suggests a big idea of measurement as being "some attributes of objects are measurable and can be quantified using unit amounts."

According to NCTM's *Principles and Standards for School Mathematics* (2000, 44), all students from prekindergarten to grade 12 should be able to do the following:

- Understand the measurable attributes of objects and the units, systems, and processes of measurement
- Apply appropriate techniques, tools, and formulas to determine measurements

The NCTM's focal points (2006) related to the area of measurement in each of the grades are described in the Focal Points table.

Most likely, no other strand in mathematics more commonly applied than measurement. We use it daily for telling time, reading a calendar, cooking, shopping, planting, and redecorating. Yet it is far too common for a school district's overall weakness on a standardized math test to be in measurement. This has been confirmed by the National Center for Education Statistics international assessments (1996). In our experience, one of the contributing factors is that, in fear of moving on in the curriculum when everyone does not "get it," teachers have a tendency to not be able to finish their curriculum for the year, therefore skipping units that they either feel are simpler or that they do not have the materials on hand to teach. Measurement falls into both of these categories. In the primary years, teachers often underestimate the complexity inherent in learning measurement. This unit also requires myriad tools that teachers often do not have, or do not have time to collect. In some curricula it may show up at the end, and teachers simply do not get to it.

Another important factor in the poor results in measurement is that "it tends to focus on the procedures of measuring rather than the concepts underlying them" (Stephan and Clements 2003). These authors explain that this is probably because the typical focus of measurement is how to measure, not what measurement means. For students to be successful in this area, teachers need to know the concepts behind measurement and the developmental processes students go through.

Measurement involves estimation, precision, and accuracy (Chapin and Johnson 2000; Kennedy, Tipps, and Johnson 2008). Children struggle with estimation because they do not have enough experience with different units. Giving them plenty of opportunities to repeatedly work with units helps them establish benchmarks and improve their estimations over time. When we measure, we are looking for approximate, not exact, answers. Even measurements

NCTM FOCAL POINTS

Kindergarten	First Grade	Second Grade	Third Grade
Children use measurable attributes, such as length or weight, to solve problems by comparing and ordering objects. They compare the lengths of two objects, both directly (by comparing them with each other) and indirectly (by comparing both with a third object), and they order several objects according to length.	Children strengthen their sense of number by solving problems involving measurements. They measure by laying multiple copies of a unit end to end and then counting the units by using groups of tens and ones, which supports children's understanding of number lines and number relationships.	Children develop understanding of the meaning and processes of measurement, including such underlying concepts as partitioning (the mental activity of slicing the length of an object into equal-sized units) and transitivity (e.g., if object A is longer than object B and object B is longer than object C, then object A is longer than object C). They understand linear measure as an iteration of units and use rulers and other measurement tools with that understanding. They understand the need for equal-length units, the use of standard units of measure (centimeter and inch), and the inverse relationship between the size of a unit and the number of units used in a particular measurement (i.e., children recognize that the smaller the unit, the more iterations they need to cover a given length).	Students strengthen their understanding of fractions as they confront problems in linear measurement that call for more precision than the whole unit allowed them in their work in grade 2. They develop their facility in measuring with fractional parts of linear units. They develop measurement concepts and skills through experiences in analyzing attributes and properties of two-dimensional objects. They form an understanding of perimeter as a measurable attribute and select appropriate units, strategies, and tools to solve problems involving perimeter.

(Continued on following page.)

(NCTM Focal Points, continued)

Fourth Grade	Fifth Grade	Sixth Grade
Students recognize area as an attribute of two-dimensional regions. They learn that they can quantify area by finding the total number of same-sized units of area that cover the shape without gaps or overlaps. They understand that a square that is one unit on a side is the standard unit for measuring area. They select appropriate units, strategies (e.g., decomposing shapes), and tools for solving problems that involve estimating or measuring area. They connect area measurement to the area model that they have used to represent multiplication, and they use this connection to justify the formula for the area of a rectangle.	Students recognize volume as an attribute of three-dimensional space. They understand that they can quantify volume by finding the total number of same-sized units of volume that they need to fill the space without gaps or overlaps. They understand that a cube that is one unit on an edge is the standard unit for measuring volume. They select appropriate units, strategies, and tools for solving problems that involve estimating or measuring volume. They decompose three-dimensional shapes and find surface areas and volumes of prisms. As they work with surface area, they find and justify relationships among the formulas for the areas of different polygons. They measure necessary attributes of shapes to use area formulas to solve problems. Students recognize volume as an attribute of three-dimensional space.	Problems that involve areas and volumes, calling on students to find areas or volumes from lengths or to find lengths from volumes or areas, are especially appropriate. These problems extend the students' work in grade 5 on area and volume and provide a context for applying new work with equations.

that appear to be exact usually are not. The level of exactness depends on the tool. The smaller the unit, the more precise the answer. Some fields such as medicine, require more precise measurements than others. Accuracy, on the other hand, depends on the individual taking the measurements. The more experience and understanding children have using different tools, the more accurate they can become.

Metric versus U.S. Customary System

It is ironic that a superpower such as the United States is the only country that has not culturally given in to the use of the metric system. Maybe this is an overall reflection of our mathematical stubbornness, also seen in the inflexible way we use algorithms. There are, however, increasing numbers of areas in which we use the metric system. Pharmaceutical companies, NASA, and the military are among those that have adopted metric units.

The original "foot" was the length of the foot of King Henry I, who lived from 1069–1131. He also determined that a yard was the measurement from the tip of his nose to the tip of his finger on his outstretched arm. King Henry VII was the one to eventually determine that 1 yard would be 3 feet, which he inscribed on a brass rod (Kennedy, Tipps, and Johnson 2008).

Although the idea of the metric system was first thought of by Simon Stevin (1548–1620), it was not created until 1791, when the French Academy of Sciences was directed by the National Assembly of France to create a standard for measures and weights. Their motivation was to rid themselves of a system that was part of the recently overthrown monarchy. At that time, the meter was defined as being one ten-millionth of the distance from the equator to the North Pole, but it is now most accurately defined as 1,650,763.73 wavelengths of the orange-red line of the krypton-86 atom (Chapin and Johnson 2000; Kennedy, Tipps, and Johnson 2008).

Besides Celsius, there are only three base units: meter, gram, and liter. All amounts are indicated by adding a prefix to the base unit. Greek prefixes are used to represent amounts more than one base unit, and Latin prefixes are used to represent amounts less than the base. The metric system parallels the base 10 system, which makes it an easy system to calculate conversions. Despite its ease, Americans have trouble with this system because we have difficulty creating mental benchmarks for the base units. For example, most of us know how far a mile is. Many of us have run a mile, some even 26.2 miles. However, as we run a 10K, it is hard to judge our time because we are unsure how the kilometer compares to the mile.

Whereas in the U.S. customary system there is no consistent relationship or ratio between consecutive units or capacity and linear measures, the metric system was devised with these relationships. A gallon, pound, and foot are not related, whereas a cubic centimeter, milliliter, and gram are.

Take a small centimeter cube from the base 10 blocks. That is a cubic centimeter. If you stack 10 high, 10 long, and 10 deep, you have just built a 1,000 cube, or a cubic decimeter. If your structure were hollow (some measurement kits have ones that are), you would be able to fill it with a liter of water. Because there were 1,000 centimeter cubes in the structure, 1 centimeter cube would hold a milliliter of water. If the temperature of the water was 4°C (the point at which water is most dense), then it would weigh a gram. Therefore, a cubic centimeter and a milliliter are equivalent. So are a liter, cubic decimeter, and a kilogram (when measuring water). You might have heard of pharmacies dispensing liquid medication using CCs, or cubic centimeters.

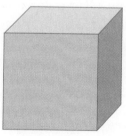

1 cubic centimeter
Holds 1 milliliter of water
weighs 1 gram

1,000 cubic centimeters = 1 cubic decimeter
1,000 milliliters of water = 1 liter of water
1,000 grams = 1 kilogram

Metric conversions	
kilo	1000
heca	100
deca	10
Meter, liter, gram (base)	
deci	0.1
centi	0.01
milli	0.001

Note some other metric measures:
1,000 kilograms =
    1 metric ton
1,000 square meters =
    1 hectare

	milli-	centi-	deci-	**base**	deca-	heca-	kilo-
milli-	1	10	100	1,000	10,000	100,000	1,000,000
centi-	0.1	1	10	100	1,000	10,000	100,000
deci-	0.01	0.1	1	10	100	1,000	10,000
base	0.001	0.01	0.1	1	10	100	1,000
deca-	0.0001	0.001	0.01	0.1	1	10	100
heca-	0.00001	0.0001	0.001	0.01	0.1	1	10
kilo-	0.000001	0.00001	0.0001	0.001	0.01	0.1	1

Figure 14.8. Relationships of different metric units.

Older students who are learning about the metric system can complete a partially filled out conversion chart (figure 14.8) by analyzing the relationships between each unit. This is a powerful activity for discovering patterns and relationships inherent in the metric system.

It is much easier for an American to learn the metric system than for a foreigner to learn our system. The units and conversions of the U.S. customary system are conventions and must be memorized. Figure 14.9 contains conversions for a variety of measures.

Comprehension Check

- Why are a cubic centimeter (cc) and milliliter (ml) the same amount?
- What is the relationship each of the following unit pairs?
  a. A centimeter to a meter
  b. A centimeter to a decimeter
  c. A decimeter to a centimeter
  d. A centimeter to a kilometer
  e. A kilometer to a centimeter

Measuring in the Early Years

When we measure, we are comparing or evaluating something against another standard. Therefore, the earliest experiences need to be comparing and developing the language used to describe those comparisons.

Making Comparisons

In kindergarten, children first begin comparing amounts when they are lined up next to one another. When describing the differences between the amounts, they should be using words like *shorter than*, *longer than*, *more than*, and *less than*. Often they are comparing amounts by creating cube trains and laying them side

Linear Measures for the U.S. Customary System			
12 inches	1 foot		
36 inches	3 feet	1 yard	
63,360 inches	5,280 feet	1,760 yards	1 mile

Area Measures for the U.S. Customary System				
144 square inches	1 square foot			
1,296 square inches	9 square feet	1 square yard		
		4,840 square yards	1 acre	
			640 acres	1 square mile

Capacity Measures for the U.S. Customary System					
3 teaspoons	1 tablespoon				
	2 tablespoons	1 fluid ounce			
		8 fluid ounces	1 cup		
		16 fluid ounces	2 cups	1 pint	
		32 fluid ounces	4 cups	2 pints	1 quart
		128 fluid ounces	16 cups	8 pints	4 quarts	1 gallon

Figure 14.9. Some conversions of the U.S. customary system.

by side. They also need to take an object and compare it with something else—for example, a pencil, a train of three cubes, or a string the length of their foot. They should be using language such as "The book is longer than the pencil." At this point, they are not trying to see how many pencils long an object is.

Children should be exploring not just length but capacity and weight as well. Centers can be set up in the classroom where different objects are compared. In *Mathematics Their Way* (1995), Mary Baratta-Lorton suggests comparing weights of a variety of small objects using a milk-carton scale, comparing weights of large objects with a homemade teeter-totter, comparing lengths with different pieces of string, and comparing the volume of different-size jars by filling them with the same amount of rice.

A concept that young children have to grapple with is that something can be big and little at the same time, depending on the referent. Activities in which an object might be big compared to one object and small compared to another object are important in helping develop this early idea that measuring is comparing one thing to another. Units such as inches or feet are not yet used to measure; Baratta-Lorton (1995, 139) explains that at first, when making comparisons, the focus needs to be on the gross differences of objects and not on the numbers:

> At this early stage, numbers *interfere* rather than enhance the development of the concept. At this stage, we want children to experience the *whole*, and the numbers focus the child's attention on the particular difference in measurement. . . . Using standard measurements of centimeters or inches is a much later step and should only be used after the children have had an opportunity to create their own standard and fully explore the idea of measurement.

Measuring Time

Another area of measurement children begin to explore in kindergarten and first grade is that of time. Understanding the passing of time is developmental and is usually solidified by second or third grade, although many children may still not know how to read an analog clock as late as sixth grade.

In these grades, daily calendar exercises are essential. This usually includes identifying the date and day of the week, identifying what the previous day was and what the next day will be, and identifying the season. In addition to the traditional bulletin board–style calendars posted in most classrooms, students need access to a large yearlong flip calendar. This helps develop the idea that the months are not random. Some children can develop the sense of time sooner than others, and a flip calendar helps them learn to anticipate events further out than the current month. Teachers also usually have some kind of system to record the number of days in school. All these activities help children see patterns in the sequence of days and help give them a better feel for time in days, weeks, and months.

Time within a day is difficult for young children to grasp and is something that needs to be addressed daily. Teachers need to record the times of the various activities and always note what time it is. The class can even record shadows of an object at different times of the day to relate time to the passing of the sun. Children need benchmarks for 1, 5, 15, 30, and 60 minutes. They can be quite comical when trying to describe how much time has passed. One method we have found helpful for children trying to develop some benchmarks is to repeatedly time students doing different activities for 1 minute. Here are some ideas for such activities:

- Write your name as many times as you can in a minute
- Touch your toes as many times as you can in a minute
- Walk around the room for a minute
- Run around the track and stop in 1 minute
- Close your eyes, and raise your hand when you think a minute is over

Teach students how to read the minute hand on a clock. Most have no idea that the red hand on a school clock goes around one time in a minute. Time other activities for longer lengths—set a timer so that you do not forget.

Teaching kindergartners and first graders how to tell time to the nearest hour is usually uneventful. After all, they are only paying attention to the smaller hand. But telling time to the 30 minutes brings the minute hand into play, and that is where the trouble begins. Learning to read an analog clock can be difficult, and state standards may be set too high on this one. So what are the best ways to teach telling time?

First, start with a large, nongeared demonstration clock that children can see well (or a small one on a document camera). Take the minute hand off the clock so that the hour hand is the only one on the clock. Focus on the movement of the hour hand and what it does as it moves from hour to hour. Begin to develop language related to half an hour. Ask students where they think the hand should be when it is halfway between two o'clock and three o'clock (figure 14.10). This also elicits good discussion on fractions and how they relate to the clock.

Using a picture of a clock and cutting and opening it so that it lies flat can create a more linear model that might be helpful to children who are having trouble relating to the rotation. Place an arrow at different points on the line and ask what time they think it should be based on where the hour hand is (see figure 14.10). At first, do this with only the hour and half hour, but later, when it is necessary to teach to 15 minutes you can draw in tick marks to identify 15, 30, and 45 minutes).

Now do activities with both hands and allow students to have their own geared clocks so that they can explore how one hand affects the other. They also need their own clocks to make an hour that you present. Whenever you have to teach more difficult amounts, go back to the one-handed clock. Usually, by the time students understand 45 after, they are able to easily understand to

Figure 14.10. Using a clock with just an hour hand to determine the time.

5 minutes (as long as they can count by fives or there are fives printed on their clocks). The part where students get tripped up with telling time is the last 15 minutes, when the hour hand is close to the next hour. That is why the preceding exercise is helpful; it assists students with reasoning the position of the hour hand.

It is not uncommon for upper-grade students to not know how to tell time. Just because second or third grade may be the last time it appears in the state standards does not mean that all students have mastered it. Upper-grade teachers may no longer find telling time in their curriculum but can find it extremely beneficial to take a week and create focused routines for telling time. Usually, it finally clicks for the students who did not get it before. It is well worth the investment in time, no pun intended.

Comprehension Check

- Describe activities that young children should experience to lay foundations for understanding measurement.

Measuring Size

What are the underlying concepts and the developmental steps that children tend to move through when learning to use standard units for measuring size, including length, area, and surface area?

First, consider an overview of what is learned throughout the elementary years (figure 14.11).

Typical Grade Explored	Type of Measurement	How Measured
Kindergarten	Linear	Compare amounts
Kindergarten, 1, 2	Linear	Nonstandard units
1, 2	Linear	Standard units
2	Perimeter	Nonstandard units
3	Perimeter	Standard units
3	Area of quadrilateral	Making arrays
3	Identifying types of angles: acute, obtuse, right	Comparing
3	Volume	Counting cubes
4	Perimeter	Developing or using formula
4, 5	Area of quadrilateral	Developing or using formula
4, 5	Area of triangle	Developing or using formula
5	Surface area	Developing or using formula
5	Volume	Developing or using formula
5	Measuring types of angles	Standard units
5	Parts of a circle: diameter, radius, midpoint	Standard units
5	Circumference of a circle	Developing or using formula
6	Area of a circle	Developing or using formula
6	Sum of angles in triangle, quadrilateral	Developing or using formula

Figure 14.11. The typical grade at which certain areas of measurement of size are explored.

Linear Measurement or Length

Stephan and Clements (2003) and Barrett et al. (2003) describe seven concepts in understanding linear measurement: partitioning, unitization, unit iteration, transitivity, conservation of size, accumulation of distance, and relationship between number and measurement.

Partitioning	The realization that an object can be mentally cut into smaller, equal-sized parts
Unitization	The ability to bring a shorter object to compare it to another object
Unit iteration	The ability to take a smaller object, or unit, and see how many times it fits next to a larger object
Transitivity	The ability to use a third object, such as a pencil, to compare two different objects, such as a door and a window
Conservation of size	A Piagetian term describing when children understand that if an object is moved the length does not change
Accumulation of distance	Through unit iteration, what is being measured is the distance from the beginning of the first unit to the end of the last
Relationship between number and measurement	The realization that measuring is essentially counting but in continuous, not discrete, units.

There is disagreement in the literature as to which of these concepts needs to be in place first to develop others. Piaget, Inhelder, and Szeminska (1960) believed that conservation must be in place before they could have transitivity because to a child, once an object is moved, the length changes. Boulton-Lewis et al. (1987) further argued that students must be able to reason transitively before measurement concepts can be understood, concluding that the ruler is useless until this reasoning has been set. However, more recently, Clements (1999) argued that transitivity and conservation do not need to be developed to be able to learn some ideas about measurement. This is supported by Stephan et al. (2001), who showed that children as young as 6 years were able to develop the concept of accumulation of distance, provided that they received meaningful instruction. A complete understanding of measurement may not be fully developed for several years, but children can benefit from meaningful instruction at an early age. Although there is still question as to the order in which these concepts develop, researchers agree that all must be developed before full understanding of measurement can be achieved (Stephan and Clements 2003).

When working with standard units, we want children to become familiar with the different units so that they are able to select an appropriate unit when measuring. We also want students to develop an understanding of the relationships between units and between the size of the unit and number of units. They also need to be able to think of the whole unit and parts of another unit (Grant and Kline 2003).

Developing Benchmarks

Benchmarks are "having a 'feel' for units of measurement and possessing a set of meaningful reference points or benchmarks for these units" (Joram 2003, 57).

It is important that students have experiences to help them develop benchmarks for different units. Hope (1989, 15) states that "a wide variety of everyday measurement references . . . is the foundation for good measurement sense as well as good number sense."

Children see a ruler often enough that they probably can tell you how big a foot is and may even be able to estimate how long an inch is. But what about 10 feet? 100 feet? 1 mile? Children have little experiences related to longer distances and have no concept to how long they might be. The width of a pinky is the common benchmark for centimeter. Some students may use hands and arms to consider other measurements. But caution must be given to the use of growing body parts to establish secure benchmarks. We may clearly remember in grade school that a yard or meter came to about our noses and may still have that impression every time we think about how long a meter is, but we have to remember to adjust down because of growth.

Have your students measure the dimensions of the classroom (including the height) to help them establish what 10 feet and 20 feet look and feel like and how high ceilings generally are. Another powerful activity to have children internalize longer distances is to take a 100-foot tape measure and open it across the playground. Have two students walk together and stop every 10 feet. After about 30 feet, one student closes his eyes and walks what he feels should be 10 feet. When he stops he can open his eyes to see whether he was correct. Have them continue for the entire 100 feet. This helps them internalize 10 feet and 100 feet.

Measure the distance around the track or playground at your school and figure out how many laps would total a mile. Give students frequent opportunities to run a mile to begin to feel how long that is.

Common Misconceptions about Measuring

One of the biggest concepts that our students seem to miss throughout elementary school is that when measuring length they are looking for the amount of space, or distance, between two points. Ask a student where 5 inches is on a ruler, and more than likely she will point to the number 5. Students think of measuring like finding the mark. This is the same problem that arises when working with fractions on a number line; they think ½ is the point in the middle. Students have to be reinforced from the beginning that what they are measuring is the amount of space from point A to point B. This notion is critical when students get into area, because many have no clue that what is being counted is the space inside of the figure. Stephan et al. (2001) show that this concept can be constructed by children as young as 6 years.

Another extremely common error children make is starting at one rather than zero. This may be partly because, generally, in the younger grades, counting starts at "one." But the underlying factor behind this mistake is that children do not know what is being measured. Again, they think they are counting something but they do not understand what.

Young children also may mistake the number of units for the total length of an object. For example, a stack of cubes (that measure 12 inches total) is seen as longer than two 6-inch pencils lying end to end because there are more cubes.

Struggling Learner

Think of as many ways you can to make math as kinesthetic as possible for your struggling students. They often have different learning styles and need the movement to help them internalize mathematics.

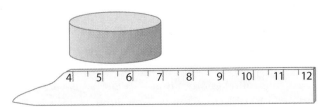

Figure 14.12. A broken ruler exercise.

Activities to Help with Measuring Misconceptions

Using a broken ruler is a good way to get children to think about how to use a ruler and what they are measuring. If a ruler does not have the first few numbers, whether it is broken or faded, the child is forced to begin with a different number and the answer can no longer be the final number (figure 14.12).

If the child says that the preceding cylinder is 7 inches, provide him with a few different broken rulers to see whether he keeps saying the end number or he begins to realize that it cannot be a different answer because the size has not changed. This indicates whether or not he understands what he is finding out. Usually, this makes him realize that he has to start with the first number and count up.

This leads to the second misconception: starting with one rather than zero. We have to use a lot of caution when we advise children to start at the end of the ruler. A few years ago, California state testing used rulers for which the zero was not flush to the edge. Whether or not that was done on purpose, many students miscalculated their measurements because they started from the edge of the ruler and not the zero. This taught us that there is more to measuring than teaching the procedure of how to use a ruler. These students seemed to know "how" to use a ruler, but they did not understand what they were measuring.

Children might align an object with the ruler starting with one (figure 14.13). However, when making their own recordings or measurements, they may design a measurement tool to begin at one (figure 14.14).

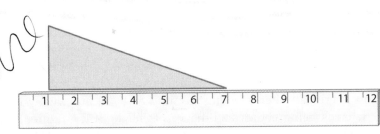

Figure 14.13. A typical misconception of starting with 1 on a ruler.

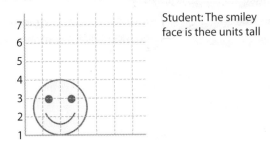

Student: The smiley face is thee units tall

Figure 14.14. A typical student-designed measurement tool.

This is where strategic questioning comes in. You want the children to realize that this does not make sense, but telling them to start at zero does not help them make sense of what they are doing. When sharing as a whole group, there are bound to be some conflicting ideas, and having those with opposing views try to convince one another is powerful. But we want to make sure that students change their mind because they understand, not because they just believe their peers. You should challenge your students to draw an object that is one unit high and compare that with the one in question. This should stimulate enough discussion that the need to start at zero is obvious.

Tricky Language Related to Measuring Length

Students always seem to have problems with the language related to comparing lengths. Teachers tend to ask, "How long is ____?" but not "How much longer is ____ than ____?" Just as with *more than*, the *longer than* questions seem to be difficult, especially for our English-language learners.

If there is a picture of two objects being measured by the same ruler and the question is "How much longer is the green arrow than the blue arrow?" it is common for students to answer "8 inches" (figure 14.15). This is because they are just looking for the green arrow and seeing how long it is. These are the types of multiple-choice questions that trip up children. They know that one is longer, but they are not attending to the language of the question. Teachers need to be explicit about what they are asking in these types of questions.

To train children to differentiate various types of questions related to figure 14.15, interchangeably ask the following:

Which is longer, the green or the blue arrow?

How long is the green arrow?

How short is the blue arrow?

How much longer is the green arrow than the blue arrow?

How much shorter is the blue arrow than the green arrow?

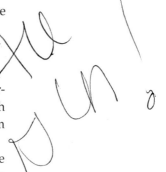

Language Tip

Always ask many different questions about the same diagram so that students must attend to the language structure of the question.

Area and Perimeter

Area describes how much surface the shape takes up in square units. *Perimeter* is the measurement in units of length of the outer edge of an area. The two seem to be related, but they are indeed different measures. Every upper-grade teacher knows the perils of teaching area and perimeter.

Why are these two concepts so difficult? First, they tend to come up at the same time in the curriculum. There may be 2 days on perimeter and 2 days on area, back to back. Students know that both have to do with measuring a figure, but they can never keep the two straight.

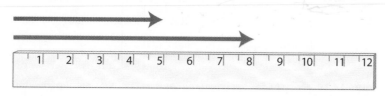

Figure 14.15. Using a ruler to compare the lengths of two different objects.

It can be helpful, from as early as kindergarten, to reinforce the language in natural contexts. Invite your students to sit on the perimeter of the rug when you want a circle or rectangle and on the area when you want a closer group of children, perhaps during a readaloud.

Second, we propose that the early experiences with area should be taught and reinforced during the multiplication unit. Area is initially taught through arrays and developing counting strategies for finding the total square units needed to build these arrays. The same experiences are used in multiplication. When teaching multiplication through the building of arrays with square units, use the language "What is the area of our rectangle?" even if you are not formally introducing the vocabulary. We feel that if the notions of area and perimeter were separated in the curriculum (area with multiplication and perimeter with measurement), at least initially, then some confusion might be avoided.

Third, to create understanding of the difference between the two, have students study the actual words and their etymology. When introducing the vocabulary, discuss what *peri-* and *meter* mean to help make sense of the words.

Same Area, Same Perimeter?

It is important that students have time to explore the relationships between perimeter and area. They need to know that not all shapes with the same area have the same perimeter, and vice versa.

Same Perimeter, Different Area Take a string of a given length, say, 12 inches. Now take a piece of graph paper with 1-inch squares. Tracing the squares with the string, how many different closed figures can you make with a 12-inch perimeter? Which kinds of figures have the greatest area? Which kinds of figures have the least? Making only rectangular arrays, which kinds of arrays yield the greatest and least area?

Same Area, Different Perimeter An area can be reconfigured to many different shapes, but the perimeter depends on how much surface area is exposed. Take the two shapes in figure 14.16.

Both of these shapes have an area of nine square units. Which one has a larger perimeter? What kind of shape do you think has the shortest perimeter? Have your students create as many different configurations using 12-square tiles (or 24 as an extension) and chart which tables would be able to seat the most people and which would be able to seat the least. All tiles must be completely sharing a side, not corners. You may want to discuss how a shape, such as the second one in figure 14.16, may not be conducive for eating because the chairs would be in one another's way.

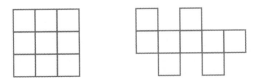

Figure 14.16. Two shapes depicting the same area but different perimeters.

Calculating Area and Perimeter

It is important that students go through informal to formal processes when learning about these concepts. Because area is typically taught heavily in fourth grade, upper-grade teachers often fail to provide concrete support for students. The following processes, over time, are used to represent area and perimeter problems:

- Building figures with square tiles
- Drawing these models with one-to-one corresponding pictures using graph paper
- Using open arrays or sketches and labeling them with numbers

It is far too common for students to be solving problems from a book that look like the one in figure 14.17.

Most students do not have enough experience with these concepts to know what to do with the numbers. If they are lucky, they might remember a formula presented in class, but those are easily mixed up.

Children need to build the shape in figure 14.17 with tiles and discuss what they are finding. Most do not understand why the answer is in square feet, for example, until they realize that they are counting the number of square tiles that fit inside the shape. When recording, they need to use graph paper so that they are reinforcing the idea that they are counting the number of squares. Because this stage usually parallels what they are learning in multiplication ideas, students are developing counting strategies for finding the total. The terms *width* and *length* can be compared and connected to the words *rows* and *columns*. If they are going through this process after they have explored and understood multiplication, then they quickly develop the formula themselves by realizing that the width and the length can simply be multiplied to come up with the result. After a while, as with any other mathematical strand, they wean themselves off the tiles because they become too cumbersome.

Once the understanding is solid, children no longer need to draw a picture on graph paper and they can simply create a sketch with labels, because they have attached the meaning of what to do with the numbers.

Calculating perimeter comes with its own set of misconceptions. Young students may use nonstandard units for finding out how far it is around an object. There is a caution regarding what types of tools to use or not use. Many classrooms use square tiles as the nonstandard unit of measure. When calculating straight length, this does not seem to pose a problem until perimeter. Take the scenario in figure 14.18.

A child wanted to find the perimeter of the inside rectangle. She used color tiles to measure all around. What do you think her response was? Why do you think she got 26 inches instead of 22 inches? This child counted the tiles on the corners, which are not touching the interior rectangle. This shows that she might have an understanding that perimeter goes around a shape but is counting square units, not the sides of those squares that are touching the rectangle.

Paperclips or other objects might be more supportive nonstandard units for initial experiences related to perimeter; however, even if tiles are used, a rich mathematical conversation can surface about what perimeter is measuring compared to what is being measured in the preceding example.

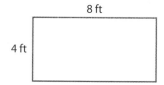

Find the area and perimeter for the above figure.

Figure 14.17. A typical textbook problem related to area.

Figure 14.18. Using square tiles to calculate the perimeter of a rectangular object.

As with area, students derive a formula for finding perimeter when they are in about fourth grade. Some formulas may be as follows:

l + l + w + w
(l × 2) + (w × 2)
2l + 2w

It is also helpful for students to explore the relationship between lengths and total area. What happens to the area when the length of one side is doubled? Halved? When both sides are doubled? Tripled?

Squares When exploring squares, students realize that the perimeter is adding the side four times and therefore generate the following:

s + s + s + s
s × 4
4s

For area, they may come up with the following:

s × s
s^2

It is important to help students make connections between all formulas that are generated. This helps them later realize that a formula can have the same information but be written in different ways.

Triangles A big idea is to understand that a triangle is half the area of a square. But this idea has to be explored in a concrete way, not just through the formula. This is most commonly explored through geoboards. On a geoboard, there are 16 square units. When they make a triangle, it is easy to count the square units and half squares to find the area (figure 14.19).

Many triangles should be explored to prove that this works for all triangles. A formula that children make is as follows:

length times width divided by two
l × w ÷ 2

The teacher would want to show how this can also be notated as follows:

$$\frac{l \times w}{2}$$

The terms *base* and *height* as they relate to triangles need to be defined; therefore, change the preceding formula to the following:

$$\frac{b \times h}{2}$$

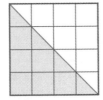

Student: The area of this triangle is six full square units and four half squares to equal eight square units.

Figure 14.19. Exploring the area of triangles by cutting squares in half.

This formula makes a lot more sense to children than $\frac{1}{2}b \times h$, although in many cases the latter can be derived while looking at patterns and the relationships between the area of the triangle and that of the rectangle.

Figure 14.20. A parallelogram.

Parallelograms It may seem simple enough that the area of the parallelogram is base multiplied by height, but why? After students understand how to find an area of a rectangle, square, and triangle, they can then combine their understandings to develop the formula for a parallelogram. Look at figure 14.20.

How can we prove that base multiplied by height is the formula for finding the area of this parallelogram? Is there a way to break this shape into smaller parts? That is just what children do.

They first notice that they can create a rectangle by creating two triangles from the ends (figure 14.21).

They then cut one triangle and put it next to the other triangle, creating one large rectangle (figure 14.22).

Figure 14.21. Dividing the parallelogram into different sections.

Students then derive that the length multiplied by the width of this rectangle would find the area and that the parallelogram must be the same because no area is lost. Compared to the original parallelogram, the width would be the height; therefore, the formula is now base multiplied by height.

This bigger idea of taking a shape and breaking it up to find the area of smaller shapes compliments what students should already know regarding multiplication and its arrays.

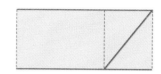

Figure 14.22. Moving one triangle over to create a complete rectangle.

Surface Area Surface area seems hard for students because it is usually presented in a disconnected way. They are usually looking at a drawing in a book and asked to calculate the surface area of a diagram. Children need something more concrete and connected to a real-life context to understand what is being asked.

Presenting problems of how much wrapping paper would be needed to cover a three-dimensional block, or box, that they have in front of them, would be much more accessible to them. They just need to make the connection that all they are doing is finding the area of all faces of the object. It is then no longer so mysterious.

Comprehension Check

- Create a figure of 9 square units that has a perimeter of 12 units, 20 units, and 36 units. What type of figure has the smallest perimeter?

- Imagine you have a cube with lengths of three units. Derive a formula for surface area that you think a child would consider.

Measuring Volume and Capacity

We might use or hear the terms *volume* and *capacity* interchangeably, but there is a difference between them. *Capacity* is the amount a container holds. *Volume* also describes this amount but refers to the size of the object as well. A rock has volume but no capacity. Volume is measured in cubic units and capacity is measured in liters, gallons, or another liquid measure.

Volume

Whereas the concepts of area and surface area are difficult to understand, volume is nearly impossible for some students to grasp. Again, it is because of an inability to conceptualize what is being asked. In California, there is a written state standard for volume in third and fifth grades but not in fourth grade. Therefore, fourth-grade teachers generally do not teach it. They do not realize how critical it is to try to bridge the gap between what is expected in third

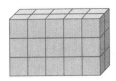 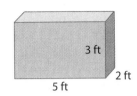

Figure 14.23. The ways volume is present in third grade (left) and fifth grade (right) in the California state standards.

grade and in fifth grade. The third-grade standard expects students to find volume based on a counting strategy for counting all cubes within a shape. The fifth-grade standard expects students to use the formula (figure 14.23). In fifth grade, students are usually given a shape with dimensions but not pictures of the individual cubes. This is a big leap from the last time they saw volume in third grade.

Take the shape in figure 14.23. On paper, some students can tell that 30 cubes make up this entire shape. However, many students do not have the visual skills to know what is being asked. Many students attempt to count every face that they see. In some cases, it might be the same answer. In figure 14.23, counting all faces would yield an answer of one more than all cubes. It is important to know that children struggle with this.

To strengthen this visual skill, it is important to have a model made of the picture. Show the model and, without letting them touch it, ask students to tell you how many cubes are in the shape. You might be surprised that some still count the faces. If there are more than two layers, many cannot visualize how many cubes are hidden inside the figure. It likely will be necessary to take apart the model to prove how many cubes there are and then reassemble it. Have students identify in their picture all parts that are in the model. For example, point to a face in the picture and ask them to show you where that face is in the model. They have to realize that they cannot see all the cubes in the picture and have to imagine that they are there.

Older students struggling to understand volume may need to go back and build models using the dimensions given to them. This helps them derive the formula $l \times w \times h$. They usually find the number of cubes in one layer and then multiply that by the number of layers (or use repeated addition).

Capacity

Most of us do not have a good sense of capacity and have not developed benchmarks for this besides a cup and gallon. Do you know how many gallons should fill the bathtub or swimming pool? Children have an even weaker sense of capacity. It is important to give opportunities for them to fill many different-size and different-shape containers and compare them with one another. When trying to help your students make the connection between 1 cubic centimeter and 1 milliliter, make a small, hollow centimeter cube using tag board and packaging tape. Have students use a measurement dropper to fill the cube so that they can see the connection.

Measuring Angles and Circles

Angles

Usually in third and fourth grades, students are classifying angles as being a right angle, greater than a right angle, or smaller than a right angle. They may even have to know the terms *right, obtuse,* and *acute* (figure 14.24). Learning the general meaning for obtuse, and other ways to use the word, helps them remember which type of angle it is referring to.

Making students create these angles by using straws connected with a twist tie, popsicle sticks, or even just their arms, helps them internalize these different types. This is going to be critical later when they begin to use a protractor.

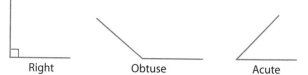

Right   Obtuse   Acute

Figure 14.24. Three types of angles.

Using the Protractor

One of the most frustrating parts of learning to use the protractor is that there is usually never enough time carved out in the curriculum. It is not an easy tool to use, but there are a few steps you can do to make the process easier.

Understanding the notion of degrees is a different kind of unit that students have used in the past. To help them understand the connection between degrees and a shape, show them a circle divided into 360° so that they see what they are measuring.

Make a protractor out of wax paper. Cut a square from the wax paper and fold it twice in half and then twice diagonally. Trim the excess off the top to create a circular figure (figure 14.25).

This homemade protractor can be folded in half if necessary. By not having any numbers on it, it serves the same purpose as nonstandard units. The students are only focusing on how many lines fill an angle they are measuring and are not worrying about the numbers for now.

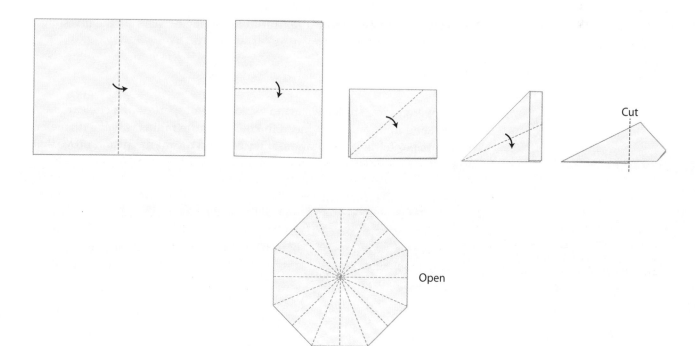

Figure 14.25. Making a homemade protractor.

By the time the students use a standard protractor, some of the reasoning should be in place. The issue with protractors is that there are numbers going both directions. Many students state that the angle is 20° when it should be 160°. This shows the teacher that they are not estimating first. Before measuring, students should always tell themselves whether it is going to be less than 90° or greater than 90°. This way, they can catch themselves when they are using the wrong numbers.

Another issue with using the protractor is starting at zero. Sound familiar? Maybe children who struggle with starting at zero while using a protractor still have misconceptions about using a ruler. They forget to align the protractor at the zero and therefore get an incorrect measurement. The more time they have to explore with the homemade protractor, the fewer errors they should make later when using the standard one.

Total Number of Angles in a Triangle and a Quadrilateral

A big idea in sixth grade is understanding that the sum of the angles of a triangle totals 180° and the sum of those of a quadrilateral totals 360°.

To get students to discover this concept, you could have them measure the angles in many different triangles or quadrilaterals and chart them as shown in figure 14.26.

The class could compare the data and see what they discover. Unfortunately, at this point, there are too many issues with accuracy when children are measuring these angles. Few students actually end up with 180°. Perhaps this is where a great virtual manipulative website can be handy.

Another popular activity is to tear off the angles of a triangle or quadrilateral and glue them next to one another (figure 14.27). Students can then see that they always equal a straight angle (for those in a triangle) or a circle (for those of a quadrilateral).

This is a powerful lesson, but it is not free of challenges. If students cut the corners off too straight, it is hard to tell which angle of the torn piece is the angle they were trying to measure. We strongly suggest marking the tips somehow so that this does not happen.

Circles

In the upper grades, students start to explore the properties of a circle: radius, diameter, and midpoint. They need to know that the radius is half a diameter. Through paper-folding explorations, they can find the midpoint and prove that

Triangle no.	Angle A	Angle B	Angle C	Total degrees
1	90°	60°	30°	180°
2	30°	30°	120°	180°
3				

Figure 14.26. Charting the measurements of angles of a triangle to notice that all total 180°.

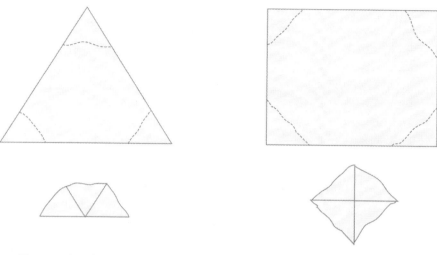

Three angles of a triangle   Four angles of a quadrilateral

Figure 14.27. Tearing off the corners of triangles and quadrilaterals to prove that the total degrees are 180 and 360, respectively.

the radius is the same no matter where it is on the circle. They can even generate an equation that states the following:

$$2r = d$$
$$\tfrac{1}{2}d = r$$

The circumference is like the perimeter of a circle. There is an awesome book called *Sir Cumference and the Dragon of Pi* by Cindy Neuschwander (see the "Lit Link" section at the end of this chapter). This is the best book we know of that explains what pi is and how it is related to diameter (it takes 3.14 diameters to make a circumference, which is pi). However, before reading the book, there are some good explorations students can do to discover relationships on their own, which we describe in the next sections.

Everyone is likely easily deceived by how long around the circumference is. Take a cylinder, such as a toilet paper roll. First estimate which is going to be larger, the circumference or the height. Now measure the circumference with a string and compare that string with the height. More often than not, you will be surprised with what you have found. This is a sure way to capture the attention of your students.

Relationships of Circumference to Height and Diameter

We always want to encourage students to discover whether there is a relationship between two different quantities. Have students take several cylindrical objects and find the circumference with a string and compare it with the height. Have them record their findings on a T-chart (figure 14.28). Have them calculate the ratio and determine whether there is a relationship between the two measurements. *Note:* Yarn is stretchy and thus not an accurate measuring tool. Try

Item	Circumference in Inches	Height in Inches	Ratio
Paper towel roll			
Toilet paper roll			
Glass jar			

Figure 14.28. A chart on which to record ratios between circumference and height.

Item	Circumference in Inches	Diameter in Inches	Ratio
Paper towel roll			
Toilet paper roll			
Glass jar			

Figure 14.29. A chart on which to record ratios between circumference and diameter.

Comprehension Check

■ Gather at least three cylindrical objects. Using a piece of chord or string, compare the circumference with the diameters and fill in figures 14.28 and 14.29. Which measurements have a relationship? What is that relationship?

to use something, such as packaging ribbon, that has no elasticity and therefore can produce more precise measurements.

Then have them make the same chart for the circumference and the diameter (figure 14.29).

What do you think the results are going to show? After discovering that there is no relationship between circumference and height yet there is one between circumference and diameter, have your students discuss why this is true.

Using Inquiry to Teach Measurement

Exploring Capacity Using Milliliters and Liters

Launch cycle 1	The teacher asks (holding a 50-ml plunger that students are familiar with), "Would it be efficient to measure a liter of water using the plunger? Knowing what we know about the metric system, discuss with a partner how many of these it should take to fill a liter."
Explore cycle 1	Students draw a diagram to show how many plungers it would take to fill a liter.
Summarize cycle 1	As a class, students discuss how many milliliters should go into a liter. If the plunger is 5 ml, what fraction would this be?
Launch cycle 2	The teacher gives directions for the explore activity.
Explore cycle 2	Students find several containers on their tables (including a homemade hollow centimeter cube). First they estimate the capacity of each object; then they test their estimates by using one of the tools: a 50-ml plunger, a graduated cylinder, a dropper, or any other capacity tool they may have.
Summarize cycle 2	Students discuss their results and which tools they used to measure the different objects. They also make the connection between a cubic centimeter and a milliliter of water and how 1,000 cubic centimeters equal a cubic liter.

Using Nonstandard Units to Measure Length

Launch	The teacher has an object taped to the board and asks students which is longer, the object or a block. Students agree that the object is longer. The teacher asks them how they can figure out how many blocks long it is. A couple of students come up to demonstrate how they could measure the object using blocks. The teacher makes sure that the students understand that the blocks have to be touching because we are trying to figure out how many blocks fit on the object.

Explore	Partnerships get a bag with different measuring objects, such as a paper clip, an unsharpened pencil, a feather, a color tile, and a button. They are instructed to measure objects around the room using each of these tools and to record it on a chart the teacher provided.
Summarize	Students come together to discuss what they measured. The teacher picks one object a partnership measured and has them show how they used the different tools to measure it. The teacher poses the following questions to the class: "Are there going to fit more square tiles or more pencils on this object? Why do you get a big answer when you use this object but get a little answer when you use that object? The generalization to be made is that the smaller the unit, the more of them that are used when measuring.

Finding the Volume of Rectangular Prisms

Launch cycle 1	The teacher gives students 12 connecting cubes with which they create rectangular prisms.
Explore cycle 1	Students create a rectangular prism using all 12 of their cubes.
Summarize cycle 1	Students compare the different rectangular prisms they were able to make and note the dimensions, which the teacher writes on the board. They discuss how the dimensions are different yet the total volume is the same.
Launch cycle 2	Each small group is given 36 connecting cubes with which they create various rectangular prisms. Explain that they should record the prisms they create by drawing them and labeling the dimensions.
Explore cycle 2	Students build different prisms with all 36 cubes. They complete a chart of four columns: length (cubes in one row), width (rows in one layer), height (layers in prism), and volume.
Summarize cycle 2	Students add their data to a class chart and analyze it to determine what they do to the numbers (length, width, and height) to find the total volume. Students discover, and then discuss why, all numbers need to be multiplied together to arrive at the total number of cubes.

Deriving the Area of a Quadrilateral

Launch cycle 1	The teacher shows a picture of a quadrilateral made from graph paper on a whiteboard or overhead. The teacher asks students to discuss with their partner how many square units are inside the quadrilateral.
Explore cycle 1	Students discuss with a partner.
Summarize cycle 1	As a class, students share answers and strategies of how they figured it out. Most likely, some counted, some used repeated addition, and some used multiplication. The teacher introduces the vocabulary of *length* and *width*.
Launch cycle 2	The teacher states that the students are going to figure out a strategy that they can use with any rectangle, even if they do not know what the measurement of the sides are. The teacher hands the small groups several quadrilaterals that they can explore.
Explore cycle 2	Students work in small groups to find the areas of their quadrilaterals and try to generalize a way to find the area of any quadrilateral.
Summarize cycle 2	As a class, students discuss that they notice they are multiplying one side times the other side, or length times width, in each figure. When asked to write an equation to show this, they write "length $\times$ width = area". The teacher further asks them to write the equation using letters to stand for the words, so students derive the following: "$l \times w = a$."

CONCLUSION

A meaning-centered classroom is a safe place for students to take intellectual risks and to be in a state of disequilibrium as they dig deeply into mathematics and construct understanding. Rigorous mathematical content, strong teaching, high achievement, and a rich learning environment are all evidence of a meaning-centered classroom.

Engagement is a key indicator of the learning environment. Students cannot learn if they are not engaged in the learning at hand. Oftentimes, it appears that all students are engaged when in actuality many are not. Lesson design, teaching, learning behavior, management, physical environment, and charts are all areas that need to be thoughtfully considered when trying to maximize engagement of all students.

Engagement is heightened by the use of concrete tools, and measurement is a perfect venue for tool use. Measurement is such a fundamental application of mathematics, yet the children in our schools are not performing well in this strand. We need to ensure that, for their entire elementary experience, they have plenty of opportunities to explore what measurement means before applying any kind of procedure. Even using a ruler is often a procedure for which no meaning is attached to what they are trying to find out.

▶ Interview Video with an Eye on Content

Watch some student interviews around areas of measurement. Note the child's response and what his understanding or misconception is around the area. Think about what the next steps might be for teaching this child.

Focus of the interview. What area of measurement is being assessed?	
What understandings and generalizations does the student exhibit?	
If you were to teach this child, what would your next steps be?	

▶ Interview a Child

1. Design and conduct a student interview related to a concept of measurement that is appropriate for the grade level of the student you will be working with. When considering your questions, think of the big ideas and most common misconceptions children have.

2. Write an overall summary about how your student did. Include recommendations you would make for the child's teacher or what would you do with this child if you were to continue to work with him.

▶ Classroom Video with an Eye on Pedagogy

Watch the classroom lessons. What evidences are there of a meaning-centered classroom?

Focus for the lesson		
Evidences of a meaning-centered classroom.	Content	
	Teaching and learning	
	Environment	

▶ Classroom Application

1. Observe your cooperating teacher and note how the teacher encourages all students to be engaged.

2. Collaboratively design and teach a lesson related to an area in measurement. Consider how you will engage your students, as well as how you will create an intellectual community.

▶ Resources

Pedagogy

The Essential 55, Ron Clark (2003)

A Framework for Understanding Poverty, Ruby K. Payne (1996)

Content

Learning and Teaching Measurement: 2003 Yearbook, National Council of Teachers of Mathematics (2003)

▶ Lit Link

Literature Books to Support Geometric Reasoning

Title	*Author*
Archimedes and the Door of Science	Jeanne Bendick
Big and Little	Steve Jenkins
Biggest, Strongest, Fastest	Steve Jenkins

Title	Author
Can I Go?	Rozanne Lanczak Williams
Drop of Water, A: A Book of Science and Wonder	Walter Wick
Earthshine	Theresa Nelson
G is for Googol: A Math Alphabet Book	David M. Schwartz
Holes	Louis Sachar
How Big Is a Foot?	Rolf Myller
How Much Is a Million?	Davis M. Schwartz
How Much, How Many, How Far, How Heavy, How Long, How Tall Is 1,000?	Helen Nolan
How Tall, How Short, How Far Away	David A. Adler
Icebergs & Glaciers	Seymour Simon
Inch by Inch	Leo Lionni
Inchworm and a Half	Elinor J. Pinczes
Insects Measure Up!	Jennifer Schieber
Is a Blue Whale the Biggest Thing There Is?	Robert E. Wells
Jim and the Beanstalk	Raymond Briggs
Just Right!	Maria Kathe
Measuring Up	J. E. Osborne
Missing Piece, The	Shel Silverstein
Morning Rush, The	Rozanne Lanczak Williams
My Map Book	Sara Fanelli
Pig is Big, A	Douglas Florian
Princess Rock and the Royal Inches	Marlene Perez
Sir Cumference and the Dragon of Pi	Cindy Neuschwander
Sir Cumference and the First Round Table	Cindy Neuschwander
Sir Cumference and the Great Knight of Angleland	Cindy Neuschwander

Title	Author
Spaghetti and Meatballs for All! A Mathematical Story	Marilyn Burns
Telling Time: How to Tell Time on Digital and Analog Clocks!	Jules Older
Teotihuacan: Designing an Ancient Mexican City	Lynn George
Tweet and Chirp	Barbara Glover
Village of Round and Square Houses, The	Ann Grifalconi
Weight	Henry Pluckrose
What's Smaller Than a Pygmy Shrew?	Robert E. Wells

 Tech Tools

Websites

NCTM: Illuminations, Web Links—Measurement, http://illuminations.nctm.org/WebResourceList.aspx?Ref=2&Std=3&Grd=0

National Library of Virtual Manipulatives, http://www.nlvm.usu.edu/

NCTM: Investigating the Concept of Triangle and the Properties of Polygons—Making Triangles, and Learning Geometry and Measurement Concepts by Creating Paths and Navigating Mazes (e-examples 4.2 and 4.3) http://standards.nctm.org/document/eexamples/

Software

Measurement in Motion, Learning in Motion (for fifth grade and up; http://www.learn.motion.com/produts/measurement/index.html)

Differentiating Instruction in the Regular Classroom, Diane Heacox (a CD-ROM filled with student questionnaires to help the teacher and student recognize which kind of learner that student is)

Technology Integrations and Data Analysis and Probability

PEDAGOGICAL CONTENT UNDERSTANDINGS

Pedagogy   *Technology Integrations*

- Technologically Supported Tasks During Launch
- Using Technological Tools During Explore
- Using Technological Tools During Summarize
- WebQuests: Tools for Supporting All Inquiry

Content   *Data Analysis and Probability*

- What Is Statistics?
- Early Experiences with Analyzing Data
- What Is Probability?
- Theoretical and Experimental Probability

....

"Once a new technology rolls over you, if you're not part of the steamroller; you're part of the road."

Stewart Brand

CONVERSATION IN MATHEMATICS

Imagine a fourth-grade classroom in which each child has a Texas Instruments Explorer calculator. The teacher presents this problem:

In our six-inning class kickball game, the pitcher on the winning team rolled about seven pitches per inning. How many total pitches?

One child grabs his calculator and types +7; then he presses the CONST button.

He pushes 0; then he pushes the CONST button six times. The calculator produces this sequence of numbers after each strike of the CONST button:

1   7   *(first strike)*

2   14   *(second strike)*

3   21   *(third strike)*

4   28   *(fourth strike)*

5   35   *(fifth strike)*

6   42   *(sixth strike)*

He gleefully blurts out, "42."

Teacher: How'd you get 42?

Student: I knew that we were adding 7 every time, so I told the calculator to add 7 over and over again by using the constant key. I could keep track of how many sevens were being added by looking at the first number.

Teacher: How does the calculator screen compare with the times table?

Student: The first number is like the first number on each row. The second number is the result when multiplying the first number on the row by 7.

Teacher: Can you think of a multiplication sentence for each calculator reading?

Student: Yeah, 1 × 7 = 7, 2 × 7 = 14, and so on.

One of the unbalanced results of the reform movement in mathematics was the idea among some extremists that because of calculators and technology children no longer needed to be able to perform fundamental computations. Not only is such an idea dangerous, it caused the use of calculators and technology in general to be viewed poorly among some mathematics educators and the public. Such a position is also dangerous, particularly considering the role of technology in our society. Children are living in a technological age, and the appropriate use of technology, as shown in the preceding "Conversation in Mathematics," not only bolsters mathematical understanding but also implicitly communicates to children the need to think "technologically" as they prepare for their adult lives.

Data analysis and probability are two of many areas in math that lend themselves to the use of technology. It is important that we give children plenty of opportunity to collect, organize, analyze, and interpret data so that they can learn how to make informed personal decisions. Technology can be an effective tool for accomplishing this. With the level of technology available to us today, students can gather information from the computer and Internet, easily calculate central tendencies, and quickly display data in a variety of graphs. If we are to prepare our students for the technological age, then they need to have quality experiences beginning in elementary school.

PEDAGOGY — *Technology Integrations*

Learning Theory

The *Principles and Standards for School Mathematics* (NCTM, 2000, 24–25) states a clear vision for the use of technology in enhancing mathematical conceptualization:

> **Electronic technologies—calculators and computers—are essential tools for teaching, learning, and doing mathematics. They furnish visual images of mathematical ideas, they facilitate organizing and analyzing data, and they compute efficiently and accurately. They can support investigation by students in every area of mathematics, including geometry, statistics, algebra, measurement, and number. When technological tools are available, students can focus on decision-making, reflection, reasoning, and problem solving.**
>
> **Students can learn more mathematics more deeply with the appropriate use of technology. . . . Technology should not be used as a replacement for basic understandings and intuitions; rather, it can and should be used to foster those understandings and intuitions.**

The *Principles and Standards* (2000, 25) goes on to provide a list of ways that technology can enhance mathematical learning:

- **Calculators and computers (enable students to) examine more examples or representational forms than are feasible by hand, so they can make and explore conjectures easily.**
- **The computational capacity of technological tools extends the range of problems accessible to students and also enables them to execute routine procedures quickly and accurately, thus allowing more time for conceptualizing and modeling.**
- **Students' engagement with, and ownership of, abstract mathematical ideas can be fostered through technology.**
- **Technology enriches the range and quality of investigations by providing a means of viewing mathematical ideas from multiple perspectives.**
- **Students' learning is assisted by feedback, which technology can supply.**
- **Technology offers teachers options for adapting instruction to special student needs.**

Priscilla Norton and Debra Sprague (2001, 5–6) describe the types of learning technology can support (see also Jonassen 1995):

- *Active.* Learners are engaged by the learning process in mindful processing of information and are responsible for the result.

- *Constructive.* Learners can accommodate new ideas into prior knowledge in order to make sense or make meaning or reconcile a discrepancy, curiosity, or puzzlement.

- *Collaborative.* Learners work in learning and knowledge-building communities, exploiting one another's skills while providing social support and modeling and observing the contributions of each member.

- *Intentional.* Learners are actively and willfully trying to achieve a learning objective.

- *Conversational.* Learning is inherently a social, dialogical process in which learners benefit from being part of knowledge-building communities both in and out of school.

- *Contextualized.* Learning tasks are situated in meaningful real-world tasks or simulated through some case-based or problem-based learning environment.

- *Reflective.* Learners articulate what they have learned and reflect on the processes and decisions that were part of the process.

Application to the Learning and Teaching of Mathematics

If you can see the forest through the trees to any degree, you saw mathematical inquiry written all over the developmental rationale for incorporating technology in your mathematics instruction. And by incorporating, we are talking about children putting their hands on the technology in a way that supports their own inquiry. This means that if we are talking about inquiry then we are talking about technology supporting the launch–explore–summarize cycle. In the next three sections, we talk about how you can use technology to enhance the "worthwhileness" of the tasks you present in your launches, to empower children to solve those tasks as they explore, and to facilitate their communication during the summarize stage.

Technologically Supported Tasks During Launch

Powerful launches provide a sense of authenticity to the task or problem that is presented. This is part of the notion of *worthwhile*. Computers can be an excellent way of creating that sense of authenticity through computer-based simulations, games, problem-solving software, and data sources—which may or may not be specifically designed for mathematical learning purposes.

First look at simulations. Many of us have invited our students to "play" the social studies–history simulation *The Oregon Trail.* It is quite difficult to engage in a real pioneer trail traveling experience, but thanks to the com-

puter, students can be placed in a simulated one that can be an effective means for students to experience some trials and difficulties of pioneer traveling. As it turns out, there is a great deal of mathematics inherent in that simulation. When each pioneer company outfits for the trip, it must manage its resources in acquiring needed supplies. Then while traveling, there is a constant report available to the travelers about the distances they travel, the elapsed days of travel, and the status of their supplies.

All of this information is mathematical and provides a rich context for problematic tasks—for example, computing miles per day or graphing elapsed distances per day.

Games are a second way that technology can be used to create authentic tasks to present during your launch. A great game that involves using a calculator to conceptualize place value is called *Broken Keys.* Students are invited to make a certain number appear on the calculator display but are only allowed to use certain keys. For example, grab a calculator and try to make 35,648 appear on the display with only the 1, 0, and + keys.

Problem-solving software creates lifelike contexts in which problem-solving opportunities are provided. For example, *Math Shop* allows students to engage in various computational contexts related to a variety of retail stores.

The Internet provides an almost infinite source of data that is mathematical in nature and therefore can be used in presenting tasks to children. For example, if fifth-grade students are studying earthquakes, they could be invited to visit the Earthquake Hazards Program website of the U.S. Geological Survey, where an updated list of earthquakes and their respective intensities are listed. Children could then be invited to examine that data to look for patterns and make comparisons before displaying their findings.

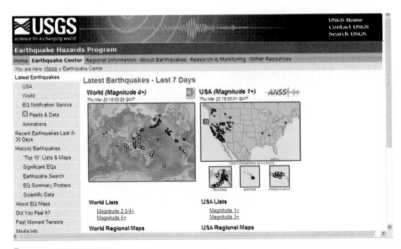

From www.usgs.gov

Using Technological Tools During Explore

Whether a task is presented with the support of technology or not, there are great technological tools to enhance the quality of mathematical exploration.

Suppose you wanted third graders to think about the relationship between addition and multiplication and the role of each of the numbers in a multiplication sentence. The CONST key on an Explorer calculator could be useful. For example, think about 3 × 7, which can be thought of as 3 seven times. On an Explorer calculator, press +3 CONST 0. Then push CONST once, then twice, and then several more times. You can read those screens as 1 three is 3, 2 threes is 6, and so on.

On an Explorer calculator, press ⊕ 3 [CONST] then ⓪ .

a. Then push [CONST] once,

b. then twice

You can read those screens as one 3 is 3, two 3's is 6, etc.

Graphing calculators and spreadsheets can also be useful for older children as they make simple graphs of data. For example, you might invite them to conduct a simple survey about their class members' favorite ice cream flavors. They can create tables and choose various graphing options to display the data. They can even change the graph configurations to examine the effects of scale size, intervals, and so on. See figure 15.1 for an example.

Special Needs

Students with special needs tend to perform exceptionally well with technology, such as a computer, because games and programs give instant feedback to performance. However, the teacher needs to be aware that it may appear that students have mastered certain skills but have actually just memorized the order in which the questions are asked. When assessing understanding, try to use programs that pose random questions.

Flavor	Number
Vanilla	7
Strawberry	8
Chocolate	10
Mint chocolate chip	5

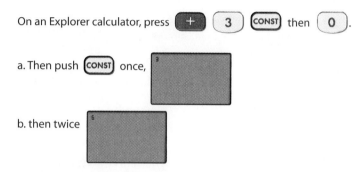

Figure 15.1. Using technology to display data collected in class.

Another source of technological support for student exploration is virtual manipulatives. A great resource for these that is free of charge is the National Library of Virtual Manipulatives website.

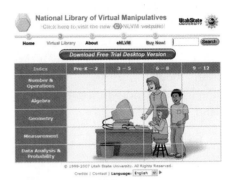

Reprinted by permission of Utah State University and National Science Foundation.

Here is a list of the manipulatives available from the website in data analysis and probability for elementary children:

- *Bar Chart.* Create a bar cart showing quantities or percentages by labeling columns and clicking values.
- *Box Model.* Randomly select and display letters drawn from a box.
- *Coin Tossing.* Explore probability concepts by simulating repeated coin tosses.
- *Hamlet Happens.* Verify that rare events happen by drawing letters from a box.
- *Histogram.* Summarize data using a histogram graph.
- *Loan Calculator.* Explore how to pay off a loan and how interest affects payment.
- *Pie Chart.* Explore percentages and fractions using pie charts.
- *Savings Calculator.* Explore how savings, with or without regular deposits, grow over time.
- *Spinners.* Work with spinners to learn about numbers and probabilities.
- *Stick or Switch.* Investigate probabilities for sticking with a decision or switching.

Here is a page that promotes two different pictorial representations of fractions:

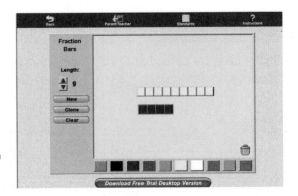

Reprinted by permission of Utah State University and National Science Foundation.

In this case, children can make sense of the measurement division of fractions by counting the number of yellow halves that fit into ⅞, using the number line to help determine the fractional part of the answer.

To use these virtual manipulatives in your teaching, simply make them available to children as one of their possible tools as they explore the problem you presented in your launch.

A second source of virtual manipulatives that also provides problematic tasks is the NCTM Illuminations website.

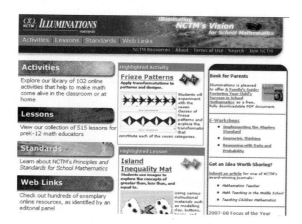

Here is a page that provides both virtual manipulatives and tasks as children explore the notion of combinations.

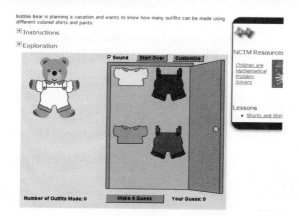

As children explore the number of outfits possible by matching shirts and shorts, they develop an important conceptualization of multiplication.

Using Technological Tools During Summarize

All technological tools discussed in the previous section would also be useful during the summarize stage of your lesson for at least two reasons: First, if a child used a technological tool to solve the problem, she would probably need to use the same tool to communicate and justify the strategy used. Second, you may want to invite all children to engage themselves in that strategy by inviting them to use the same tool the sharing child used.

If you think about the summarize stage of your lesson as a series of presentations, then it is easy to see how technology, particularly authoring systems and multimedia, would be useful in enhancing children's sharing. For example, you might place students in groups during the explore stage to solve a problem together and then invite them to create a poster to describe their thinking. You should then consider inviting them to create a simple PowerPoint or Keynote presentation, or even a word processing document with large fonts, that includes graphical representations. Such presentations would make great additions to a child's mathematics portfolio.

WebQuests: Tools for Supporting All Inquiry

No technology chapter would be complete without a reference to WebQuests. For ready-made WebQuests, try one of these two sites:

http://bestwebquests.com

http://webquest.org/index.php

What are WebQuests? The second website, housed at San Diego State University, describes WebQuests in this way:

> **A WebQuest is an inquiry-oriented lesson format in which most or all the information that learners work with comes from the Web. The model was developed by Bernie Dodge at San Diego State University in February 1995, with early input from SDSU/Pacific Bell Fellow Tom March, the Educational Technology staff at San Diego Unified School District, and waves of participants each summer at the Teach the Teachers Consortium.**
>
> **Since those beginning days, tens of thousands of teachers have embraced WebQuests as a way to make good use of the Internet while engaging their students in the kinds of thinking that the 21st century requires. The model has spread around the world, with special enthusiasm in Brazil, Spain, China, Australia, and Holland.**

Comprehension Check

■ List some different technological tools that can be integrated into the math lesson.

CONTENT *Data Analysis and Probability*

● Big Ideas and Focal Points

Some of the bigger ideas specific to data analysis and probability, as defined by Randall Charles (2005, 20–21), are as follows:

- *Data Collection.* Some questions can be answered by collecting and analyzing data. The question to be answered determines the data that needs to be collected and how best to collect it.
- *Data Representation.* Data can be represented visually using tables, charts, and graphs. The type of data determines the best choice of visual representation.
- *Data Distribution.* Special numerical measures describe the center and spread of numerical data sets.
- *Chance.* The chance of an event occurring can be described numerically by a number between zero and one inclusive and can be used to make predictions about other events.

NCTM FOCAL POINTS

Kindergarten	First Grade	Second Grade	Third Grade
Children sort objects and use one or more attributes to solve problems. Counting is used when comparing data collected.	Children represent discrete data in picture and bar graphs, which involves counting and comparisons.		Students use computation to represent and analyze data, and they solve problems by using frequency tables, bar graphs, picture graphs, and line plots.
Fourth Grade	**Fifth Grade**	**Sixth Grade**	
Students continue to solve problems by using frequency tables, bar graphs, picture graphs, and line plots; they also incorporate place-value knowledge to create stem-and-leaf plots.	Students apply their understanding of whole numbers, fractions, and decimals as they construct and analyze double-bar and line graphs and use ordered pairs on coordinate grids.		

Reprinted with permission from *Curriculum Focal Points for Prekindergarten Through Grade 8 Mathematics: A Quest for Coherence*, copyright 2006 by the National Council of Teachers of Mathematics. All rights reserved.

According to NCTM's *Principles and Standards* (2000, 48), all students from prekindergarten to grade 12 should be able to do the following:

- Formulate questions that can be addressed with data and collect, organize, and display relevant data to answer them.
- Select and use appropriate statistical methods to analyze data.
- Develop and evaluate inferences and predictions based on data.
- Understand and apply basic concepts of probability.

The Focal Points table details the NCTM focal points related to data analysis and probability throughout the elementary grades.

It is interesting to note that there is nothing specified by the NCTM for second and sixth grades. This does not mean that data is not taught in these grades; rather, skills from previous grades are reinforced and expanded upon at these grade levels.

Data Analysis

What Is Statistics?

According to *The Merriam-Webster Dictionary* (2008), *statistics* is a branch of mathematics dealing with the collection, analysis, interpretation, and presentation of masses of numerical data. The data to be collected comes from real-life questions and problems to be answered. The way data is presented can influence the way it is interpreted. Oftentimes, the presentation of data is exaggerated to persuade the reader to draw certain conclusions.

B-day Chart

Early Experiences with Analyzing Data

Sorting and Classifying Data

Children as young as prekindergarten begin analyzing data through sorting and classifying activities. Small children begin by sorting by one or more attributes. An *attribute* describes a property of an object, like red, round, or hot. We want children not only to notice and sort by attributes but also to be able to articulate these attributes when describing their groups. These activities help them notice and compare how a group of objects are the same or different and develop flexibility in their reasoning skills. "Children need to learn to categorize things in different ways in order to learn to make sense of real-world data" (Van de Walle 2004, 389).

The earliest experiences should include a set of objects for which the attributes are clear. Commercially produced attribute sets have objects that can be sorted by shape, color, size, or thickness. Alternatively, attribute cards can easily be created by teachers. Students begin by sorting by one attribute, but different students may choose to sort by different attributes (figures 15.2 and 15.3). When sharing their results, students should explain how they sorted. At this early stage, the teacher may need to begin modeling how to describe what has been sorted. This helps students think of different ways in which objects can be classified.

"I sorted my shapes by size: medium, large, and small."

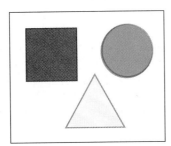 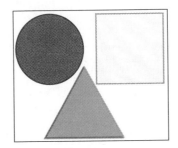 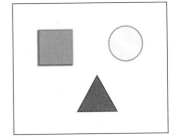

Figure 15.2. An attribute sort by size.

"I sorted my shapes by color: red, blue, and yellow."

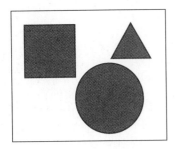 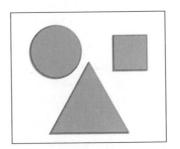 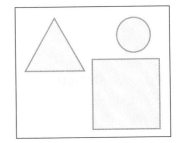

Figure 15.3. An attribute sort by color.

Later, we want students sorting objects for which the attributes are not so clear. Have you ever dumped out a junk drawer with the intention of cleaning it out? Chances are that you had to think about how you were going to sort the items in that drawer so that it could be organized. Taking a box in the classroom where the toys are mixed up and giving the children the task of sorting them and then articulating the reason for their sort helps develop higher-level thinking skills. As students become more familiar with reading genres, the classroom library could be dumped out periodically throughout the year and re-sorted by the students. In the beginning, this may just look like fiction and nonfiction. By the end of the year, children may be sorting into many different genre types.

Students should also be given experiences of finding items that do not belong and articulating why. For example, consider the following:

F   H   I   G   L

Which one does not belong, and why? One might argue that the "G" does not belong because it is not composed of all straight lines. Another might argue that the "I" does not belong because it is a vowel and the rest are consonants.

A fun game for children is to play *Guess My Rule.* This is where the teacher decides on an attribute he is going to use to sort but does not tell the class. The teacher begins sorting the objects into groups based on the secret attribute and then takes the next object and asks the students where they think it should go and why. This game is most engaging when the students are the ones to be sorted. The teacher might decide to sort based on an article of clothing, gender, hair color, and so on.

Venn diagrams are ways to classify information using more than one attribute. Objects that share more than one characteristic can be categorized in overlapping circles. Objects outside the circles do not fit any category (figure 15.4).

As the focus shifts from physical attributes to numerical data, students begin to shift the organization of their data from piles to rows, or towers, where they notice that the objects are more easily compared for numerical relation-

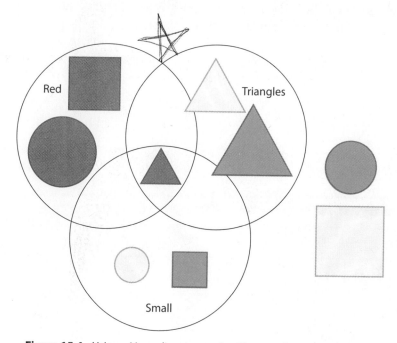

Figure 15.4. Using a Venn diagram to classify more than one attribute.

ships. In *Mathematics Their Way* (1995, 143), Mary Baratta-Lorton gives us a clear hierarchy of how young children develop the ability to read and organize data into graphs.

Type of Graph	Number of Groups Compared
Real graph	Compare two groups
	Compare three groups
Picture graph	Compare two groups
	Compare three groups
Real graph	Compare four groups
Picture graph	Compare four groups
Symbolic graph	Compare two groups
	Compare three groups
	Compare four groups

Real graphs are made when objects are used. Suppose that the class wants to compare how many boys and girls are in the class. They would get up and form two lines and talk about whether there are any girls or boys without a partner. If they wanted to take their tub of small animals and compare how many are four-legged compared to two-legged animals, they would make two rows of each and compare the lengths.

Young children, however, do not always have one-to-one correspondence or conservation of number, so it is essential that work mats be used for placing the objects. They would place one object in a predrawn square on the mat. When children make rows of objects without a work mat, one row may be more compacted than another, causing one row to look longer than it really is (figure 15.5).

Putting tape down on the rug can create a large enough mat for children to stand in or to use to compare large objects.

Picture graphs help students make the connection between an object and a more abstract symbol. The pictures that children can identify most are those of themselves. Many teachers in the primary years have students place their pictures on a daily graph, such as attendance, lunch count, or activity choice. These topics are meaningful to the students, and they stimulate frequent discussion on the relationships of the different groups.

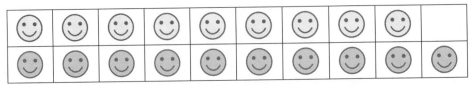

Figure 15.5. Comparing data with and without a work mat.

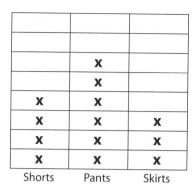 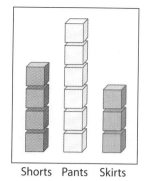

Figure 15.6. Symbolic graphs.

Symbolic graphs are harder for our youngest students to interpret because they have to understand that one abstract object or mark represents a different concrete object. An example of symbols would be an X, tally, cube, or written name (figure 15.6). Careful attention needs to be made to be sure that students are properly making the connections between the symbol and what it is representing; otherwise, in the head of a child, she may just be comparing groups of Xs or different-colored blocks.

Language Tip

The terms that the teacher should emphasize while comparing the different groups are *alike, not alike, different, same, longer, shorter, more than, less than, one more or one less than,* **and** *difference.* **These comparing words are difficult for all children and even more so for English-language learners. The language needs to be modeled by the teacher, and he needs to demand its use by the students by setting up the situation to use it.**

Collecting Data

Data collection procedures should be modeled in the classroom from an early age. Many teachers have a specified area in their classroom where they post a question for data collection purposes. This is typically done weekly throughout the year but may be more frequent if the class is studying data analysis and graphing. One quick method for colleting the data is for students to write their name on a sticky note and place it on the corresponding choice. They may have a prelabeled clothespin or magnet with their picture on it (figure 15.7). If students know that every Monday, say, there is a new question, then part of settling in to class may be answering that week's question.

Students in all grades should be involved in the process of data collection. If not carefully orchestrated, however, this could be a chaotic event. Students are usually asked to all come up with a different question and then rotate around the room to ask all other students to answer their question. One problem is that children do not know how to make up good questions and students do not have any strategies for how to know that everyone has

Comprehension Check

■ Describe some early experiences children can have to develop their sorting, classifying, and comparing skills.

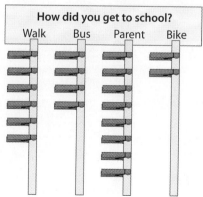

Figure 15.7. Figure graph for which students use clothespins to answer.

answered their question or that they did not ask the same friend twice. Another issue is that upper-grade students are most often witnessed doing these activities and teachers do not adjust the level for higher thinking skills.

Primary students tend to generate questions such as "What is your favorite food?" "What is your favorite TV show?" or "What is your favorite pet?" The problem that arises with these questions is that they do not realize that they have to provide a limited amount of choices or else 25 students may say 25 different things. They should more appropriately ask, "What is your favorite of these three foods: apples, oranges, or carrots?"

Children do not really know what to ask and often get stuck on the "what is your favorite" question. One reason for this is that they do not ask questions to solve real problems. They tend to be doing these activities out of context or just to learn about the process. Perhaps the class should practice generating authentic questions that the students indeed want to solve. These questions may be more superficial at the primary grades and increase in depth in the upper grades. As students get older, they should have experiences with random sampling of students or adults outside their own class. This helps stimulate discussions about whether there is a difference between adult and child, gender, or age group responses within the school. Examples of authentic questions might be as follows:

- What genre of book should our teacher read next?
- What game should we play during P.E.?
- What types of treats should we sell at our class bake sale?
- Where should we go on our next field trip?
- What type of community service projects should we do?

It is also important that children have the opportunity to collect data over time and watch how it changes. This might be keeping track of the weather, the number of lost teeth in the year, or the percentages on their spelling tests.

When collecting data through a poll, children have to decide how they are going to record the responses. In elementary school, this is typically done on a *tally chart* (figure 15.8). Even young students, who do not yet know that the fifth tally lays diagonal over the other four, can make a tally chart of just vertical lines. These tally marks are converted into a *frequency table*, where the tallies are totaled, and then a decision has to be made about how to best record the data. They also have to decide whether their question is going to have a limited or an unlimited amount of choices. For example, the question might be "What is your favorite vegetable?" It might be impossible to list all vegetables that peo-

Favorite vegetables	
Broccoli	///
Tomato	卌 //
Corn	/
Pea pods	
Cucumber	//

Favorite vegetables	
Broccoli	3
Tomato	7
Corn	1
Pea pods	0
Cucumber	2

Figure 15.8. A tally chart and a frequency table after a poll to find out what kinds of vegetables students like.

ple might like. In this case, students may either decide to list some vegetables and put lots of extra spaces for extras that come up during the polling or, if the poll is only among classmates, students may choose to list all their friends' names, write the vegetable next to the name, and later create a tally chart to include all vegetables that were recorded.

Organizing and Presenting Data

Over the course of the elementary school years, children learn how to present their data in different ways. If we look at the preceding example, the tally table is practically a form of a line plot graph and can be easily linked to bar graphs. Later, students learn to create pictographs, line graphs, histograms, circle graphs (or pie charts), and coordinate grids.

Line plot graphs and bar graphs are used to display categorical data. An example of both a line plot graph and a bar graph for the kinds of pets children in a class have is shown in figure 15.9.

Line plot graphs are easily gathered even without frequency tables. Earlier in the chapter, we discussed how teachers can gather weekly data from the class. When students put their name on a sticky note and place it up on the graph, it creates a form of a line plot graph. One difference between a line plot graph and a bar graph is that in a line plot graph there is a one-to-one correspondence between the X and what it represents. In a *bar graph,* one tick mark, or interval, can also represent larger numbers.

Pictographs, or *picture graphs,* are also similar to line plot graphs in that one picture can stand for an amount. Younger children start by using one picture to stand for one response, or tally. In about second or third grade, children begin to allow the picture to represent more than one. In the preceding pet example, a picture of one cat would represent one cat. But if the class were to poll their entire grade level, this would cause the graph to be too large and the picture would need to represent more than one. The issues here are whether children are able to skip count and what to do when the number that is being counted by is not an even number. For example, if one picture of a cat represented 4 cats, what happens if there are 10 cats? The child would then have to

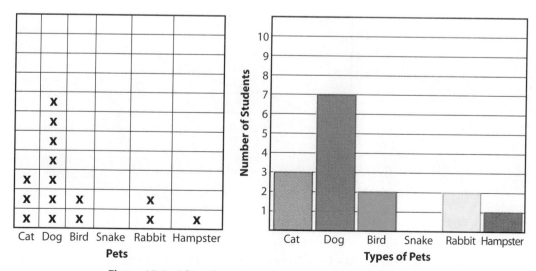

Figure 15.9. A line plot and bar graph for the pets students have.

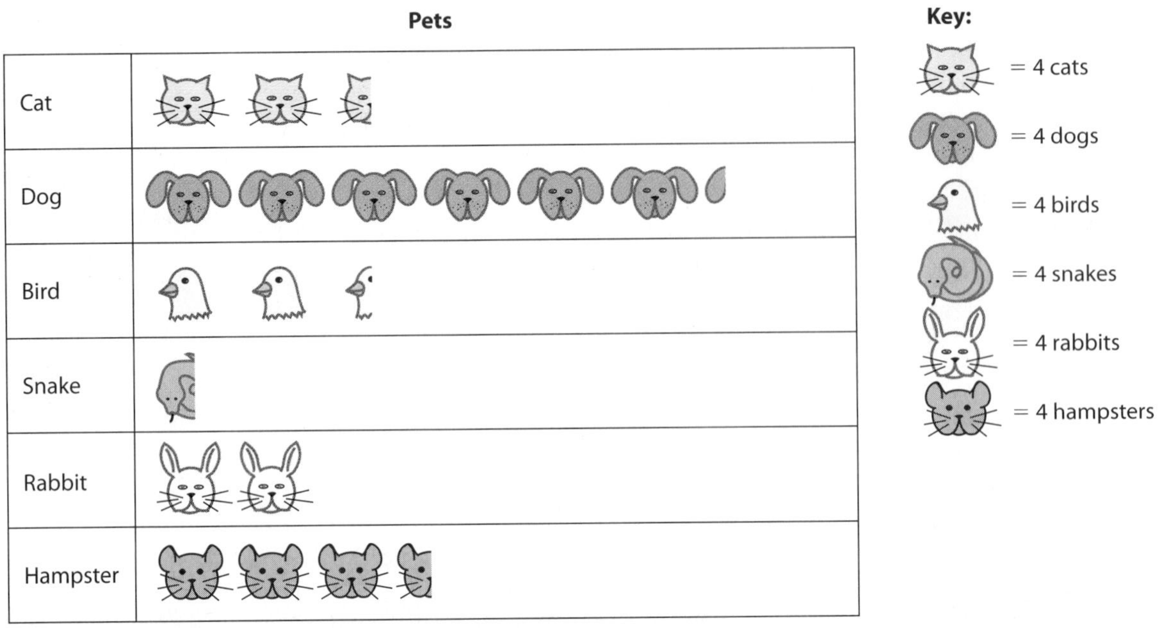

Pets
Cat
Dog
Bird
Snake
Rabbit
Hampster
Key:
= 4 cats
= 4 dogs
= 4 birds
= 4 snakes
= 4 rabbits
= 4 hampsters

Figure 15.10. A pictograph for the pets students have.

draw a half a cat. In general, the area of the picture shown represents the fractional amount intended. So, in this case, one-fourth of a cat would represent one cat (figure 15.10).

A *line graph* is used to represent continuous data. A line graph is often mistaken for merely a graph that connects the dots of discrete data. For example, we cannot create a line graph with the pet example. We cannot merely place a dot on the top value and then connect them, because lines indicate that there are values between the dots. Line graphs can be created for data such as weather, age, and growth, where there are suggested values between each point (figure 15.11).

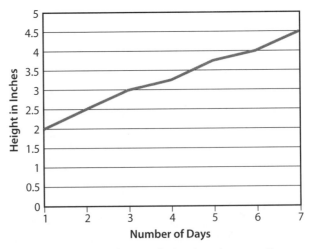

Plant Growth in Inches
Height in Inches
0
0.5
1
1.5
2
2.5
3
3.5
4
4.5
5
1
2
3
4
5
6
7
Number of Days

Figure 15.11. A line graph showing plant growth.

A *histogram* is a graph that is similar to a bar graph but is measuring the frequency of a group of data, such as an age range or a period of time. In a histogram, unlike a bar graph, the bars are always touching because the categories are continuous. For example, if we were graphing the average temperature over the last century, we would possibly have a category for each of two decades, but because the decades continue, the bars would be touching.

The ability to create and interpret a *circle graph*, or *pie chart*, depends on the students' understanding of fractions and percentages. This type of graph shows percentages of a whole, and children often have trouble knowing what is the whole and then creating percentages from their collected data (figure 15.12). Drawing correct slices is also quite difficult, and it is best to present students with circles with tenth slices already drawn. This helps keep students from having to convert the percentages into degrees when using a protractor. Nowadays, it is probably easiest to have students enter their data into a spreadsheet program that creates the graphs for them. Then they only need to manipulate the data to see how it affects the appearance of the graph.

The most common issue students have in creating their own graphs after collecting their data is remembering to label their graphs. If students spent time trying to analyze one another's graph, they would realize that not having labels can cause confusion because there is not enough information. There is also a lot of difficulty choosing the correct interval and knowing how large the graph should be. Students need experiences that help them make good decisions rather than tell them what to do. At first, this might include a lot of trial and error. Students may try counting by twos and realize that they ran out of paper. It may be painful to watch, but it is a necessary step in developing better judgment. It is also important that students understand that the distance between the intervals must be even. They may just label points for the different data and not pay attention to the relationships.

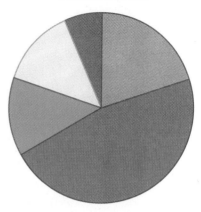

The Pets We Have

Figure 15.12. A pie chart, or circle graph for the pets students have.

Comprehension Check

- Referring to one of the questions you designed in the last section, which graph do you think would best represent the data your students collect? Would they make a graph with a one-to-one correspondence, or do you think they would have to consider using a different interval? What might the considerations be for deciding on the necessary interval?

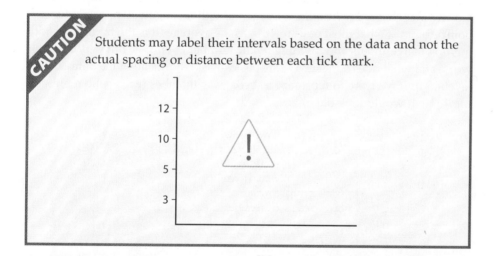

CAUTION Students may label their intervals based on the data and not the actual spacing or distance between each tick mark.

Data analysis and algebra are related, because algebra is a way to describe the relationship between two related variables. An example of this would be rate (feet per second). These variables are recorded and graphed on a *coordinate grid*. An in-depth look at coordinate grids and graphing can be found in chapter 8.

Analyzing and Interpreting Data

Children have to learn that the purpose of graphs is to visually present information in a way that provides a quick picture of the data. They also need to learn that different graphs are different ways to organize the same data and that they may give different perspectives. From the earliest experiences, children need to be asked questions such as "What is this graph trying to tell us?" They need lots of practice interpreting the information on the graph.

We have noticed that, generally, the experience of the child in school is to create simple graphs by manipulating data but not reading or interpreting them. In an average curriculum, children may only have a couple days per academic year upon which they have lessons related to reading a graph. Older children do not usually have experiences collecting meaningful data, displaying it in different types of graphs, and making decisions about which graph would best represent what they are trying to illustrate. Students should be interpreting not only real-world graphs but also one another's graphs. This helps students develop stronger skills related to creating graphs.

Creating and reading double-line graphs and double-bar graphs helps children make comparisons between two sets of data. Even younger children could interpret a double-line graph for weather from two different U.S. cities. They could even draw conclusions regarding which would be a better place to visit during certain times a year. First graders, when recording the growth of their bean plant, could compare the growth rate to that of the plants of other students in the class.

Older students need to begin to analyze the relationships of the numbers in the data. One of the most common analyses in elementary school is that of central tendency, or average. However, you can also expose young students to the idea of averaging by asking them what they think is "typical." In the pet example earlier, a child may say that it is most typical that a student has a dog for a pet because "more kids have dogs." This beginning idea can help support older students when have to find the average through mean, median, or mode.

The *mean* is what most of us refer to as the average. It is the traditional adding up of all numbers and dividing by the number of entries. But why does this work, and what does it mean? We are basically spreading all of the data out and leveling it. If we were to represent test scores with cubes (each cube representing 10%), it would look like this:

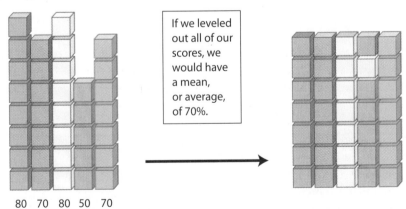

If we leveled out all of our scores, we would have a mean, or average, of 70%.

80 70 80 50 70

If we try to model what is happening with the algorithm, we could add up all the cubes and then split (or divide) them by the number of scores (five), as shown in figure 15.13.

Figure 15.13. Using cubes to model and understand the meaning of average, or mean.

Not all data can level off this nicely. Unless the next test score was 70%, we would have to split some cubes so that they would evenly level out. In real life, averages typically have a fractional answer and students need to understand that the average is not necessarily one of the pieces of data but could be another number altogether. Giving them experiences to understand what average is and guiding them to develop an algorithm, or a way to solve it, helps them remember how to calculate it in the future.

To increase the cognitive demand on problems involving mean, consider the following problems (unknown source):

- The mean weight of 12 boulders is 25 pounds. Adding another boulder increases the mean weight to 29 pounds. How much does the 13th boulder weigh?

- The mean of a list of seven numbers is 45. If two numbers are added to the list, the mean becomes 37. What is the mean of the two numbers added to the list?

- Construct a set of 10 numbers with a mean of seven.

The *median* is another way to describe central tendency. We often hear of the median salary or the median price of a house in a neighborhood. Medians are useful because they are not influenced by *outliers,* or extreme pieces of data. A multimillion-dollar house in the neighborhood of mostly $250,000 houses would skew the data if the mean were calculated. To find this center amount, the pieces of data need to be organized in ascending or descending order. Like the mean, the median does not necessarily have to be one of the pieces of data, although it often is. If there is an even number of pieces of data, then the median falls between the two middle numbers, or the average of the two. The median of the preceding test scores would be:

50, 70, ⟨70⟩ 80, 80

A test score of 0 would have severely affected the mean (58%), whereas the median score would still be 70%.

The *mode* is what children tend to naturally use when they describe "typical." This describes the number or response that occurs most often. In long strings of data, it is most helpful that the pieces are arranged in order to easily see which number appears most often. In the example of the test scores, the 70 and the 80 are both considered the mode because they both occurred more than once and they tied for most often. If every piece of data occurs only once, then it is considered to not have a mode. However, if all pieces of data occur the same number of times, then they are all the mode.

Having the data arranged in order is also helpful when trying to easily identify the *range* of the data. This is the difference between the smallest number and the largest number. The range is useful in determining the spread of something, like test scores, salaries, and house values. It tells you how diverse something is.

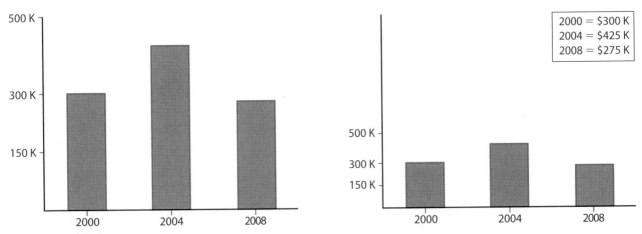

Figure 15.14. How intervals can influence bias.

It is important not only to be able to calculate the mean, median, and mode but also to know which would make sense for a particular set of data or for drawing a certain type of conclusion. The media uses different calculations depending on what kind of bias it wants to create for a set of data. If it wants to make people think that the economy is doing well, then perhaps it would use the mean salary if there are some extremely high salaries to skew the information. The media also creates bias by adjusting the intervals on bar graphs or histograms. A small interval causes exaggerations between bars, whereas a large interval causes the bars to appear much closer (figure 15.14). When do you think it would be advantageous to use either one?

Probability

What Is Probability?

Probability is the way we measure uncertainty and the likelihood that certain events occur. It is data used to drive risk. When we collect data, depending on some factors, such as the tool we use, there is an element of chance that our data is not completely accurate. Therefore, the conclusions that we make in regard to that data may also not be accurate.

Two kinds of probability are mathematical and historical. The mathematical probability of an event occurring is proved through theoretical probability. People who use historical probability look at trends and history when making predictive statements. Examples of historical probability are predicting the weather, making investment choices, opting for a certain medical procedure, and asking parents' permission to participate in an activity. Even young children have experience with this kind of probability in their daily lives at home. Children behave in ways that will most likely let them get what they want. If they have the experience that telling their parents "no" has serious consequences, then they are probably not going to continue doing that. However, if they have experienced that in a store if they keep pestering their parents for a toy they will eventually get it, then they are more likely to continue the behavior.

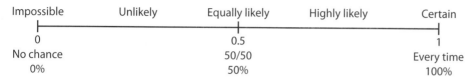

Impossible · Unlikely · Equally likely · Highly likely · Certain

0 · 0.5 · 1
No chance · 50/50 · Every time
0% · 50% · 100%

Figure 15.15. A probability chart.

Theoretical and Experimental Probability

The experience that teachers expect children to receive in elementary school is that of experimental and theoretical probability, with more emphasis on the former than on the latter. To give students lots of experience in testing odds, you first want to have some key tools in a probability kit, including spinners, coins, dice, two-sided counters, color tiles, paper lunch bags, and a box with colored marbles with a corner cut out to act as a peep-hole.

These give students lots of different experiences and allow them to make connections with different tools and apply understandings from one tool to another.

The primary grades focus on possible outcomes using words such as *certain, likely, unlikely,* and *impossible.* The following are some questions to ask young children:

Sample tools to include in a probability kit.

- What is the chance that it will be sunny tomorrow?
- What is the chance of rolling a 2?
- What is the chance that the sun will be up at midnight?

Even though the focus at this time is not yet on the numerical outcome, there should be a large model drawn somewhere in the classroom to resemble the one shown in figure 15.15.

This chart can be added to as students develop vocabulary related to probability and chance. This will also indirectly support the connection between fractions, decimals, and percentages.

Language Tip

A probability chart is a strong support for English-language learners in developing their vocabulary for these concepts.

> **CAUTION** It is important to note that there is a difference between the terms *chance* and *odds. Chance* refers to the number of times the event might happen compared to the total number of outcomes. *Odds* is a ratio of the number of times the event might happen in comparison to the event not happening. Therefore, the chance of getting heads is ½ (or one in two), but the odds are 1:1 (or one to one).

Simple Events

A beginning activity in experimental probability is flipping a coin or two-sided counter. When doing so, students will need to have some way of collecting their data and recording their results, such as a tally chart and bar graph. Students should take the data of their individual tosses and compile it with those of all the members of their group onto a larger tally chart or bar graph. Someone from each group could go up to the board to add the totals to a larger class graph. The discussions should revolve around the differences between the individual, small group and the entire class data and what they think might happen if they were to do 1,000 flips. The theoretical probability begins to surface as a result of these conversations. This is when you might want to teach the convention of how to record this chance as a fraction.

The probability of an event is the number of specified, or target, outcomes divided by the total number of outcomes:

$$P(E) = \frac{\text{Number of specified outcomes}}{\text{Total number of outcomes}}$$

With younger children, we tend to use the language *out of*, as in "one out of two." Later, as their understanding of fractions develops, they can use a fractional notation.

Other beginning activities include the following:

- *Single Spinner.* Provide a variety of spinners divided into different number of parts (some spinners with equal parts and some not) and have students record all their spins. *Hint:* To create a homemade spinner, lift up one end of a paper clip and, from the bottom of the spinner, poke it straight up through the spinner. Place another paper clip over the raised end and spin.

- *Peep-Hole.* Using small boxes or milk cartons, cut a hole in one corner of each box. Place a different combination of colored marbles inside each box, seal it shut, and label the boxes A, B, and so on. Students shake a box and record which marble comes to the corner. After a specified number of shakes, the student has to estimate the color combination of the marbles in each box.

- *Bag of Tiles.* Make several bags of a different combination of color tiles. Students pull a tile, record their pull, and replace it in the bag. After a specified number of pulls, the students have to estimate the color combination of the tiles in the bag.

At the end of these activities, students should be able to make more accurate predictions of similar activities using appropriate vocabulary and begin to tie those predictions with numerical descriptors (3 out of 12 pulls). It is also important to begin conversations about whether they think there are any factors that might affect a particular event. Sometimes students think that one side of the coin might show more often because the picture on one side is heavier than the image on the other. The discussion should begin as a prediction and continue after a large enough sample has been pulled.

Independent and Dependent Events

An *independent event* occurs when one event does not affect another. For example, when two coins are tossed, the result of the first coin does not have anything to do with the result of tossing the second coin. They both have equal chance of getting either heads or tails. A *dependent event* occurs when the first event does affect the second. For example, if there is a bag of six color tiles (three blue, two red, and one green), the probability of pulling a blue tile would be three out of six, or ½. However, if I do not return that tile to the bag, my chances of pulling a blue again change. Now the probability would be ⅖.

Third graders can begin by doing experiments on two independent events, such as tossing two pennies. The challenge is to figure out what the possible outcomes will be so that they can properly record their data. Depending on the

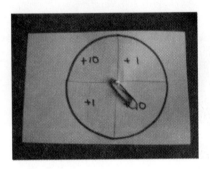
Homemade spinner.

Connecting Probability to Fractions, Decimals, Percentages, and Graphing

We want students to walk away from our classroom understanding the connections that one area of mathematics has with another. When working with theoretical probability, students should be incorporating their knowledge of fractions, decimals, percentages, and graphing. One activity to explicitly bring these together is to take an event and record its outcomes using all these forms.

It is a good idea to play a game for which students have to use their probability skills. One common example is a two-dice toss. In this game, the students have a work mat with the numbers 1–12 written on the bottom. Each student is given 12 tiles and is allowed to place them in any column they wish. They may have more than one in any column. The teacher rolls the dice and announce the sum. If a student has a tile in that column, she may remove it. The student with all tiles removed first wins. Initially, a work mat may look like the one in figure 15.20.

After a couple of rounds, the teacher will notice that students are changing their strategies. Now their mats may look like the one in figure 15.21.

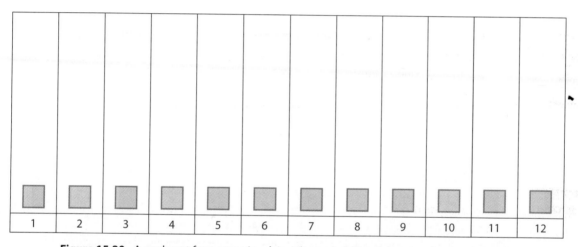

Figure 15.20. A work mat for a game involving the probability of the sum of a two-dice toss.

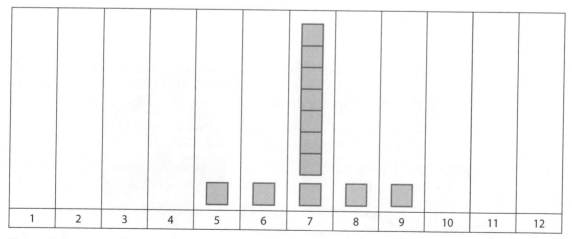

Figure 15.21. A typical work mat for a game involving the probability of the sum of a two-dice toss after several rounds have been played.

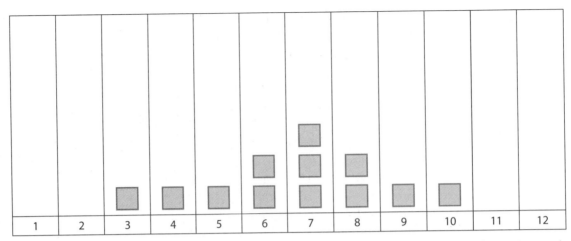

Figure 15.22. A typical work mat resembling more the actual probability for a two-dice toss after many rounds have been played.

If you ask students why they have changed their strategy, they will comment that they realize that 7 is a common sum, so they are putting most of their chips on 7. However, after a while, they realize that although 7 is called often it is not exclusively rolled. After a few more rounds, student's mats begin to look like the one in figure 15.22.

Students quickly come to the conclusion that getting a 1 is impossible and that a 2, 11, and 12 are less likely than the other sums. They still feel like 7 is rolled the most, so they want a few more tiles there.

					1 + 6					
			1 + 5	2 + 5	6 + 2				
		1 + 4	2 + 4	3 + 4	3 + 5	6 + 3			
	3 + 1	2 + 3	3 + 3	4 + 3	4 + 4	5 + 4	6 + 4		
1 + 2	2 + 2	3 + 2	4 + 2	5 + 2	5 + 3	4 + 5	5 + 5	5 + 6	
1 + 1	2 + 1	1 + 3	4 + 1	5 + 1	6 + 1	2 + 6	3 + 6	4 + 6	6 + 5	6 + 6
1	2	3	4	5	6	7	8	9	10	11	12

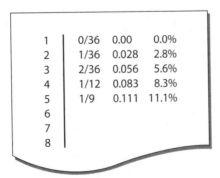

Probablility of sums of two dice

1	0/36	0.00	0.0%
2	1/36	0.028	2.8%
3	2/36	0.056	5.6%
4	1/12	0.083	8.3%
5	1/9	0.111	11.1%
6			
7			
8			

Figure 15.23. Determining the total possible sums for a two-dice toss and recording them as a fraction, decimal, and percentage. These calculations are then used to create a pie chart.

This is a good time to have students chart all the ways to make a sum. On their same mat, they can fill each column with all the ways to make that sum using two dice. When they are done, they can see a bell curve similar to the one some students made on their own with the tiles. Having students record the fraction, decimal, and percentage of the likelihood of getting each sum reinforces their computational skills. The oldest students can continue by creating a pie chart of the probabilities of getting all the different sums (figure 15.23). The pie chart can easily be made in programs such as Microsoft Excel.

Comprehension Check

■ What would the possible outcomes be if we tossed a coin, rolled a die, and spun a spinner with three equal parts colored red, blue, and yellow? Draw a tree diagram showing these outcomes. What would the likelihood be of getting heads, 4, and red?

■ Continue creating Pascal's triangle from figure 5.19. List four different patterns that you notice.

Using Inquiry to Teach Data Analysis and Probability

Attribute Sort

Launch	The teacher provides each partnership with a pile of attribute shapes.
Explore	The teacher asks students come up with their own way to sort the shapes and to explain their sort to a partner using specific vocabulary of size, color, or thickness.
Summarize	As a class, students discuss the different ways they sorted their shapes.

Interpreting Graphs

Launch cycle 1	The teacher displays a bar graph without a title or any supporting labels except for numbers. The teacher asks students what this graph could be telling them.
Explore cycle 1	Partnerships come up with a title and labels to add to the graph.
Summarize cycle 1	Students discuss their ideas, including which ones would be most likely and why.
Launch cycle 2	The teacher displays data in three different graphs. Students are asked to determine which graph is the best representation of the data and why.
Explore cycle 2	Students use previously collected data from surveys and as a small group determine how to best display their data.
Summarize cycle 2	Students discuss which types of graphs they chose for displaying their data and why.

Mystery Bags

Launch	The teacher explains the activity by first distributing partnerships bags of six tiles each and recording sheets. Students are not to peek inside their bags.
Explore	Students pull a tile and record its color on the recording sheet. They put it back and pull again. After every 5 pulls, they make a prediction about the configuration of color tiles in their bag. After 30 pulls, they record their experimental probabilities using fractions, decimals, and percentages. They can also draw a pie chart to show the probability of each pull.
Summarize	Students look inside their bags and compare the actual colors with their predictions. As a class, students discuss the differences between their predictions after 5, 10, 15, 20, 25, and 30 pulls. Did they guess the right color combinations after just 5 or 10 pulls?

CONCLUSION

If you have taken time to explore the options and suggestions of this chapter, then maybe you had a fraction of the fun we had writing it. These technological supports are engaging, exciting, and best of all, they help children learn more mathematics. Research has consistently demonstrated that when properly used, technology enhances mathematical learning in the classroom. Simultaneously, it sends a clear message to children that technology is an important component of mathematical proficiency in our day and age.

The act of collecting and interpreting data should be connected to meaningful questions and activities and lends itself nicely to the use of technology. When students are merely handed 10 numbers for which they must find the mean, median, and mode, they are not able to make judgments about which calculation may be most appropriate for the particular set of numbers because they are not connected to anything. Situations in commercial textbooks are usually disconnected from students' lives, which causes them to become passive in their interactions with them. Science is the real-life application of mathematics and therefore the best place to incorporate data collecting and graphing. When children are trying to find out how something works scientifically, they have reasons to need to collect, record, and interpret data.

Probability is an area where graphs are put to practical use. Through experiments, students can see how data is naturally distributed. Lots of classroom discussion should be centered on the interpretation of results and whether other factors might be playing a role in the outcomes. A thorough understanding of probability and statistics allows students to be able to interpret information they read in the media or on the computer and discern the validity of the conclusions being drawn.

▶ Interview Video with an Eye on Content

Watch some student interviews around data analysis and probability. Note the child's response and what his understanding or misconception is around each area. Think about what the next steps might be for teaching this child.

Focus of the interview. What area of data analysis and probability is being assessed?	
What understandings and generalizations does the student exhibit?	
If you were to teach this child, what would your next steps be?	

▶ Interview a Child

1. Design and conduct a student interview related to a concept of data analysis or probability that is appropriate for the grade level of the student you will be working with. When considering your questions, think of the big ideas and most common misconceptions children have.

2. Write an overall summary about how your student did. Include recommendations you would make for the child's teacher or what would you do with this child if you were to continue to work with him?

▶ Classroom Video with an Eye on Pedagogy

Watch the video segment of the classroom lesson. As you watch, determine which stage of the lesson—launch, explore, or summarize—is being supported by technology. Afterward, decide on the nature of the technology being used and the specific way in which it is used.

1. What stage of the lesson is being supported by technology?

_____

_____

_____

2. What specific technology is being used?

_____

_____

_____

3. How is it used?

_____

_____

_____

▶ Classroom Application

1. Observe your cooperating teacher and note how the teacher incorporates technology into math lessons.

2. Collaboratively design and teach a lesson related to an area in data analysis or probability. Consider how you could incorporate the use of technology into your lesson.

3. Alternatively, collaboratively design and teach a lesson related to any content area discussed in this text that incorporates the use of technology into your lesson.

▶ Resources

Math by All Means: Probability Grades 1–2, Bonnie Tank (1996).

Math by All Means: Probability Grades 3–4, Marilyn Burns (1995).

Navigating through Data Analysis and Probability in Grades 3–5. NCTM (2003).

Lit Link

Literature Books to Support Data Analysis and Probability

Title	Author
Anno's Hat Tricks	Akihiro Nozaki
Berries, Nuts, and Seeds	Diane L. Burnes
Button Box, The	Margarette S. Reid
Chimp Math: Learning about Time from a Baby Chimpanzee	Ann W. Nagda and Cindy Bickel
Drop of Water, A: A Book of Science and Wonder	Walter Wick
Fantastic Book of 1,001 Lists	Russell Ash
Martha Blah Blah	Susan Meddaugh
Phantom Tollbooth, The	Norton Juster
Probability Games and Other Activities: Games of Combinations, Permutations, Predictions, Luck and Chance	Ivan Moscovich
So You Want to Be President	Judith St. George
Tell-Tale Heart and Other Writings, The	Edgar Allan Poe
Ten Sly Piranhas: A Counting Story in Reverse	William Wise
Toys, The	Sarah Holliday
Tikki Tikki Tembo	Arlene Mosei
Wilma Unlimited: How Wilma Rudolph Became the World's Fastest Woman	Kathleen Krull

▶ Tech Tools

Websites

NCTM: Illuminations, Web Links—Data Analysis & Probability, http://illuminations.nctm.org/WebResourceList.aspx?Ref=2&Std=4&Grd=0

National Library of Virtual Manipulatives, http://nlvm.usu.edu/en/nav/vlibrary.html

Census Bureau, http://www.census.gov

NCTM: Assessing and Investigating Data Using the World Wide Web, http:// standards.nctm.org/document/eexamples/chap5/5.4/index.htm

NCTM: Comparing Properties of the Mean and the Median through the Use of Technology, http://standards.nctm.org/document/eexamples/chap6/6.6/index .htm

Graphing the Weather, http://score.kings.k12.ca.us/lessons/graphweather.html

National Security Agency: Data Analysis Learning Units, http://www.nsa .gov/teachers/teach00011.cfm

Software

Math Shop, Scholastic

The Oregon Trail, The Learning Company

PHASES

Emergent Phase	Matching Phase	Quantifying Phase
• Know numbers signify quantity • Rote count to 10 with words in order • Identify by sight 1–5 objects • Begin to write numerals • Know numerals are different from letters • Know more, less, and same and that a change results in either bigger or smaller (but not know by how much)	**Counting** • Rote count to double digits • Count lots of collections • Know one-to-one correspondence — Keep track through moving, touching, and then pointing — Get a particular quantity — Remember how many after counting • Count all or use direct modeling in problem solving • Know the cardinality principle (last number counted stands for total amount; it is not just a label) • Know what things can be discretely counted versus continually counted **Number Relationships** • Know more, less, and same • Figure out how many more or less or how many to make the same amount • Know one more and one less without counting • Know spatial relationships and beginning estimation • Relate one number to another (when changing numbers) — Know if more need to be added or take away — Put more or remove extras	**Counting** • Count on, count back • Skip count (in groups) — Realize repeated addition or subtraction results in same total as counting by ones • Know ordinal numbers **Number Relationships** • Develop a sense of quantity and reasonableness • Understand part–part–whole relationships — Know numbers are within numbers — Understand number combinations • Combine by using relationships, using doubles and near doubles, and just knowing • Use benchmarks of 5 and 10 • Know how many to add or subtract (to change a number) • Relate one number to another — Know how many to add or subtract • Have conservation of number • Write number sentences (equations) • Understand greater than, less than, and equal to • Understand that when dealing all groups are the same • Use concrete materials to model tens and ones and to add tens

(Continued on following page.)

Partitioning Phase	Factoring Phase	Operating Phase
Counting • Count by tens starting with any number (e.g., 34) • Skip count while keeping track of number of groups counted (double counting) **Number Relationships** • Use part–part–whole relationships without seeing objects • Know any number is made with other numbers • Understand and use inverse operations for addition and subtraction • Compare whole numbers using patterns that do not concretely represent amounts (e.g., 100 chart) **Numbers as Tens and Ones** • Recognize numbers as tens and ones • Combine and separate tens and ones —— Tell how many to make the next 10 —— Add by making tens —— Subtract by breaking apart tens and restructuring remainder into tens and ones • Know 10 more or less for any two-digit number • Know place value for two-digit numbers • Know and use expanded notation **Fractional Understanding** • Believe equal halves can look different • Divide numbers into fractions • Know ⅓ is greater than ¼	**Numbers as Hundreds, Tens, and Ones** • Know place value for three-digit numbers and larger • Read, write, and say whole numbers beyond thousands **Multiplication and Division** • Use arrays to represent multiplication • Understand inverse operation for multiplication and division • Decompose and recompose factors without changing quantity • Understand and use the commutative property of multiplication • Think additively and multiplicatively • Understand different models for division • Use other language to interpret $\times$ and $\div$ signs (*groups of, shared by,* etc.) **Fractional Understanding** • Represent fractions with models and pictures and compare their like and unlike denominators • Split fractions and decimals into whole and parts • Relate fractions to division	**Counting, Place Value, and Number Relationships** • Count by tenths, hundredths, and thousandths over the whole • Use understanding of relationships between successive places to order decimal numbers **Multiplication and Division** • Make multiplicative comparisons and deal with proportional situations • Understand that when multiplying by a factor less than one, the product is smaller • Understand that when dividing by a divisor less than one, the quotient is larger **Fractional Understanding** • See any number can be thought of as a unit that can be repeated or split up a number of times • Represent common and decimal fractions on a number line • Partition decimal numbers • Understand that two fractions are being compared to same whole • Compose and decompose fractions visually or mentally • Write number sentences (equations) for multiplication and division of whole numbers, fractions, and decimals

Compiled from Western Australia's Department of Education and Training (Willis et al 2006) and Kathy Richardson's *Developing Number Concepts* (1999 a–c).

NCTM PROFESSIONAL TEACHING STANDARDS

- Tasks
- Discourse
  — Teacher's role
  — Student's role
  — Tools for enhancing discourse
- Environment
- Analysis

Standard 1
Worthwhile Mathematical Tasks

- *The teacher of mathematics should pose tasks that are based on*
  — sound and significant mathematics;
  — knowledge of students' understanding, interest, and experiences;
  — knowledge of the range of ways in which diverse students learn mathematics;

- *and that*
  — engage students' intellect;
  — develop students' mathematical understandings and skills;
  — stimulate students to make connections and develop a coherent framework
    for mathematical ideas;
  — call for problem formulation, problem solving, and mathematical reasoning;
  — promote communication about mathematics;
  — represent mathematics as an ongoing human activity;
  — display sensitivity to, and draw on, students' diverse background experiences
    and dispositions;
  — promote the development of all students' disposition to do mathematics.

Standard 2
The Teacher's Role in Discourse

- *The teacher should promote classroom discourse by*
  — posing questions and tasks that elicit, engage, and challenge each student's
    thinking;
  — listening carefully to students' ideas;
  — asking students to clarify and justify their ideas orally and in writing;
  — deciding what to pursue in depth from the ideas that students bring up
    during a discussion;

— deciding when and how to attach mathematical notation and language to students' ideas;

— deciding when to provide information, when to clarify an issue, when to model, when to lead, and when to let students struggle with a difficulty;

— monitoring students' participation in discussions and deciding when and how to encourage each student to participate.

Standard 3
Students' Role in Discourse

- *The teacher should promote classroom discourse in which students*
  — listen to, respond to, and question the teacher and one another;
  — use a variety of tools to reason, make connections, solve problems, and communicate;
  — initiate problems and questions;
  — make conjectures and present solutions;
  — explore examples and counterexamples to investigate a conjecture;
  — try to convince themselves and one another of the validity of particular representations, solutions, conjectures, and answers;
  — rely on mathematical evidence and argument to determine validity.

Standard 4
Tools for Enhancing Discourse

- *The teacher, to enhance discourse, should encourage and accept the use of*
  — computers, calculators, and other technology;
  — concrete materials used as models;
  — pictures, diagrams, tables, and graphs;
  — invented and conventional terms and symbols;
  — metaphors, analogies, and stories;
  — written hypotheses, explanations, and arguments;
  — oral presentations and dramatizations.

Standard 5
Learning Environment

- *The teacher of mathematics should create a learning environment that fosters the development of each student's mathematical power by*
  — providing and structuring the time necessary to explore sound mathematics and grapple with significant ideas and problems;
  — using the physical space and materials in ways that facilitate students' learning of mathematics;
  — providing a context that encourages the development of mathematical skill and proficiency;
  — respecting and valuing students' ideas, ways of thinking, and mathematical dispositions;

- *and by consistently expecting and encouraging students to*
  — work independently or collaboratively to make sense of mathematics;
  — take intellectual risks by raising questions and formulating conjectures;
  — display a sense of mathematical competence by validating and supporting ideas with mathematical argument.

Standard 6
Analysis of Teaching and Learning

- *The teacher of mathematics should engage in ongoing analysis of teaching and learning by*
  — observing, listening to, and gathering other information about students to assess what they are learning;
  — examining effects of the tasks, discourse, and learning environment on students' mathematical knowledge, skills, and dispositions;

- *in order to*
  — ensure that every student is learning sound and significant mathematics and is developing a positive disposition toward mathematics;
  — challenge and extend students' ideas;
  — adapt or change activities while teaching;
  — make plans, both short range and long range;
  — describe and comment on each student's learning to parents and administrators, as well as to the students themselves.

Compiled from National Council of Teachers of Mathematics. (1991). *Professional Standards for Teaching Mathematics.* Reston, VA: National Council of Teachers of Mathematics.

CURRICULUM FOCAL POINTS AND CONNECTIONS FOR KINDERGARTEN

The set of three curriculum focal points and related connections for mathematics in kindergarten follow. These topics are the recommended content emphases for this grade level. It is essential that these focal points be addressed in contexts that promote problem solving, reasoning, communication, making connections, and designing and analyzing representations.

Kindergarten Curriculum Focal Points	Connections to the Focal Points
Number and Operations: Representing, comparing, and ordering whole numbers and joining and separating sets Children use numbers, including written numerals, to represent quantities and to solve quantitative problems such as counting objects in a set, creating a set with a given number of objects, comparing and ordering sets or numerals by using both cardinal and ordinal meanings, and modeling simple joining and separating situations with objects. They choose, combine, and apply effective strategies for answering quantitative questions, including quickly recognizing the number in a small set, counting and producing sets of given sizes, counting the number in combined sets, and counting backward.	**Data Analysis:** Children sort objects and use one or more attributes to solve problems. For example, they might sort solids that roll easily from those that do not. Or they might collect data and use counting to answer such questions as, "What is our favorite snack?" They re-sort objects by using new attributes (e.g., after sorting solids according to which ones roll, they might re-sort the solids according to which ones stack easily).
Geometry: Describing shapes and space Children interpret the physical world with geometric ideas (e.g., shape, orientation, and spatial relations) and describe it with corresponding vocabulary. They identify, name, and describe a variety of shapes, such as squares, triangles, circles, rectangles, (regular) hexagons, and (isosceles) trapezoids presented in a variety of ways (e.g., with different sizes or orientations), as well as such three-dimensional shapes as spheres, cubes, and cylinders. They use basic shapes and spatial reasoning to model objects in their environment and to construct more complex shapes.	**Geometry:** Children integrate their understandings of geometry, measurement, and number. For example, they understand, discuss, and create simple navigational directions (e.g., "Walk forward 10 steps, turn right, and walk forward 5 steps"). **Algebra:** Children identify, duplicate, and extend simple number patterns and sequential and growing patterns (e.g., patterns made with shapes) as preparation for creating rules that describe relationships.
Measurement: Ordering objects by measurable attributes Children use measurable attributes, such as length or weight, to solve problems by comparing and ordering objects. They compare the lengths of two objects both directly (by comparing them with each other) and indirectly (by comparing both with a third object), and they order several objects according to length.	

CURRICULUM FOCAL POINTS AND CONNECTIONS FOR GRADE 1

The set of three curriculum focal points and related connections for mathematics in grade 1 follow. These topics are the recommended content emphases for this grade level. It is essential that these focal points be addressed in contexts that promote problem solving, reasoning, communication, making connections, and designing and analyzing representations.

Grade 1 Curriculum Focal Points	Connections to the Focal Points
Number and Operations and Algebra: Developing understandings of addition and subtraction and strategies for basic addition facts and related subtraction facts Children develop strategies for adding and subtracting whole numbers on the basis of their earlier work with small numbers. They use a variety of models, including discrete objects, length-based models (e.g., lengths of connecting cubes), and number lines, to model "part–whole," "adding to," "taking away from," and "comparing" situations to develop an understanding of the meanings of addition and subtraction and strategies to solve such arithmetic problems. Children understand the connections between counting and the operations of addition and subtraction (e.g., adding two is the same as "counting on" two). They use properties of addition (commutativity and associativity) to add whole numbers, and they create and use increasingly sophisticated strategies based on these properties (e.g., "making tens") to solve addition and subtraction problems involving basic facts. By comparing a variety of solution strategies, children relate addition and subtraction as inverse operations.	**Number and Operations and Algebra:** Children use mathematical reasoning, including ideas such as commutativity and associativity and beginning ideas of tens and ones, to solve two-digit addition and subtraction problems with strategies that they understand and can explain. They solve both routine and nonroutine problems. **Measurement and Data Analysis:** Children strengthen their sense of number by solving problems involving measurements and data. Measuring by laying multiple copies of a unit end to end and then counting the units by using groups of tens and ones supports children's understanding of number lines and number relationships. Representing measurements and discrete data in picture and bar graphs involves counting and comparisons that provide another meaningful connection to number relationships. **Algebra:** By identifying, describing, and applying number patterns and properties in developing strategies for basic facts, children learn about other properties of numbers and operations, such as odd and even (e.g., "Even numbers of objects can be paired, with none left over"), and zero as the identity element for addition.
Number and Operations: Developing an understanding of whole number relationships, including grouping in tens and ones Children compare and order whole numbers (at least to 100) to develop an understanding of and solve problems involving the relative sizes of these numbers. They think of whole numbers between 10 and 100 in terms of groups of tens and ones (especially recognizing the numbers 11 to 19 as one group of ten and particular numbers of ones). They understand the sequential order of the counting numbers and their relative magnitudes, and they represent numbers on a number line.	
Geometry: Composing and decomposing geometric shapes Children compose and decompose plane and solid figures (e.g., by putting two congruent isosceles triangles to together to make a rhombus), thus building an understanding of part–whole relationships, as well as the properties of the original and composite shapes. As they combine figures, they recognize them from different perspectives and orientations, describe their geometric attributes and properties, and determine how they are alike and different, in the process of developing a background for measurement and initial understandings of such properties as congruence and symmetry.	

CURRICULUM FOCAL POINTS AND CONNECTIONS FOR GRADE 2

The set of three curriculum focal points and related connections for mathematics in grade 2 follow. These topics are the recommended content emphases for this grade level. It is essential that these focal points be addressed in contexts that promote problem solving, reasoning, communication, making connections, and designing and analyzing representations.

Grade 2 Curriculum Focal Points	Connections to the Focal Points
Number and Operations: Developing an understanding of the base 10 numeration system and place-value concepts Children develop an understanding of the base 10 numeration system and place-value concepts (at least to 1,000). Their understanding of base 10 numeration includes ideas of counting in units and multiples of hundreds, tens, and ones, as well as a grasp of number relationships, which they demonstrate in a variety of ways, including comparing and ordering numbers. They understand multidigit numbers in terms of place value, recognizing that place-value notation is a shorthand for the sums of multiples of powers of 10 (e.g., 853 as 8 hundreds + 5 tens + 3 ones).	**Number and Operations:** Children use place value and properties of operations to create equivalent representations of given numbers (e.g., 35 represented by 35 ones, 3 tens and 5 ones, or 2 tens and 15 ones) and to write, compare, and order multidigit numbers. They use these ideas to compose and decompose multidigit numbers. Children add and subtract to solve a variety of problems, including applications involving measurement, geometry, and data, as well as nonroutine problems. In preparation for grade 3, they solve problems involving multiplicative situations, developing initial understandings of multiplication as repeated addition.
Number and Operations and Algebra: Developing quick recall of addition facts and related subtraction facts and fluency with multidigit addition and subtraction Children use their understanding of addition to develop quick recall of basic addition facts and related subtraction facts. They solve arithmetic problems by applying their understanding of models of addition and subtraction (e.g., combining or separating sets or using number lines), relationships and properties of number (e.g., place value), and properties of addition (commutativity and associativity). Children develop, discuss, and use efficient, accurate, and generalizable methods to add and subtract multidigit whole numbers. They select and apply appropriate methods to estimate sums and differences or calculate them mentally, depending on the context and numbers involved. They develop fluency with efficient procedures, including standard algorithms, for adding and subtracting whole numbers; understand why the procedures work (on the basis of place value and properties of operations); and use them to solve problems.	**Geometry and Measurement:** Children estimate, measure, and compute lengths as they solve problems involving data, space, and movement through space. By composing and decomposing two-dimensional shapes (intentionally substituting arrangements of smaller shapes for larger shapes or substituting larger shapes for many smaller shapes), they use geometric knowledge and spatial reasoning to develop foundations for understanding area, fractions, and proportions. **Algebra:** Children use number patterns to extend their knowledge of properties of numbers and operations. For example, when skip counting, they build foundations for understanding multiples and factors.
Measurement: Developing an understanding of linear measurement and facility in measuring lengths Children develop an understanding of the meaning and processes of measurement, including such underlying concepts as partitioning (the mental activity of slicing the length of an object into equal-sized units) and transitivity (e.g., if object A is longer than object B and object B is longer than object C, then object A is longer than object C). They understand linear measure as an iteration of units and use rulers and other measurement tools with that understanding. They understand the need for equal-length units, the use of standard units of measure (centimeter and inch), and the inverse relationship between the size of a unit and the number of units used in a particular measurement (i.e., children recognize that the smaller the unit, the more iterations they need to cover a given length).	

CURRICULUM FOCAL POINTS AND CONNECTIONS FOR GRADE 3

The set of three curriculum focal points and related connections for mathematics in grade 3 follow. These topics are the recommended content emphases for this grade level. It is essential that these focal points be addressed in contexts that promote problem solving, reasoning, communication, making connections, and designing and analyzing representations.

Grade 3 Curriculum Focal Points	Connections to the Focal Points
Number and Operations and Algebra: Developing understandings of multiplication and division and strategies for basic multiplication facts and related division facts Students understand the meanings of multiplication and division of whole numbers through the use of representations (e.g., equal-sized groups, arrays, area models, and equal "jumps" on the number lines for multiplication, as well as successive subtraction, partitioning, and sharing for division). They use properties of addition and multiplication (e.g., commutativity, associativity, and the distributive property) to multiply whole numbers and apply increasingly sophisticated strategies based on these properties to solve multiplication and division problems involving basic facts. By comparing a variety of solution strategies, students relate multiplication and division as inverse operations.	**Algebra:** Understanding properties of multiplication and the relationship between multiplication and division is a part of algebra readiness that develops at grade 3. The creation and analysis of patterns and relationships involving multiplication and division should occur at this grade level. Students build a foundation for later understanding of functional relationships by describing relationships in context with such statements as, "The number of legs is four times the number of chairs."
Number and Operations: Developing an understanding of fractions and fraction equivalence Students develop an understanding of the meanings and uses of fractions to represent parts of a whole, parts of a set, or points or distances on a number line. They understand that the size of a fractional part is relative to the size of the whole, and they use fractions to represent numbers that are equal to, less than, or greater than one. They solve problems that involve comparing and ordering fractions by using models, benchmark fractions, or common numerators or denominators. They understand and use models, including the number line, to identify equivalent fractions.	**Measurement:** Students in grade 3 strengthen their understanding of fractions as they confront problems in linear measurement that call for more precision than the whole unit allowed them in their work in grade 2. They develop their facility in measuring with fractional parts of linear units. Students develop measurement concepts and skills through experiences in analyzing attributes and properties of two-dimensional objects. They form an understanding of perimeter as a measurable attribute and select appropriate units, strategies, and tools to solve problems involving perimeter.
Geometry: Describing and analyzing properties of two-dimensional shapes Students describe, analyze, compare, and classify two-dimensional shapes by their sides and angles and connect these attributes to definitions of shapes. Students investigate, describe, and reason about decomposing, combining, and transforming polygons to make other polygons. By building, drawing, and analyzing two-dimensional shapes, students understand attributes and properties of two-dimensional space and the use of those attributes and properties in solving problems, including applications involving congruence and symmetry.	**Data Analysis:** Addition, subtraction, multiplication, and division of whole numbers come into play as students construct and analyze frequency tables, bar graphs, picture graphs, and line plots and use them to solve problems. **Number and Operations:** Building on their work in grade 2, students extend their understanding of place value to numbers up to 10,000 in various contexts. Students also apply this understanding to the task of representing numbers in different equivalent forms (e.g., expanded notation). They develop their understanding of numbers by building their facility with mental computation (addition and subtraction in special cases, such as 2,500 + 6,000 and 9,000 − 5,000), by using computational estimation, and by performing paper-and-pencil computations.

CURRICULUM FOCAL POINTS AND CONNECTIONS FOR GRADE 4

The set of three curriculum focal points and related connections for mathematics in grade 4 follow. These topics are the recommended content emphases for this grade level. It is essential that these focal points be addressed in contexts that promote problem solving, reasoning, communication, making connections, and designing and analyzing representations.

Grade 4 Curriculum Focal Points	Connections to the Focal Points
Number and Operations and Algebra: Developing quick recall of multiplication facts and related division facts and fluency with whole number multiplication Students use understandings of multiplication to develop quick recall of the basic multiplication facts and related division facts. They apply their understanding of models for multiplication (i.e., equal-sized groups, arrays, area models, and equal intervals on the number line), place value, and properties of operations (in particular, the distributive property) as they develop, discuss, and use efficient, accurate, and generalizable methods to multiply multidigit whole numbers. They select appropriate methods and apply them accurately to estimate products or calculate them mentally, depending on the context and numbers involved. They develop fluency with efficient procedures, including the standard algorithm, for multiplying whole numbers; understand why the procedures work (on the basis of place value and properties of operations); and use them to solve problems.	**Algebra:** Students continue identifying, describing, and extending numeric patterns involving all operations and nonnumeric growing of repeating patterns. Through these experiences, they develop an understanding of the use of a rule to describe a sequence of numbers or objects. **Geometry:** Students extend their understanding of properties of two-dimensional shapes as they find the areas of polygons. They build on their earlier work with symmetry and congruence in grade 3 to encompass transformations, including those that produce line and rotational symmetry. By using transformations to design and analyze simple tilings and tessellations, students deepen their understanding of two-dimensional space.
Number and Operations: Developing an understanding of decimals, including the connections between fractions and decimals Students understand decimal notation as an extension of the base ten system of writing whole numbers that is useful for representing more numbers, including numbers between 0 and 1, between 1 and 2, and so on. Students relate their understanding of fractions to reading and writing decimals that are greater than or less than one, identifying equivalent decimals, comparing and ordering decimals, and estimating decimal or fractional amounts in problem solving. They connect equivalent fractions and decimals by comparing models to symbols and locating equivalent symbols on the number line.	**Measurement:** As part of understanding two-dimensional shapes, students measure and classify angles. **Data Analysis:** Students continue to use tools from grade 3, solving problems by making frequency tables, bar graphs, picture graphs, and line plots. They apply their understanding of place value to develop and use stem-and-leaf plots.
Measurement: Developing an understanding of area and determining the areas of two-dimensional shapes Students recognize area as an attribute of two-dimensional regions. They learn that they can quantify area by finding the total number of same-sized units of area that cover the shape without gaps or overlaps. They understand that a square that is one unit on a side is the standard unit for measuring area. They select appropriate units, strategies (e.g., decomposing shapes), and tools for solving problems that involve estimating or measuring area. Students connect area measurement to the area model that they used to represent multiplication, and they use this connection to justify the formula for the area of a rectangle.	**Number and Operations:** Building on their work in grade 3, students extend their understanding of place value and ways of representing numbers to 100,000 in various contexts. They use estimation in determining the relative sizes of amounts or distances. Students develop understandings of strategies for multidigit division by using models that represent division as the inverse of multiplication, as partitioning, or as successive subtraction. By working with decimals, students extend their ability to recognize equivalent fractions. Students' earlier work in grade 3 with models of fractions and multiplication and division facts supports their understanding of techniques for generating equivalent fractions and simplifying fractions.

CURRICULUM FOCAL POINTS AND CONNECTIONS FOR GRADE 5

The set of three curriculum focal points and related connections for mathematics in grade 5 follow. These topics are the recommended content emphases for this grade level. It is essential that these focal points be addressed in contexts that promote problem solving, reasoning, communication, making connections, and designing and analyzing representations.

Grade 5 Curriculum Focal Points	Connections to the Focal Points
Number and Operations and Algebra: Developing an understanding of and fluency with division of whole numbers Students apply their understanding of models for division, place value, properties, and the relationship of division to multiplication as they develop, discuss, and use efficient, accurate, and generalizable procedures to find quotients involving multidigit dividends. They select appropriate methods and apply them accurately to estimate quotients or calculate them mentally, depending on the context and numbers involved. They develop fluency with efficient procedures, including the standard algorithm, for dividing whole numbers; understand why the procedures work (on the basis of place value and properties of operations); and use them to solve problems. They consider the context in which a problem is situated to select the most useful form of the quotient for the solution, and they interpret it appropriately.	**Algebra:** Students use patterns, models, and relationships as contexts for writing and solving simple equations and inequalities. They create graphs of simple equations. They explore prime and composite numbers and discover concepts related to the addition and subtraction of fractions as they use factors and multiples, including applications of common factors and common multiples. They develop an understanding of the order of operations and use it for all operations. **Measurement:** Students' experiences connect their work with solids and volume to their earlier work with capacity and weight or mass. They solve problems that require attention to both approximation and precision of measurement. **Data Analysis:** Students apply their understanding of whole numbers, fractions, and decimals as they construct and analyze double-bar and line graphs and use ordered pairs on coordinate grids. **Number and Operations:** Building on their work in grade 4, students extend their understanding of place value to numbers through millions and millionths in various contexts. They apply what they know about multiplication of whole numbers to larger numbers. Students also explore contexts that they can describe with negative numbers (e.g., situations of owing money or measuring elevations above and below sea level).
Number and Operations: Developing an understanding of and fluency with addition and subtraction of fractions and decimals Students apply their understandings of fractions and fraction models to represent the addition and subtraction of fractions with unlike denominators as equivalent calculations with like denominators. They apply their understandings of decimal models, place value, and properties to add and subtract decimals. They develop fluency with standard procedures for adding and subtracting fractions and decimals. They make reasonable estimates of fraction and decimal sums and differences. Students add and subtract fractions and decimals to solve problems, including problems involving measurement.	
Geometry, Measurement, and Algebra: Describing three-dimensional shapes and analyzing their properties, including volume and surface area Students relate two-dimensional shapes to three-dimensional shapes and analyze properties of polyhedral solids, describing them by the number of edges, faces, or vertices, as well as the types of faces. Students recognize volume as an attribute of three-dimensional space. They understand that they can quantify volume by finding the total number of same-sized units of volume that they need to fill the space without gaps or overlaps. They understand that a cube that is one unit on an edge is the standard unit for measuring volume. They select appropriate units, strategies, and tools for solving problems that involve estimating or measuring volume. They decompose three-dimensional shapes and find surface areas and volumes of prisms. As they work with surface area, they find and justify relationships among the formulas for the areas of different polygons. They measure necessary attributes of shapes to use area formulas to solve problems.	

CURRICULUM FOCAL POINTS AND CONNECTIONS FOR GRADE 6

The set of three curriculum focal points and related connections for mathematics in grade 6 follow. These topics are the recommended content emphases for this grade level. It is essential that these focal points be addressed in contexts that promote problem solving, reasoning, communication, making connections, and designing and analyzing representations.

Grade 6 Curriculum Focal Points	Connections to the Focal Points
Number and Operations: Developing an understanding of and fluency with multiplication and division of fractions and decimals Students use the meanings of fractions, multiplication and division, and the inverse relationship between multiplication and division to make sense of procedures for multiplying and dividing fractions and explain why they work. They use the relationship between decimals and fractions, as well as the relationship between finite decimals and whole numbers (i.e., a finite decimal multiplied by an appropriate power of 10 is a whole number), to understand and explain the procedures for multiplying and dividing decimals. Students use common procedures to multiply and divide fractions and decimals efficiently and accurately. They multiply and divide fractions and decimals to solve problems, including multistep problems and problems involving measurement.	**Number and Operations:** Students' work in dividing fractions shows them that they can express the result of dividing two whole numbers as a fraction (viewed as parts of a whole). Students extend their work in grade 5 with division of whole numbers to give mixed number and decimal solutions to division problems with whole numbers. They recognize that ratio tables not only derive from rows in the multiplication table but also connect with equivalent fractions. Students distinguish multiplicative comparisons from additive comparisons.
Number and Operations: Connecting ratio and rate to multiplication and division Students use simple reasoning about multiplication and division to solve ratio and rate problems (e.g., "If 5 items cost \$3.75 and all items are the same price, then I can find the cost of 12 items by first dividing \$3.75 by 5 to find out how much one item costs and then multiplying the cost of a single item by 12"). By viewing equivalent ratios and rates as deriving from, and extending, pairs of rows (or columns) in the multiplication table, and by analyzing simple drawings that indicate the relative sizes of quantities, students extend whole number multiplication and division to ratios and rates. Thus, they expand the repertoire of problems that they can solve by using multiplication and division, and they build on their understanding of fractions to understand ratios. Students solve a variety of problems involving ratios and rates.	**Algebra:** Students use the commutative, associative, and distributive properties to show that two expressions are equivalent. They also illustrate properties of operations by showing that two expressions are equivalent in a given context (e.g., determining the area in two different ways for a rectangle whose dimensions are $x + 3$ by 5). Sequences, including those that arise in the context of finding possible rules for patterns of figures or stacks of objects, provide opportunities for students to develop formulas. **Measurement and Geometry:** Problems that involve areas and volumes, calling on students to find areas or volumes from lengths or to find lengths from volumes or areas and lengths, are especially appropriate. These problems extend the students' work in grade 5 on area and volume and provide a context for applying new work with equations.
Algebra: Writing, interpreting, and using mathematical expressions and equations Students write mathematical expressions and equations that correspond to given situations, they evaluate expressions, and they use expressions and formulas to solve problems. They understand that variables represent numbers whose exact values are not yet specified, and they use variables appropriately. Students understand that expressions in different forms can be equivalent, and they can rewrite an expression to represent a quantity in a different way (e.g., to make it more compact or to feature different information). Students know that the solutions of an equation are the values of the variables that make the equation true. They solve simple one-step equations by using number sense, properties of operations, and the idea of maintaining equality on both sides of an equation. They construct and analyze tables (e.g., to show quantities that are in equivalent ratios), and they use equations to describe simple relationships (e.g., $3x = y$) shown in a table.	

abstract A developmental stage related to representation in which a child can use abstract symbols to support thinking.

accommodate Making a new category in a schema for new information.

accuracy The student uses careful recording, a knowledge of basic number combinations, and concern for double-checking results.

additive principle Number systems with this principle have digits that can be added together to determine the quantity.

algorithm A set of rules for solving a particular kind of problem.

alternative algorithm Usually an invented algorithm that is different from the standard algorithm.

alternative assessment An assessment consisting of newer alternatives, such as open-ended questions or performance.

assimilate Fitting a new idea into an existing schema.

backward design Beginning with "the end in mind" by determining the role of assessment throughout the lesson.

behaviorism A psychological position based on the proposition that all things organisms do—including acting, thinking, and feeling—can and should be regarded as behaviors and, as such, can be described scientifically without reference to either internal physiological events or constructs such as the mind.

BICS basic interpersonal communication skills; language proficiency in informal and social settings.

Bloom's taxonomy A way of thinking about, or classifying, objectives according to the level of cognitive complexity they elicit.

CALP cognitive academic language proficiency; language proficiency in academic settings.

cardinality principle The last number counted represents the total number in the set.

compare problem A problem that encourages comparison between two distinct sets.

compensating A strategy in which a child deliberately changes the problem to simpler numbers and then compensates for them at the end.

complex instruction A small group strategy in which students are interdependent within their group and all students are accountable.

composing Combining smaller quantities to compose a larger quantity, such as a ten. Also referred to as *regrouping*.

conceptual knowledge The quality of a student's knowledge of mathematical concepts and ideas.

concrete A developmental stage related to representation in which a child requires solid objects to support thinking.

constant The numerals in the expression that do not change.

constructivism A psychological position that states individual learners must actively "construct" knowledge and skills from the world in which they live.

content goal An objective that describes what the student should know (conceptual and procedural).

context-embedded environment An environment rich in linguistic supports, such as modified speech, print-rich strategies, and total physical response.

context-reduced environment An environment that is more abstract, more formal, and less personal than a context-embedded environment. This often reflects the academic setting.

continuous counting Counting things that cannot be counted discretely.

counting all Counting both sets of numbers (e.g., $3 + 4$ would be counted as, "1, 2, 3, 4, 5, 6, 7").

counting back A backward counting sequence that begins with the larger of a pair of numbers and continues according to the other number (e.g., $8 - 3$ could be counted as "8, 7, 6, 5"). Also referred to as *counting down*.

counting on A forward counting sequence that begins with one of two pairs of numbers and continues according to the second number (e.g., $3 + 5$ could be counted as "3, 4, 5, 6, 7, 8").

counting on to A forward counting sequence that begins with the smaller of a pair of numbers and continues until the second number is reached (e.g., $3 + \_\_\_ = 8$ could be counted as "3, 4, 5, 6, 7, 8," so the number in the blank is 5).

decomposing Taking apart a quantity into two or more component quantities. Also referred to as *regrouping*.

derived fact A problem-solving strategy that involves using a known fact to derive the answer to an unknown fact.

direct instruction Teaching by telling a student what to do.

direct modeling Acting out the situation in a problem to find an answer.

discrete counting Counting things using numbers.

disequilibrium A person's state of mental unbalance because a new idea does not fit into an existing schema.

disposition goal An objective that describes how the lesson improves the student's habitual inclination to see mathematics as sensible, useful, and worthwhile, coupled with a belief in diligence and self-efficacy.

efficiency The student can carry out problems easily, keeping track of subproblems and using intermediate results to solve the problem.

emergent A developmental phase in which skills with numeracy emerge and numbers signify quantity.

equilibrium A person's state of mental balance.

explore After the launch period, students work on the proposed task, either in small groups or with a partner.

flexibility The student knows there is more than one approach to solving a particular kind of problem.

formative assessment An often informal assessment used to inform teachers.

hierarchy of numerical complexity Numbers and operations at which a child is capable of problem solving.

higher-level demand task A task in which a student is doing mathematical procedures, making connections, and exploring relationships among representations.

hypothetical learning trajectory A potential curricular sequence to guide instruction adjusted by the assessment of student thinking.

illusion of learning When a student seems to know and understand but does not.

incrementing A strategy in which the child begins with one of the two numbers in the problem, without having to create it mentally through counting or modeling, then incrementally adds or removes the second number.

informal learning Vygotsky's view that there is some adult intervention in learning but that the child is still in control of the activity.

inquiry instruction The discovery of concepts guided by the teacher.

integer A whole number used to count discrete quantities.

internal chatter The internal talk that we have about what a problem means and how to solve it.

join problem A problem that involves adding additional elements to a given set.

joining all A direct modeling strategy that involves using objects to represent addends and counting the union of two sets.

joining to A direct modeling strategy that involves beginning with an initial quantity and adding objects until a given total is reached.

launch The part of the lesson in which the teacher sets up the task to be explored and all students meet as a group.

lower-level demand task A task in which a student is memorizing and practicing procedures without connections.

manipulative A physical object used to demonstrate a mathematical idea and construct mathematical understanding. Also referred to as a *mathematical tool.*

matching A developmental phase in which a student exemplifies one-to-one correspondence for sharing and counting.

matching A direct modeling strategy that involves creating a one-to-one correspondence between two quantities until the smaller quantity is removed.

mean A measure of central tendency consisting of an arithmetic average.

measurement division A type of division problem in which the number of groups is unknown.

median A measure of central tendency that represents the middle number of a set of data arranged from least to greatest.

missing addend The number that must be added to one given number to equal another given number.

mode The number or response that occurs most often.

multiplicative principle Number systems in which numerals to the left of one another have a greater value, depending on the base. In the base 10 system, each numeral is 10 times greater than the numeral to the right of it (e.g., in 333, 300 is 10 times greater than the 30 to the right, which in turn is 10 times greater than the 3 to the right).

naturalistic learning Piaget's view that the adult role is to provide an interesting environment and the child chooses the activity and actions.

number sense Good intuition about numbers and their relationships.

number system A way a society records and communicates ideas about numbers.

number talk An ongoing, purposeful mathematical routine in which the student is expected to look at numbers, determine how they relate to one another, and make conjectures and generalizations about how the numbers work.

operation sense A deep understanding of the meanings and uses of operations.

ordinal number A number used to tell order or position (e.g., 1, 2, 3 . . .).

partial quotient An algorithm in which the student tries to pull as many groups out of the divisor as possible. The student then subtracts the amount removed from the total and continues pulling out groups until there are no more numbers or only a remainder is left.

partitioning A developmental phase in which a student thinks in tens and ones.

partitive division A type of division problem in which the number in each group is unknown.

part–part–whole problem A problem in which the student examines the relationship between a set and its two subsets.

part–set fraction A type of fraction in which the denominator refers to the number of objects in one whole set.

part–whole fraction A type of fraction in which the denominator refers to one whole object divided into sections.

probability The way we measure uncertainty and the likelihood that certain events will occur.

procedural knowledge A student's knowledge of the symbols used to represent mathematical ideas and knowledge of the rules and procedures for solving mathematical problems.

process goal An objective that describes what the student should be able to do.

Pythagorean theorem The formula to finding the length of the hypotenuse of a right triangle.

quantifying A developmental phase in which a student uses part–part–whole relations for numerical quantities.

range The difference between the smallest and the largest number.

reliability The degree of consistency the results obtained from an assessment possess.

residue Learning that takes place from solving problems.

routine A whole-class, purposefully structured activity that helps children develop procedural fluency, as well as reasoning and problem-solving skills, through meaningful practice.

scaffolding Giving the student just enough supportive information to solve the question without help.

semiconcrete A developmental stage related to representation in which a child requires pictures to support thinking.

separate problem A problem that involves removing elements of a given set.

separating from A direct modeling strategy that involves representing a larger quantity and removing a smaller quantity from it.

social goal An objective that teaches or improves proper social interaction in the mathematics class setting.

standard algorithm The algorithm most commonly used in the United States. Other algorithms are standard in other nations.

statistics A branch of mathematics that deals with the collection, analysis, interpretation, and presentation of masses of numerical data.

structured learning Vygotsky's view that the adult is in control of the learning activity and gives direction to the child's action.

summarize After the launch and explore stages, students get back together as a whole group to discuss their findings and share their strategies, like mathematicians.

summative assessment An assessment administered at the end of the learning.

talk move An intentional move a teacher uses to orchestrate discourse in the classroom.

task An activity that a student engages in during a math lesson.

traditional assessment An assessment consisting of various time-honored techniques, such as short-answer and multiple-choice questions.

trial and error A problem-solving strategy that involves trying various number combinations.

validity The degree to which an assessment measures what the teacher thinks it measures.

variable The unknown quantity that is to be solved for and can change.

WebQuest An inquiry-oriented lesson format in which most or all information that learners work with comes from the Web.

zero pair A number created when a negative and a positive are combined.

zone of proximal development The distance between the most difficult task a child can do alone and the most difficult task a child can do with help.

Ambrose, R., L. Clement, R. Philipp, and J. Chauvot. 2004. Assessing prospective elementary school teachers' beliefs about mathematics and mathematics learning: Rationale and development of a constructed-response-format beliefs survey. *School Science and Mathematics* 104 (2):56–69.

Anderson, G. 1995. *The 22 non-negotiable laws of wellness: Take your health into your own hands to feel, think and live better than you ever thought possible.* New York: HarperCollins.

Australian Association of Mathematics Teachers. 2002. *Standards for excellence in teaching mathematics in Australian schools.* Adelaide, South Australia: Australian Association of Mathematics Teachers.

Bahr, D. L. 2007. Creating mathematics performance assessments that address multiple student levels. *The Australian Mathematics Teacher*, 1 (63):33–40.

Bahr, D. L., and R. Sudweeks. 2008. Teacher-developed mathematics performance assessments in the context of reform-based professional development. *Focus on Learning Problems in Mathematics* 1 (30):12–33.

Bahr, D. L., and S. Truscott. Research in progress. Curricular thinking informed by student thinking in the context of multiplying and dividing fractions.

Ball, D. L. 2006. Definitions Powerpoint.

Ball, J. 2005. *Go figure: A totally cool book about numbers.* New York: DK Publishing.

Baratta-Lorton, M. 1995. *Mathematics their way.* New York: Addison-Wesley.

Barnett-Clarke, C., and A. Ramirez. 2004. Language pitfalls and pathways to mathematics. In *Perspectives on the teaching of mathematics: 66th yearbook*, 56–66. Reston, VA: National Council of Teachers of Mathematics.

Baroody, A., Y. Feil, and A. Johnson. 2007. An alternative reconceptualization of procedural and conceptual knowledge. *Journal for Research in Mathematics Education* 38 (2):115–131.

Barrett, J., G. Jones, C. Thornton, and S. Dickson. 2003. Understanding children's developing strategies and concepts for length. In *Learning and teaching measurement: 2003 yearbook*, 17–30. Reston, VA: National Council of Teachers of Mathematics.

Beldock, D., L. Reggett, and G. Winters. 2005. Teacher observation guide (unpublished program designed for observations of intellectual communities by principals within San Diego Unified School District).

Bell, M., J. Bell, J. Bretzlauf, A. Dillard, R. Hartfield, A. Isaacs, J. McBride, K. Pitvorec, and P. Saecker. 2007. *Everyday mathematics: Student reference book* (5th grade). Chicago: Wright Group/McGraw Hill.

Bickmore-Brand, J. 1990. *Language in mathematics.* Portsmouth, NH: Heinemann.

Blanton, M. L., and J. J. Kaput. 2005. Characterizing a classroom practice that promotes algebraic reasoning. *Journal for Research in Mathematics Education* 36 (5):412–446.

Bloom, B. 1956. *Taxonomy of educational objectives. Handbook I: Cognitive domains.* New York: Longman.

Boulton-Lewis, G. 1987. Recent cognitive theories applied to sequential length measuring knowledge in young children. *British Journal of Educational Psychology* 57:330–342.

Bottage, B. A. 1999. Effects of contextualized math instruction on problem solving of average and below-average achieving students. *Journal of Special Education* 33 (2):81. *Academic OneFile.* Gale. Brigham Young University–Utah. http://find.galegroup.com.erl.lib.byu.edu/itx/start.do?prodId=AONE (accessed September 2007).

Bragg, M. 2006. *History in our time.* Online radio program from the BBC. March 9. http://www.bbc.co.uk/radio4/history/inourtime/inourtime_20060309.shtml (accessed October 2007).

Bresser, R. 2003. Helping English-language learners develop computational fluency. *Teaching Children Mathematics* 9 (6):294–298.

Bresser, R., and C. Holtzman. 1999. *Developing number sense: Grades 3–6.* Sausilito, CA: Math Solutions.

Bresser, R., and C. Holtzman. 2006. *Minilessons for math practice: grades k–2.* Sausalito, CA: Math Solutions.

Brodesky, A. R., F. E. Gross, A. S. McTigue, and C. C. Tierney. 2004. Planning strategies for students with special needs: A professional development activity. *Teaching Children Mathematics* 11 (3):146–154.

Bruner, J. S. 1966. *Toward a theory of instruction.* Cambridge, MA: Belknap Press.

Burns, M. 1994. *Math by all means: Place value grades 1–2.* Sausalito, CA: Math Solutions.

Burns, M. 1995a. *Math by all means: Probability grades 3–4.* Sausalito, CA: Math Solutions.

Burns, M. 1995b. Timed Tests. *Teaching Children Mathematics.* March 1995: 408–409.

Burns, M. 1998. *Math: Facing an American phobia.* Sausalito, CA: Math Solutions.

Burns, M. 2000. *About teaching mathematics: A K–8 resource*, 2nd ed. Sausalito, CA: Math Solutions.

Burns, M. 2001a. *Teaching arithmetic: Lessons for introducing fractions, grades 4–5.* Sausalito, CA: Math Solutions.

Burns, M. 2001b. *Teaching arithmetic: Lessons for introducing multiplication, grade 3.* Sausalito, CA: Math Solutions.

Burns, M. 2003a. *Teaching arithmetic: Lessons for extending fractions, grade 5.* Sausalito, CA: Math Solutions.

Burns, M. 2003b. *Teaching arithmetic: Lessons for multiplying and dividing fractions.* Sausalito, CA: Math Solutions.

Burns, M. 2006. Marilyn Burns on the language of math. *Instructor* April: 41–43.

Burns, M., and R. Silbey. 2000. *So you have to teach math? Sound advice for K–6 teachers.* Sausalito, CA: Math Solutions.

Butterworth, B., and D. Yeo. 2004. *Dyscalculia guidance.* David Fulton Publishers: London.

Campbell, D. 1998. *The Mozart effect.* New York: Avon.

Campbell, P. 1995. *Project IMPACT: Increasing mathematics power for all children and teachers,* phase 1, final report. College Park: Center for Mathematics Education, University of Maryland.

Cardoso, S. H. 2000. Our ancient laughing brain. *Cerebrum: The Dana Forum on brain science* 2 (4). http://www.cerebromente.org.br/n13/mente/laughter/laughter1.html (accessed July 2008).

Carnine, D. 1997. Instructional design in mathematics for students with learning disabilities. *Journal of Learning Disabilities* 30 (2):134–141.

Carpenter, T. P., E. Fennema, M. L. Franke, L. Levi, and S. Empson. 1999. *Children's mathematics: Cognitively guided instruction.* Portsmouth, NH: Heinemann.

Carpenter, T. P., and M. L. Franke. 2001. Developing algebraic reasoning in the elementary school: Generalization and proof. In *Proceedings of the 12th ICMI Study Conference: The future of the teaching and learning of algebra,* ed. H. Chick, K. Stacey, J. Vincent, and J. Vincent, 155–162. Melbourne, Australia: University of Melbourne.

Carpenter, T. P., M. L. Franke, and L. Levi. 2003. *Thinking mathematically: Integrating arithmetic & algebra in elementary school.* Portsmouth, NH: Heinemann.

Carr, M., and D. L. Jessup. 1997. Gender differences in first-grade mathematics strategy use: Social and metacognitive influences. *Journal of Educational Psychology,* 89:318–328.

Carroll, L. 2004. *Alice's adventures in wonderland.* New York: Sterling Publishing Co., Inc.

Casey, B., P. Paugh, and N. Ballard. 2002. *Sneeze builds a castle.* Chicago, IL: The Wright Group/McGraw-Hill.

Casey, B., E. Pezaris, K. L. Anderson, and J. Bassi. 2004. Research rationale and recommendations for spatially based mathematics: Evening the odds for young girls and boys. In *Challenging young children mathematically,* an NCSM monograph series volume 2, ed. C. Greenes and J. Tsankova, 28–39. Golden, CO: National Council of Supervisors of Mathematics.

Casey, M. B., R. Nuttall, E. Pezaris, and C. P. Benbow. 1995. The influence of spatial ability on gender differences in mathematics college entrance test scores across diverse samples. *Developmental Psychology,* 31:697–705.

Casey, M. B., R. Nuttall, and E. Pezaris. 1997. Mediators of gender differences in mathematics college entrance test scores: A comparison of spatial skills with internalized beliefs and anxieties. *Developmental Psychology,* 33:669–680.

Cathcart, W. G., Y. M. Pothier, J. H. Vance, and N. S. Bezuk. 2001. *Learning mathematics in elementary and middle schools,* 2nd ed. Upper Saddle River, NJ: Merrill Prentice Hall.

Cazden, C. B. 2001. *Classroom discourse: The language of teaching and learning,* 2nd ed. Portsmouth, NH: Heinemann.

Chambers, D. L. 1999. Direct modeling and invented procedures: Building on students' informal strategies. In *Reflecting on practice in elementary school mathematics,* ed. Anne R. Teppo. 36–39. Reston, VA: National Council of Teachers of Mathematics.

Chambers, D. L. 2002. Direct modeling and invented procedures: Building on students' informal strategies. In *Putting research to practice,* ed. Donald L. Chambers, 12–15. Reston, VA: National Council of Teachers of Mathematics.

Chapin, S. H., and A. Johnson. 2000. *Math matters: Understanding the math you teach.* Sausalito, CA: Math Solutions.

Chapin, S. H., A. Koziol, J. MacPherson, and C. Rezba. 2003. *Navigating through data analysis and probability in grades 3–5.* Reston, VA: National Council of Teachers of Mathematics.

Chapin, S. H., C. O'Connor, and N. C. Anderson. 2003. *Classroom discussions: Using math talk to help students learn. Grades 1–6.* Sausalito, CA: Math Solutions.

Chapman, C., and R. King. 2005. *Differentiated assessment strategies: One tool doesn't fit all.* Thousand Oaks, CA: Corwin Press.

Charles, R. 2005. Big ideas and understandings as the foundation for elementary and middle school mathematics. *NCSM Journal* Spring/Summer: 9–21.

Charlesworth, R., and K. Lind. 2007. *Math and science for young children.* Clifton Park, NY: Thomson Delmar Learning.

Chase, W. G., and H. A. Simon. 1973. The mind's eye in chess. In *Visual information processing,* ed. W. G. Chase, 215–281. New York: Academic Press.

Civil, M. 1993. Prospective elementary teachers' thinking about teaching mathematics. *Journal of Mathematical Behavior* 12:79–109.

Clark, C. M., and P. L. Peterson. 1986. Teachers' thought processes. In *Handbook of research on teaching,* 3rd ed., ed. M. C. Wittrock, 255–296. New York: Macmillan.

Clark, R. 2003. *The essential 55.* New York: Hyperion.

Clements, D. 1999. Teaching length measurement: Research challenges. *School Science and Mathematics* 99:5–11.

Clements, D. H., and S. McMillen. 1996. Rethinking "concrete" manipulatives. *Teaching Children Mathematics* 2 (5):270–279.

Cobb, P. 1997. Instructional design and reform: A plea for developmental research in context. In *The role of contexts and models in the development of mathematical strategies and procedures,* ed. M. Beishuizen, K. Gravemeijer, and E. van Leishout, chap. 12. Utrecht, The Netherlands: Freudenthal Institute.

Coggins, D., D. Kravin, G. D. Coates, and M. D. Carroll. 2007. *English language learners in the mathematics classroom.* Thousand Oaks, CA: Corwin Press.

Cohen, D. 1987. Behaviorism. In *The Oxford companion to the mind*, ed. R. L. Gregory, 71. New York: Oxford University Press.

Cohen, E. G. 1994. *Designing groupwork: Strategies for the heterogeneous classroom*. New York: Teachers College Press.

Confer, C. (1994). *Math by all means: Geometry grades 1–2.* Sausalito, CA: Math Solutions.

Cooney, T. J., B. E. Shealy, and B. Arvold. 1998. Conceptualizing belief structures of preservice secondary mathematics teachers. *Journal for Research in Mathematics Education* 29:306–333.

Covey, S. 2004. *The seven habits of highly effective people.* New York: Free Press.

Cummins, J. 1979. Linguistic interdependence and the educational development of bilingual children. *Review of Educational Research* 49:222–251.

Cummins, J. 1981. The role of primary language development in promoting educational success for language minority students. In *Schooling and language minority students: A theoretical framework*. Sacramento: California State Department of Education.

Cummins, J. 1984. *Bilingualism and special education: Issues in assessment and pedagogy*. San Diego: College Hill.

Cummins, J. 1994. Primary language instruction and the education of language minority students. In *School and language minority students: A theoretical framework*, 2nd ed., ed. California State Department of Education. Los Angeles: California State University, Los Angeles.

Dacey, L. S., and R. Eston. 1999. *Growing mathematical ideas in kindergarten*. Sausalito, CA: Math Solutions.

De Avila, E. A., and S. E. Ducan. 1981. *A convergent approach to oral language assessment: Theoretical and technical specification of Language Assessment Scales (LAS), form A.* San Rafael, CA: Linguametrics.

de Jong, T., and M. G. M. Ferguson-Hessler. 1996. Types and qualities of knowledge. *Educational Psychologist* 31:105–113.

Doise, W., and G. Mugny. 1984. *The social development of the intellect*. New York: Pergamon.

Duckworth, E. 1987. *The having of wonderful ideas and other essays on teaching and learning*. New York: Teachers College Press.

Dunbar, S. B., and E. A. Witt. 1993. Design innovations in measuring mathematics achievement. In *Measuring what counts: A conceptual guide for mathematics assessment*, ed. Mathematical National Research Council. Washington, DC: National Academy Press.

Dunn, R., and K. Dunn. 1987. Dispelling outmoded beliefs about student learning. *Educational Leadership* 44 (6):55–61.

Ebbinghaus, H. 1885. *Über das gedchtnis. Untersuchungen zur experimentellen Psychologie.* Leipzig: Duncker & Humblot; the English edition is Ebbinghaus, H. 1913. *Memory. A contribution to experimental psychology.* New York: Teachers College, Columbia University.

Ellis, A. B. 2007. Connections between generalizing and justifying: Students' reasoning with linear relationships. *Journal for Research in Mathematics Education* 38 (3):194–229.

English, L., and E. Warren. 1995. General reasoning processes and elementary algebraic understanding: Implications for instruction. *Focus on Learning Problems in Mathematics* 17 (4):1–19.

Ernest, P. 1989. The knowledge, beliefs and attitudes of the mathematics teacher: A model. *Journal of Education for Teaching* 15:13–34.

Falkner, K. P., L. Levi, and T. P. Carpenter. 1999. Children's understanding of equality: A foundation for algebra. *Teaching Children Mathematics* 6:232–236.

Fennema, E., M. L. Franke, T. P. Carpenter, and D. A. Carey. 1993. Using children's mathematical knowledge in instruction. *American Educational Research Journal* 30 (3):555–583.

Ferchmin, P. A., E. L. Bennett, and M. R. Rosenzweig. 1978. Direct contact with enriched environment is required to alter cerebral weights in rats. *Journal of Comparative and Physiological Psychology* 88:360–367.

Firestone, W. A., and R. Y. Schorr. 2004. Introduction. In *The ambiguity of teaching to the test*, ed. W. A. Firestone, R. Y. Schorr, and L. F. Monfils, 1–18. Mahwah, NJ: Lawrence Erlbaum.

Fosnot, C. T., and M. Dolk. 2001a. *Young mathematicians at work: Constructing multiplication and division.* Portsmouth, NH: Heinemann.

Fosnot, C. T., and M. Dolk. 2001b. *Young mathematicians at work: Constructing number sense, addition and subtraction.* Portsmouth, NH: Heinemann.

Fosnot, C. T., and M. Dolk. 2002. *Young mathematicians at work: Constructing fractions, decimals, and percents.* Portsmouth, NH: Heinemann.

Freire, P. 2003. *Pedagogy of the oppressed.* New York: Continuum.

Franco, J. 2005. Isn't English a trip? In *Changing the faces of mathematics: Perspectives on Latinos*, 21–22. Reston, VA: National Council of Teachers of Mathematics.

Fuller, F. 1969. Concerns of teachers: A developmental conceptualization. *American Educational Research Journal* 6 (2):207–226.

Fuson, K. C., M. Kalchman, and J. D. Bransford. 2005. Mathematical understanding: An introduction. In *How students learn: History, mathematics, and science in the classroom*, ed. M. S. Donovan, and J. D. Bransford, 217–256. Washington, DC: National Academies Press.

Gardner, H. 1983. *Frames of mind: The theory of multiple intelligences.* New York: Teachers College Press.

Garnett, K. 1998. Math learning disabilities. *Learning Disabilities Journal of CEC.* http://www.ldonline.org/article/5896 (accessed October 2007).

Garrison, L., O. Amaral, and G. Ponce. 2006. UnLATCHing mathematics instruction for English learners. *NCSM Journal* 9 (1):14–24.

Garrison, L., and J. K. Mora. 2005. Adapting mathematics instruction for English-language learners: The language–concept connection. In *Changing the faces of mathematics: Perspectives on Latinos*, 35–47. Reston, VA: National Council of Teachers of Mathematics.

Geary, D. C. 2004. Mathematics and learning disabilities. *Journal of Learning Disabilities* 37:4–15.

Gibbons, P. 1993. *Learning to learn in a second language.* Portsmouth, NH: Heinemann.

Gibbons, P. 2002. *Scaffolding language, scaffolding learning: Teaching second language learners in the mainstream classroom.* Portsmouth, NH: Heinemann.

Glaser, R., K. Raghavan, and G. P. Baxter. 1992. *Cognitive theory as the basis for design of innovative assessment: Design characteristics of science assessments,* CSE Technical Report No. 349. Los Angeles: University of California, National Center for Research on Evaluation, Standards, and Student Testing.

Grant, T. J., and K. Kline. Developing the building blocks of measurement with young children. In *Learning and teaching measurement: 2003 yearbook,* ed. D. Clements and G. Bright, 46–56. Reston, VA: National Council of Teachers of Mathematics.

Greenes, C., and J. Tsankova. 2004. Artful guidance: The pedagogy of creating powerful mathematical learning environments for young children. In *Challenging young children mathematically.* 2:57–70. Golden, CO: National Council of Supervisors of Mathematics/Houghton Mifflin.

Gregorc, A. F. 1982. *Inside styles: Beyond the basics.* Columbia, CT: Gregorc.

Gregory, G. H., and C. Chapman. 2002. *Differentiated instructional strategies: One size doesn't fit all.* Thousand Oaks, CA: Corwin Press.

Griffin, S. A., R. Case, and R. S. Siegler. 1994. Right-start: Providing the central conceptual prerequisites for first formal learning of arithmetic to students at risk for school failure. In *Classroom lessons: Integrating cognitive theory and classroom practice,* ed. K. McGilly, 25–49. Cambridge, MA: MIT Press.

Gronlund, N. and R. Linn. 1990. *Measurement and Evaluation in Teaching.* 6th edition. Upper Saddle River, NJ: Prentice Hall.

Gunter, M. A., T. H. Estes, J. Schwab. 2006. *Instruction: A models approach.* Boston: Allyn and Bacon.

Hallinan, M. 1994. School differences in tracking effects on achievement. *Social Forces* 72:799–820.

Hannell, G. 2005. *Dyscalculia: Action plans for successful learning in mathematics.* New York: David Fulton.

Hiebert, J., T. P. Carpenter, E. Fennema, K. Fuson, D. Wearne, H. Murray, A. Oliver, and P. Human. 1997. *Making sense: Teaching and learning mathematics with understanding.* Portsmouth, NH: Heinemann.

Hiebert, J., and P. Lefevre. 1986. Conceptual and procedural knowledge in mathematics: An introductory analysis. In *Conceptual and procedural knowledge: The case of mathematics,* ed. J. Hiebert, 1–27. Hillsdale, NJ: Lawrence Erlbaum.

Hiebert, J., and D. Wearne. 1993. Instructional tasks, classroom discourse, and students' learning in second-grade arithmetic. *American Educational Research Journal* 30:393–425.

Hiebert, J., and D. Wearne. 1996. Instruction, understanding, and skill in multidigit addition and subtraction. *Cognition and Instruction* 14:251–283.

Hill, D. 2004. The mathematics pathway for all children. *Teaching Children Mathematics* 11 (3):127–133.

Hogan, J., K. Murcia, and J. van Wyke. 2004. *Numeracy across the curriculum.* Canberra, ACT, Australia: Numeracy Research and Development Initiative.

Hope, J. 1989. Promoting number sense in school. *Arithmetic Teacher* 36:12–16.

Howden, H. 1989. Teaching number sense. *Arithmetic Teacher* 36 (6):6–11.

Jensen, E. 1998. *Teaching with the brain in mind.* Alexandria, VA: Association for Supervision and Curriculum Development.

Johnson, J. 1991. Constructive processes in bilingualism and their cognitive growth effects. In *Language processing in bilingual children,* ed. Ellen Bialystok, 193–221. Cambridge: Cambridge University Press.

Jonassen, D. 1995. Supporting communities of learners with technology: A vision for integrating technology with learning in schools. *Educational Technology* 35:60–63.

Joram, E. 2003. Benchmarks as tools for developing measurement sense. In *Learning and teaching measurement,* eds. D. H. Clements and G. Bright, 57–67. Reston, VA: National Council of Teachers of Mathematics.

Kamii, C. K. 1984. Autonomy: The aim of education envisioned by Piaget. *Phi Delta Kappan* 65 (6):410–415.

Kamii, C. K. 1985. *Children reinvent arithmetic.* New York: Teachers College Press.

Kamii, C. K. 2004. *Young children continue to reinvent arithmetic: 2nd grade, implications of Piaget's theory.* New York: Teacher's College Press.

Kamii, C. K., and L. L. Joseph. 1989. *Young children continue to reinvent arithmetic.* New York: Teachers College Press.

Kamii, C. K., L. Kirkland, and B. A. Lewis. 2001. Representation and abstraction in young children's numerical reasoning. In *The roles of representation in school mathematics: 2001 yearbook.* Reston, VA: National Council of Teachers of Mathematics.

Kaput, J. 1999. Teaching and learning a new algebra with understanding. In *Mathematics classrooms that promote understanding,* ed. E. Fennema and T. Romberg, 133–155. Mahwah, NJ: Erlbaum.

Karp, K., and P. Howell. 2004. Building responsibility for learning in students with special needs. *Teaching Children Mathematics* 11 (3):118–126.

Kennedy, L. M., S. Tipps, and A. Johnson. 2008. *Guiding children's learning of mathematics.* Belmont, CA: Thompson.

Kilpatrick, J., Swafford, J., and Findell, B., ed. 2001. *Adding it up: Helping children learn mathematics.* Washington, DC: National Academy Press. http://www.nap.edu/catalog/9822.html (accessed September 2008).

Knapp, M. S., N. E. Adelman, C. Marder, H. McCollum, M. C. Needels, C. Padilla, P. M. Shields, B. J. Turbull, and A. A. Zucker. 1995. *Teaching for meaning in high-poverty schools.* New York: Teachers College Press.

Knuth, E. J., A. C. Stephens, N. M. McNeil, and M. W. Alibali. 2006. Does understanding the equal sign matter? Evidence from solving equations. *Journal for Research in Mathematics Education* 37 (4):297–312.

Krashen, S., and T. Terrell. 1983. *The natural approach.* Hayward, CA: Alemany Press.

Krathwohl, D. R., B. S. Bloom, and B. B. Masia. 1964. *Taxonomy of educational objectives. Handbook 2: Affective domain.* New York: Longman.

Labinowicz, E. 1980. *The Piaget primer.* Menlo Park, CA: Addison-Wesley.

Labinowicz, E. 1985. *Learning from children: New beginnings for teaching numerical thinking.* Menlo Park, CA: AWL Supplemental.

Labinowicz, E. 1987. One point of view: Children's right to be wrong. *Teaching Children Mathematics* 2:20.

Lamon, S. J. 1999. *Teaching fractions and ratios for understanding.* Mahwah, NJ: Lawrence Erlbaum Associates.

Lawrence, A. and C. Hennessy. 2002. *Lessons for algebraic thinking: Grades 6–8.* Sausalito, CA: Math Solutions.

Lee, L. 1996. An initiation into algebraic culture through generalization activities. In *Approaches into Algebra*, ed. N. Bednarz, C. Kieran, and L. Lee, 87–106. Dordrecht, The Netherlands: Klewer.

Leff, R. 2004. Vive la Difference! Gifted kindergartners and mathematics. *Teaching Children Mathematics.* 11 (3):155–157.

Lesh, R. A., T. R. Post, and M. J. Behr. 1987. Representations and translations among representations in mathematics learning and problem solving. In *Problems of representation in the teaching and learning of mathematics*, ed. C. Janvier, 33–40. Hillsdale, NJ: Lawrence Erlbaum.

Linn, M. C., and A. C. Peterson. 1986. A meta-analysis of gender differences in spatial ability: Implications for mathematics and science achievement. In *The psychology of gender: Advances through meta analysis*, ed. J. S. Hyde and M. C. Linn, 67–101. Baltimore: The Johns Hopkins University Press.

Lovin, L., M. Kyger, and D. Allsopp. 2004. Differentiation for special needs learners. *Teaching Children Mathematics* 11 (3):158–167.

Lyon, G. R. 1995. Research initiatives in learning disabilities: Contributions from scientists supported by the National Institute of Child Health and Human Development. *Journal of Child Neurology* 10 (Suppl. 1):S120–S126.

Ma, L. 1999. *Knowing and teaching elementary mathematics: Teachers understanding of fundamental mathematics in China and the United States.* Mahwah, NJ: Lawrence Erlbaum.

Maier, E., and L. Linnen. 2008. *Algebra through visual patterns: A beginning course in algebra, volumes 1 and 2.* Salem, OR: The Math Learning Center.

Mastropieri, M. A., T. E. Scruggs, and S. Shiah. 1991. Mathematics instruction for learning disabled students: A review of research. *Learning Disabilities Research & Practice* 6:89–98.

Maybin, J., N. Mercer, and B. Stierer. 1992. Scaffolding learning in the classroom. In *Thinking voices: The work of the National Oracy Project*, ed. K. Norman. London: Hodder and Stoughton.

McCarthy, B. 1990. Using the 4MAT system to bring learning styles to schools. *Educational Leadership* 48 (2):31–37.

McMillan, J. H. 2004. *Classroom assessment: Principles and practice for effective instruction.* Boston: Pearson.

Mercer, C., L. Jordan, and S. Miller. 1996. Constructivistic math instruction for diverse learners. *Learning Disabilities Research & Practice* 11 (3):147–156.

Messick, S. 1989. Validity. In *Educational measurement*, 3rd ed., ed. R. Linn, 13–103. New York: American Council on Education / Macmillan.

Mewborn, D., and P. Huberty. 1999. Questioning your way to the standards. *Teaching Children Mathematics* 6 (4):226–246.

Miller, S., and C. Mercer. 1997. Educational aspects of mathematics disabilities. *Journal of Learning Disabilities* 30 (1):47–56.

Miller, S. P. 1996. Perspectives on mathematics instruction. In *Teaching adolescents with learning disabilities*, ed. D. Deshler, E. Ellis, and B. K. Lenz, 313–368. Denver: Love.

Montis, K. K. 2000. Language development and concept flexibility in dyscalculia: A case study. *Journal for Research in Mathematics Education* 31 (5):541–556.

Mooney, C. 2000. *Theories of childhood: An introduction to Dewey, Montessori, Erikson, Piaget, & Vygotsky.* St. Paul, MN: Redleaf Press.

Morgan, C. 1998. Assessment of mathematical behaviour: A social perspective. In *Mathematics education and society*, ed. P. Gates, 277–283. Proceedings of the First International Mathematics Education and Society Conference (MEAS 1). Nottingham: Nottingham University.

National Center for Education Statistics. 1996. Pursuing excellence: Initial findings from the Third International Mathematics and Science Study, NCES 97198. Washington, DC: U.S. Government Printing Office. http://nces.ed.gov/pubsearch/pubsinfo.asp?pubid=97198 (accessed July 2008).

National Center for Learning Disabilities. 2006. Fact sheet: Dyscalculia. http://www.ldonline.org/article/13709/ (accessed October 2007).

National Clearinghouse for English Language Acquisition and Language Instruction Educational Programs. 2006. How many school-aged English language learners (ELLs) are there in the U.S.? http://www.ncela.gwu.edu/expert/faq/o1leps.html (accessed December 2007).

National Council for the Social Studies. 1994. *Expectations for excellence: Curriculum standards for the social studies.* Silver Spring, MD: Author.

National Council of Teachers of Mathematics. 1989. *Curriculum and evaluation standards for school mathematics.* Reston, VA: National Council of Teachers of Mathematics.

National Council of Teachers of Mathematics. 1991. *Professional standards for teaching mathematics.* Reston, VA: National Council of Teachers of Mathematics.

National Council of Teachers of Mathematics. 2000. *Principles and standards for school mathematics.* Reston, VA: National Council of Teachers of Mathematics.

National Council of Teachers of Mathematics. 2003. *Learning and teaching measurement: 2003 yearbook.* Reston, VA: National Council of Teachers of Mathematics.

National Council of Teachers of Mathematics. 2006. *Curriculum focal points for prekindergarten through grade 8 mathematics: A quest for coherence.* Reston, VA: National Council of Teachers of Mathematics.

National Research Council. 2000a. *How people learn: Brain, mind, experience and school.* Washington, DC: National Academy Press.

National Research Council. 2000b. *Inquiry and the national science education standards: A guide for teaching and learning.* Washington, DC: National Academy Press.

Nichols, M. 2006. *Comprehension through conversation.* Portsmouth, NH: Heinemann.

Nolte, J. 1988. *The human brain.* St. Louis: C.V. Mosby.

Norton, P., and D. Sprague. 2001. *Technology for teaching.* Needham Heights, MA: Allyn and Bacon.

O'Connor, J., and E. F. Robertson. 2003. *Nine chapters on the mathematical art.* http://www-groups.dcs.st-and.ac.uk/~history/HistTopics/Nine_chapters.html (accessed June 2008).

O'Keefe, J., and L. Nadel. 1978. *The hippocampus as a cognitive map.* Oxford, UK: Clarendon.

Pajares, M. F. 1992. Teachers' beliefs and educational research: Cleaning up a messy construct. *Review of Educational Research* 62:307–332.

Parkay, F., E. Anctil, and G. Hass. 2005. *Curriculum planning: A contemporary approach.* Boston: Allyn and Bacon.

Parker, R. 2000. *The algebra that students entering high school should know and understand.* Mathematics Education Collaborative, public session No. 5, March.

Parker, R. 2002. *Mathematically powerful students.* Handout provided at a professional development training. San Diego, CA.

Payne, R. K. 1996. *A framework for understanding poverty.* Highlands, TX: Aha! Process.

Pegg, J. 2003. Assessment in mathematics: A developmental approach. In *Mathematical cognition,* ed. J. Royer, 227–259. Greenwich, CT: Information Age.

Perkins, D. 1992. *Smart schools.* New York: Simon & Schuster.

Perret-Clermont, A. N. 1980. *Social interaction and cognitive development in children.* London: Academic Press.

Pesek, D. D., and D. Kirshner. 2000. Interference of instrumental instruction in subsequent relational learning. *Journal for Research in Mathematics Education* 31:524–540.

Philipp, R. A., R. Ambrose, L. C. Lamb, J. T. Sowder, B. P. Schappelle, L. Sowder, et al. 2007. Effects of early field experience on the mathematical content knowledge and beliefs of prospective elementary school teachers: An experimental study. *Journal for Research in Mathematics Education* 38 (5):438–476.

Piaget, J. 1965. *The moral judgment of the child.* New York: Free Press.

Piaget, J., B. Inhelder, and A. Szeminska. 1960. *The child's conception of geometry.* New York: Basic Books.

Pilar, R. 2005. Spanish–English language issues in the mathematics classroom. In *Changing the faces of mathematics: Perspectives on Latinos,* 23–33. Reston, VA: National Council of Teachers of Mathematics.

Poplin, M. S. 1988. The reductionistic fallacy in learning disabilities: Replicating the past by reducing the present. *Journal of Learning Disabilities* 21:389–400.

Pressley, M., and K. R. Harris. 1990. What we really know about strategy instruction. *Educational Leadership* 48 (1):31–34.

Rectanus, C. (1994). *Math by all means: Geometry grades 3–4.* Sausalito, CA: Math Solutions.

Reinhart, S. 2000. Never say anything a kid can say. *Mathematics Teaching in the Middle School* 5 (8):478–483.

Reys, R. E., and N. Nohda, ed. 1994. *Computational alternatives for the twenty-first century: Cross-cultural perspectives from Japan and the United States.* Reston, VA: National Council of Teachers of Mathematics.

Rezba, R. J., C. R. Sprague, J. T. McDonnough, and J. J. Matkins. 2007. *LEARNING and assessing science process skills,* 5th ed. Dubuque, IA: Kendall/Hunt.

Richardson, K. 1999a. *Developing number concepts. Book 1: Counting, comparing, and pattern.* Parsippany, NJ: Dale Seymour.

Richardson, K. 1999b. *Developing number concepts. Book 2: Addition and subtraction.* Parsippany, NJ: Dale Seymour.

Richardson, K. 1999c. *Developing number concepts. Book 3: Place value, multiplication, and division.* Parsippany, NJ: Dale Seymour.

Richardson, K. 1999d. *Understanding geometry.* Bellingham, WA: Lummi Bay.

Richardson, K. 2003a. *Assessing math concepts: Concept 1, counting objects.* Bellingham, WA: Mathematical Perspectives.

Richardson, K. 2003b. *Assessing math concepts: Concept 2, changing numbers.* Bellingham, WA: Mathematical Perspectives.

Richardson, K. 2003c. *Assessing math concepts: Concept 3, more/less trains.* Bellingham, WA: Mathematical Perspectives.

Richardson, K. 2003d. *Assessing math concepts: Concept 4, number arrangements.* Bellingham, WA: Mathematical Perspectives.

Richardson, K. 2003e. *Assessing math concepts: Concept 5, combination trains.* Bellingham, WA: Mathematical Perspectives.

Richardson, K. 2003f. *Assessing math concepts: Concept 6, hiding assessment.* Bellingham, WA: Mathematical Perspectives.

Richardson, K. 2003g. *Assessing math concepts: Concept 7, ten frames.* Bellingham, WA: Mathematical Perspectives.

Richardson, K. 2003h. *Assessing math concepts: Concept 8, grouping tens.* Bellingham, WA: Mathematical Perspectives.

Richardson, K. 2003i. *Assessing math concepts: Concept 9, two-digit addition and subtraction.* Bellingham, WA: Mathematical Perspectives.

Ridgeway, J. 1998. From barrier to lever: Revising roles for assessment in mathematics education. *NISE Brief* 2 (1):1–9.

Roney-Dougal, C. 2006. Guest speaker on *History in our time.* Online radio program from the BBC. March 9. http://www.bbc.co.uk/radio4/history/inourtime/inourtime_20060309.shtml (accessed October 2007).

Rosenzweig, M. R., and E. L. Bennett. 1972. Cerebral changes in rats exposed individually to an enriched environment. *Journal of Comparative and Physiological Psychology* 80:304–313.

Ross, S. 1989. Parts, wholes, and place value: A developmental view. *Arithmetic Teacher* 36 (6):47–51.

Ross, S. 1990. Children's acquisition of place-value numeration concepts: The roles of cognitive development and instruction. *Focus on Learning Problems in Mathematics.* 12 (1):1–15.

Russell, S. J. 2000. Developing computational fluency with whole numbers. *Teaching Children Mathematics* November: 154–157.

Schoenfeld, A. 1992. Learning to think mathematically: Problem solving, metacognition, and sense-making in mathematics. In *Handbook for research on mathematics teaching and learning,* ed. D. Grouws, chap. 15, pp. 334–370. New York: Macmillan.

Schroyer, J., and W. Fitzgerald. 1986. *Mouse and elephant: Measuring growth.* Menlo Park, CA: Addison-Wesley.

Secada, W. 1992. Evaluating the mathematics education of limited English proficient students in a time of educational change. In *Focus on Evaluation and Measurement,* ERIC Document Reproduction Service, No. ED 349 828. Washington DC: U.S. Department of Education, Office of Bilingual Education and Minority Languages Affairs.

Seligman, M. E., and A. Altenor. 1980. Coping behavior: Learned helplessness, psychological change, and learned inactivity. *Behaviour Research and Therapy* 18:459–512.

Sierpinska, A. 1994. *Understanding in mathematics.* London: Falmer Press.

Silver, E. A., and M. K. Stein. 1996. The QUASAR Project: The "revolution of the possible" in mathematics instructional reform in urban middle schools. *Urban Education* 30:476–521.

Simon, M. 1995. Reconstructing mathematics pedagogy from a constructivist perspective. *Journal for Research in Mathematics Education* 26:114–145.

Skolnick, J., C. Langbort, and L. Day. 1997. *How to encourage girls in math and science.* Palo Alto, CA: Dale Seymour.

Smith, M., and J. O'Day. 1991. Systemic school reform. In *The politics of curriculum and testing: The 1990 yearbook of the Politics of Education Association,* ed. S. Fuhrman and B. Malen, 233–267. New York: Falmer Press.

Sowell, E. J. 1989. Effects of manipulative materials in mathematics instruction. *Journal for Research in Mathematics Education* 20:498–505.

Starr, J. 2005. Reconceptualizing procedural knowledge. *Journal for Research in Mathematics Education* 36 (5):404–411.

Statistics. 2008. In Merriam-Webster Online Dictionary. http://www.merriam-webster.com/dictionary/statistics (accessed July 2008).

Stein, M. K., M. S. Smith, M. A. Henningsen, and E. A. Silver. 2000. *Implementing standards-based mathematics instruction: A casebook for professional development.* New York: Teachers College Press.

Stephan, M., and D. H. Clements. 2003. Linear and area measurement in prekindergarten to grade 2. In *Learning and Teaching Measurement: 2003 yearbook,* 3–16. Reston, VA: National Council of Teachers of Mathematics.

Stephan, M., P. Cobb, K. Gravemeijer, and B. Estes. 2001. The role of tools in supporting students' development of measurement conceptions. In *The roles of representation in school mathematics: 2001 yearbook,* ed. Al Cuoco, 63–76. Reston, VA: National Council of Teachers of Mathematics.

Stevenson, H. W., and J. W. Stigler. 1992. *The learning gap: Why our schools are failing and what we can learn from Japanese and Chinese education.* New York: Simon & Schuster.

Suydam, M. 1984. Research report: Manipulative materials. *Arithmetic Teacher* 31 (5):27.

Tank, B. 1996. *Math by all means: Probability grades 1-2.* Sausalito, CA: Math Solutions.

Tash, B. 2005. Extended day mathematics intervention program: Grades 3–6 (unpublished program designed for the teachers in the San Diego Unified School District to use with struggling students in the upper elementary grades).

Tombari, M., and G. Borich. 1999. *Authentic assessment in the classroom: Applications and practice.* Columbus, OH: Merrill.

Tomlinson, C. A. 2001. *How to differentiate instruction in mixed-ability classrooms.* Alexandria, VA: Association of Supervision and Curriculum Development.

University of Washington. Instructional design approaches. http://depts.washington.edu/eproject/Instructional%20Design%20Approaches.htm (accessed July 2008).

Usiskin, Z. 1988. Conceptions of school algebra and uses of variables. In *The ideas of algebra, K–12,* ed. A. F. Coxford, 8–19. Reston, VA: National Council of Teachers of Mathematics.

Utah State Math Standards. http://www.uen.org/core/math/index.shtml (accessed July 2008).

Vacc, N. N., and G. W. Bright. 1999. Elementary preservice teachers' changing beliefs and instructional use of children's mathematical thinking. *Journal for Research in Mathematics Education* 30:89–110.

Van de Walle, J. A. 2004. *Elementary and middle school mathematics: Teaching developmentally,* 5th ed. Boston: Pearson.

Van de Walle, J. A. 2006. *Teaching student-centered mathematics: Grades 3–5.* Boston: Pearson.

Van de Walle, J. A. 2007. *Elementary and middle school mathematics: Teaching developmentally,* 6th edition. Boston: Pearson.

Vaughn, S., C. S. Bos, and J. S. Shumm. 1997. *Teaching mainstreamed, diverse, and at-risk students in the general education classroom.* Needham Heights, MA: Allyn and Bacon.

Villasenor, A., and H. S. Kepner. 1993. Arithmetic from a problem-solving perspective: An urban implementation. *Journal for Research in Mathematics Education* 24:62–70.

Von Rotz, L., and M. Burns. 2002. *Lessons for algebraic thinking: Grades K–2.* Sausalito, CA: Math Solutions.

Vygotsky, L. S. 1978. *Mind in society: The development of higher psychological processes,* ed. M. Cole, V. John-Steiner, S. Scribner, and E. Souberman. Cambridge, MA: Harvard University Press.

Walter, T. 1996. *Amazing English: How-to handbook.* New York: Addison-Wesley.

Walter, T. 2004. *Teaching English language learners: The how-to handbook.* White Plains, NY: Pearson Education.

Wearne, D., and J. Hiebert. 1989. Cognitive changes during conceptually based instruction on decimal fractions. In *Number concepts and operations in the middle grades,* ed. J. Hiebert and M. Behr, 220–235. Reston, VA: National Council of Teachers of Mathematics.

Wickett, M., and M. Burns. 2001. *Lessons for extending multiplication: Grades 4–5.* Sausalito, CA: Math Solutions.

Wickett, M., and M. Burns. 2003. *Lessons for extending division: Grades 4–5.* Sausalito, CA: Math Solutions.

Wickett, M., K. Kharas, and M. Burns. 2002. *Lessons for algebraic thinking: Grades 3–5.* Sausalito, CA: Math Solutions.

Wiggins, G., and J. McTighe. 1998. *Understanding by design.* Upper Saddle River, NJ: Prentice Hall.

Wood, T., B. S. Nelson, and J. Warfield, ed. 2001. *Beyond classical pedagogy: Teaching elementary school mathematics.* Mahwah, NJ: Lawrence Erlbaum.

Wright, R. L. 2007. Literacy is not content knowledge. http://www.lifescied.org/cgi/content/full/4/3/189 (accessed July 2007).

Yakimanskaya, I. S. 1991. *The development of spatial thinking in schoolchildren.* Soviet studies in mathematics education, vol. 3. Reston, VA: National Council of Teachers of Mathematics.